Australia for everyone

Australia for everyone

A MODERN GUIDE

Osmar White

WREN PUBLISHING PTY LTD
33 Lonsdale Street, Melbourne 3000

First published 1968
by William Heinemann, Melbourne
as *Guide to Australia*
2nd edition 1974
Set by Trade Composition Pty Ltd, Melbourne
Printed and bound by Wilke and Company Limited,
Clayton, Victoria
Designed by Derrick I. Stone

National Library of Australia
Cataloguing-in-Publication data

White, Osmar
Australia for Everyone/a modern guide/
[by] Osmar White. – [2nd ed.] – Melbourne:
Wren, 1974.
Index.
ISBN 0 85885 103 2.
ISBN 0 85885 104 0 Paperback.

1. Australia – Description and travel –
Guide-books.
I. Title

919.404

Contents

List of Illustrations

List of Maps

Acknowledgements

Permission to reproduce most of the colour and black-and-white photographs in this guide was given generously by the Australian Tourist Commission and the Australian News and Information Bureau. The cover transparency was kindly supplied by General Motors-Holden's. The Shell Company of Australia has been particularly cooperative in making available to us their most up-to-date material for all except one of the maps in this book—the map of Sydney, which came from the New South Wales Tourist Bureau.

The book itself could not have been written without the interest, skill and hard work of my researchers, Mrs H. F. Newton-John and Miss Sally White, who devoted many months to the compilation and classification of information from diverse sources.

I am also deeply grateful to my wife for the ingenuity, patience and stamina which she summoned up to provide an index and to help solve formidable editorial and design problems.

Osmar White

Author's Note

The primary aim of this book is to provide information which will be of general interest and practical value to everyone who travels to or within Australia, either on business or for pleasure. While I hope that it will encourage people overseas to visit a vast, richly diverse and beautiful continent and help them to understand it, and that it will stimulate native Australians to make new journeys of discovery in their own country, it is *not* propaganda for tourism. Its publication was not inspired or sponsored by the travel industry or any section of it. The facts contained in *Australia for Everyone* are basic, uncoloured by commercial considerations, and have not been selected with any 'promotional' end in mind.

The first editions of the book appeared in 1968 under the title *Guide to Australia*. The original text has been revised, re-organised for easier reference, up-dated and supplemented in many areas. In others, however, there have been fairly substantial deletions. For instance, this edition does not quote currency exchange rates, fares, accommodation tariffs, or give estimates of other travel costs. These omissions are, regrettably, unavoidable.

Like most countries in a monetarily unstable modern world, Australia in the 1970s is experiencing severe domestic inflation. The dollar cost of most goods and services is rising—and at an unpredictable rate. Furthermore, the value of the Australian dollar in relation to other world currencies could be subject to arbitrary but unpredictable re-adjustment. In consequence there seems little point in giving figures which could soon be outdated and tend to mislead rather than offer reliable guidance. Intending travellers would be wiser to depend on the up-to-date information which can be supplied by travel bureaux and agencies.

A comparable but less fundamental difficulty has been encountered in deciding what hotels, motels and restaurants to recommend. With increase of leisure the domestic travel industry is growing apace. Almost every day new hotels, motels and eating houses are opening and the managements of old-established ones are changing. Standards therefore vary rapidly, both for better and for worse.

The recommendations are made on the basis of the situation as it was at the beginning of 1974 and are confined to establishments which at that time enjoyed a more or less long-standing reputation for providing accommodation and services of good quality. A few may since have declined, and no doubt there are many newcomers of notable merit. But in preparing this text it seemed undesirable to enter into speculation about what the situation would be by the time it was published.

A word of warning to campers and caravaners: Many tourist parks in Australia are excellently sited, equipped and managed. Many are not. But the overall standard is improving. The term 'all facilities' does not necessarily indicate that the facilities are well maintained, so it is advisable to check thoroughly before moving in.

MELBOURNE, 1974.

AN INTRODUCTION TO AUSTRALIA AND AUSTRALIANS

Face of a Continent

In old-fashioned geography books Australia was often described as the world's largest island. It would have been more accurate to describe it as the smallest of the continents, isolated from other great land masses on earth by the vast Pacific and Indian Oceans, and geologically and topographically unique because of this isolation. Its area of nearly 800 million hectares makes it almost as large as the United States of America, four-fifths the size of Canada, nearly three-quarters the size of all Europe, and twenty-five times the size of the British Isles.

Stand on the summit of Ayers Rock, gargantuan sandstone monolith, nearly 400 metres high, sited almost exactly in the geographical centre of the continent, and you will have to travel 1 600 kilometres in any direction to reach the sea.

It stands to reason that so vast a land mass, stretching almost from the equator to the Roaring Forties and its shores washed by three oceans, should possess a great variety of physical characteristics; that the scenery, climate, vegetation and general conformation of its regions should be equally diverse.

'Typically Australian' is a misleading term. This is a land of contrasts and contradictions. In the mountains of the south-east a traveller who had become lost could freeze to death in a blizzard in the same season of the year as another traveller lost in the mountains of the north-west, could perish of thirst and heat exhaustion.

Two-fifths of the continent lie north of the Tropic of Capricorn. But a tropical vista in Australia may be one of parched treeless plains even more frequently than it is of palm-fringed beaches, jungle-covered mountains, or coral islets.

Australia is the driest continent on earth but in parts of it the average annual rainfall exceeds 375 cm. It is the flattest continent, but its mountains, from the snow-capped peaks of south-western Tasmania to the blazing red domes and pinnacles of the Macdonnell Ranges in the Northern Territory, are scenically magnificent.

For innumerable Europeans and Americans the term 'Australian bush' conjures up visions of a vast, featureless plain covered by dreary gum trees which somehow affords subsistence to large numbers of sheep and kangaroos. In reality the Australian bush can be anything from dense forest dominated by giant conifers to rolling, open savannah—from vine-festooned jungle to sombre, barren heathland. There are enormous areas of Australia in which sheep have never grazed and equally enormous areas through which one can travel for days on end without sighting a kangaroo or any other marsupial animal.

It is, however, true that the great variety of terrain to be found in Australia occurs mainly in the coastal regions of the east and south-east and the north and north-west. The heartland of the continent is a huge plateau of arid and semi-arid land on which vegetation is sparse and where the predominant earth colour is red to reddish-brown and tan.

The breathtaking monotony of this country is here and there relieved by mountainous ridges of rock, some of which reach an elevation of more than 1 600 metres above sea-level, and by huge salt and mud pans described on maps as 'lakes'. Some of them are below sea-level and they contain water only after heavy rain—which falls rarely.

The 'rivers' which drain this irregularly eroded plateau are also dry most of the time. They appear as aimlessly wandering runnels on the face of the desert, but rain can transform them, too. After heavy falls they become raging yellow torrents, burst their banks, and spill out over thousands of square kilometres of countryside.

Before the days of high-flying jets, air travellers on the Perth-Sydney or Darwin-Adelaide routes saw cross-sections of Australia from an altitude of about 2 000 metres. The crude anatomy of the continent was clearly revealed—its thin green skin of forest and farmland near the sea, its broken carapace of mountains, the irregular mosaic of grainfields and improved pastures on their landward slopes and finally the overwhelming red desolation of the Outback flowing on and on for more than 2 500 kilometres until the coastal pattern is repeated in reverse.

Unfortunately, modern passenger aircraft fly much too high to permit any detailed observation of geography. From an altitude of 10 000 metres one part of the earth's surface is apt to look very much like any other. The globe-trotter who wishes to boast that he has actually seen how Australia is put together must either charter a light aircraft for his crossings or travel by road or rail.

Along the entire east and south-east coast of Australia a band of highlands extends from Cape York in the far north to Cape Howe in the south, where it turns westward and extends half-way across the State of Victoria. This mountain system is geologically very complicated and made up of rocks of varying origins and age, but loosely speaking it was formed by a great wrinkling of the earth's crust many millions of years ago—a wrinkling which has since been smoothed out by water and wind and alternating heat and cold over the ages.

The Great Dividing Range, as these highlands are known, runs more or less parallel with the seashore for a distance of over 4 000 kilometres and is broken only by a few low gaps. On the seaward side its slopes are steep and drained by fast-flowing rivers. Landward the slopes are much more gradual and merge almost imperceptibly into the central plateau.

The coastal strip, which contains the best watered and most fertile land of the continent, is between 50 and 400 kilometres wide and it supports most of the population.

The profile of the range is flat—one might almost describe it as an interlocked series of tablelands into which the rivers have cut a complicated pattern of deep gorges, many with vertical sides. The mountaintops reach elevations much above 1 600 metres only in the south-east, where the highest peak, Mount Kosciusko, rises above 2 300 metres; in northern Queensland at the 17th parallel; and in Tasmania which was once linked with the mainland and where a spur of the main range constitutes the island State's central core.

Australia's eastern and south-eastern regions receive liberal and reasonably regular rainfall because of the configuration of the land. It ranges from 250 centimetres in parts of the far north to 75 centimetres in the south. Severe droughts do occur but they are not frequent and the country supports a lush and varied native vegetation. Thus the coastal plains are, by Australian standards, closely settled and agriculturally developed. In the north they produce crops of sugar-cane, tropical fruits, cereals such as maize and sorghum, peanuts and oil seeds. In the south they are given over chiefly to dairying, meat-raising and mixed farming.

The mountains themselves are in the main densely wooded, although the nature and quality of the forest differs greatly according to latitude, aspect and soil type.

Some of the mightiest trees in the world, *Eucalyptus regnans*, grow in dense stands on Victorian and Tasmanian hillsides. They attain a height of more than 100 metres. Throughout the entire length of the range, irrespective of latitude, isolated areas of rain forest are found. To the lay eye they present much the same appearence as the jungles of Asia, Africa or tropical America—although the botanist will detect fascinating differences. Mostly, however, the highlands are covered by a mixed vegetation of smaller trees in which the eucalyptus and acacia genera predominate. Indeed, these families dominate the tree cover of the entire continent. The subdued greyish-green of their leaves is basic to the colouration of almost all Australian woodlands; their smaller species, adapted to drought and fierce heat, provide an insistent, harsh complement to the red earths and stones and sands of the inland.

The eastern and south-eastern coast and hinterland is pleasant country, often strikingly beautiful and always different, to the eyes of a traveller from other parts of the world. The region offers tourists a magnificent diversity of scenery and outdoor recreation in appropriate seasons of the year. The beaches along the coast of New South Wales and southern Queensland are among the finest in the world for surfing and surfboard riding. Usually set between rocky headlands, they are crescents of pale golden sand on which the long swells of the Pacific roll in unbroken by reefs or contrary currents. The water is warm and clear the year round.

On a small-scale map this seaboard appears rather featureless, but it is in fact indented deeply by many river estuaries and there are large expanses of sheltered water ideal for yachting, boating, fishing and aquatic sports of every kind.

North of the Tropic of Capricorn the coast of Queensland is flanked by the world's largest coral formation, the Great Barrier Reef, which stretches 2 000 kilometres southward from Torres Strait almost to the 25th parallel. This enormous buttress of brilliantly coloured coral heads and ledges, wooded islands and blue lagoons is rightly described by the travel brochures as a wonderland for lovers of the sea and the sea's creatures.

Long stretches of the main range in these latitudes are also scenically superb, with great waterfalls and rapids in the gorges. But they are perhaps less spectacular than the mountain country farther south where the rivers have cut a maze of ravines and hidden valleys through sandstone escarpments more than 900 metres thick. In the Blue Mountains area, west of Sydney, the precipitous ramparts of the range foiled for more than 30 years repeated efforts by early explorers to conquer them.

Still farther south the highlands assume a quasi-Alpine character. For three or four months every year—or longer at altitudes above 1 600 metres—the tops are covered by deep snow and are ideal for skiing and other winter sports. This country is also attractive in summer and autumn when the high plains are spangled with wildflowers and there is fine trout-fishing in the streams and artificial lakes created by national water conservation projects. The south-eastern mountains are the most important rainfall catchment in the Commonwealth and they are the source of hydro-electric power supplies for the great industrial cities of Sydney and Melbourne. The storages also irrigate large areas of intensively cultivated farmland in the valleys of the Murray-Murrumbidgee river system.

Although the Great Dividing Range is by far the most extensive mountain area in Australia, highlands of considerable extent and elevation occur in Central Australia, the remote and relatively inaccessible north-west of Western Australia and Arnhem Land in the Northern Territory.

The Macdonnell and Musgrave-Warburton Ranges of Central Australia, and the Hamersleys in the north-west are particularly spectacular. The vegetation they support is sparse but unique in form. Their rock towers and canyons are often sculpted by sand and wind into fantastic shapes. Their ground colours are of incredible intensity and range from deep blue-black and rich brown hues to brilliant reds, yellows and purples.

The great saw-toothed ridges and towering mesas of the Australian desert are like no other mountains on earth. As communications improve under the stimulus of the rich mineral discoveries made in this country during recent years, they are attracting more and more tourists during the mild, cloudless winter months.

There is little physical similarity between coastal Australia and the stupendously spacious and lonely inland. Maps tend to mislead, to convey a false impression of terrain, the density of settlement and the nature of man-made communications. Cartographers are notoriously loath to leave empty spaces and most maps they make of the inland are 'decorated' with place names which often indicate nothing more than the existence of a small homestead or mining camp which may or may not still be inhabited. Boldly traced rivers may not have flowed for years and primitive vehicular tracks are sometimes shown as roads or even highways.

Australia's density of population, now a little more than seven persons per 1 000 hectares, is the lowest of any inhabited continent—about one-sixth the density of South America and Africa, one twenty-fifth that of North America, one sixty-sixth that of Europe, and one fifty-fifth that of Asia, excluding the USSR. But even this measure of emptiness is apt to deceive, because four out of five Australians live in cities and towns on or near the coast and the rural population is mainly concentrated in regions of relatively high rainfall near the mountains.

Twin tyrannies have dictated the pattern of settlement—the tyranny of distance and the tyranny of climate.

THE CLIMATES OF AUSTRALIA

The range of climatic variation found in Australia is fairly wide and the climatic pattern itself is complicated, but it is true as a generalization that most of the continent is hot and dry and that the farther one goes inland the hotter and drier it becomes. Its average annual rainfall is only about 420 millimetres compared with a world average of 660 millimetres, and the total annual flow of all Australian rivers, if spread evenly over the land surface, would cover it to a depth of only 38 millimetres. In North America the corresponding figure would be 228 millimetres.

The rainfall is uneven in distribution and areas on the seaward side of the coastal mountain ranges receive the heaviest falls. Vast tracts of desert in the Centre and near the head of the Great Australian Bight receive an average of less than 127 millimetres a year—and achieve that mean only because of torrential falls from freak thunderstorms which occur every few years. At the other end of the scale, averages exceed 250 centimetres in parts of the West Tasmanian highlands and the North Queensland ranges and reach 127 centimetres on the coastal strip all the way from Cape York to the border of New South Wales and Victoria.

In the tropics, summer and autumn are the wet seasons and substantial falls are rare in winter and spring. In the north-eastern segment the rain is the product of the north-west monsoon, and in the north-west of an erratic 'cyclone season'. In the temperate south, falls are distributed much more evenly but generally winter and spring are wet and summer and early autumn dry. The climate somewhat resembles that of the western Mediterranean seaboard of Europe.

Except in the high country of the south-east and in Tasmania, severe winter cold spells are very unusual. Even then screen temperatures do not drop much below freezing point. Sub-zero readings are confined to the depth of winter and to the peaks and plateaux over 1 800 metres. No permanently inhabited region experiences winters comparable in severity with those of North America and Europe.

Again excepting the south-east and the extreme south-west, summers are hot to extremely hot. Maximum shade temperatures above 38°C are common in most inland centres from November to mid-March. The highest shade temperature ever recorded at an official weather station in Australia was 53°C at Cloncurry in Western Queensland on 16 January 1889; but the most consistently hot inhabited region is about the little mining town of Marble Bar in Western Australia, where maxima of 50°C are fairly common. In 1923-24 Marble Bar experienced 160 consecutive days on which the temperature climbed above 38°C.

In the southern States the hottest months are January and February. In a normal year the capital cities have a few days of torrid weather, and heatwaves in which the thermometer records maxima above 32°C for perhaps a week or 10 days at a time. Otherwise the summer climate is pleasant and sunny.

November and December are the hottest months in the far north. Then the arrival of the monsoon cools the air, but discomfort increases as humidity builds up. From late April to late August the weather is usually mild, with cloudless, warm days and cool nights. The diurnal variation in the dry season is most marked in inland districts where temperatures as low as 4·5°C are often experienced just before dawn when the earth's heat loss from radiation is at its highest. September and October are usually warm, rather windy months and dust can make conditions unpleasant.

In the wet season the northern third of the continent is occasionally visited by severe cyclones with wind velocities exceeding 160 kilometres an hour. They are mostly accompanied by rains which result in severe flooding. The rivers burst their banks, inundate large areas of countryside and disrupt road, rail and air communications. These great storms often cause heavy property damage and occasional loss of life in the settled areas of the Queensland coast and the north-west, but many of them penetrate far inland and give a new lease of life to tens of millions of hectares of marginal desert.

The 'Wet' is a season of capricious violence throughout the entire north, and no time to be travelling for pleasure. In the south, winter and spring storms can also cause destructive flooding and wind damage, but rarely are these disturbances comparable with the winter gales which lash Europe and North America.

PEOPLE OF AUSTRALIA

The population of Australia is just over 13 million people, of which about three-quarters are native-born. Ethnically, the vast majority of Australians are of Caucasian origin, Anglo-Saxon and Celtic strains from the British Isles predominating. Since the second world war, however, there has been a considerable influx of European migrants and Australian society has assumed a much more cosmopolitan character than hitherto. Nevertheless, the cultural and political traditions of the nation are essentially British. The language is English. Foreign-language groupings of recent European immigrants have now put in an appearance in the larger cities, but they are not as yet socially significant.

The number of full-blood aborigines—the primitive, nomadic people who inhabited the continent before the coming of white men—is not precisely known, but is estimated at about 40,000, with about 100,000 people of mixed blood who claim aboriginal descent.

The aboriginal population is highest in remote rural areas of Queensland, Western Australia and New South Wales and in the Northern Territory. Only a few hundred desert-dwellers continue to live as their ancestors did, observing the strict and elaborate tribal laws and winning their subsistence as nomadic hunters. The rest have been detribalized.

Most white Australians are, contrary to popular belief in other parts of the world, confirmed town and city dwellers. More than four-fifths of them live in State capital cities or in the large provincial centres, most of which are on or near the coast. Few of them have any real experience of country life—although they are fond of outdoor living—and fewer still have ever set foot on a big cattle or sheep station. Their society is urban and industrial and their culture derivative from Western European civilization. They are a technologically advanced people who enjoy a high level of material prosperity and of political stability.

Superficially, Australian social attitudes are almost aggressively egalitarian. It is customary to avoid any form of address or attitude implying difference in social status or a master-servant relationship. An Australian taxi-driver, shop assistant or service-station attendant may—or may not—address his clients as 'sir' or 'madam' while actually transacting business; the same courtesy may be accorded a managerial executive by an employee during working hours. But in any other situation acknowledgement of status differences is rare.

This convention, however, is apt to be deceptive. In reality Australians are much more class-conscious than their manners indicate. The stratification of their society is dictated more by vocation than by considerations of inheritance,

Whitsunday Passage from Shute Harbour (Q)

AUSTRALIA PHYSICAL

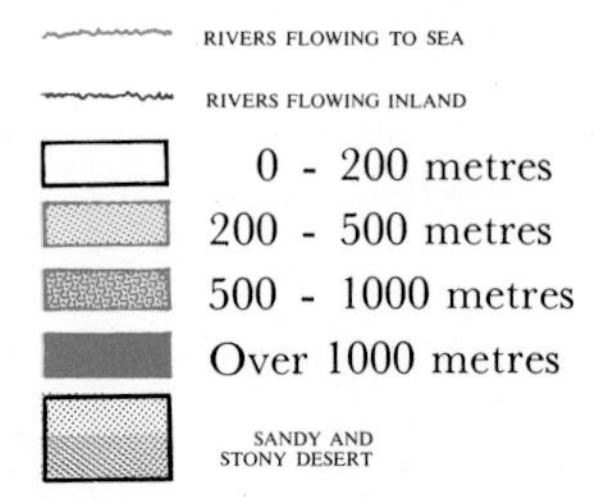

SEA
Torres Strait
Cape York
C. Arnhem
Arnhem Land
Gulf of Carpentaria
Groote Eylandt
Roper R.
Cape York Pens.
Princess Charlotte Bay
CORAL SEA
140
Mitchell R.
Cooktown
Wellesley Is.
Gilbert R.
Cairns
ATHERTON PLATEAU
Normanton
Great Barrier Reef
PACIFIC OCEAN
Magnetic Is.
Barkly Tableland
Leichhardt R.
Flinders R.
Gregory Ra.
TOWNSVILLE
Burdekin R.
150
20
Mt. Isa
Cloncurry
Richmond
Selwyn Ra.
GREAT
Belyando R.
QUEENSLAND
Rockhampton
Longreach
ALICE SPRINGS
GREAT AUSTRALIAN BASIN
Thompson R.
Simpson Desert
Birdsville
Dawson R.
Bundaberg
DIVIDING
Lake Eyre Basin
Oodnadatta
McGregor Ra.
Warrego R.
Roma
SOUTH AUSTRALIA
Darling Downs
Moreton Bay
BRISBANE
L. Eyre
Sturt Desert
Toowoomba
Macpherson Ra.
Culgoa R.
C. Byron
Lismore
Grey Ra.
Barwon R.
Bourke
RANGE
New England Ra.
Grafton
Flinders Range
Darling
Liverpool Ra.
30
Broken Hill
NEW SOUTH WALES
Port Macquarie
PORT AUGUSTA
Streaky Bay
Gawler Ra.
Whyalla
Port Pirie
Mt. Lofty Ra.
Maitland
NEWCASTLE
MURRAY RIVER BASIN
Lachlan R.
Bathurst
Blue Mtns.
Renmark
Mildura
SYDNEY
Bight
Port Lincoln
ADELAIDE
Murrumbidgee R.
Wollongong
TASMAN SEA
St. Vincents Gulf
Murray R.
Riverina
Albury
CANBERRA
Kangaroo Is.
Encounter Bay
Bendigo
AUSTRALIAN ALPS
VICTORIA
Ballarat
Mt. Gambier
MELBOURNE
Cape Howe
GEELONG
Sale
C. Otway
Port Phillip B.
Wilson's Prom.
140
40
King Is.
Bass Strait
150
Flinders Is.
40
LAUNCESTON
Queenstown
TASMANIA
HOBART

Sydney from the air

Blue Mountains, N.S.W.

power, wealth or education. Medical practitioners, lawyers and bank managers, for instance, rank higher in the popular estimation than Members of Parliament, academics or creative artists. The cohesion of the wealthy classes is probably less marked in Australia than it is in other parts of the Western world.

Class distinction carried to the length of overt snobbery is more marked in rural than in urban communities. 'Graziers' or 'pastoralists' who raise sheep and cattle on large holdings are considered superior to other categories of farmers, irrespective of the income they derive from working their land. Residual attitudes of 19th-century English society persist among large landholders. Titles and aristocratic connections are respected and conventions more strictly observed among the declining 'squattocracy'—the large pastoral landowners—than among other privileged elements.

The subtle illogicalities of the Australian class structure need be of little concern to the overseas visitor, except insofar as they affect the quality of the personal service he receives in the course of his travels. It is enough to remember that an authoritarian manner does not command good service or willing co-operation in Australia. Polite request achieves more than command.

Some degree of race and colour prejudice exists among native Australians, but it is grossly apparent only in rural communities where educational standards and the level of sophistication are low.

For more than half a century the much-debated 'White Australia Policy' has restricted immigration of coloured people and prevented the establishment of ethnic and cultural minorities within the social complex. Most Australians, and particularly those of the younger generation, genuinely deplore racial discrimination and in personal contacts behave accordingly. Nevertheless, in country towns and far-northern districts in which an appreciable proportion of the population is of aboriginal blood, racial friction exists and is sometimes publicly manifest.

URBAN LIFE

The point has already been made that Australians are mainly an industrial and mercantile people alienated from country life. The two largest cities, Sydney and Melbourne, each have populations of about three millions. Both are growing rapidly and are in the process of redevelopment. The standardized modern skyscraper and the traffic engineering of the automobile age are rapidly obliterating their original architectural character, which was predominantly mid-Victorian.

Sydney, the most populous and sophisticated metropolis in the Commonwealth, strongly reflects American influence. It is a bustling, vital city and supports a varied and colourful night life. Melbourne, the capital of Victoria, the most highly industrialized and wealthiest State, is notably more conservative and 'English' in atmosphere. It is regarded as the nation's financial capital.

The smaller State capitals, Brisbane, Adelaide, Perth and Hobart, still retain something of their Victorian character and are more recognizably the product of an Australian environment. The national capital, Canberra, is an elaborately planned model city sited in fertile and beautiful country on the western slopes of the Great Dividing Range roughly half-way between Sydney and Melbourne.

Even the largest of Australian cities are not, by comparison with Europe,

America or Asia, overcrowded. Melbourne, for instance, has a metropolitan area of about 200 000 hectares. This characteristic sprawl has grave economic disadvantages, but it is the basis of much which is unique and attractive in the Australian way of life. The average citizen lives in a detached suburban house which he owns himself, enjoys the pleasures of a small private garden, and spends a good deal of his time in the open air playing or watching competitive sports.

Serious air and water pollution, excessive noise and the sort of sociological problems created by crowded tenement dwelling are only now becoming matters which immediately and urgently concern city dwellers. Areas of substandard housing do exist and slum clearance and redevelopment of rundown residential districts is going forward in all large centres, but a relatively small proportion of the population is affected.

RURAL COMMUNITIES

The pattern and flavour of life in all but the largest provincial towns and cities differ substantially from the pattern and flavour of life in the capitals. The great majority of rural settlements in Australia exist simply as utilitarian service centres for primary producers. Some decentralization of secondary industry has occurred, mainly in the populated south-east of the continent and along the coastal strip in Western Australia and Queensland and prosperous, civically integrated communities have grown up in closely settled irrigation areas. The more progressive of these are, in architecture and atmosphere, somewhat similar to towns of comparable size in southern parts of the United States. The inland centres of population, however, are still frontier settlements which have little to commend them aesthetically.

For many years there has been a steady drift of population from the country to the cities. Pastoral and agricultural industries in Australia are highly mechanized and in relation to their productivity do not employ a large labour force. Young people find career opportunities more easily in the cities than in the 'bush' and find little to hold them in even the well-developed country towns where living conditions are pleasant.

The spectacular growth of the mining industry over the past decade has not done a great deal to correct the population imbalance. Developmental works have attracted considerable forces of temporary labour to the Outback, but the mining operations themselves are, like farming, highly mechanized and the new towns created by, for instance, iron-ore and bauxite quarrying are merely small, self-contained company settlements accommodating, at the most, a few hundred technicians and their families.

Immigration has to some extent slowed down depopulation of remote rural areas. The traveller encountered on a lonely outback track these days is more likely to be an Italian, a German, a Pole or a Yugoslav than a third or fourth-generation Australian. But even if the inflow of migrants continues the nature of economic development now occurring suggests that the growth of the agricultural and pastoral industries will take some time to match the rate of expansion in other segments of the national economy. Australia's great open spaces remain unpopulated, even if the great Australian loneliness has to some degree been conquered by the technology of 20th-century transport and communication.

POLITICAL SYSTEM

The Commonwealth of Australia comprises six sovereign States and seven Territories. The States are: New South Wales, Victoria, Queensland, South Australia, Western Australia and Tasmania. The Territories are: The Australian Capital Territory, the Northern Territory, Norfolk Island, Cocos Island, Christmas Island, Heard and Macquarie Islands and Australian Antarctic Territory. The last two Territories are not permanently occupied.

Federation of the six sovereign States was achieved in 1901. Previously they had been colonies of Great Britain although they had for many years before the establishment of the Commonwealth had representative self-government and virtual political autonomy.

The link between the Commonwealth and the United Kingdom is constitutional recognition by both nations that the Crown is an essential element of Parliament—a recognition which today means only acknowledgment of common political and legal tradition. The Sovereign is represented in the Commonwealth by a governor-general and in each of the States by a governor. The Sovereign's representatives are appointed on the advice of the Federal or State governments in power at the time the offices became vacant.

The system of Federal government is bi-cameral, both Houses of Parliament, the Senate and the House of Representatives, being elected by adult franchise. The system of State government is also bi-cameral, except in Queensland, where the Upper House was abolished in 1922. Members of the Lower Houses of State legislatures are elected by adult franchise, but the membership of Upper Houses is determined by the vote of electors with age, residential, property or other qualifications which vary somewhat between State and State.

In general and approximate terms, the Federal Government has legislative and executive power in all provinces affecting the welfare of the Commonwealth and its citizens as a whole. Matters of purely domestic significance are more the province of the State governments, although the Commonwealth Government, as principal taxing authority since the second world war, controls pensions and has had to engage itself increasingly in the fields of social services and education. The States' power to raise taxes is limited and their governmental work is financed largely by Commonwealth grants.

Political ideologies and political rivalries do not play a very important part in the lives of ordinary Australians. The level of material prosperity has remained high for many years. Except for brief periods of major economic depression in the 1890s and 1930s, unemployment has been kept at a low level. No large section of Australian society is so underprivileged or depressed that its condition arouses a passionate desire for radical change. Poverty does exist, but certainly not to the extent that it exists in both industrial and rural sectors of the United States and Western Europe.

Some conflict of sectional interests exists at the political and industrial level—mainly between management and trade union-organized labour. Disputes about wages, working hours and conditions are common, and strikes and lockouts occur. But thanks to a system of industrial conciliation and arbitration established in the early years of this century, they have seldom been prolonged. Outbreaks of civil disorder caused by industrial unrest are extremely rare in Australian history.

Despite its internal political stability, the Australian Commonwealth has been deeply involved in the two world wars in this century and has committed combat forces to the conflicts in Malaysia, Korea and Vietnam. But the Australian continent itself has never experienced enemy invasion, although the Japanese air force raided far-northern settlements during the second world war. Nevertheless, most Australians are proud of the reputation for efficiency, initiative and courage won by their expeditionary forces on foreign battlefields. Martial tradition remains a significant element in Australian national sentiment.

DISCOVERY AND SETTLEMENT

Australia, for long described rather meaninglessly in school geography books as the island continent, was the last great habitable land mass on earth to be surveyed, penetrated and colonized by Europeans.

Nobody can say for sure who discovered it. References to *Terra Australis*, the Great South Land, were made by geographers of the second century and many maps and manuscripts of the Middle Ages indicate a knowledge—or perhaps supposition—of its existence. Arab, Indonesian or even Chinese mariners may have sighted or landed on its northern coast centuries before the arrival of the first European ship. But there is no direct evidence of this, and it must be assumed that Portuguese were the first civilized men to make a landfall on the shores of a continent which for more than 300 years was regarded as so desolate and inhospitable that even the greedy empire-builders of the sixteenth and seventeenth centuries did not covet it.

Very probably Portuguese shipmasters exploring the archipelagos of the East Indies came within sight of the Australian coast before 1542. Torres, the Spaniard, passed through the strait between New Guinea and the mainland in 1606. The same year the Dutch East India Company ship, *Duyfken*, sailed down the west coast of Cape York peninsula; and during the next 30 years no fewer than nine Dutch navigators made voyages from which the whole northern and western coastline, from Cape York to the head of the Great Australian Bight, was roughly plotted.

In 1642, Abel Janszoon Tasman set out from Batavia to survey the extent of the continent and discovered Tasmania and New Zealand. Two years later he cruised in the north and the west, confirming the observations of his predecessors.

The English did not put in an appearance until nearly half a century later when the pirate ship, *Cygnet*, anchored off the coast north of where the little town of Broome now stands. *Cygnet's* crew included William Dampier, an intelligent and observant swashbuckler, who returned to the area some eleven years later in command of HMS *Roebuck* and for the first time carried out systematic explorations ashore.

Dampier published a fascinating and colourful account of his voyages when he returned to England. He did not much like what he saw of Australia and described its aboriginal inhabitants as 'the miserablest people on earth', but his observations of the terrain and the strange birds, animals and plants he encountered are extraodinarily accurate.

Thereafter, *Terra Australis* was ignored by Europeans for three-quarters of a century. It was too far away and, by the accounts of the early voyagers, too poor a land to be of any interest to the powers struggling for territory and trade supremacy in Asia.

In 1769 James Cook, in HMS *Endeavour*, set sail from England with a party of scientists bound for the South Seas, ostensibly to observe the transit of the planet Venus from a favourable vantage point on the island of Tahiti. The secondary object of the expedition was to determine whether or not the Great South Land was part of a super-continent extending almost from the Equator to the South Polar regions.

The astronomical assignment complete, Cook sailed south-east, circumnavigated both the North and the South Islands of New Zealand, crossed the Tasman Sea and sighted the Australian mainland on 20 April 1770. Nine days later he landed at Botany Bay, made observations, and then followed the coast northward for some 1 300 miles.

In June *Endeavour* grounded on a coral reef near Trinity Bay in North Queensland and was so severely damaged that repairs took two months. She then continued to follow the land, and turned westward through Torres Strait in August, when Cook formally proclaimed British sovereignty over the whole east coast of the continent 'from latitude 38° S to this place 10½° S'.

Two years later Cook returned to the South Seas with the ships *Resolution* and *Adventure* in an effort to discover the answer to the riddle of the Antarctic continent and was able to satisfy himself that if such a continent did exist it was not connected with the Australian mainland and lay too far south to be of any use for trade and settlement.

Cook undertook a third voyage in 1776, and by the time he met his death at the hands of hostile natives in the Sandwich Islands three years afterwards practically the whole coast of Australia had been at least cursorily explored. It remained only for Bass and Flinders to discover the existence of a strait between Tasmania and the mainland in 1798, 10 years after the first settlement had been established at Sydney Cove by Captain Arthur Phillip. Phillip commanded a fleet of eleven ships commissioned by the British Government to transport from English gaols and prision hulks some 700 convicts to the territory annexed by Cook.

On 26 January 1788 Phillip raised the Union Jack over the first encampment on the rocky shores of Port Jackson and proclaimed British sovereignty over the whole eastern half of the continent. The western half was not formally annexed until 1829 when a company of free settlers had already been established for two years on King George Sound and when further settlement was contemplated on the Swan River in the vicinity of Perth.

JOURNEY TO AUSTRALIA

Travel by Air

A journey to Australia from other continents is no longer the time-consuming —and by inference—the expensive business it was only a few years ago. These days jet aircraft travel from London to Sydney in a little more than 30 hours and from the west coast of North America in a little less than 20. Before inter-continental flying became commonplace, the fastest mail steamers travelling the shortest route took between 21 and 28 days to make the voyage from the United Kingdom to Australia.

By 1973 international airlines were flying 200 scheduled flights a week in and out of Australian airports, providing direct links with the major cities of Western Europe, North America, Asia, South Africa and New Zealand. No Australian city is today more than 48 hours travelling time from any national capital throughout the world. Supersonic flight may substantially reduce this time (for passengers willing to pay premium fares) during the next few years.

Cabin accommodation and service on passenger aircraft flying scheduled routes to Australia are generally of high standard. Differentiation between one airline and another can be made only on a basis of personal preference.

Service and accommodation on unscheduled charter flights is generally of lower standard than that provided on scheduled flights.

Where economy and time are not of paramount importance, travellers to Australia from the Northern Hemisphere should consider breaking the journey at one or more stops en route, particularly if they are not accustomed to long distance air travel. Individual reaction to factors of noise, vibration, changes in atmospheric pressure and normal living rhythms varies, but the majority of people are fatigued by flights lasting more than six or eight hours and, additionally, find some difficulty in adjusting to rapid climatic changes. Stopovers, even of short duration, reduce the physical and psychological strains of long journeys made at jet speeds.

There are at present five international airports in Australia—Sydney, Melbourne, Brisbane, Perth and Darwin. Internal air services are not specifically co-ordinated with the arrival of overseas aircraft, but their flight frequency in most cases assures that passengers bound for other destinations in Australia do not have to wait long for connecting aircraft.

Health, immigration and Customs formalities are not usually prolonged in the cases of air passengers whose travel documents are in order. The courtesy and efficiency of Australian officials compares favourably with that of their British, American and European counterparts. It should, however, be noted that the Australian authorities are more than ordinarily diligent in the enforcement of quarantine restrictions and Customs regulations affecting the importation of unacceptable literature and films.

Clothing. The strain and discomfort of travelling half around the world in a day and a half can be appreciably diminished by the selection of suitable travelling attire. It is well to remember that a long, hot summer in the Northern Hemisphere can easily be simultaneous with a long, cold winter in the Antipodes and vice versa; and that transition from one to the other is by way of the tropics.

Modern aircraft are air-conditioned to maintain constant cabin temperature and humidity, a necessity rather than a luxury, which does little to help the human body adjust to an unnaturally quick transition from, say, the climate of New York to that of Sydney or Brisbane.

Discomfort can be very considerably lessened by wearing light-weight, loosely fitting garments as basic attire and carrying a warm topcoat and pullover or cardigan jacket to alleviate the effects of a cold beginning or end to the journey. The plight of the inexperienced traveller sweltering in woollen underwear in Singapore or Nadi—or shivering in tropical kit while his baggage is being unloaded at Kingsford Smith airport in Sydney on a bitterly chilly July day—is sad indeed, but avoidable. While it is true that the Australian climate is temperate in the southern States, the cold of winter and spring months can be unpleasant if one is not suitably dressed for it.

Loosely fitting travelling slippers are a comfort on a long flight. They are well worth the space they occupy in the overnight bag or topcoat pocket.

Air Sickness. Air sickness is not nearly so common in the jet age as it was in the days of propeller-driven aircraft. The jets climb quickly and cruise at altitudes above ordinary air turbulence. Some people, however, are especially prone to gastric disturbances from travel motion. Most of these can be helped by the mild sedatives which are marketed under proprietary names and can be supplied by pharmacists without medical prescription.

Gratuities. Airline employees are forbidden to accept gratuities from passengers.

Travel by Sea

Twelve companies operate passenger ship services to Australian ports from the United Kingdom, Europe, North America and the Far East. Ships from Europe travel via South Africa or via the Panama Canal. According to the line, the voyage from European ports to Sydney takes from four to six weeks via South Africa and from four and a half to seven weeks via Panama. Two weeks is the average length of the voyage from Hong Kong or Japanese ports to Sydney.

Shipboard travel has much to commend it if time is not an important consideration and the traveller enjoys the leisured social life still to be found on passenger liners. It should be remembered, however, that the outright cost of passage by ship to Australia is nowadays almost as high as passage by air in excursion and economy class brackets—and higher in the first class. Incidental expenses on shipboard are naturally heavier.

Passengers embarking for Australia at British or European ports should make bookings well in advance, particularly if they are travelling on tourist class or one-class liners. Tens of thousands of migrants are travelling from Europe to Australia every year and most go by ship. Conditions for tourist class passengers can at times be trying on crowded ships carrying large numbers of children. On the Europe-Australia run service and cuisine standards are not high on ships manned by British and European crews. Passengers are much better off on runs from Far Eastern and US ports. The trans-Pacific and Asian passenger liners depend mainly on tourist traffic and do not transport large numbers of migrants.

Clothing. The liberal free baggage allowance made by all shipping lines to passengers eliminates most of the problems about wardrobe which air travellers encounter. Cabin baggage should include a range of clothing adequate to assure comfort in the extremes of climate likely to be encountered on the voyage. It should again be stressed that Australian climates range from the tropical to the temperate—the latter term implying that, while summers are warm to hot in the southern States, winters can be uncomfortably chilly if not freezingly cold as in northern Europe, America and Asia.

Gratuities. It is customary to offer gratuities to cabin and saloon stewards providing efficient personal service during the voyage.

FORMALITIES FOR ENTRY INTO AUSTRALIA

PASSPORTS AND VISAS

Citizens of New Zealand and citizens of other Commonwealth countries who have been granted permission to reside indefinitely in New Zealand do *not* require passports or visas for travel to Australia *direct from New Zealand.*

Citizens of Commonwealth countries and Eire, who are of European descent do *not* require *visas*, but on arrival should hold valid passports, be in sound health, of good character and be able to support themselves. Citizens of Cyprus, Malta, Mauritius and residents of the Seychelles Islands require an entry authority similar to a visa.

Holders of Commonwealth diplomatic or official passports and their spouses or dependent relatives do not require visas whether travelling to Australia officially or privately.

All other people must have a valid travel document and a visa which is obtainable from the nearest Australian or British Government representative. Visas indicate the authorized length of stay. Applications for extensions may be made at any office of the Department of Immigration in Australia.

Visas are issued free to all British subjects requiring them, diplomatic personnel on official business, United Nations and Red Cross officials, wives of Australian servicemen and ex-servicemen, assisted passage migrants, refugees travelling under the auspices of the United Nations High Commissioner for Refugees and nationals of the following countries:

> Austria; Belgium; Brazil; Federal Republic of Germany; Finland; France; Greece; Iceland; Israel; Italy; Japan; Liechtenstein; Denmark; Luxembourg; Mexico; Monaco; The Netherlands; Norway; The Philippines; Portugal; Spain; Sweden; Switzerland; Turkey; United States of America; Yugoslavia.

Students People other than British subjects of European descent must seek approval from an Australian Government representative before enrolling in an educational institution. Students are normally admitted for an initial period of 12 months.

Transit Non-British people (whether of European or non-European descent), citizens of Malta, Cyprus and Mauritius, residents of the Seychelles Islands and British subjects of non-European descent (New Zealand citizens of Maori descent excluded), must have a valid transit visa, passport endorsement or Letter of Authority issued by an Australian or British Government representative. Except for stateless people or nationals of communist countries, transit visas are not required for people who are direct transit passengers travelling from one country to another via Australia in the same vessel, or who, when travelling by air, depart within 72 hours.

Tourist Visas A person who intends to visit Australia solely as a tourist may obtain a tourist visa immediately on completion of a simple application form and production of evidence of having paid for a return or onward ticket, a valid passport and a declaration that he or she has sufficient funds to support a stay in Australia. Normally, an entry permit for up to three months is granted, but applications for a longer stay will be considered on merit. Holders of tourist visas are not permitted to accept employment in Australia.

The time which may elapse between application and issue of a visa varies considerably from country to country. Many visas are issued on the same day if all relevant documents are available but residents of Communist countries may have to wait from about three months to two years for the visa to be issued. This is generally because exit permits etc from their own countries are not forthcoming and if visas to enter Australia were issued too soon they would have expired before the traveller arrived in Australia.

HEALTH REQUIREMENTS

Persons over the age of 12 months arriving in Australia must be vaccinated against smallpox *unless they have come from Canada or the United States after having spent at least 14 days in one or both of those countries; or unless they have travelled by sea for 14 days.*

Visitors from areas in which cholera is endemic (eg India, Pakistan, Indonesia and South-East Asia generally) must be inoculated against cholera.

Visitors from Central Africa and the north of South America must be inoculated against yellow fever.

Travellers by sea undergo a cursory examination of hands, forearms and face within 24 hours of berthing in the first Australian port. This examination is carried out either by the ship's doctor or by a Commonwealth medical officer where the vessel has no doctor. Travellers are also required to tender their current international medical card with its record of inoculations etc or documents relating to exemption.

Travellers entering the country by air must produce their international health cards before going to Immigration and Customs. International aircraft are treated with an insecticide spray on touchdown at the first international airport they reach in Australia.

Visitors who remain in Australia longer than six months are normally required to have an X-ray for TB. This is a State regulation and not a Federal one, but it is administered by the Commonwealth Health Department.

CUSTOMS REGULATIONS

Passengers to Australia by air or sea are required to make a declaration to clear Customs. Forms are supplied by the shipping or air service company. False declarations may be heavily penalized, including forfeiture of articles not correctly declared.

All goods imported are, technically speaking, subject to inspection and assessment for duty; but concessions are made which, in effect, permit visitors to import bona fide personal effects free of charge, provided those personal effects are not prohibited imports.

Duty-free personal effects include wearing apparel, jewellery and toilet articles, binoculars, cameras (still and cine), portable typewriter, portable battery-operated radio or radio-gramophone (one set not weighing more than 2 kg to each passenger aged 10 years or older), tape recorder or similar device (one recorder not weighing more than 6 kg to a family).

Personal sporting requisites and camp equipment also are admitted free. BUT *it should be noted that the importation of firearms and ammunition is restricted. All firearms and ammunition must be produced for the examining officer at the port of entry.*

Firearms and ammunition are the province of State police authorities and regulations governing admissibility vary somewhat between State and State. Visitors planning to hunt game in Australia should make specific inquiries about the admissibility of their personal sporting firearms before embarking.

Riding saddles require quarantine clearance and must be declared.

Tradesmen's hand tools and portable instruments and equipment used in their trade or profession by employed workers are admitted duty-free.

Each passenger aged 18 years or older is entitled to bring into the country duty-free: 200 cigarettes, *or* 250 g cigars *or* tobacco; *and* one litre of spirituous beverage.

Gifts and Souvenirs In addition to the concessions outlined above, each passenger aged 18 years or older may bring in duty-free $A100 worth of goods intended as gifts, and additional goods to the value of $A160 dutiable at the rate of 25 per cent of their value. These particular concessions apply to passengers under the age of 18 years if they are *not* accompanied by a parent. Where accompanied, each child is entitled to duty-free admission of $A50 worth of goods and admission of an additional $A80 worth at 25 per cent.

All goods in excess of the values above are dutiable at normal commercial rates.

It should be noted that concessions in respect of gifts do *not* apply to tobacco products, liquor, fur apparel, radios, cameras, tape recorders etc, or vehicles of any kind.

Cars and Private Aircraft Cars which are brought into Australia by a tourist or temporary resident are not subject to Customs duty or sales tax if the importer can guarantee he intends to export the car again.

This can be done in two ways. Probably the simpler is to obtain a triptyque (valid for one country) or a carnet (valid for a number of countries) from one's home country automobile association. These are issued by all countries party to the international agreement and are accepted by the Australian Customs in lieu of Customs documentation. You must obtain the triptyque or carnet before departure.

The alternative is to provide Customs documentation at entry. Two documents are required—a normal Customs entry and Form 46 which is a record of importation and subsequent exportation. The Customs entry implies either a cash or documentary guarantee (from a bank or insurance firm etc) that the vehicle will not be sold in Australia.

Private aeroplanes come under the same system of Customs entry declaration. It is advisable to check with the Australian embassy or consulate in the country of origin concerning specific regulations (eg recognition of pilots' licences etc).

Prohibited Imports Included in a long list of imports prohibited by Australian law are: Dangerous weapons (including spring-bladed knives, swordsticks, coshes etc); essences of wines and spirituous liquors; narcotic drugs; works or articles deemed by the Customs Department to be blasphemous, indecent or obscene; plants and plant products subject to quarantine; animals and animal products; birds; insects; seeds; semen; germ cultures etc.

It should be noted that importation of books and cinematograph films are subject to strict censorship regulations and that Australian Customs standards are more conservative than those of most other nations of the Western world.

Travellers requiring Customs information more detailed than that given above can obtain it from:

Europe: The Australian Customs Representative,
Canberra House,
Maltravers Street, off Arundel Street,
Strand, LONDON, WC2, UK.

America: The Australian Customs Representative,
636 Fifth Avenue,
NEW YORK, N.Y. 10020 USA.

Asia: The Australian Customs Representative,
Sankaido Building
9–13 Asasaka 1—Chome,
MINATO-KU, TOKYO, JAPAN.

Australia: The Collector of Customs at the State capital city of entry; or at Darwin, NT.

CURRENCY

Australian money is in dollars and cents. Coins are issued in pieces of one cent, two cents, five cents, 10 cents, 20 cents and 50 cents. Treasury notes are issued in denominations of one dollar, two dollars, five dollars, 10 dollars, 20 dollars and 50 dollars.

A traveller to Australia may bring into the country an unlimited amount of currency of any type. Those who remain for no longer than six months are able to take out financial reserves up to the limit of the amount brought in. Provision is made to keep a check on this by a sticker attached to travellers' passports on arrival.

A person remaining in Australia for more than six months can take $100 in Australian currency out of the country. Of that amount not more than $4 should be in coin.

TRAVEL AND TOURISM

CHOOSING WHAT TO SEE AND DO

The point has already been made that Australia is an immense and diverse country offering visitors a great variety of interesting things to see and do. Even a year's carefully planned travelling would not suffice to explore all its natural beauties or traverse the full range of its elemental difference from other parts of the world. In planning an itinerary in Australia the overseas tourist is, therefore, wise to allocate priorities of interest and not try to take in too much. It is also important to take climatic factors into consideration. For instance, only those thoroughly acclimatized to the tropics should consider travelling in northern Australia in the summer months—or, for that matter, in late spring or early autumn.

The tourist industry is still relatively undeveloped in Australia and is more oriented to pleasing domestic holidaymakers than overseas visitors. However, package-deal conducted tours of scenic regions or other areas of special interest are becoming popular. There are now many to choose from. They are organized mainly by domestic airlines and tourist-coach companies in collaboration with tourist authorities and offer substantial fare and accommodation economies. The standard of service is by no means de luxe but it is efficient and provides basically comfortable travelling at cut rates.

At the time of writing there is no package-deal tour purporting to present a cross-section of the whole Commonwealth or, indeed, of any single State. The key localities from which most travellers will begin their exploration of Australia are:

SYDNEY

Climate: Warm temperate. Australia's oldest and most sophisticated city built around the shores of Port Jackson (Sydney Harbour). Several large hotels of international standard. Gay night life. Many notably beautiful surf beaches and marine resorts in or near the metropolitan area. Architecturally and historically interesting but in the process of rapid re-development. Base for short tours of the Blue Mountains, the valley and estuary of the Hawkesbury River, the South Coast, the vineyards and pasture lands of the Hunter River valley, and for many air-coach tours of sheep stations etc. Best season: Spring, early summer, autumn.

CANBERRA

Climate: Cool temperate. The carefully planned national capital with superb tree-plantations, parks and gardens. Interesting and sometimes distinguished architecture in public buildings. Beautifully situated in rolling pasture lands on the western slopes of the Great Dividing Range. Base for tours of the fascinating water storages and hydro-electric power stations of the Snowy Mountains water conservation and utilization project. Close to Mount Kosciusko National Park, winter sports resorts, densely timbered mountains, trout streams etc. Best season: Late spring, autumn.

MELBOURNE

Climate: Temperate, changeable. Regarded as the Commonwealth's financial capital. Conservative in mood and vaguely English in atmosphere. Historically and architecturally interesting, but like Sydney in the throes of re-development. Notably good restaurants. The National Arts Centre of Victoria houses a magnificent art collection in a modern gallery of unique architectural and ultilitarian merit. The Royal Botanic Gardens are rated among the finest in the world. The classic horse race, the Melbourne Cup, is run every year in early November. Melbourne is a convenient base for excursions to the historic goldfields towns of Ballarat and Bendigo and to the fine mountain scenery of the nearby ranges. The Sir Colin Mackenzie Wild Life Sanctuary near Healesville, 58 kilometres north-east, contains the finest collection of native birds and animals in Australia. Best season: Late summer, autumn.

BRISBANE

Climate: Sub tropical. A progressive city pleasantly situated about 20 kilometres from the mouth of the Brisbane River on Moreton Bay. A base for excursions to the much publicised Gold Coast beach resorts (80-100 kilometres south) and their mountainous, scenically magnificent hinterland. The Sunshine Coast, extending northward to Gympie (200 kilometres) also has fine beaches and sheltered inlets for aquatic sports. Some of Australia's most productive agricultural and pastoral land is on the Darling Downs, 130 kilometres west of Brisbane. Best season: April-November.

ADELAIDE

Climate: Warm temperate. Dry. Well planned, civically active capital of South Australia, noted for its beautifully kept parks and gardens but otherwise scenically undistinguished. It is, however, close to areas of particular interest to tourists—the picturesque vineyard areas of the Barossa Valley and the Southern Vales, the lower reaches of the Murray River with their prolific bird and animal life (paddle steamer cruises available); and the beach and fishing resorts of Kangaroo Island and the Eyre Peninsula. Adelaide is also the logical jumping-off place for sight-seeing expeditions to the Flinders Ranges, the most accessible of Australia's brilliantly coloured desert mountain chains. Best seasons: For excursions inland, May-October. For Adelaide and environs, spring and autumn.

PERTH

Climate: Warm temperate. Dry. A small, beguilingly charming city nearly 3 000 kilometres west of Australia's main centres of population, it is unrivalled as a holiday resort for people who enjoy sunshine and outdoor living. Base for trips to the great mountain and coastal forests of the South-West, a region famous for its unique wildflowers in spring and the beauty of its coastline; to the semi-arid nickel and goldfields, about Kalgoorlie (480 kilometres east) and to the spectacular Murchison Coast (500 kilometres north). Perth is also a convenient point of departure for those wishing to visit the extremely colourful iron ore country of the Pilbara, the Hamersley Ranges, and the Ord River Development project in the Kimberley cattle country (all more than 1 750 kilometres north). Best season: For Perth and the South-West, August-November. For northern areas, May-October.

HOBART

Climate: Cool temperate. Capital of the island state of Tasmania, separated from the mainland by Bass Strait where the Indian and Pacific Oceans merge. It is a small city of predominantly maritime character at the mouth of the Derwent River—still unspoiled by 20th-century 'development' although a large and lush gambling casino has recently been opened there. Has many buildings and relics of early colonial days and is close to truly unique and impressive mountain scenery. Base for excursions which can encompass the entire island in a few days. Best season: December-April.

DARWIN

Climate: Tropical. Administrative capital of the Northern Territory. A small, modern city, almost completely re-built since the second world war in which it was severely damaged by Japanese air raids. It has become extremely popular with Australian holidaymakers in winter. The tropical bush near Darwin abounds with wild life and game and the fishing in both river and coastal waters is excellent. A base for 'safari' camping tours to Arnhem Land and other interesting coast and hinterland excursions which can occupy anything from a few days to a few weeks. Its attractions appeal particularly to physically active, adventure-minded visitors. Accommodation standards in town are good—out of town primitive. Best season: May-October.

AREAS OF PARTICULAR INTEREST

GREAT BARRIER REEF

Australia's most widely publicized tourist attraction—a coral rampart off the coast of Queensland extending more than 2 000 kilometres from Torres Strait southward to below the Tropic of Capricorn. There are numerous offshore islands and cays, many of which have been developed as resorts. Recreations include swimming, scuba diving, reef and big game fishing, launch and sail-boat cruising etc. Bird and marine life is abundant. Accommodation standards vary. Access: Southern sectors from Gladstone and Rockhampton; central sections (the most popular) from Mackay and Proserpine; northern sections from Townsville and Cairns which are also bases for trips by road, rail or air into the hinterland. Domestic air services to all these centres from Brisbane, the nearest international airport, are frequent.

CENTRAL AUSTRALIA

Alice Springs, originally a small service settlement and telecommunications centre halfway between Adelaide and Darwin, has in recent years become very popular as a holiday resort. It has a magnificent winter climate and is a base for sightseeing in nearby desert mountain ranges, and at Ayers Rock, the world's largest monolith, 400 kilometres to the south west. The countryside is brilliantly colourful and supports an abundance of wild life. Numerous coach and aerial tours which visit unusual beauty spots, aboriginal mission stations and pastoral properties operate from 'the Alice' where comfortable accommodation for tourists is now available. Best season: May-October. Summer is torrid.

MURRAY VALLEY

The Murray River—Australia's 'Old Man River'—rises in the Australian Alps and flows west and south for 2 600 kilometres through a widely varied terrain to join the sea at Lake Alexandrina in South Australia. Good motor roads flank the stream from source to mouth, passing through practically every type of country to be found inland in south-eastern Australia from dense mountain forests through marshlands to treeless, arid plains. The water is stored in dams and weirs at various points to irrigate rich orchards, citrus groves, vineyards and mixed farms. Rural communities thrive in the valley and the riverbank towns are interesting, sometimes picturesque, places. Best season: March-May, September-November. (Winters are chilly and summers hot and humid.)

PUBLIC TRANSPORT

AIR SERVICES

Considering the low population density and the long distances between major cities and towns, facilities for rapid, comfortable travel within the Commonwealth are surprisingly well developed. All State capitals and most important provincial cities and towns are linked by thoroughly efficient and frequent air services every day of the week. Australians are an air-minded people and it is the rule rather than the exception to make inter-capital journeys by plane.

Only two airlines operate the interstate services—Trans-Australia Airlines, which is owned by the Commonwealth Government, and the privately owned Ansett Airlines of Australia. On trunk routes both operate modern jet aircraft as the basis of their fleets. There is little to choose between them. On a passenger-mile calculation their safety record is as high as or higher than any in the world. The standard of accommodation and personal service provided passengers, both in the air and on the ground, is excellent. (Intrastate air services are dealt with in sections devoted to the States.)

INTERSTATE RAIL SERVICES

All capital cities (with the exception of Darwin in the Northern Territory and Hobart in Tasmania) are linked by Commonwealth and State-owned railways which operate an inter-system passenger express service daily between eastern capitals, five times a week between Adelaide and Perth and twice a week between Sydney and Perth, via Broken Hill.

One of the unfortunate legacies inherited by the Commonwealth when federation of the six autonomous Australian colonies was achieved in 1901 was State rail systems each of which operated on a gauge different from that of its neighbours. Transhipment of passengers and freight was therefore necessary between one system and another. Work, however, has been proceeding with gauge unification for many years and in 1970 a standard gauge link was established between Sydney and Perth on the Indian Pacific route. The journey takes about 60 hours. Through services also run between Sydney and Brisbane, Sydney and Melbourne, and Sydney and Adelaide.

The existing inter-capital expresses are comfortable, but by no means first class or speedy when compared with the accommodation and service provided by crack European and American 'flyers'. The financial position of the Australian railways has been unsatisfactory for many years, and difficulties have been experienced in recruiting, training and holding first-class staff and labour. Competition by airways and to a lesser extent by motor coach services has cut heavily into passenger revenue.

However, train travel is much cheaper than air travel. The cost of a first-class train ticket with seat reservation and, where necessary, a sleeping berth, is roughly two-thirds that of a first-class air fare. Trains are therefore popular at holiday times and reservations for holiday periods should be made, in most cases, weeks or even months in advance. An additional disadvantage of travelling at these times is that supplementary or 'second division' expresses are made up of antiquated rolling stock. Except where economy is a prime consideration (or, perhaps, curiosity about railway conditions 40 or 50 years ago) second division expresses should be avoided.

Travellers would also be well advised to leave, where possible, the complexities of making all forms of rail reservation in Australia to tourist bureaux or private travel agencies. In most States, and particularly in Victoria, the system of reservation is intolerably ponderous.

In addition to the inter-capital, inter-system services, the Commonwealth Government Railways run a train between Port Augusta, South Australia, and Alice Springs, 1 778 kilometres north of Adelaide. The train, known as The Ghan,* runs twice a week and comprises air-conditioned day and sleeping coaches, with a number of flatcars to accommodate automobiles. The road between Port Augusta and Alice Springs is so rough that the majority of motorists, whether bound north or south, prefer to ship their vehicles over the section.

The Ghan is a tolerably comfortable train, even if something less than luxurious. Changes, caused by break of gauge, must be made at Hawker and Marree. Like the Transcontinental Express between Port Pirie and Kalgoorlie it traverses a route fascinating to those who respond to the almost hypnotic repetition of form and colour throughout great distances which so characterizes the Outback.

The Ghan has only one serious disadvantage. It runs on a cheaply engineered roadbed in country which is subject to serious flooding when the ordinary dry rivers it crosses are swollen by occasionally heavy rains. The train can be flood-bound or held up for days, or even weeks, at a time by washouts. Travelling by it always has the tang of novelty and adventure, but it cannot honestly be recommended to travellers preoccupied by time limits. (To a lesser extent the same observation applies to the Transcontinental and the Indian Pacific which from time to time are held up for long periods when heavy rains fall on the Nullabor Plain.)

MOTOR COACH SERVICES

Three major motor coach companies, Pioneer, Panther and Greyhound,

* 'Ghan', a contraction of 'Afghan'. Camel teams, usually driven by Pathans or Afghans, supplied settlers and miners in The Centre before the railway was built.

operate tourist and/or express services on various routes between Brisbane, Sydney, Melbourne, Adelaide, Perth and Darwin. Several express coaches run daily between the eastern capitals. They are the cheapest form of interstate travel. The tourist coach fares include overnight accommodation at points between the capitals.

Motor coach companies also conduct numerous package tours of Central, Northern Australia and north-western Australia during the dry season. Details of routes, schedules and fares (which usually include accommodation costs) are obtainable from all Government tourist bureaux and from travel agencies.

PASSAGES ON SHIPS

Interstate passages on overseas liners calling at major Australian ports can often be obtained. Schedules can be obtained from tourist bureaux and travel agencies.

The Australian National Line operates a thrice-weekly service between Melbourne and Devonport, Tasmania, with the 12,000-ton passenger/vehicle ferry *Empress of Australia* and a twice-fortnightly service to Tasmanian ports with the 8 500-ton *Australian Trader*

CAR RENTALS

Rent-a-car services now operate in all State capitals, most large provincial centres and major tourist resorts. Generally speaking the vehicles are recent models, well maintained and mechanically reliable, but the hirer should make a point of inspecting the car provided to spot minor malfunctions and have them adjusted, and—particularly in peak tourist season—take it for a trial run before setting out on a long journey.
Main companies are:

Avis Rent-a-Car System,
Hertz of Australia Ltd,
Budget Rent-a-Car System,
Kays Rent-a-Car,
Bewglass Empire Drive Yourself Pty Ltd (Tasmania only)

All companies offer substantial concessions for long rentals, stated mileage being included in the quoted rate. Avis offers a convenient 'fly one way, drive the other' plan in conjunction with the domestic airlines.

Hirers must be 21 years of age, and have personal reference if under the age of 25.

The 'rent-it-here, leave-it-there' system operates between all capitals (excepting Perth and Darwin) and within Tasmania. There is no charge. But if the car is left other than in eastern capital cities or Tasmanian towns, a re-positioning fee is charged. Insurance against collision damage is available.

ACCOMMODATION STANDARDS AND TARIFFS

The tourist industry in Australia is still in its infancy and the highly specialized (and expensive) luxury services provided by holiday resorts in North America, Europe and the Far East are available only at a very few establishments in the major cities. It is, however, possible to get entirely comfortable accommodation, adequate if not elaborate service, and good European cuisine in the first-class hotels and motor hotels of the State capitals, Canberra, and the main provincial centres. In these, air conditioning, telephone, radio, television, refrigeration and private toilet facilities are now standard amenities. Swimming pools are often provided by many of the better establishments for the use of their guests. Express laundry and valet services are less common. Top bracket hotels and motor-hotels provide room service and are fully licenced to serve alcoholic liquors in public rooms, restaurants and guest quarters.

The tariff scale for de luxe accommodation varies slightly between State and State and locality and locality.

There is a wide range of choice among first-class but less glamorous establishments and an even wider choice among economy bracket motels-hotels which may not be air-conditioned, provide room service etc. or have an attached restaurant.

Small private hotels, motels and guest houses offer even cheaper accommodation for the visitor travelling on a tight budget.

In most popular holiday resorts guest-houses and tourist motel tariffs are loaded in peak seasons—Christmas and Easter in the south and winter-spring in the north (May-October). Forward reservation is essential.

Off-the-beaten track enthusiasts should note that hotel and motel accommodation in remote country centres is often spartan, but the austerities and informalities of the bush pub are often mitigated by the genuine hospitality offered strangers who are not over-demanding.

HEALTH

There are few health hazards in travelling in any part of Australia. Standards of hygiene are high by world standards in the preparation of food for sale to the public, and reticulated water supplies are pure. *It is perfectly safe to drink the tap water in any Australian town*, although minor gastric upsets may be caused to sensitive people by high mineralization of the supplies in inland areas. It is quite unnecessary to exercise the great care in choosing what to eat and drink which is advisable for travellers in Central and South America, Asia, Africa and Southern Europe.

The incidence of endemic tropical diseases such as malaria, cholera, bacillary and amoebic dysentery is negligible and the extremely rare outbreaks are very quickly contained and controlled.

Visitors from cold-climate countries should guard against too much exposure to the Australian sun, particularly on beaches at whatever latitude.

Hospital and medical fees in Australia are high. Overseas visitors should seriously consider the advantages of insurance.

CLOTHING

Heavyweight clothing of the kind essential for North American, North European and North Asian winters is unnecessary except for winter sports enthusiasts; but visitors to the southern States between May and November will find a use for light woollen underwear, cardigan jackets etc, and medium-weight topcoats. Suffice to say that large areas of southern Australia experience winter frosts and cold, moist winds even at sea level. Tropical clothing of lightweight wool, cotton, etc (with a little supplementary gear in case of cold snaps) is adequate for northern Australia in any season and for southern Australia between November and early May.

Australians do not, generally speaking, dress formally—particularly in hot weather. Men wear evening kit only on special occasions of an official or ritual nature; a business suit is usually acceptable for theatre, opera, concert and private social engagements. 'Darwin rig'—dark slacks, long-sleeved shirt and tie—is now considered correct attire at even formal parties in the tropics. For day wear, shorts with three-quarter hose, long sleeved shirt with cravat or tie are approved in hot weather.

Some hotels and restaurants—usually those declining in popularity and attempting to hold an ageing and conservative clientele—require jackets and ties to be worn in the dining-room. Women are entirely free to choose the apparel which seems suitable to them for the occasion.

POINTERS FOR TRAVELLERS

Tipping Offering gratuities for service is not officially countenanced in Australia and is certainly not an inbuilt part of tourist industry economics. But tactfully offered tips are appreciated and accepted by drink and food waiters in hotels and better class restaurants. Ten per cent of the bill is adequate, but if the service has been particularly good 15 per cent is appropriate. Ship and rail terminal porters have a fixed scale of charges and hotel porters are happy with a tip of 20 cents and doormen at the more fashionable hotels and restaurants with 20 or 30 cents for calling taxis etc. Taxi drivers do not *expect* tips but appreciate a gratuity—say 10 per cent of the fare for courteous and efficient service. It is not necessary but customary to tip sleeping-car conductors on the railways. Do NOT offer tips to shop assistants, hairdressers, airline employes, public car park attendants, traffic officers and police. Do NOT tip at all if service has been unsatisfactory.

Hotel and Motel Reservations If travelling on a fixed itinerary, it is convenient to make reservations with travel agents or State Government tourist bureaux who will be able to advise fairly accurately on standards of accommodation. If not travelling on a fixed itinerary, consult the RAA official accommodation guide, a specialist publication which is revised annually but even so cannot monitor with entire accuracy changing standards due to managerial and staffing problems which plague the industry in Australia. Major hotel and motel chains have telex facilities which enable immediate confirmation of forward bookings at establishments in the group—but the association does NOT necessarily indicate uniformity of quality.

Outdoors Small bush flies are a great pest in the Australian countryside during warm weather. They do not carry disease but often greatly diminish enjoyment of a day in the open. Carry a small can of aerosol insect repellent. There are many satisfactory brands on the market, available at supermarkets and pharmacies. They are also effective protection against mosquitoes, midges and sandflies which in some areas can be troublesome.

Motoring in Australia

Motoring in settled parts of Australia does not present any particular hazards or problems for a competent overseas driver who takes the precaution of familiarizing himself with basic road rules and drives with particular caution until he has acquired the 'feel' of local traffic movement.

Because the continent is so large and so sparsely populated, Australians cannot yet afford the standard of road engineering they would, as a highly motor-minded people, like to have. The mileage of expressways and freeways in the Commonwealth is small, but the south-eastern States are served by a network of good roads, most of which are sealed and maintained in fair condition. The main inter-capital highways between Brisbane, Sydney, Melbourne and Adelaide carry a large volume of traffic. Beyond the developed south-east, however, road conditions are variable. Visitors would be well advised to make a study of the detailed touring maps available from automobile club offices or from service stations before undertaking a long journey inland or to the far north or west.

Motorist organizations affiliated with the Automobile Association of Australia are highly efficient, courteous and willing to help overseas visitors, particularly if they are members of motorist organizations in their own countries and carry the usual credentials. Route maps and reports on current road conditions are kept punctiliously up-to-date and club officers are able to help in many other ways with advice and service in the event of mechanical breakdown or other mishap.

All main routes and most secondary ones are adequately provided with filling and service stations, except in sparsely populated regions, where a careful note of mileages should be taken and a reserve of fuel carried.

Petrol is marketed in Australia in two grades—Standard (89 octane) and Extra or Super (98 octane). Price varies marginally between the States and between city and country.

Registration Visitors are exempt from the payment of vehicle registration fees during the currency of their home registration up to a maximum period of one year, but visitors importing their own cars should check on arrival to make sure that all formalities have been correctly completed, that they have the necessary documents, and that *they are covered by compulsory Third Party Insurance.*

Driving Licences In most cases, overseas driving licences, valid for the class of vehicle being driven and for a period of one year, are recognized by the Australian authorities. *It is preferable that a visitor should have an International Driving Permit*, a document which is recognized in all States and Territories. Licences or permits should be carried at all times for production on demand by the police.

Motor Vehicle Insurance Foreign insurance policies are not valid in Australia. *No vehicle may be driven or trailer or caravan towed without Third Party Insurance having been taken out.* Premiums vary according to the horsepower and classification of the vehicle. Comprehensive insurance policies in addition to Third Party Insurance are available, and motorists are strongly advised to arrange this cover.

Rules of the Road Each of the Australian States and Territories makes its own traffic regulations and driving rules. There is not yet completely uniform traffic law in the Commonwealth. Therefore it is essential that a visiting driver should obtain and study a copy of the *Highway Code* in each State or Territory in which he is travelling. Copies are available from the police and from motoring organizations. Certain rules, however, apply generally.

(**1**) Vehicles must be driven on the *left hand side of the road*, except when overtaking or where clearly marked traffic lanes are provided.

(**2**) Drivers are required to signal, *either by hand or by approved signalling device*, their intention to stop, reduce speed, or turn right. (Hand signals: To slow down or stop—upper right arm level with shoulder, forearm and hand vertically upwards outside car. To turn right—arm and hand at shoulder level extended horizontally outside car.)

(**3**) At intersections, the vehicle or vehicles *approaching on the right have right of way* but some intersections or road junctions have 'Stop' or 'Halt' signs. Obey them and proceed only if the way is clear. Other intersections have 'Give Way' signs, in which case you must give way to *all* vehicles on the road ahead.

(**4**) **Overtaking** Vehicles, other than trams, or animals going in the same direction, must be overtaken on the right, except where there are traffic lanes or the driver of the vehicle ahead has indicated his intention to turn right, in which case he may be passed on the left. *Tramcars must be overtaken on the left* and they may *not be overtaken* while they are embarking or disembarking passengers. Overtaking on intersections, bends or blind crests on main roads marked by a double line is an offence.

(**5**) **Right-hand turns** must be made by signalling intention to turn, drawing over to the right-hand side of the road *but to the left of the centre line*. Left-hand turns must be made as close as possible to the left kerb.

(**6**) **Pedestrian, school and rail crossings** are clearly marked and must be approached with care. Pedestrians have absolute right of way on any crossing.

(**7**) **Traffic control lights** are used in all cities and many towns. **Red:** Stop. **Green:** Go. **Amber** (following green): Stop. **Red and Amber together:** Prepare to go on following green. **Flashing red:** Rail crossing or other hazard—stop while flashing. **Flashing amber:** Proceed with caution.

(**8**) **Vehicle lighting** regulations vary slightly between State and State. Visitors should have their lights checked on arrival.

(**9**) **Speed Limits** (at March 1974) New South Wales and Victoria, 100 kilometres per hour, prima facie. South Australia and Queensland, 96 kilometres per hour, prima facie. Western Australia, 104 kilometres per hour, absolute. Tasmania and Northern Territory, no prescribed limit except as indicated by road sign. Australian Capital Territory, as indicated by road sign. Speed limits in built up areas (i.e. areas provided with street lighting) vary, but are usually clearly indicated by sign. Check the statutory speed limit of any city you are driving in.

(**10**) **Accidents** In the event of any accident, *the driver must stop.* Procedure in reporting varies between State and State, but if there is any personal injury, or possibility of injury or damage to the person, *the accident must be reported to the police and the insurers.*

(**11**) **Road Signs** are not standard throughout Australia, but their intention is always clear. Study the diagrams of road signs given in your copy of the *Highway Code* for the State or Territory you are driving in.

(**12**) **Parking** In general, city or town traffic authorities control parking. Regulations vary, but it is an offence to leave a vehicle on any public highway in a position which may cause obstruction to traffic. Vehicles must be parked as close as possible to the kerb or edge of the road, but in some localities angle and median strip parking is permitted. Double parking is not permitted and vehicles may not be parked within prescribed distances of 'Stop' lines, fire hydrants, intersections, safety zones, tram and bus stops etc. In the principal cities and towns there are parking time limits and, in some cases, total prohibition. In congested urban areas parking meters are usually installed. Time limits and charges are clearly indicated. Off street parking space is often provided. Be alert to observe and obey parking notices.

Left-hand Drive Vehicles may be imported temporarily by bona fide visitors and driven in all States and Territories, provided they carry a sign 'Left-hand drive' in three inch letters on a white background, in a conspicuous position at the rear of the vehicle, and are provided with approved signalling devices.

Road Dangers The road accident rate in Australia is high. Analysis has shown that a high proportion of serious accidents occur on country roads and that excessive speed for road conditions is an important contributory factor. Distances are great and fatigue causes loss of caution and judgment. Alcohol is also a cause of many accidents.

Australian drivers are, on the whole, less courteous and disciplined than they are in Great Britain, most countries of Western Europe, and the United States.

Travel in the outback

The most economical, comfortable and safe way to see the vast, sparsely populated and fascinating parts of Australia known vaguely as 'the Outback' is to travel on one of the many organized motor coach, air, or air-and-coach tours which are now run from the capital cities of all States. These tours are competently conducted and they cover regions of great scenic interest.

Most coaches are air conditioned, dust-proof and well appointed. Stopover accommodation may not always be luxurious, but it is adequate.

On the debit side, road coach tours cover long distances every day, often over bad roads. They must observe schedules, they are fatiguing and they pass through many hundreds of kilometres of country remarkable only for its desolate monotony. Where minimum outlay on transportation is not a prime consideration, a combined air-and-coach tour is preferable. Travellers with more leisure should also consider the merits of 'Safari' tours.

This section of the *Guide*, however, is addressed mainly to travellers who wish to explore the Outback on their own initiative, to taste the flavour of personal adventure and pursue their own interests in their own time. For all practical purposes, it is addressed to people who want to travel in their own or in a rented motor vehicle.

Some general observations are valid for those who plan to do their exploring mainly in Northern or Central Australia but will make the departure point of their expedition in the south-eastern States. The unmade sections of the Stuart Highway from south to north are simply not worth the trouble of driving over, unless the motorist has special interests—such as opal fossicking at Coober Pedy or Andamooka. The same comment applies to highways in Western Queensland.

In the long run it is far less expensive, in terms of vehicle deterioration alone, to freight your car on the railway from Port Augusta or Marree to Alice Springs or to rent a vehicle in Darwin.

All that can be said in favour of the unmade sections of the trans-Australian highways is that it is now practically impossible to get lost on them. Bad as they are, they carry heavy commercial traffic—and a procession of private motorists who perversely prefer to do things the hard way.

All roads marked as unsealed highways or main routes on the many tourist maps published by the major oil companies can be negotiated by conventional vehicles, except after heavy rain. But many of them are rough, dusty or stony, and entirely unsuitable for high speed cruising.

Hazards such as sharp bends, sudden dips, creek crossings etc are rarely signposted. The unpredictability of the bush signposting is a trap for the unwary. Cattle stops—in the form of barred crossings—are often constructed on main routes instead of gates and the crossing may not be flushed with the surface of the road. An approach at speed is highly dangerous.

On loose surfaces, stones thrown up by wheels can easily smash windscreens, so give other cars or trucks on the track as wide a berth as possible without leaving the formation or running the risk of damaging tyre walls on rock ledges or weather-hardened stumps concealed in sand or dust.

The speed build-up to which inexperienced drivers on straight, monotonous stretches of road are especially prone is probably the greatest single cause of accidents or serious damage to vehicles. Therefore cultivate the routine of regularly checking the speedometer, especially when the going seems to be good. Deep potholes, ledges or bad patches of sand or dust have a habit of appearing with wicked suddenness.

On no account continue to drive when feeling drowsy or when vision and judgement seem affected by mirage or by rapidly alternating bands of light and shadow on the surface of the track. Pull up and take a few minutes' rest.

If possible, avoid driving in the very early morning or late afternoon in country where kangaroos are numerous. The animals have a literally suicidal disregard of moving cars, so that any avoiding action is entirely up to the driver. 'Roos are hard to see in half light and they do most of their travelling just after dawn or just before nightfall. Even a small kangaroo can easily smash a headlight, crumple a wing or catapult through a windscreen, if hit at speed. If you think such a hazard is negligible, count the number of dead kangaroos on or beside the roads, particularly in South Australia, Western Australia, parts of the Northern Territory, and western New South Wales and Queensland.

Night driving should be avoided unless you have been over the road before and remember its idiosyncracies. Stock and—in the north—pests such as wild donkeys and horses frequent the track at night, so if you have a reason for night driving, reduce speed.

Unless thoroughly experienced in outback conditions, the motorist who averages more than 500 kilometres a day, even on main roads, is pushing his car and his luck—and probably not seeing much of the countryside anyway.

Secondary and Tertiary Roads No map can be trusted to indicate if a secondary or tertiary road is negotiable by a conventional drive vehicle. Its condition may have changed radically since the map was made. Therefore always seek local advice before setting off on a side-track. The tracks indicated on maps by dotted lines are suitable for four-wheel drive vehicles. Cross country travel is safe only for thoroughly experienced drivers and navigators.

Anywhere in inland Australia, never drive off the formation without making certain that you are not in danger of becoming stuck in sand, dust or mud.

On no account yield to the very human temptation of pulling off an abominably rutted or stony road to travel on the blissfully smooth surface of a salt or claypan—unless you can clearly see the tracks of somebody who has travelled ahead of you and got away with it, either because of luck or local knowledge. Remember that getting a car towed out of a bog in the middle of nowhere is very expensive—if it can be arranged at all.

Even the most prudent drivers occasionally get stuck in sand, or the curse of outback travelling, bulldust. Bulldust is dust as fine as talcum powder, all-pervading and diabolically dangerous if more than a few inches thick. It often masks hazards such as deep potholes, stumps and rocky bars which can smash the bottom out of a sump or break the axle of any vehicle moving faster than about 25 kilometres an hour. Slow down whenever there is sand, bulldust or mud ahead. However small the patch may appear to be don't charge it and hope to get through. Shift into low gear, travel slowly and steadily, and resist the desire to try to 'rev' out of trouble.

The most effective way to get out of deep sand is to deflate the tyres to about one half the normal pressure, or less. This greatly increases tread traction and will usually get you through a sandy patch unless you have been recklessly unobservant and run into an axle-deep soft spot. In that case you will probably have to jack up the driving wheels, dig energetically and use anything from brushwood cut from the nearest mulga clump to your spare shirts to give the tyres something to bite on. Seasoned bush motorists usually carry a block of metal or timber to provide a firm foundation for the jack and a few sacks, lengths of coir or wire netting to act as 'sand mats'. They are well worth the little space they occupy.

Blacksoil mud, often encountered after freak dry season rainfall in the Kimberley or on the plains of western New South Wales and Queensland, is even more difficult than sand to negotiate. A motorist travelling in the season when there is risk of early or late rain should always take the precaution of carrying chains. If stuck, or unable to steer the car safely on a blacksoil surface, only patience can help you. Be prepared to wait until the track has dried out sufficiently to allow you to travel. That may take anything from a few hours to a day or two, but there is nothing you can do about it.

Very few creeks or rivers crossed by outback roads are bridged or have adequate and permanent viaducts. Never attempt to cross a flowing water-course without ascertaining the depth and the nature of the streambed. Where the water is likely to cover the exhaust but not likely to wet spark plugs or distributor, a length of rubber hose attached to the exhaust and fixed so that its end will not submerge often assists in making a critical crossing.

If stalled in deep water it sometimes works to remove the spark plugs, engage low gear, and use the starter motor to get you out—provided the engine and starter motor are not submerged. But only bad luck or carelessness will get you into situations where such radical methods need be tried.

Scrupulous servicing of vehicles travelling long distances on outback roads pays handsomely. Grease and oil should be changed at half the normal intervals. Bulldust and sand are insidious enemies of the internal combustion engine. If driving a car with an air-cooled motor check the air filter daily to see that it has not become clogged. Be meticulous in checking radiator levels and the circulation of water-cooled motors.

Beware of road-trains, particularly in the cattle country of the north. Don't attempt to pass one until the driver gives an all clear signal.

Preparing the car Anyone who starts a motoring trip in the outback with a car in anything less than first class mechanical order is asking for trouble. Engine, transmission, steering, brakes, tyres, electrical circuits, cooling system and fuel lines should be thoroughly checked and all worn or suspect parts replaced. Furthermore, the more completely the car can be made dust-proof the happier you are likely to be on your journey.

If intending to travel off main roads, fitting a steel plate to protect the sump is a worthwhile precaution. A kangaroo guard or 'bull-bar' to protect the radiator and wings can also be attached to most cars satisfactorily. They provide cheap insurance, and are used by almost all old hands who drive in kangaroo country or where wandering stock could be encountered at night.

In making preparations, remember that in the really remote parts of the country there may not be a repair garage, a service station, or even a refuelling point, in hundreds of miles. Even a minor accident can be at worst dangerous and at best uncomfortable—and expensive if you have to call for help to get moving again.

Do not on any account undertake a long trip outback unless at least one member of the party is competent to diagnose the more common mechanical malfunctions of a car and carry out running repairs.

This means that you must carry an adequate tool kit and a reasonable range of spare parts such as plugs, points, fuses, headlight globes, top and bottom radiator hoses, gaskets, fan belt and a fully charged extra battery. A liberal length of tow rope, a spare wheel with sound tyre, a second spare tyre and tyre repair and changing gear are essentials. So are a compact shovel, axe and short crowbar.

Normal fuel consumption varies greatly according to terrain and road conditions. Never make 'fine' calculations of how far you will travel on a full petrol tank. On really lonely roads carry enough spare fuel in metal containers to give you an extra 320 kilometres range under normal running conditions. *Never carry extra fuel in a plastic container.*

A supply of water for the radiator and a small quantity of distilled water for the battery cells are, of course, obvious necessities in dry country.

Emergencies A mechanical breakdown which cannot be repaired on the spot is the greatest inconvenience which an outback motorist can experience. Barring violent collision or capsize, it can also be the greatest danger.

If a breakdown occurs on a road classified as primary or secondary on a reliable tourist map (or something more precise), there is little cause for worry on grounds of personal safety. In an hour or two—or in exceptional circumstances, a day or two—some other vehicle is bound to come along. The danger occurs on tertiary tracks where traffic is very infrequent and in hot, dry weather. The risk can, however, be minimized or eliminated if certain rules are observed.

1 If your map indicates that a region is sparsely settled and you are in any doubt about it carrying daily traffic, seek competent advice before setting out. Police and station owners are helpful. *Inform them where you are going and when you expect to arrive. Report in when you do arrive.* If you don't turn up, a search will be made after reasonable time has elapsed.

2 Carry enough drinking water in a secure container for at least three or four days even under conditions of extreme heat—and if anything goes wrong, ration it from the start. Allow at least 1½ litres a day per person, preferably more.

3 Do not under any circumstances abandon your vehicle. A car is far easier to find in the desert than a man—both from the air and on the ground.

4 Don't move about in the heat of the day. Remain as motionless as possible in any available shade to conserve body fluids. Heat thirst can be relieved by adding a small quantity of salt to part of the water ration, or by sucking a pebble. If you feel you *must* be active, confine your activity to the cool hours of the morning or evening.

5 Resist the temptation to go looking for water unless you are an experienced bushman, know where to look, can accurately gauge your own physical capacity, and know you can find your way back.

Observe these rules rigidly and the chance of suffering more than a scare and some discomfort from a breakdown are remote. However, in some circumstances it may be impossible to observe all rules. For instance, a capsize might cause the loss of reserve water. In this case, remember that there is water in the radiator of the car and that you will drink the foul stuff gladly when you are thirsty enough.

If the water situation is really desperate, and there is a dry creekbed nearby, try digging a deep hole in the sand of any likely looking depression. (Kangaroos often dig for water and their scratchings are always a pointer to where to look.) Small pools often occur in solid rock outcrops. Thicker vegetation than usual indicates the presence of water in arid regions.

Another emergency procedure which is tedious but effective is to dig a neat hole about one metre deep and at least one metre in circumference, place a billy can or similar container in the centre of the hole and firmly pack around it any live vegetable matter you can gather—mulga leaves, spinifex, saltbush etc. Stretch a sheet of plastic material as smoothly as possible across the top of the hole and secure it tightly with sand, rocks or anything that comes to hand. Then gently weight the centre of the stretched plastic with a pebble, directly above the billy can. The heat of the sun will distill the moisture from the live vegetable matter, water will condense on the under side of the plastic sheet, gently run down and drip into the can. With any sort of luck you should be able by this method to distill more than half a litre of potable water every 24 hours.

Finding the Way Anyone who intends to travel on tertiary or station roads should have reliable maps and a reliable compass. Know how to use them—and make a habit of using them. Sometimes it is difficult in the back country to determine the surveyed route amid a confusion of stock pads and old wheel tracks leading off in all directions. Remember that at some time or other a mechanical grader has probably been put over the 'road' and it is not hard to detect the characteristic marginal ridges a grader blade leaves. If in any doubt at all, never depart far from the graded line. Where the going is not clear, check your direction of travel at regular intervals and keep an eye on the speedometer and the fuel gauge. Never be tempted to 'drive blind' beyond the point of no return as indicated by your fuel reserves.

General Equipment Much of the pleasure of outback travel depends on the traveller being equipped to camp for a day or two in some attractive place, or to spend a night in the open beside the car without undue discomfort. There can be no detailed rules about what to take and what not to take. Everyone has his own ideas about what constitutes camp comfort, but balance the labour of unloading and loading gear against the benefit you are likely to get from the use of elaborate equipment. However hot it may be by day, desert nights can be bitterly cold, so carry warm clothing and bedding.

It should go without saying that no long distance motorist should be without an adequate first aid kit, and if untrained in first aid techniques should keep a small, *modern* manual of directions in some handy place such as the glove box.

A cool drink is a great luxury on a long, hot, dusty drive. Most outback people carry a stout canvas water bag attached to the front of the car as high as possible so as to avoid damage from flying stones. Evaporation keeps the water at a pleasantly cool temperature, but it is well to remember that water wastage from a bag is fairly high. A compact foam plastic (not metal) ice container, large enough for canned liquids such as beer or fruit juice, is a luxury in which even the hardiest outback motorists these days indulge.

Dangers Off the Track No warm blooded animals native to Australia are dangerous to man, but in the north buffalo and range cattle (which are, to all intents and purposes, wild) should be treated with caution. They should not on any account be approached closely on foot.

Venomous snakes are the only denizens of the Australian wilds which are really dangerous. The snake population of the continent is probably fairly high, so that every bush walker and camper should know how to minimize the risk of snakebite and how to treat it if it occurs. The basic rules are:

1 Wear adequate protection for the feet and lower legs if walking in undergrowth and long grass.

2 Watch where you are going and where you are putting your hands, particularly when gathering wood for the campfire or any other purpose.

3 Don't move about camp at night with bare feet and legs. Snakes are night travellers.

4 If you see a snake, leave it alone unless you are quite certain you know how to deal with it—and that certainly is justified only after you have had some expert instruction and experience. Most snakes are just as scared of you as you are of them and bite only when molested. Only one species, the taipan found in north-eastern Australia and New Guinea, deserves its reputation of being aggressive. Fortunately, taipans are not a numerous species. Their venom is lethal, they are large and their fangs are long. Another species, the death adder, is a nasty customer—not because it is aggressive but because it is protectively coloured and sluggish. It won't be bothered to get out of the way. The best way to clear away any snakes that may be concealed in the vicinity of a campsite is to 'beat about the bush' vigorously. Snakes have no external ears and sense approaching danger by terrestrial vibration and sight.

5 If bitten, don't panic. Kill the snake if possible to aid certain identification of the species. Clean the excess venom from the wound, using spittle or urine if water is not available. If bitten on a limb, apply a tourniquet tightly between the wound and the heart and loosen it for a half minute every 20 minutes to prevent atrophy. Promote free bleeding by sucking the bite vigorously. Keep as quiet as possible. Don't take alcoholic stimulants. Get medical help as soon as you can. There are effective antivenenes for all types of snake venom, and bush aid posts and hospitals stock them.

Those who have a morbid fear of snakes—and there are many people who have—can take some consolation in the thought that death from snakebite is very rare in Australia. The careless wanderer in the Australian bush is in infinitely less danger of coming to an untimely end than the inattentive driver on any Australian road.

Much the same observation could be made, and with equal truth, about the danger of sharks in all Australian waters and of crocodiles and poisonous creatures like stone-fish and sea wasps in tropical waters. Still, the danger does exist and only the foolish ignore it.

Do not swim anywhere, particularly in estuarine waters, without taking reliable local advice about possible danger. Sea bathing is inadvisable anywhere in the Australian tropics during 'the wet', except in protected enclosures. In the temperate zone the shark danger is highest in late summer and autumn, especially in deeply indented coastal inlets.

Bushfire Risks In southern States restrictions are placed on the lighting of fires anywhere in the open air during the hot, dry summer months. For most of the time it is legal to light fires in prepared fireplaces at picnic and camping spots, or in trenches at least 75 cm deep in cleared areas where prepared fireplaces are not available. Some days, however, are declared days of total fire ban.

It is the duty of travellers to inform themselves of fire restrictions. Heavy penalties are imposed for breach of the law—with complete justification. *The greatest danger in the Australian bush is fire.* Recklessness and carelessness by travellers on the roads and in the bush has cost the country scores of lives and hundreds of millions of dollars in property and stock losses.

Observe meticulously the well publicized rules about lighting fires in the open. They are necessary rules. They do not err on the side of over-caution.

Never, anywhere or at any time in populated areas or out of them, build a fire larger than is necessary to cook your food or keep you warm. And never leave a campsite with a fire still burning. Extinguish it, or it may end up extingushing you or some innocent person.

If caught on the road by fire, don't panic, leave the vehicle and run for it — unless you can see an absolutely secure refuge. Close the windows, cover yourself with any protective fabric available, crouch on the floor and wait until the fire front has passed. This takes only about half a minute in the case of grass fires and rarely more than three or four minutes in undergrowth fires. Your tyres may catch fire in this time, but it is extremely unlikely that your petrol tank will explode or the interior trim of the car ignite. When the front has passed, get out of the vehicle and stay on burnt-over ground. Observe these rules and your survival without serious injury is highly likely.

Courtesy in the Bush Once upon a time outback people were noted for their hospitality to travelling strangers. That came to an end with the advent of the mass produced cars and the creation of a network of motor roads.

The nature of outback people hasn't changed—but they are heartily tired of tourists battening on their good nature, causing loss of stock or property damage through carelessness or ignorance or sheer lack of consideration.

There are certain Do's and Don'ts to observe if you want courteous treatment and co-operation.

DO remember that lonely stations are not roadhouses where you can demand to buy petrol, fill up with water, or get yourself pulled out of a bog. If you are in real trouble, explain your position courteously and you will get help. Offer tactfully to pay for the commodity or service you require, but keep in mind the fact that you haven't got the *right* to buy it.

DO make a point of leaving gates as you found them—open or shut as the case may be. Controlling the pasturage of stock is an essential part of a station manager's business. A gate left open when it should be closed can result in unnecessary hard work for the station workers or stock losses.

DO make a point of considering the interests of the man through whose property you may be passing by reporting stock at an empty trough or a windmill which may have broken down. Report seemingly recent damage to fences, or sick or injured stock.

DON'T shoot on any station property without first having obtained permission—and don't resent it if permission is refused. The station manager or owner has probably had bitter experience with trigger-happy passers-by.

DON'T fail to ask permission to camp anywhere near homesteads. The courtesy is appreciated, and you may well be offered reciprocal courtesy and information which will allow you to see much more in the locality than you would otherwise have seen.

DON'T forget that station roads are private property and you should have permission to travel on them.

DON'T enter native reserves without permission from the appropriate authorities. Aborigines appreciate their privacy just as keenly as white men, and their reserve is their home.

The Australian Outback is enormous—and very, very empty—but remember you don't own it.

Finally, a personal appeal to all outback travellers, seasoned or unseasoned. Please refrain from disfiguring even the unfriendly face of the desert with hard garbage. Observe and reflect on the state in which yahoos on wheels have left even the most beautiful oases in the Never Never.

THE STATES
AND
TERRITORIES

Australian Capital Territory

When Federation of the Australian States was achieved in 1901, the Constitution provided for the establishment of a Seat of Government on a site to be selected in New South Wales, at a distance of more than 160 kilometres from Sydney.

After prolonged investigations, an area of highland on the western slopes of the Great Dividing Range about 310 kilometres from Sydney and 660 kilometres from Melbourne was chosen, and in October 1909 a total of 235 000 hectares was transferred from State to Commonwealth jurisdiction. In 1915 a further area of 23 200 hectares on the shores of Jervis Bay was ceded to the Commonwealth to provide it with independent control of seaport access. These two tracts of land now constitute Australian Capital Territory.

CANBERRA

(Population 156 334)

Australia's capital, Canberra, is built on an undulating plain in an amphitheatre of the Australian Alps, 309 kilometres by road south-west of Sydney. The Molongolo River, a tributary of the Murrumbidgee, intersects the city and has been dammed to create Lake Burley Griffin, now one of the most beautiful features of an urban complex which has been landscaped with great ingenuity and at great expense to exploit the advantages of a superb natural setting.

Mountains within the boundaries of the Australian Capital Territoty include three peaks above 1 800 metres and two above 1 500 metres. The climate is dry, with a mean annual rainfall of 560 millimetres. It is warm to hot in summer, and cold and bracing in winter. Rainfall in the mountain catchment area on which the city depends for its water supply is considerably higher than in the valley.

Canberra was conceived and developed as a seat of national government and administration—a showplace and a symbol of Australian creative talents. Its architecture and its atmosphere are unique and stimulating. Of all Australian cities it is the most calculated, the most self-conscious, and the most handsome.

Its population is growing more rapidly than that of any other city in Eastern Australia (12½ per cent a year) and it is expected that 250 000 people will be living in the A.C.T. by 1984. To cope with the expected increase, a multi-million dollar development project is under way at Woden Town Centre, 10 kilometres south-west of the present centre of the city. A second satellite city, Belconnen, has been built 10 kilometres to the north-west.

Extraordinary care has been lavished on the development of public parks, gardens and recreation areas. More than two million native and exotic trees have been planted in the streets and reserves of the city and its suburbs. The area was originally cleared pasture land and its appearance has undergone complete transformation in little more than a decade. Since 1957 planning and supervision have been solely the responsibility of the National Capital Development Commission.

Service and light industries have grown vigorously in the A.C.T. in the last few years, but government in all its aspects is still the prime reason for

CANBERRA
MILES
KILOMETRES
0
½
1
CANBERRA COLLEGE OF ADVANCED EDUCATION
SOUTHWELL PARK TENNIS COURTS
CANBERRA RIDING CLUB
CANBERRA RACECOURSE
SHOWGROUND
DRIVE-IN THEATRE
Commodore
Canberra Lakes Carotel
Horse Era Museum
Billabong Park
YOWANI GOLF LINKS
Clubhouse
SPORTS GROUND
Travelodge
Noah's Inn
Y.H.A. HOSTEL
BRUCE
LYNEHAM
DOWNER
WATSON
HACKETT
DICKSON
O'CONNOR
AINSLIE
TURNER
BRADDON
REID
CAMPBELL
RUSSELL
ACTON
CITY
City Hill
PARKES
ARANDA
Mt Majura 2920'
Lookout
Pines
Girl Guide Association Camp
Mt Ainslie 2762'
Steep Grade
Tip
RIFLE RANGE
RIFLE CLUB
Woolshed
Black Mountain 2664'
TV Transmitters
Black Mountain Lookout
BOTANIC GARDENS
PICNIC AREA
AUSTRALIAN NATIONAL UNIVERSITY
Tourist Bureau
Motor Village
Dickson Swimming Pool
Downer Shops
Watson Shops
Hackett Shops
Dickson Shops
Lyneham Shops
O'Connor Shops
Ainslie Shops
Canberra North
"Rex at Canberra"
Aston Inn
All Saints Church
St Patrick's Church
Kurrajong Pt
Black Mountain Pen
Acacia Inlet
WESTON PARK
COMMONWEALTH NURSERY
Water Police
Tarcoola Reach
Yarramundi Reach
Lake Burley Griffin
General Bridge's Grave
Duntroon
SPORTS GROUND
Sullivans
Jamison Centre
BELCONNEN WAY
HAYDON DRIVE
WEETANGERA RD
ARCHIBALD ST
STIRLING AVE
NORTHBOURNE AVENUE
BARRY DRIVE
CLUNIES ROSS STREET
BLACK MTN DRIVE
LADY DENMAN DRIVE
DRYANDRA STREET
MONASH DRIVE
FAIRBAIRN AVENUE
LIMESTONE AVE
CONSTITUTION AVE
PARKES WAY
LONDON CIRCT
COMMONWEALTH AVE
WAKEFIELD AVE
MACARTHUR AVE
MORPHETT ST
COWPER ST
MAJURA ST
ANTILL ST
MELBA ST
SWINDEN ST
BRADFIELD ST
HIGINBOTHAM ST
WINDEYER ST
KNOX ST
PHILLIP ST
MADIGAN ST
MACKENZIE ST
HAWDON ST
OFFICER CRES
TYSON ST
BONNEY AVE
DUFFY ST
FOVEAUX ST
PATERSON ST
EBDEN ST
CHISOLM ST
WOLSELEY DR
DONALDSON ST
AINSLIE AVE
CURRONG ST
CORANDERRK ST
ANZAC PDE
BLAMEY CRES
WHITE CRES
TRUSCOTT ST
GENERAL BRIDGES DR
GIRRAHWEEN ST
IPIMA ST
COOYONG ST
MASSON ST
CONDAMINE ST
DAVID ST
MILLER ST
BANKSIA ST
BOROONIA DRIVE
SCRIVENER ST
BIGALOW ST
MACKENNAL ST
WATTLE ST
Goodwin St
Dumaresq St
Davenport
Blacket St
Dickson
Atherton
A'Beckett St
Irvine St
Rivett St
Maitland St
Aspinall St
Dunsmore St
Tate St
Moorhouse St
Clianthus St
Banambila St
Wangara St
Wattle
BINDUBI ST
BINDEL ST
BANDJALONG CRES
Mirning Ct
Beraba
Walu St
BOWMAN ST
TLETON CRES
Holmes Cr
Hopkins
Rd
6
3
23

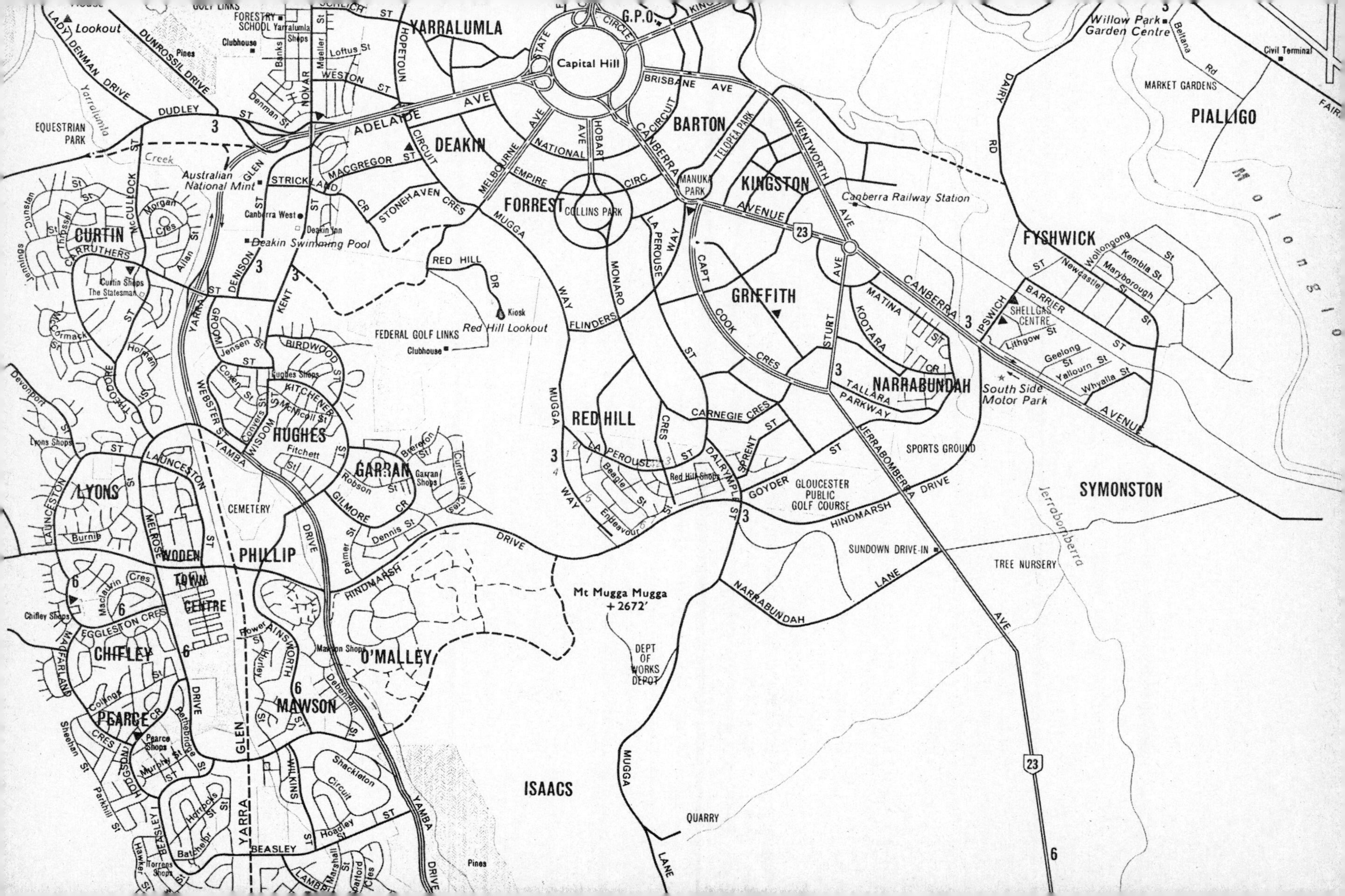

Lookout
LADY DENMAN DRIVE
DUNROSSIL DRIVE
Pines
FORESTRY SCHOOL
Clubhouse
Yarralumla Shops
Banks
Mueller St
Loftus St
WESTON ST
NOVAR
HOPETOUN
YARRALUMLA
G.P.O.
CIRCLE
STATE
Capital Hill
BRISBANE AVE
Willow Park Garden Centre
Beltana Rd
Civil Terminal
MARKET GARDENS
PIALLIGO
DAIRY RD
Molonglo
EQUESTRIAN PARK
Yarralumla
DUDLEY ST
Denman St
ADELAIDE AVE
CIRCUIT
DEAKIN
BARTON
TELOPEA PARK
WENTWORTH AVE
Creek
Australian National Mint
GLEN
STRICKLAND
MACGREGOR ST
NATIONAL
HOBART AVE
CANBERRA
CIRCUIT
EMPIRE
MELBOURNE AVE
CIRC
MANUKA PARK
KINGSTON
Canberra Railway Station
AVENUE
McCULLOCK
Morgan Cres
Canberra West
Deakin Inn
Deakin Swimming Pool
STONEHAVEN CRES
CR
FORREST
COLLINS PARK
MUGGA
LA PEROUSE
WAY
23
FYSHWICK
Wollongong
Kembla St
Newcastle
Maryborough St
Dunstan
Jennings
Thrussel
CURTIN
CARRUTHERS
Allan St
DENISON
3
KENT
RED HILL DR
MONARO
CAPT COOK CRES
GRIFFITH
MATINA
KOOTARA
CANBERRA
IPSWICH
BARRIER
SHELLGAS CENTRE
Lithgow
Geelong St
Yallourn St
Whyalla St
Curtin Shops
The Statesman
GROOM
YARRA
Kiosk
Red Hill Lookout
FLINDERS
FEDERAL GOLF LINKS
Clubhouse
STURT
NARRABUNDAH
TALLARA PARKWAY
South Side Motor Park
AVENUE
McCormack
Holman
Jensen St
BIRDWOOD ST
Hughes Shops
KITCHENER
McNicoll St
THEODORE
Devonport
Cohen St
Conyers St
WISDOM
WEBSTER ST
HUGHES
MUGGA WAY
RED HILL
CARNEGIE CRES
SPRENT ST
Lyons Shops
LAUNCESTON
YAMBA
Fitchett
Brereton St
Curlewis Cres
GARRAN
Garran Shops
Robson St
LA PEROUSE
Red Hill Shops
DALRYMPLE ST
JERRABOMBERRA DRIVE
SPORTS GROUND
GOYDER
GLOUCESTER PUBLIC GOLF COURSE
HINDMARSH DRIVE
SYMONSTON
Jerrabomberra
LYONS
CEMETERY
GILMORE CR
Beagle St
Endeavour
Burnie
MELROSE
WODEN
TOWN
CENTRE
PHILLIP
DRIVE
Palmer St
Dennis St
SUNDOWN DRIVE-IN
TREE NURSERY
Maclaurin Cres
Chifley Shops
EGGLESTON CRES
HINDMARSH
Mt Mugga Mugga +2672'
NARRABUNDAH LANE
AVE
MACFARLAND
CHIFLEY
Fower
AINSWORTH
Hurley
Mawson Shops
O'MALLEY
DEPT OF WORKS DEPOT
Collings
PEARCE
CR
Pethebridge St
MAWSON
Debenham
Sheehan St
CRES
Pearce Shops
Murphy St
HODGSON
GLEN
WILKINS
Shackleton Circuit
ISAACS
MUGGA
Parkhill St
BEASLEY
Hawker St
Torrens Shops
Hotchkiss St
Batchelor
YARRA
Hoadley
Marshall St
Bradford Cres
LAMBERT
YAMBA DRIVE
Pines
QUARRY
LANE
6

Canberra's privileged civic existence. Tourism, however, has become very important. It is estimated that about 1 000 000 non-official visitors come to see the national capital every year and their presence is beginning to inject an element of informality and vitality into the hitherto constrained and rigidly stratified social life of the resident community.

Spring and late autumn are the seasons in which to see Canberra in its most colourful and charming moods—although both are apt to be windy.

HISTORY Dr Charles Throsby was the first European to explore the locality. During his Lake George expedition of 1820 he followed the course of the Yass River, named Limestone Plains and crossed into the present Territory. The following year, he passed over the site of the future city and reached the Murrumbidgee River between Pine Island and the Point Hut crossing. His overseer, Wild, examined the country for its pastoral possibilities in 1823 and may have introduced stock into the valley, although this is not authenticated.

Robert Campbell, merchant, banker and pastoralist, received a grant of 4 000 acres of land in 1825 and established Duntroon station where the Royal Military College, founded in 1911, now stands.

The name Canberra, widely held to be the local aboriginal term for 'meeting place', was first used about 1836. Other spellings were Kamberra, Kembury and Canberry. The first resident landholder in the district was John Macpherson (a son of the Victorian Premier in 1869-70), who received a grant of 640 acres as a reward for capturing a bushranger on Black Mountain.

When the land on which the city is now built was acquired by the Commonwealth Government in 1911, it contained only two small villages, Hall and Tharwa, which served a sparsely populated pastoral area. The site had been decided only after prolonged wrangling between State and Federal authorities. Albury, Armidale, Bombala, Tumut, Lake George and Orange-Bathurst had been considered and rejected. The commission in charge of selection then proposed Dalgety near the Victorian border to the south, but again no agreement could be reached until 1908 when the actual area to be ceded was finally chosen and defined. The townsite was selected the following year and an international competition for a city plan was won by the distinguished American architect, Walter Burley Griffin, of Chicago.

In 1913, the name Canberra emerged from thousands of ingenious suggestions —which included Sydmeladperbrisho and Wheatwoolgold! Construction of the first public buildings was begun the same year and in 1914 a rail service for goods was opened between Sydney and the embyro capital. War delayed development for many years. It was not until 1927 that the Federal Parliament could transfer from its temporary seat in Melbourne.

Depression and the second world war slowed down building construction, but siteworks continued steadily over the next 20 years. The rate of progress has been spectacular since the mid 1950s.

Notable Buildings and Memorials

Australian War Memorial, east of the central city, is Canberra's greatest single tourist attraction. More than 750 000 people visit it every year. The cloisters, galleries and halls surrounding the Pool of Reflection in the courtyard contain a vast and fascinating collection of relics, paintings, sculptures, photographs and records of the wars in which Australian soldiers have served, from the Sudan campaign to the present day. The central Hall of Memory has beautiful mosaic walls and stained glass windows and contains a Roll of Honour, inscribed with the names of more than 100 000 servicemen killed in action or died on active service. Open 9 am to 4.45 pm daily.

Australian-American Memorial, at the head of King's Avenue, is an aluminium spire of 79 metres with an eagle superimposed. It commemorates the contribution of the people of the United States to the defence of Australia during the second world war.

Parliament House, home of the Commonwealth Parliament since 1927 (soon to be transferred to a new building on another site). The imposing entrance, King's Hall, contains paintings of famous Australian politicians and a painting of the opening of the first Parliament to meet in Canberra. Conducted tours are available when neither the House of Representatives nor the Senate is in session. Only King's Hall is open to the public during sittings.

National Library, a notably beautiful and dignified building of contemporary design overlooking Lake Burley Griffin near Commonwealth Bridge. It is Australia's first great national reference library, housing more than one million volumes, vast collections of newspapers and periodicals, microfilm records, documents of historical value, maps, photographs, cinema films and sound recordings. Open 9 am to 10 pm Monday to Friday. Saturday, Sunday and public holidays, 9 am to 4.45 pm.

Australian Academy of Science, Edinburgh Avenue, an unusual building featuring a copper dome 46 metres in diameter resting on arches set in an annular pool. The interior is not generally open for inspection. The Academy was founded by Royal Charter in 1954.

Institute of Anatomy, opposite the Academy of Science, houses two museums, one featuring specimens of Australian fauna and the other exhibits of the culture of the Australian aborigines and the natives of Papua and New Guinea. Open 9 am to 5 pm Monday to Friday, 2 pm to 5 pm Saturday and Sunday.

St John the Baptist Anglican Church (and adjacent schoolhouse, now a museum of ecclesiastical and educational history), Constitution Avenue, is built of volcanic material from the hills to the north, Black Mountain sandstone and cedar from the north coast of New South Wales. Consecrated in 1845 by Bishop Broughton.

Acton House, now used as courthouse and police station, was erected about 1826.

Government House, Yarralumla, official residence of the Governor-General. Not open for inspection, but a view of the house and grounds may be obtained from a point near the entrance gates.

Blundell's Cottage, Wendouree Drive, a restored settler's cottage dating from 1858 is on its original site in a small reserve. Furnished as a museum. Open for inspection daily from 2 pm to 4 pm and on Wednesday mornings.

Duntroon Station Homestead, in grounds of Royal Military College.

All Saints' Church, Ainslie, erected in 1958 from carved masonry preserved after the demolition of the Mortuary Railway Station at Rookwood, Sydney. The Mortuary Station was built in 1886.

Places of Interest

Lake Burley Griffin. Created in 1964 by the damming of the Molonglo River at Yarralumla. The shoreline totals 36 kilometres and the average depth of water is 5 metres. The lake waters, which have been liberally stocked with trout, are used for rowing and sailing, but swimming is inadvisable. Power boats are prohibited. Development of the foreshores is going on and the **Commonwealth Gardens** have been established on 32 hectares overlooking the lake. Ninety-minute ferry cruises on the lake are available.

Memorial Water Jet, which sends a huge column of water 140 metres above the surface, and the **Carillon Tower** (on Aspen Island), a gift of the United Kingdom.

Botanic Gardens, on slopes of Black Mountain. Forty hectares containing 6 000 native plants of 2 000 species. Open 9 am to 5 pm daily. Conducted tours by arrangement.

Development Commission Display, Regatta Point, features photographs and models of the city's present and projected development.

Royal Australian Mint, Deakin. Large plate glass windows in the visitors' gallery permit an excellent view of continuous operations. Open Monday to Friday 9 am to 4 pm (public holidays excepted) and Sunday 11.15 am to 4.30 pm.

Billabong Park Horse Era Museum, Stirling Avenue, Watson. A colonial style coach house, containing horsedrawn vehicles and exhibits including Hamilton Hume's buggy and a Cobb & Co. freight wagon of 1869. Open daily 9 am to 5 pm.

Australian National University (School of General Studies and Institute of Advanced Studies). Tours, 3 pm Monday to Friday (except public holidays). Visitors must provide their own transport.

Space Tracking Stations at Orroral Valley, Honeysuckle Creek and Tidbinbilla (56 kilometres south-west). Inspections can be arranged. There is a **fauna reserve** at Tidbinbilla. Inquire Canberra Tourist Bureau.

Mount Stromlo Observatory (16 kilometres west off Cotter Dam Road). Visiting hours 11 am to 3 pm Monday to Friday, 2 pm to 4 pm Saturday, Sunday and public holidays.

Civic and Theatre Centre. Spacious well-planned complex of buildings about a pleasant square, with a statue of Ethos, representing the spirit of the community.

Panoramic Lookouts at Black Mountain, Red Hill and Mount Pleasant (access by road) and Mount Ainslie (access by footpath) for fine view of city against background of Brindabella Range.

Cotter Dam (23 kilometres west) and **Mount Franklin.**

Sports

Canberra has many beautifully situated recreation reserves which cater for golf (three 18-hole courses), lawn and hard court tennis, bowls, croquet, squash, swimming (two major pools), pistol and rifle shooting, horse racing etc. Rowing and sailing are popular on Lake Burley Griffin and there is excellent trout fishing in nearby mountain streams. The city is within easy reach of some of the finest ski runs in the Australian Alps.

Entertainment

Major legitimate theatrical productions are presented in the **Canberra Theatre Centre** and at the **Riverside Repertory Theatre,** and there are several auditoriums suited for performances of music etc. **Cinemas:** Capital, Center and Civic.

Accommodation

Canberra City and Environs: Eleven **hotels.** Recommended: Canberra, Acton; Canberra Rex, Northbourne Avenue, Braddon; Deakin Inn, Kent Street, Deakin; Wellington, National Circuit and Canberra Avenue, Forrest; Jamieson Inn, Bowman Street, Macquarie.

Fifteen **motels.** Recommended: Travelodge Canberra City, Northbourne Avenue; Park Royal, Northbourne Avenue, Braddon; Manuka Travelodge, Griffith.

Three **caravan parks** near city, all facilities.

Transport

Air, rail and **road** services linking with State and interstate transport systems. The city and suburbs are served by public **buses.** Metered **taxis, hire cars, rental cars** and **air charters** are available. Numerous **motor coach tours** of the city, its environs and the nearby Snowy Mountains Hydro-electric Project can be made.

Business Hours

Shops are open 9 am to 5.30 pm Monday to Friday, from 6.30 pm to 9 pm on Friday, and from 9 am to 11.30 am on Saturday.

Banks are open 10 am to 3 pm Monday to Thursday and 10 am to 5 pm on Friday.

Miscellaneous

Tourist inquiries, Canberra Tourist Bureau, London Circuit and West Row.

National Roads and Motorists' Association (NMRA), 29 Lonsdale Street.

Emergencies: Police, telephone 49 7444; Ambulance, telephone 49 8133; Fire, telephone 7 2244.

Academy of Science, A.C.T.

Emu flock, Tidbinbilla Reserve, A.C.T.

Kangaroo

New South Wales

New South Wales is the oldest and most populous State in the Australian Commonwealth. In the early days of settlement it covered more than one half of the continent, but as the other colonies one by one gained administrative autonomy its area was reduced to about 80 million hectares, roughly one-tenth of Australia. Its population now exceeds 4 500 000.

Geographically and economically, it falls into four natural divisions which run approximately north and south. These are: (1) The coastal lowlands, for the most part narrow, fertile and well watered. (2) The tablelands of the Great Dividing Range. An almost unbroken series of plateaux 48 to 160 kilometres wide rises to average elevations of about 1 200 metres in the north and somewhat less than 760 metres in the south. The southern region has, however, the highest mountains in Australia, several of them above 2 100 metres. (3) The western slopes of the range, comparatively well watered. (4) The semi-arid plains of the far west, which receive less than 178 millimetres of rain a year.

The State's principal rivers are the Murray (1 930 kilometres in NSW) and its tributaries, the Darling (2 560 kilometres), the Murrumbidgee (1 500 kilometres), the Lachlan (1 480 kilometres), the Macquarie (860 kilometres) and the Namoi (850 kilometres). The main coastal rivers are the Hawkesbury, the Hunter, the Macleay, the Clarence and the Shoalhaven.

The climate is as varied as the topography. The western plains and the lower areas of the western slopes experience dry summer heat with maxima above 38°C fairly common. The mountain regions have warm, sunny summers and briskly cold winters during which frosts are frequent. But only in the very high country of the Australian Alps do screen temperatures fall much below freezing point in winter and early spring. The climate of the coastal strip (1 500 kilometres long) is sub-tropical as far as Sydney, and south of that may be described as temperate in all seasons.

ECONOMY There are three major areas of secondary industry on the New South Wales coast—the great metropolis of Sydney itself, Newcastle at the mouth of the Hunter River, and Wollongong-Port Kembla just over 80 kilometres south of the capital.

Vast deposits of high quality black coal under the Hunter Valley, the Illawarra Coast and the Blue Mountains provide an abundant source of cheap fuel and power which largely account for the establishment of the important iron and steel industries in the two big industrial cities on Sydney's flanks. This central coastal region generally is the heart of industrial Australia and vastly significant to the national economy. Its mines, mills and factories are modern, technologically sophisticated and on the whole efficient. Wages scales are high and the workforce enjoys an enviable living standard in an environment less affected by dense concentration of population and industry than in most other parts of the world where the nature and volume of production are similar.

The primary production of New South Wales is very diversified. A relatively small area of the north coast produces tropical crops—mainly sugar and bananas. The rest of the coastal strip is chiefly devoted to dairying and mixed farming, with some production of timber. Cool climate fruits are widely grown on the central western slopes. Wool, cereal crops, and meat are the mainstays of most areas west of the mountains, with diversification into fruit, rice, viticulture and

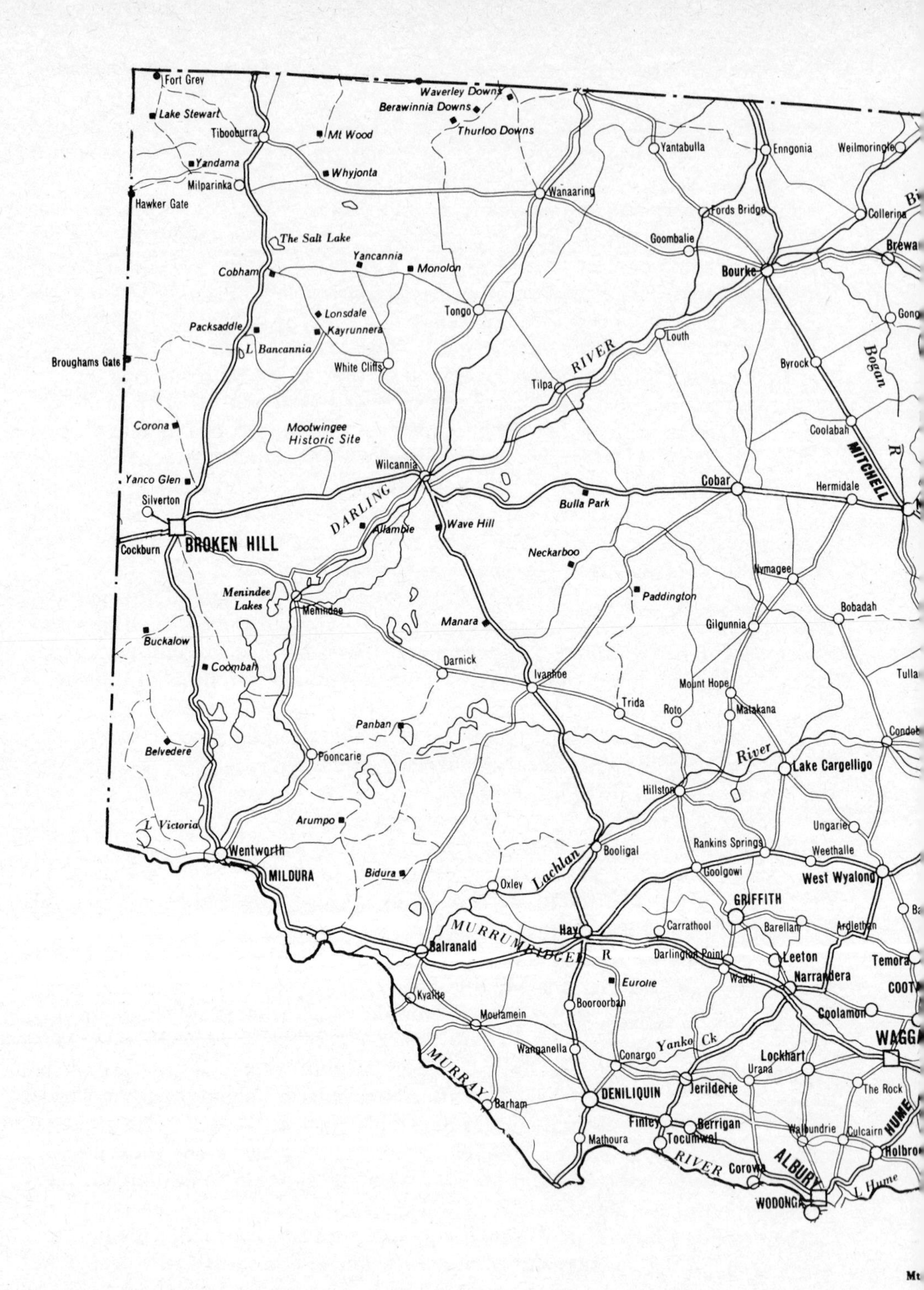
Fort Grey
Lake Stewart
Tibooburra
Mt Wood
Waverley Downs
Berawinnia Downs
Thurloo Downs
Yantabulla
Enngonia
Weilmoringle
Yandama
Milparinka
Whyjonta
Hawker Gate
Wanaaring
Fords Bridge
Collerina
The Salt Lake
Goombalie
Brewa
Yancannia
Monolon
Cobham
Bourke
Tongo
Lonsdale
Gong
Packsaddle
Kayrunnera
L Bancannia
Louth
Bogan
Broughams Gate
White Cliffs
RIVER
Byrock
Tilpa
Corona
Mootwingee
Historic Site
Coolabah
MITCHELL
R
Wilcannia
Yanco Glen
Cobar
Hermidale
Silverton
Bulla Park
DARLING
Allambie
Wave Hill
Cockburn
BROKEN HILL
Neckarboo
Nymagee
Menindee
Lakes
Menindee
Paddington
Bobadah
Manara
Gilgunnia
Buckalow
Coombah
Darnick
Ivanhoe
Mount Hope
Tulla
Trida
Roto
Matakana
Panban
Condob
Belvedere
Pooncarie
River
Lake Cargelligo
Hillston
Arumpo
Ungarie
L Victoria
Rankins Springs
Weethalle
Booligal
Wentworth
Goolgowi
MILDURA
Bidura
Lachlan
West Wyalong
Oxley
GRIFFITH
MURRUMBIDGEE
Hay
Carrathool
Barellan
Ardlethan
Balranald
R
Darlington Point
Leeton
Temora
Waddi
Narrandera
Euroley
COOT
Kyalite
Booroorban
Moulamein
Coolamon
WAGGA
Wanganella
Yanko Ck
Conargo
Lockhart
MURRAY
Urana
Jerilderie
The Rock
DENILIQUIN
Barham
HUME
Finley
Berrigan
Walbundrie
Culcairn
Mathoura
Tocumwal
Holbro
RIVER
Corowa
ALBURY
L Hume
WODONGA

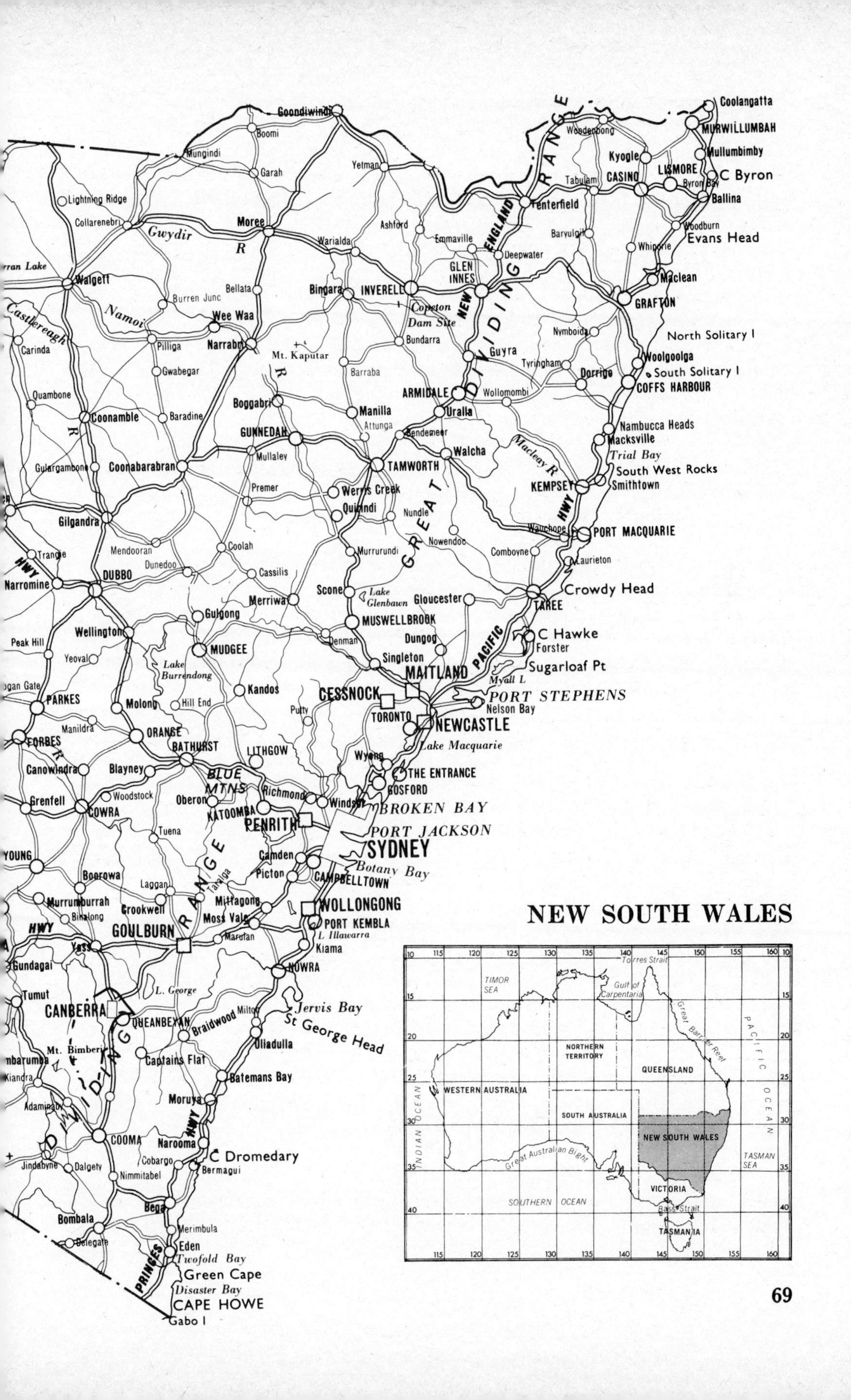
NEW SOUTH WALES
Goondiwindi
Boomi
Mungindi
Garah
Yetman
Lightning Ridge
Collarenebri
Moree
Gwydir
R
Ashford
Warialda
Emmaville
Deepwater
GLEN INNES
Walgett
Bellata
Burren Junc
Bingara
INVERELL
Copeton Dam Site
Namoi
Wee Waa
Castlereagh
Carinda
Pilliga
Narrabri
Mt. Kaputar
Bundarra
Gwabegar
Barraba
Quambone
Boggabri
Manilla
Coonamble
Baradine
GUNNEDAH
Attunga
Gulargambone
Coonabarabran
Mullaley
TAMWORTH
Premer
Werris Creek
Quirindi
Nundle
Gilgandra
Trangie
Mendooran
Coolah
Murrurundi
Nowendoc
HWY
Narromine
DUBBO
Dunedoo
Cassilis
Scone
Lake Glenbawn
Gloucester
Merriwa
MUSWELLBROOK
Gulgong
Wellington
Denman
Dungog
Peak Hill
MUDGEE
Yeoval
Singleton
MAITLAND
Lake Burrendong
Kandos
CESSNOCK
PARKES
Molong
Hill End
Putty
TORONTO
NEWCASTLE
Manildra
FORBES
ORANGE
BATHURST
LITHGOW
Lake Macquarie
Wyong
Canowindra
Blayney
BLUE MTNS
THE ENTRANCE
GOSFORD
Grenfell
Woodstock
Oberon
KATOOMBA
Richmond
Windsor
BROKEN BAY
COWRA
PENRITH
PORT JACKSON
Tuena
SYDNEY
YOUNG
Camden
Botany Bay
Boorowa
Laggan
Taralga
Picton
CAMPBELLTOWN
Murrumburrah
Crookwell
Mittagong
WOLLONGONG
Binalong
Moss Vale
PORT KEMBLA
GOULBURN
Marulan
L Illawarra
Yass
Kiama
Gundagai
NOWRA
L. George
Tumut
Jervis Bay
CANBERRA
QUEANBEYAN
Braidwood
Milton
St George Head
Mt. Bimberi
Ulladulla
Captains Flat
Kiandra
Batemans Bay
Adaminaby
Moruya
COOMA
Narooma
C Dromedary
Jindabyne
Dalgety
Cobargo
Bermagui
Nimmitabel
Bega
Bombala
Merimbula
Delegate
Eden
Twofold Bay
PRINCES
Green Cape
Disaster Bay
CAPE HOWE
Gabo I
Coolangatta
MURWILLUMBAH
Woodenbong
Mullumbimby
Kyogle
LISMORE
Byron Bay
C Byron
Tabulam
CASINO
Ballina
Tenterfield
NEW ENGLAND
Baryulgil
Woodburn
Evans Head
Whiporie
Maclean
GRAFTON
North Solitary I
Nymboida
Guyra
Woolgoolga
Tyringham
South Solitary I
Dorrigo
COFFS HARBOUR
ARMIDALE
Wollomombi
Uralla
Nambucca Heads
Bendemeer
Macksville
Walcha
Macleay R
Trial Bay
South West Rocks
KEMPSEY
Smithtown
GREAT DIVIDING RANGE
Wauchope
PORT MACQUARIE
Comboyne
Laurieton
Crowdy Head
TAREE
PACIFIC
C Hawke
Forster
Sugarloaf Pt
Myall L
PORT STEPHENS
Nelson Bay
TIMOR SEA
Torres Strait
Gulf of Carpentaria
Great Barrier Reef
PACIFIC OCEAN
NORTHERN TERRITORY
QUEENSLAND
WESTERN AUSTRALIA
INDIAN OCEAN
SOUTH AUSTRALIA
NEW SOUTH WALES
Great Australian Bight
TASMAN SEA
VICTORIA
SOUTHERN OCEAN
Bass Strait
TASMANIA
10
15
20
25
30
35
40
115
120
125
130
135
140
145
150
155
160

intensive mixed farming in irrigated areas of the Riverina and Murray Valley.

Mining of coal is, of course, still extremely important in the Hunter River and Illawarra (south coast) areas, and the vast silver-lead-zinc deposits in the Barrier Range 1 125 kilometres west of Sydney support the thriving city of Broken Hill with a population of about 30 000. Broken Hill is a classical example of how the harsh environment of the inland can be conquered by human ingenuity when a profit motive is strong enough.

Apart from coal and silver, lead and zinc, the mineral resources of New South Wales appear to have been largely depleted, although modern exploration methods may yet establish the existence of ore bodies in the vicinity of old strikes which are as yet undiscovered. There has, for instance, been a revival of copper mining at Cobar and new interest is being shown in the mineralized Northern Tablelands. Rutile-zircon sands are mined on the North Coast and an energetic search is being made for oil and natural gas.

EXPLORATION AND SETTLEMENT A brief account of the discovery and exploration of the eastern seaboard of Australia is given in the general section on Australia. The section on Sydney deals with the first settlement by Europeans.

Extensive further exploration of the coastline of the continent was made by George Bass, Matthew Flinders and other navigators at the end of the 18th and beginning of the 19th centuries, but very little was known about the interior until 1813. Between 1793 and 1806 a number of expeditions failed to penetrate the forbidding sandstone ramparts and gorges of the Blue Mountains about 65 kilometres west of Sydney to find what lay beyond, but they examined the coastal strip fairly thoroughly and discovered large tracts of fertile land suitable for grazing and agriculture.

In 1813, Gregory Blaxland, William Lawson and William Charles Wentworth, all of whom had an interest in finding new pastures for sheep and cattle, at last crossed the great, stony barrier and glimpsed the Bathurst plains beyond.

Now that the key to the interior had been turned, progress in both exploration and settlement was rapid. George Evans, Governor Macquarie's surveyor, penetrated as far west as the Lachlan River in 1815. In 1817 and 1818 John Oxley investigated the middle reaches of the Macquarie River and on his return journey discovered fine country on the Liverpool Plains and the New England tablelands.

By 1821 Hamilton Hume had pushed south-westward to the Murrumbidgee River. The squatters—pastoralists who grazed their herds and flocks on Crown land as yet unsold—followed hard on the heels of the explorers. The colony expanded with extraordinary rapidity once the breakthrough into the interior had been made. Allan Cunningham discovered a pass connecting the Bathurst plains with the Liverpool plains and the Hunter River Valley in 1823. The same year, Captain Currie reached the Monaro plains in the south-east and the following year, 1824, Hume and Hovell made the journey overland to Port Phillip.

Thereafter the work of exploration was taken up by such men as Charles Sturt and Thomas Mitchell who between them solved the remaining major riddles of geography in the south-eastern sector of the continent and, incidentally, ushered in what is often called the 'squatting age' in Australia. For many years the great landholders were to dominate the politics and economy of the entire colony.

The discovery of gold on the western slopes of the mountains in 1851 brought a spectacular increase in population. Tens of thousands of immigrants flooded into the country from all over the world. Inevitably most of them were to be disappointed in their quest for quick fortunes, but many stayed on to become farmers or to work in the secondary industries being established in and about Sydney and Newcastle.

The last half of the 19th century saw the rise of a powerful merchant class and gradual diminution of the relative influence of the great landholders. Merchant influence was largely responsible for the excessive centralization of population and industry which is so characteristic of Australia today.

However, Australia was to remain primarily an agrarian country until after Federation in 1901, when protection was given local industry as a matter of national policy and the value of manufactures began at last to overhaul the value of foodstuffs and raw materials. The need to attain some degree of economic self-sufficiency was sharply pointed up by the two world wars of the 20th century which powerfully stimulated Australian technology.

TOURING IN NEW SOUTH WALES Of all the Australian States New South Wales has the greatest variety of interests to offer the tourist—the sophisticated diversions of its large capital city, many hundreds of miles of magnificent ocean beaches, superb river, lake, and mountain scenery and the harsh but fascinating spaciousness of the interior.

An enterprising traveller can find within the State places which are either unique, or approximately representative of the continent's scenic spectrum—excluding the Great Barrier Reef, the mountains of the centre, and Western Australia.

The far North Coast is sub-tropical—indeed almost tropical—in climate and atmosphere. The highlands 1 300 kilometres south of it are snow-covered for much of the year and are claimed by skiers of international experience to provide some of the finest running in the world. Between these extremes there is a bewildering variety of choice for sightseers and holidaymakers.

As in most of southern Australia, travelling conditions are best in spring or autumn. Dust, heat and flies make the Australian bush unpleasant in summer, particularly west of the ranges. Mosquitoes and sandflies, although rarely in plague numbers, can be troublesome in the lake and river country at lower altitudes.

Much of the most interesting and beautiful country in New South Wales is within 200 kilometres of Sydney—the Blue Mountains and Jenolan Caves, the Hawkesbury River and Broken Bay, the Illawarra coast, and the historically fascinating settlements of the southern highlands. Comfortable, well organized motor coach tours of from two to seven days duration cover these beauty spots for the visitor without private transport but it is more rewarding to travel with a flexible schedule. Neither the Blue Mountains nor the Hawkesbury can be fully appreciated during a perfunctory tour of lookouts and wildlife parks. Weeks or months of exploration will not exhaust their attractions. It is probably preferable to stay in an attractive resort long enough to get to know it well rather than to try to sample too much in a short time.

Given good weather, however, one can see most of the spectacular scenery in the Blue Mountains and take in the Jenolan Caves as well in about four days; and get at least the flavour of the Hawkesbury in three days of launch or ferry cruising. These regions should have high priority for overseas visitors to New South Wales with limited time at their disposal. It is also possible for the foreign tourist to get a fleeting glimpse of the 'traditional' Australia by making one of the air and coach tours to western sheep properties at mustering and shearing time.

Farther afield from Sydney, the Snowy Mountains Hydro-electric Project and the Kosciusko State Park have much more to show than the fascinating complexity of the nation's most spectacular and important engineering achievement. There is also mountain, lake, river and forest scenery of memorable individuality and beauty. Although the trip from either Sydney or Melbourne to Cooma, the base for most Snowy tours, is never boring, the traveller in a real hurry can save time by flying. There are frequent air services to and from both cities.

For those who like to get off the beaten track and are prepared to put up with whatever inconvenience a lack of formal tourist amenities may imply, the Warrumbungle and Nandewar Ranges of the north-west can be strongly recommended. They, and the more easily accessible New England highlands, have for some unaccountable reason so far been overlooked as districts of enormous scenic appeal.

If you are seeking the real Outback, far western New South Wales has less flavour than far western Queensland, Central Australia or Western Australia. But the adventurous motorist who travels the lonely road from Bourke down the Darling River to Wilcannia and thence down the Barrier Highway to Broken Hill and either Adelaide or Mildura can justifiably boast that he has had more than a fleeting introduction to the Australian backblocks. The river and the countryside can be very beautiful when the roads have dried out after good rain. Broken Hill is certainly a city well worth visiting—a distinctive urban oasis in some of Australia's harshest country.

Almost any coastal resort in New South Wales will please lovers of the sea. Very little of the State's 1 300 kilometre coast line could be classed as dull. The beaches and inlets of the far South Coast are ideal for summer holidays.

PUBLIC TRANSPORT **Rail.** The New South Wales Government operates more than 10 000 kilometres of standard gauge railway within the State. There are few rural centres of any consequence which cannot be reached by rail. The standard of the service provided by intercapital expresses and long-haul expresses is tolerably good, and very good on electrified lines in the vicinity of Sydney. Otherwise it hardly if at all surpasses the Australian average, which is lamentable.

Road. Efficient and comfortable motor coach or bus services operate in most rural areas where rail services are inadequate.

Air. Kingford Smith Airport, Sydney, is the major international flight terminal in Australia. It also handles the majority of interstate and intrastate flights. The following country towns have scheduled flights to and from the capital, by either Airlines of New South Wales, East-West Airlines or feeder services: Albury, Armidale, Ballina, Baradine, Bathurst, Bega, Bombala, Bourke, Brewarrina, Broken Hill, Casino, Cobar, Coff's Harbour, Collarenebri, Condobolin, Coolah, Cooma, Coonabarabran, Coonamble, Corowa, Corryong, Deniliquin, Dubbo, Eden, Gilgandra, Glen Innes, Goodooga, Goulburn, Grafton, Griffith, Grenfell, Gunnedah, Inverell, Hay, Kempsey, Khancoban, Leeton, Lismore, Moree, Moruya, Mudgee, Newcastle, Orange, Parkes, Port Macquarie, Tamworth, Taree, Temora, Wagga, Walgett.

Ferry Services ply on Sydney Harbour and on the Hawkesbury River and Broken Bay.

Boats and **launches** for cruising and fishing can be hired at major sea and lakeside resorts.

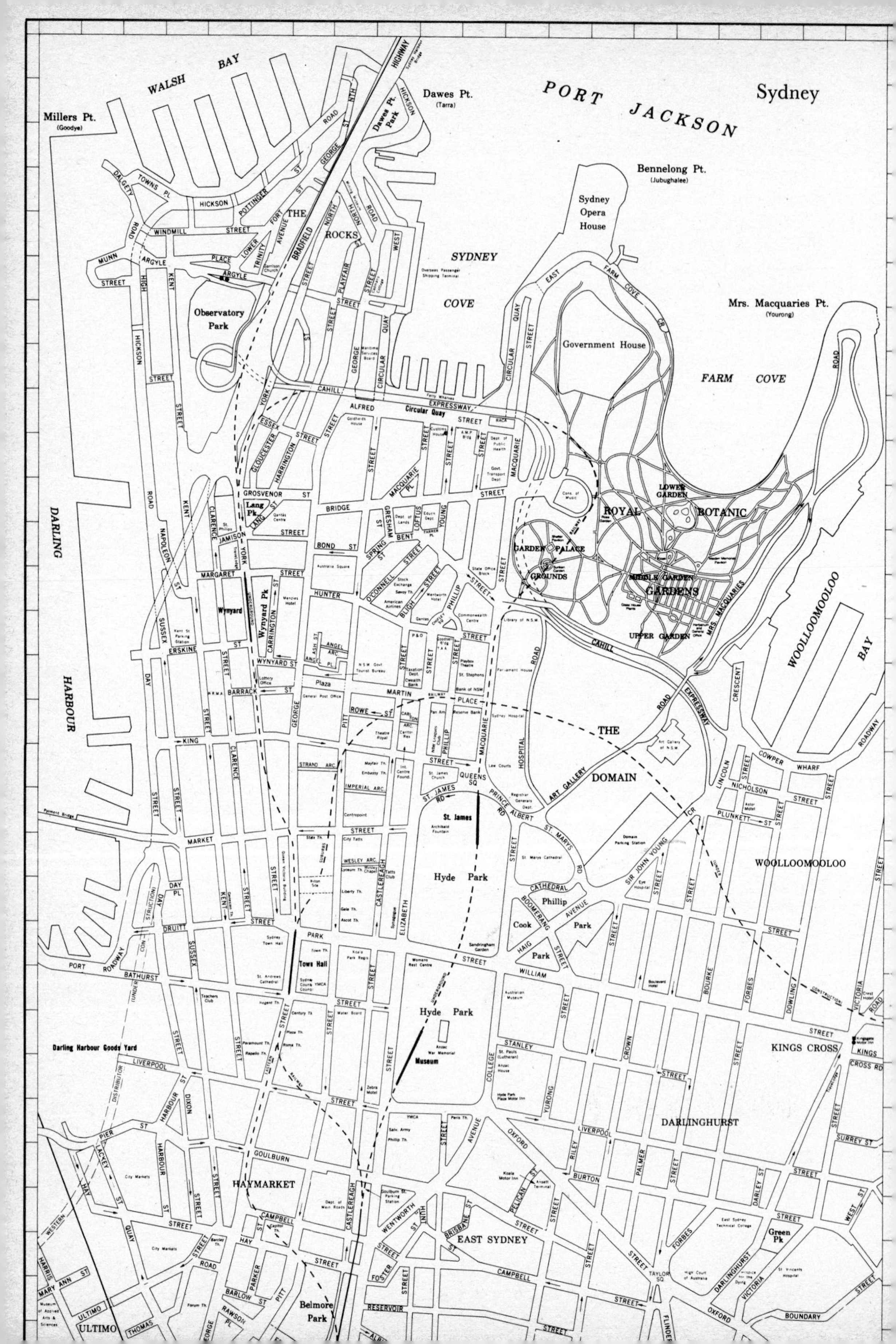
Sydney
PORT JACKSON
WALSH BAY
Millers Pt.
(Goodye)
Dawes Pt.
(Tarra)
Dawes Pt. Park
Bennelong Pt.
(Jubughalee)
Sydney Opera House
SYDNEY COVE
Mrs. Macquaries Pt.
(Yourong)
FARM COVE
Government House
THE ROCKS
Observatory Park
Circular Quay
ROYAL BOTANIC GARDENS
LOWER GARDEN
MIDDLE GARDEN
UPPER GARDEN
GARDEN PALACE GROUNDS
WOOLLOOMOOLOO BAY
DARLING HARBOUR
Wynyard
Wynyard Pk
Lang Pk
THE DOMAIN
St. James
Hyde Park
Town Hall
Museum
Cook Park
Phillip Park
WOOLLOOMOOLOO
KINGS CROSS
DARLINGHURST
Darling Harbour Goods Yard
HAYMARKET
EAST SYDNEY
Green Pk
Belmore Park
ULTIMO

SYDNEY

(Population 3 000 000)

Sydney, the capital of New South Wales, the first city of the Commonwealth and its busiest seaport, is built about the shores of Port Jackson, a deep and topographically complicated indentation in the east coast of Australia at a latitude of 33°52′ South and a longitude of 151°12′ East. The city proper, on the southern shores of the inlet, has an area of about 2 900 hectares, though its boundaries have never been precisely defined. The metropolitan complex covers some 183 000 hectares, extending far inland and for many kilometres up and down the coast on either side of Sydney Heads. The built-up area is on undulating lowlands south and west of the city, on steeply scarped sandstone plateaux north of the harbour and along to suburbs facing the ocean (to an elevation of more than 200 metres) and on a plateau south of Botany Bay (to an elevation of 150 metres). Beyond the urban area to the west is the Cumberland Basin, flanked on the west by the Blue Mountains and on the south by the northern foothills of the Southern Tablelands.

The harbour is regarded as one of the most beautiful in the world and one of the best from a utilitarian point of view. The entrance between North and South Heads is 1.2 kilometres wide at its narrowest and 9 metres deep at low tide. It has an area of 5 500 hectares with 240 kilometres of foreshores. The passage of the heads is safe and the harbour itself suffers little siltage and requires little dredging. Large ships can berth close to the commercial centre of the city proper, at Circular Quay, Darling Harbour and Wooloomooloo Bay.

Sydney is a city of pronounced maritime character, its appearance dominated by the many bays and inlets of its harbour. Its most prized commercial and residential sites overlook either the ocean or enclosed water.

Of all the Australian State capitals it is the most cosmopolitan and sophisticated. Although it is still vaguely Victorian in architectural atmosphere, this characteristic is rapidly diminishing as the centre of the city is re-developed with multi-storey buildings of modern design. The predominant influence is 20th century American. It has now almost obliterated the distinctive Australian character which the city had acquired by the early years of the 20th century.

The commercial and social elements of Sydney life run fairly parallel to those of a city of comparable size in the southern United States. The industrial pace is more leisured because Australian workers have not experienced really keen competitive conditions on the labour market for more than 35 years.

Sydney boasts a lively night life—much more lively than any other Australian city. Its numerous night clubs, cabarets and restaurants rarely achieve the standards of service, entertainment or cuisine available to patrons of similar establishments in Western Europe, the Americas or the Far East, but they are colourful, gay and increasingly cosmopolitan

Sydney is undoubtedly the capital for the performing arts in Australia. It supports a symphony orchestra of world class and numerous other groups of distinguished performers in the various fields of popular entertainment. It has an architecturally spectacular Opera House, a State art gallery, fine public libraries and a number of small but enterprising semi-commercial theatres.

The city's night life is mainly if not by any means wholly concentrated in the King's Cross area east of the central city. 'The Cross' has become legendary in Australia—an antipodean equivalent of New York's Greenwich Village, London's Soho, or Montmartre in Paris.

The fashionable residential areas of the city are along the foreshores of Port Jackson, mainly to the east of the Sydney Harbour Bridge and along the coast north of Narrabeen Lake. Some older residential areas, like Paddington and Hunter's Hill near the mouth of the Lane Cove and Parramatta Rivers are finding favour again and being restored or redeveloped.

CLIMATE Sydney enjoys a mild and agreeable climate—even if not quite as ideal as its propagandists protest. Its mean summer temperature is 21.4°C and its mean winter temperature 12.6°C. Extremes range from 38°C+ down to about 4°C. On the whole humidity tends to be high and rainfall at 1 142 millimetres a year is well above the average for the continental coast. Generally speaking, January, February and March are uncomfortablly warm and humid months. Winters can be chilly, but are rarely severe. The sun shines—at one time or another—on 342 days out of the 365 in the year; but this statistic is also apt to be a little deceptive and is more quoted by the promoter than the recipient of the city's climatic favours. The best measure of the meteorological realities is that frost-sensitive plants and tropical genera are readily acclimatized if given sheltered positions in domestic gardens.

Possibly the truly unique virtue of Sydney compared with other big cities in the world is that the population can readily escape into a natural environment which is largely unspoiled and always stimulating and beautiful. Its surf beaches, and the mountains and rivers which can be reached by a short journey from the metropolis, are the priceless heritage of its citizens.

COMMERCE AND INDUSTRY Sydney is still mainly a commercial city and dependent on its busy port for much of its prosperity. Its chief exports are wool, wheat, coal, flour and meat. The volume of cargo shipped from Port Jackson annually is now approaching 5 million tonnes.

Industrial production is predominantly of consumer goods, although important industries located in the metropolitan area are associated with shipbuilding, chemicals, earth-moving and agricultural equipment, railway rolling stock, paper, electrical and communications equipment, aircraft manufacture and maintenance and oil refining. The industries are grouped into two major zones—the first from the dockland suburbs southward to Botany Bay and the second from Rhodes, Rydalmere and Parramatta south-westwards to Liverpool. There are also important satellite industrial areas about St Mary's in the west and Sutherland to the south. Since the second world war there has been a tendency to move from the crowded inner suburbs to the roomier areas to the west and south and, to a lesser extent, to suburbs north of Manly.

HISTORY In 1787, 11 ships under the command of Captain Arthur Phillip left England to establish a settlement at Botany Bay in New Holland, as Australia was then known. They carried 1 000 men, women and children, of whom more than 700 were convicts. They had been dispatched to found the new colony in large part to relieve the intolerable congestion in British prisons which were crammed to overflowing with political prisoners and petty offenders sentenced to transportation under the harsh criminal code of the day.

The site of the new penal colony had been chosen by Joseph Banks, Captain James Cook's botanist, who—despite the fact that he described the region as the barrenest spot on earth—apparently felt that it was a suitable place to contain Britain's malcontents and criminals.

Phillip found Botany Bay to be barren indeed—so much so that he decided immediately to move his cargo of sick and desperate prisoners to Port Jackson, further north, where at least some of the land appeared to give promise of becoming productive under cultivation. He chose as a landing place a small bay on the southern side of the main inlet where a stream of fresh water entered the sea.

Phillip named the place Sydney Cove and set up an encampment there on 26 January, 1788. He apparently intended to call it Albion, but for some unknown reason the name was never adopted—nor was it ever named Sydney officially.

The appalling hardships suffered by Phillip and his unwilling colonists have become legendary in Australian history. Although starvation threatened when supply ships from England were delayed or wrecked, Phillip hung on and set about building a village and planning a town. Clay deposits were discovered near the present site of the Haymarket and the convicts were set to work shaping and firing bricks. In June 1789 the first Government House was built in brick on a site near the present intersection of Bridge and Phillip Streets.

Because insufficient fertile land was discovered near the settlement to sustain it, Phillip dispatched parties of explorers into the bush to look for areas where animals could be pastured and grain crops planted. Good river flats were found about 20 kilometres away at Rose Hill (Parramatta) and farther afield at the mouth of the Hawkesbury River. By the end of 1790, the first farms in the new colony had begun to produce a little food to supplement the rotting supplies shipped out with the first fleet.

When Phillip was forced by illness to return to England in 1792, the worst of the crisis was over and development could have proceeded on the orderly lines laid down by the first Governor if it had not been for the corruption and greed of the military corps which had accompanied the convicts as guards. The officers banded together to monopolize the colony's trade. They set themselves up on great estates, practically self-supporting now that agriculture was firmly established, worked by convict labour. Phillip's carefully considered plans for the development of the town were scrapped. It grew into a disorderly collection of huts interspersed with more solid buildings ranged on either side of wandering cart tracks. (The chaotic tangle of streets in the centre of modern Sydney is an inheritance from those days.) Far worse, the military contrived an extraordinary barter system in which rum was widely used instead of currency and virtually destroyed the judicial system.

The careers of three governors succeeding Phillip—Captain John Hunter, Philip Gidley King and the redoubtable Captain William Bligh of *Bounty* fame—were wrecked before the power of the Rum Corps, as the New South Wales regiment was known, was broken by its recall to Britain in 1809.

The colonel of the regiment which replaced the Rum Corps, the 73rd Regiment of Highlanders, was Lachlan Macquarie, a man of unusual energy and competence who found Sydney in a 'state of shameful dilapidation' when he arrived. He immediately set about restoring order, cleaning up the town, improving its roads and communications and allocating land for community use. Macquarie, indeed, should be regarded as the city's real founder. The emancipist Francis Greenway, an architect of genius, was his protege. Greenway was responsible for many of the simple, elegant buildings built in the late Georgian style which are Sydney's pride today.

Macquarie's term of office ended in 1821, but under his successors steady progress was made as the interior was opened up to settlement and the city became a major shipping and trading centre for the south-west Pacific.

Transport services were greatly improved in the 1830s and 1840s. Ferry services on Sydney Harbour proliferated and the first horse-drawn omnibuses began running in 1842. By 1861 the first horse-drawn trams were operating in Pitt Street.

The discovery of gold in 1851 had a galvanic effect on the city's economy, just as it did in the case of Melbourne, Victoria's capital. In the middle and late 19th century, Sydney acquired many public and private buildings which bear witness to the prosperity of the era, but unhappily they are by no means all architecturally or aesthetically commendable.

In 1858 the first electric telegraph began operation and during the 1890s electric lighting replaced gas lamps in the streets.

In the 20th century the city has undergone rapid industrialization and within living memory has changed radically in appearance and social character.

Sydney's Historic Streets

George Street. The oldest street in Australia. Originally called High Street, but renamed in 1810. It was the site of the colony's first gaol and execution place. During the 1850s it was part of Sydney's Chinatown. Now a typically metropolitan thoroughfare of banks, department stores, office buildings and cinemas.

Pitt Street. Built on reclaimed land over a buried village at the northern end. It began as a row of convict huts and developed into a brothel district. It now contains most of Sydney's major insurance buildings.

Macquarie Street. Sydney's 'Harley Street'. It is one of the few streets in central Sydney which has an air of spaciousness. When Macquarie arrived in 1810, it was only a bridle track beside the Domain. He planned for the whole east side to be occupied by official buildings. The western side was later lined with the town houses of wealthy citizens.

Bridge Street, now the administrative centre of NSW, was so named because it was the site of the first bridge ever built on Australian soil—across the Tank Stream which supplied early Sydney with water.

Places of Interest

Opera House, Bennalong Point. This striking, extremely controversial building was designed by the Danish architect, Joern Utzon, who in 1956 won a world-wide competition which attracted 223 entries. Work began in March 1959. The concrete shell roofing the structure, a series of peaked vaults, weighing in all 21 000 tons and of a form which is said to have been suggested by the sails of yachts on the harbour, presented enormous problems of construction. Costs rose far beyond original estimates, and problems associated with making the interior of the building functional as an opera house and centre for the performing arts caused a quarrel between the NSW Government and the architect who was dismissed when the building was less than half completed. Other architects were appointed to modify the design and finish the project. The building costs, totalling more than $A100 million, were met from the profits of big State lotteries. The Opera House was officially opened in October 1973 by the Queen and is now the venue of regular performances of music and drama.

Sydney Harbour Bridge, spanning Port Jackson from Dawes Point to Milson's Point. Second largest single-span bridge in the world, linking Sydney with northern suburbs. Measures 500 metres from pylon to pylon, rising 135 metres above the water. Width, with approaches, 4 kilometres. Built between 1923 and 1932 by Dorman Long & Co. at a cost of $A20 230 000. Average daily traffic flow 110 000 vehicles. Motorists are charged a toll for crossing. A lookout and restaurant are situated on the south-west pylon. Open 9 am to 6 pm (admission charge).

Australia Square Tower, George and Pitt Streets, is Australia's tallest building. It is a strikingly modern cylindrical structure of 50 floors which rises 183 metres above street level. Its features include a plaza with trees and a fountain, and a revolving roof-top restaurant, the 'Summit', with views of the city and harbour (inspection tours by arrangement with Lend Lease Corporation Ltd.).

Australian Museum, corner of College and William Streets. Open 10 am to 5 pm, Tuesdays and Saturdays and public holidays; noon to 5 pm, Mondays (school holidays 10 am to 5 pm); Sundays 2 pm to 5 pm.

Art Gallery of New South Wales, Domain. Open 10 am to 5 pm, Mondays to Saturdays, 2 pm to 5.30 pm, Sundays.

Public Library of New South Wales, Shakespeare Place. Contains general reference library and **Mitchell Library** of Australian books, manuscripts etc. Also **Dixon Library, Shakespeare Tercentenary Library** and **Mitchell and Dixon Galleries.** Public Library opens 10 am to 10 pm, Monday to Saturdays; 2 pm to 6 pm, Sundays and public holidays. Closed Christmas Day and Good Friday.

Museum of Applied Arts and Sciences, Harris Street, Ultimo (near Central Station), containing **Planetarium** etc. Open 10 am to 5 pm, weekdays, Saturdays and public holidays, 2 pm to 5 pm, Sundays. Closed Christmas Day, Good Friday.

Mining Museum, 28 George Street North. Outstanding collection of geological specimens, ores, fossils, gemstones etc.

Sydney Town Hall, George Street, contains auditorium with seating for 2 500 and one of the world's finest pipe organs. May be inspected 9 am to 5 pm, weekdays.

Cenotaph, Martin Place, war memorial. Ceremonial mounting of the guard 12.30 pm, Thursdays.

Stock Exchange, O'Connell Street. Public Gallery open during trading hours, 10 am to 3.30 pm.

Paddy's Market, Haymarket. Fridays only, 11 am to 5.30 pm. Colourful and amusing.

Observatory, Flagstaff Hill. Open to public 2 pm to 4 pm Wednesdays.

Fort Denison ('Pinchgut'), Sydney Harbour. Originally used to imprison refractory convicts, later converted to fort. Inspection permits required. Charges and details from Room 120, Maritime Services Building, Circular Quay.

AMP Building, Circular Quay, for high level views of city and harbour. Conducted tours 11 am and 2.30 pm. Observation platform open 9 am to 5 pm, Monday to Saturday, 10 am to 5 pm Sundays, 7 pm to 10 pm Saturdays and Sundays. Admission charge, except for pensioners with travel card and organized school groups.

Captain Cook's Landing Place, Kurnell Peninsula. Access from Princes Highway via The Boulevarde and Captain Cook Drive south of George's River bridge.

Main Parks and Gardens

Botanic Gardens, Farm Cove. There are 24 hectares of lawns, gardens and plantations, with hot-houses of orchids and ferns to water's edge. Open daily 8 am to sunset.

The Domain, open parkland, adjoining Botanic Gardens. Soap box orators on Sundays.

Hyde Park, Most central of city's parks, extending from Liverpool Street to Queen's Square, and College to Elizabeth Streets. Features include **Archibald Memorial,** commemorating French and Australian alliance in first world war; **F. J. Walker Family Fountain** (commemorating pioneer family); **Busby's Bore Fountain** at site of Sydney's first water supply; **Anzac Memorial** and **Sandringham Garden,** in memory of King George V and King George VI.

Taronga Park Zoological Gardens, across harbour on north shore of Port Jackson. A really magnificent collection of animals, birds, reptiles and fish in beautiful 20-hectares parkland setting. Open daily 9.30 am to 5 pm. Accessible by road and ferry.

Notable Historic Buildings

St James' Church, King Street and Queen's Square. Built 1819. Designed by Francis Greenway. Fine proportions and spire.

Hyde Park Barracks, Queen's Square. Now law courts. Built 1817. Designed by Greenway, who received for the work free pardon from Macquarie for the forgery offence for which he was transported. Sadly altered from the original.

Conservatorium of Music, formerly Government House stables, is now centre of musical instruction for the State.

Elizabeth Bay House, in Regency style, now being restored by State Planning Authority.

The Old Mint, Macquarie Street, fine example of colonial style. Built 1811-16. Architect unknown.

Parliament House, Macquarie Street. Central part built 1811-16 as part of Rum Hospital. Open weekdays.

Richmond Villa, behind Parliament House, facing Domain. Victorian Gothic, 1849. Now headquarters of the NSW Parliamentary Country Party. Architect, Mortimer Lewis.

Royal College of Physicians, Macquarie Street. Two storeys built about 1848, others an addition.

General Post Office, Martin Place. Begun 1865, completed 1887. Renaissance style. Architect, James Barnet, who also designed the Customs House and the Australian Museum.

Great Hall, University of Sydney, Parramatta Road. Designed by Edmund Blackett, exponent of Gothic revival architecture. It has a magnificent hammer beamed roof.

St Andrew's Cathedral (Anglican), Bathurst Street. Architect, Blackett.

St Mary's Cathedral (Roman Catholic), Cathedral Street. Architect, William Wardell.

Darlinghurst Court House, Taylor Square. Greek revival. Designed by Mortimer Lewis, 1837.

Vaucluse House, Wentworth Avenue, Vaucluse, former home of William Charles Wentworth, father of the NSW Constitution. (Open for inspection 10 am to 4.45 pm.)

The Rocks. Historic area on the western shores of Sydney Cove containing many fine old houses and terraces which can be viewed by walking from Church Hill to Argyle Place and Lower Fort Street. In this area the first settlers built their huts. Later, substantial houses were built here by the wealthy, but fashions changed and the Rocks became a notorious slum. Extensive restoration and redevelopment is now being undertaken.

City Churches

Baptist, 619 George Street. **St Andrew's Cathedral** (Anglican), George Street. **St James'** (Anglican), King Street. **St John's** (Anglican), Darlinghurst Road. **St Mary's Cathedral** (Roman Catholic), Cathedral Street. **St Paul's** (Lutheran), 3 Stanley Street. **St Philip's** (Anglican), Church Hill, York Street. **St Stephen's** (Presbyterian), Macquarie Street. **Salvation Army,** 140 Elizabeth Street. **The Great Synagogue,** Elizabeth Street. **Wesley Chapel** (Methodist), Castlereagh Street.

Sports

Sydney's recreation areas cater for practically every kind of organized sport. There are excellent public club golf links and golf practice ranges within a short distance of the city; hard and lawn tennis courts at White City, Rushcutters Bay; squash courts, bowling and croquet greens; ten-pin bowling centres; riding schools; swimming pools. Small craft for boating, cruising, yachting, angling, deep-sea and game fishing may be hired at many waterfront resorts in the harbour, river or Broken Bay areas. Information may be obtained from the classified telephone directory, the classified advertising columns of the daily newspapers, or from the Tourist Bureau.

Major race meetings are held at Randwick, Canterbury, Rosehill and Warwick Farm racecourses. Championship **tennis** at White City, Rushcutters Bay. Test and Sheffield Shield **cricket** at Sydney Cricket Ground, Moore Park. There is a **motor racing** circuit at Warwick Farm. **Greyhound racing** is held at Wentworth Park.

Main Surf Beaches

North of Sydney Heads: Manly, Freshwater, Curl Curl, Dee Why, Long Reef, Collaroy, Narrabeen, Warriewood, Mona Vale, Bungan, Newport, Bigola, Avalon, Whale Beach, Palm Beach. **South of Sydney Heads:** Bondi, Bronte, Clovelly, Coogee, Maroubra, Malabar, Cronulla, Marley, Wattamolla.

Surf carnivals with spectacular marches and lifesaving competitions between various clubs are held at main beaches during weekends.

Entertainment

Theatres: Capitol, 13 Campbell Street; Her Majesty's, Quay Street; Music Hall, 156 Military Road, Neutral Bay; Ensemble Theatre in the Round, 78 McDougall Street, Milson's Point; Drama Theatre, Opera House; Richbrooke, 150 Elizabeth Street; Nimrod, Nimrod Street, Kings Cross; Genesian, 420 Kent Street.

Theatre Restaurants: Bonaparte's, 152 William Street; Amado's Spanish Fiesta, 85–91 Oxford Street; Macleay, Chevron Hotel, Macleay Street; The Cockney's Pride, Bay Lodge Arcade, Double Bay; Tabou, 24 Darlinghurst Road; Les Girls (all male revue) 1–11 Oxford Street, Paddington; The Military Tattoo, Spit Road, Mosman; Whiskey, 152 William Street; The Barrell, 24 Bayswater Road (burlesque); Carousel, Roslyn Street, Kings Cross.

Street scene, Sydney

City Cinemas: Ascot, 246 Pitt Street; Barclay, 681 George Street; Century, 586 George Street; Embassy, 79 Castlereagh Street; Forum, 747 George Street; Gala, 236 Pitt Street; Liberty, 232 Pitt Street; Lyceum, 210 Pitt Street; Mayfair, 75 Castlereagh Street; Paramount, 525 George Street; Paris, 205 Liverpool Street; Plaza, 600 George Street; Rapallo, 527 George Street; Regent, 487 George Street; Roma, 628 George Street; Savoy, 29 Bligh Street; State, 49 Market Street; Town, 303 Pitt Street.

Restaurants

Recommended: Chelsea, 119 Macleay Street; Caprice, Sunderland Avenue, Rose Bay; Prunier's Chiswick Gardens, 65 Ocean Road, Woollahra; Gaslight, Carlton Rex Hotel, 58 Castlereagh Street; Fisherman's Lodge, Watson's Bay; La Taverne, 122–28 New South Head Road, Edgecliff; Macquarie Inn; Mme Defarge, 107 Queen Street, Woollhara; Summit, Australia Square (revolving restaurant); Texas Tavern, 44 Macleay Street; French Restaurant, Taylor's Square, Darlinghurst; Garden Court, Wentworth Hotel, Phillip Street; Top of the Cross, 110, Darlinghurst Road; Bourbon and Beefsteak Bar, 24 Darlinghurst Road.

Accommodation

Recommended Hotels: Boulevard, 90 William Street; Carlton Rex, 56 Castlereagh Street; Chevron, Macleay Street; Crest, Darlinghurst Road, Kings Cross; Gazebo, 2 Elizabeth Bay Road; Menzies, 14 Carrington Street; Kingsgate Hyatt, King's Cross Road; Sebel Town House, 23 Elizabeth Bay Road; Wentworth, Phillip Street.

Recommended motels: Chateau Commodore, 14 Macleay Street; Cosmopolitan Motor Inn, Knox Street, Double Bay; Koala Park Regis, Castlereagh Street; Koala Motor Inn, Oxford Street; Travelodge, 110 Darlinghurst Road, Rushcutter's Bay; Travelodge, 13 Blue Street, North Sydney.

Serviced Apartments: Balyarta, 358a Victoria Street, Kings Cross; Florida Motor Inn, 1 McDonald Street, Kings Cross; The Rembrandt, 31 Bayswater Road, Kings Cross.

Note. Reservations may be made with the NSW Government Tourist Bureau in licensed and private hotels, guest houses and motels anywhere in the State. In the Sydney area furnished apartments, flats and holiday cottages are available for rent on a weekly basis, but bookings must be made through estate agencies, a list of which will be found in the classified Sydney Telephone Directory.

Annual Events of Note

Waratah Spring Festival (carnival, parades, art exhibitions and displays). First week in October.

New Year's Eve Mardi Gras celebrations at Manly, Kings Cross, Coogee and Bondi.

Royal Easter Show. Exhibitions of prize stock, agricultural produce, manufactures etc. Spectacular ring events, sideshows etc.

Carols by Candlelight. Massed choirs sing in Hyde Park on Christmas Eve.

Main department stores, city

Centrepoint, Pitt and Market Streets; Coles, George, King and Pitt Streets, Liverpool Street, Oxford Street; David Jones', Elizabeth, George and Market Streets; Farmer's, Pitt, Market and George Streets; Gowing's, corner Market and George Streets; Grace Bros., Broadway; Hordern Bros., Pitt Street; Lowes, George Street and Rawson Place; Mark Foys, Liverpool Street; Woolworths, Park Street, George Street and Liverpool Street.

Business hours

Normal banking hours, 9.30 am to 3 pm Monday to Thursday, and 9.30 am to 5 pm Friday. Banks close on Saturday. Shopping hours, 9 am to 5.30 pm weekdays, 9 am to 12 noon Saturdays. Hotel bars open at 10 am and close 10 pm Monday to Saturday.

Public Holidays are observed on New Year's Day, 1 January; Australia Day, 27 January; Easter, Good Friday to following Tuesday; Anzac Day, 25 April; Queen's Birthday, 16 June; Bank Holiday, 4 August; Labour Day, 6 October; Christmas Day, 25 December; Boxing Day, 26 December. (These dates were decreed for 1973.)

Transport

The inner city and the suburbs are served by **diesel buses,** but a short loop of **underground railway** runs north and south beneath the central city, considerably reducing congestion of through passenger traffic to and from the north shore suburbs. It connects with suburban lines to the north, west and south.

Rail. All **country and interstate trains** arrive at and depart from Central Railway Station.

Opera House, Sydney

Suburban rail services pick up and drop passengers in the city at Museum, Town Hall, St James, Wynyard and Quay stations.

Harbour Ferries. Regular **ferry services** run from Circular Quay to Manly, Taronga Park Zoo and other harbourside suburbs. There are **ferry tours** of Port Jackson and an ocean cruise by ferry to Broken Bay. Two **hydrofoil ferries** operate on the run to Manly and north shore suburbs and on harbour cruises.

Air. International, interstate and country **air services** use Kingsford Smith airport. **Air charter** and **taxi flights** and **aerial tours** are available.

Overseas. The overseas **shipping passenger** terminal is at Circular Quay.

All registered **taxis** carry meters and standard rates are clearly displayed in each car.

Coach tours

More than 20 half and full day coach tours of Sydney and its environs are now available. There are also regular ferry and launch cruises on the harbour. These are a convenient and inexpensive way of seeing the city and visiting beauty spots in the nearby mountains and along the coast. *Not all run daily.* A booklet is available from, and booking should be made through:

The New South Wales Government Tourist Bureau
8 Martin Place, Sydney 2000. Telephone 2 0136.

Day tours by air to sheep stations and farms in inland NSW are run by East-West Airlines and Airlines of NSW. Bookings may be made through the bureau.

Visiting Motorists

One-way Traffic in Central Sydney. Traffic flow: north only in Castlereagh, Clarence, Crown, Sussex Streets; south only in Pitt, York, Kent, Palmer, Bourke Streets; each way in Elizabeth, George Macquarie Streets, Cross-streets; east only in King, Bathurst, Albion Streets; west only in Market, Liverpool, Foveaux Streets; each way in other main streets.

Street numbers in the city run from north to south and from east to west.

Emergency Telephone Numbers

For Police, Fire, Ambulance: **Dial 000.**

OUTER SUBURBS OF NOTE

PARRAMATTA (On Great Western Highway 21 kilometres)

(Population 84 000)

Parramatta, now merged with the metropolitan complex of Sydney, was the second European settlement on the Australian continent. It was selected as a farming area for Sydney in 1788 when, at a distance of 15 miles from the village on the shores of Sydney Cove, it was regarded as the 'interior' of the colony.

The first land grant issued in Australia was made to James Ruse, an ex-convict who showed marked talent in farming the unfamiliar soil. Influential pioneers such as Surgeon John Harris and John Macarthur had estates in the district. It gradually lost its agricultural significance as the much more extensive and rich lands of the Hawkesbury were opened up, but it remained an important staging post on the road to the west. A regular coach service between Sydney and Parramatta was begun in 1823. For more than a century thereafter it remained a favoured residential area, a virtual dormitory suburb of the rapidly growing capital. In recent years it has been increasingly industrialized.

Historic Buildings

Roseneath Cottage, built in 1837 by Janet Templeton, early importer of Saxon-merino sheep. Now a private residence.

Old Government House, remodelled in 1815-16 on the base of an older building constructed in 1790 when it seemed that Governor Phillip might remove permanently from Sydney to Rose Hill (as Parramatta was then known). The portico is attributed to Greenway. Open for inspection Tuesday, Wednesday, Thursday, Sunday and public holidays.

St John's Church, with twin towers, built under the supervision of Lieutenant John Watts in 1820 and remodelled in 1855. It contains plaques in memory of early citizens and its graveyard is the oldest cemetery in Australia still in use.

Elizabeth Farm House, built in 1793 by John Macarthur and believed to be the oldest farmhouse in Australia. Privately owned but may be seen from adjoining reserve.

Hambledon Cottage, built for the governess to Macarthur's children. Open for inspection at weekends.

Experiment Farm Cottage, built on the site of John Ruse's land grant in 1798. Open for inspection daily.

The **Lancer Barracks,** designed by John Watts, aide-de-camp to Macquarie. Some alterations.

LIVERPOOL (On Hume Highway)

(Population 32 000)

This outer suburb of Sydney on George's River and the main southern railway line was named after Lord Liverpool, afterwards Lord Hawkesbury, who became Prime Minister of England. It was expected to become a seaport. Schooners of up to 40 tons could navigate the river as far as the town in the early days, but silting eventually closed the waterway to ships. It is today heavily industrialized but the surrounding district is used for mixed farming, dairying and grape growing. The district is the site of a large military training establishment, set up before the first world war. The town was declared a municipality in 1872 and a city in 1906.

Historic Buildings

Greenway's **Church of St Luke,** built between 1818 and 1824. **State Hospital and Asylum,** one of the finest pieces of colonial architecture surviving attributed to Greenway, was built in 1824-30 and is now a technical school. **Lansdowne Bridge,** 6.44 kilometres from Liverpool on the Hume Highway, built by David Lennox (also responsible for the original Princes Bridge in Melbourne) for the amazingly small cost of £1000.

Warwick Farm Racecourse which incorporates one of the finest motor racing tracks in Australia is at Liverpool. The city has the usual sports facilities. Several good golf courses.

SUTHERLAND-ROYAL NATIONAL PARK

(Princes Highway 25 kilometres)

Sutherland gives access to the Kurnell Peninsula where Captain Cook first landed on Australian soil in 1770. The peninsula is flanked by Botany Bay to the north and Bate Bay and Port Hacking to the south. The area is now heavily industrialized. **Royal National Park** and the adjacent **Heathcote National Park** lie to the south of Port Hacking and are pleasant areas of nature reserve traversed by Princes Highway with many attractive picnicking spots. The beaches along the coast are renowned for their surf.

CAMPBELLTOWN (On Hume Highway)

(Population 16 374)

An important dairying and fruit growing centre 53 kilometres south-west of Sydney, Campbelltown also has well developed engineering and textiles industries. The town is of considerable historical interest. The Hawkesbury area was subject to bad floods and the Campbelltown district was a vital reserve area in food production for early Sydney. Macquarie visited the area in 1810 and the town was proclaimed in 1820. It achieved great prosperity during the mid-19th century and numbers of handsome and substantial buildings were constructed, many in the Georgian style.

Campbelltown is associated with the legend of Fisher's Ghost. In 1826 a convict named Worral murdered Fisher, a settler, and threw the body into a creek. Three months later a farmer named Farley claimed to have seen Fisher's ghost and the body was found. Worral, who had said that Fisher had returned to England under a false name, leaving him in charge of the farm, was arrested. Inquiries in England showed that the story was untrue. The legend is the subject of an opera by John Gordon and a verse play by Douglas Stewart.

Historic Buildings. Town: **Church of St Peter** (early period), somewhat altered then returned in 1962 to original simplicity. **Glenalvon,** Lithgow Street, early publican's house, bold and pleasing architecture. **Denham Court House,** begun in 1812 and the original cottage later incorporated. Georgian section designed by noted architect, John Verge, who also designed Camden Park House and Elizabeth Bay House. **Macquarie Fields,** near Glenfield. Built in Regency style about 1840, for John Hosking, first Mayor of Sydney. Recently renovated by National Trust and open for periodical inspection. Architect unknown. **Glenfield,** built for Dr Charles Throsby, of handmade bricks. Fine barn. **Campbellfield,** built for Dr Redfern about 1810, of handmade bricks with rough stone walls. Named after Lady Macquarie, wife of Governor. **Varronville,** Campbelltown-Cowpastures Junction. Built before 1827 and reputedly improved by later alterations.

Sports. Golf course. Tennis, bowls etc. Olympic swimming pool.

HORNSBY—KU-RING-GAI CHASE

Ku-ring-gai Chase is a national park of about 16 200 hectares of bushland on the foreshores of Pittwater and Cowan Creek, about 23 kilometres from the G.P.O. The Pacific Highway and northern railway line skirt its western boundary from Hornsby north to the Peat's Ferry Bridge across the Hawkesbury River. Its south-western corner is traversed by Ku-ring-gai Chase Road, Farrer Avenue and Bobbin Head Road; and by the eastern and northern segments of Mona Vale and Commodore Heights Roads. Still farther to the east lies the long spit of sandy land on which the fashionable beach suburbs of **Newport, Avalon** and **Palm Beach** have grown up. The historic Barrenjoey lighthouse is at the tip of this peninsula.

Ku-ring-gai was the name of the group of aborigines who originally occupied the area. It was declared a national park in 1894.

Ferry Services in Broken Bay Area. Palm Beach to Kangaroo Point and Bobbin Head (Cowan Creek), summer only. Also to Coasters Retreat, The Basin, Currawong and Great Mackerel beaches. **Church Point** to Scotland Island, Towler's Bay and Ewina Bay. **Patonga** to Brooklyn. Ferries also ply from **Wiseman's Ferry,** Lower Portland and Sackville down the Hawkesbury River. **Brooklyn** to Dangar Island and Spencer. **Gosford** to Woy Woy, Davistown, Killcare, Empire Bay and Kincumber.

SYDNEY'S SCENIC ENVIRONS

BROKEN BAY AND THE LOWER HAWKESBURY

The Hawkesbury River is an important waterway which rises in the Great Dividing Range near Crookwell, 278 kilometres south-west of Sydney, flows north and then turns sharply east into its estuary at Broken Bay.

The stream is known by two different names—the Nepean in its upper reaches and the Hawkesbury in the lower, because these sections were discovered at different times in the early history of the Colony and it was not realized that they were part of the one river system. The entire system is between 480 and 630 kilometres long and drains an area of some 332 000 hectares.

With the exception of the rocky terrain about the estuary, the valley is rich agricultural country and Sydney in its early days was largely dependent on its produce for subsistence. Most of the land once used to grow wheat and maize is now devoted to mixed farming, market gardening and fruit-growing (particularly citrus).

Much of the country through which the lower tidal reaches of the river pass is very beautiful. The famous English novelist, Anthony Trollope, who visited

Australia in the 1870s, wrote: 'Govett's Leap [a spectacular lookout in the Blue Mountains] astonished me very much, but not so much as the scenery of the Hawkesbury River. . . . The lower part of the river—that between Wiseman's Ferry and Broken Bay—is very much finer than the upper reaches. . . . The banks rise suddenly, sometimes covered with timber and sometimes bald, sometimes sloping and sometimes precipitous . . . broken here and there into lateral valleys which give to the imagination the idea that the glory of the scene is far spread and would repay pursuit. . . . To me [it was] more enchanting than those [waters] of either the Rhine or the Mississippi. . . .'

The description is just as valid today as when Trollope wrote it. The lower Hawkesbury is undoubtedly the most beautiful reach of river on the Australian continent, if one excepts the much smaller but blazingly spectacular Katherine Gorge in the Northern Territory and Giekie Gorge in the Kimberley.

One of the most delightful holidays Australia can provide is a leisurely few days or weeks spent cruising on the hundreds of miles of clear, sheltered water of Broken Bay's three long narrow branches—Pittwater, Cowan Creek and Brisbane Water. Pittwater, the southern branch, was named by Governor Phillip who described it as 'the finest piece of water I ever saw'.

'Live-aboard' launch cruises on the Hawkesbury have become very popular and a number of firms, most of which advertise in the classified pages of the Sydney telephone directory, charter craft capable of accommodating from four to nine people at surprisingly reasonable rates. The best cruisers are supplied with bottled gas, electric lighting, showers and toilets, cooking utensils, bed linen and crockery.

There are of course, many pleasant tourist resorts on the foreshores, where accommodation ranging from luxury hotels and motels to modest beach cottages can be obtained readily in all but the peak of the season, for which it is necessary to book well ahead.

The New South Wales Government Tourist Bureau can provide full details of facilities, accommodation and costs.

HISTORY In 1789 Governor Phillip and a party sailed up the river as far as Richmond Hill and two years later overlanded from Rosehill (Parramatta) to explore its banks. Settlement began in 1794 when 22 settlers were given 12 hectare grants of good land on the south bank. For many years all produce was sent to Sydney by boat, which accounts for the early development of a boat-building industry on Brisbane Water, where excellent timber was available. Many of the locally built craft were large enough to enter the sealskin trade in Bass Strait, which is notorious for its rough weather.

The white settlers soon came into conflict with the aborigines and by 1796 Governor Hunter was forced to station a military detachment at Windsor (then known as Green Hills) to maintain order. A vehicular road between Parramatta and Windsor and Richmond was completed in 1797.

During the next 30 or 40 years agriculture and forest industry flourished. The rich river flats were at first cultivated with hand hoes, then with bullock-drawn wooden ploughs and finally with horsedrawn iron ploughs. Early crops were almost exclusively wheat, maize and hops.

The timber-milling industry began about 1820. The saws were at first water-driven, then horses were used and finally, in the 1830s, steam was introduced. By the end of the century, however, most of the forests were cut out and the dairying industry had established itself. More recently fruit-growing—first peaches, apricots and plums, then citrus fruits—has taken over and the orchardists run poultry farms as well to control insects and weeds in the groves. Market gardening and mushroom-growing (particularly in abandoned railway tunnels on the old route of the western line into the mountains) are well established. Urban industry is chiefly associated with packing and processing the produce.

Main Towns, Resorts

GOSFORD

(Population 38 093)

The tourist centre of beautiful Brisbane Water, Gosford is 85 kilometres north of Sydney. It is also the main town of an extensive mixed farming, fruit and vegetable-growing district noted for the excellence of its citrus orchards and passionfruit plantations. Some timber is cut in the locality and building stone quarried. Its secondary industries are geared to fruit-packing and processing, but bricks, pipes and fibrous plaster also are produced.

History. The town was surveyed in 1839 and named by the Governor, Sir George Gipps, after his colleague, the second Earl of Gosford. About the same time, a rich Sydney tea merchant, Samuel Peek, built a private town at East Gosford. Both were incorporated into a single municipality in 1886. In 1854 the Peat's Ferry road was built, halving the time of travel from Sydney, and the town and district thereafter progressed rapidly. Citrus-growing was begun in 1885 by immigrants from Finland, and was from the first successful. In 1889 the opening of the Hawkesbury River Bridge allowed the town to be directly linked by rail with Sydney.

Places of Interest. Eric Worrell's **Reptile Park** (1.61 kilometres north). Worrell, an eminent herpetologist and naturalist, set up an aquarium at Ocean Beach, Woy Woy, where he also displayed a number of Australian reptiles. In 1960 he transferred to Gosford and now has the largest collection of reptiles in the Commonwealth. About 5 000 snakes are 'milked' for their venom in the park every year to supply the Commonwealth Serum Laboratories and other scientific institutions working on antivenenes. Visitors are welcome at the park and may watch the snakes being milked. There are a number of tame wombats and kangaroos in the enclosures open to the public. **Floraland Sanctuary** and Native Plants Nursery (8 kilometres west). **Henry Kendall's cottage** and orchard, West Gosford, is preserved as a memorial to the famous Australian poet, and now houses a museum of local history. **Kendall's Rock** (below the highway). **Somersby Falls** (11 kilometres north-west). A nature trail runs from the falls to Girrabool. **Mount Elliott Lookout** (11 kilometres north-east). **Mangrove Mountain** (24 kilometres north-west), citrus district. **Staples Lookout** (about 16 kilometres south-west). Panoramic views.

Sports. Racing and trotting (monthly meetings). Golf course. Bowls. Tennis. Yachting and water-skiing. Fishing (best months October to June). Olympic pool.

Accommodation. Three **hotels.** Recommended: Broadwater, Mann Street. Two **motels.** Recommended: Galaxy, Pacific Highway. One **private hotel.** Good **caravan and camping park,** all facilities.

Transport. **Electric train** service from Sydney. Local **bus** services.

WOY WOY-ETTALONG (Population 12 206)

About six kilometres south of Gosford. Boating, fishing, swimming etc. Headquarters of district **bus** and **ferry** services to many other resorts.

Accommodation. Three **hotels.** Recommended: Ettalong, The Boulevarde. **Guest houses.** **Caravan and camping park** (with stationary caravans for hire) at Ettalong.

TERRIGAL (Population 4 450)

Fine coastal and bush scenery. Matcham Ferneries (8 kilometers). Surfing and most other sports.

Accommodation. Two **hotels.** Highly recommended: Florida, The Esplanade. Four **motels.** Recommended: Clan, Ocean View Road. **Caravan and camping park,** all facilities.

PATONGA AND PEARL BEACH

Within Brisbane Water National Park, south of Woy Woy. Relatively secluded and unspoiled stony country. Fine fishing and impressive scenery on approaches. Noted for waratahs during spring flowering season.

Accommodation. **Caravan and camping park,** all facilities. **Holiday cottages** available. **Transport.** **Bus** services to Woy Woy and Gosford. **Ferry** service to Palm Beach.

ERINA PENINSULA

South of Terrigal. Beautiful wild country. Magnificent views and good fishing.

Accommodation. **Camping area** at MacMaster's Beach.

UPPER HAWKESBURY AND NEPEAN

As Anthony Trollope noted, the upper reaches of the Hawkesbury and Nepean lack the memorable quality of the lower reaches and the foreshores of Broken Bay, but the countryside is still charming, much of it intensively cultivated despite the fact that it is periodically subjected to severe flooding.

Main towns

PENRITH

(Population 27 461)

An historic town on the Nepean River and the Great Western Highway, 55 kilometres from Sydney and almost absorbed by the metropolis. The district produces beef cattle and dairy produce, maize, fruit and vegetables and fodder crops. Secondary industries are well developed and include engineering and electrical workshops, textile, plastics and aluminium-foil factories, and plants for the production of building material and concrete products.

History. The district was explored by Watkin Tench and William Dawes in 1789. It was at first known as Evan and later Castlereagh, but after the opening of the Blue Mountains road in 1815, a courthouse and small gaol were built and a grazing paddock established for travelling stock. It was then called Penrith after the English town. The early pioneers of the area were the Cox family and Henry Fulton, a transportee chaplain.

Warragamba Dam. A major source of water for the city of Sydney, Warragamba Dam is about 19 kilometres south of Penrith, across a bottleneck gorge below the junction of the Cox and Wollondilly Rivers. It occupies an area of 8 770 hectares and has an average depth of 27 metres. It backs up into the preciptously walled Burragorang Valley for a distance of 55 kilometres on the main southern arm, and contains about four times the volume of water in Sydney Harbour. The dam is 124 metres high and 335 metres long. It was constructed in about four years, between 1955 and 1959.

The great lake can be approached from either Penrith or through Liverpool or Cabramatta to the east, but its shores are difficult of access and it is best viewed from the air.

Other Places of Interest. Australia's first **lion reserve** opened at Warragamba Dam in 1968. More than 60 lions and cheetahs, none of them born free, range over 36 hectares of bushland, surrounded by double wire fences. Visitors pass through gates on Springsure Road, 7 kilometres from the village of **Wallacia.** They are warned not to leave their cars during a drive-through safari. Open daily. **Bullen's Animal World,** Wallacia, a **zoo** for children. **St Thomas's Church of England,** built in 1836. **'Fernhill',** home of Edward Cox, a son of William Cox, is still standing.

Accommodation. Several **motels** and **hotels.** Recommended: Log Cabin Motor Inn, Nepean Avenue (1.5 kilometres west of Penrith).

WINDSOR (Population 4 523)

One of Australia's oldest towns, Windsor is 56 kilometres north-west of Sydney and 21 kilometres from Parramatta. It is centre of a fertile agricultural and fruit-growing area. The first settlers arrived in 1794 and the district was then called Green Hills. The name was changed by Governor Macquarie in 1810. Macquarie took a particular interest in the settlement and personally selected the sites of its early churches and major residential allotments. A coach service from Sydney was started in 1832 and in 1864 the railway reached the town.

Historic Buildings. **Claremont Cottage** is on the site originally granted to John Pugh in 1796, but the cottage was not built until 1822. **Hawkesbury District Hospital,** Macquarie Street. Erected as convict barracks by Macquarie in 1820, it was converted into a convict hospital, then into an asylum and district hospital in 1823. The buildings were entirely remodelled in 1911. **St Matthew's Anglican**

Church, Moses Street, designed by Francis Greenway and built by convict labour with hand-made bricks. Construction began in 1817. **Macquarie Arms,** Thompson Square, built by an emancipist, R. Fitzgerald, at the request of Macquarie in 1815. It was used as an officers' mess between 1835 and 1840, then as a private home until 1874, when it became the Royal Hotel. The name has now been changed back to the original. The building is substantially unaltered. **St Matthew's Roman Catholic Church** and Rectory, Tebbutt Street, built about 1840—exceptionally fine buildings of the period. **Tebbutt's Observatory,** built for the distinguished astronomer John Tebbutt (1834-1916) who discovered the comet which bears his name; built in 1863 and extended about 1890. **Doctor's Terrace,** Thompson Square, built 1830, is excellently preserved. It was used as the town's post office during the 1850s. **Toll House,** Bridge Street, was probably built between 1814 and 1816. The keeper collected tolls on the Fitzroy Bridge until 1887. **Hawkesbury Museum,** Thompson Square. A colonial brick building on the site of John Howe's general store and ferry service. It later became the Daniel O'Connell Inn. (The museum is open from 10 am to 5 pm at weekends, and will be opened on request during the week.) **Court House,** Court Street. Built by William Cox in 1820-21 and designed by Greenway, it is an exceptionally fine example of design and craftsmanship.

Sports. Golf course. Bowls etc. Olympic swimming pool.

Accommodation. Two **hotels.** Preferred: Colonial, George Street. One **motel. Camping and caravan park,** no information on facilities.

RICHMOND (Population 3 809)

Sister town of Windsor and about 8 kilometres west of it. Richmond Hill was sighted and named by Phillip in 1789. The town, however, was not proclaimed until 1810.

Historic Buildings. Hobartville, Chapel Street, is the former home of William Cox junior, son of the Paymaster of the NSW Corps who built the road over the Blue Mountains in 1814 and also carried out minor exploration. It was built in 1828 to the design of Francis Greenway, the architect of many of Sydney's finest early buildings, in an elegantly Georgian style with 'bushranger-proof' doors, stone flagged verandahs, barred cellars and cedar woodwork. **Toxana House,** Windsor Street, was built in the 1860s for William Bowman, a member of the first NSW Parliament, whose family were pioneers on the Hawkesbury. It is now used as an historical museum. **St Peter's Anglican Church,** built 1837-41. **Woolpack Inn,** North Richmond. First known as Travellers' Rest and built in the 1830s. **School of Arts,** built about 1866. **'Belmont',** St John of God Hospital, North Richmond.

Also of Interest. Hawkesbury Agricultural College (1.5 kilometres south) on a holding of 1 400 hectares. It was founded in 1891, but the present building was constructed in 1895. The college accommodates 250 residential students. There are divisions for beef and dairy cattle, sheep, horses, pigs and poultry. **Richmond RAAF Base** (on road to Windsor). An airfield used for civilian flying training in 1915, it was taken over by the RAAF in 1927. **Australiana Village,** Wilberforce (about 5 kilometres north). Reproduction of an old-time rural settlement in the valley, with carefully restored furniture, implements, vehicles etc. The oldest surviving timber building in Australia, 'Rose Cottage' built in 1798, is on the site. **Ebenezer Presbyterian Church,** Portland Head (10 kilometres north), built in 1809 and the oldest church in Australia in which services are held regularly. **Lookout Points** commanding panoramic views: Terrace Park (about 5 kilometres west on Wilberforce-Kurmond Road; Vale of Avoca (10 kilometres west on Grose Vale Road); Cherry Park, near Kurrajong Heights. *Note:* Some of the finest bush walking in NSW is to be had in the mountains west of Windsor and Richmond and in the valley of the Grose River to the south-west.

Accommodation. One **hotel,** one **motel.** Motel preferred. At Wilberforce, one recommended **hotel-motel.**

TUGGERAH LAKES

The Tuggerah Lakes (Munmorah, Budgewoi and Tuggerah) are about 64 kilometres north of Sydney and cover an area of about 3 450 hectares. They have about 72 kilometres of foreshore. The narrow channels which separate them are spanned by bridges, giving access to the seaside resorts of The Entrance, Toukley and Budgewoi. The main town in the area is Wyong, on the railway line from Sydney to Newcastle. It is 4 kilometres up Wyong Creek and 106 kilometres from Sydney.

The chief industry of the region is tourism, but prawning and fishing fleets operate profitably from lake bases and citrus fruit, vegetable and mixed farming is carried on in the district.

THE ENTRANCE (Population 6 000)
At the ocean entrance of Tuggerah Lakes, it is a well-developed tourist town with facilities for all popular sports and visitors can enjoy good fishing and prawning. There are many entertainments—cinemas, dancing, carnivals etc.

Accommodation. Three **hotels.** Recommended: The Entrance, Gosford Road. Five **motels.** Recommended: Jetty, The Entrance Road. Many **guest-houses, holiday cottages** and **cabins. Caravan and camping parks,** all facilities, at Bateau Bay, Blue Lagoon, Long Jetty and Toowoon Bay

WYONG (Population 2 579)
Wyong is 23 kilometres north of Gosford. A number of small manufacturing industries have been established in the town and rutile-zircon is mined in the neighbourhood. The surrounding countryside is particularly attractive in spring and the sheltered waters of the lakes are suitable for all kinds of water sports.

History. The district was first sparsely settled in 1823, mainly by timber-getters who established camps and semi-permanent hamlets in the dense cedar forests. In 1854, Edward Hargreaves, who discovered gold at Summer Hill Creek near Bathurst, and began the great goldrush in 1851, built himself a house near the present site of Noraville, 19 kilometres east. The first citrus orchards were planted in 1887, but the settlers turned to agriculture only when the forests had been cut out.

Places of Interest. State forests of Wyong, Ongley and Orimbah. Large thermal **power stations** at Vales Point and Munmorah. **Burbank Horticultural Demonstration Farm** (of great appeal to gardeners). **Kangy Zoo** (6 kilometres south). **Scenic drive** through Yarramalong Valley to Kulnura, returning via Dog Trap Road to Orimbah forest.

Sports. Horse racing and trotting and greyhound coursing at the Wyong showground. Good golf course. Tennis, bowls etc. Swimming.

Accommodation. Two **hotels.** Preferred: Grand, Pacific Highway. Two **motels.** Preferred: Central Coast, Pacific Highway and Central Drive. **Guest-houses.** Two **caravan and camping parks,** limited facilities.

Other Resorts in Area

TOUKLEY
At junction of Tuggerah and Budgewoi Lakes with nearby settlements at Charmhaven, Canton Beach, Gorokan, Norah Head, Buff Point.

Places of interest include famous Norah Head lighthouse, Edward Hargreaves' homestead at Noraville. An annual aquatic festival is held. Good fishing and surfing.

Accommodation. One **motor hotel.** Five **caravan and camping parks,** all facilities. Numerous **guest-houses, holiday flats** and **cottages** available.

BUDGEWOI
Between Budgewoi and Munmorah Lakes in a very beautiful reserve noted for the abundance of its bird life. Good sports facilities. Fishing.

Accommodation. Caravan and camping park, all facilities.

THE BLUE MOUNTAINS

The Blue Mountains, a segment of the Great Dividing Range with an area of 141 000 hectares, begin about 64 kilometres west of Sydney. They contain some of the most spectacular mountain scenery in eastern Australia—tremendous sandstone precipices ringing densely wooded valleys which, viewed from a distance, are of an intense cobalt blue.

For nearly a century the plateau, bounded on the north by the Grose River and on the south and south-west by Cox's River and their tributaries, has been a favourite holiday place for the people of Sydney. It has been intensively developed for tourism and is now criss-crossed by more than 1 100 kilometres of roads, most of which are first class. The terrain, however, is so broken by deep gorges that considerable areas are still rarely visited, except by skilled bush-walkers and rock climbers.

Unfortunately much of the area has been repeatedly devastated by bushfires, but over the past few years fire-control measures have been so improved that the forest is being slowly regenerated, although the once prolific wildlife has been slower to recover.

The pure hue of the haze from which the mountains get their name is believed to be due to extremely small droplets of oil from eucalyptus forests (concentrated in the air above the enclosed valleys) intensifying the light refraction phenomenon called Rayleigh Scattering, which causes distant objects to appear blue.

The highest part of the Blue Mountains are about 1 100 metres above sea level. The winter months are cold, but for most of the year the climate is invigorating. The soil is stony and infertile.

Twenty-four towns and villages, almost all of them mainly dependent on the tourist trade for their existence, are now incorporated in the City of the Blue Mountains.

HISTORY The towering cliffs west of the Nepean River resisted all efforts by early explorers to break out of the narrow plains about Sydney until 1813 when Lieutenant William Lawson, William Charles Wentworth, Acting-Provost Marshal, and Gregory Blaxland, a free settler, found a ridge route which led them across the first of the two main ranges of the divide which separates the coastal tract from the plains of the interior. Later the same year the Assistant Surveyor-General, G. W. Evans, completed the crossing to the Bathurst Plains and discovered that large tracts of fertile, well-watered land suitable for grazing and agriculture lay beyond the barrier.

Governor Macquarie, anxious to make use of the newly discovered country and encourage further exploration of the interior, authorized the building of a road across the mountains. The job was begun by convicts and soldiers under the supervision of William Cox, a former military paymaster turned landowner, in the winter of 1814. It was completed as far west as the Macquarie River early in 1815. In April of that year the Governor, his wife and a party of 35 crossed the range, and formally founded and named a settlement at Bathurst.

The road, the survey of which is fairly closely followed by the modern highway, was a lifeline to the pastoralists of the west. It became even more important when gold was discovered near Bathurst in 1851 and the series of great rushes began.

Sydney people, however, did not discover the merits of the scenery and climate until the late 1870s, when rich men in Sydney began to build themselves elaborate holiday homes in the hills to escape the discomforts of summer on the plains.

Cobb and Co. ran a coach service between Sydney and the western goldfields from 1862 onwards until it was displaced by the railway which reached Bathurst in 1876.

Transport. The mountain towns are now served by a fast **electric train** service from Sydney, the journey between Sydney and Mount Victoria taking about two hours. There are numerous **motor coach** services from the city to Blue Mountains beauty spots. There are two main roads—the Great Western Highway (linking with the Olympic Way to Melbourne, at Bathurst) and the Bell's Line road which crosses the mountains to the north, via Windsor, Richmond and Kurrajong to Mount Victoria.

Main Towns

SPRINGWOOD

On Great Western Highway, at an altitude of 371 metres, 80 kilometres from Sydney. Named by Governor Macquarie. Good shopping centre. Pleasant year-round climate.

Places of Interest. Numerous scenic walks and lookouts, particularly Hawkesbury and Yellow Rock Lookouts on the road north to Richmond; St Martin's View, Sassafras Park; Flying Fox Home of the late Norman Lindsay, famous Australian artist.

Sports. Good golf course. Tennis, bowls, swimming. Miniature rifle range.

Accommodation. One **motel.** Several **guest-houses.**

Smaller Towns Nearby. Faulconbridge, Linden, Woodford. (Convicts' cell and whipping post preserved at Ball's Camp, Woodford). Lapstone and Glenbrook.

HAZELBROOK

At an altitude of 674 metres, 93 kilometres from Sydney.

Places of Interest. Lyre Bird Glen (1.61 kilometres from town) for native ferns and flowers. Horseshoe and Burgess Falls (north). Meeting of the Waters and Terrace Falls (south).

Accommodation. Caravan and camping park, limited facilities.

LAWSON

Altitude 732 metres, 92 kilometres from Sydney. Named after William Lawson, one of the first party to cross the mountains. The town was originally called 'Blue Mountain'. The area offers pleasant walks, including Empire Pass and Frederica Falls.

Sports. Golf, tennis, bowls, croquet. Swimming pool.

Accommodation. Guest-houses. Caravan and **camping park,** limited facilities. Holiday **cabins** available.

WENTWORTH FALLS

Altitude 854 metres, 113 kilometres from Sydney. The town was first known as 'The Weatherboard Hut' but later named after W. C. Wentworth of the original exploring party.

Places of Interest. National Pass (scenic walk), via Weeping Rock and Queen's Cascades to Valley of the Waters. Wentworth Falls (275 metres drop). King's Tableland bushwalking track.

Sports. Golf, tennis, bowls. Swimming pool.

Accommodation. Guest-houses.

KATOOMBA-LEURA

(Population 14 000)

Katoomba, and the smaller town Leura with which it is now merged, is the tourist centre of the Blue Mountains. It is entirely dependent economically on the traffic of holidaymakers and travellers from Sydney and western New South Wales or Victoria, via the Olympic Way. The Blue Mountains City Council estimates that in the course of a year at least half a million people visit the area it administers.

Katoomba and Leura are towns of pleasant appearance and have a number of attractive parks besides the magnificent mountain lookouts and bush walks which are their chief attraction.

History. Katoomba came into being in 1879, when J. G. North and T. S. Mort opened a small coal mine in the Jamieson Valley three kilometres from the centre of the present town. At the same time a number of prominent people in Sydney discovered the magnificence of the Blue Mountains scenery and the bracing, pleasant climate during the hot months of the year. They built elaborate holiday homes in choice sites and before long an extraordinary real estate boom occurred. Where the elite led, the proletariat followed and before long hotels and guest-houses were mushrooming along the road which had hitherto been regarded simply as a utilitarian access to the goldfields and pasture lands of the west.

Katoomba and Leura, being within short walking distance of some of the finest panoramic lookouts, outstripped rival settlements in growth. Despite the failure of the coal mine and the ups and downs of fashion in holiday resorts, they survive as very prosperous communities—the more so because they have now become almost dormitory towns for Sydney since the completion of the fast electric railway service from the city.

Katoomba was named after an aboriginal word meaning 'waterfalls' and Leura is believed to have got its name because of a slip in the official printing of the name Laura.

Places of Interest. Echo Point, a lookout commanding one of the most beautiful mountain panoramas in Australia, overlooking Jamieson and Burragorang Valleys and the Three Sisters (an extraordinary rock formation). **Mount Solitary, the Ruined Castle, Sublime Point, King's Tableland** etc. **Katoomba Falls** and **Orphan Rock, Leura Cascades** and **Bridal Veil** (waterfall). (Note: Leura Cascades, the Three Sisters, Katoomba Falls and the Orphan Rock are floodlit at night between 7 and 9 o'clock.) **Malaita Point,** overlooking Jamieson Valley. **Cyclorama Point,** overlooking Megalong and Jamieson Valleys, and **Narrow Neck** (separating the valleys), the highest point in the area. (In clear weather it is possible to see Mount Gibraltar at Bowral, and Mount Jellore, more than 97 kilometres distant). **Gordon Falls** and reserve and **Fairy Dell,** south of Leura township. **Everglades,** 5-hectare garden property, Denison Street, Leura. It was acquired by the National Trust as a national garden and arboretum.

Drives. Most vantage points and features listed above can be viewed from Cliff Drive, which begins on the Western Highway, just west of the town and skirts the precipitous walls of the tableland from Cyclorama Point to Leura Falls. There are, of course, many other scenic drives to places of interest in the district which are listed under individual towns. Roads are on the whole good.

Walks. The Blue Mountains provide splendid walking of all grades—from the gentle to the highly strenuous. Prince Henry's Cliff Walk (about 11 kilometres in all and split into three well-graded sections) follows the line of the precipices from Katoomba Falls to Gordon Falls via Echo Point and Leura Falls. Federal Pass, from Katoomba Falls to Leura Falls (about 6.5 kilometres) skirts the same cliffs at their base and traverses interesting stands of rain forest and tree ferns. Access is by approximately 2 200 steps cut into the cliff faces and talus slopes at both ends of the 'pass', but they are well graded and offer no difficulty for an ordinarily fit walker. Minnehaha Falls, about five kilometres north of the town, makes an interesting walk for those genuinely interested in Australian mountain bush, but it is not a particularly spectacular route.

Novelties. Scenic Railway and Skyway, operating from a spot near Katoomba Falls, with revolving restaurant commanding a view of the valleys. The railway runs through the access tunnel of the abandoned coal mine to the floor of the valley, a distance of 400 metres, and the skyway runs on a cable strung between cliff faces and travels at a height of 300 metres above the valley for a distance of 460 metres.

Entertainments. One **cinema.** Hotel and guest-house **cabarets.**

Sports. Golf courses at Katoomba and Leura (the latter excellent). Tennis courts. Bowling and croquet greens etc. Swimming pools. Motor racing on Catalina circuit in Frank Walford Park. Trotting track. Riding schools. Rock climbing.

Accommodation. One **hotel.** Eight **motels.** Highly recommended: Echo Point, Echo Point Road, Katoomba; Leura, Fitzroy Street, Leura. Innumerable **guest-houses** and **private hotels. Camping and caravan park** (Katoomba Falls Reserve), all facilities. Furnished holiday **flats and cottages** available. At Medlow Bath, 6.5 metres north-east of Katoomba, one **hotel,** the historic Hydro Majestic.

Tours. Motor coach and **car tours** to all mountain resorts and beauty spots and to the nearer towns of central New South Wales are available from Katoomba and from Sydney. **Aerial sightseeing tours** from Katoomba Aerodrome.

BLACKHEATH (Population 2 226)

Altitude 1064 metres, 120 kilometres from Sydney.

Places of Interest. Megalong Valley (scenic drive). Evans Lookout and Grand Canyon Track to Neate's Glen (the latter a moderately strenuous walk). Govett's Leap Lookout and Rodriguez Pass (also strenuous) to Evans Lookout or Neate's Glen.

Sports. Good golf links. Tennis courts. Bowling greens. Riding schools. Blackheath celebrates a Rhododendron Festival in November every year.

Accommodation. Four **motels.** Recommended: High Mountains, Great Western Highway. Several **guest-houses.** Holiday **cabins.** Furnished **flats** and **cottages** available. **Caravan and camping park,** all facilities.

MOUNT VICTORIA

Altitude 1 064 metres, 127 kilometres from Sydney.

Places of Interest. Mount York (with commemorative pavilion opened in 1913). Mitchell's Lookout, at head of Victoria Pass, fine views of Kanimbla Valley and tablet to the memory of Sir Thomas Mitchell who supervised the building of the road through the pass. Scenic drives to Mount Wilson (fine avenues of elm, chestnut and walnut trees). Hartley village, historic settlement with old Court House and inn. Victoria Falls, lookout.

Accommodation. One **hotel.** One **motel. Guest-houses.** Holiday **cabins** and **cottages.**

JENOLAN CAVES

The Jenolan Caves, 188 kilometres west of Sydney and 77 kilometres south-west of Katoomba, are the best known and most spectacular limestone caves in Australia. They are situated in extremely rugged mountainous country in a 2 428-hectare wildlife reserve. There are eight 'dark' caves, approached through three enormous open arches, which have been developed for tourists and are now elaborately lit by electricity to display the fantastic forms and subtle colours of the calcite deposits within—stalactites, stalagmites, pillars, shawls, canopies and nodules.

Geologists estimate that the water erosion of the elevated limestone and marble strata which formed the caves began about half a million years ago and is still continuing. The whole system has not yet been completely explored by speliologists.

More than 150 000 tourists visit the Jenolan Caves every year. The eight caves open to guided inspection are: The Imperial Cave (discovered 1879); the Chifley Cave (1881); Lucas Cave (1860); Skeleton Cave (1903); Orient Cave (1904); Temple of Baal (1904); Ribbon Cave (1904); River Cave (1903).

Regular inspection hours are: Morning, 10, 10.15, 10.30 and 11. Afternoon, 1.30, 1.45, 2 and 4. Evening, 8. Inspection fees vary from 70c to $A1 (children under 15, half price). Restriction is made on the size of parties in the Ribbon and Skeleton Caves (eight persons) and the Orient and Ribbon Caves and Temple of Baal (25 persons).

At least two days—preferably three—are necessary to see and enjoy the best that Jenolan has to offer. Opinions vary, but travellers who have only one day to spare would probably be well advised to give the Imperial Cave and the Temple of Baal preference.

Photography inside the caves is permitted only at 11 am and 4 pm (one cave each day) without extra charge. Special photographic tours may be arranged.

History. The aborigines undoubtedly used the caves long before the arrival of white men. The first European to discover them was a bushranger named James McKeown who terrorized and robbed settlers on the Great Western Road in the early 1830s. In 1838 one of his victims, James Whalan, tracked McKeown through previously unexplored country to the Devil's Coachhouse, one of the great open arch caves at Jenolan. He discovered that the bushranger had established himself on a small, carefully cultivated farm in the valley. The following day Whalan returned with his brother, Charles, and two troopers. They surprised the bushranger in a large cavern now known as McKeown's Hideout.

The Whalan brothers guided visitors to the area for many years. In 1866 the NSW Government declared the caves and their environs a reserve and appointed a regular 'keeper', Jeremiah Wilson. Development was hastened after the completion of a good motor road from the Western Highway in the 1920s.

Accommodation is at **Jenolan Caves House,** a licensed hotel run by the NSW Government Tourist Bureau. The standard is good. A billiards room, ballroom, table tennis room and tennis court are provided for the use of guests.

Other attractions include walks through the nature reserve with its great variety of birds and animals and a 40-kilometre drive to **Kanangara Walls** from which the panorama of wild mountain bush is spectacular.

LITHGOW

(Population 13 135)

Lithgow is an important coalmining and manufacturing city on the north-western fringes of the Blue Mountains 123 kilometres from Sydney. A large State mine and several smaller private mines are working the Western Coalfield, which extends from the valley of the Grose River to Kandos and Ulan. The seam is estimated to contain about 400 million tonnes of black bituminous coal.

The secondary industries of Lithgow include the Commonwealth Small Arms Factory, a large power station, a textile mill, clothing factories, a brick works and a brewery. The urban area is not attractive but the surrounding countryside is noted for its beauty.

History. Lithgow—originally Lithgow Valley—was named after William Lithgow (1784-1874), at one time Auditor-General of New South Wales. Flour and woollen mills were established in the valley by Andrew Brown in 1858 and fuel for them was mined at Bowenfels. After the extension of the western railway in 1869, four mines were opened and the village expanded rapidly. T. S. Mort, the early Australian industrialist, opened Australia's first meat chilling works at Bowenfels in 1873. Two years later an ironworks and blast furnace, founded by James Rutherford, began operations and by 1880 two copper smelters were in commission. In 1894 a sheet steel rolling mill began production and in 1900 the first open hearth steel furnace was completed. In 1908 the ironworks was bought by G. and C. Hoskins who founded Australian Iron and Steel Pty Ltd. Major operations were transferred to Port Kembla in 1928.

Until 1910 the railway descended the mountains east of Lithgow by the famous Zig Zag on which two locomotives, one pushing and the other pulling, were required for each train.

Places of Interest. Defunct **kerosene shale works** at Wolgan and Capertree Valleys. Nearby **Mount York, Mount Blaxland** and **Hartley Vale. Zig Zag National Reserve.**

Sports. Usual facilities.

Accommodation. Two **hotels.** Recommended: Commercial. Two **motels.** One **caravan and camping park,** all facilities.

SOUTHERN HIGHLANDS

(Traversed by Hume Highway)

The Southern Highlands district comprises about 258 000 hectares of mountainous, picturesque country south and west of Sydney, less than two hours drive from the centre of the city, and approached through Liverpool.

The Gib Rock (Mount Gibraltar, 853 metres) and Mount Jellore dominate the landscape and from their tops magnificent panoramas may be seen. These mountains are believed to be the denuded plugs of old volcanoes, the lava from which has formed the mineral-rich soil of a district in which there are fine farmlands and stands of rain forest supporting abundant wildlife. Large areas of the more remote mountains have been declared sanctuaries. The highlands are drained by the Wollondilly River flowing north, and the Shoalhaven flowing from west to east.

Very little is now known about the original natives of the region, but from descriptions by early settlers they seem to have been nomadic people wearing skin garments, and decorated with beads made of reeds, headcloths of net and quills thrust through their noses. Some tribes violently resisted the white invasion of their territory and all were skilled mountaineers. Their most famous leader, Cannabygal, was killed in 1816 in a native rising. The pure bloods died out very quickly. By 1870 none were left.

Exploration of the district was stimulated even before the end of the 18th century when Irish convicts escaped into the bush from the Sydney district, spurred by the notion that China was only 250 kilometres away over the mountains. This curious belief was so persistent that Governor Hunter sent out a party of convicts under guard to see the fallacy of it for themselves. The expedition left Parramatta in 1798, led by John Wilson, an emancipist who lived with the aborigines and had learned something of their bushcraft. The reports he brought back were the first authentic information about the district to reach the Government.

By 1815 most of the land about Camden and Campbelltown had been taken up, and two years later Dr Charles Throsby, of Glenfield Park, led an expedition which closely examined the Berrima district. Later Throsby was responsible for the building of the first road from Picton to the Goulburn Plains.

The new land was attractive, but conditions of life were hard. The first crops were taken from hand-hoed fields of wheat and maize. Dairying—which is the mainstay of the region today—began in mid-century after wheat crops suffered major damage from rust and smut. (Much of Sydney's milk supply still comes from Berrima farms.)

The district suffered from the depredations of such notorious bushrangers as Ben Hall and Jack-jacky who, based on the Burragorang Valley, repeatedly held up travellers and raided lonely settlements.

So dense was the forest in the Yarrawa and Wingecarribee areas that the country remained virtually a no-man's-land until towards the end of the century.

CAMDEN (Population 5 357)

Birthplace of the merino sheep industry in Australia, Camden is a pleasant, rural town on the banks of the Nepean, 64 kilometres south-west of Sydney. It is now the centre of a district mainly devoted to dairy farming, viticulture and fruit growing.

History. In 1795 two convicts discovered wild cattle, the descendants of strays, grazing on the river flats and called the area Cowpastures. In 1805 John Macarthur received a 2 000-hectare grant which he named Camden Park after the Secretary of State for the Colonies who issued the land grants. Macarthur ended up by owning about 12 000 hectares in the district. It was here he carried out his experiments in merino woolgrowing and sheep breeding which were continued on the estate until the 1860s. Camden Park homestead is still owned by descendants of John Macarthur.

Dairying began in the district in 1826 and became the chief industry when smut and rust began to affect wheat crops. The village was surveyed in 1836 and the municipality proclaimed in 1889.

Places of Interest. **Camden Park** homestead. Churches of **St John,** Camden (begun 1840, completed 1849) and **St Paul,** Cobbity.

Accommodation. One **motel.**

Transport. **Rail** services on main southern line.

PICTON (Population 1 512)

Historic small town, 80 kilometres south-west of Sydney, on southern railway and Hume Highway. Nearby features include Nepean, Avon and Cordeaux dams.

Accommodation. One **hotel.**

MITTAGONG (Population 3 620)

A commercial and tourist centre near the Nattai River, 124 kilometres south-west of Sydney, Mittagong serves a district producing mixed farm crops, milk, vegetables and poultry. Coal and trachyte and building marble are mined, and the town has a malting works, a veterinary research station and other light industries.

History. The district was discovered in 1802 by the explorer F. Barratier, but the first settlers did not arrive until 1821, when W. Charker (or Chalker) received a 81-hectare grant. A village grew up in the late 1820s to serve travellers on their way to 'The New Country' to the south. In 1833 iron ore was found west of the town and between 1848 and 1880 iron was smelted at the Fitz Roy Ironworks, where a second village first named Nattai and then New Sheffield sprang up. Kerosene shale was also mined in the region between 1878 and 1902, but operating costs and labour trouble caused the work to be closed. Mittagong means 'little mountain'.

Places of Interest. **Frencham School** and **Sturt Educational Centre** (Australian experiment in progressive education). **Mount Alexandra** and **Lake Alexandra,** scenic walk in November when waratahs are in flower. **Sixty Foot Falls.** Lookouts at **Mount Gibraltar** and **Mount Alexandra. Joadja** ghost town, site of old-time shale mine.

A Dahlia Festival is held annually.

Sports. Golf course. Bowls, tennis etc. Olympic swimming pool.

Accommodation. Four **motels.** Recommended: Poplars, Hume Highway. **Guest-houses. Holiday cottages. Caravan and camping park,** all facilities.

Transport. **Rail** services on southern line.

BOWRAL (Population 5 913)

Main town of a productive dairying, fruit-growing and mixed farming district, Bowral lies 129 kilometres south-south-west of Sydney. Trachyte is quarried in the hills. The town and its surroundings are picturesque and attract many holidaymakers.

History. First exploration was carried out in 1798 by a party under John Wilson. John Oxley applied for a cattle run in the district but did not complete payment of the purchase money. However, the estate was awarded to his sons as a gift in recognition of their father's services to exploration of the colony. The estate was subdivided and surveyed for a townsite which was proclaimed in 1863. It became a fashionable tourist resort for Sydney's well-to-do families in the 1880s. Bowral is the aboriginal name for Mount Gibraltar.

Places of Interest. **Mount Gibraltar (The Gib) Reserve,** a 24-hectare bird and animal sanctuary. Scenic drives to **Fitzroy, Belmore** and **Carrington** waterfalls (east of Moss Vale). **Wombeyan Caves** (74 kilometres west-north-west) comprising three fine limestone caves, **Wollondilly, Kooringa** and **Junction,** which are open for inspection by guided parties. No accommodation is available at caves site, but there is an excellently equipped **caravan and camping park** with tennis courts available. The reserve has been planted with many flourishing exotic trees and shrubs.

Bowral celebrates a Tulip Festival in October and its annual Horse Show in January draws horse breeders from all over Australia.

Sports. Trotting track, riding schools, tennis courts, golf course etc.

Accommodation. Three **hotels.** Recommended: Craigieburn, Centennial Road. One **motel. Guest-houses.** Furnished **cottages.**

Transport. **Rail** services on southern line. **Aerial scenic tours** on Saturdays from Glenquarry aerodrome.

MOSS VALE (Population 3 233)

Moss Vale is 140 kilometres south-south-west of Sydney on the Highland Way, which detours from the Hume Highway at Mittagong and rejoins it at Marulan, east of Goulburn. It is the market town for a district which produces beef cattle, fat lambs, dairy produce, blood horses and fruit and vegetables. Limestone and granite are quarried in the area. There is a large cement works in town.

History. The region was first settled by a nephew of Dr Charles Throsby, of Liverpool. He built a homestead, Throsby Park, between 1834 and 1837, and the house still stands. The town, proclaimed in 1861, was named for Throsby's herdsman, Jemmy Moss. A municipality was proclaimed in 1888, but the district was adversely affected by the depression of the early 1890s and it was merged with the Wingecarribee Shire.

Places of Interest. **Throsby Park House** (proclaimed for preservation by the National Trust and occasionally open for inspection). **Moreton National Park,** 20 235 hectares of bushland with deep gorges, waterfalls, and many forestry tracks of interest to naturalists and bushwalkers. Scenic drives (especially at blossom time) through Bundanoon to **apple orchards of Penrose, Wingello, Tallong. Cambewarra Mountain. Kangaroo Valley,** to south-east, a picturesque village in charming bush setting on road to Nowra.

Moss Vale celebrates a Festival of Flowers in October and organizes a championship rodeo on New Year's Day when leading rough riders compete.

Sports. Championship golf course. Tennis, bowls. Greyhound racing track. Swimming pool.

Accommodation. One **hotel.** Two **motels.** Recommended: Bong Bong, Argyle Street. **Guest-houses. Caravan park,** all facilities.

Transport. **Rail** services on southern and Illawarra lines.

BERRIMA (Population 596)

The small town of Berrima, 137 kilometres south-west of Sydney on the Hume Highway and 10 kilometres north-west of Moss Vale, is a 'must' for any traveller interested in Australian history. It is an extremely important relic of early colonial life in New South Wales—a village which has been preserved as it was in the early 19th century, entirely Australian in character and built of local materials to suit local conditions. It contains a number of exceptionally fine sandstone buildings which will greatly appeal to students of architecture.

A Berrima Village Trust was set up in 1963 to protect and preserve all lands and buildings of beauty and cultural or historical interest. The Trust comprises representatives of local and State government departments, the National Trust, the Royal Australian Institute of Architects, the Royal Australian Historical Society, the Berrima District Historical Society and local residents. Berrima means 'black swan'.

History. The district was discovered in 1798 by John Wilson's party, and re-discovered by the Hume brothers in 1814. The townsite was selected in 1829 by Thomas Mitchell, Surveyor General of New South Wales, and surveyed by Hoddle, who later surveyed the site of Melbourne. The town was proclaimed in 1831 when it was intended that it should become the principal centre of the new farming areas on the highlands then being opened up.

Historic Buildings. **Court House,** built 1838, last used for hearings in 1900 and now the Berrima School of Arts. **Berrima Gaol,** built 1835-39, enlarged 1866, closed in 1909 and used as an internment camp in first world war, remodelled and opened again in 1949 as a training centre for the rehabilitation of young prisoners. **Surveyor General Inn,** named for Major Mitchell, and claimed to be the oldest continuously licensed public house in Australia. The first license was granted to James Harper on 29 June 1835. **Church of Holy Trinity,** designed by Edmund Blackett, one of the most distinguished architects of the early days; foundation stone laid in 1847. St Francis Xavier's **Roman Catholic Church,** built on site of old convict stockade, 1849. **Presbyterian Church. 'Harper's Mansion.' Coach and Horses Inn. 'Allington',** residence first built as Victoria Inn. **White Horse Inn Motel,** first built as coaching inn.

Accommodation. One **motel** with licensed restaurant. **Caravan and camping park,** limited facilities.

Transport. **Rail** services on southern line to Moss Vale, then **road** coaches.

BUNDANOON (Population 748)

On the edge of the plateau overlooking the Kangaroo and Shoalhaven River valleys, Bundanoon is a small farming town and tourist resort, about 160 kilometres from Sydney on the Highland Way. The mountain scenery in the locality is superb.

History. The area was first sighted by Wilson's party in 1798, but the first mention of the name Bundanoon (then spelt Bantanoon) occurs in Charles Throsby's Journal for 1818. Selectors began to take up land in the district after 1861 and the little town flourished during the tourist boom of the 1880s. It was proclaimed in 1870 and incorporated in the Wingecarribee Shire in 1933 The name means 'deep gullies'.

Places of Interest. Glow Worm Glen. Echo Point lookout. **The Amphitheatre. River View** and the **Grand Canyon.** Several **wildlife sanctuaries,** noted for beauty of spring flowers. At nearby village of Exeter, **St Aidan's Church** (fine stained glass windows) and **'Invergowrie'** private garden, open at times for public inspection.

Sports. Golf course. Tennis, bowls etc. Polo-crosse, Olympic swimming pool. Riding school.

Accommodation. One **hotel.** Three **motels, guest-houses. Camping and caravan park,** all facilities.

Transport. Rail services on southern line.

GOULBURN

(Population 21 568)

A prosperous provincial city at the junction of the Wollondilly and Mulwaree Rivers and on the Hume Highway 209 kilometres south-west of Sydney, Goulburn is, strictly speaking, beyond the Southern Highlands but it is a convenient base from which to explore them. The district grows wool, wheat, potatoes, stone and pome fruits, and produces stud cattle and horses. Secondary industries include railway workshops, a tannery, abattoirs, flour mills and factories making woollens, footwear, clothing and chenille fabric. Goulburn stock and wool sales are important in the NSW economy.

History. The first white man to cross the site of the present city was John Oxley in 1820. The town was proclaimed in 1833 and for many years had a military garrison while the main southern road was being built by convicts based on Towrang Stockade (east of city), the main penal settlement of the southern districts. Police and parties of soldiers based on Goulburn patrolled the country from Lake Bathurst in the south to Oberon in the north in search of bushranging gangs who plagued the roads until well into the 1870s. The city was gazetted in 1863. It was named after Henry Goulburn, Secretary of State for War and the Colonies.

Historic Buildings. Goulburn Court House. Cathedrals of **St Saviour** and **SS Peter and Paul.**

Places of Interest. Town: **War Memorial and Museum** on Rocky Hill, from which good views of the city are obtained. **Black Swan Sanctuary** on river. **Belmore** and **Victoria Parks.** District: **Bungonia Look Down.**

Sports. Golf course. Greyhound racing and trotting tracks. Bowls, tennis etc. Squash and basketball courts.

Goulburn celebrates a Lilac Time Festival in October.

Accommodation. Four **hotels.** Highly recommended: Rana Astor, Hume Highway. Nine **motels.** Highly recommended: Travelodge Central, Auburn and Verner Streets. Two **caravan and camping parks,** all facilities.

Transport. Rail services on southern and Canberra and Crookwell lines. 'Wool tours' and scenic tours of the district by **road coach** are available (inquiries, Goulburn Town Hall).

THE ILLAWARRA COAST

(Traversed by Princes Highway)

The coastal region south of Sydney bounded on the west by the Southern Highlands and on the south by Bateman's Bay is known as the Illawarra, a corruption of the aboriginal word *alowrie*, meaning 'a high and pleasant place by the sea'.

Its attractions include fine surfing beaches and magnificent panoramic views along the whole coastline, water sports, and prawning and fishing in many inlets including Lake Illawarra, rugged and beautiful lake and mountain scenery in the Illawarra and Canbewarra Ranges, and inspection of heavy industries at Wollongong and Port Kembla. The summer climate is pleasant and the standard of accommodation and sports facilities at the various resorts good.

HISTORY Captain Cook's logbook mentions an unsuccessful attempt to land on the coast in 1770, and Lieutenant Richard Bowen in 1791 sighted and named Jervis Bay. The first Europeans to examine the area at close quarters were Bass and Flinders who noted the name given to it by the natives.

In 1797 survivors from the wreck of the ship *Sydney Cove*, making their way back to Port Jackson, reported finding coal at Coalcliff, just south of Stanwell Park. George Bass was dispatched to verify the account and on a second voyage discovered Kiama Harbour and the inlet at the mouth of the Shoalhaven River. The Government Surveyor, James Meehan, visited the district in 1805 and reported the existence of dense cedar forests. The first settlers moved large herds of cattle into the new country after Charles Throsby opened up a land route on to the plains in 1816.

The cedar forests of the area were vigorously exploited in the 1820s and agriculture was established during the next decade when the main crops were wheat, maize and potatoes. Dairying began in 1840 when butter was made on the farms for sale in Sydney. In 1887 the first co-operative butter factory in New South Wales was started at Kiama. About the same time the famous Illawarra Shorthorn breed of cattle was developed.

Coalmining began at Mount Keira, north of Wollongong, in 1849. Large mines were in production by 1880 and secondary industries began to develop. Today the city is Australia's second largest producer of iron and steel.

WOLLONGONG—PORT KEMBLA

(Population 198 768)

The city of Greater Wollongong, 82 kilometres south of Sydney, is a fusion of numbers of settlements which developed more or less independently until an era of great industrial expansion began after the second world war. Wollongong is now the third largest city in New South Wales and the seventh largest in the Commonwealth. The rural industries on which the prosperity of the Illawarra used to be based are declining as secondary industries continue to expand, but dairying is still carried on in the south and a fishing fleet still operates from the original harbour.

Wollongong produces high-grade coking coal (8 000 000 tonnes annually), pig iron, strip and billet steel, wire, tinplate, machinery and various steel products, copper, lead and zinc concentrates, industrial chemicals, fertilizers, bricks, textiles, clothing and many other manufactures. Ore for the blast furnaces and steelworks is imported from Western Australia and from Whyalla in South Australia. The heavy industries are concentrated in the port area.

History. A village was established near Wollongong proper in 1816 but a town was not planned for more than 30 years. The Surveyor-General, Thomas Mitchell, approved the site because of its proximity to a good harbour and the town was proclaimed in 1843. The first coalmine at Mount Keira was opened by James Schoobert in 1849 and another mine at Belambi was producing by 1857. Underground mining of the high-grade coal measures beneath the eastern slopes of the Illawarra Range proved very profitable and Belmore Basin, an enlargement of the natural harbour, was constructed between 1861 and 1868 with convict labour to accommodate the increased shipping. The tonnage shipped from the basin declined later when an artificial harbour at Port Kembla was developed to handle export coal for Asian countries and the railway from Sydney was completed.

In 1865 Wollongong produced the first kerosene made in Australia from local shale, and in 1876 the first metallurgical coke was manufactured. Development of the harbour at Port Kembla was authorized in 1898 and two breakwaters were completed in 1900-01.

Places of Interest. Lake Illawarra (6 700 hectares of shallow water between Port Kembla and Shellharbour and the foothills of the Illawarra Range). Good prawning and fishing grounds. Seventeen surf beaches extending northwards to the boundaries of metropolitan Sydney. **Botanic Gardens,** Kieraville. **Flagstaff Hill and lighthouse. Scenic reserves** at Avon, Cataract, Cordeaux, Nepean and Woronora dams, west and north of the city. **Lookouts** on Princes Highway to the north including Sublime Point, Mount Keira and Mount Ousley (among the finest coastal panoramas in Australia). **St Michael's Anglican Church** (built 1859). **Port Kembla Steelworks** (inspections Monday to Friday, free of charge, public holidays excepted). The Visitors' Reception Centre shows documentary films. *Note:* Visitors must wear closed footwear for inspections. Sandals or thongs not permitted.

Sports. Three excellent public golf courses. Racecourse. Greyhound racing. Yachting. Bowls, tennis courts etc. Tenpin bowling alleys, ice skating rink. Squash courts. Sea and lake fishing. Water skiing.

Accommodation. City: Six directory-listed **hotels.** Recommended: Harp, Corrimal Street. Five **motels.** Recommended: Downtown, Crown Street. Environs: Recommended: Berkeley Hotel,

Devon Street, Berkeley. Cabbage Tree Motel, Fairy Meadow. **Camping and caravan park,** all facilities.

Note: There is a hotel and guest-house accommodation at Austinmer and Thirroul.

Transport. Frequent **rail** service to Sydney and Nowra. Local **bus** services.

SHELLHARBOUR (Population 6 073)

A popular holiday resort and residential town south of Lake Illawarra, 106 kilometres south of Sydney and 24 kilometres from Wollongong, Shellharbour is one of the oldest Illawarra settlements. It was used as a port in the 1830s when a jetty and stone breakwater were built. Early industries were blue metal quarrying and beach-sand goldmining. After the opening of the South Coast railway the port declined, but the town was so pleasantly situated that it prospered as a seaside holiday centre for the people of Wollongong. Local government headquarters are at Albion Park, 8 kilometres west.

Places of Interest. **Macquarie Pass, Jamberoo Falls,** Windang Peninsula **beaches.**

Sports. Tennis. Bowls. Fishing and boating. Good surfing.

Accommodation. One **hotel.** One **motel. Camping and caravan park.** Holiday **flats** and **cottages.**

Transport. **Rail** services to Wollongong and Nowra. (*Note:* Railway station is 5 kilometres from town.)

KIAMA (Population 3 308)

A town in a lovely setting near the Minnamurra River, Kiama is the centre of a prosperous dairying and mixed farming district 118 kilometres south of Sydney. Its harbour, suitable only for small vessels, was found by Bass in 1797 and used by cedar-getters from 1815 onwards. The land on which the town now stands was reserved by John Oxley in 1826.

Kiama was surveyed in 1838 and gazetted a town the following year. It then comprised about a dozen huts surrounded by swamps infested with black snakes and forest in which giant stinging-trees thrived, but within the lifetime of the first generation of settlers it was transformed into a model settlement which resembled a village in Devonshire, according to writers of the time.

In the early days the quarrying of blue metal was a very important industry in the district.

Harbour improvement works were carried out between 1861 and 1876 and a lighthouse built in 1886. In 1954 the municipality was enlarged to include the nearby towns of Jamberoo and Gerringong. The aboriginal word *kiahama* is said to mean 'the sea makes a noise'.

Places of Interest. **The Blowhole,** on a rocky headland near the town. When high seas are running, spray is forced high into the air like a gigantic fountain. Coloured searchlights are used to illuminate it. Barren Grounds **Wildlife Reserve,** 1 740 hectares on the heights above Jamberoo Valley, is 16 kilometres west. **Saddleback Mountain** and **Mount Pleasant Lookouts** have particularly fine panoramic views. **Minnamurra Falls** and **Wildlife Reserve,** a natural rainforest area where interesting species of trees including the now rare red cedar are labelled. **Gerringong** and **Werri Beach** (11 kilometres south) are popular for surfing and fishing.

Sports. Olympic and rock swimming pools. Golf course. Tennis courts, bowling greens etc.

Accommodation. Two **hotels.** Recommended: Tory's, Terralong Street. Five **motels.**Recommended: Brigdale, Princes Highway. Three **caravan and camping parks,** all facilities. Holiday **flats, cottages** and **cabins** for rent.

Transport. **Rail** services to Nowra and Wollongong. Local **road** services.

Smaller resorts nearby. Berry (hotel accommodation), Bombo, Gerroa and Minnamurra.

NOWRA

(Population 12 866)

Nowra is the principal town of the Shoalhaven River district, 163 road kilometres south of Sydney. The region produces hardwood timbers, maize, pigs, vegetables and dairy produce and the town has a paper mill and rubber goods factory, but it is more importantly the focal point of the big and still growing tourist industry. It is ideally placed for holidays of exploration. The gorges of the Shoalhaven River are rugged and fascinating and the ranges still covered with dense forests.

History. The district was first settled in 1822 but the town was not officially established until 1857 when, at the first land sale, it was discovered that the Government 'planners' had made no provision for public institutions or buildings. However, as a bakery, hotel, church and school had already been erected, the population was not greatly disturbed. The town was incorporated with the Shire of Shoalhaven in 1948. The South Coast railway terminates at Bomaderry, about three kilometres away. The name derives from the aboriginal word meaning 'black cockatoo'.

Places of Interest. **Kangaroo Valley** (23 kilometres north-west) provides magnificent country for bush-walking, riding, fishing, canoeing etc. **Hotel** and **guest-house accommodation** is available. It is an especially attractive resort in the spring wildflower season. **Fitzroy Falls,** 39 kilometres north-west. **Belmore Falls,** 47 kilometres north-north-west. **Hanging Rock** and **War Memorial,** near town (fine lookout). **The Grotto,** an immense cavern (four kilometres from town). **Flat Rock Reservoir. Ben's Walk,** from Hanging Rock to a suspension bridge over Nowra Creek, said to be the first of its kind constructed in Australia. **Cambewarra Lookout. Fleet Air Arm Base** (HMAS *Albatross*), 11 kilometres south.

Nowra celebrates an annual Lyrebird Festival in October.

Sports. Fine golf course. Public tennis courts, bowling greens and croquet lawn. Racecourse. Surfing. Surf, rock and river fishing nearby. Speedboat racing. Olympic swimming pool. Canoeing on the Shoalhaven River.

Accommodation. One **hotel.** Five **motels.** Recommended: Vlademere, Princes Highway, and Travelodge, Kinghorne Street. Several **guest-houses.** Three **caravan and camping parks,** all facilities. **Cabins** at Gypsy Point (eight kilometres).

Transport. **Rail** services to Sydney from Bomaderry. **Road** services to far south coast towns.

Smaller resorts nearby. Crookhaven Heads, Culburra, Currarong (game fishing), Erowal Bay, Greenwall Point (hotel-motel), Orient Point, Kangaroo Valley village (guest-house), Shoalhaven Heads. Camping facilities, cottages and cabins are available at all these settlements.

ULLADULLA (Population 2 773)

A small fishing and farming town on Princes Highway 230 kilometres south of Sydney, Ulladulla is steadily gaining popularity as a summer holiday resort. The fishing fleet based on its artificial boat harbour supplies an appreciable proportion of Sydney's fresh fish. Dairying and timber-getting are the district's chief rural industries.

The village was established in the 1820s about an anchorage used by small craft taking loads of cedar to Sydney. One of the earliest settlers was the Reverend Thomas Kendall, grandfather of the poet, Henry Kendall. The townsite was surveyed in 1837.

Ulladulla and the nearby township of **MILTON** are at the northern end of a stretch of 60 kilometres of coastal lakes and lagoons with white sand beaches backed by a hinterland of fascinating mountains and secluded river valleys.

Places of Interest. **Lake Conjola** (north) is one of the most beautiful expenses of water on the coast. It has a well-equipped camping ground. **Lake Burrill,** a popular fishing, oystering and camping spot (south) has a good motel, three camping and caravan parks, and boats may be hired. **Pebbly Beach,** a secluded camping spot where wallabies come to feed on the reserve at nightfall: good rock and sea fishing; gemstone fossicking on the gravel. **Mollymook,** north of town, for surfing, golf on a good links, and excellent fishing. (Motels and guest-houses.) **Narrawallee** Inlet and beach, east of Milton. **Pigeon House Mountain** and **Castle Rock Mountain,** good climbs for novice mountaineers. **Yatte Falls,** in one of the most southerly stands of sub-tropical rainforest in Australia. At certain times of the year enormous flights of bats are seen at sunset. **Blackburn's Point,** for fine panoramas. **Durras Lake,** for good prawning, fishing, bushwalking (three camping grounds).

Sports. Golf course, surfing, water-skiing etc. River fishing as well as rock and surf fishing.

Accommodation. **Ulladulla:** One **hotel.** Four **motels.** Recommended: Town, South Street. Two **caravan and camping parks,** all facilities. **Milton:** Two **hotels.** Preferred: Marlin.

Transport. **Road** services to far south coast and **railhead** at Bomaderry.

JERVIS BAY

Jervis Bay, one of Australia's best natural ports, is an inlet on the south coast of New South Wales, 198 kilometres from Canberra and 203 kilometres from Sydney. It is part of the Australian Capital Territory, because the Seat of Government Act of 1908 which defined the site of the Federal capital stipulated that it must have sea access. In 1915, 11 600 hectares of Jervis Bay were transferred from New South Wales to Commonwealth jurisdiction. In the same year the Royal Australian Navy set up a training eollege there but in 1930, for economy reasons, the establishment was transferred to Flinders in Victoria. In 1958, the navy moved back.

The bay was sighted and named by Cook in 1770, and explored by Lieutenant Grant in 1801. Governor Macquarie visited the area in 1811 and favoured establishing a settlement there, but land access was found to be too difficult.

The port has never been developed commercially.

There are a number of small, picturesque holiday resorts on the shores. They include: **Huskisson,** for swimming (in sharkproof enclosures) and fishing; accommodation at one hotel and two caravan and camping parks. **Sussex Inlet,** for game fishing, swimming, golf, bowls etc; accommodation in guest-house, caravan and camping parks, flats, cottages and cabins. **St George's Basin,** in heavily wooded country, for fishing and boating. **Vincentia,** in Gurumbi wildlife sanctuary. **Currarong,** sometimes venue of State and Commonwealth underwater spear fishing championships; accommodation in camping area, cottages and cabins.

NEWCASTLE AND HUNTER RIVER DISTRICTS

The Hunter River Valley, roughly 160 kilometres north of Sydney, comprises an area of about 258 000 000 hectares, bounded on the east by the sea and on all other sides by precipitous and sometimes very rugged mountain ranges. It contains extensive coal measures which have been mined for 150 years and have been the basis of many heavy industries established in or near Newcastle, the State's second largest city. Its rich alluvial lands are used for intensive dairy farming, market gardening, fruit-growing, viticulture and the pasturage of beef cattle, fat lambs and bloodstock. Some of Australia's finest wines come from its vineyards.

The river is 560 kilometres long. It rises in the Mount Royal Range, flows south-west to the Denman district and then south-east to the Pacific near Newcastle, at its mouth. Its main tributaries are Wollombi Brook and the Paterson and Williams Rivers. Three-fifths of the land in the upper valley is too steep for agricultural use and cultivation is restricted to the small and very rich alluvial flats, but at Singleton the river emerges into wide plains.

The Hunter is subject to severe flooding. More than 30 major floods have been recorded since 1930. This is largely due to the rapacity with which the rich timber resources of the valley were exploited in the 19th century. Destruction of forest cover has resulted in rapid run-off from the catchment, and extensive erosion and silting. A succession of New South Wales Governments were inexplicably dilatory in instituting flood control and reclamation measures, but a long-term plan for reafforestation, soil conservation and flood control is now under way. A flood mitigation committee was established in 1945 and a Hunter Valley Research organization is active. One major flood-control dam has been built at Glenbawn and other storages are proposed.

The valley is traversed from south-east to north-west by the New England Highway and by the railway from Sydney (via Newcastle, Maitland, Singleton and Muswellbrook) to Wallangarra on the Queensland border.

A modern expressway links Newcastle with Sydney.

Both north and south of the river mouth there are deep inlets and large salt lakes of great beauty, on the shores of which there are many flourishing holiday resorts.

NEWCASTLE

(Population 249 962)

Newcastle, the most important industrial city in the Commonwealth after the State capitals, is at the mouth of the Hunter River, 171 kilometres north of Sydney. The area of the city proper is 15 700 hectares and of the entire urban area 24 500 hectares. It is the third export port in Australia, dispatching cargoes of coal, steel and iron products, general manufactures, wool, wheat, frozen meat, timber and dairy products to the rest of the Commonwealth and many other parts of the world.

Although situated in scenic countryside, close to excellent ocean beaches and provided with fine civic amenities, the concentration of heavy industry in Newcastle is too intense for the city to be superficially attractive. However, a spectacular view of its complex of industrial plants, factories and transport depots, and of its congested inner suburbs, may be obtained from the lookout hill at King Edward Park, south-west of Newcastle surf beach. The outlook is particularly impressive at night.

Like Sydney and Melbourne the city is now in the process of extensive redevelopment. It is an important educational centre with a university and many technical schools and colleges.

Like many industrial towns founded in the 19th century, Newcastle owes its prosperity to coal. It is situated on a large, saucer-shaped deposit of hard black coal extending as far as Wollongong on the coast, 240 kilometres south-south-west, and encompassing the inland fields of Maitland, Cessnock and Lithgow. Many of the seams are of unusually high quality and as much as 10 metres thick. The first mines were worked on the site of the present city.

For nearly a century Newcastle was primarily a coal town and port of clearance for the agricultural and pastoral produce of the Hunter River Valley and the Liverpool Plains. Its industrial diversification began when the great Broken Hill Proprietary Company's steelworks went into production in 1915.

Other large concerns operating in Newcastle now include the Commonwealth Steel Corporation, largest producer of special steels in Australia; John Lysaght Ltd, largest producer of galvanized iron in the British Commonwealth; and Ryland Bros (Aust) Pty Ltd, who operate the largest wire mills in the southern hemisphere. Other major products include industrial gases, electrical goods, superphosphate, industrial chemicals, cement, firebricks, synthetic and natural fibre yarns, clothing, fibre board, flour, processed foods and clothing.

The port has facilities for the bulk handling of oil, wheat, wool and coal and for the victualling, servicing and repairing of large ships. A floating dock accommodates vessels of up to 15 000 tonnes and shipbuilding is carried on at the Carrington State Dockyards.

History. First permanent settlement in the valley was at Newcastle in 1804, when convicts and guards were transferred from Sydney to 'Coal River'. It was not until the convict establishment was abolished in 1820 that free settlers moved inland and began to establish themselves as pastoralists.

The history of Newcastle may be divided into four periods: (1) 1801-24: The period of penal settlement; (2) 1825-40: The period of economic stagnation under the monopoly of the Australian Agricultural Company; (3) 1840-1915: The age of competitive coal mining; (4) 1915 onwards: The age of steel-making and heavy industry.

Nobby's Island (now connected to the mainland by a huge breakwater) was recorded by Captain Cook on his survey of the east Australian coast. In 1791 a party of convicts led by William and Mary Bryant escaped from Port Jackson in a small boat and on their voyage northwards touched at Port Hunter where they probably sighted its prominent outcrops of coal. Six years later Lieutenant Shortland, in search of a second party of escapees, explored the mouth of the Hunter River and named it after the Governor. On his return Shortland reported the coal deposits and in 1801 Hunter's successor, Philip Gidley King, dispatched Lieutenant-Colonel W. Paterson to examine the area. Paterson landed on Nobby's Island and named it Coal Island. He also discovered workable deposits of limestone.

King decided to establish a settlement for recalcitrant convicts in the district and after a false start in 1801 the first permanent establishment was set up in 1804. The convicts sent there were employed as cedar-cutters, miners and lime-burners. The most troublesome were put to the lime-burning and the more docile employed in the bush where they felled trees and rafted the lumber downriver.

During the next 20 years 'Coal River'—first named King's Town and later Newcastle, after Newcastle in England—gained its well-deserved reputation for being the 'Hell of New South Wales'. The conditions under which the convicts worked and the disciplinary measures taken against them were indescribably horrible.

In 1820, however, the penal settlement was abandoned and the prisoners transferred to Port Macquarie farther up the coast. In 1825, the Government leased the coal mines to the Australian Agricultural Company, which maintained this and other monopolies over pastoral lands in the interior until the middle of the century.

Coal was exported overseas as early as 1814, when shipments were sent to Calcutta and exchanged for Bengal rum. A trade with California began in 1849.

Newcastle was proclaimed a town in 1849 and a municipality in 1859. It was gazetted as a city in 1885 and four years later, after the completion of a bridge across the Hawkesbury River, was connected with Sydney by rail.

In 1911, the Broken Hill Proprietary Company began work on the reclamation of land at Stockton for its steelworks, which were commissioned in 1915. In 1914 a dockyard was established at Walsh Island. After a prosperous start during the war years, the enterprise failed but, again under the stimulus of war, was revived at Carrington in 1941. The industry is now firmly established.

Places of Interest. **War Memorial Cultural Centre,** Laman Street, overlooks Civic Park and houses City Art Gallery, reference library and Conservatorium of Music. (Guided tours for parties.) **City Hall,** King Street, is an impressive freestone building surmounted by a 44-metre clock tower, and is the administrative centre of Greater Newcastle. The concert hall seats 1 000. **Civic Park** nearby with illuminated fountain sculpted by Margel Hinder. **Christ Church Anglican Cathedral,** Church Street. **Nobby's Head,** beach and lighthouse with convict-built breakwater. (Inspection of the lighthouse can be arranged.) **The Obelisk,** above **King Edward Park,** was erected as an aid to navigation in 1850. It commands an excellent panorama. **Bogey Hole,** on the shore by King Edward Park, was built as a bathing place for prisoners and soldiers by the notorious commandant of convict days, Morisset. It is now used as a public swimming pool. **Police Station,** Hunter Street, is one of the few really old buildings left in the city. **Building Centre,** Watt Street, contains exhibitions of modern building materials. **Ocean Beaches** at Mereweather, Stockton, and at the foot of Hunter Street, the city's main thoroughfare. **New Lambton Heights Lookout** (8 kilometres south-west of city). **Blackbutt Nature Reserve** (8 kilometres). **Scenic Highway** to Mereweather Heights.

Tours of Industrial Plants

BHP Steelworks, 10 am and 2 pm Monday to Friday, holidays excepted (two hours).

John Lysaght (Aust) Pty Ltd. 10.30 am and 2 pm Monday to Friday, holidays excepted (90 minutes).

Stewarts and Lloyds (Aust) Pty Ltd. 10 am and 2 pm Monday to Friday, holidays excepted.

Commonwealth Steel Corporation. By arrangement.

Ryland Bros (Aust) Pty Ltd. By arrangement.

State Dockyards. By arrangement.

Note: Children under the age of nine years are not admitted on industrial tours and those between the ages of nine and 14 must be accompanied by an adult. Women are requested not to wear high-heeled shoes.

Entertainments. Theatres: Dungeon, Union Street; Roxy and Roma (amateur, semi-professional, films). Ten **cinemas.** Two **drive-ins.**

Restaurants. Oliver's Unicorn, 506 Hunter Street; Villa Franca, 2 Scott Street; Mimosa, 767 Hunter Street; The Coachhouse, 141 Scott Street; Danilo's, 66 Beaumont Street.

Sports. Newcastle has facilities for horse-racing, trotting, golf, bowls, ice skating, squash, tennis. Surfing and swimming. Yachting and boating. There is good sea fishing along the coast.

Accommodation. Ten directory-listed **hotels.** Recommended: Great Northern, Scott Street. Eleven directory-listed **motels** in the city and environs. Recommended: Travelodge, Shortland Esplanade; Hospitality Motor Inn, Martland Road, Mayfield. Nine **caravan and/or camping parks.**

Transport. Frequent **rail** and **air** services (Williamtown airport) to Sydney and Brisbane. Numerous **road coach** tours and passenger road services to Hunter Valley, Lake Macquarie and coastal resorts. Inquiries from the NSW Government Tourist Bureau or from the Hunter Valley Tourist and Information Centre, Hexham.

NEWCASTLE'S ENVIRONS

LAKE MACQUARIE

The largest seaboard lake in Australia, Lake Macquarie has an area of about 64 square kilometres and 170 kilometres of winding foreshore. It is only 27 kilometres south of Newcastle and industrial and residential development on the northern shores has been heavy in recent years, but the lake itself is still a pleasant expanse of sheltered water suitable for sailing and all kinds of water sports. The main resorts are **BELMONT, SWANSEA** and **TORONTO,** all of which have better than average **accomodation** in hotel, motel or guest-house and well appointed caravan and camping parks. Facilities for **sports** are good—golf (at Belmont), tennis and bowling greens, surfing on ocean beaches, swimming, yachting and fishing on the lake, entrance channel and deep water offshore. Boats and launches may be hired.

Places of Interest. Wangi Wangi and Vales Point **power stations** (inspection of latter by arrangement). Sulphide Corporation **zinc smelters and plant,** Boolaroo. **Heaton's** and **Hunter Lookouts** in the Wattagan Mountains, west of the lake (there are picnic grounds at the forestry station on the mountain top).

Transport. Road services from Newcastle.

RAYMOND TERRACE (Population 6 000)

A pleasant town of great historical interest 25 kilometres north-west of Newcastle and 196 kilometres north of Sydney. It is on the Pacific Highway and close to the junction of the Hunter and William Rivers and is rapidly being industrialized. The district produces citrus fruit, fodder crops, vegetables, dairy produce and broom millet. A large sawmill, a building board factory and the Tomago rayon factory are located near the town.

History. Raymond Terrace was built to a plan drawn up in 1837, four years after the pioneer, James King, established a pottery and planted the first vineyard in the district. During the 1840s it became an important wool-shipping centre and in 1894 was gazetted a municipality. In 1937 the municipality was merged with the Shire of Port Stephens.

Historic Buildings. Court House, built in 1838 and still in use. **Irrawang,** built in 1830 as the homestead of James King. Church of England **rectory,** built in 1831, and **church,** built in 1836, both of hand-hewn Muree sandstone.

Of Interest. Tomago sandbeds, 26 800 hectares of water-bearing sands replenished entirely by rainfall, being developed by the Hunter District Water Board as a major source of Newcastle's water supply.

Sports. Good golf course. Olympic swimming pool.

Accommodation. One **hotel.** Two **motels.** Recommended: Terrace Colonial, Pacific Highway. **Camping and caravan park,** all facilities.

MAITLAND

(Population 24 530)

Maitland is a coal-mining and market town on the Hunter River, 28 kilometres north-west of Newcastle on the New England Highway. Besides coal the surrounding district produces pigs, vegetables, fruit, fodder crops and sheep. Industries include an abattoir, tobacco factories, timber-mills, engineering and railway workshops, rayon and cotton mills, clothing, footwear and confectionery factories, pottery and milk-processing works, and thermal power house. The city has a number of buildings of historical interest. A booklet listing them is issued by the Maitland City Council.

The town is low-lying and is extremely susceptible to damage by floods. All new residential development is now directed towards the hillier suburbs. Levees have been built to give some protection.

History. Settlement began between 1818 and 1821 when a number of convicts were put to work in the area as cedar-getters. What is now West Maitland was originally known as The Camp, then as Molly Morgan's Plains and Wallis' Plains after the commandant at Newcastle. The town was proclaimed in 1836 and after this the terms East Maitland and West Maitland were used to distinguish twin centres of development. The origin of the name Maitland is uncertain but it was the family name of the Earl of Lauderdale. Coal mining on the South Maitland seams began in 1890. The two towns were officially combined and incorporated in 1944. Tremendous property damage and some loss of life were caused by severe floods in 1933, 1944 and 1955. In the last flood 2 000 houses were inundated.

Places of Interest. **Grossman House,** Church Street, a two-storey brick house built in 1860 as a residence and used for some years as a girls' school; it was presented to the Hunter Regional Trust in 1963 and is now used as a folk museum. The house is open to inspection for a small donation. **Aberglasslyn,** which was built in Regency style in 1842 and classified by the National Trust. **Bolwarra Flats,** where particularly rich dairy and vegetable farms can be seen. **Upper Hunter Mines** (visits can be arranged).

Sports. Good facilities for most games.

Accommodation. Three **hotels** directory listed. Recommended: Imperial. Two **motels.** Recommended: Siesta, New England Highway. One **camping and caravan park,** some facilities.

Transport. **Rail** services to Sydney, Brisbane and New England centres. **Air** services through Williamtown airport. **Road** services on the New England Highway.

CESSNOCK—KURRI KURRI

(Population 35 000)

Cessnock, 32 kilometres west of Newcastle and south of the New England Highway, is a city whose prosperity is built on strangely diverse commodities—coal and wine. The vineyards, orchards and pastures surrounding it are above the great South Maitland coalfields which have made an enormous contribution to the Australian economy for nearly 70 years.

The city itself is not particularly attractive but it is industrially progressive—and the more so because mechanization of the mines has forced diversification to absorb surplus labour. It has unlimited water and cheap fuel and power to attract the industrialist and its potteries, pipeworks, brickyards, sawmills and clothing factories are busy.

Most of the wine of the district comes from long-established vineyards in the Pokolbin area, a few kilometres north-west, where most of the leading Australian winemakers have estates. Hunter River table wines, both red and white, are undoubtedly among the best produced in Australia. Inspection of the cellars and wineries is now an established tourist attraction.

Kurri Kurri, 14 kilometres from Cessnock proper, is a satellite coal town with a population of about 12 000. A large alumina smelting plant and refinery in the town has a production capacity of 40 640 tonnes of aluminium a year.

History. The city has grown on a grazing property originally granted to James Campbell, a Scottish pioneer who named his run 'Cessnock', possibly after the poem by Robert Burns, 'On Cesnock's Banks'. The village was founded in 1853. Coal was discovered in 1856, but the discovery was not followed up until T. W. Edgeworth David found and reported on the Greta coal seam in 1886. The colliery was opened in 1891 and a private rail link with Maitland built. Another famous mine, Aberdare Extended, opened in 1904. In 1923, an explosion at the Bell Bird colliery killed 21 miners. Industrial conflict in 1929 led to the Rothbury riot in which one life was lost.

Places of Interest. **Vineyards** and **wineries** (inspections arranged). **Allandale Geriatric Hospital,** a model institution for the care of the aged. **Mount View, Mount Heaton** and **Quorrobolong Mountain** (scenic drives). Cessnock celebrates a Vintage Festival in February, every second year.

Sports. Racecourse. Trotting and greyhound racing tracks. Golf course. Tennis courts. Bowling greens.

Accommodation. Two **hotels** directory listed. Preferred: Cessnock, Wollombi Road. Two **motels.** Preferred: Hunter Valley, Allandale Road. **Caravan and camping park,** no information.

Transport. **Rail** and **road** services to Maitland.

PORT STEPHENS (Population 2 950)

Forty-eight kilometres north of Newcastle, Port Stephens is one of the most attractive and unspoiled seaside holiday areas on the NSW coast. Its 2 300 hectares of clear, calm water are ringed by beaches and mangroves. Its inshore fishing is excellent and it is within reach of some of the best big-game fishing water off the coast. The NSW game-fishing championships are held here every year in February and the spear-fishing championships at Easter.

The inlet, which is the partly drowned estuary of the Karuah, Myall and Ward Rivers, extends about 24 kilometres inland. The outer harbour is 18 metres deep, but the main channel is about 800 metres wide and 9 metres deep. It is divided by a promontory called Soldiers' Point, so named because in convict days it was a guard point to intercept escaped convicts.

Main resorts are **Nelson Bay, Shoal Bay, Soldiers' Point** and **Lemon Tree Passage** on the south shore and **Karuah** and **Tea Gardens** on the north.

The climate is pleasant for most of the year and water sports may be enjoyed even in winter. There are also many interesting bush and coast walks, particularly on Tomaree Headland (permission from Tourist Organization at Nelson Bay is required).

Sports facilities include golf (nine-hole course) at Nelson Bay, bowls at Nelson Bay and Soldiers' Point, tennis at Shoal Bay, Nelson Bay and Soldiers' Point, squash at Shoal Bay. There is good surf at Fingal Bay, south of the entrance, and at Zenith, Box, Anna Bay, One Mile and Fisherman's Beaches. Only Fingal Beach is patrolled.

Accommodation. One **hotel** at Shoal Bay (very good) and at Nelson Bay and Tea Gardens. **Motels** at Shoal Bay, Nelson Bay, Tea Gardens and Karuah (all of satisfactory standard). **Holiday flats** at Shoal Bay, Nelson Bay, Dutchman's Bay, Sandy Point, Salamander Bay, Wanda Beach, Soldiers' Point and Fingal Bay. **Furnished cottages** at Shoal Bay, Tea Gardens, Nelson Bay, Lemon Tree Passage and Soldiers' Point. **Caravan and camping parks** with all facilities at Tea Gardens, Shoal Bay, Nelson Bay, One Mile Beach, Lemon Tree Passage, Soldiers' Point and Karuah.

Transport. Road service (via Stockton ferry) to Newcastle. **Rail** and **bus** services to Sydney. **Air** (Williamtown airport) and **taxi** service to Newcastle. **Information** from Tourist Organization, Nelson Bay, Port Stephens.

DUNGOG (Population 2 119)

The centre of a sound dairying and cattle-raising district, Dungog is 233 kilometres north of Sydney and 72 kilometres from Newcastle on the upper reach of the Williams River. The town, established in 1838 as a military post to help put down bushranging, is on one of the main access routes to Barrington National Park, Chichester State Forest and Chichester Dam. Dungog is a corruption of an aboriginal word meaning 'bare hills'.

Barrington Tops is an extensive and extremely rugged plateau at an elevation of about 1 600 metres on the edge of the Mount Royal Range, north-west of the town. This hill country is the source of many rivers, including the Williams, the Manning, the Gloucester and the Paterson, and is noted for the density of the vegetation which covers it. It contains many unique flowering species, snow gums and Antarctic beeches. The area provides magnificent bush-walking, riding and trout-fishing. Accomodation is available in the heart of the area at Barrington Guest House, 42 kilometres from Dungog at the foot of Barrington mountain.

Places of Interest. The Knob (750 metres), on a forest reserve, is known for fine panoramic views (27 kilometres on Main Creek Road). **Chichester Dam** (23 kilometres north) and **Williams River Gorge** and **Allyn Valley** are worth a visit.

Sports. Golf course. Bowling greens. Tennis courts. Seasonal shooting. Fishing.

Accommodation. Town: Two **hotels.** Preferred: Royal, Dowling Street. One **motel. Caravan and camping park,** limited facilities.

Transport. Rail services to Sydney and Brisbane (on the main northern line).

STROUD (Population 650)

Stroud, 72 kilometres north of Newcastle, is a quiet country town famous for its annual international brick-throwing contest between a local team and those of three other centres named Stroud in England, Canada and the United States. The women of the four Strouds compete in a rolling-pin throwing contest. The teams, of course, throw on their home ground and distances are compared to decide the winner. Stroud, NSW, celebrates (on agreed day in July) with street parades, sky-diving displays and dancing.

Also of Interest. St John's Church, built in 1833 of bricks hand made by convicts and furnished with solid, pit-sawn cedar pews.

Other small settlements attractively sited: **Paterson** (46 kilometres), **Gresford** (74 kilometres) and **Clarencetown** (51 kilometres).

MIDDLE AND UPPER HUNTER

SINGLETON (Population 7 500)

Singleton is an important coal-mining town on the upper Hunter River, 76 kilometres west of Newcastle. Annual production of high-grade coal is more than one million tonnes. It is also the market and manufacturing centre for a district which produces milk for Sydney, and dairy produce, fat cattle and lambs, wine grapes, and vegetables for the Newcastle market. Its secondary industries include timber milling and the manufacture of cheese, butter, cordials and wine.

History. The town is one of the oldest in New South Wales. John Howe settled in an area which he called St Patrick's Plain in 1820. The town was named after B. Singleton who arrived in the district some two years later. It was proclaimed in 1836 and became a municipality and headquarters for the Shire of Patrick Plains in 1866.

Of Interest. Historical **museum** in the town's original court house.

Sports. Golf course. Tennis, bowls, swimming. Fishing. Seasonal shooting.

Accommodation. Two **hotels.** Recommended: Agricultural, Munro Street. One **motel.**

Transport. **Rail** and **road** services.

MUSWELLBROOK (Population 7 250)

Muswellbrook uses both open-cut and underground methods of coalmining, and is situated in the upper Hunter Valley, 294 kilometres north of Sydney. The district is also noted for its dairy produce, stud cattle, blood horses, merino sheep and fodder crops. A large thermal power station is currently under construction at Liddell.

Much of the country around Muswellbrook is irrigated from small tributaries of the Hunter and water conservation schemes planned to develop small agricultural holdings. The village was founded in 1827 and the town proclaimed in 1833. The derivation of the town's name is of interest. The first settlers gave the name Muscle Brook to the district after finding a number of small shellfish resembling mussels in a local creek. The town was gazetted under that spelling although Muswellbrook subsequently came into general use and the change was officially approved in 1949.

Of Interest. The **Dalwood Park winery** at Wybong, 25 kilometres west. **Apex Lookout,** Waterworks Hill.

Sports. Racecourse. Greyhound racing. Motor-cycle and cycle tracks. Golf course. Bowls and tennis. Olympic swimming pool.

Accommodation. One **hotel.** Two **motels.** Recommended: Plaza, Bridge Street. Two **caravan and camping parks,** all facilities.

Transport. **Rail** and **road** services.

SCONE (Population 3 257)

On the New England Highway 319 kilometres north of Sydney, Scone is an attractive little town in beautiful countryside which produces bloodstock, wool, fruit, vegetables, fodder crops and walnuts. It is an important stock-selling centre and headquarters of soil and water-conservation authorities.

History. The district was opened up in the 1830s. The pioneer settler, Hugh Cameron, presented a petition to the Governor, Major Mitchell, that the area be named after the valley of Strathearn in Scotland where the ancient Abbey of Scone was located. The village was, however, gazetted as Invermein in 1837, but for some unexplained reason the Colonial Secretary then ordered the name to be changed to Scone. The municipality was incorporated in 1888.

Places of Interest. **Glenbawn Dam,** 13 kilometres east, and Hunter Valley **Museum of Rural Life.** The dam has been developed as a water sports resort (launches, boats for hire and modern cabins to let). **Mount Wingen,** 17 kilometres north, where a deep coal seam has been burning very slowly for a period estimated at 2 000 years. It was originally mistaken for a volcano. (*Wingen* is the local aboriginal word for 'fire'.) The 'mountain' is on private property but may be inspected by appointment.

Sports. Racecourse. Golf course. Bowls, croquet and tennis. Olympic swimming pool.

Accommodation. Two **hotels.** Recommended: Royal Motor Inn, Kelly Street. Three **motels.** Recommended: Florida Airlie, New England Highway.

Transport. **Rail** and **air** services to Sydney. **Road** services on the New England Highway.

MURRURUNDI (Population 925)

Situated on Pages River in the Liverpool Ranges 359 kilometres from Sydney, Murrurundi is an old-established town in high-class beef and wool country. It is possibly the most picturesque settlement in the Hunter River district, being surrounded in its lush and sheltered valley by precipitous mountainsides. It began its life as a police post and lively bush trading centre, but the construction of the New England railway caused its commercial decline.

Places of Interest. The burning mountain, **Wingen** (see Scone) is 19 kilometres south; **Timor Limestone Caves,** 43 kilometres east; **Chillot's Creek,** where the huge diprotodon remains now in Sydney Museum were found; a very old **church** containing 1 000 pieces of Italian marble; and an exceptionally attractive motor camp at **Wilson Memorial Park** by the river.

Accommodation. Two **motels.** Preferred: Valley View, New England Highway. **Caravan and camping park,** all facilities.

Transport. Rail services to Newcastle, Sydney and New England centres. **Road** services on the New England Highway.

THE NORTH COAST

(Traversed north-south by the Pacific Highway and east-west by the Oxley, Gwydir and Bruxner Highways.)

In popular conception the North Coast of New South Wales extends from the Hastings and Manning Rivers in the south to the Queensland border in the north. It is a relatively narrow strip of fertile land between the sea and the eastern spurs of the Great Dividing Range. The main rivers crossing it are (from south to north) the Manning and the Hastings; the Macleay, the Nambucca, Bellinger and Clarence; and the Richmond and Tweed.

Each valley is a distinct physical unit, with a rugged, wooded upper region, an open, hilly middle portion with narrow flood plains, and a lower portion of level flood plains varying in width and ending in marshes or shallow lagoons. Although the rivers carry a considerable volume of water, navigation is made difficult by bars at their mouths.

The climate of the coast is warm at lower altitudes, and bracing in the hills where frosts are common in winter. Rainfall varies between 1 000 and 1 800 millimetres a year and is fairly evenly distributed. The countryside is at its best in late autumn, winter and spring.

Although flourishing secondary industries exist in some of the larger towns, the economy of the region is predominantly rural. The great sub-tropical forests which once clothed the valleys have now largely been cleared of their valuable softwoods, especially red cedar, and the farmlands carry large dairy herds and beef cattle and produce tropical fruit, sugar, maize, fodder crops and vegetables. Valuable timber is still obtained from the hill country where forests are being conserved by modern methods of management.

Attractions. An excellent climate except in summer. Good to excellent surf beaches. River, coastal, forest and mountain scenery which cannot be matched for sheer variety elsewhere in the south-east of the continent. River, estuary and deep sea fishing, bettered only in the remote and unfrequented areas of the north and north-west. A good if not distinguished standard of accommodation in major resorts. All in all, the North Coast of New South Wales is Australia at its gentlest and best.

The standard of main roads and of public transport services is satisfactory.

FORSTER-TUNCURRY (Population 3 682) are twin towns on opposite sides of Lake Wallis, a long established holiday and fishing area of the Great Lakes district 378 kilometres north of Sydney. Wallis Lake is 26 kilometres long and 9½ kilometres wide at its widest. It offers exciting fishing for flathead, bream, whiting and blackfish and is renowned for its oysters and prawns. Launches and boats may be hired for lake, inshore and deep sea fishing. Tuncurry is the base for a fishing fleet which supplies large quantities of fish to the Sydney market. It also ships out a great deal of timber logged in the hinterland. The two towns are now connected by a bridge completed in 1959. Sports facilities in both are exceptionally good.

Accommodation. One **hotel.** Six **motels.** Recommended: Forster Motor Inn, Wallis Street, Forster. Four **caravan and camping parks,** some facilities. Several **guest-houses. Flats** and **cottages** for rent.

Transport. Bus from Taree and Newcastle. **Air** service to Wallis Island from Sydney.

TAREE

(Population 11 914)

Main commercial and manufacturing town of the prosperous Manning River district, Taree is 340 kilometres from Sydney on the Pacific Highway. The district produces butter, cheese, maize, timber and fish. Besides dairy factories, the town has sawmills, a dowelling factory, a broom factory, fibrous plaster works, light engineering shops, joinery factories, pipe works and small shipbuilding yards. The urban area is well laid out with attractive parks, gardens and public and commercial buildings. There are many fine surfing beaches on the coast about 16 kilometres away, and the mountains to the west are spectacular, with many waterfalls and panoramic lookouts. The upland streams are liberally stocked with rainbow and brown trout.

History. Taree stands on a land grant made to William Wynter, the first settler on the Manning, about 1831. Laid out a private town in the early 1850s, it was incorporated as a municipality in 1885. It is today the headquarters of the Manning Shire.

Places of Interest. Resorts at **Black Head, Old Bar, Harrington** and **Crowdy Head. Vincent's Lookout** in the Manning River National Forest, (north). **Kiwirrak State Forest,** (south). **Mount Kaoaraoa** for fine panoramas. **Ellenborough** and **Bulga Falls** on scenic Bulga Plateau (north west).

Taree has an Aquatic Carnival every January and a district show in March.

Sports. Racecourse. Dog track. Golf courses. Bowls, tennis, croquet. Squash courts. Sea and river fishing. Water skiing, boating etc. Olympic swinmimg pool.

Accommodation. Ten **motels.** Recommended: Pacific, Riverview and Manning River, Pacific Highway, Caravilla. Three **caravan and camping parks,** all facilities.

Transport. Rail and **road** services. Daily **air** service from Sydney.

WINGHAM (Population 2 917) is 13 kilometres up river from Taree. It is the oldest town on the Manning River, having been surveyed in 1843. The **Wingham Brush** is an unusual park of seven hectares of bushland which has been preserved in its original state as an example of the vegetation which covered large areas of the North Coast a century ago. The town has the usual sports facilities. It is a good base for visitors interested in exploring the Comboyne and Bulga Plateaux.

Accommodation. Two **hotels.** Preferred: Australian. **Camping area.**

Transport. Road services.

GLOUCESTER (Population 2 012), 72 kilometres west of Taree, is a peaceful township under the shadow of a range of peaked mountains known as the Gloucester Buckets. It stands at the junction of three tributaries of the Manning River. Excellent sports facilities, and fine trout and perch fishing. Good shooting.

Accommodation. One **hotel.** One **motel. Caravan and camping park,** all facilities.

Transport. Mainline **rail** services. **Road** services.

PORT MACQUARIE

(Population 9 562)

Port Macquarie, at the mouth of the Hastings River, 430 kilometres north-east of Sydney, is the commercial centre of an agricultural, timber-getting and mining district and a favoured holiday resort. The district produces butter, bacon, fruit, iron oxide, arsenic ore and rutile, zircon and ilmenite from beach sands. The town is one of the oldest in New South Wales, having been founded as a convict settlement in 1821, and many of its historic buildings have been intelligently preserved. Its hinterland of densely timbered mountains cut through by swift streams is scenically fascinating. The town is proud of the high standard of its tourist accommodation.

History. The convict settlement at Port Macquarie was established on the recommendation of John Oxley, who noted its fine forests and rich soil and believed that the district would be suitable for the cultivation of tropical crops. Economically the settlement succeeded almost immediately, although the frosts which occurred after areas of forest had been cleared dashed hopes of raising sugar, coffee, cotton and pineapples. Wheat and maize were introduced instead and the cedar-getting industry flourished. In 1830 the penal settlement was abandoned and free settlers moved in. Among the early arrivals were Jeremiah Warlters, who had introduced the Hereford breed of beef cattle into Australia, and the colourful pioneer industrialist, banker and farmer, Major Archibald C. Innes.

Port Macquarie soon became a shipping outlet for the produce of the New England tablelands after an inland road had been built in 1840. It was proclaimed a municipality in 1887.

Historic buildings. St Thomas' Church of England, designed by Francis Greenway. The interior panelling displays the district's famous red cedar. The box pews are probably the only ones remaining in an Australian church. **Hastings District Historical Society Museum,** originally built as a store in 1835. It now contains an impressive collection of convict and pioneer relics. **Lake Innes,** remnants of Major Innes' home. **Old gaol. Two cottages** in Short Street, one the 'town house' of Jeremiah Warlters, the other the residence of the Overseer of Works in the 1820s.

Places of Interest. Sea Acres, nature sanctuary. **Observatory. Aquatic Gardens. Transit Hill,** for views of district (6 kilometres from town). **Comboyne Plateau** and Mitchell, Glenmore, Rawson, Bonavista, Diamond, Electric Light and Bridal Veil **waterfalls** (all in rainforest country). **Bulga Plateau.**

A Carnival of the Pines is held every Easter.

Sports. Golf. Tennis courts. Bowls and croquet. Squash courts. Mini golf. Rifle range. Water skiing and other aquatic sports. Riding and hiking. Exceptionally good fishing, particularly when the bream run in winter. Oystering.

Accommodation. Two **hotels.** Preferred: Royal, Horton Street. Twenty-four **motels.** Highly recommended: Travelodge, Buller Street. Holiday **flats.** Four **caravan and camping parks,** all facilities.

Transport. Rail and connecting **road** services from Brisbane and Sydney. **Air** services from Sydney and Taree daily; from Kempsey (six days a week) and from Forster (twice a week).

WAUCHOPE (Population 3 351) is 19 kilometres from the mouth of the Hastings River. The Oxley Highway passes through the town, which is the centre of a timber-getting, beef cattle, pig raising and mixed farming district, with bee-keeping also an important industry. Nearby is the Bellangry State Forest, claimed to have the biggest stands of blackbutt (esteemed for veneering and cabinet making) in Australia. The town has plywood, veneer and box making factories. Deposits of tin, manganese, copper, gold and other minerals have been located in the area, but they have not yet been fully exploited. Good sports facilities.

Accommodation. One **hotel.** One **motel.**

Transport. Rail services from Brisbane and Sydney. **Road** services. **Air** and connecting **bus** services via Port Macquarie.

CAMDEN HAVEN is a complex of three settlements—Laurieton, Dunbogan and North Haven—44 kilometres south of Port Macquarie, noted for good angling and game fishing in the waters offshore. Oysters, lobsters and crabs may be gathered in the lagoons and lakes. Aquatic sports include surfing, water skiing, speed boat racing and skin diving. The hinterland has many fine bush-walking tracks and mountain lookouts in the **Comboyne Plateau** area, which is particularly beautiful in the spring wildflower season.

Accommodation. One **motel.** Several **guest-houses.** Holiday **flats and cottages. Caravan and camping parks.** No information on facilities.

Transport. Road services from Port Macquarie, Wauchope and Taree.

KEMPSEY

(Population 8 867)

Kempsey is the main commercial and industrial town in the fertile Macleay River valley, 480 kilometres north of Sydney. It is situated 31 kilometres from the mouth of the river in pleasant countryside given over mainly to dairying and the growing of maize, lucerne, beef cattle and pigs. Timber is logged in the ranges to the west. The town's factories produce butter, cheese, processed milk, bacon, plywood and veneer, cordials, plaster and furniture, and there are brick and pipe works.

History. Kempsey is built on land that was once the property of Enoch Rudder, one of the earliest pioneers in the valley. The first subdivision was made in 1836. Communications were poor and the district received supplies and dispatched produce mainly by sea, the ships using Trial Bay as a harbour. One of Australia's first national (secular) schools was established in Kempsey in 1849. Over the years the settlement has suffered severe flooding as a result of the upland forests being ruthlessly cut out. Flood mitigation works have been undertaken only in recent years. The town was gazetted as a borough in 1886.

Places of Interest. Chapple Memorial Park, with fine swimming pool. **Apex Park,** commanding panoramic views of town and district. Resorts of **South West Rocks** (37 kilometres), **Crescent Head** (19 kilometres) and **Trial Bay,** where the ruins of the old gaol have been converted into a picnic spot. (The port now has large bulk oil installations.)

Kempsey has a Festival of Spring in October, and organizes a big rodeo at the same time. A district show is held in April.

Sports. Golf course. Racecourse. Tennis courts. Bowls and croquet. River fishing. Aquatic sports.

Accommodation. Two directory listed **hotels.** Recommended: Kempsey, Belgrave Street.

Eight **motels.** Recommended: Stardust Travelodge, Macleay River and City Centre, Pacific Highway. Four **caravan and camping parks,** all facilities. **Holiday cabins** available.

Transport. Frequent **rail** services from Brisbane and Sydney. **Road coach** service from Queensland. **Air** services.

NAMBUCCA HEADS (Population 2 712)

A small, beautifully situated township at the mouth of the Nambucca River, 552 kilometres north of Sydney, Nambucca Heads is famous for Yarrahapini Lookout which commands one of the most colourful and impressive panoramas on the coast of New South Wales. The district produces bananas, beef, maize, timber, butter and vegetables. It derives considerable extra income from the increasing tourist traffic.

The river was discovered in 1818, but its valley was not settled until 1842 when cedar-getters began to exploit the forests. The timber lasted 30 years, after which dairy farmers occupied the denuded river flats. The village of Nambucca (the name means 'entrance of waters') was founded in 1885. It was incorporated with the shire in 1915.

Places of Interest. Shelley Beach, northern bay of the lookout headland. **Sturt Island,** linked by a causeway with the mainland. Nearby resorts of **Macksville** (upriver), **Bowraville** and **Scott's Head. Yarrahapini State Forest.**

Sports. Golf, bowls, tennis, fishing etc.

Accommodation. One **hotel-motel.** Eight **motels.** Recommended: Miramar, Blue Dolphin and Hacienda, Pacific Highway. Two **camping and caravan parks,** all facilities. **Flats, cabins.**

Transport. Rail, road and **air-road** services (from Coff's Harbour).

COFF'S HARBOUR

(Population 10 107)

Coff's Harbour, which claims to be the biggest timber port in Australia, is 580 kilometres north of Sydney on the Pacific Highway. It is a progressive town which has more than doubled its population within the last decade. The surrounding district produces bananas, timber, sugar, vegetables (especially tomatoes), dairy produce and fish. 'Coff's', as it is known on the North Coast, is really two towns—one situated on the highway and the other, Jetty Town, near the artificial harbour and the railway station.

History. J. Korff, after whom the harbour was named, was the first settler in the district. He arrived in 1847 and a village grew up on his property to serve the cedar-getters in the dense forests of the hinterland. For some years it was known as Brelsford, but was referred to as 'Coff's' Harbour after 1861. In time it became the principal shipping outlet for the produce of the Bellingen, Dorrigo and Orara districts. The town was incorporated in the Dorrigo Shire in 1886. The port's trade diminished after the railway was extended from Raleigh in 1915, but it retains its importance for the handling of bulky cargoes. Banana growing began in 1929.

Places of Interest. 'The Biggest Banana in the World', an amusing publicity gimmick, stands on McCauley's Head plantation on the Pacific Highway about three kilometres north of town. It is made of reinforced concrete on a wooden frame and visitors can walk through it and see illuminated colour slides depicting all aspects of the banana industry. They are also welcome to inspect the plantation itself, on which there is a lookout commanding fine panoramic views of the town and coast. **Banana Bowl,** at Hills Beach (private golf course, lake and riding school). **Sapphire Gardens** (8 kilometres north). **Moonee Beach** (13 kilometres north), fishing and swimming.

Sports. Good golf course. Tennis, bowls etc. Racecourse. Sailing. Estuary and deep sea fishing. (Launches for hire.)

Accommodation. Five **hotels**. Recommended: Pier, High Street. Nineteen **motels**. Recommended: Allambie Court, Camperdown Street; Town Lodge, Pacific Highway; Zebra, Graffin Street. Holiday **flats and cottages.** Ten **caravan and camping parks,** all facilities, near town. One **caravan park** at Moonee Beach.

Transport. Rail and **road** services. Daily **air** services to Sydney.

SAWTELL, 8 kilometres south of Coff's Harbour just off the Pacific Highway, is close to good beaches and has facilities for golf, bowls, tennis and croquet.

Accommodation. One **hotel,** several **guest-houses,** holiday **flats and cottages. Caravan and camping park,** all facilities.

WOOLGOOLGA, 26 kilometres north of Coff's Harbour, charming seaside town near a lake where the whiting fishing, crabbing and prawning are reputedly the best on this section of the coast. Good surf beach. Water skiing.

Places of Interest nearby include **Barcoongerie State Forest, Woolgoolga State Forest Nursery** and the resorts of **Red Rock, Emerald Beach, Mullaway, Corindi** and **Arrawatta.**

Accommodation. Four **motels.** Recommended: Ocean Beach, Beach Street. **Caravan and camping park,** all facilities.

DORRIGO is an important timber town 72 kilometres west of Coff's Harbour with magnificent forest, river and mountain scenery in State Park and good sports facilities. Excellent trout fishing.
Accommodation Two **hotels.** Preferred: Commercial. One **motel.**
Transport. **Road** services.

BELLINGEN, on banks of Bellinger River, south of Coff's Harbour within easy reach of Dorrigo State Park and picturesque river and forest scenery. A lush farming area for fruit and maize.
Accommodation. One **hotel. Camping areas.** All facilities.

URUNGA, 32 kilometres south of Coff's Harbour, is a popular family holiday resort with first-rate fishing for bream, whiting, tailor and snapper.
Accommodation. Four **motels.** Preferred: Westella, Pacific Highway. **Camping park, flats. cabins.**

GRAFTON

(Population 16 354)

Main centre of the rich Clarence River district, Grafton is 665 kilometres north of Sydney on the Pacific Highway at its junction with the Gwydir Highway. The city is famous for broad streets lined with magnificent jacaranda, wheel and flame trees, silky oaks and bauhinias. Its sub-tropical climate and rich soil make it genuinely a 'garden city'. In the first week in November it celebrates a Jacaranda Festival which is so colourful and full of entertainment that it attracts many thousands of visitors from all parts of Australia. The festival was first held in 1935—probably the first carnival week of its type in the Commonwealth.

The district's chief industries are dairying and farming a variety of crops including peanuts and potatoes. Coal, asbestos and limestone are mined in the area, which also produces timber, scale fish, prawns and oysters. The secondary industries of the city are geared to the processing of its primary produce.

History. The Clarence River was first explored by Richard Craig in 1831 and timber-getters moved into its great cedar forests in 1838. Two settlements grew up on opposite sides of the river and were regarded as entirely separate until 1932 when the stream was spanned by a double deck bridge, carrying rail traffic on one level and motor traffic on the other. The municipalities, previously known as The Settlement and Woolport and later as North and South Grafton (after the Duke of Grafton), were merged into the City of Grafton in 1956.

Places of Interest. Scenic drives through the **Orara Valley Road,** to Macpherson's Crossing and Bawden's Bridge. **Susan Island,** in midstream opposite the city, a recreation reserve covered with rainforests containing giant fig trees and stinging trees. It is rich in bird life.

Sports. Golf course. Racecourse (Grafton Cup meeting, July). Bowls and tennis etc. Olympic swimming pool. Sailing and water skiing. Estuary fishing.

Accommodation. **North:** Two directory listed **hotels.** Recommended: Grafton, Fitzroy Street. Four **motels.** Recommended: Camden Lodge, Villiers Street and Key Lodge, Fitzroy Street. Four **caravan and camping parks,** all facilities. **South:** Two directory listed **hotels.** Recommended: Good Intent, Armadale Road. Six **motels.** Recommended: Caravilla, Pacific Highway. **Caravan and camping park,** all facilities.

Transport. **Rail** services north and south. Network of **road** services to New England towns etc. **Air** services to Sydney (daily) and Kempsey (daily except Sunday).

MACLEAN, YAMBA AND ILUKA (Total population 3 974)

On the delta of the Clarence River about 740 kilometres north of Sydney, Maclean, Yamba and Iluka serve a prosperous sugar farming area and are gaining favour steadily as holiday resorts. The climate is unusually equable and mild and the countryside and coast are full of interest. Much of the district's sugar cane is grown on large islands in the mouth of the river which are inundated and fertilized by silt in periodical floods. Maize, bananas, mixed farm crops and potatoes are also grown under intensive cultivation. Large fishing and prawning fleets are based on the three settlements and it is estimated that they catch between 16 and 20 per cent of the State's seafood. The industry was founded on the Clarence by John Wallace in 1884.

Places of Interest. **Sugar mill** on Harwood Island. **Iluka Rainforest.** Blue pool (fresh water) and surfing beaches at **Angourie.** Resorts of **Woody Head, Brooms Head, Big Lake and Sandon River** (camping facilities only).

Sports. Golf courses. Tennis courts. Bowling clubs. Surfing, swimming and water skiing. Boating, fishing and oystering (public oyster leases).

Accommodation. Maclean: One **hotel.** One **motel.** One **caravan park,** all facilities. **Yamba:** One **hotel.** Four **motels.** Recommended: Moby Dick, Yamba Road. Holiday **flats and cottages.** Two **caravan and camping parks,** all facilities. **Iluka:** One **hotel.** Holiday **flats and cottages. Caravan park,** all facilities, and **camping areas,** limited facilities.

Transport. **Rail** from Sydney and Brisbane to South Grafton, thence **road** services. **Road** service from Lismore, and Maclean to other resorts. **Ferry** services to many islands.

LISMORE

(Population 20 901)

The city of Lismore, 821 kilometres north-north-east of Sydney and on the north arm of the Richmond River, is the largest centre of population on the North Coast of New South Wales. The surrounding district is claimed to be the most closely settled and intensively cultivated rural area in Australia. It produces sugar, butter, cheese, bacon, bananas and pineapples, beef cattle, maize, lucerne and other fodder crops. Timber-getting is still a significant industry on the upper reaches of the river. Besides its large dairy factories, Lismore has sawmills, engineering and steel fabricating works, a sugar mill and factories producing clothing, furniture, brooms and other manufactures. It is well known for its imaginatively designed and beautifully tended public parks and gardens.

History. Captain H. Rous discovered the Richmond River in 1828. Fifteen years later Ward Stephens (one of the founders of the Sydney Morning Herald newspaper) established a station which was later occupied by William Wilson, the first permanent settler. He named it Lismore, after the island on Loch Linnie, Argyleshire. The town was surveyed in 1855 and gazetted the following year. It did not develop greatly until the 1870s and 1880s when bridges replaced the ferry punts across the river and a port was developed. Sugar was by this time a highly profitable crop and several mills were built. The town was proclaimed a municipality in 1879 and a city in 1946.

Lismore celebrates a Floral Carnival in September and a Music Festival in August-September. The North Coast Agricultural and Industrial Show is held in mid-October, and a river regatta at Easter.

Places of Interest. Near city: **Richmond River Museum. Lismore Art Gallery.** City: **Spinks, Currie** and **Nesbitt Parks. Rotary Park,** a tract of jungle preserved in its natural state, with specimens of cedar trees etc. **Lions' Commemorative Fountain,** near City Hall. **Robinson's Lookout,** with panoramic views of city and river. **Girard's Hill. King George VI Memorial Drive.** District: **Rocky Creek and Minyon Falls** (72 kilometres). **Nightcap National Forest,** containing three State forests with an area of 13 000 hectares.

Sports. Racecourse. Bowling and croquet greens. Tennis courts. Squash courts. Golf course. Archery range. Greyhound track. Water skiing and other aquatic sports, Olympic pool. River fishing.

Accommodation. Six **hotels.** Recommended: Canberra, Molesworth Street. Five **motels.** Recommended: Karinga, Molesworth Street. **Camping and caravan park,** all facilities.

Transport. **Rail** services (from Casino Junction to Murwillumbah). **Road** services. **Air** services to Casino and connecting buses.

CASINO (Population 9 048)

A road and rail junction on the North Coast, 32 kilometres west of Lismore and 810 kilometres north-north-east of Sydney, Casino is an important commercial and manufacturing centre on the middle reaches of the Richmond River. It has a large butter factory, meatworks and timber yards. Its airport serves a wide segment of the north-east.

History. The name of the town derives from the Cassino cattle station, settled by two pioneers, Clay and Stapleton, because of some association they had had with Monte Cassino in Italy. A court house was built on the site in 1846 and a police barracks in 1853, but the town was not gazetted until 1855 when the present spelling of its name was used. For many years Casino was the chief settlement on the Richmond because the only track from the Clarence valley to Ipswich and Moreton Bay ran through it. It was proclaimed a municipality in 1880. The bridge across the river, opened in 1876, was named after Clyde Irving, who took over the original run from Clay and Stapleton.

Sports. Racecourse. Greyhound track. Golf course. Tennis and squash courts. Bowling and croquet greens. Olympic swimming pool. Rifle range. River fishing.

A Bushman's Carnival (rodeo) is held in May.

Accommodation. Four **hotels.** Recommended: Royal, Walker Street. One **motel,** Trade Winds (recommended). **Camping and caravan park,** all facilities.

Transport. Mainline **rail** services. Branch line services to Murwillumbah via Lismore, Byron Bay etc. **Road** services. **Air** services to Sydney and Brisbane.

KYOGLE (Population 3 000)

Kyogle is the urban centre of a dairy and mixed farming area, regarded by many experts in agriculture as the richest land in New South Wales. It is 840 kilometres north of Sydney on the upper reaches of the Richmond River.

The production of the local butter factory averages almost 3 000 000 kilograms a year. Veneer and plywood manufacture is also a major secondary industry, quantities of fine timbers coming from the ranges and the Nightcap National Forest to the north-east. The town is well laid out and has a good shopping centre. It is a convenient base for visitors wishing to explore the mountains in the vicinity of Mount Lindesay on the Queensland border, a region of rare and spectacular beauty.

History. The first explorers were Patrick Logan and Allan Cunningham in 1828. Timber-getters moved in during the 1830s and the first squatters arrived in 1839, taking up such large runs as Kyogle, Wiangaree and Kuralaki. These estates were subdivided during the early years of the 20th century and the first butter factory was opened in 1905. The shire was founded in 1906 and the town proclaimed in 1909. It suffers from occasional severe flooding. The name derives from an aboriginal word meaning 'plains turkey's egg'.

Places of Interest. Attractive **picnic spots** at Moore Park, Border Gate, Toolem Falls, Wynedin, Unumbar and Poor Bullock Range. **Dourigan's Gap,** panoramic lookout. **Forest Nursery** at Rosebery. **Nimbin Rocks** scenic area. **Fairymount,** for views of town. **Rocky Creek Falls.** The **veneer** and **butter factories** in town may be inspected.

Sports Golf course. Bowls, croquet, tennis. Rifle range. Swimming and river fishing.

Accommodation. One **hotel.** One **motel.** Several **guest-houses. Caravan park,** all facilities.

Transport. Mainline **rail** services. **Road** services.

BALLINA (Population 6 133)

Situated at the mouth of the Richmond River. 31 kilometres from Lismore and 824 kilometres north of Sydney, Ballina is a progressive industrial, fishing and tourist town which also serves a rich dairy farming and tropical fruit growing district. A fishing fleet of more than 100 vessels is based on the port and there are fish and fruit canning factories in town. Two shipyards also operate. One of them, the Ballina Slipway and Engineering Company, is the largest in NSW outside the Newcastle-Sydney-Wollongong complex. There are many fine surfing beaches on the nearby coast, and enclosed water in the river encourages boating and aquatic sports. Large public oyster leases, where the shellfish may be opened and eaten but not taken away, are situated on the waterfront. (Best months December to March.)

History. The town was founded by cedar-getters in 1842-3 when its port became the shipping centre for the output of the whole Richmond valley. In 1860 gold was discovered in the beach sands and a short-lived rush ocurred. During the 1880s breakwaters were built to improve the port. Boom years followed, but as the timber trade declined so did the importance of the town. The name is said to mean 'place where oysters are plentiful'.

Places of Interest. **Shelly Beach,** formed entirely of shell fragments. **Shaws Bay** with sheltered, safe swimming. **Lighthouse Surf Beach** and fine lifesavers' club house. **Pioneer Memorial Park** and **Memorial Wall,** East Ballina. **Minyon Falls.** Bagot's **old timber mills,** established in 1884.

Sports. Racecourse (Christmas and New Year racing carnival, informal and well attended). Golf course. Bowls and croquet. Tennis and squash. Surfing and water skiing. Beach and river fishing.

Accommodation. Two **hotels.** Recommended: New Lobster Pot, River Street. Twelve **motels.** Recommended: All States and Colonial, Pacific Highway. Several **guest-houses.** Holiday **flats.** Four **camping and caravan parks,** all facilities.

Transport. **Road** services on Pacific Highway and to Lismore.

CORAKI, 32 kilometres south-east of Casino, once a bustling port on the Richmond, but now an aquatic sports resort known for water skiing. Golf. Bowls. Fishing.

Accommodation. Two **hotels. Camping areas.**

EVANS HEAD (Population 1 313), 48 kilometres south-east of Lismore, is renowned for excellent fishing—both for professionals who make large catches of scale fish and king prawns, and for amateurs operating from rocky headlands, surf beaches and small boats on the river. It has a highly recommended **seafood restaurant,** the owner of which runs his own trawler. Golf course. Bowling greens. Tennis courts.

Accommodation. One **hotel.** One **motel.** One **caravan park,** all facilities. Three **camping areas,** all facilities.

Transport. **Road** services from Ballina and Lismore etc. **Air** services to Brisbane and Sydney daily. (Evans Head was a large RAAF training base during the second world war.)

BYRON BAY (Population 2 370)

The most easterly settlement on the Australian mainland. Byron Bay is 885 kilometres north-east of Sydney and 193 kilometres south of Brisbane. The district produces butter, bacon, beef cattle, maize and tropical fruit. Rutile and zircon are recovered from beach sands along the nearby coast. Other industries include a meatworks and a fish processing and storage plant. Australia's most powerful lighthouse is on Cape Byron. It is a 25 metre tower which houses a three million candlepower reflector visible 43 kilometres out to sea.

History. Captain Cook named both Cape Byron and Byron Bay after John Byron (grandfather of the poet Lord Byron) who commanded HMS *Dolphin* on a voyage of discovery in 1764-66. The town was founded as a timber port in 1860 and its first butter factory was established in 1895. The town was gazetted in 1896 and incorporated in a shire in 1906. Its surf lifesaving club, one of the oldest in Australia, was formed in 1907.

The first enterprise to exploit mineral sands by the flotation process was pioneered in the Byron Bay area in 1932. A whaling station was established in 1954, but high operation costs and the reduction of the whale population by Antarctic fleets caused its abandonment after a few years.

Places of Interest. Watego's beach, under Cape Byron, one of the best surfboard riding beaches on the east coast because of its northerly aspect. **Suffolk Beach,** five kilometres south.

An Oleander Festival is celebrated in October.

Sport. Golf course. Bowls and croquet. Tennis and squash. Rifle range. Fishing. Surfing.

Accommodation. One **hotel.** Three **motels.** Preferred: Beacon, Bay Street.

Transport. Rail services to Lismore and Murwillumbah. **Road** services.

BRUNSWICK HEADS (Population 1 197)

Brunswick Heads is reputedly one of the best fishing resorts on the North Coast. It is at the mouth of the Brunswick River, 171 kilometres south of Brisbane and 850 kilometres from Sydney. The surrounding countryside produces tropical fruit, macadamia nuts, peanuts, mixed crops, timber and dairy produce. A large commercial fishing fleet is based on its boat harbour.

Places of Interest. Minyon Falls. Rocky Creek Dam (also accessible from Lismore). **Cape Byron Lookout. Peach Mountain Lookout. Mount Nardi.**

Sports. Bowls. Tennis. Water skiing. Fishing (boats and canoes for hire). Surfing.

Accommodation. One **hotel.** Two **motels.** Recommended: Brunswick, Pacific Highway. Holiday **flats** Five **caravan and camping parks,** all facilities.

Transport. Road services.

TWEED HEADS

On the NSW-Queensland border, 105 kilometres south of Brisbane, Tweed Heads is the twin town of Coolangatta, most southerly centre of the Gold Coast of Queensland. Primarily a tourist resort, it has fishing and fish processing industries. It used to be an important timber port.

Sports. Golf (two courses). Bowls. Tennis. Swimming and surfing. Water skiing etc.

Places of Interest. Porpoise Pool with performances by trained dolphins. **Razorback,** lookout with 360 degrees panorama. **Point Danger,** where Cook nearly wrecked *Endeavour* in 1770. **Terranora Lakes. Kingscliff** resort, on Pacific Highway south of town.

Accommodation. One **hotel,** the Dolphins (highly recommended). Four **motels.** Holiday **flats. Camping and caravan park,** all facilities.

Transport. Road services connecting with Gold Coast and North Coast towns. **Air** services to Coolangatta.

MURWILLUMBAH (Population 7 374)

Murwillumbah is 32 kilometres from the mouth of the Tweed River, close to the Queensland border and 914 kilometres north of Sydney. It is the centre of a picturesque district which grows bananas and sugar cane, and supports a flourishing dairy industry. The town has butter, clothing, casein and agricultural seed-cleaning factories, sugar and timber mills and joinery and stockfood processing works. (The sugar mill is open for inspection.)

The town has a Tweed Banana Festival in August-September.

History. Sugar growing began in the Tweed valley in 1869 and the townsite was surveyed in 1872, but its development was slow until the railway was extended from Lismore in 1894. In 1907 a disastrous fire practically wiped out the town which was substantially rebuilt the following year. Banana plantations were established in the early years of this century but the bunchy-top disease destroyed many of them in the 1920s. The pest has since been eliminated by chemical sprays. The town has at times been subject to bad floods, but control works have since proved effective. The meaning of the aboriginal name is obscure. It is popularly held to mean 'camp site' or 'possums' camp'.

Sports. Golf course. Bowls and croquet. Tennis. Four swimming pools. River fishing. Aquatic sports.

Accommodation. Three **hotels,** no preference. Two **motels.** Preferred: Tweed River, Pacific Highway. **Caravan and camping park,** all facilities.

Transport. Rail service via Lismore. **Road** services to Brisbane.

THE NEW ENGLAND TABLELANDS

(Traversed north-south by New England Highway)

New England is an extensive but not precisely defined area of northern New South Wales consisting of the plateau stretching from the Moonbi Range near the town of Tamworth north to the Queensland border, a distance of about 320 kilometres. It is the largest area of highland in Australia, 1 320 000 hectares lying at an altitude of more than 900 metres. The highest peaks are: Round Mountain (1 615 metres), Point Lookout, Mount Bajimba, Ben Lomond, Capoompeta and Chandler's Peak (all about 1 500 metres).

The countryside is varied and scenically lovely. Considerable areas of it are heavily wooded, and there are many fast, clear streams in the mountain gorges with spectacular cascades and waterfalls. The high features often command broad panoramas of mountain forests, rivers and rich, cultivated valleys.

Unlike many highland districts in Australia, the northern tablelands of New South Wales have very wide areas of rich soil and in the vicinity of the main settlements these are intensively farmed. The average rainfall of the whole area is about 760 millimetres a year. The main primary industries are mixed farming, sheep and cattle grazing, fruit-growing and the breeding of bloodstock. A romantic but not as yet economically important industry is the mining of industrial diamonds, sapphires, emeralds and semi-precious gemstones in streams near Glen Innes. It is wonderful country for the 'rockhound'. Some alluvial gold is dredged. The mineralization occurs at the junction of granite and basaltic intrusions of the original sedimentary rock.

Roads in the district are, on the whole, good. The New England Highway traverses the plateau from north to south, and the Oxley, Gwydir and Bruxner Highways give access from the coast and lead into the western districts of the State.

The best time to visit New England is in spring and autumn. Winters are usually wet, windy and cold.

History. John Oxley's expedition crossed the southern end of the tableland in 1818 on its journey east from the Macquarie River to Port Macquarie on the coast. The first settler is believed to have been H. C. Sempill of Belltrees, Scone, who established a station which he called Wolka, near the present town of Walcha. By 1837 there were about 30 squatters in the district and two years later the Land Commissioner, George Macdonald, fixed the administrative headquarters of the district at Armidale, which was gazetted a town 10 years later in 1849. The name New England was applied to the region generally in 1836, but for a number of years Scottish settlers persisted in referring to it as New Caledonia.

A revealing glimpse of the conditions in the early days is given by John Henderson in his *Excursions and Adventures in New South Wales* (1851). He wrote: 'New England is studded with stations at a distance of 10 or 15 miles from each other, and is chiefly or entirely occupied by young men of respectabliity and education. . . . In this respect it is much superior to the Liverpool Plains [where leaseholders] live within the bounds of the colony and leave their establishments to be managed by. . . overseers. . . often procured from the iower or emancipated orders. Within the last two years one or two ladies have found their way into the New England district. . . and when wives can be found the comfort of the stations and the respectability of the district will be much increased.'

Prominent in the history and legend of the district is the bushranger Frederick Ward, better known as 'Captain Thunderbolt', who preyed on travellers in the area between 1864 and 1870. He was shot dead at Uralla in 1870 and buried in the town cemetery where his grave is still tended. Tin and gold discoveries in the 1870s boosted the regional economy. Many parts of the highlands produce minerals, including coal, phosphates and silver-lead ores.

'New State' sentiment was high in the area for many years, the residents alleging that the district had been neglected by a succession of State governments because of its geographical remoteness from Sydney. Plebiscites, however, never resulted in the percentage of 'yes' votes required for political separation.

ARMIDALE

(Population 18 137)

Regarded as New England's 'capital', Armidale is 566 kilometres north of Sydney at an altitude of 1 000 metres in the New England Ranges. It is roughly halfway between Sydney and Brisbane. The surrounding district produces high quality merino wool, fat lambs, beef, apples, pears and stone fruit, cereals and vegetables.

The city is a pleasant tourist and holiday resort, centred as it is on a region of great scenic and historical interest, but it is largely dependent on commerce generated by its educational institutions although some light industries have been established. It is the nearest thing Australia has to a 'university town'. It is the seat of the University of New England, the Armidale Teachers' College, a technical college and State high school, Armidale School (a noted private secondary school) and a number of other similar establishments. It has particularly fine ecclesiastical, educational and commercial buildings, the last often displaying fine iron lace decoration.

History. William Dumaresq, a relative by marriage to the Colonial Secretary, Alexander MacLeay, squatted on a tract of land on the Beardy Plains in 1835. (The Beardy Plains derive their name from two of Captain Dumaresq's stockmen named Duval and Chandler, who wore distinctive black beards and possessed an intimate knowledge of the back country.) In 1839 a village was founded about eight kilometres from the Dumaresq homestead and was proclaimed a town in 1849. It reached municipal status in 1863 and was gazetted a city in 1885, two years after the railway from Sydney had been opened to traffic.

Places of Interest. City: Cathedrals of **St Peter's** and **St Mary's.** Hinton Benefaction **Art Gallery** (in Teachers' College) reputed to be the most valuable provincial collection of art in Australia. **Educational Museum,** also in the grounds of the Teachers' College—a mid-Victorian school re-erected. **Folk Museum,** containing relics of pioneering times. **Central Park,** containing fountains, war memorial statuary etc. (and a large relief map of the district which is valuable to visitors). **Apex Lookout** on ridge overlooking city about three kilometres north. Environs: **Wollombi Falls,** near village of the same name 48 kilometres east; the Chandler River plunges over a 350 metre precipice with a series of falls and cascades below. **Ebor Falls,** still farther east in the Doughboy and Dorrigo Ranges, three horseshoe-shaped tiers with a total drop of water of 450 metres. **Dangar Falls. New England National Park,** of 22 663 hectares, containing stands of rainforest and the impressive **Point Lookout** (81 kilometres east, at an altitude of 1 600 metres overlooking coastal plains). Scenic drive along **Arding** lanes between Armidale and Uralla (especially in spring when orchards are in blossom). **Big Hill,** panoramic lookout on Kempsey Road. **Dutton Fish Hatchery** on Serpentine River. **Hillgrove,** old mining settlement with buildings still intact (26 kilometres east off the road to the national park). **Oaky River Hydro-electric** scheme, east of city (inspections 2.30 pm Sundays).

Sports. Golf course. Tennis courts. Dog racing track. Gun club. Trout fishing (season, October-April). Duck and quail shooting (other game protected). Wild pig hunting.

Accommodation. Two **hotels.** Recommended: Tattersalls, Beardy Street. Eight **motels.** Recommended: Halfway House, Marsh Street. Two **camping and caravan parks,** all facilities.

Transport. Frequent **air** and **rail** services to Sydney and Brisbane. Daily **bus** services to Inverell via Guyra, twice weekly to Coff's Harbour via Dorrigo, weekly to Port Macquarie via Uralla and Walcha. **Bus** tours of city. **Scenic flights** from aerodrome.

Small Towns in District

URALLA (Population 1 140) was the village where the bushranger Captain Thunderbolt was shot dead in 1870.

Places of Interest. Thunderbolt's Lookout and grave. **Alma Park,** in town. Kentucky Soldiers' Settlement **orchards. Reservoir Lookout.**

Sports. Golf, tennis, bowls, swimming etc.

Accommodation. Two **hotels.** Recommended: Coachwood and Cedar. Two **motels.** Recommended, Altona, New England Highway. **Camping and caravan park,** some facilities.

WALCHA (Population 1 603) was the first town from which aerial crop dusting was carried out in Australia.

Places of Interest Folk Museum, open 11 am-4 pm weekends (a pioneer home maintained by the local historical society). **Tia Falls.** (36 kilometres east of town off the Oxley Highway and difficult to locate). **Apsley Falls,** in John Oxley Park (20 kilometres east), discovered by John Oxley in 1818. Total drop 300 metres. Plaque at the picnic spot where the explorer camped.

Sports. Golf, bowls, tennis. Water skiing. Wild pig shooting. Duck shooting (seasonal). Good trout streams.

Accommodation. Two **hotels.** Preferred: New England.

GUYRA (Population 1 682) is one of the highest towns in NSW, its altitude being 1 300 metres. The name is derived from an aboriginal word meaning 'fish may be caught'. Excellent trout and eel fishing in local streams.

Places of Interest. Chandler's Peak, for panoramic views. **Ebor Falls** and picnic reserve. Balancing rock formations such as **The Mushroom** at Backwater and **The Haystack,** east of Backwater. The road east leads to New England National Park.

Accommodation. One **hotel.**

INVERELL

(Population 9 700)

Inverell is 668 kilometres north of Sydney on the Gwydir Highway and the junction of the Swanbrook and MacIntyre Rivers. The surrounding land is very fertile and produces grain, potatoes, fruit, maize, wine grapes and fodder crops. There are also many dairy farms on the river flats where some wool, fat lambs and pigs are raised. The area is particularly rich in minerals; tin, industrial diamonds, sapphires and zircons are mined and deposits of silver, phosphates and bauxite have been located.

Secondary industries include timber mills, brickworks, engineering shops, abbattoirs, butter, bacon, cheese and smallgoods factories.

An annual Floral Festival is held in October and the district show, which maintains an exceptionally good standard, is held in February.

History. Alexander Campbell established Inverell station, of 20 235 hectares, in 1848. The name in Gaelic means 'meeting of the swans' and Campbell chose it because of the numerous swans he saw on the nearby rivers. The district was also known during the 1850s as Green Swamp. The townsite was surveyed in 1858. Rich tin discoveries were made at Tingha in the early 1870s, and in 1890 a diamond mine was worked at the Copeton diggings. In 1902 the town was connected with Sydney by rail, but the route is so circuitous (via Narrabri and Moree) that it is more than 160 kilometres longer than by road.

Places of Interest. Campbell and Victoria Parks. McIlveen Park, with 'million acre panoramic view' on outskirts. **Inverell station** homestead; original building incorporated as one wing.

Sports. Racecourse. Golf course. Tennis courts. Bowling greens. Olympic swimming pool.

Accommodation. Three **hotels.** Preferred: New Royal. Two **motels.** Recommended: Inverell, Otho Street.

Transport. Daily **rail** and **air** services to Sydney; weekly **air** services to Coolangatta and Brisbane.

Small Towns in District

DELUNGRA (Population 387), 30 kilometres west of Inverell, contains the Yaralla private zoo and gardens. Visitors welcome Wednesday, Thursday and weekends.

Accommodation. One **hotel.**

TINGHA (Population 258) is an old mining town 26 kilometres south-east of Inverell with tin dredge still operating at Cope's Creek. Private mineral museum open to public. Swimming pool. Potato crisp factory.

Accommodation. One **hotel.**

ASHFORD (Population 709) is the centre of tobacco-growing district, 56 kilometres north-west. Caves on Limestone Creek not yet fully explored. MacIntyre River Falls. Severn River Dam. River fishing, golf, tennis.

Accommodation. One **hotel. Camping park.**

WARIALDA (Population 1 294) is 53 kilometres west of Inverell. The district is well known for stud farms. Racecourse. Golf, bowls, tennis. Shooting and fishing.

Accommodation. One **hotel.**

BINGARA (Population 1 401) is an enticing town 42 kilometres south of Warialda. Fascinating for geologists and specimen collectors. Glacial area at **Rocky Creek** (32 kilometres). Coral and fish fossils. Hill of serpentine. Diamonds, sapphires, tourmalines can be found in local creeks and rivers. River fishing and sports facilities. The district is well known for its bloodstock. **Historic homestead** of 'Keera' (construction began in 1858) was the birthplace of the NSW Country Women's Association in 1922. A memorial to pioneers overlooks it.

Accommodation. One **hotel.** One **caravan and camping park.**

GLEN INNES (Population 5 762)

A beautifully situated mountain town (altitude 1 073 metres) on the Gwydir and New England Highways 671 kilometres from Sydney and 111 kilometres from the Queensland border, Glen Innes is the progressive centre of a rich dairying and mixed farming district. It is remarkable for civic pride and its fine public and private gardens. A Rose Festival lasting a week is held in October-November every year. The climate is cool (cold in winter) and bracing. Industries include bacon and butter factories, timber mills, brick and concrete pipe works, tannery, boot factory, vegetable processing (snap freezing) works. Sapphire mining is carried out on a full-time basis in the area.

History. The town began as a store and village on Furracahad station in 1851 and took its name from the pioneer settler Archibald Clune Innes, one of the first pastoralists to establish himself in New England. It was proclaimed a municipality in 1872. Bushrangers were very active in the district in the early days.

Sports. Racecourse. Golf course. Tennis courts. Bowling greens. Aero club. Rifle club. Swimming pool.

Places of Interest (environs). **Gibralter Range National Park,** on Gwydir Highway to Grafton; noted for wildflowers, including tree orchids, waratahs and Christmas bells, ferns and stands of rainforest. **Waterloo Valley Lookout,** 15 kilometres west of the town, offers exceptionally fine views. Spectacular **waterfalls** on the Mitchell, Mann and Henry Rivers. **Balancing rock formations** at Stonehenge (11 kilometres south, on private property but can be seen from the road) and at **Stonehenge Recreation Reserve.** Shannon Vale **Agricultural Experiment Farm** and animal nutrition station.

Accommodation. Three **hotels.** Recommended: Boomerang, Grey Street. Six **motels.** Recommended: Amalgamated, Church Street; Alpha and Glen, New England Highway. Three **caravan and camping parks,** all facilities.

Transport. Rail service from Sydney and to Queensland rail system. **Road** services to surrounding towns. **Air** service (several times weekly) to Sydney and Brisbane.

TENTERFIELD (Population 3 232)

At the junction of the Bruxner and Mount Lindesay Highways 760 kilometres north of Sydney and 277 kilometres from Brisbane, Tenterfield is the market town for a district known for its high quality dairy produce, beef and fat lambs, tobacco, apples, maize and honey. Tin is mined in the district. Its secondary industries include killing and freezing works, a butter factory and timber mills. It is also an important stock-trucking centre.

The surrounding countryside has many unusual scenic attractions. The town celebrates a Festival of the Willows, following the district agricultural show, in February-March.

History. The first settlers arrived in the district about 1840, a village was established in 1848, the town gazetted in 1851 and the municipality in 1871. In 1886 the railway from Sydney to Wallangarra reached the town. In 1889 the Australian statesman, Henry Parkes, made a speech at the Tenterfield School of Arts which is regarded as having launched the political movement for the federation of the Australian States.

Places of Interest. Town: **School of Arts,** taken over by the National Trust as a memorial to Sir Henry Parkes and now used as a public library. The section of the building in which the famous speech was delivered is preserved as a museum of records and relics associated with Parkes. **Centenary Cottage,** historical museum run by local historical society. **'House of Dolls',** Railway Street, a private doll collection open for inspection 9 am to 5 pm daily. Environs: **Boonoo Boonoo Falls** (pronounced bunna-bernoo), 32 kilometres north, are spectacular but the access road is fairly rough, crossing shallow streams and traversing virgin bush. **Bald Rock,** a large granite monolith on private property 6½ kilometres from the Mount Lindesay Highway; the access road is very rough indeed. **Ghost Gully,** a fantastically eroded gully not far from town, is of great interest to photographers. **Long Gully,** 64 kilometres east, contains fascinating stands of palm trees, ferns and rainforest. **Boorook,** near Long Gully, has a fine waterfall and an old aboriginal corroboree ground.

Sports. Golf course. Bowling and croquet greens. Tennis courts. Swimming pool. Fishing in Mole and Severn Rivers.

Accommodation. Three **hotels.** Recommended: Commercial, Rouse Street. Four **motels.** Recommended: Tally Ho, New England Highway. Three **caravan and camping parks,** all facilities.

Transport. Rail services to Queensland and Sydney. Daily **road** services from Brisbane, via Warwick, Stanthorpe and Wallangarra. Daily **bus** to Lismore (except Sunday).

URBENVILLE (Population 309) is 135 kilometres north of Tenterfield in scenically interesting country. Attractions include State forests at Yabbra, Mandle and Beaury; Crown Mountain for panoramic views; Toolem Falls and Lookout in luxuriant tropical forest country.

Accommodation. One **hotel.**

NORTH-WESTERN SLOPES

The north-western slopes of the Great Dividing Range in New South Wales, roughly comparable in area with Scotland, comprise a region of remarkable geographical contrasts. The eastern section, under the shadow of the massive New England tablelands, is a land of timbered slopes and green river valleys broken here and there by dramatic mountain ranges like the Warrumbungles, near the little town of Coonabarabran, and the Nandewars east of Narrabri. The western section falls gradually away into the great plains of the inland—the wide, brown, sun-blistered country of meandering rivers and mirage and heat and dust.

The black soil plains of the north-west are particularly fertile in good seasons. But when drought or flood hits this country it hits hard.

In autumn and spring particularly the north-west has a great deal to offer sightseers and holidaymakers. The mountains and marshy areas on the west-flowing rivers abound in wildlife of all kinds and are of enormous appeal to field naturalists and sportsmen. The terrain also is of absorbing interest to geologists and prospectors, particularly in the hilly sections where a great variety of mineral specimens, gemstones and fossils may be collected.

The roads, with the exception of the Newell and Castlereagh Highways serving the more populated areas, are by no means good, but in dry weather they can be negotiated without difficulty by motorists whose prime consideration is not speed. After rain, particularly in the black soil areas, they are treacherous and travellers should always make a point of inquiring locally about conditions ahead if the weather has been wet or is threatening.

The north-west is not geared as yet to tourism, but clean and fairly comfortable accommodation is almost always available at the hotels in larger towns. And, of course, modern-type motels conform to acceptable standards.

TAMWORTH

(Population 24 694)

Situated at the foot of the Moonbi Range in the rich Peel River Valley, 451 kilometres north of Sydney, Tamworth is a solid, prosperous city with pleasant public and commercial buildings and attractive parks and gardens. The district produces wool, fat lambs and cereals, dairy produce, table poultry and eggs, fruit, vegetables, honey and some tobacco. Secondary industries are butter and smallgoods factories, timber mills, egg grading and packing, an abattoir and a freezing works, flour mills, wheat and grain-processing plants, a brewery and furniture and clothing factories. It is also the headquarters of East-West Airlines which flies a network of internal passenger and freight services in New South Wales and southern Queensland.

History. John Oxley discovered the Peel River valley in 1818. In 1839 a village was founded at Goonoo-Goonoo on land granted to the Australian Agricultural Company, a monopolistic organization formed in London in 1824 to develop the fine-wool industry and cultivate grapes, flax, olives and other produce usually imported by Britain from Mediterranean countries. The town of Tamworth, named after the home of the British statesman, Sir Robert Peel, was proclaimed in 1850. Philip Gidley King, grandson of Governor King, was its first mayor.

By the 1860s the settlement had become an important coaching station and several manufacturing industries had been developed. The municipality was gazetted in 1876, and in 1888 the construction of a steam power house gave it the distinction of being the first country town in Australia to be lighted by electricity.

Places of Interest. Town: **City Art Gallery** (of higher standard than usual in Australian provincial cities). **Town Hall. Oxley Park Lookout.** Environs: **Oxley's Anchor Memorial** 8 kilometres north-north-west. **Moonbi Lookout** 24 kilometres north-east. **Nundle** township, reached by a good road through precipitous mountain scenery to the south of the city, is an old goldmining centre in picturesque surroundings, with hotel and camping accommodation. **Hanging Rock Lookout** 8 kilometres south of Nundle. **Keepit, Dungowan** and **Sheba Dams.**

The Tamworth district is particularly good tourist territory. Its scenery is varied and spectacular and the climate is pleasant for most of the year. The city celebrates its annual Festival of Light in October-November when a variety of entertainments—celebrity concerts, sports carnivals, flower shows, parades and art and industrial exhibitions—is organized.

Sports. Golf, bowls, tennis etc.

Accommodation. Five **hotels.** Recommended: Good Companions, Brisbane Street. Ten **motels.** Recommended: Travelodge, New England and Oxley Highways; Flag Motor Inn, New England Highway; Tamworth Motor Lodge, Marius Street. Two **caravan and camping parks,** all facilities.

Transport. Rail, road and **air** services to Sydney and other centres.

Small Towns in District

MANILLA (Population 1 616). The centre of a wheat and mixed-farming area, 37 kilometres north-west of Tamworth, and 37 kilometres east of **Keepit Dam** on the Peel River, which was originally built to regulate the flow of the Namoi River and provide water for irrigation, Manilla is these days being developed as a tourist attraction. It is in charming country and has facilities for picnics, bathing and water sports of all kinds. Amenities include a kiosk, store, post office and cafe and a caravan park is being built. A second aquatic centre on the dam is **Manilla Ski Gardens,** off the main road from Manilla, 21 kilometres from town. Fishing in the district is excellent.

Accommodation. One **hotel.**

Transport. Rail and **road** services from Tamworth.

BARRABA (Population 1 579). On the Manilla River in the Nandewar Range 90 kilometres north of Tamworth, Barraba is the centre of a productive agricultural and pastoral area. The region also produces diatomite clay which is mined by open-cut methods. The town has good sports facilities and on New Year's Eve and New Year's Day holds a bushmen's carnival or rodeo at Upper Horton (32 kilometres north) which creates great interest throughout the north-west. Barraba is an excellent base from which to explore the eastern part of **Nandewar Mountains,** a spur range branching off the New England Plateau, which is the watershed of the Namoi and Gwydir Rivers. The range is volcanic in origin and its highest peak is Mount Kapatur (1 526 metres). The panorama from the summit reached by good road from Narrabri is breathtaking, taking in a vista of eight million hectares. The area was reserved as a national park in 1925. Other notable peaks are Mount Grattai (1642 metres), Mount Lindesay (1 442 metres) and Yalludunida (1 280 metres), a crater mountain overlooking tremendous gorges cut by erosion of the massif. This region is only now beginning to come into its own as tourist country. The mountain scenery is as fine as anything the State has to offer.

Accommodation (at Barraba). Two **hotels.** Preferred: Central, Queen Street. At the national park there are **caravan and camping facilities** and three holiday **cabins.** (Inquiries, Secretary, Mount Kaputar National Park Trust, Maitland Street, Narrabri, NSW 2390.)

GUNNEDAH

(Population 8 219)

Central town of the rather vaguely defined Liverpool Plains district of New South Wales, Gunnedah is 477 kilometres north-west of Sydney (and 76 kilometres west of Tamworth) at the junction of the Namoi and Mooki Rivers. The name is derived from an aboriginal word meaning 'white stones'.

The black soil country of the plains grows good wheat, fat stock, wool and fodder crops and two coal mines are worked in the district which also produces cypress pine timber from its forested areas. The town has one of the largest stock-marketing and killing centres in NSW. There are also thriving flour mills. A soil conservation and research station was established there some years ago.

History. The Liverpool Plains were discovered by Oxley in 1818. He recognized the region to be highly fertile country, but it was not until Allan Cunningham found Pandora's Pass through the western end of the Liverpool Range in 1823 and later when Henry Dangar found a practicable route from the Hunter Valley that the area became accessible to settlers. By 1827 three stations had been established there, but then the holders were displaced by the powerful Australian Agricultural Company (granted 1 000 000 acres at peppercorn rental by Royal Charter in 1824). The company maintained its monopoly over the best of the Liverpool Plains land until 1850, when the agreement with the Imperial Government was dissolved and the land sold to comparatively small holders. Gunnedah was proclaimed a town in 1856 and a municipality in 1885. Today it is quiet, prosperous settlement which has taken a good deal of pride in developing its civic amenities. The climate is uncomfortably hot in summer.

Sports. Golf course. Racecourse. Greyhound-racing track. Tennis, bowls etc. River fishing.

Accommodation. Four **hotels.** Recommended: Regal, Conadilly Street. Three **motels.** Recommended: Gunnedah, Conadilly Street. **Two camping and caravan parks,** all facilities.

Transport. Daily **rail** and **air** services to Sydney. Local **road** services.

NARRABRI

(Population 5 875)

On the Liverpool Plains 573 kilometres north-north-west of Sydney, Narrabri lies between the tall and spectacular Nandewar Range and the vast and sombre Pilliga Scrub country to the west. The district produces the usual fat stock and cereals of the north-west, but recently cotton has become an important crop. More than 20 000 hectares are under cultivation. There are also productive dairy and mixed farms on the Namoi River flats. Rutile is mined in the locality and a search for oil is under way. The town has a freezing works, timber and flour mills, and an engineering plant. Four cotton gins and an oil seed crushing plant have been established at Wee Waa, 41 kilometres north-west.

History. The town was surveyed in 1859 and the first land sales took place the following year, but its progress was slow until communications were improved and water-conservation projects began. It was proclaimed a municipality in 1883. The name is a corruption of the aboriginal word for 'big creek'.

Places of Interest. World's first stellar intensity **interferometer,** (20 kilometres). The instrument is designed to measure the stars. Solar heliograph, a huge camera for taking radio pictures of the sun, is now operating at Culgoora. The observatory is open for public inspection between 2 pm and 4 pm Sunday. Two other scientific stations of interest are the **Irrigation Experimental Farm,** 24 kilometres west and the **North-Western Wheat Research Institute,** five kilometres from town. Drive to **Mount Kaputar Lookout** (20 kilometres east).

Narrabri celebrates a Cotton Festival each year in late May. Inspection of farms and gins is part of the programme.

Sports. Golf course. Bowling greens. Tennis courts. Olympic swimming pool.

Accommodation. Four **hotels.** Preferred: Namoi, Maitland Street. Three **motels.** Recommended: Nandewar Motor Inn, Dangar Street. Two **caravan parks,** all facilities.

Transport. Daily **rail** and **air** services to Sydney.

MOREE

(Population 9 114)

On the Gwydir River, 666 kilometres north-north-west of Sydney, Moree is the centre of a wool, wheat and beef-producing district first settled in 1848 by James Cox who established a station of the same name (an aboriginal word meaning 'rising sun'). The Gwydir is subject to serious flooding and the town has three times suffered serious damage—in 1910 and in 1928, after which the central section had to be rebuilt, and in 1955.

The town is well known for its artesian water baths which are reputed to give relief to rheumatic and arthritic conditions. Nearby Broadwater Creek, between the Gwydir and Mehi Rivers, is believed to be unique. When the water level is low it flows into the Mehi, when it is high into the Gwydir. There is no other instance known of a stream having two directions of flow.

Sports. Racecourse. Greyhound racing track. Olympic swimming pool. Bowls, golf, tennis etc.

Accommodation. Three **hotels.** Recommended: Royal, Heber Street. Two **motels.** Recommended: Artesian, Newell Highway. Two **caravan and camping parks,** all facilities.

Transport. **Rail** service to Sydney. **Air** services to Brisbane, Tamworth and Sydney.

COONABARABRAN (Population 3 045). A wheat, sheep and timber town on the Castlereagh River, Coonabarabran (meaning obscure) lies 491 kilometres north-west of Sydney. Diatomite, a mineral substance used for filtering and insulation, is mined in an open cut nearby. Numerous fossils are found in the area.

Places of Interest. **Timor Rock** and a recently constructed dam (good scenic views) on the Castlereagh. **Mount Stromlo** field observatory at Siding Spring Mountain with the world's second largest optical telescope; on a spur road off the Renshaw Parkway to the Warrumbungles, 24 kilometres west. A $A2 000 Cup Meeting is held on the local racecourse on the second Monday in October.

Accommodation. Two **hotels.** Preferred: Coonabarabran, John Street. Three **motels.** Recommended: Coonabarabran Motor Lodge, Newell Highway. **Caravan and camping park,** all facilities.

Transport. **Rail** and **air** services to Sydney and other centres.

WARRUMBUNGLE NATIONAL PARK

The Warrumbungle Ranges, about 488 kilometres north-west of Sydney near Coonabarabran, contain some of the most spectacular and extraordinary mountain peaks in Australia. They are ancient volcanic plugs which rise suddenly from the surrounding plain in much the same way as the Glasshouse Mountains of southern Queensland. The Warrumbungles are larger and more impressive and they contain deep gorges and precipitous rock faces which provide mountaineers with some of the finest rock climbing to be found in Australia. The main peaks in the group are Belougery Spire, The Needle, Crater Bluff and Tonduron Spire. The north wall of Crater Bluff rises 300 metres sheer from the floor of the valley.

One of the strangest rock formations in the Warrumbungles is The Breadknife—a gargantuan, upended sliver of rock 90 metres high, only one and a half metres wide at the top and little wider at the base. The rock was originally cast in a volcanic fissure of harder substance than the mountain, which has since eroded away and left the intrusion exposed.

The reserve, however, has more attractions than its eerie peaks. The 5 660 hectares now reserved are a sanctuary for an amazingly diverse range of native vegetation and wildlife. Snow gums flourish alongside grasstrees and Port Jackson figs. Twenty-two varieties of wattle, 29 flowering peas and 17 orchids have been identified in the area. The deep gullies contain trigger plants and rare ferns and mosses and the cover forest of kurrajongs, river oaks and eucalyptus shelters 120 different species of birds from wedgetailed eagles, with a wing span of more than two metres, to tiny finches and wrens. Terrestrial animals include koalas, kangaroos, several kinds of wallabies, spiny ant-eaters (echidnas) and possums. Regrettably, motorists speeding on the access roads have taken a heavy toll of them. The locality is of interest to lapidarists. Silver, gold, opal and fossilized wood can be found.

History. John Oxley first sighted the range in 1818 and called it the Arbuthnot Range, but in documents dating from 1830 they are referred to as the Warrumbungles (aboriginal for 'broken mountains'). The area was known only to local bushmen and settlers until the early 1930s when rock-climbing was established as an organized sport in Australia. In 1953, about 2 200 hectares were proclaimed as a national park and sanctuary. A local landowner, Alfred Pincham, gave his property to increase the area and there is a memorial cairn to him at Canyon Camp, the park's headquarters.

Plans are now being made to acquire more country in the Wombelong Valley. The best time of the year to visit the Warrumbungles is between May and September.

Access. The main access road is from Tooraweena, off the Oxley Highway north-east of Gilgandra, but an indirect route is available from Bugaldie, south-west of Coonabarabran. A new sealed highway from Coonabarabran has recently been completed. Walking tracks have been formed to key vantage points. The old access roads are rough and may be impassable after heavy rain.

Accommodation. Six corridor-type trams have been fitted out as **lodge** accommodation for visitors. Each has two units accommodating four adults. Electricity, hot and cold showers and sanitation are provided.

GILGANDRA (Population 2 554). On the Castlereagh River and at the junction of the Oxley, Newell and Castlereagh Highways, 449 kilometres from Sydney, Gilgandra serves a district growing cereal crops, wool and cypress pine and hardwood timber. Good sports facilities. The Gilgandra Gift, one of the richest professional footraces held in New South Wales, is run here every year.

Accommodation. One **hotel.** Two **motels.** Preferred: Silver Oaks, Newell Highway. **Caravan and camping park,** all facilities.

Transport. **Rail** service to Sydney. **Motorcoach** service to Dubbo for **air** connections. Local **road** services.

COONAMBLE (Population 3 152)

Near the western margins of the Pilliga Scrub country, 518 kilometres north-west of Sydney, Coonamble is in an area of fertile country which suffers badly in drought seasons from an inadequate supply of ground water. It is an artesian basin, but depletion of the reservoirs has resulted in the use of the bore water being restricted to stock and domestic supplies. Previously high yields of rice and lucerne were obtained at the local experiment farm, but development in this direction now awaits water-conservation works on the Castlereagh River. In good years the district produces high-grade wool, fat lambs, beef cattle and wheat. The town celebrates a Wool Festival in October.

The completion of the railway from Coonabarabran to Gwabegar, north-east of Coonamble, has encouraged exploitation of the timber resources of the Pilliga Scrub, an area of nearly 890 000 hectares in which cypress pine and ironbark eucalypts grow prolifically. Roughly one-third of the area is State Forest. The agricultural potential of the Pilliga has been doubted for many years, but wheat is now being successfully established.

Adjacent to Coonamble Shire are the **Macquarie Marshes,** an enormous breeding ground for birds and a region rich in unusual plant life.

Sports. Good racecourse. Olympic swimming pool. Tennis, bowls etc.

Accommodation. Two **hotels.** Preferred: Tattersall's, Castlereagh Street. Two **motels.** Preferred: Cyprus, Castlereagh Highway. **Caravan and camping park,** all facilities.

Transport. Rail and **air** services to Sydney and other centres.

WALGETT (Population 1 700) and Lightning Ridge

The terminus of the north-west railway line and near the junction of the Namoi and Barwon Rivers, Walgett is a small pastoral town on the margin of the semi-arid, sparsely populated far-western plains of New South Wales. Some wheat and fodder crops are grown, but most of the countryside is given over to sheep-farming. The town and most of the properties in the area are dependent on artesian bores for domestic and stock water.

The town is of interest to tourists mainly because it is the nearest sizeable settlement to the famous **Lightning Ridge** opal fields, 75 kilometres north. Large-scale mining has revived in recent years with the introduction of mechanical excavators.

The black opal found at Lightning Ridge is of great depth and brilliance and is today extremely valuable. It is classed by jewellers as a precious gemstone and, unlike other kinds of opal, is sold by the carat rather than by the ounce. It occurs not in bands but in small, ovoid shapes encased in soft white sandstone.

The first big strike of black opal was made at Lightning Ridge by a prospector, Jack Nettleton, in 1901. He was investigating stories that opal had been found in the locality some 20 years earlier. Conservative Sydney jewellers were not at first interested in the new, fiery-coloured stones but when the first specimens were sent to Europe they caused a sensation and a rush ensued. Hundreds of 'gougers' flocked to the Ridge, and a few of them—like their goldmining brethren—made fortunes. Probably the most valuable stone ever found on the field was Queen of the Earth, which would today be valued at about $A150 000.

Active mining continued on the field for more than 20 years, after which the deposits yielded fewer and fewer stones of value. The miners drifted off to new strikes of seam opal at Coober Pedy in South Australia and elsewhere.

Today the ground about the tiny township of Lightning Ridge is pockmarked with innumerable mine shafts up to 21 metres deep and lucky finds can sometimes be made by visitors picking over the waste material on the workings.

The whole area is highly mineralized and attracts gem fossickers from all over Australia. Even if they fail to pick up opal they may discover good specimens of white and blue topaz and other semi-precious stones in the dry creekbeds.

Lightning Ridge is to some extent restoring its fortunes with tourism. Special tours to the fields have been run from Sydney, and the small hotel, caravan park and old tram cars converted as lodges are usually crowded in the cool months between May and September. A summer visit can be recommended only to the very hardy. However, the settlement now has electric light and an adequate water supply which it lacked for many years.

Walgett is a convenient base for visits to the ridge. The town has a swimming pool and the usual facilities for sports. There is good fishing and pig-shooting in the district.

Accommodation. One **hotel.** Two **motels.** Recommended: Coolabah, Wee Waa Street.

Transport. Rail service to Sydney. Local **road** services.

THE CENTRAL WEST

The Central West of New South Wales comprises mainly gently rolling country on the western slopes of the Great Dividing Range. It has always been noted for wheat and woolgrowing but it has become much more prosperous since the construction of great water storages such as the Burrendong Dam (31 kilometres south-east of Wellington at the confluence of the Macquarie and Cudgegong Rivers) and the Wyangala Dam on the Lachlan River, 42 kilometres upstream from Cowra. Irrigation of the fertile river flats has in recent years greatly diversified and increased production.

The countryside is on the whole pleasant, but it is scenically attractive only in the east where the foothills run up into the high tablelands of the range proper. It will, however, appeal to travellers interested in the techniques of pastoral and agricultural industry in Australia. One-day air tours from Sydney to properties in the Dubbo district, to watch shearing, mustering etc, are favoured by overseas tourists. Longer holidays on some central-western stations can also be arranged. Inquiries should be made from the New South Wales Government Tourist Bureau in Sydney.

Roads through the region are mostly good. Motorists should note that the Olympic Way, now a popular alternative to the Hume Highway between Sydney and Melbourne, passes through the major towns of both the Riverina and the Central West.

Spring and autumn are the best seasons in which to tour. Summers are dry, hot and dusty and winters—particularly at higher elevations such as Bathurst—can be uncomfortably cold.

Accommodation of reasonably good standard is available in all the larger towns, many of which are attractively situated and substantial. Most are served by the intrastate rail and air networks.

BATHURST

(Population 17 169)

Australia's oldest inland city, Bathurst is 209 kilometres west of Sydney, on the Macquarie River. It is the centre of a long-established pastoral and grain-growing district which also produces fruit and vegetables. Urban secondary industry includes railway and precision engineering workshops, canning and can-manufacturing plants, flour mills, brick, pipe and cement works, and factories for the manufacture of office furniture and footwear.

Bathurst has been accurately described as a sedate city of red brick and blue granite in a setting of carefully planned and well-maintained plantations, parks and gardens. Many distinctive buildings face King's Parade, its central square.

History. In 1813 the explorers Blaxland, Wentworth and Lawson crossed the Blue Mountains and the same year the Surveyor-General, George Evans, named the Bathurst Plains after the then Secretary of State for the Colonies, Henry Bathurst, who took an active and intelligent interest in the new colony and encouraged investigation of its potential.

Two years later, in 1815, William Cox built the first road over the mountains and Governor Macquarie, who took nine days to travel over it, chose the site for the first settlement on the western slopes of the Great Dividing Range. The following year the settler William Lee moved the first flock of sheep into the new country, but little was done to make land available to the small farmer immigrant whom Macquarie had hoped to encourage.

Nevertheless, Bathurst developed as an outpost and became the base for many expeditions to explore the inland. Evans, Oxley, Cunningham, Mitchell and Sturt all made it the point of departure for journeys into the interior of the continent.

The 1820s were turbulent years for the little settlement. The aborigines strongly resisted the infiltration of white men into their tribal lands and in 1824 the position of settlers had become so insecure that the authorities proclaimed martial law in the district and offered a reward of 500 acres of land for the capture of the native ringleader, Saturday. In 1830 violent rioting broke out among convicts in the Bathurst goal and when order was restored 10 prisoners were hanged for their part in the disorders.

The first coach service to Parramatta was opened in 1824 and in 1833 a new townsite was surveyed to a design by J. B. Richardson, who was later to have a hand in the planning of Melbourne and Adelaide.

Progress, however, was still very slow until 1851 when gold was discovered at Summer Hill Creek, near Orange, 48 kilometres north-west, and a nugget weighing 48 kilograms was unearthed. Thousands of prospectors rushed the area—followed by the bushrangers Gardiner, Gilbert, Hall and others. As was the case with many other Australian goldmining towns, the diggers stayed on to become farmers and tradesmen after the mines declined.

Bathurst was the birthplace of J. B. Chifley, Prime Minister of Australia from 1945 to 1949. The Chifley Housing Settlement in the city is his memorial.

Notable Buildings and Monuments. **Civic Centre.** **Court House** (reputedly built to a plan prepared for a court house in Gambia, North-West Africa, and sent to NSW by mistake; the court house in Gambia was intended for Bathurst). It also contains the city post and telegraph office and Public Works Department offices. **Holy Trinity Church,** in the suburb of Kelso, was the first church built west of the Blue Mountains and its churchyard contains the graves of many prominent pioneers. **No 1 George Street** (Macquarie House), one wing of which was built in 1817, houses a **folk museum.** **The Singing Tower,** a carillon housing 35 bells, was erected as a memorial to the dead of two world wars (30 metres high); it is played every Wednesday and Friday afternoon, 4.30 to 5 o'clock. **South African War Memorial** (opened by Lord Kitchener in 1910) and **George Evans Memorial,** King's Parade.

Other Places of Interest. Town: **Machattie Park,** with fine begonia house. Environs: **Mount Panorama** motor-racing circuit and **McPhillamy Park.** **Pioneer houses** in suburb of Eglinton, including 'Strath', the residence of Major-General Sir William Stewart (1769-1854), Lieutenant-Governor of New South Wales. **Abercrombie Caves** (74 kilometres south), the hideout of the bushranger Ben Hall (guides available). **Hill End** (about 84 kilometres north and west), proclaimed a national historic village; the town originally had a population of 30 000 and 52 hotels; the huge Beyers and Holtermann nugget was found here in 1872. **Ben Chifley Dam** (43 kilometres). **Old mining towns** of Sofala and Wattletree, and **Capertree scenic drive** (due north).

Annual events at Bathurst include the Carillon Tourist Festival in March, an eisteddfod in October, the District Show a week after Easter, motor-racing meetings on the Mount Panorama circuit at Easter and in October and a Lions' Club Fun Festival on New Year's Eve.

Sports. Trotting track (night) at showground. Greyhound racing track. Olympic swimming pool. Bowling greens, croquet lawns, tennis courts etc. Excellent golf course, gun club.

Accommodation. One **hotel.** Eight **motels.** Recommended: Bathurst Motor Lodge, Durham Street. One **caravan and camping park,** all facilities.

Transport. **Rail** services (on main western line) to Sydney etc. Daily **air** services to Sydney, Orange, Dubbo, Cowra (except Sunday) and Parkes. Local **road** services.

ORANGE

(Population 24 154)

The prosperity of Orange, situated on the eastern slopes of Mount Canobolas (1 285 metres), 259 kilometres west-north-west of Sydney, is rooted in the rich, red volcanic soil which has made the district one of the most productive fruit-growing areas in New South Wales. It is noted for the excellence of its cherries, apples, pears and peaches but, despite its name, it would be difficult to find an orange tree in the entire region, which is subject to sharp winter frosts. Fat cattle and lambs, pigs, fodder crops and vegetables are also produced on the rich farmlands.

Secondary industries include the manufacture of electrical goods—one of the State's largest plants, covering more than 12 hectares—woollen and timber mills, printing works, light engineering shops, confectionery and cordials factories and fruit-packing and processing establishments.

The town and district are particularly attractive in spring when the cherry orchards are in blossom and an annual festival is held.

History. Orange was originally known as Blackman's Swamp for reasons which are now obscure. However, it was eventually named for the Prince of Orange by the explorer and Surveyor-General, Major Mitchell. The district had been examined by both Oxley and Evans in the 1820s, but settlement was slow and the village was not gazetted until 1846. Gold was discovered by Edward Hargreaves at Ophir (Summer Hill Creek) about 16 kilometres north-west and the rush started. The prosperity created by the diggings continued throughout the 1860s, but after that the district turned to wheat-farming until the advent of the railway in 1885, after which it was possible to market the fruit which grew so abundantly in the area.

Orange reached town status in 1885 and was proclaimed a city in 1946. It was the birthplace of the celebrated Australian bush poet A. B. (Banjo) Paterson in 1864. The town was at one time seriously considered as a site for the Federal capital, but inadequate water supply at that time caused it to be rejected.

Places of Interest. **Mount Canobolas,** scenic drive and fine panoramic view. **Lake Canobolas,** scenically memorable. **Cook Park** Municipal Gardens. **Towac motor-racing circuit.** **Old goldmining town** of Ophir. **Millthorpe,** a neighbouring small town with an interesting historical museum.

Sports. Golf course. Racecourse. Bowling greens, tennis courts etc. Rifle club.

Accommodation. Three **hotels.** Recommended: Canobolas, Summer Street. Four **motels.** Recommended: Oriana, Mitchell Highway.

Transport. Daily **rail** and **air** services to Sydney and other western towns. Local **road** services.

WELLINGTON

(Population 5 534)

At the junction of the Macquarie and Bell Rivers 365 kilometres north-west of Sydney. Wellington is situated in rolling hill country which produces wool, fat cattle and lambs, fruit, vegetables and fodder crops. A gold dredge still operates in the Macquarie River gravels. The town has a plant for the production of earthmoving and farm machinery and a dairy factory.

History. John Oxley made the locality a depot for his Macquarie River exploration in 1817-18. The settlement was founded in 1823 and a convict settlement established, but this was abandoned in 1831. The town was gazetted in 1846. In the 1850s payable gold was discovered in the surrounding countryside, notably at Stuart Town and Mookerawa. The municipality was proclaimed in 1879 and in 1947 part of East Macquarie Shire and of Macquarie Shire were amalgamated to form Wellington Shire.

Places of Interest. **Cameron Park,** occupying the entire side of the main street and fronting on the Bell River; it contains an impressive War Memorial, sunken garden, swimming pool and children's playground. **Wellington Limestone Caves** (8 kilometres south), containing fine stalagmites and stalactites and the bones of fossilized prehistoric animals; Cathedral and Gaden Caves are open for inspection each day; the former contains a huge stalagmite resembling a statue of theVirgin Mary. **Museum,** on Warne and Percy Streets, in what was the original Bank of New South Wales; it contains material illustrating early history of the district. **Burrendong Dam** and national park; the dam (31 kilometres south-east on the Macquarie River) is being developed for aquatic sports.

Lapidarists should note that many of the gravels in rivers and creeks of the district contain precious and semi-precious gemstones. Gold fossicking can still be profitable.

Sports. Racecourse. Golf, tennis, bowls etc. Trotting and greyhound-racing tracks.

Accommodation. Two **hotels.** Recommended: Grand, Lee Street. Two **motels.** Recommended: Sunset, Lee Street. Two **caravan and camping parks** (one at Wellington Caves), all facilities.

Transport. **Rail** services via Orange and west to Bourke. Local **road** services.

DUBBO

(Population 17 767)

A pleasant, well-planned city on the Macquarie River, 420 kilometres north-west of Sydney, Dubbo is the centre of a district which produces wheat, wool, fat lambs and cattle, and some fruit, vegetables and poultry. Timber is logged in nearby State forest areas. The town is an important rail junction, has busy abattoirs and stock saleyards, a clothing factory and an RAAF stores depot.

History. The first settler, G. T. Palmer, moved into the area in 1824, four years after John Oxley's expedition had passed through it. A court house and police post were established in 1847 and two years later the village was proclaimed. It had grown to municipal status by 1872 and in 1966 was gazetted a city.

Places of Interest. **Victoria Park,** with playing areas and gardens, near the centre of the city. **Pioneer Museum,** Macquarie Street. **State Forests and National Aboretum.**

Sports. Golf course. Racecourse. Bowls, croquet, tennis etc. Water skiing and fishing on the Macquarie River.

Accommodation. Five **hotels.** Recommended: Amaroo, Macquarie Street. Nine **motels.** Recommended: Homestead and Golden West, Cobar Street. One **caravan and camping park,** all facilities.

Transport. **Rail, road** and **air** services.

MUDGEE

(Population 5 583)

On the Cudgegong River, 264 kilometres north-west of Sydney, Mudgee is the centre of a district noted for the production of fine wool and stud sheep as well as for cattle, cereal crops, fodder, wine grapes and honey. The town has very attractive parks and gardens. The name means 'nest among the hills'.

The Australian poet and short-story writer, Henry Lawson, spent some years of his boyhood at Eurunderee, about 8 kilometres from town, and Mudgee celebrates a Henry Lawson Floral Festival in September every year.

Sports. Golf course. Tennis courts. Bowling greens. Olympic swimming pool etc.

Accommodation. Two **hotels.** Preferred: Sydney, Church Street. Three **motels.** Recommended: Mudgee, Sydney Road. **Caravan and camping park,** all facilities.

Transport. **Rail** and **air** services daily to Sydney. Local **road** services.

GULGONG (Population 1 486)

Twenty nine kilometres north-west of Mudgee, Gulgong is an old goldmining centre known since the conversion of the Australian currency to the decimal system as 'the town on the 10-dollar note'. The reverse side of the note is designed from photographs of buildings which stood in Gulgong's main street when it was a roaring boom town in the 1870s after a rich strike at Red Hill. However, none of the buildings depicted on the note is still standing. The Gulgong goldfield is estimated to have produced 18 tons of gold in the first five years of its life. Today the only profitable mining that goes on in the locality is for high-quality kaolin clay used in the making of pottery.

There is an interesting **Pioneers' Museum,** containing an excellent collection of relics, in the town. It is open from 2 pm to 5 pm Monday to Friday and from 9.30 am to 5 pm at weekends and on public holidays.

Accommodation. Two **hotels.** Preferred: Commercial, Mayne Street.

YOUNG

(Population 6 062)

Young is a picturesque town in the western foothills of the Great Dividing Range, 395 kilometres west-south-west of Sydney. The district produces cereals, cattle, poultry and pigs, but is best known for its cherries and prunes. More than one million kilograms of cherries and 1 250 tonnes of prunes are produced by Young's orchards every year. The town's secondary industries, besides fruit-processing and packing plants, include a knitting mill, a prune brandy distillery and factories for the production of clothing, fabricated steel, tiles, magnesium oxide and flour.

The town celebrates an annual Cherry Blossom Festival in November.

History. The first settler, James White, founded Burrangong station in 1830. Suitable country in the valley of Burrangong Creek was reserved for lambing ewes and became known as Lambing Flat, on which a small settlement eventually grew up. In 1860 a prospector named Dennis Regan discovered gold and the population of Lambing Flat leapt to 20 000 in the course of twelve months. About 2 500 of the diggers were industrious Chinese who were resented by the poorer elements in the white community and violent racial riots broke out which, despite Government intervention, ended in the eviction of the Chinese. Historians hold that the Lambing Flat incidents were important in the formulation of the policy to restrict Asian immigration to Australia.

The town of Young was proclaimed in 1861 and named for the then Governor of New South Wales, Sir John Young. In local usage, however, it remained Lambing Flat until well into the 1890s. Cherries were first planted in the district by Nicole Jasprizza in the 1860s. By 1932 this orchard had grown so much that it was claimed to be the largest cherry orchard in the world.

Places of Interest. **Historic pug-mill** on Boorowa Road, restored as an example of early goldmining methods. **Chinaman's Dam,** on Kingsvale Road, with an old stone retaining wall and remains of water races for sluicing. **Great Court House** (now high school assembly hall). **Town Hall and Memorial. Churches** of St Mary and St John. **Burrangong Creek** picnic grounds, site of the original gold discovery. **Smith's Aviaries** (29 kilometres north-east on the road to Cowra), an excellent collection of native birds. **Tout Park Lookout,** panoramic views. Thuddungra **open-cut magnesium mines** (29 kilometres north-west on Bribbaree Road). **The Grange,** Kingsvale (17 kilometres south), prune-processing plant and orchards.

Sports. Night trotting. Greyhound racing. Golf course. Tennis, bowls etc. Squash courts. Olympic swimming pool.

Accommodation. Two **hotels.** Preferred: Commercial, Boorowa Street. Two **motels.** Recommended: Cherry Blossom Olympic Highway. **Caravan and camping park,** all facilities. **Cabins.**

Transport. **Rail** services (Blayney-Harden line). **Air** service via Cowra (connecting coach). Interstate **road** coaches on Olympic Way route.

COWRA

(Population 7 282)

Cowra, on the Lachlan River, 365 kilometres west of Sydney, is the centre of a highly productive pastoral and agricultural district which has in recent years benefited greatly from the construction of the great Wyangala Dam, about 42 kilometres upstream to the south-east. The valley has for a long time produced good wool, wheat and fat lambs, but now that water is available for seasonal irrigation more emphasis is being laid on fruit-growing, market gardening and mixed farming. Asparagus is an increasingly important crop grown on the rich flats. One of the largest canneries in the State operates in the town. Other secondary industries include a freezing works, stock-food factories, engine reconditioning and light engineering plants and brick, tile and cement works.

History. The district was first settled in 1831 and in the 1840s a village grew up on a station owned by the Reverend Henry Fulton and named 'Cowra Rocks'. It was gazetted as a town in 1849 and as a municipality in 1888. During the second world war a concentration camp was built near the town to accommodate Japanese prisoners of war. On the night of 4 August 1944 they made a mass attempt to escape and in the fighting four Australian guards and 230 Japanese died—many of the Japanese committing suicide. The Japanese War Cemetry, built at the expense of the Japanese Government to honour the memory of the 518 Japanese servicement who died in Australia during the war, was officially opened at Cowra in November 1964.

Places of Interest. **Japanese War Cemetry. War Memorial Park,** on the Lachlan River, with many sports facilities. **Asparagus canning factory** (inspections may be arranged in season). **Bellevue Hill Lookout. Experiment Farm** and soil conservation station (William Farrer worked here while experimenting with wheat strains). **Woodstock** (24 kilometres north-east off highway), a village which preserves the style of early days. **Scenic drives** in market gardening country to Canowindra; through flowering wattle groves to Gooloogong (early spring); to Mount Collins, for panoramic views. Cowra celebrates a Lachlan Valley Festival in March-April.

Sports. First class racecourse. Trotting and greyhound racing. Olympic swimming pool. Excellent golf course. Bowls, tennis etc.

Accommodation. Two **hotels.** Recommended: Coach House, Kendal Street. Two **motels.** Recommended: Caravilla, Macquarie Street. **Caravan and camping park,** all facilities.

Transport. Branch **rail** services, connecting for Sydney and Melbourne. Frequent **air** services to Sydney. Interstate **road** services on Olympic Way.

WYANGALA NATIONAL PARK

Wyangala National Park, 55 kilometres from Cowra, is well worth visiting. It is served by a good bitumen road which passes through scenically attractive country. The area is being developed for water sports of all kinds and the fishing in the district is good. **Holiday cabins** can be rented in the area, which also has a good **caravan and camping park.** (Inquiries to Secretary, Wyangala National Park, Box 71, Cowra, NSW 2794.)

GRENFELL (Population 2 912)

A small but historically interesting wheat town on the Mid-Western Highway, 377 kilometres west of Sydney, Grenfell is named for John Granville, a bank manager killed by bushrangers soon after the discovery of gold in 1866. Henry Lawson, the famous author and poet, was born in the district in 1867 and his parents' reminiscences of the early days and his own experiences as a boy provided the raw material for many of his stories and verses.

When mining declined and wheat farming began, George H. Greene, one of the chief landowners in the region, devised a scheme of co-operative share farming to increase the productivity of the land. It was highly successful and his Iandra Estate became an experimental showplace which greatly influenced farming practice in the western wheatlands. It was used for the first large-scale testing of Farrer's highly successful strain of smut and drought-resistant wheat, Federation. Iandra Mansion (on the Greenthorpe-Tyagong Road), a bizarre 'castle' built for Greene in the late 19th century, is now used as a Methodist home for boys.

Grenfell celebrates a Henry Lawson Festival in June and poetry and art awards are made.

Places of Interest. **Historical Museum** in the municipal library. **Ben Hall's Lookout** (21 kilometres north of Forbes Road), reputedly a haunt of the notorious bushranger. **Lawson Memorial Obelisk** at the now-abandoned diggings where the writer is believed to have been born.

Sport. Golf course. Bowling greens etc.

Accommodation. One **hotel.** One **motel. Caravan park,** all facilities.

Transport. **Road** services.

PARKES

(Population 8 849)

Parkes is the commercial and industrial centre of an agricultural and pastoral area which in an average year produces more than seven million bushels of wheat and five million kilograms of wool, in addition to large quantities of maize, oats, barley, fruit and poultry. It is 364 kilometres west of Sydney on the

Perisher Valley, Australian Alps

Coogee Beach, Sydney

Radio telescope, Parkes, N.S.W.

Newell Highway. Its secondary industries include iron foundries, steel fabricating works, sawmills, joinery plants, railway workshops and factories for the production of agricultural machinery of all kinds. It is also an important railway centre from which branch lines serving the central and far western parts of the State radiate.

History. Parkes was first settled in 1862 when reef gold was discovered and worked for about five years. It was incorporated as a municipality in 1883, having been named after the Australian statesman, Sir Henry Parkes, who had strongly advocated federation of the Australian colonies before, during and after his five successive terms as Premier of New South Wales between 1871 and 1891. Parkes was an enormously energetic reformer who introduced free compulsory education, redesigned the functions of local government bodies and improved the hospitals system. He is regarded by many historians as the 'Father of Federation'. (The town had originally been called Bushman's.)

Parkes today is particularly well known as the town near the giant **radio telescope,** installed by the Commonwealth Scientific and Industrial Research Organization at Alectown (24 kilometres north) in 1961, which is said to be one of the largest and most accurate instruments of its type in the world. The 'dish' of the instrument (64 metres in diameter) is supported by a concrete-based tower as high as an 18 storey building. It is, in essence, an enormous radio antenna which picks up the radio signals emitted by distant stars and permits radio astronomers to plot the outer limits of the universe with extraordinary accuracy. Every Sunday, observation programme permitting, inspections of the installation may be made between 2 pm and 4 pm. On special open days during the school holidays, radio astronomers guide visitors through the control tower and up to the track-turret section.

Places of Interest. Shrine of Remembrance, on the Hill of Memory (in the centre of the town). Aboriginal **boomerang factory,** Peak Hill (45 kilometres). **Historical relics room,** municipal library, at Civic Centre. **Sir Henry Parkes private library,** municipal library. **Bumberry Dam,** lookout on Mount Conambro, water sports on the dam. **Old Phoenix goldmine** and obelisk erected over the mine's 274 metre shaft. **Curra aboriginal reserve,** with colourful rock formations. **Eugoura** (32 kilometres south-east and more easily accessible from Forbes), with a plaque commemorating the greatest gold-escort robbery in the history of bushranging, when Ben Hall and Frank Gardiner robbed the coach of 2719 ounces of gold and £3 700 in cash on 15 June 1862.

Inspection of farm properties in the district may be arranged for genuinely interested visitors. (Inquiries from Civic Chambers, Clarinda Street.) Shearing, crop-dusting, sheep dogs at work etc.

Sports. Racing, night trotting. Olympic swimming pool. Golf, bowls, squash etc.

Accommodation. Three **hotels.** Recommended: Coach House, Welcome Street. Three **motels.** Recommended: Parkview, Forbes Road. Four **caravan and camping parks,** all facilities.

Transport. Rail services from Sydney and Melbourne direct. Twice-daily **air** services from Sydney.

FORBES

(Population 7 467)

The typical central-western town of Forbes is situated 302 kilometres west of Sydney on the Lachlan River. It serves a district which produces grain, dairy produce, beef cattle and fat lambs, honeys, wine grapes and fruit. The town's industries include a meatworks, butter factories, cannery, flour mill, and cement and light engineering works.

History. Gold was discovered near Forbes in 1861 and a small village on the Cunumbla station founded by Arthur Rankin mushroomed into a boom town of 28 000 inhabitants. The mines did not last long and Forbes, named after Sir Francis Forbes, Chief Justice of New South Wales from 1823 until his death in 1841, became a ghost town until further development of the good pastoral land in the valley restored its commercial importance. The bushranger Ben Hall was shot dead by police at Bogan Gate, north-west of the town, in 1865. He was buried in the local cemetery, where his grave is still tended.

Places of Interest. Lake Forbes, ornamental lagoon. **King George Memorial Park,** with swimming pool. **Bundaburra Creek,** aquatic sports. Lachlan River **irrigation scheme.**

Sports. Racecourse. Golf course. Tennis courts. Bowling greens etc. River fishing.

Accommodation. Two **hotels.** Preferred: Victoria, Lachlan Street. Two **motels.** Recommended: Plainsman, Sherrif Street.

Transport. Rail and **road** services. **Air** services from Parkes. **Coach** connection.

NARROMINE (Population 2 724)

A pastoral and agricultural town on the Macquarie River, 457 kilometres from Sydney, Narromine was the site of an important wartime RAAF training school and its large aerodrome is still used for training civil airline pilots and as an international airport when Sydney Airport is closed.

Accommodation. Two **hotels.** Preferred: Narromine, Dandaloo Street. One **motel.**

Transport. Rail and **road** services.

SOUTHERN NEW SOUTH WALES

FAR SOUTH COAST

(Traversed by Princes Highway)

The Far South Coast of New South Wales extends from Bateman's Bay 290 kilometres south of Sydney to the Victorian border, a narrow plain between the mountains and the sea drained by numerous short rivers. The countryside is scenically attractive and the climate good except during late winter and early spring when it tends to be wet and cold. The coast is one of the finest areas for fishing in southern Australia. Bermagui is a world famous centre for big game fishing, the main species taken being black marlin, bluefin tuna and hammerhead shark. There is good rock and beach fishing for bream, tuna, whiting, groper, blackfish, rock cod, snapper and salmon. Spear fishermen get exciting sport at Point Perpendicular, Tollgate Island, Montague Island and many other localities. Prawning is good in most of the shallow inlets and crayfish can be taken off rockier sections of coast. Most of the settlements are within easy reach of trout and perch water in the hills. There are exceptionally fine surf beaches, most of which are patrolled in summer on holidays and during weekends, and many natural and man-made rock pools for swimmers. Boats of all kinds can be hired at most of the major resorts.

Sports facilities generally are good—particularly the golf courses and bowling greens.

Captain Cook sighted and named the most prominent coastal features in 1770, and Bass re-examined the area in 1827, but settlement did not get under way until the 1820s when squatters pushed down through Araluen and the Moruya River valley. The district developed very slowly until gold was discovered at Araluen and Braidwood in the 1850s. One of the richest of the fields was at Nerrigundah, now virtually a ghost town except for its timber mills.

In the latter half of the century agriculture, fruit-growing and dairying became well established and supplemented the revenue of the prosperous timber and tan-bark industry. Poor communications, however, handicapped large-scale economic development until well into the 20th century when the Princes Highway and a number of modern motor roads with adequate bridges had been constructed.

BATEMAN'S BAY (Population 2 214)

At the estuary of the Clyde River, 294 kilometres south of Sydney, Bateman's Bay is a small, charmingly situated resort town which has become very popular with Canberra people since the road linking Princes Highway with the Monaro Highway was improved a few years ago. The district produces timber, vegetables, maize and excellent cheese, but tourism is becoming increasingly important. The bay is famous for its oysters and crayfish.

History. The inlet on which the town stands was sighted by Cook in 1770 and named after Captain Bateman of the ship *Northumberland.* The region was settled in the 1830s and the village at Bateman's Bay was less important than that at Broulee, farther south, which for some decades was an important timber port at which vessels from Sydney and whalers from the Jervis Bay fleet called almost daily. Broulee, however, declined with the coastal shipping and the timber trade and population moved to the more convenient Bateman's Bay.

Places of Interest. Tollgate Island, wildlife reserve; frequented by penguins and an excellent spot for spear fishing. **Araluen,** an old mining town in the hills to the north-west.

Sports. Claimed to have one of the finest bowling clubs in the State. Golf at Catalina Country Club. Tennis courts. Swimming and surfing. Water-skiing.

Accommodation. Three **motels.** Recommended: Clyderiver Lodge, Clyde Street. One **guest-house.** Five **caravan and camping parks,** all facilities. Holiday **cottages** and **cabins.**

Transport. **Road** services to Canberra, Sydney. **Air** services via Moruya, 29 kilometres south.

Smaller resorts nearby: **Batehaven** (cabins available but no camping) and **Broulee.**

MORUYA (Population 1 650)
Situated on the Moruya River 322 kilometres from Sydney, Moruya is a dairying, timber and oyster-farming centre with a growing bias towards tourism. Silver-lead deposits were discovered in the nearby hills in 1839, but the town did not grow until it became the gateway to the Araluen and Braidwood gold diggings. After the gold was worked out many famous dairying estates were founded in the district, including T. S. Mort's 'Bodalla' and John Hawdon's 'Howlong'. Excellent granite has been quarried in the district, particularly that used in the construction of the pylons of the Sydney Harbour Bridge and the base of the Cenotaph in Martin Place, Sydney.

Places of Interest. **Historic cemetery** at Moruya Heads. **Coomerang House** and **Bodalla** (south of town), home of Thomas Sutcliffe Mort (1816-1878), one of the most diversely successful industrialists in Australian history who founded a famous stock and station agency, ran a 12 000 hectare model dairy farm, built shipyards at Balmain, established the Hunter River Steam Navigation Company, pioneered refrigerated cargo ships and promoted successful goldmines. **Mort Memorial Church,** Bodalla (designed by E. Blackett). **Merrigundah** (to south-west), a picturesque old goldmining town in beautiful surroundings, with memorial to a police constable murdered by the infamous Clarke bushranging gang in the 1860s. **Public oyster reserve.**

Sports. Bowling greens and tennis courts. Duck and pigeon shooting, fishing, surfing etc.

Accommodation. Two **hotels.** Preferred: Pearl Shells, Princes Highway. One **motel.** Two **caravan and camping parks,** all facilities. **Cabins** for rent at Moruya Heads.

Transport. **Air** service from Sydney. **Road** services from Canberra, Melbourne and **railhead** at Bombaderry.

NAROOMA (Population 1 551)
An extremely popular holiday and fishing resort at the mouth of the Wagonga River and on Princes Highway, Narooma is 360 kilometres south of Sydney. Its name is a corruption of the aboriginal word *noorooma*, meaning 'clear, blue water'. The town is built on the site of the original Narooma homestead on a cattle station established in the 1860s. The town became particularly well known after the publicity given it by the American novelist and big game fisherman, Zane Grey. It is also famous for its mud oysters.

Places of Interest. **Tuross** and other **lakes and inlets** both north and south of the town. **Montague Island** (big game fishing). **Mystery Bay,** near Lake Corunna (south), with coloured sands and strange rock formations.

Sports. Sporting golf course (tee shot from third is across a narrow canyon between sea cliffs). Bowling greens and tennis courts. Fishing. Prawning (in season).

Accommodation. Two **hotels.** Preferred: Hylands, Princes Highway. Ten **motels.** Recommended: Famboro, Highway, Holiday Lodge, Top of the Town, Princes Highway. Three **camping and caravan parks,** all facilities.

Transport. **Air** services to Moruya, thence bus. **Road** services from Melbourne and **railhead** at Bombaderry.

BERMAGUI (Population 429)
A small port and tourist village, Bermagui is 13 kilometres from Princes Highway and 391 kilometres from Sydney. The surrounding district produces whole milk, butter, maize and timber. Like Narooma, Bermagui was publicized for its excellent fishing grounds by Zane Grey in the 1930s. In 1880 it was the centre of a short-lived goldrush to the Montreal diggings, where a Canadian prospector discovered a little payable colour. The name derives from an aboriginal word meaning 'like a canoe'.

Bermagui is mainly of interest to game fishermen, but it has good facilities for golf, bowls and other games, and the rock pools on the coast are very beautiful. The town celebrates a Tuna Festival in October, in conjunction with its well-known horse show.

Accommodation. One **hotel.** One **motel.** One **guest-house.** Two **caravan and camping parks** (good facilities).

BEGA
(Population 4 146)

Known as the capital of the far South Coast, Bega is the centre of a rich dairying, mixed farming and pastoral district specially noted for its output of high-quality cheese. As well as factories for dairy produce, the town has fish canneries, sawmills and plants which manufacture furniture, fibrous plaster and tiles. The town itself is undistinguished, but it is probably one of the few places in the world where a tourist can enjoy first-rate surfing in the morning and first-rate skiing in the afternoon, for no more trouble than a three-hour drive between beach and mountains. It is within easy reach of the best Kosciusko State Park snow resorts.

The town was gazetted in 1851 within the boundaries of Biggah cattle station, established by Peter Imlay in 1839.

Places of Interest. **Kameruka Cheese Factory** and Kameruka dairy estate. (Inspection by arrangement.) **Dr George Lookout** (8 kilometres) and **Bega Valley Lookout,** for fine panoramic views. **Wallagoot Lake,** for aquatic sports. **Brown Mountain,** hydro-electric project (50 kilometres west in mountain).

Sports. Racing and trotting tracks (Bega Cup is a provincial classic). Golf, tennis, bowls etc. Good fishing, water-skiing and surfing.

Accommodation. Three **hotels.** Recommended: Bega, Carp Street. Three **motels.** Recommended: Grand, Princes Highway. Two **caravan and camping parks,** all facilities.

Transport. **Road** services.

MERIMBULA (Population 1 434)

A small but beautiful sea and lakeside resort 473 kilometres south of Sydney, Merimbula and its sister village, Pambula, offer visitors first-class surfing, boating, fishing and prawning. There is a number of memorable scenic drives on the inland routes to Bombala, Wyndham and Burragate. Sports facilities include tennis courts and bowling greens. Boats are for hire.

Accommodation. Merimbula: One **hotel.** Two **motels,** highly recommended: Black Dolphin, and Hillcrest Motor Inn, Princes Highway. Two **caravan and camping parks,** all facilities. **Pambula:** One **hotel. Caravan and camping park,** all facilities.

Transport. **Road** and **air** services to Sydney and Melbourne.

EDEN (Population 2 210)

Eden is a quiet but prosperous little town on Twofold Bay, 512 kilometres south of Sydney. Its primary industries are fishing, timber-getting and some mixed farming, with pastoral country in the hinterland. It has an unusually fine natural harbour. There have been repeated moves to develop it as an outlet for the produce of the Monaro plains, but so far nothing has come of them.

History. In 1842 two settlements were established on Twofold Bay, one at Boydtown by the pioneer banker, whaler and pastoralist, Benjamin Boyd, and the other at the Government approved site at Eden. Boyd had grandiose plans to make his town the capital of Australia, erected many buildings and established a steamship service to Sydney. In 1850, however, he got into financial difficulties and left the settlement, never to return. Thereafter it steadily declined. Some time later he disappeared while on a voyage to the Pacific Islands. A subdivision of Boydtown was planned in 1920, but it was not until the 1930s that it was to an extent resuscitated as a tourist resort. Eleven kilometres away, the rival town of Eden survived. For some years its population was swelled by miners on their way to the Kiandra goldfields, but when the diggings were worked out it reverted to a quiet pastoral, farming and fishing village. Its importance has grown recently with the establishment of a bulk oil terminal at the port and a modern fish cannery.

Places of Interest. Eden **Museum.** Ruins of **Boydtown. Sea Horse Inn** (restored) and nearby **lighthouse. Lake Curala** oyster beds. **Wonboyn Lake,** to the south off Princes Highway. **Nadgee Fauna Reserve** (11 656 hectares) between Disaster Bay and the Victorian border.

Sports. Golf course. Tennis courts. Bowling greens etc.

Accommodation. Two **hotels.** Recommended: Australasia, Imlay Street. Three **motels.** Recommended: Halfway, Princes Highway.

Transport. **Road** services.

KOSCIUSKO STATE PARK

Kosciusko State Park, an area of more than one million hectares embracing the highest plateau in the Australian continent in the south-eastern corner of New South Wales, is a national asset of incalculable value. It is the most reliable source of water on the mainland and the birthplace of the great Murray and Murrumbidgee Rivers, from which some of the most productive agricultural land in southern New South Wales and Victoria is irrigated (see Riverina and Murray Valley). It is also the source of the Snowy River, a short, rapid stream passing through relatively unproductive mountain country in north-eastern Victoria and flowing southward into the Tasman Sea.

In one of the most ingenious and intricate civil engineering projects of the 20th century, the waters of the Snowy River system have been diverted through the crest of the watershed into the Murray-Murrumbidgee system to provide water for the irrigation of an additional 530 000 hectares of farmland. At the same time, the water has been harnessed in a series of huge hydro-electric generating stations to produce five million kilowatt hours of power every year to meet the peak-load demands of the great industrial cities of Sydney and Melbourne.

This vast project has involved the construction of more than 160 kilometres of highways and 1 000 kilometres of secondary and access roads through 975 000 hectares of mountain country which was previously inaccessible. A secondary but by no means unimportant result of the undertaking has been the opening up to tourism of a majestically beautiful region of highlands, often more than 1 800 metres above sea level. Five 'peaks' in the area—Kosciusko, Twynham, Townshend, North Ramshead and Carruthers—attain an altitude of more than 2 100 metres. Kosciusko (2 238 metres) is the highest mountain of the continent.

Much of this country, of course, is under heavy snow for five or six months of the year, and the development of access roads has greatly increased the area which can be used for winter sports. Additionally, sixteen major dams built to conserve and control the river waters have created large artificial lakes in the mountains. Many have been liberally stocked with fish and some are being developed as aquatic sports resorts. The combination of lakes, streams, mountains, forests and alpine heathlands is unique in Australia. Tens of thousands of holidaymakers go to the Kosciusko resorts every winter and more than 60 000 visitors make conducted tours, mostly in summer and autumn, of the dams and power stations of the Snowy Mountains hydro-electric project. The number is growing each year as the facilities and standards of accommodation improve.

The area is just as enticing in summer as in winter. Since the high country was declared a sanctuary in 1944—grave damage had previously been caused by uncontrolled grazing and burning-off—both forest and heathland have been regenerated and now sustain a tremendous variety of native bird and animal life. There is probably no better place in Australia for the nature lover to observe the whole spectrum of plant and animal life in the temperate zone of the continent. Nearly 325 000 hectares of country surrounding the summit of Mount Kosciusko have been declared a Primitive Area, in which all forms of human interference with the native environment are strictly prohibited. Throughout the whole reserve the use of firearms, the picking of wildflowers or the taking of any native plant or animal is forbidden. Penalties for infringement are heavy.

Fishing, however, is permitted—from September to April in the streams and minor lakes and all the year round in Lake Eucumbene. Both brown and rainbow trout have acclimatized excellently. It is not unusual for anglers in the lake to land rainbow trout of 3 kilograms weight. It is probably the most rewarding trout water in the Commonwealth. More rarely native trout and freshwater crayfish are taken in the streams.

WHEN TO TOUR. Snow persists on the southern faces of mountains above 2 000 metres for all or most of the year. The snow sports season generally starts in late May or early June and continues until mid or late October. Thereafter the period of thaw until Christmas tends to be unpleasant. January is the month in which the wildflowers—buttercups, alpine and everlasting daisies, orchids and multicoloured heaths—are at their best on the high plains. February, March and April are also fine months for touring. During summer and autumn, however, the sensitive tourist may prefer to avoid such 'developed' ski resorts as Perisher Valley and Thredbo. They are picturesque when snow-covered, but depressingly unsightly when the thaw reveals the architectural monstrosity of the scores of public and private ski lodges which disfigure the hillsides. Fortunately the country is big enough and rugged enough to permit the traveller to get out of sight of them quickly. Generally speaking, the area controlled by the Snowy Mountains Authority has been far more intelligently developed than that which has been administered by the New South Wales Government through the Kosciusko State Park Authority.

MISCELLANEOUS. Although the Australian Alps may not experience sub-zero weather, conventional winter-resort clothing of the type worn elsewhere in the world is necessary in the snow season. There can also be severe cold snaps with occasional snowfalls in the summer. Usually the weather is mild and sunny by day, but even during January tourists should include warm, windproof clothing and sunglasses in their luggage.

Private motorists on the access roads during the snow season need rear wheel chains and should take the usual overnight precautions against freeze-up. Put anti-freeze mixture in the radiator (or drain it) and leave the wheels chocked and the brakes off when parked.

Winter Sports Resorts

Thredbo Alpine Village (Crackenback), 90 kilometres from Cooma (altitude 1 256 metres). Access road from Cooma kept open all the year. Good ski runs. Three chair lifts, five T-bars. Skating. Summer attractions include bowls, swimming, riding, trout fishing and tennis. **Accommodation.** Two **hotels.** Thredbo Alpine. Highly recommended: Ten commercial **lodges.** Additional facilities include kindergarten, baby-sitting service, ski instruction, hire service for equipment, mini bus tours, etc.

Perisher Valley, 90 kilometres from Cooma (altitude 1 676 metres). Winter access by road coach from Cooma to Smiggin Holes, thence by snow vehicle. Excellent ski runs. Thirteen T-bars and chair lifts. Ski instruction. Summer attractions include drift skiing as well as the usual sports. **Accommodation.** Three **hotels.** Recommended: Man from Snowy River (open all the year round); The Valley Inn (winter). Fifteen **lodges, chalets** or **guest houses.**

Pipers' Gap (between Smiggin Holes and Perisher proper). Poma lift and T-bar. **Accommodation.** One **motel.** One **lodge.**

Smiggin Holes, 89 kilometres from Cooma (altitude 1 676 metres). Road kept open all the year (limited parking for private vehicles). Poma lifts and T-bars. Ski instruction and equipment hire. Summer attractions include usual sports, drift skiing and golf (5 kilometres). Name from Scottish means shallow hole tramped by cattle. **Accommodation.** One **hotel** (Smiggins, highly recommended). One **lodge.**

Charlotte Pass, 92 kilometres from Cooma (altitude 1 349 metres). Motor coach to car park and service station on Alpine Way, thence chair lift. Chair lift and ski tours. Ski school, equipment hire. **Accommodation.** Kosciusko **Chalet.**

Wilson's Valley, 77 kilometres from Cooma (altitude 1 463 metres). Ski school and equipment for hire. **Accommodation.** One **motor hotel.**

Kiandra, 90 kilometres north-west of Cooma (altitude 1 256 metres). T-bar and rope tow, skis for hire. **Accommodation.** One **hotel.** One **ski lodge. Caravan** park.

Diggers Creek, 80 kilometres from Cooma (altitude 1 300 metres). Ski lift. **Accommodation,** One **guest-house,** with licensed restaurant.

Other Holiday Centres

Sawpit Creek, 74 kilometres from Cooma. Six-berth **cabins. Caravan park,** all facilities. Run by Kosciusko State Park Trust. Applications required six months in advance.

Adaminaby, 53 kilometres from Cooma. One **hotel.** One **motel. Caravan and camping park,** all facilities.

Berriedale, 43 kilometers south-west of Cooma, on shores of Lake Eucumbene. **Hotel-motel. Camping and caravan park,** all facilities. **Cabins.**

Buckanderra, 43 kilometres north-west of Cooma, on shores of Lake Eucumbene. **Caravan and camping park,** all facilities. Boat and cruiser hire; marina service.

Jindabyne, 57 kilometres from Cooma, is increasingly popular with tourists. Four **motels.** Highly recommended: Commodore. **Caravan and camping park,** all facilities.

THE SNOWY RIVER PROJECT

The Snowy River Irrigation and Hydro-electric Project is Australia's greatest public work for the conservation of water and the generation of power. It has involved the construction of 16 major dams (and many smaller ones), 7 power stations, 160 kilometres of tunnels, and 130 kilometres of aqueducts. When completed—probably before 1975—it will provide about two million acre feet of water for irrigation and the annual value of the energy produced by the power stations will approximate $A50 million.

The total cost of the scheme will be about $A800 million, all of which will have been covered, including the interest on borrowed capital, by the sale of the generated electricity. The increase in the value of primary production made possible by the additional water for irrigation has been estimated at about $A60 million a year.

The scheme in its first phase diverted the waters of the Eucumbene River, a tributary of the Snowy River, through the mountains to the Tumut River, a tributary of the Murrumbidgee; and diverted the Upper Murrumbidgee River to the Eucumbene River and the Tooma River (in the Murray catchment) to the Tumut River. In its second phase it diverted the Snowy River into the Murray River. Provision has been made to supply the conserved water into whatever system is most in need.

The major dams are: Eucumbene main storage (3 860 000 acre feet capacity, the largest earth and rock fill dam in the world); Tumut Pond (43 000 acre feet); Tantangara (206 000); Tooma (23 000); Tumut 3 (86 000); Tumut 4 (138 000); Blowering (846 000); Geehi (17 300) and Jindabyne (560 000).

Major power stations: Tumut 1-4; Murray 1-2; Guthega. Others are under construction or consideration.

Tours. The Snowy Mountain Authority encourages inspection of the scheme and provides experienced and specially trained guides for parties of visitors. Tours from **Cooma** daily. Inquiries from the New South Wales Government Tourist Bureau, Martin Place, Sydney. Pioneer Tours conduct numerous coach tours from **Sydney** and **Melbourne**. Weekly tours are also run from **Brisbane** and **Adelaide**. Package air-coach-accommodation tours are available from **Melbourne**. From **Cooma** Pioneer conducts three and four-day tours. Information centres at Cooma and Khancoban.

Other Transport. Cooma, the centre from which most tours of the Snowy begin, has a **twice daily air** service from Sydney and a **daily air service** from Melbourne.

Rail from Sydney: Air conditioned daylight express (daily return except Sunday). Night train, Tuesday, Thursday, Friday and Sunday (about 10 hours).

Rail from Melbourne: Mainline express services to Goulburn, New South Wales. Five hour wait for Cooma connection. Sleepers are available.

Road Routes. From Sydney: Hume, Federal and Monaro Highways through Canberra to Cooma (425 kilometres). **Or** Princes Highway to Bateman's Bay, thence Braidwood and Canberra to Cooma (557 kilometres). **Or** Princes Highway to Bega, thence Nimmitabel to Cooma (561 kilometres). **From Melbourne:** Princes Highway to Orbost, thence Bonang Highway to Bombala, Nimmitabel to Cooma. **Or** Hume Highway to Wodonga, thence Corryong, Kiandra, Adaminaby to Cooma. (Examination of road maps will indicate interesting variations of routes.)

COOMA

(Population 7 784)

In the foothills of the Snowy Mountains at the junction of the Monaro and Snowy Mountains Highways, Cooma is 418 kilometres from Sydney. During the years in which the great hydro-electric and irrigation project was under construction it was regarded as the most cosmopolitan town in Australia. Immigrants from 50 nations were employed on the engineering works. The population leapt from less than 2 000 to more than 10 000.

The town is not so polyglot today, but tourism is to some extent substituting for the construction boom. Cooma is the base for most visits to the Snowy River Project and to the rapidly growing snow resorts of the Australian Alps. Before the boom, it was a sleepy service centre for the large pastoral district of the Monaro plains, first settled as early as 1826, but not developed until after 1850. Today it is a town of modern shops, impressive public buildings and up-to-date hotels and motels.

On the contrary, the little village of **Kiandra** to the north-west, now only a ski resort, was the scene in the 1890s of a frenzied gold rush to rich alluvial diggings in the beds of snow-fed streams. Kiandra is claimed to have had the first ski club in Australia and to have organized races long before skiing became popular as a sport in Europe.

Accommodation. One **hotel** (Snowy Mountains, recommended). Thirteen **motels.** Recommended: Marlborough, Salmon, and Travelodge, Sharp Street. Two **caravan and camping parks,** most facilities.

Transport. Rail, road and **air** connections with Sydney and Melbourne. Snowy Mountains and resorts **tours by road coach** are available in Cooma (inquiries from Cooma Visitors' Centre, Centennial Park) and from Sydney and Melbourne. (Inquiries, State Tourist Bureaux.) Airlines run extra flights from Sydney and Melbourne at weekends during the ski season.

THE RIVERINA

The name Riverina has been variously applied to areas of southern New South Wales but is now taken generally to include the country bounded by the Murray River in the south and south-west, the Lachlan in the north and the north-west and by a line drawn roughly between Condobolin and Albury, including the towns of Wagga Wagga and Junee. It is no longer simply applied to the land which lies between the two main rivers.

The land of the eastern Riverina gives high yields of good quality wheat and the land to the west is farmed for its excellent merino wool and sheep studs. In the heart of the region is the Murrumbidgee Irrigation Area, nearly 81 000 hectares, which produces large quantities of rice, stone and citrus fruits and wine and table grapes. The scheme depends mainly on water conserved in the Burrinjuck Dam on headwaters of the river fed by rainfall and the melting snows in the Australian Alps. This land is among the most productive in the continent.

The climate in winter is invigorating, with clear, sunny days and crisp nights. The summer is hot, with the thermometer often reaching 38°C or more, but the humidity is low except in the enclosed river valleys.

Apart possibly from the Murray Valley itself and the mountainous country of the extreme east, the Riverina has little to offer in the way of conventional tourist attractions, but it is intensely interesting to people who travel to sse more than scenery. It exemplifies the sort of life and productivity which scientific water conservation and farming can create in many inland regions of Australia as yet undeveloped. Over much of the country there is good rough shooting and the streams and dams provide sport for fishermen.

Travel in the Riverina is uncomplicated. It is crossed with major highways—by the Hume Highway between Sydney and Melbourne, the Cobb and Midwestern Highways, the Olympic Way from north to south, and the Sturt and Riverina Highways from east to west. The main towns have regular air services linking them with Sydney, Melbourne and Adelaide. The trunk railway line between Melbourne and Sydney cuts across the south-eastern corner.

HISTORY. John Oxley crossed the northern part of the region in 1817, but settlement did not begin until after Hume and Hovell made their epic overland journey from Sydney to Port Phillip in 1824 and Charles Sturt made his whaleboat voyage down the Murrumbidgee in 1829.

Land-takers moved into the hilly sections of the eastern Riverina in 1830 and established themselves mainly on river frontages, but the arid hinterland remained unoccupied until wells were dug and dams built to provide domestic and stock water supplies.

In the 1840s and 1950s large numbers of sheep and cattle were moved from Queensland and New South Wales into Victoria and enterprising settlers established stock ferries at the river crossings. Many of the villages which grew up round these places grew into large and prosperous towns. Cultivation of wheat began in eastern Riverina after the railway from Sydney reached Narrandera in 1881.

For many years the southern Riverina was primarily dependent on river traffic for transportation of essential supplies and marketable produce. The navigability of the Murray was regarded in South Australia as highly important and in the 1850s the State Government offered a reward of £2 000 for the first two iron steamers to pass up the river from Goolwa, near its mouth, to its junction with the Darling, a distance of 896 kilometres. The prize was won by Francis Cadell in a river boat, *Lady Augusta*, which he had had specially built in Sydney. Cadell actually reached Howlong, near Albury, and received £2 500. The navigators of a smaller wooden boat, the *Mary Ann*, which travelled even farther upstream, received a consolation prize of £600. Cadell then floated the Murray River Navigation Company and the great boom in paddle steamers began. In 1860, George Bain Johnston, a director of the company, took the *Edward R* up the Darling and Namoi Rivers to Walgett, a distance of 896 kilometres. Two years earlier his paddle wheeler *Albury* had reached the settlement of the same name on the Murray.

The river trade reached its peak in the 1870s, but thereafter declined when a series of droughts made the waterways impassable and railways, built by the State governments eager to capture the trade in Riverina wool, made the steamers obsolete. By the 1950s the last of them was being used for novelty tourist cruises.

SOUTHERN RIVERINA

ALBURY-WODONGA

(Population 37 916)

On the north bank of the Murray River 596 kilometres from Sydney and 307 kilometres from Melbourne, Albury is the Riverina's largest city and an important distribution centre for the region's produce—wheat, wool, oats, barley, meat, wine grapes, fruit and honey. Under the Commonwealth Government's decentralization plan which provides for the establishment of an inland metropolis, it has merged with the twin town of Wodonga on the southern (Victorian) bank of the river.

Albury-Wodonga is attractively situated in hilly country and has many fine public and commercial buildings in tree-shaded streets. It is culturally active and supports an annual ABC concert series and music and drama groups. A Floral Festival is held in March and a noted Sheep Show in June.

Secondary industrial development has been vigorous. There are woollen mills, clothing factories, wool classing, treatment and selling establishments, dairy factories, a tinplate and canister works and plants for processing meat and honey, manufacturing electrical goods and fabricating steel.

History. Hume and Hovell crossed the Murray near the present site of Albury in 1824. By 1838 a police post had been established on the river to protect overlanders between Sydney and Port Phillip. The following year a townsite was surveyed and named after Albury in Surrey, England.

In 1840 German immigrants began viticulture in the district but progress in agriculture was very slow because of distance from markets. Punt services across the river were established in 1849 and as the paddle steamer traffic from South Australia developed, Albury became a flourishing river port. In 1859 the municipality was proclaimed and two years later the first permanent bridge across the river was built. In 1883 the rail link with Melbourne was completed and Albury was gazetted a city in 1946.

Wodonga was first settled in the 1830s by C. H. Ebden and the Huon brothers who took up the Bonegilla and Wodonga sheep runs. A township was gazetted in 1852 and called Belvoir. But in 1876 the shire was proclaimed and the name changed to the aboriginal place name which means 'edible nut'.

Places of Interest. War Memorial, Monument Hill (30 metres high, 90 metres above the city and floodlit at night). **Music Bowl,** Monument Hill. **Civic Centre. Noreuil Park,** with nearby river gum marked by the explorer Hovell. **Botanic Gardens. Folk Museum** at Turk's Head Hotel. **Lake Hume** (a major water storage of the Murray) is extensively developed for aquatic sports. The dam is 13 kilometres from town.

Sports. Racecourse (Gold Cup meeting is a big event of the Australian turf). Golf courses. Bowling and croquet greens. Tennis courts. Olympic swimming pool.

Accommodation. Eight **hotels.** Highly recommended: New Albury, Kiewa Street. Recommended: Astor, Hume Highway; and Boomerang, Albury North. Fourteen **motels.** Highly recommended: Travelodge, Elizabeth Street. Three **caravan and camping parks,** all facilities. Two **camping areas. Holiday cottages** available at Lake Hume.

COROWA-WAHGUNYA (Population 3 308)

On the Murray River 56 kilometres downstream from Albury. A pleasant town reached by the Riverina Highway. The district is famous for its wine grapes and wineries. It has excellent sports facilities including lawn tennis courts, golf course, swimming pool etc. Fishing and boating on the river.

Accommodation. One **hotel.** Two **motels.** Preferred: Macambo. **Caravan and camping park,** all facilities.

Transport. Rail and **road** services.

MULWALA (Population 830)

Near Corowa on Lake Mulwala, a resort for boating and aquatic sports enthusiasts. At a highly recommended **motel-boatel**, Cypress Gardens, boat-owners can moor craft beneath their suites. Duck and rabbit shooting can be had, and golf at Yarrawonga across the river in Victoria.

WAGGA WAGGA

(Population 27 639)

A well-to-do city which is focus for an extensive agricultural area consisting mainly of small holdings, Wagga Wagga is on the Murrumbidgee River 517 kilometres south-west of Sydney on the Sturt Highway. It is a centre of agricultural and soil conservation research and has historical associations with the wheat-breeding pioneer, William James Farrer, who did valuable work on the rust-resistant strains at a time when the Australian industry was in serious difficulties with the disease. He also developed early-maturing and drought resistant-types, including Federation.

There are many important educational and research establishments at Wagga Wagga, including teachers' training and agricultural colleges. Kapooka Army Camp and the RAAF Forest Hill Training Base are near the city.

The surrounding farms produce wheat, fat lambs, beef, pigs, poultry and dairy produce and urban factories make rubber goods, flour, bacon, butter and milled timber. There is also an abattoir and an iron foundry. The stock saleyards are the biggest in the State outside Sydney.

The city has many fine public parks and buildings. An annual eisteddfod is held in October. An affiliation with the city of Leavenworth, Kansas, USA, was established in 1962.

History. Landseekers appeared in the area in the mid-1920s but the first land permanently occupied was probably the holding of the pioneering pastoralist R. H. Best. In 1847 a court house was built in the locality, but the town site was not surveyed and proclaimed until 1849. The railway from Sydney reached the settlement in 1878, after which the district began to develop rapidly. The city was gazetted in 1946. The name is from the aboriginal for 'meeting of crows', but it is commonly shortened to Wagga.

Places of Interest. Victory Memorial and **Botanic Gardens** at Wollundry Lagoon in the centre of the city. **Cabarita Riverside Park** and beach. **Agricultural College and Research Institute. Lake Albert,** for water skiing, speedboat racing and sailing etc. **Civic Centre,** theatre and library. Historical Museum.

Sports. Two good golf courses. Racecourse. Trotting track. Dog racing track. Rifle and archery ranges. Bowling and croquet greens. Tennis courts. Olympic swimming pool.

Accommodation. Six **hotels.** Recommended: Astor, Sturt Highway. Eight **motels.** Recommended: Koala, Tompson Street. Two **caravan and camping parks,** all facilities.

Transport. Rail and **air** services to Sydney, Melbourne etc. Local **road** services.

Small Towns Nearby

The Rock (32 kilometres south). Unusual scenery and fascinating nature reserve.

Lockhart (64 kilometres west). A picturesque little 'bush' town almost totally unspoiled by redevelopment.

DENILIQUIN

(Population 6 604)

On the Edward River, a branch of the Murray, 771 kilometres south-west of Sydney and 48 kilometres from the Victorian border, Deniliquin is the commercial centre of the Berriquin, Denimein, Deniboota and Wakool irrigation areas which form the largest complex of its kind in Australia, aggregating nearly 750 000 hectares. The Water Conservation and Irrigation Commission, the Commonwealth Scientific and Industrial Organization, the Department of Main Roads and the Murray River County Council are all established in the town.

The northern part of the district is famed for merino sheep studs such as Wanganella and Boonoke.

Wool is still the dominant industry, but as more intensive cultivation is practised the emphasis is changing to the production of beef, fat lambs, dairy produce, rice, fruit and tobacco. Grain also is grown. There is commercial fishing for Murray cod in the river and irrigation channels. Secondary industries in town include butter, cheese and cordials factories, timber mills, brick and fibrous plaster factories, iron and steel fabricating, seed processing.

History. In 1845 Benjamin Boyd established a property named Deniliquin from the aboriginal *denilocoon*, meaning 'wrestlers' ground'. After a punt was installed on the river, the station became an important crossing for stock. The town was founded in 1848 and was at first known as The Sandhills. The name was changed when it was gazetted in 1850. In 1861 George Peppin Hall and his sons bred the Peppin strain of merino at Wanganella, a significant milestone in the history of the Australian wool industry. Deniliquin was declared a municipality in 1868 and was linked with the Victorian rail system by a private transport company in 1876. The line was taken over by the Victorian Government in 1923.

Of Interest. Inspection of some larger **sheep studs** and **irrigated properties** may be arranged.

Sports. Racecourse. Golf, tennis, bowls. Squash courts. Water skiing. River fishing.

Accommodation. Two **hotels.** Recommended: Coach House, End Street. One **motel. Caravan and camping park,** all facilities.

Transport. Rail services, connecting with NSW and Victorian systems. **Air** services to Sydney and Melbourne. Local **road** services.

JERILDERIE (Population 1 000)

On Newell Highway between Deniliquin and Narrandera, Jerilderie is the centre of the largest merino stud area in NSW. Some cotton is grown. A museum devoted to relics of the Kelly gang of bushrangers who once held the town for two days, locked the police in goal and cut the telegraph wires, is of interest.

Accommodation. One **motel. Caravan park.**

Transport. Rail to Sydney via Narrandera, to Melbourne via Tocumwal. Local **coach** services.

HAY (Population 3 206)

On the Murrumbidgee River at the junction of Cobb and Sturt Highways in the far south-west of NSW, 763 kilometres from Sydney. Hay is the commercial town for an enormous area of semi-arid grazing country, some of which has been brought under irrigation and produces fruit and dairy produce. The population of the town has been constant since the 1880s.

History. Sturt passed close to the present townsite on his journey down the Murrumbidgee to the Murray. In 1840 the locality became known as Lang's Crossing and Cobb and Co. established a coach staging-post there. In 1858-59, the town was surveyed and after the river boats began to run, it became a busy outback 'port'. In 1877 the construction of the Hay Waterworks began and the town claims to be the first rural centre in NSW to have a reticulated water supply and sewerage. It was certainly the cradle of Riverina irrigation as water was taken to farmland from the storage long before the Murray irrigation scheme got under way.

Places of Interest. Famous **sheep studs** of Mundugal, Uardry and Wonga. **Boer War Memorial,** Hay Park. Excellently equipped War Memorial **High School,** built by public subscription in 1922. Cobb and Co. **Coach Factory.**

Sports. Bowls, golf, tennis etc. Gun Club conducts annual clay target shooting championships at Easter. In season duck shooting and pig hunting in marshes and forests near the junction of the Murrumbidgee and Lachlan Rivers.

Accommodation. Two **hotels.** Preferred: New Crown, Lachlan Street. Two **motels.** Recommended: Commodore, Lachlan Street. **Caravan and camping park.**

Transport. Rail service, through Junee. **Air** services to Sydney, Melbourne, Canberra and Adelaide.

NORTHERN RIVERINA

CONDOBOLIN (Population 3 214)

The northernmost centre of the Riverina, 475 kilometres west-south-west of Sydney and on the banks of the Lachlan River, Condobolin is the focus of a red-soil plains district irrigated by water from Wyangala Dam. It produces wool, fat lambs, mixed-farm produce, fruit, pigs, poultry and fodder crops. Wheat is also being grown increasingly in the area. The town's secondary industries include sawmilling, sleeper-cutting, a freezing works and stock-selling yards.

History. The word Condobolin means 'hop scrub'. There were two stations of that name in the 1840s, one owned by William Lee, the first settler, and the other by Benjamin Boyd. It is unclear on which property the town was founded and proclaimed in 1859. The municipality was gazetted in 1890.

Sports. Race and trotting clubs. Golf course. Tennis courts. Bowling greens. Olympic swimming pool.

Accommodation. Several **hotels.** Preferred: Condobolin, Bathurst Street. One **motel.** One **caravan and camping park,** all facilities.

Transport. Rail services to Sydney and Broken Hill. **Air** service to Sydney.

LAKE CARGELLIGO (Population 1 095)

A small agricultural and pastoral township on a lake of the same name, it is 568 kilometres west of Sydney and has considerable tourist potential. The district is a major producer of magnesite. The lake has an area of 1 400 hectares and an average depth of three metres. It is controlled by the Water Conservation Board and is a wildlife sanctuary, although an open season for certain types of game is often declared.

An artificial lake used for boating and swimming has been created at Ballyrogan, 40 kilometres from town. A range of impressive peaks rises sheer from the south-western-shore.

A Festival of the Lakes is held every January at Australia Day weekend.

Accommodation. One **hotel.** One **motel.** Lakeside **caravan and camping park.**

Transport. **Road** services from West Wyalong, Condoblin etc.

WEST WYALONG (Population 3 438)

West Wyalong is the business centre of three associated areas of settlement. It is 480 road kilometres west of Sydney at the junction of the Mid-West and Newell Highways. The surrounding area produces wheat and mixed-farm crops and the towns have flour and sawmills, brick and fibrous plaster works and a eucalyptus oil distillery.

History. •`ich gold strikes were made in the Wyalong district in 1893. Although Wyalong proper was surveyed several kilometres away, West Wyalong became known as the 'Main Camp'. It was proclaimed a town in 1900. More than 445 000 ounces of gold were taken from the reefs between 1894 and 1921, when the last of the old mines closed down.

Sports. Trotting track. Golf course. Tennis courts, bowling greens etc. Basketball and hockey clubs. Olympic swimming pool. Fishing. Rabbit and kangaroo shooting.

Accommodation. Two **hotels.** Preferred: Metropolitan, Main Street. Four **motels.** Recommended: Charles Sturt, Neeld Street. **Caravan and camping park,** some facilities.

Transport. **Rail** and **air** services to Sydney.

ARDLETHAN (Population 800)

On the Newell Highway south of West Wyalong, a tin-mining town with treatment works of interest to mining engineers and technicians.

TEMORA (Population 4 469)

Temora is an important rail storage centre for the rich wheatlands of the northern and western Riverina. Large quantities of oats and barley also are produced in the district, as well as fat lambs, pigs and cattle. The town has a freezing works, a flour mill, an egg storage depot and plaster and brick works. It is the headquarters of the Northern Riverina County Council and the Narraburra Shire.

History. The district was first settled in the 1840s but did not greatly progress until the discovery of gold in 1879. About 150 000 ounces were won from the field, including the Mother Shipton nugget of 258 ounces. The mines declined after 1886. During the goldrush period the town was known as Watsonforde, but the local people preferred the name of the original station. Temora is thought to have derived from the Celtic word meaning 'an eminence commanding a wide view'.

Of interest is the **Rock and Mineral Museum.**

Sports. Golf course, bowling greens, swimming pool, tennis courts.

Accommodation. Two **hotels.** Recommended: Shamrock, Hoskins Street. Two **motels.** Recommended: Broadvilla, Wagga Road.

Transport. **Rail** and **air** services from Sydney.

COOTAMUNDRA (Population 6 630)

Highly productive pastoral and agricultural country surrounds Cootamundra which is on the main Sydney-Melbourne railway, 61 kilometres north of Gundagai and 427 kilometres from Sydney. It is an important rail junction for branch lines serving central New South Wales and is a stock-selling centre. The town has flour and rice mills, a butter factory and abattoirs. Some gold is mined at the nearby settlements of Cullinga and Muttama. The town's water supply comes from the Burrinjuck Dam.

History. John Hurley established a station which he called Cootamondra in 1830. The aboriginal meaning of the name is obscure but the word is thought to indicate a swamp or a low-lying place. In 1861 the town was proclaimed and called Cootamundry—and the spelling persisted until 1952 when officialdom bowed to usage. The highly ornamental wattle of the same name was first found in the district. Cootamundra was the birthplace of the famous Australian cricketer, Sir Donald Bradman.

Sports. Usual country town facilities and in addition greyhound racing, trotting and motor cycling clubs, hockey fields and rifle club.

Accommodation. One **hotel.** Three **motels.** Recommended: Cootamundra Gardens. **Caravan park,** all facilities.

JUNEE (Population 3 765)

On the south-western slopes of the Great Dividing Range 482 kilometres west-south-west of Sydney, Junee is an important railhead and railway workshops town and the commercial centre of a district producing fat lambs, wheat, wool, wine grapes and poultry products. The NSW Egg Board depot in town handles three million eggs a year.

From Junee, itself pleasantly situated and interesting for several historic buildings, a scenic road to Mount Ulandra (609 metres) has recently been opened.

History. 'Jewnee' was gazetted as a village in 1863 on a site held by stockmen under a licence to F. L. de Salis and another, Smyth, issued in 1847. The railhead from Sydney reached the settlement in 1883, when it was variously known as Jewnee Junction or Loftus. The present spelling of the name (which means 'speak to me' or 'frog') was adopted when the municipality was incorporated in 1886.

Sports. Golf, bowls. Olympic swimming pool.

Accommodation. Two **hotels.** Preferred: Commercial. **Caravan and camping park,** all facilities.

Transport. **Rail** and **road** services (on Olympic Way).

EASTERN RIVERINA

GUNDAGAI (Population 2 061)

A progressive and prosperous little town on the Hume Highway, 402 kilometres south-west of Sydney, Gundagai is known all over Australia for the songs and verses in which its name has featured. The most famous of them is 'Nine miles from Gundagai', a set of verses written about the turn of the century by Jack Moses, a travelling wine salesman who was inspired by an old bush doggerel about teamsters and the dogs who guarded their possessions on the track. Jack O'Hagen's 'Along the Road to Gundagai' also has become an Australian folk song.

In 1932 a Pioneer Monument in the form of a dog sitting on a tuckerbox (tucker is Australian slang for food) was erected beside the highway at Five Mile Creek, a camping ground used by the teamsters in the old days.

The Gundagai district produces wool and wheat, and large quantities of fruit and vegetables are grown on the Murrumbidgee river flats near the town.

History. Pioneer brothers named Stuckey established a sheep run at Willia Ploma in 1825 or 1826 and are credited with having introduced to the district the Murrumbidgee strain of willows said to have been grown from cuttings taken from trees near Napoleon's grave on St Helena. The town, however, took its name from the property of another early settler, 'Sugar' O'Brien, who called his station by the aboriginal word meaning 'going upstream'. Sections of the settlement grew on both north and south banks of the river. They were connected by ferry until a permanent bridge was opened in 1867. The town was first surveyed in 1840. Four years later the little settlement suffered severe damage from floods and in 1852 it was the scene of the worst flood disaster in Australian history when 89 residents were trapped and drowned by the raging river. One of the heroes of that tragedy was an aborigine, Yarrie, who saved many townspeople in his bark canoe.

In the 1860s Gundagai was plagued by the bushrangers Gardiner and Peisley, and later by Ben Hall, Gilbert and Dunn. In the late 1860s the even more notorious Captain Moonlight and his gang were active in the district, but they were eventually captured and brought to trial in the local court house in 1870.

The activities of the bushrangers were in part due to the discovery of gold at Spring Flat in 1861. Miners continued to work in the area until 1875 when the field petered out. A new rush occurred, however, in 1894 when amendments to the mining law liberalized the conditions under which miners could operate on private property. The fields produced 135 000 ounces in all before the last mine closed in 1942.

In 1903 the railway bridge and line to Tumut were opened. Gundagai and Adjungbilly Shire were merged to form Gundagai Shire in 1923.

Places of Interest. Town: **Historical Museum,** Homer Street, pioneer and bushranging relics, aboriginal curios. **Old blacksmith's shop,** Punch Street. **Bell Tree** at St Paul's Church (the bell sounds when the wind blows). **Marble carving** by an artist named Rusconi, comprising 20 945 pieces of NSW marble, took 25 years to build and is on view at Tourist Information Centre, near corner of Sheridan and Homer Streets. **Graves** of police killed by the bushranger Gilbert in a gun battle in 1860. Environs: **Dog and Tuckerbox Memorial,** 8 kilometres north (sculpted by Rusconi). **Shearing sheds** of stations in district when shearing is in progress (visits can be arranged). Abandoned **goldmines** at Reno and Adelong (lapidarists and fossickers find the district interesting). **Lookouts** at Mount Kimo, Brummy's Hill, and Reno Hill. **Asparagus farm,** five kilometres south. **Historic inn** at Jugiong, 37 kilometres north (Australia's oldest hotel to retain licence in one family. Issued to J. P. Sheahan in 1844).

Sports. Golf course. Bowls and tennis. Racecourse. Fishing and swimming in river. Olympic pool.

Accommodation. Two **hotels.** Preferred: Criterion, Sheridan Street. Five **motels.** Recommended: Sunset, Hume Highway. **Holiday cabins** available. **Caravan and camping park,** all facilities.

Transport. **Rail** services to Sydney and Melbourne. **Air** via Wagga Wagga airport (bus connecting). **Road** services (interstate road-coach passengers picked up or set down).

YASS (Population 4 240)

On the Yass River 296 kilometres south-west of Sydney, Yass is the centre of a pastoral district noted for superfine wool, farmlands which produce wheat and oats, and orchards which yield high-quality apples, pears, cherries and other fruit. Silver, lead and bismuth are mined in the district.

The town is situated in singularly beautiful rolling hill country on the western watershed of the Great Dividing Range. It has many attractive public and commercial buildings.

History. The Yass plains were discovered by Hume and Hovell in 1824 and the town was founded in 1837. In the early 1840s, a time of exceptional drought and financial depression when sheep were selling for sixpence each, many pastoralists were saved from ruin by the establishment of the tallow industry. The method of boiling down carcases for tallow was pioneered and publicized by Henry O'Brien, a pioneer of the Yass district. Tallow exports from New South Wales grew from 4 735 tonnes in 1843 to 130 048 tons in 1850. Yass is the aboriginal word for 'running water'.

Places of Interest. Town: Yass **Historical Museum. Graves** of explorers Hamilton Hume and Henry O'Brien in local cemetery. **Cooma Cottage,** built by Hume in 1830. He lived there until his death in 1873. Environs: **Burrinjuck Dam,** fishing and aquatic sports (32 kilometres south-west). **Taemas Bridge,** for trout fishing (22 kilometres south-south-west). **Wee Jasper** and **Micalong Creeks,** for trout fishing. **Caley's Cave,** Wee Jasper, open on Sunday and Wednesday afternoons. Grave of bushranger John Gilbert at Binalong.

Sports. Swimming pool. Polo ground. Golf course. Bowls. Tennis and squash courts.

Accommodation. Three **hotels.** Recommended: Australian, Comur Street. Three **motels.** Recommended: Yass, Hume Highway. **Caravan and camping park,** all facilities.

Transport. Rail and **road** services to Sydney and Melbourne (motorists note that Yass is five kilometres from highway turnoff to Canberra).

TUMUT (Population 5 250)

Tumut is known for the beauty of the countryside surrounding it and for fine plantations of European trees. It is the northern gateway of the Mount Kosciusko snow resorts and the Snowy Mountains Hydro-electric Project. The town is 31 kilometres from the Hume Highway and 399 kilometres south-west of Sydney. It is a small but vigorous manufacturing centre and the local factories produce butter, eucalyptus oil, brooms, processed fruit and milled timber. The soil of the surrounding district is highly fertile and grows beef, wool, millet, fruit, vegetables, tobacco and fodder crops. Granite is quarried in the district.

Tumut people celebrate the Festival of the Falling Leaves in late April and a bushman's carnival in January every year.

History. The Tumut River and its rich valley were discovered by Hume and Hovell in 1824 and the first settlers arrived in the 1830s. A pioneer, Thomas MacAlister, established a station named Dalbalara where he bred the well-known breed of Dalbalara Shorthorn beef cattle. The townsite was surveyed in 1848 and named for an aboriginal word meaning 'campsite by a river'. The municipality was proclaimed in 1887 but later merged with the Tumut Shire. Harnessing the waters of the Tumut River into which the Eucumbene, Tooma and Upper Murrumbidgee have been diverted is an integral part of the Snowy Mountains Hydro-electric and Irrigation Project.

Places of Interest. Environs: **Yarrangobilly Caves** (35 kilometres south-south-east). Four large limestone caverns electrically lit and open for inspection. Thermal pool in which the water is a constant 29.4 °C is near the Caves House which provides accommodation for visitors. Nearby **Cooleman Caves** are not yet developed but are of interest to speliologists. The caves were discovered in 1834 but were not generally known until after the Kiandra gold strike in 1859.

Sports. Racecourse. Motor cycle circuit. Golf course. Bowling greens. Tennis and squash courts. First class trout fishing in 193 kilometres of accessible streams from the Gaden hatchery at Jindabyne.

Accommodation. Three **hotels.** Recommended: Woolpack and Royal, Wynyard Street. Two **motels.** Recommended:Ashton, Wynyard Street. **Caravan park,** all facilities.

Transport. Rail from Sydney. **Road** services.

TUMBARUMBA (Population 1 391)

A small town in the district which produces timber, fruit, wool, fat cattle, dairy produce and vegetables, Tumbarumba is 505 kilometres south-west of Sydney, in the foothills of the Australian Alps. It is the base for excursions to the mountains and the Upper Murray bush-holiday resorts, and the scenery is very fine indeed.

History. The district was settled in 1839 and gold was discovered in the local streams in the 1850s. In 1854 the bushranger Dan Morgan raided the town and shot Sergeant McGinty. Nothing very exciting has happened since. In October a Festival of the Mountain Gums is held, and on New Year's Day a rodeo.

Places of Interest. Paddy's River Falls (16 kilometres south on Tooma Road), a spectacular 60 metre cascade. **Granites Lookout.**

Sports. Golf course. Bowls and tennis. Swimming pool. Racecourse. Polo ground. Pony club. Trout fishing.

Accommodation. One **hotel.** One **motel,** recommended.

Transport. **Rail** service to Sydney. Local **road** services.

Small Towns in District

HOLBROOK (Population 1 068) is a convenient overnight stopping place for travellers on the Hume Highway. It is 521 kilometres south-west of Sydney and 74 kilometres north-east of Albury. A noted stock-breeding centre first called Ten Mile Creek and then Germantown, it was renamed during the first world war after Norman Holbrook RN, who while commanding a submarine in the Mediterranean dived under five rows of mines and torpedoed a Turkish battleship. He received the Victoria Cross. The town is also a convenient stop for tourists to the Upper Murray resorts leaving the main Sydney-Melbourne railway line at Culcairn.

Sports. Racecourse, tennis, bowls, Olympic swimming pool. Trout fishing.

Accommodation. Two **hotels.** Recommended: Riverina, Hume Highway. Three **motels.** Recommended: Byer Flag Motor Inn, Hume Highway.

Transport. **Rail** and **road** services.

BATLOW (Population 1 403) is a small timber-milling and fruit-packing town in the foothills of the Great Dividing Range, south of Tumut. The district produces apples, pears and berry fruits. Hardwood and pine are milled from 40 470 hectares of carefully managed forest in the hills. There is an Apple Blossom Festival in October.

Places of Interest. **Buddong Falls. Paddy's River Dam,** built by Chinese miners after a gold strike in the 1850s. **Memorial Park,** developed by community effort.

Sports. Golf, bowls and trout fishing.

Accommodation. One **hotel.**

Transport. **Rail** from Sydney via Cootamundra.

ADELONG 20 kilometres north-west of Tumut, is a picturesque little town in a region noted for rural beauty and the excellence of its trout fishing.

Accommodation. One **hotel. Caravan park,** all facilities.

MURRUMBIDGEE IRRIGATION AREA

The Murrumbidgee Irrigation Area, about 122 000 hectares of intensively cultivated land both north and south of the Murrumbidgee River, is just under 644 kilometres south-west of Sydney. Its water is supplied from the Burrinjuck Dam storage (supplemented by water diverted from the Snowy River) and distributed by canals and channels to farms which grow citrus and stone fruits, wine and table grapes, fodder crops, fat lambs, wool, rice and cotton. A large area is also under wheat.

The irrigation project was undertaken largely as a result of the example and influence of the late Sir Samuel McCaughey, who migrated from Ireland in 1855 at the age of 20, bought a property near Narrandera, and built up a famous merino stud. In 1899 he bought North Yanco station on the banks of the river and constructed a dam and pump to irrigate 16 000 hectares on which he grew lucerne and other fodder crops. His success encouraged the NSW Government to proceed with the construction of Barren Jack (later Burrinjuck) Dam. It was completed in 1912 (and enlarged in 1957) and its water is used to generate power for Port Kembla, Canberra and Yanco.

Rice has become a particularly important crop in the MIA, where selective breeding of strains originally imported from California and improved methods of cultivation have achieved the highest yields per hectare in the world. The total area under rice is about 12 100 hectares. This cannot be increased

Brush-tail possum

Tasmanian Devil

Koalas

substantially until more water from the Snowy River diversion is available. The rice is sown in September-October and harvested in April-May. Mills are located at Leeton, Griffith, Yenda, Cootamundra and Echuca. After the grain is polished the residue is used for stock food, the hulls for packing and polishing material, cellulose and fuel, and the straw for packing and paper making. Grain is exported to Japan, Malaysia and Great Britain.

Cotton is also grown successfully under irrigation.

The Colleambally Irrigation Area, to the south of the MIA proper, is being vigorously developed. It now has about 200 farms. The Blowering Dam on the Tumut River, now complete, will increase the number to about 850.

Note. Visitors are not permitted to bring fruit, vegetables or plants into the Murrumbidgee Irrigation Area. This quarantine regulation is strictly enforced.

GRIFFITH
(Population 11 015)

Griffith, on the main irrigation canal of the Murrumbidgee Irrigation Area, is the district's largest town. It is 647 kilometres west-south-west of Sydney on the crossroads of highways leading to Sydney, Melbourne, Adelaide and Canberra. It was developed as a model settlement on a town plan by the famous American architect, Walter Burley Griffin, who designed the layout of the Federal capital, Canberra, and of Griffith's sister settlement in the MIA, Leeton.

The streets of Griffith are planted with shade trees and lawns and its public and commercial buildings are architecturally good. Its secondary industries are associated with the produce of the countryside—flour and rice mills, starch and fruit-processing plants, canneries, wineries and packing sheds.

History. The explorer John Oxley sighted the district from Mount Binya in 1817 and described it as barren and desolate—and barren and desolate it remained until the first water came from Burrinjuck after the completion of the dam in 1912. The boundaries of the town were surveyed in 1916 and it was named after Arthur Griffith, Minister for Works in NSW, who officially opened the irrigation project. After the first world war returned servicemen were successfully settled on many small farms in the area.

Places of Interest. **Fruit and vegetable canneries** and **wineries** (inspections can be arranged). Yenda **rice mill. Lake Wynangan** (6 kilometres from town), for water sports. **Scenic Hill,** for panoramic views of town and distant McPherson Ranges and Binya and Cocoparra Hills. Exterior mural mosiac at the **Ex-servicemen's Club.**

Sports. Facilities for most sports including golf and horse racing. Duck shooting in season.

Accommodation. Two **hotels.** Preferred: Area, Banna Avenue. Three **motels.** Recommended: Irrigana, Banna Avenue. **Caravan and camping park,** all facilities, at Lake Wynangan.

Transport. **Rail** services to capital cities and Broken Hill. **Air** services to Sydney, Melbourne and Adelaide. Sightseeing **charter flights** available at airport. **Road** coach services to Melbourne and Sydney. **Coach tour** from Sydney in season.

LEETON
(Population 6 638)

On the main canal in the southern section of the MIA, Leeton is 615 kilometres from Sydney. The nearby irrigated lands are used mainly for growing stone, citrus and vine fruits, rice and dairy produce. The town is proud of the fact that it has the largest cannery in the southern hemisphere, where more than half a million cans of fruit are processed daily during the December-March season. Conducted tours of the plant can be made four times daily. The rice mills and fruit-packing sheds may be inspected twice daily.

Leeton was established in 1912 and the first rice crops were harvested in the district in 1924-25.

Places of Interest. **Agricultural Research Station** (inspection on weekdays). **McCaughey Lookout,** for views of town and Corbie Hill citrus area. **Golgeldrie Weir** (25 kilometres south-west). **Yanco township** (6 kilometres south) with homestead of Samuel McCaughey, agricultural college and research station.

Sports. Usual facilities plus night trotting track. Duck shooting.

Accommodation. Two **hotels.** Preferred, Hydro. Two **motels.** Leeton and Riverina, both recommended. **Caravan and camping park,** all facilities.

Transport. **Road** and **rail** services (see Griffith).

NARRANDERA

(Population 4 825)

Near the intersection of the Sturt and Newell Highways 580 kilometres south-west of Sydney, Narrandera is an old-established pastoral and wheat town at the gateway of the irrigation area. It was named in 1880, when the township was gazetted, after the station property on which the settlement had slowly been growing up since 1863. The name means 'lizard'. In 1885 the borough was proclaimed and in 1960 the Shire of Narrandera was formed, incorporating the municipality and the old Shire of Yanco.

Places of Interest. Sturt's Beach and Narrandera **Parks** (small zoo in latter). **Lake Talbot Reserve,** bird sanctuary. **Forestry Commission** tree nursery. **Yanco Weir** (16 kilometres). **Berembed Weir. Inland Fisheries Research Station.**

Sport. Racecourse. Golf course. Tennis courts. Bowling greens. Good fishing.

Accommodation. Two **hotels.** Recommended: Charles Sturt, East Street. Two **motels.** Recommended: Koala, East Street. **Caravan and camping park,** all facilities.

Transport. **Rail** and **air** services. **Road** coach services to Sydney and Melbourne.

FAR WESTERN DISTRICT

The far west of New South Wales is aptly described by promoters of tourism in Australia as a fascinating and forbidding region—a region where the centres of population are separated by vast distances and the red monotony of seemingly endless plains is broken only here and there by low, rocky ranges and slow-flowing, meandering rivers. Despite its harshness, the far west creates no small proportion of the State's wealth. It carries more than two million sheep which produce fine quality merino wool. It is rich in mineral wealth, specially silver, lead, zinc and copper. There is every reason to believe that modern prospecting methods will disclose even greater resources than those already exploited.

The main highways leading from the State capitals of Sydney, Melbourne and Adelaide to the great mining city of Broken Hill are reasonable if not first class motorways, but secondary roads are rough, mostly unsealed, and must be negotiated with particular care after both long dry spells and rain. Broken Hill and Bourke (and towns en route) are served by reliable and comfortable rail services, but probably the best way to see the country is by air taxi, except for the traveller with the time and desire to delve below superficialities. Air taxi rates are reasonable, with concessions for small groups.

Travel for pleasure is not recommended between November and March, when heat, dust and flies can be trying. The winter climate is bracing and pleasant.

BROKEN HILL

(Population 29 743)

Broken Hill is a modern, progressive city built to service workers in the fabulously rich silver-lead-zinc mines of the Barrier Range in far western New South Wales. The mines produce two million tonnes of ore a year and can continue their output for 50 more years. The city is 1 170 kilometres by road (1 125 kilometres by rail) west of Sydney, situated in some of the most forbidding, arid country in the Australian continent where the average rainfall is less than 178 millimetres a year and the annual evaporation nearly 2½ metres. The mean winter temperature is 18°C. In summer the daily maximum often exceeds 38°C, but humidity is low.

Broken Hill is an example of the extraordinary resource shown by human beings in escaping the dangers and discomforts of hostile nature by creating an artificial environment. Although surrounded by a vast area of sunblistered wasteland, it is a place of bright gardens, green parks and sportsgrounds. Its water comes from local conservation schemes and from a dam on the Darling River, 112 kilometres east, which has been further developed as an aquatic sports resort.

Architecturally, Broken Hill is not distinguished despite a number of well designed public and private buildings. Its distinction lies in the unusual nature of the community which has evolved out of the isolation of its locale and the richness of the mineral resources that are exploited. The mining companies and their employees have rejected the system of arbitration and conciliation which regulates industrial relations in other parts of Australia. They have their own system of negotiating wages scales and working conditions. In 1925 all unions of workers in Broken Hill affiliated in the Barrier Industrial Council, a body now so powerful that it controls practically every aspect of the city's civic life.

History. The explorer Charles Sturt was in the area in 1844—and nearly died of thirst. He named the hump-backed range Broken Hill and returned to examine it more closely on a second journey the following year. In 1867 the white quartz reefs of the range led to a disastrous goldrush in which many diggers lost their lives. The silver ore outcropping was not recognized. However, in 1875 silver-lead was discovered at Thackaringa and specimens were sent to London for assay but had to be jettisoned when the ship carrying them ran through a bad storm. In 1880 further specimens were sent. The assays were so high that a rush began at Thackaringa and present day Silverton.

In 1883 a German-born boundary rider at Mount Gipps station, Charles Rasp, discovered what he thought was a tin outcrop near the present city. With a syndicate of six others he pegged out a 16 hectares claim. Specimens obtained of silver assayed at an incredible 600 oz to the ton. Rasp and his associates then formed the Broken Hill Proprietary Company, the stock of which was valued at £1 520 000 in the first year of its existence and paid £64 000 in dividends. A tremendous boom ensued and BHP shares at one stage were quoted at £412 each in London. Other companies moved into the area and, despite the inevitable bursting of the speculators' bubble, the Barrier mines were soon producing about one-third of the world's silver. Rasp's original discovery turned out to be a lode almost 6 kilometres long and 155 metres wide.

BHP withdrew from mining in the area in 1939 and transformed itself into a gigantic iron, steel and shipbuilding concern. The Barrier lodes are today worked by four major companies, North Broken Hill, Broken Hill South, New Broken Hill and the Zinc Corporation. More than 100 million tonnes of ore have been extracted from the mines.

In 1885 and 1886 blast furnaces were opened at several of the mines but 12 years later they were transferred to Port Pirie in South Australia.

Broken Hill is, it will be noted, economically and geographically oriented to South Australia rather than to New South Wales, despite completion of the standard rail link with Sydney in 1927.

Serious industrial unrest occurred on the Barrier in 1892, 1908, 1916 and 1919, but since the advent of the Barrier Industrial Council and the introduction of the 'lead bonus' on wages, disputes between management and labour have greatly diminished. A strike in 1968 affected production.

It is worth comment that Broken Hill is a city in which serious crime is practically unknown.

Places of Interest. In or near city: **Royal Flying Doctor Base,** established 1939 and open to public every weekday at 4 pm. **School of the Air,** begun by NSW Department of Education in 1956, broadcasts lessons to children of the Outback; children's answers to teachers' questions transmitted on station transceivers. (Visitors welcome.) **Museum of Applied Arts and Sciences,** at Technical College. **Cathedral of the Sacred Heart,** restored in recent years, built originally of local stone and roofed with copper. (Fine Italian marble altar and sanctuary, and stained glass windows.) **Afghan Mosque,** built in late 19th century when Afghans ran numerous camel trains supplying outback stations and mining camps. **Sturt's Memorial,** at **Stephens Reservoir,** the first water storage constructed for the city in 1892. **Umberumberka Reservoir** (28 kilometres north-west). **Protective tree plantations,** established by amateur botanist Albert Morris with help from the mining companies on the south-west margins of the city to protect it from dust storms. **Charles Rasp Memorial Library.** Patton Street, Duff Street, Queen Elizabeth Street, Keast, See, Duke of Cornwall and Sturt **Parks** (all run by City Council with some aid from mining companies). **Twin Lakes Project,** on southern approaches of the city. **Imperial Lake** (north-east). **Repertory Theatre. Visitors' Information Centre,** Palace Hotel, Argent and Sulphide Streets.

In district: **Menindee Lakes Scheme,** 112 kilometres, a 16 000 hectares stretch of water developed for aquatic sports and incorporated in **Kinchega National Park. Mootwingee Ranges,** 131 kilometres north-east, an aboriginal tribal ground now proclaimed a national historic site. The area is rich in rock carvings, drawings etc, and native birds and animals, but has been made unsightly by litterbugs and vandals. The access road is poor. **Yanco Glen Hotel,** 30 kilometres north, where an excellent collection of native artifacts may be seen. **Euriowie,** 69 kilometres north, unusual rock formations and aboriginal 'intaglios' (permission to visit is required from Bijerkerno station homestead).

Sports. Two golf links with unusual oiled sand greens. Two swimming pools. Three bowling clubs. Racecourse and trotting track. Greyhound track. Squash courts. Yachting, water skiing etc on Menindee lakes. The city boasts five general sports ovals.

Broken Hill stages a Silver City Festival every five years.

Accommodation. Three directory listed **hotels.** Recommended: Royal Exchange and Mario's. Five **motels.** Recommended: Crystal and Lodge, Crystal Street. **Caravan and camping park,** all facilities. (Good **camping park** also at Menindee lake.)

Transport. **Rail** services from Sydney, Melbourne, Adelaide and Perth. Direct **air** services from Sydney, Melbourne, Adelaide. **Air Taxi** services. **Coach** tours from eastern capitals from March to October. **Coach** tours from Broken Hill through far north-west, taking in major places of interest and extending into Queensland and South Australian Outback.

WHITE CLIFFS (Population 150)

The old opal mining town 1 085 kilometres west of Sydney is now only a collection of bleached weatherboard shacks surrounded by innumerable shallow shafts and heaps of mullock.

History. Two kangaroo shooters discovered the first opal in the area in 1890 and a rush followed. In 1902 gems worth £140 000 were found and the town had five hotels and a population of 4 500. By 1916 the field seemed worked out though several minor strikes from time to time have temporarily revived interest. A few gougers are now working in the area with earth moving machinery. Amateur prospectors and tourists sometimes pick up opal in the mullock heaps, particularly after rain when the flash of colour can be more easily seen.

Accommodation. One **hotel** (for the hardy traveller only).

Transport. Mail service by **road** from Wilcannia.

BOURKE (Population 3 620)

Claimed to be the largest railhead for wool shipment in the world, Bourke is 797 kilometres north-west of Sydney on the Darling River. It is the service centre of a vast area of outback sheep country, where about 300 runs varying in size from 5 000 and 40 000 hectares produce between 50 000 and 60 000 bales of wool a year. It has a meatworks and wool scouring plant. Some country close to the town is irrigated from the Darling and grows citrus fruit and fodder crops and fattens cattle.

History. In 1829 Sturt passed the present site of Bourke on his way down the Darling, and in 1835 T. L. Mitchell built a log stockade against possible aboriginal attack and called it Fort Bourke after Governor Bourke of NSW. The area was later given to the Royal Australian Historical Society and dedicated as a historical reserve in 1914. It is about 11 kilometres from the present town which was surveyed in 1862. By 1881 it had become a prosperous port for the paddle steamers plying on the river. The first bridge across the Darling was built in 1883.

Sports. Olympic pool, and swimming in river. Golf course. Tennis courts. Bowling club. Good fishing for bream, Murray cod and perch in the river. Rodeo championships are held annually, in late winter when the climate is at its best.

Accommodation. Two **hotels.** Preferred: Royal, Mitchell Street. **Caravan and camping park.** No information on facilities.

Transport. **Rail** service from Sydney. **Air** service from Sydney, via other western towns.

NYNGAN (Population 2 478)

Nyngan is the centre of a wool growing district on the Bogan River, 603 kilometres north-west of Sydney. The rainfall in the region is unreliable, but in favourable seasons wheat is grown. Thomas Mitchell explored the area in 1835, but settlement was held up for many years because of the hostility of the aborigines. Many early stations had to be abandoned. However, after the rail was pushed through from Dubbo in 1882, the town grew rapidly and was declared a municipality in 1891. The name means 'many streams'.

Places of Interest. **Bird Sanctuary** in the Macquarie Marshes, 64 kilometres north. **Water supply scheme** for the town of Cobar, 134 kilometres west, where large-scale copper mining has been resumed by the Broken Hill South Company.

Accommodation. Three **hotels.** Highly recommended: Overlander, Pangee Street. One **motel.**

Transport. **Rail** services to Sydney and Bourke. **Air** services to Sydney.

COBAR (Population 3 744)

An old mining town on the Barrier Highway, 723 kilometres north-west of Sydney, Cobar has been given a new lease of life by the re-opening and development of its copper mines which were worked continuously between their discovery in 1871 and their closure because of high running costs in 1952.

Accommodation. Two **hotels.** Recommended: Sundowners' Great Western. One **motel.**

Transport. **Rail, road** and **air** services.

BREWARRINA (Population 1 444)

There is excellent sport for anglers and fishers around Brewarrina, a cattle, wool and river-fishing town 811 kilometres north-west of Sydney.

Settlement followed soon after the explorer Edmund Kennedy crossed the Warrego River west of the town in 1847. The town was laid out in 1861 and became established as a river crossing for stock when a punt and pontoons were built in 1888. In those days the wool clips of the district were dispatched by river to Adelaide. The name means 'good fishing'.

Accommodation. One **hotel.** One **motel. Caravan park,** all facilities.

Transport. Air services to Sydney.

BALRANALD (Population 1 425)

On the Murrumbidgee River (and the Victorian railways system), Balranald is 438 kilometres from Melbourne. The nearest NSW railhead is Hay, 125 kilometres east. The district produces wool, cattle, wheat, fruit (on irrigated land) and timber.

The first permanent settler arrived in 1847 and the town was gazetted in 1851 when it was thought it would become an important river port. Burke and Wills passed through it in 1860. It was declared a municipality in 1882 and the shire was established in 1957.

The first telephone in Australia was installed at Yanga homestead near the town by the nephew of A. G. Bell. The town police once captured four bushrangers who had been troubling the district after riding 284 kilometres in 34 hours.

Accommodation. One **hotel.** Two **motels.** Recommended Capri, Market Street. **Caravan and camping park,** all facilities.

Transport. Rail services to Melbourne. **Road** services. **Air** services.

WENTWORTH (Population 1 154)

Wentworth is a small town named after William Charles Wentworth, 1 056 kilometres west-south-west of Sydney, near the junction of the Murray and Darling Rivers (576 kilometres from Melbourne). It is the centre of three old established irrigation settlements, Pomona, Curlwaa and Coomealla, which grow citrus and vine fruits. The mainstay of the district is wool, but timber and fat lambs are also produced. The town has sawmills and brickworks.

History. Wentworth was the terminal point of Sturt's journey down the Darling in 1829. In 1859 the River Murray Steam Navigation Company set up a store at the townsite and between 1890 and 1900 it became one of the largest river ports in Australia. As many as 400 boats used it in a year. The town was proclaimed a municipality in 1879 and the area became a shire in 1957.

Places of Interest. Wentworth **Folk Museum and Arts Centre. Sturt's Trees** at Caravan Park (marked by explorer). **Old Court House,** reputedly built in the 1840s and restored by local service club. **Old gaol,** with stretching rack and whipping stool used for punishment of prisoners. **Wentworth Lock,** and site of projected **Chowilla Dam.**

Accommodation. Two **hotels.** Recommended: Royal, Darling Street. **Caravan and camping park,** all facilities.

Transport. Road services to Mildura (31 kilometres west). **Rail** service.

LORD HOWE ISLAND

The largest of 13 islands of the Lord Howe Group in the Tasman Sea 480 kilometres east of Port Macquarie, Lord Howe Island is 640 kilometres north-east of Sydney. It is of volcanic origin, crescent shaped, about 11 kilometres long and roughly one kilometre in width. Its total area is 1 300 hectares, but it is dominated by two peaks, Mount Gower (860 metres) and Mount Lidgbird (763 metres), so that only about 120 hectares are suitable for cultivation. The soil, however, is extremely rich and will produce all kinds of subtropical crops.

The interior of the island has dense vegetation, the larger species being Kentia palms, pandanus and banyan trees. The banyans are often huge and a single tree can cover a hectare of ground. Imported Norfolk Island pines also thrive in the soil. The terraced slopes of Mount Lidgbird are riddled with the burrows of the rare Bighill mutton bird and the commoner species have rookeries in the palm forests on the eastern side of the island.

Off the western shore a coral reef enclosing a large lagoon is the most southerly in the world, and its marine life is very similar to that of the Great

Barrier Reef. The climate of the island is equable and mild the year round, the temperature rarely rising above 26°C in the summer or dropping below 10°C in the winter. The scenery is memorably beautiful.

There are now about 250 permanent residents on the island. They sustain themselves by fishing, vegetable growing and handcrafts but are mainly dependent on the tourist trade. At any time the island has a floating population of between 100 and 200 visitors who arrive by Sandringham flying boat from Sydney, and are accommodated in guest-houses owned and run by islanders. There is no hotel, but liquor may be bought from a store operated by the Lord Howe Island Board.

The coastal waters teem with fish and the beaches have excellent surf. The lagoon is a happy hunting ground for shell collectors, water skiers and snorkellers (equipment may be hired.) Launches are available for deepsea fishing excursions.

History. The island was discovered in 1788 by Lieutenant H. Lidgbird Ball, of HMS *Supply* while on his way from Port Jackson to establish a penal colony on Norfolk Island. He named it in honour of the First Lord of the Admiralty. The island had remained undiscovered by the Polynesians on their migrations throughout the Pacific and was uninhabited. The first settlers arrived in 1834 and grew fruit and vegetables which they traded with whalers. Turtles were also an abundant source of food.

For many years the only cash source of income for the islanders was from the sale of Kentia (Howea) palm seeds which were marketed all over the world, but the tourist industry, which began in the 1930s when passenger vessels called at the island regularly, received a great boost from the establishment of the flying boat service after the second world war.

Rats, accidentally introduced to the island from a wrecked vessel in the early years of this century, became such a pest that several times in the 1920s they nearly caused the abandonment of the settlement. With the cats brought in a vain endeavour to control them, they almost wiped out terrestrial bird life, reducing the number of species from 40 to 10. The island's small flora also suffered grave damage from the rats, and from domestic pigs run wild.

Note: All birds, animals and plants on the island are strictly protected.

Administration. Lord Howe Island is a dependency of the State of New South Wales. It is administered by the Lord Howe Island Board, with headquarters in Sydney, and represented on the island by a Superintendent who is himself advised by an elected Island Committee of four. It is included in the State electorate of King and the Commonwealth electorate of West Sydney. Civic works on the island are financed by a levy of 10c per day on tourists. There are no police stationed on Lord Howe.

Sport. Bowling club (one good green). Tennis courts. Water skiing, skin diving, fishing.

Accommodation. There are several **guest-houses** of moderately good standard on the island. None could be ranked in the luxury class. Preferred: Leanda Lei.

Transport. Three times weekly **air** service from Sydney. Local **bus** service. **Bicycles** may be hired. (The Board and the Department of Civil Aviation which maintains a meteorological station on the island use motor vehicles.)

Victoria

Victoria, with an area of 22 775 004 hectares, is the smallest State on the Australian mainland. It is in the south-eastern corner of the continent and enjoys the advantages of a relatively temperate climate, fertile soil and a rainfall (about 635 millimetres) which is substantially above the Australian average, calculated on a State-area basis.

Although it occupies somewhat less than three per cent of the land area of the Commonwealth, its population of three and a quarter million represents about 28 per cent of the total population. About one third of the gross national product has for many years come from Victoria. It is the most closely settled and highly industrialized part of the continent. Only in the far north-west does its topography resemble that of the inland.

The proportion of mountains to flat land is higher in Victoria than in any other State except Tasmania. The highlands are mainly in the east and south-east and a large proportion of them are at an altitude of more than 1 500 metres. Seven peaks rise above 1 830 metres. The highest is Mount Bogong (1 987 metres). About 230 600 hectares of the country are snow-covered from June to October. This is the catchment which feeds the great Murray-Murrumbidgee river system, the waters of which have been harnessed to supply the cities of Melbourne and Sydney with power and to irrigate large areas of the Riverina—the land which lies between the two rivers—and central and north-western Victoria.

The Murray is the State's northern boundary and the east-west extensions of the Great Dividing Range are its major watershed. The valleys of tributaries running northward through central Victoria and southward through Gippsland contain the State's most productive agricultural, dairying and fruit-growing land, much of which has the benefit of seasonal irrigation.

The western half of Victoria, with the exception of districts close to the Otway Ranges, is given over mainly to wool and grain growing. The far north-west is a semi-arid region which produces good wheat but which is arable only because farms can be supplied with water from the Murray. The fully irrigated areas are extremely productive.

Geographically and scenically Victoria is an interesting part of Australia. Its mountains and the forests clothing them are noble, much of the coastline west of Port Phillip Bay resembles that of Cornwall in its wild and rugged beauty, and in the enclosed valleys of the north-east one finds Australia in a rare mood of gentle, green charm.

The overseas traveller in search of the essential 'Down-Under' should consider a tour of the Murray Valley from Mildura to Albury, returning to Melbourne by way of the alpine highway across the Bogong High Plains and East Gippsland. The route will not reveal all that Victoria has to offer, but it will cut a surprisingly representative cross-section of southern Australia—through the 'big sky' country of the dry plains, the gum-fringed reaches and backwaters of the great river which contributes so much to the nation's prosperity, and the rolling, blue uplands laced by turbulent streams which Australians seem so often to forget when describing their country to strangers.

ECONOMY The total annual gross value of Victoria's primary products is more than $A4 000 million. A significant feature of the rural scene is the

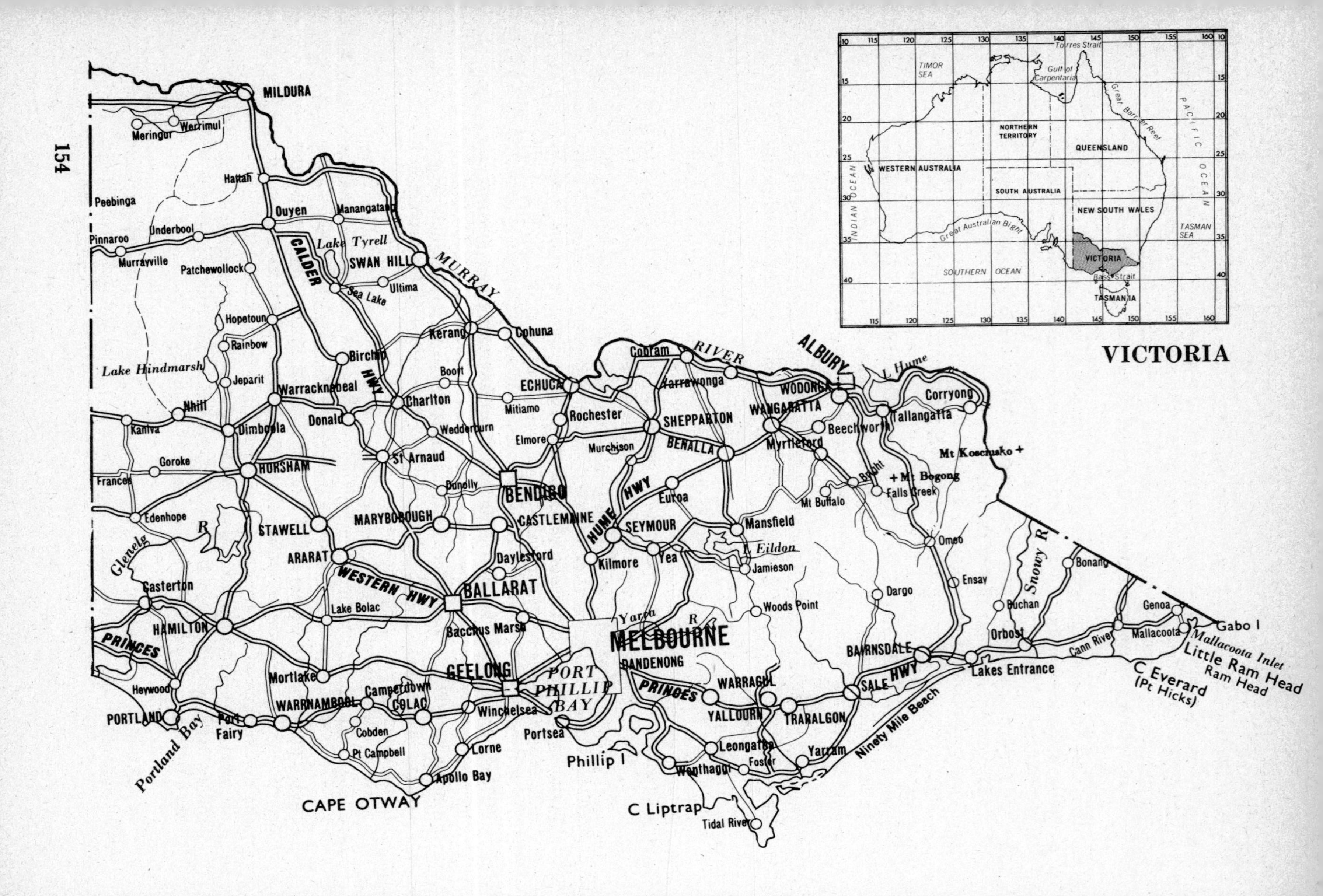
VICTORIA
PACIFIC OCEAN
TASMAN SEA
TIMOR SEA
INDIAN OCEAN
SOUTHERN OCEAN
Great Australian Bight
Great Barrier Reef
Torres Strait
Gulf of Carpentaria
Bass Strait
NORTHERN TERRITORY
QUEENSLAND
WESTERN AUSTRALIA
SOUTH AUSTRALIA
NEW SOUTH WALES
VICTORIA
TASMANIA
MILDURA
Meringur
Werrimul
Hattah
Peebinga
Ouyen
Manangatang
Underbool
Pinnaroo
Murrayville
Lake Tyrell
SWAN HILL
CALDER
MURRAY
Patchewollock
Ultima
Sea Lake
Hopetoun
Rainbow
Kerang
Cohuna
Lake Hindmarsh
Jeparit
Birchip
HWY
Boort
ECHUCA
Cobram
RIVER
Yarrawonga
ALBURY
L Hume
WODONGA
WANGARATTA
Corryong
Tallangatta
Warracknabeal
Charlton
Mitiamo
Rochester
SHEPPARTON
Beechworth
Nhill
Kaniva
Dimboola
Donald
Wedderburn
Elmore
BENALLA
Myrtleford
Murchison
Mt Kosciusko +
Goroke
HORSHAM
St Arnaud
Bright
+ Mt Bogong
Falls Creek
Frances
Dunolly
BENDIGO
HWY
Euroa
Mt Buffalo
Edenhope
R
STAWELL
MARYBOROUGH
CASTLEMAINE
HUME
SEYMOUR
Mansfield
Omeo
Glenelg
ARARAT
L Eildon
Daylesford
Kilmore
Yea
Jamieson
Snowy R
Bonang
Ensay
WESTERN HWY
BALLARAT
Dargo
Casterton
Lake Bolac
Yarra R
Woods Point
Buchan
Genoa
Gabo I
HAMILTON
Bacchus Marsh
MELBOURNE
Orbost
Mallacoota
Mallacoota Inlet
PRINCES
DANDENONG
BAIRNSDALE
Cann River
Little Ram Head
Ram Head
Mortlake
GEELONG
PORT PHILLIP BAY
Lakes Entrance
C Everard
(Pt Hicks)
Heywood
Camperdown
PRINCES
WARRAGUL
SALE
HWY
WARRNAMBOOL
COLAC
Winchelsea
YALLOURN
TRARALGON
PORTLAND
Port Fairy
Portland Bay
Cobden
Portsea
Ninety Mile Beach
Pt Campbell
Lorne
Leongatha
Yarram
Phillip I
Foster
Wonthaggi
Apollo Bay
CAPE OTWAY
C Liptrap
Tidal River

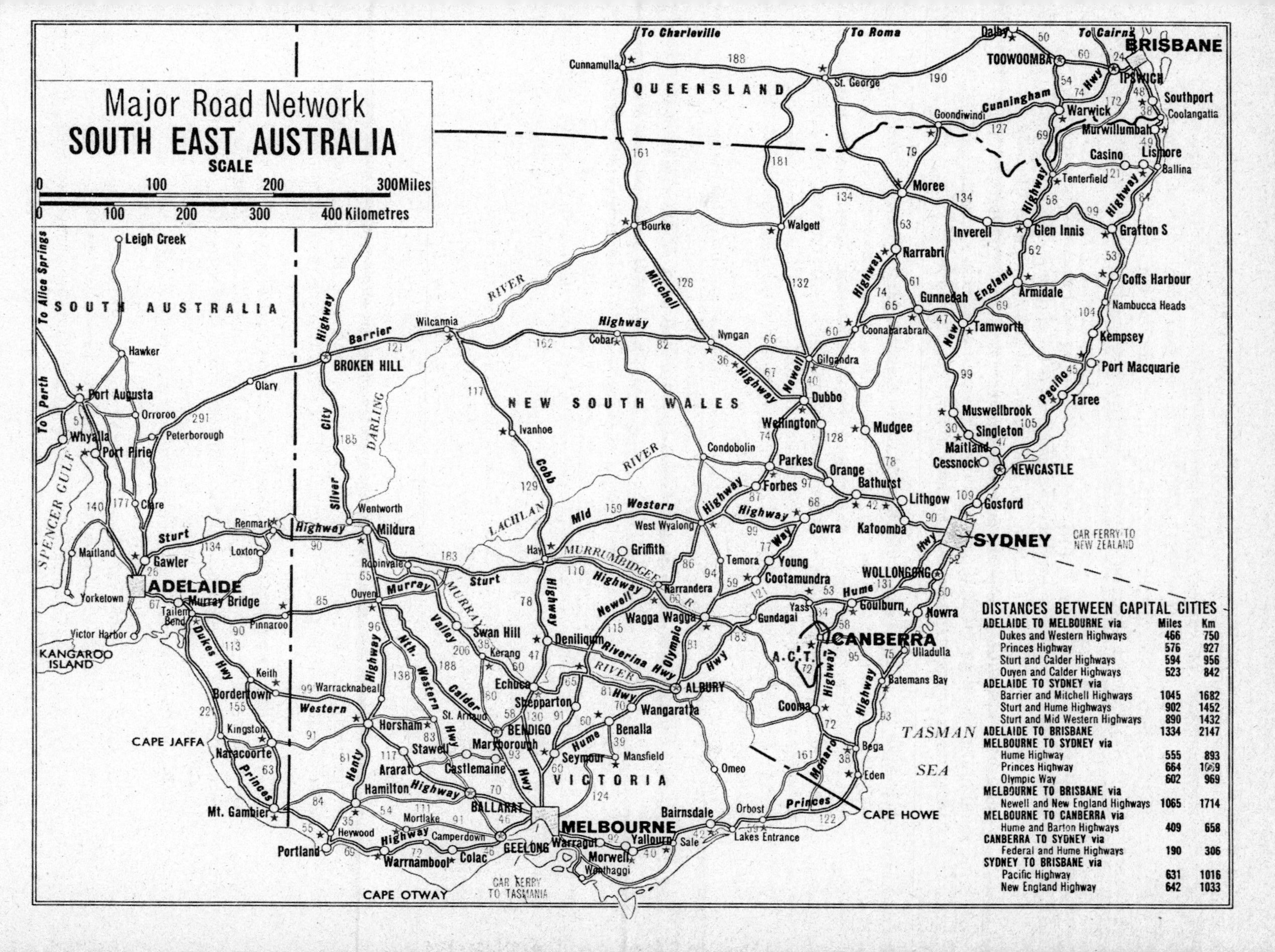
Major Road Network
SOUTH EAST AUSTRALIA
SCALE
0 100 200 300 Miles
0 100 200 300 400 Kilometres
QUEENSLAND
NEW SOUTH WALES
SOUTH AUSTRALIA
VICTORIA
A.C.T.
TASMAN SEA
BRISBANE
SYDNEY
CANBERRA
MELBOURNE
ADELAIDE
To Charleville
To Roma
To Cairns
To Alice Springs
To Perth
CAR FERRY TO NEW ZEALAND
CAR FERRY TO TASMANIA
CAPE HOWE
CAPE OTWAY
CAPE JAFFA
KANGAROO ISLAND
SPENCER GULF
DISTANCES BETWEEN CAPITAL CITIES
Miles Km
ADELAIDE TO MELBOURNE via
Dukes and Western Highways 466 750
Princes Highway 576 927
Sturt and Calder Highways 594 956
Ouyen and Calder Highways 523 842
ADELAIDE TO SYDNEY via
Barrier and Mitchell Highways 1045 1682
Sturt and Hume Highways 902 1452
Sturt and Mid Western Highways 890 1432
ADELAIDE TO BRISBANE 1334 2147
MELBOURNE TO SYDNEY via
Hume Highway 555 893
Princes Highway 664 1069
Olympic Way 602 969
MELBOURNE TO BRISBANE via
Newell and New England Highways 1065 1714
MELBOURNE TO CANBERRA via
Hume and Barton Highways 409 658
CANBERRA TO SYDNEY via
Federal and Hume Highways 190 306
SYDNEY TO BRISBANE via
Pacific Highway 631 1016
New England Highway 642 1033

extent to which irrigation is used. More then 810 000 hectares of the State's farmlands receive water from 41 large reservoirs and 265 smaller storages. It has been estimated that about one third of the average annual flow of Victorian rivers is stored or diverted for agricultural use. Most of the irrigation areas lie north of the Great Dividing Range in the valleys of the Goulburn and Murray Rivers.

In secondary industry, the State produces 57 per cent of Australia's textiles, 50 per cent of its rubber products, 45 per cent of its clothing, 35 per cent of its chemicals and 30 per cent of its industrial metals, machines and vehicles. Its industrial strength has been enormously increased by exploitation of the oil and natural gas fields discovered off the Gippsland coast. More than 19 000 factories produce goods valued at more than $A6 000 million.

HISTORY In 1770 Lieutenant Hicks, in Captain James Cook's *Endeavour*, sighted the Victorian coast at the point now known as Cape Everard, but made no investigation of the nature of the land. George Bass and Matthew Flinders surveyed the coast at much closer quarters in 1797-8, discovered the strait between Van Dieman's Land (now Tasmania) and the mainland and reported to the authorities in Sydney. This encouraged the settlement of the south-eastern parts of Australia a few years later.

Lieutenant J. Grant sailed his ship *Lady Nelson* into Port Phillip Bay in February 1802 and the following year Lieutenant D. Collins was dispatched by the Governor of New South Wales to settle the area. Collins, who was apparently a man of little initiative, chose a sandy site near the mouth of the bay. When it proved to be unsuitable, he reported unfavourably on the region and received permission to transfer to Van Dieman's Land.

More than thirty years later parties from Van Dieman's Land, unable to find suitable land, explored the south coast of the mainland for grazing country. Among them was the Henty family who in 1834 settled on Portland Bay in the far west. It was an area already well known to the crews of whaling and sealing ships. The following year John Batman and soon after him John Pascoe Fawkner investigated the good country in the valleys of the Yarra and Maribyrnong Rivers at the head of Port Phillip Bay. Batman 'purchased' about 600 000 acres (273 000 hectares) of land from natives of the Doutagalla tribe for an annual tribute of trade goods worth about $200. The transaction was subsequently repudiated by the Colonial Office, but the settlers were not to be denied and eventually the British Government recognized the *fait accompli*.

Port Phillip district developed rapidly as a squatting colony and by 1837 the white population had grown to about 500. Governor Bourke visited the new town, named it Melbourne after the British Prime Minister, and authorized his Government Surveyor, James Hoddle, to survey it to a convenient plan. In 1842 it was incorporated and the first mayor and councillors appointed.

From the beginning there was a strong sentiment in the Port Phillip District for political separation from New South Wales. The colonists wished to have nothing to do with the convict system and on two occasions forced convict transports bound for the new settlement to continue on to Sydney without landing their passengers.

Separation was at last achieved on 1 July 1851. Hardly a month later a rich gold strike was made near the hamlet of Buninyong, close to Ballarat and a great rush began. Diggers came from every part of the world to try their luck on the incredibly rich Victorian fields. Between March 1851 and December 1852 the population of the State grew from 77 000 to 168 000.

Gold strikes farther afield kept the fever high for many years, but the mining industry began to decline after 1860 and many of the immigrants who had come to look for the elusive yellow metal stayed on to establish farms or raise cattle and sheep. Many others, unaccustomed to the hard life in the Australian bush, retreated to Melbourne and found employment in urban industry which developed rapidly in the 1870s and 1880s.

Generally speaking, the State prospered greatly for 40 years after the gold-rushes. Both primary and secondary industries established on a sound basis and social and political development was rapid, both in the capital and in provincial centres. In the early 1890s, however, a serious setback was suffered when wild speculation in land ended in a financial crash which caused widespread unemployment. Nevertheless, the colony soon recovered, and immigration from Great Britain both before and after the first world war increased its population substantially.

Both world wars strongly stimulated the State's manufacturing industries and technology. Migration from Europe since 1949 has considerably increased the resources of manpower and industrial skills.

TOURING IN VICTORIA Autumn is probably the best season in which to make an all-Victorian tour. The uncomfortable heat of summer has then been tempered in the north and west and the weather is more stable in the mountains and along the coast. Snow sports and wildflower enthusiasts, however, should do their travelling in spring.

Victoria is well served by a network of good all-weather roads. Overall, its highway system is probably the best engineered and maintained in Australia. There are few parts of the State of any interest to tourists which cannot be reached in motoring comfort, although off the main routes formations tend to be narrow. There are about 160 000 kilometres of public roads (used by more than 1 300 000 motor vehicles) of which about 24 000 kilometres are surfaced with concrete or bitumen. About 7 200 kilometres are classed as State Highways and 14 400 kilometres as main roads.

The Government Railways have about 6 400 kilometres of track in operation. The services are of economic value to Victorians, but of only theoretical interest to most tourists. Most of the passenger trains, with the exception of the fast intercapital expresses and trains on electrified suburban lines, are made up of antiquated rolling stock, are slow and have few amenities for the comfort of travellers. Road-coach travel is preferable.

Intrastate air services ply between Melbourne and major provincial centres on the Murray and in the western districts and East Gippsland.

First class hotel accommodation in Melbourne is slightly better than in Sydney, particularly in the matter of service and cuisine, but there is not quite so wide a choice. Tariffs are about the same.

In the larger provincial towns, the leading hotel is usually of fair standard and the rest unpredictable. (Staff turnover is high.) For the traveller not on a strictly limited budget, motels are undoubtedly preferable for short or overnight stops.

Tourist resorts in Victoria are generally much less competitively and successfully developed than they are in Queensland, New South Wales and Tasmania, but inexpensive and reasonably comfortable accommodation is available at beach and mountain guest houses. Where economy is a consideration, peak holiday periods should be avoided. During these periods surcharges are levied and service standards decline.

MELBOURNE

(Population 2 388 941)

Capital of Victoria, second city of the Australian Commonwealth and fifth in the Commonwealth of Nations, Melbourne is situated near the mouth of the Yarra River at the head of Port Phillip Bay, a large, deeply indented and almost landlocked expanse of water extending northward from Bass Strait. The metropolitan area comprises 38 individually administered local government areas designated as cities and covers an area of 218 700 hectares.

The terrain is mostly flat or gently undulating and settlement has developed in a series of rectangles modified only by the contours of the bay's foreshores and the course of the Yarra and its tributary, the Maribyrnong. The northern and eastern suburbs are within sight of the Great Dividing Range and the Dandenong Ranges.

Central Melbourne is at present in the process of extensive redevelopment, many of its older buildings being demolished and replaced by multi-storey office blocks, but the city still retains much of its 19th century character and a number of fine public buildings designed in neo-classical style. A proportion of contemporary structures replacing those condemned by the march of progress are also of architectural merit, but the personality of the new city which is replacing the old is as yet unformed. The inner-ring suburbs are not yet so obviously affected by redevelopment and are strongly late Victorian and Edwardian. Outer suburbs—extending up to 30 or more kilometres from the heart of the city—are dominated by the styles of modern, standardized, low-cost housing.

Despite its extraordinary and occasionally comical architectural inconsistencies, Melbourne is a city of dignity and beauty—a dignity and beauty conferred largely by its wide, tree-shaded streets and avenues and its truly magnificent public parks and gardens, which have been developed with great emphasis on the acclimatization of European species of trees, shrubs and grasses. These, combined with qualities of climate and light, have given Melbourne the reputation of being the most 'English' of all the Australian State capitals. The likeness to an English or European city, however, does not extend far beyond the area of original settlement where the landscape is dominated by deciduous trees. The grey-greens, blues and ochre tints typical of the country side in temperate zone Australia are once more dominant a few kilometres from the inner city.

The climate of Melbourne can be shown by meteorological statistics to be mild and sunny, with no extremes of cold in winter and extremes of heat in summer rare. But statistics are to some extent deceptive as a measure of comfort, for the weather of all southern Victoria is subject to rapid change as the pressure systems originating over the Southern Ocean move from west to east. Northerly air streams passing over the interior of the continent build up heat fairly quickly and a change of wind to the south-west or south can bring dramatically sudden drops in temperature. Summers are fairly short, the really hot days in which the thermometer registers 38°C or more being confined mostly to January and February, and winters are cloudy, chilly and often windy. What Australians call cold weather can be experienced in Melbourne well into

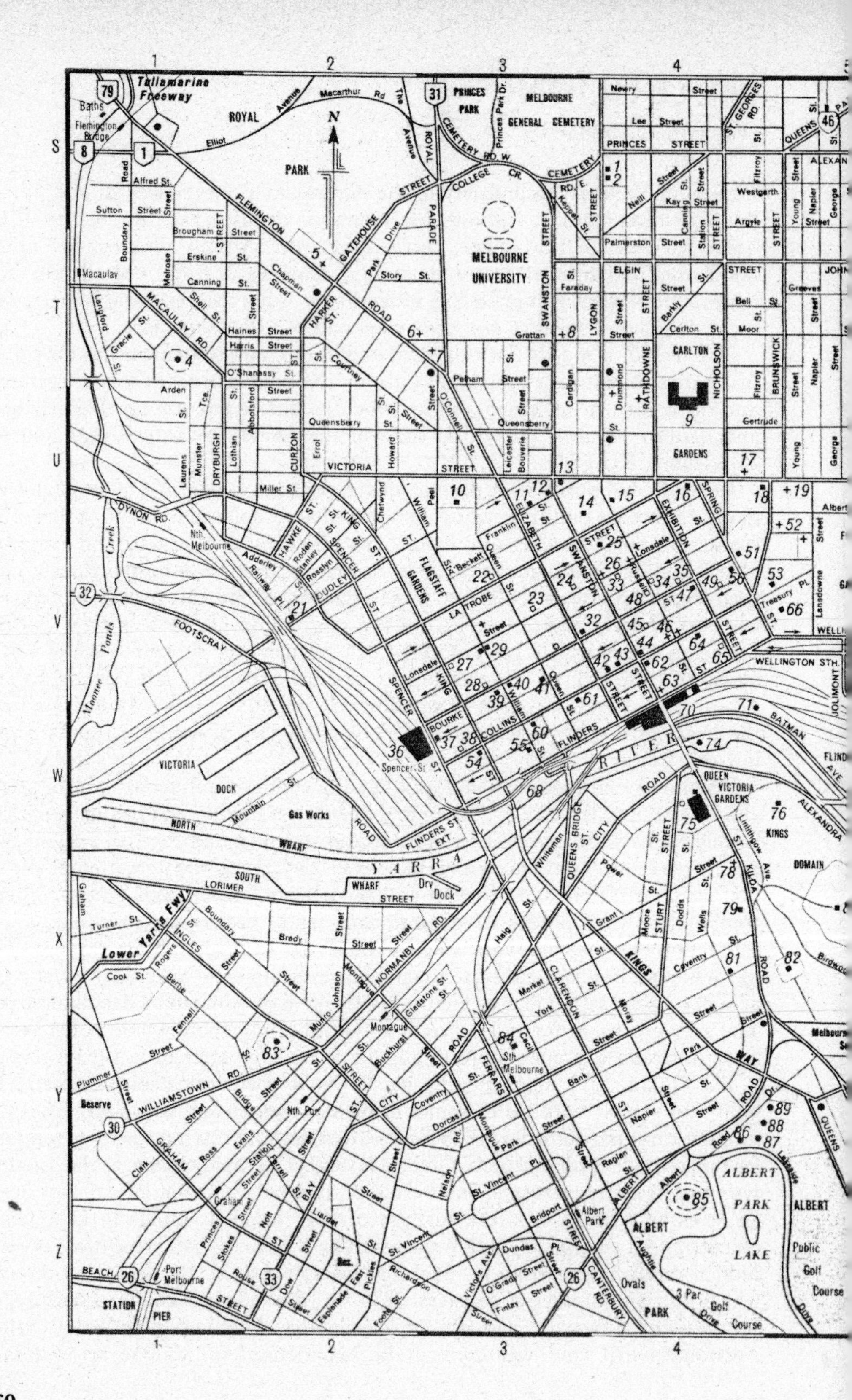
1
2
3
4
S
T
U
V
W
X
Y
Z
Tullamarine Freeway
79
31
46
8
1
32
30
26
33
Baths
Flemington Bridge
ROYAL PARK
Macarthur Rd
Elliot
Avenue
N
PRINCES PARK
Princes Park Dr.
MELBOURNE GENERAL CEMETERY
CEMETERY RD. W.
CEMETERY RD. E.
COLLEGE CR.
ROYAL PARADE
The Avenue
Nevry Street
Lee Street
PRINCES STREET
ST. GEORGES RD
QUEENS PDE.
ALEXANDRA
FLEMINGTON ROAD
GATEHOUSE STREET
Alfred St.
Sutton Street
Brougham Street
Erskine St.
Canning St.
Boundary Road
Melrose Street
Macaulay
MACAULAY RD.
Shiel St.
Langford St.
Gracie St.
Chapman Street
Haines Street
Harris Street
O'Shanassy St.
Arden St.
Munster Tce.
Laurens St.
DRYBURGH STREET
Lothian St.
Abbotsford Street
CURZON STREET
Errol St.
Courtney St.
HARKER ST.
Park Drive
Story St.
MELBOURNE UNIVERSITY
SWANSTON STREET
Grattan St.
Faraday St.
LYGON STREET
Cardigan St.
ELGIN STREET
Drummond Street
RATHDOWNE STREET
Barkly St.
Carlton St.
CARLTON GARDENS
NICHOLSON STREET
Palmerston Street
Kay Street
Canning St.
Station St.
Nelli Street
Fitzroy St.
Westgarth St.
Argyle Street
Young Street
Napier Street
George St.
Bell St.
Moor St.
Greeves Street
BRUNSWICK STREET
Gertrude St.
Pelham Street
Queensberry St.
Leicester St.
Bouverie St.
O'Connell St.
Howard St.
VICTORIA STREET
Miller St.
Chetwynd St.
William St.
Peel St.
ELIZABETH ST.
Franklin St.
Queen St.
A'Beckett St.
FLAGSTAFF GARDENS
LA TROBE ST.
EXHIBITION ST.
SPRING ST.
Lonsdale St.
Russell St.
Treasury Pl.
Lansdowne St.
Albert St.
WELLINGTON STH.
JOLIMONT
DYNON RD.
Moonee Ponds Creek
Nth. Melbourne
HAWKE ST.
Roden St.
Stanley St.
Rosslyn St.
KING ST.
SPENCER ST.
DUDLEY ST.
Adderley St.
Railway Pl.
FOOTSCRAY RD.
Lonsdale St.
BOURKE ST.
COLLINS ST.
FLINDERS ST.
Spencer St.
VICTORIA DOCK
NORTH WHARF
Mountain St.
Gas Works
ROAD
FLINDERS ST EXT.
YARRA RIVER
BATMAN AVE.
FLINDERS
QUEEN VICTORIA GARDENS
ALEXANDRA AVE.
KINGS DOMAIN
Linlithgow Ave
ST KILDA ROAD
SOUTH WHARF
LORIMER STREET
Dry Dock
QUEENS BRIDGE ST.
CITY ROAD
Whiteman St.
Power St.
STURT STREET
Grant St.
Moore St.
Dodds St.
Wells St.
Coventry St.
Birdwood
Graham St.
Turner St.
Lower Yarra Fwy.
INGLES ST.
Boundary St.
Rogers St.
Cook St.
Bertie St.
Brady Street
Montague St.
Johnson St.
NORMANBY RD.
Gladstone St.
Haig St.
CLARENDON ST.
Market St.
York St.
Munro St.
Fennell St.
Plummer Street
Beserve
WILLIAMSTOWN RD.
Bridge St.
Nth. Port
Buckhurst St.
Coventry St.
Dorcas St.
Cecil St.
Sth. Melbourne
FERRARS ST.
KINGS WAY
Park St.
Bank St.
Napier St.
Moray St.
Melbourne
QUEENS RD.
GRAHAM ST.
Ross St.
Evans St.
Clark St.
Station St.
Farrell St.
BAY ST.
Nott St.
Stokes St.
Princes St.
Liardet St.
St. Vincent Pl.
Nelson Rd.
Bridport St.
Albert Park
ALBERT RD.
ALBERT PARK LAKE
ALBERT
Lakeside Dr.
Public Golf Course
BEACH ST.
STATION PIER
Port Melbourne
Rouse St.
Dow St.
Esplanade East
Pickles St.
Richardson St.
Foote St.
Victoria Ave.
Dundas Pl.
O'Grady Street
Finlay Street
CANTERBURY RD.
Ovals
ALBERT PARK
3 Par Golf Course
Aughtie Drive
Res.

MELBOURNE CITY OUTLETS

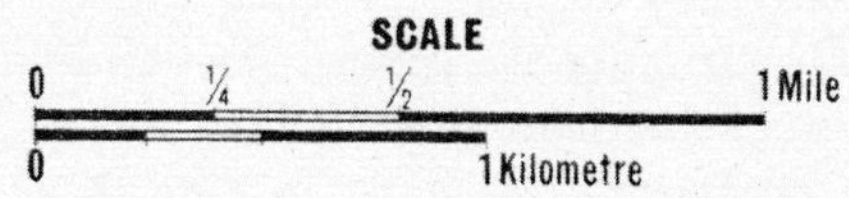

GUIDE TO SYMBOLS

Car Parks (covered)	□
Churches	+
General Features	■
Hospitals	+
Sporting Facilities	●
Motels (not indexed)	●

	No.	Feature	Ref.
●	*90*	Albert Cricket Ground	Z5
+	*92*	Alfred Hospital	Z6
■	*39*	A.M.P. & Car Park	V3
■	*12*	Ansett Terminal	U3
●	*43*	Australia Hotel	V4
●	*88*	Badminton Centre	Y5
●	*87*	Basket Ball Centre	Y5
□	*38*	Baulds Car Park	W3
●	*71*	Beaurepaire Baths	W4
■	*40*	B.H.P.House	V3
■	*67*	Capt. Cook's Cottage	V5
●	*91*	Chevron Hotel	Z5
●	*13*	City Baths	U3
□	*31*	City Car Park	V3
■	*62*	City Square	V4
□	*23*	Cobb & Co. Car Park	V3
●	*3*	Collingwood F'ball Grd.	S6
■	*16*	Commonwealth Offices	U4
■	*64*	C.R.A. Building	V4
+	*7*	Dental Hospital	T3
□	*24*	Downtown Car Park	V3
■	*18*	Eastern Hill Fire Stn.	U4
■	*9*	Exhibition Buildings	U4
+	*19*	Eye & Ear Hospital	U5
■	*54*	Federal Hotel	W3
■	*21*	Festival Hall	V2
■	*69*	Flinders St. Rly. Stn.	W4
□	*75*	Gallery Car Park	W4
■	*32*	General Post Office	V3
□	*33*	Golden Square Car Pk.	V4
■	*80*	Government House	X5
□	*45*	Grand Central Car Pk.	V4
■	*68*	Heliport	W3
■	*81*	H.S.V. 7 T.V. Station	X4
□	*49*	Kings Parkade	V4
□	*22*	La Trobe-a'Beckett C. Pk.	V3
■	*29*	Law Courts	V3
□	*27*	Lonsdale 565 Car Pk.	V3
□	*28*	Marland House Car Pk.	V3
■	*20*	Masonic Centre	U5
●	*72*	Melb. Cricket Ground	W5
■	*44*	Melb. Town Hall	V4
□	*48*	Mid City Car Park	V4
■	*2*	Motor Registration Br.	S4
■	*25*	Museum & Pub. Library	U4
■	*76*	Myer Music Bowl	W5
□	*60*	Nat. Mut. Car Park	W3
■	*60*	Nat. Mutual Centre	W3
●	*4*	Nth. Melb. Cricket Grd.	T1
●	*77*	Olympic Pool	W5
□	*35*	Palladium Car Park	V4
■	*51*	Parliament House	V4
■	*15*	Police Headquarters	U4
●	*83*	Port Melb. Cricket Grd.	Y2
+	*78*	Prince Henrys Hosp.	X4
■	*70*	Princes Bdge. Rly. Stn.	V4
■	*70*	Princes Gate Bldg.	V4
□	*70*	Princes Gate Car Pk.	V4
+	*26*	Queen Victoria Hosp.	V4
■	*41*	R.A.C.V. Building	V3
●	*73*	Richmond Cricket Grd.	W6
●	*74*	Rowing Sheds	W4
+	*5*	Royal Childrens Hosp.	T2
+	*6*	Royal Melb. Hosp.	T2
■	*14*	Royal Melb. Inst. Tech.	U3
+	*8*	Royal Womens Hosp.	T3
●	*37*	Savoy Plaza Hotel	W3
+	*46*	Scots Church	V4
■	*55*	S.E.C. Building	W3
□	*65*	Southern Car Park	V4
■	*82*	Shrine of Remembrance	X5
□	*47*	Southern Cross Car Pk.	V4
■	*47*	Southern Cross Hotel	V4
●	*85*	Sth. Melb. Cricket Grd.	Z4
■	*84*	Sth. Melb. Market	Y3
■	*36*	Spencer St. Rly. Stn.	W3
●	*86*	Squash Centre	Y4
■	*53*	State Gov't. Offices	V5
■	*61*	Stock Exchange House	V3
+	*52*	St. Patricks Cathedral	U5
+	*63*	St. Pauls Cathedral	V4
+	*17*	St. Vincents Hosp.	U4
■	*11*	T.A.A. Terminal	U3
●	*89*	Table Tennis Centre	Y5
□	*34*	Total Car Park	V4
■	*1*	Transport Reg. Board	S4
■	*66*	Treasury Gardens	V5
■	*79*	Victoria Barracks	X4
■	*10*	Victoria Market	U3
■	*75*	Vic. Arts Centre	W4
■	*42*	Vic. Govt. Tour. Bureau	V4
■	*50*	Windsor Hotel	V4

October or early November. It should be emphasized, however, that this weather does not conform to European or North American standards. A freeze at sea level is unheard of. Discomfort is caused by the instability of the climate rather than by its extremes.

Overseas visitors—particularly Americans—should be warned that air-conditioning or even central heating is a refinement of modern living which has reached Australian cities only in recent years. It will be found only in the better-class hotels and motels and in modern office blocks, shops and theatres.

Autumn is the season in which Melbourne's weather is most pleasant and reliable.

While it is true that Melbourne has a good deal to offer its citizens and visitors in the way of sophisticated pleasures, its social character is somewhat conservative. Its night life is remarkably subdued. There are relatively few places of entertainment which could be classed as night-clubs. On the other hand Melburnians are keenly appreciative of good music and ballet and performances by overseas and visiting artists are eagerly patronized. The Melbourne Symphony Orchestra, usually conducted by virtuosi of world repute in the Town Hall auditorium, is first class. The standard of choral music also is high. Art exhibitions create lively interest and discussion, and the striking new Arts Centre of Victoria is a focal point for the State's artistic development which has endowed Melbourne with enviable cultural prestige. It houses probably the best collection of paintings, statuary and *objets d'arts* in the southern hemisphere.

The fashionable restaurants of the city and inner suburbs undoubtedly provide the best-cooked food to be found in Australia. The gourmet from overseas will probably be pleasantly surprised by the variety of fare he can obtain, the excellence of its basic quality, and the modest size of his bill. But he will not yet be able to discover the culinary refinements expected in a first class restaurant on the Continent.

There are two periods of carnival in the Melbourne calendar during which the somewhat staid city becomes gay—Cup Week in late October-early November and the Moomba Festival in March. The Melbourne Cup horse race, run on the first Tuesday in November every year, is recognized internationally as a turf classic. It is the highlight of a spring racing carnival which regularly attracts thousands of racing enthusiasts from all parts of Australasia. The city's hotels and restaurants and places of entertainment are crowded and animated.

Moomba is an occasion of somewhat different flavour—a festival of street processions, sports contests, fireworks displays, beauty queen contests and other popular diversions into which a mild 'cultural' flavour has been injected with popular concerts, open-air art shows and literary competitions. Moomba, said to be an aboriginal word signifying 'let's get together and have fun', has been part of Melbourne life for some years but has yet to develop indigenous character and spontaneity.

A third gala occasion is the Royal Melbourne Show in September when the finest livestock in the State is on display and exhibits, ring events and sideshows draw huge crowds to the Agricultural Showgrounds in Ascot Vale. Judged on attendance figures, the Melbourne Show ranks among the biggest in the world although far surpassed by the enormous Royal Sydney Show at Easter.

Overseas visitors interested in spectator sports will, if they are in Melbourne during the winter months, no doubt wish to see a game of Australian Rules Football—a fast, open, strenuous game for big men to which people of the southern States are fanatically devoted. The vast amphitheatre of Melbourne Cricket Ground, main arena of the 1956 Olympic Games and regularly the scene of Test cricket as well as interstate matches for the Sheffield Shield, provides the right atmosphere for a clash between good teams.

World-class tennis may be watched at the Kooyong courts of the Victorian Lawn Tennis Association when major tournaments are in progress, and Australia's finest swimmers compete at championships in the Olympic Swimming Stadium, not far from the centre of the city.

COMMERCE AND INDUSTRY Four fifths of the manufacturing capacity of the State of Victoria is concentrated within the Melbourne metropolitan area.

The city is generally regarded as the financial capital of the Commonwealth. Its Stock Exchange lists more than 3 000 securities with a nominal value of well over $A12 000 million. Trading can be watched from a visitors' gallery. Headquarters of the Commonwealth's largest industrial and mining combines —giants such as the Broken Hill Proprietary Company and Conzinc Riotinto of Australia—are located in the city.

Major industries are heavy engineering, automobile and agricultural machinery manufacture, industrial chemicals, textiles, clothing and petroleum products.

Melbourne has never noticeably assumed the character of a maritime city, but its port is of enormous economic importance. In an average year the 107 berths provided in Hobson's Bay and within the Yarra River accommodate nearly 13 million tonnes of shipping which discharge about 7 500 000 tonnes of cargo and load about three million tonnes. The port is undergoing continual alteration to deal with containerized cargo.

The city's new Tullamarine airport receives or dispatches more than two million passengers a year, about 50 000 of whom are overseas arrivals or departures.

HISTORY The history of Melbourne is inseparable from the history of the settlement and development of the State as a whole. Readers interested in the events which led to the foundation of the city may care to refer to the brief entry covering the history of Victoria.

The first permanent settlement on the Yarra was established in 1836 by rival landseekers John Batman and John Pascoe Fawkner. It was variously known as Port Phillip, Bearbrass and Doutigalla, until the Governor of New South Wales, Sir Richard Bourke, approved its town plan in 1837 and named it in honour of the British Prıme Minister, Lord Melbourne, who had succeeded to the title his father had choosen from the small town of Melbourne in Derbyshire.

Melbourne was incorporated as a town in 1842, two years after its residents first petitioned for the separation of the Port Phillip District from New South Wales.

The population was suddenly and greatly increased by the discovery of gold in the hills about 12 kilometres inland in 1851. Two years later the University of Melbourne was founded. In 1854, Australia's first railway linked the town with Sandridge, now Port Melbourne.

The 1860s and 1870s were an era of rapid industrial expansion and Melbourne began to establish itself as a manufacturing town.

An extraordinary rate of growth was also achieved in the early years of the 20th centry after recovery from the economic depression of the 1890s, but it was not until 1933 that Melbourne's population passed the one million mark. From Federation in 1901 until the establishment of a national capital at Canberra in 1927, Melbourne was the seat of Federal Government.

Parks and Gardens

Royal Botanic Gardens and National Herbarium (off St Kilda Road). Forty three hectares of plantations, flower beds, lawns and ornamental lakes so superbly landscaped, developed and tended that they are regarded by many experts to be the equal of any similar reserve in the world. The site was selected by the Honourable Charles Joseph La Trobe in 1845. Its original development was carried out by John Arthur and his successor, John Dullachy, and it was further developed and expanded by Dr Ferdinand Mueller (later Baron Sir Ferdinand Von Mueller) who was appointed Government Botanist in 1852. He was succeeded by W. R. Guilfoyle, a landscape artist who further remodelled and expanded the gardens. A plaque on an ancient gum tree beside Lake Walk commemorates the separation of Victoria from New South Wales. The national herbarium is in the south-west corner of the reserve and is of great interest to botanists. An enormous variety of tropical, sub-tropical and temperate zone flora has been successfully cultivated. Open daily.

The gardens of Government House (about 25 hectares) are adjoining. Inspection is not permitted.

King's Domain, St Kilda Road. Comprises 43 hectares of tree-shaded lawns and contains the impressive **Shrine of Remembrance, Pioneer Womens' Memorial Gardens** (Alexandra Avenue), old **Observatory, La Trobe's Cottage** (first Government House), **Sidney Myer Music Bowl,** an unconventional aluminium and steel structure housing sound-shell, stage etc. Between 60 000 and 70 000 people can be accommodated on the lawns.

Alexandra and Queen Victoria Gardens, adjacent to Domain, 130 hectares of parkland.

Flagstaff Gardens, William Street, West Melbourne. Originally known as Burial Hill. The city's first public gardens, developed after 1840 when the cemetery was closed. A monument bears a plaque describing how the site was used as a signalling station to inform settlers of the arrival and departure of ships at Williamstown.

Treasury and Fitzroy Gardens (separated by Lansdowne Street). Near centre of city and State Government offices. Fitzroy Gardens contain a **cottage** which was associated with Captain James Cook in the village of Great Ayton, Yorkshire. It was transported from England and re-erected in 1934. The cost of operation was borne by a private citizen, the late Sir Russell Grimwade, to commemorate the city's centenary. Ivy on the walls was grown from an original slip taken at Great Ayton. Otherwise the cottage has been given sadly unimaginative treatment. Also in the gardens is a model **Tudor village** with cottages of doll's house size which is laid out near an **ancient tree trunk** carved in tiny fantasy creatures by the Australian sculptress, the late Ola Cohn.

Exhibition Gardens, Carlton. Twenty four hectares of lawns and flowers containing an insubstantial but impressive building with dome erected for the Great Exhibition of 1880. The building was for 27 years the meeting place of the Federal Parliament until the opening of Parliament House, Canberra. The grounds contain fountains, an ornamental lake and statuary of varying merit.

Melbourne Cricket Ground, Olympic Park and **Victoria Park,** sports arenas where the 1956 Olympic Games were held. The MCG has been established for more than 100 years as a venue for Test cricket, football etc. The stands now accommodate more than 120 000 people. Close by is the Olympic swimming pool (specially designed and built for 1956 Games), velodrome, soccer field and athletics arena etc.

Royal Park, north of city and west of Royal Parade, includes **Zoological Gardens** (20 hectares) and playing fields. The zoo is recently improved and contains a good section devoted to native animals. Children's entertainment includes pony and miniature train rides, merry-go-round, etc (Open 9.30 am-5 pm). Royal Park was point of departure for Burke and Wills expedition in 1860; a cairn off The Avenue marks the spot.

Albert Park and Lake (golf course, indoor sports centre, sailing etc), off St Kilda Road.

Galleries, Libraries, Museums

Arts Centre of Victoria, St Kilda Road, South Melbourne. Melbourne's cultural life achieved an exciting new dimension in August 1968 when the $14 million first stage of the Victorian Arts Centre was opened just south of the Yarra River. The air conditioned building is a huge rectangle of bluestone and concrete fronted by a moat and designed round the Oriental, Sculpture and Australian courtyards, open to the sky. The Australian courtyard, venue for all kinds of artistic, commercial and industrial shows before an audience in tiered balconies, is an extension of the spell-binding Great Hall which is roofed by the largest stained glass ceiling in the world. The radiant kaleidoscope, 50 by 15 metres, was made by Melbourne artist Leonard French, who spent five years fashioning it from inch-thick slabs of imported glass. A unique feature of the building is the storage study galleries enabling the visitor to view on demand every painting that is not on show. Also remarkable is the even distribution of light at all times which architect Roy Grounds has contrived by use of ingenious design and modern materials. To minimize 'gallery fatigue' he planned frequent changes of floor treatment, from carpet to terracotta tiles or hardwood parquetry, and comfortable lounge areas with chairs and small tables where tea and coffee can be served from the gallery restaurant. Under the gallery is an enormous car park, entered from Sturt Street. When completed the Arts Centre will cover 3 hectares including parklands and pools. The second stage, at the north end, will be a conical building surmounted by a soaring copper spire, 126 hectares high and gilded at its top. It will house auditoria for music and drama, a post-graduate art school, restaurant-cafetaria and administrative offices. The complex is still incomplete, but already the Gallery section is a mecca of international repute for visitors. Open Tuesday, 10 am to 5 pm; Wednesday, 10 am to 9 pm; Thursday to Sunday 10 am to 5 pm.

State Library, Swanston Street, contains more than 800 000 volumes and manuscripts. It includes **La Trobe Library** with state archives and a notable collection of Australiana. The reading room dome is a landmark of Melbourne. Open Monday to Friday, 10 am to 10 pm; Saturday, 10 am to 5 pm; Sunday, 2 am to 10 pm.

National Museum and **Institute of Applied Science,** Swanston Street. The former contains a fine selection on abóriginal and Pacific Island artifacts etc and fascinating exhibits devoted to mineralogy, crystalography and conchology. Good dioramas. The Institute houses a **planetarium** (afternoon and evening sessions. Phone 663 4815 for details) Open Monday to Saturday, 10 am to 5 pm; Sunday, 2 pm to 10 pm.

Victorian Artists' Society Galleries, Albert Street, East Melbourne (exhibitions not continuous).

A number of private art galleries displaying the work of contemporary artists is located in the city and suburbs.

Historical Museum, corner of Electra Street and Melbourne Road, Williamstown.

Railway Museum, Champion Road, Newport.

Notable Cathedrals, Churches

St Paul's Anglican Cathedral, Swanston and Flinders Streets. Built in 1880-91, of Melbourne bluestone and Pyrmont (Sydney) sandstone. Impressive interior. Peal of 13 bells in belfry.

St Patrick's Roman Catholic Cathedral. Regarded as one of the finest examples of 19th century Gothic revival architecture. Building started in 1863, but spires and west portal not added until 1939. Design, William Wardell.

St James Old Cathedral, Batman and King Streets. Oldest church in metropolitan area. Built 1839-51. Removed from original site and re-erected 1913-14. Architect Robert Russell.

Church of St Francis, Elizabeth and Lonsdale Streets. Built 1841. Earliest Melbourne example of Gothic revival architecture. Architect, Samuel Jackson.

Independent Church, (Congregational) Collins and Russell Streets, Romanesque style. Built 1867. Architect, Joseph Reed.

Wesley Church (Methodist) Lonsdale Street. Built during the 1850s in style of Gothic revival. Architect, Joseph Reed. Excellent statue of John Wesley at entrance.

St Peter's Anglican Church, Gisborne Street. Built 1846-50 of bricks imported from England, on bluestone footing. Architect, Charles Laing.

Scots Church, Collins and Russell Streets. Ornate Victorian Gothic. Architect James Webb, who adapted an earlier design by Samuel Jackson in 1842.

Baptist Church, Collins Street. Built 1845-61 on unusual classical design by various architects. Impressive portico designed by Joseph Reed.

Some Historic Buildings

Old Melbourne Gaol, Franklin Street. Built of bluestone and Tasmanian freestone 1841-45. Originally housed 600 prisoners, but only one wing and the entrance still stand. Recently carefully restored and furnished as a **penal museum** with relics and death mask of notorious bushranger Ned Kelly who was executed there. Open daily 10 am to 5 pm.

Exhibition Buildings, Nicholson Street, Carlton. Built for the International Exhibition of 1880 at a cost of £2 460 000. Still used for trade displays, etc. Beautiful garden setting. State Parliament met here between 1901 and 1927 when Federal Government was based on Melbourne. Note Royal Terrace (1854) opposite in Nicholson Street.

Public Library of Victoria Built 1854-1911. (See above.)

State Parliament House, Spring Street. Built in neo-classical style, of stone quarried in the Grampian Ranges, between 1856 and 1892. Designs by Peter Kerr and J. C. Knight.

Law Courts and Supreme Court Library, William Street. Plans for both buildings were based on the design of the Four Courts, Dublin. In the Renaissance style. Construction took from 1874 to 1885. Note: Library is not open to the public. It is used exclusively by members of the legal profession who are levied for its upkeep.

Former Royal Mint, William Street. The building is regarded as an architectural gem in the neo-classical style. Design by draughtsmen of the Public Works Department. Built *circa* 1868.

La Trobe's Cottage, King's Domain (see above). Brought from England in pre-fabricated sections by the first Lieutenant Governor of Victoria, Charles La Trobe, when he arrived in 1839. It was erected in Jolimont, fell into disrepair after La Trobe's departure, and was extensively restored and re-erected on its present site in 1964.

'Como', Como Avenue, South Yarra, is the headquarters of the National Trust of Victoria. It was built in stages between the late 1840s and 1859, and has been restored, furnished and equipped authentically. Open daily from 10 am to 5 pm.

Out of Town

Emu Bottom, Racecourse Road, Sunbury. Victoria's oldest homestead, built by a pioneer settler in 1836, restored and furnished with period pieces. Open Tuesday to Sunday, 10 am to 5 pm.

Schwerkolt Cottage, Deep Creek Road, Mitcham. Early settler's cottage (1860) restored by Nunawading Shire Council. Open daily 2 pm to 5 pm.

Henty Cottage, Ridge Road, Olinda. Built by pioneer Edward Henty in late 1850s. Open daily 9 am to 5 pm.

Of General Interest

Shrine of Remembrance (National War Memorial). Impressive pyramidal mausoleum (completed 1934) on a commanding site in King's Domain and in beautifully landscaped surroundings. It is the focus of numerous pilgrimages and ceremonial parades. The top galleries of the Shrine offer fine panoramic views of the city and its major parklands. Open weekdays, 10 am to 5 pm; Sundays, 2 pm to 5 pm.

Lookout, observation deck, **National Mutual Centre,** Collins Street. Open to public weekdays. Observation deck **I.C.I. Building,** Nicholson Street. Conducted tours Monday to Friday at 2.15 pm. (Ring 662 0201 for appointment.)

Airport and Astrojet Space Centre, Tullamarine.

Moorabbin Air Museum, Moorabbin Airport, Cheltenham. Displays of aircraft from first and second world wars. Open Saturday, Sunday and public holidays, 1 pm to 5 pm.

Luna Park, Lower Esplanade, St Kilda. Fun fair open from 7.30 pm on Thursdays, and Fridays; and from 2.15 pm on Saturday and Sunday. Closed in winter.

Southgate Fountain, south side of Princes Bridge.

Sports

Horse Racing, Flemington, Caulfield, Moonee Valley and Sandown Park courses.

Night Trotting (in season), Royal Agricultural Society Showgrounds, Ascot Vale.

Track Cycling, Velodrome, Batman Avenue, Brunswick Velodrome.

Dog Racing, Olympic Park and Sandown Park.

Motor Racing, Sandown Park, Calder Motor Raceway.

Cricket and Australian Rules Football, VFL Park Mulgrave. MCG and suburban sports grounds.

Soccer, Victoria Park, Royal Park, Albert Park.

Swimming, City Baths, Swanston Street; YMCA, City Road, South Melbourne; Swimming Stadium at Olympic Park. Most suburbs have a municipal pool.

Skating, St Moritz Glaciarium, Upper Esplanade, St Kilda; Iceland, Ringwood; Olympic, Oakleigh.

Boxing and Wrestling, Festival Hall, West Melbourne.

Golf. There are twenty four public courses in the metropolitan area. The most central are at Yarra Bend (Kew and Fairfield) and at Albert Park.

Tennis. Among numerous public courts, the most central are at Albert Park and Kooyong.

Squash, Badminton, Table Tennis, Basketball at Albert Park sports centres.

Entertainment

Theatres. Her Majesty's, Exhibition Street; **Comedy,** Exhibition Street; **Princess,** Spring Street; **St Martin's,** South Yarra; **Melbourne Theatre Company,** Russell Street; **Playbox,** Exhibition Street. Live shows are occassionally produced at the **Palais Theatre,** Esplanade, St Kilda, and at **Festival Hall,** West Melbourne.

Concerts. Major orchestrial concerts are usually given in the **Melbourne Town Hall** auditorium, Swanston Street, at **Dallas Brooks Hall,** East Melbourne, and at the **Myer Music Bowl,** King's Domain.

City Cinemas. Albany, 230 Collins Street; Athenaeum, 188 Collins Street; Australia Nos 1 and 2, 270 Collins Street; Barclay, 131 Russell Street; Bercy, 128 Bourke Street; Bryson, 184 Exhibition Street; Capitol, 113 Swanston Street; Chelsea, 178 Flinders Street; Cinema Centre, Nos 1, 2, 3, 140 Bourke Street; Nos 4 and 5, 200 Bourke Street; Dendy, off 241 Collins Street; East End, Nos 1, 2, 3, 100 Bourke Street; Esquire, 238 Bourke Street; Forum, 154 Flinders Street; Metro, 20 Bourke Street; Metro Collins, 167 Collins Street; Odeon, 283 Bourke Street; Rapallo, 11 Russell Street; Roma, 225 Bourke Street.

Restaurants

Recommended: **Argonaut** (converted sailing ship, Bay cruises some nights in season), No 3 South Wharf, South Melbourne; Geoff Brooke's **Steak Cave,** 7 Queen Street; **Fanny's** Garibaldi Room (de luxe cuisine) 243 Lonsdale Street; **Florentino,** 80 Bourke Street; **Mayfair Room,** Southern Cross Hotel, Exhibition Street; **Maxim's,** 100 Bourke Street; **Pickwick,** South Yarra; **Pamplemousse,** 20th floor, 447 Collins Street; **The Distillery,** Chevron Hotel, 519 St Kilda Road; **Le Chateau,** Queens Road; **Oriental Gourmet,** 112 Little Bourke Street.

Cabarets (open to 3 am) **Taboo,** St Kilda; **Los Gitanos,** South Yarra; **Top Hat,** City; **Troika,** Hampton.

Accommodation

First class city hotels include: **Australia,** 226 Collins Street; **Chevron,** 519 St Kilda Road; **Graham,** 67 Swanston Street; **Noah's Melbourne Hotel,** Cnr Exhibition and Little Bourke Streets; **Victoria,** 215 Little Collins Street; **Windsor,** 103 Spring Street.

First class motels in or near city: **Commodore Chateau,** 131 Lonsdale Street; **Commodore Downtowner,** Lygon and Queensberry Streets, Carlton; **Commodore,** 4 Queens Road; **John Batman Travelodge,** 59 Queens Road; **Lygon Lodge,** 204 Lygon Street, Carlton; **Marco Polo,** Harker Street and Flemington Road, North Melbourne; **Melbourne Town House,** 701 Swanston Street, Carlton; **Parkville Motor Inn,** 443 Royal Parade, Parkville; **Parkville Motel,** 68 Park Street Brunswick; **President Motor Inn,** 63 Queens Road; **Sheraton Motor Hotel,** 13 Spring Street; **St Kilda Travelodge,** Albert Park Road and Park Street.

Main Department Stores, City

Myer Emporium (Melbourne), Bourke Street; **Ball and Welch,** Flinders Street; **Buckley and Nunn,** Bourke Street; **Big W,** Bourke Street; **Georges,** Collins Street; **Walton's,** Bourke Street.

Transport

Rail. Electric train services to major suburbs from **Flinders Street** and **Princes Bridge Stations. Interstate** and most **country** trains from **Spencer Street Station.**

Trams and/or buses to all suburbs: north and south via Swanston Street; east and west, Flinders, Collins and Bourke Streets and Batman Avenue.

Interstate and country air services from Tullamarine Airport (22 kilometres). **Moorabbin Airport** accommodates private and charter aircraft (17 kilometres from city). Air charters available from both airports.

Sea. Large overseas liners usually berth at **Princes Pier,** Port Melbourne (five kilometres); smaller vessels at North Wharf, South Wharf or Victoria Dock, near city.

Road-coach services and tours. Inquire at the Tourist Bureau or any travel agent.

All registered **taxis** have meters and tariff rates are clearly displayed in each car. Numerous **car rental** and **hire car** firms operate.

Excellent tours of Melbourne and environs—covering major points of scenic, historical or industrial interest—are conducted by tourist coach charter companies. The Victorian Government Tourist Bureau will advise. Trips to the Dandenong Ranges, Healesville and the Upper Yarra district and to the south-western coastal resorts and the Otway Ranges can be recommended to both Australian and overseas visitors interested in general sightseeing. Port Phillip and Westernport Bay resorts and beaches will appeal to those interested in aquatic sports, but the area is not on the whole as interesting as most sections of coast in southern Australia. Surf beaches fronting Bass Strait are often excellent for board riding but not as scenically attractive as those in New South Wales, Queensland and Western Australia.

Business Hours

Banks open 9.30 am to 3 pm Monday to Thursday, and 9.30 to 5 pm Friday. Banks do not open on Saturday. **Shopping** hours, 9.00 am to 5.30 pm Monday to Thursday; to 9 pm on Fridays. 9.00 am to 12 noon Saturdays. Hotel bars close 10.00 pm.

Public Holidays. New Year's Day, 1 January; Australia Day, 26 January; Labour Day and Moomba procession, March, as decreed; Easter, Good Friday, Easter Sunday, Monday and following Tuesday; Anzac Day, 25 April; Queen's Birthday, June, as decreed; Royal Show Day, September, on Thursday, as decreed; Melbourne Cup Day, first Tuesday in November; Christmas Day, 25 December; Boxing Day, 26 December.

Miscellaneous

Information: Victorian Tourist Bureau, 272 Collins Street; **Royal Automobile Club of Victoria,** Queen Street (excellent information and map service).

Emergency Telephone Calls (police, ambulance, fire etc). Dial 000.

MELBOURNE'S ENVIRONS

MORNINGTON PENINSULA

The Mornington Peninsula is a boot-shaped promontory of about 39 000 hectares which separates Port Phillip from Westernport Bay. Its townships are now virtually outer suburbs of Melbourne, but much of its inland area retains a rural character and is used for pasturage and mixed farming. It was named after Mornington, Ireland. The countryside is picturesque and the climate milder than that of Melbourne. It is regarded as Melbourne's summer playground and is always crowded with holidaymakers at Christmas, Easter and long weekends. Suburban strip development on the western coast of the peninsula is now almost continuous from Melbourne to Port Phillip Heads.

The chief towns are:

FRANKSTON, MOUNT ELIZA

(Population 59 410)

Forty-two kilometres south of Melbourne. Miscellaneous light industries; silica, lime, brickworks and timber mills. Residential area for Melbourne commuters. Facilities for tennis, bowls, croquet and squash. Four golf courses. Rifle and yacht clubs.

Accommodation. Three **hotels.** Recommended: Vine's Frankston, Nepean Highway. One **motel.** Five **guest-houses. Caravan and camping park,** all facilities.

Transport. Electric train from Melbourne (passenger railhead). **Bus** and **coach** services to other peninsula towns.

MORNINGTON

(Population 14 289)

Fifty-five kilometres south of Melbourne. Light industries. Bay beaches. Racecourse, riding and usual sports facilities. Good yacht harbour.

Accommodation. One **hotel.** Three **motels.** Recommended: Ranch, Nepean Highway. **Camping and caravan park,** all facilities.

Transport. Co-ordinated **rail-road** from Melbourne. Road to other peninsula towns.

MOUNT MARTHA About 6 kilometres past Frankston. Good views of bay, pleasant beaches. Golf course, tennis courts.

Accommodation. One **hotel.** One **motel. Caravan and camping park,** all facilities.

Transport. Rail-road.

DROMANA At the foot of Arthur's Seat, a high feature (835 metres) commanding panoramic views of Port Phillip and Westernport. Chair lift operates throughout the year. Memorial to Matthew Flinders at summit. Restaurant. Also of interest is King's Falls national park. On foreshores, good beaches and picnic grounds. Usual sports facilities. Riding. Water ski club. Boat ramp.

Accommodation. One **hotel.** One recommended **motel. Flats** and **lodges** available. Eight **caravan and/or camping parks.** Applications for sites on council's foreshore reserve must be **mailed.**

Transport. Rail-road.

ROSEBUD Well developed bayside resort. Aquarium and marine museum. Usual sports. Golf club. Riding. Swimming pool. Name believed to have derived from *The Rosewood*, a Greek vessel wrecked off the coast in the 19th century. Day tours of peninsula available.

Accommodation. One **hotel.** Two **motels.** Recommended: Rosebud, Nepean Highway. Many **flats, cottages** and **lodges** available.

Transport. Rail-road.

SORRENTO Closely associated with early history of Victoria. Site of temporary settlement in October 1803, when Collins landed with 50 marines, 31 civilians, 299 convicts and 71 wives and children. Memorial and graves on site. Interesting examples of early building in limestone. There is a good aquarium. Usual sports facilities and first class golf course. Riding. Swimming and water sports on bay beach, surfing and surfboard riding on Back Beach, fronting Bass Strait. During the season a ferry operates between Sorrento pier and Queenscliff on the other side of the bay.

Accommodation. Three **hotels.** Recommended: Koonya, Nepean Highway. Many **holiday flats** available. Seven **caravan and camping grounds,** all facilities.

Transport. Road-rail.

PORTSEA Three kilometres west of Sorrento. Excellent, clean beaches. Chair-lift from sandhills to Back Beach where surfing is first class. Pleasant golf course. Panoramic views of Cape Schanck and coastline. Founded as a settlement for lime burners in 1842. Quarantine Station (now Army Officer Cadet School) was built in 1856 after 82 deaths from smallpox on vessel *Ticonderoga* anchored in Weeroona Bay. Visitors should make a point of seeing London Arch, an impressive rock formation near Back Beach, where the ship *Sierra Nevada* was wrecked in 1900 with loss of 23 lives.

Accommodation. Two **hotels.** Recommended: Portsea. One **camping and caravan park,** all facilities.

Transport. Rail-road.

FLINDERS On south coast of peninsula, 89 kilometres from Melbourne. Good surfing, swimming and fishing. Excellent golf course. Places of interest include Cape Schanck Lighthouse, the Blowhole, and Elephant Rock.

Accommodation. One **hotel.**

Transport. Rail-road services.

SHOREHAM Near popular surf beach at Point Leo, 80 kilometres from Melbourne, on Westernport Bay. Gemstones have been found in rocky outcrops along the shore.

Accommodation. Guest-houses. Camping ground.

SOMERS Quiet village with good beaches on Westernport Bay. Tennis and yacht clubs. Excellent fishing.

Camping ground only.

HASTINGS Fishing port, on Westernport Bay, 69 kilometres from Melbourne. Tennis, bowls and seawater swimming pool. Yacht club.

Accommodation. One **hotel. Camping ground.**

Transport. Rail-road.

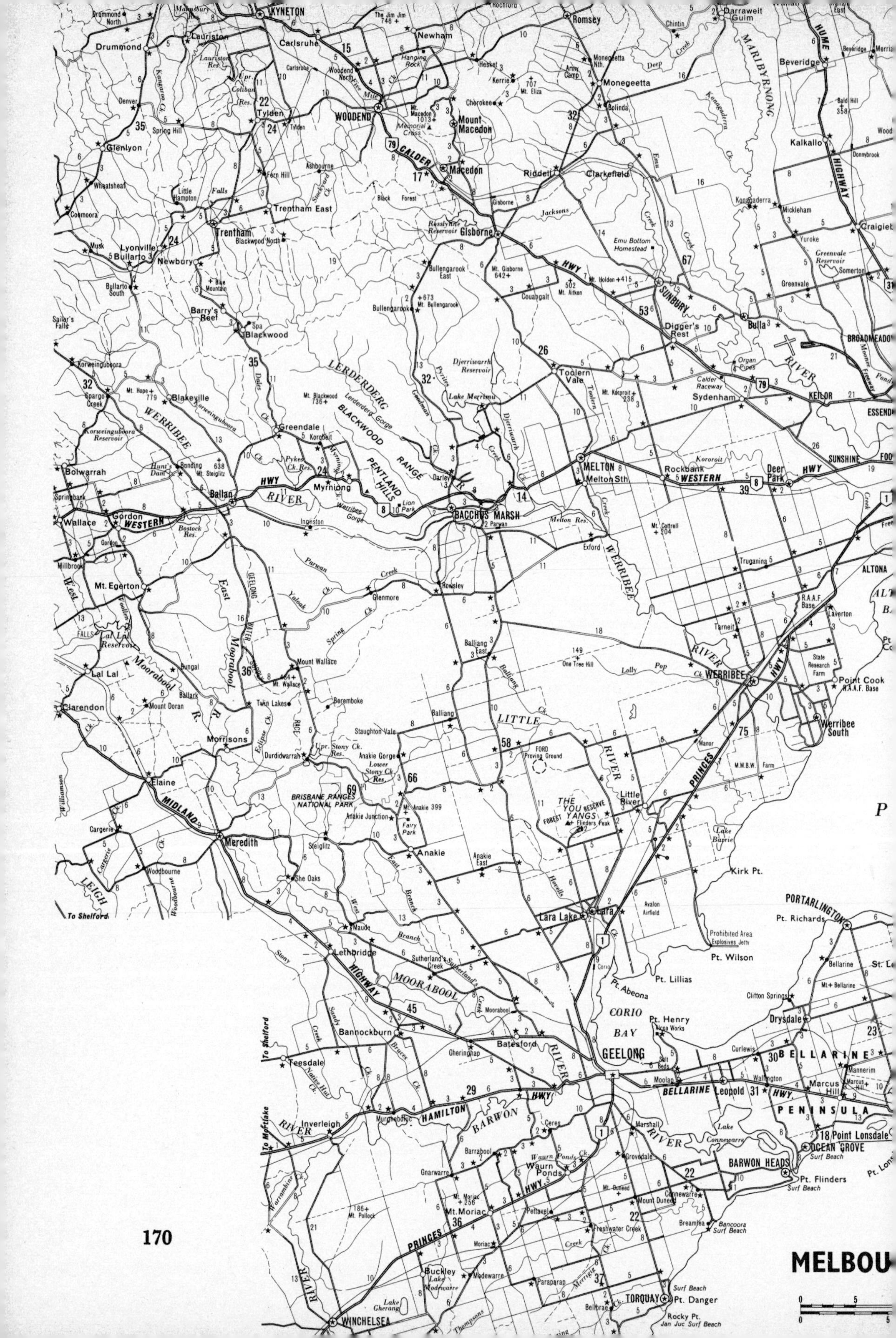
KYNETON
Romsey
Darraweit Guim
Drummond North
Malmsbury
Rochford
Drummond
Lauriston
Carlsruhe
Newham
The Jim Jim 746
Hanging Rock
Chintin
Lauriston Res.
Woodend North
Hesket
Monegeetta Nth.
Monegeetta
Army Camp
Kerrie
Mt. Eliza
MARIBYRNONG
HUME
HIGHWAY
Beveridge
Denver
Coliban Res.
Tylden
WOODEND
Mt. Macedon
Memorial Cross
Mount Macedon
Cherokee
Bolinda
Kalkallo
Donnybrook
Spring Hill
Glenlyon
CALDER
Macedon
Ashbourne
Riddell
Clarkefield
Wheatsheaf
Fern Hill
Little Hampton
Falls
Trentham East
Black Forest
Gisborne
Jacksons
Konagaderra
Mickleham
Coomoora
Trentham
Blackwood North
Rosslynne Reservoir
Gisborne
Emu Bottom Homestead
Yuroke
Craigieburn
Musk
Lyonville
Bullarto
Newbury
Bullengarook East
Mt. Gisborne 642
HWY
Mt. Holden 415
Greenvale Reservoir
Somerton
Bullarto South
Blue Mountain
Mt. Aitken
Coimadai
SUNBURY
Greenvale
Sailor's Falls
Barry's Reef
Bullengarook
Mt. Bullengarook
Digger's Rest
Bulla
Spa
Blackwood
BROADMEADOWS
Korweinguboora
LERDERDERG
Djerriwarrh Reservoir
Toolern Vale
Organ Pipes
RIVER
Spargo Creek
Mt. Hope 779
Blakeville
Lake Merrimu
Mt. Kororoit 238
Calder Raceway
Sydenham
KEILOR
ESSENDON
Mt. Blackwood 736
Lerderderg Gorge
BLACKWOOD
RANGE
WERRIBEE
Korweinguboora Reservoir
Greendale
Korobeit
PENTLAND HILLS
Pykes Ck. Res.
Bunding
Hunt's Dam
Mt. Steiglitz 638
MELTON
Melton Sth
Rockbank
WESTERN
Kororoit
Deer Park
HWY
SUNSHINE
Bolwarrah
Myrniong
Darley
Ballan
RIVER
Springbank
Gordon
WESTERN
Lion Park
Werribee Gorge
BACCHUS MARSH
Parwan
Melton Res.
Wallace
Ingliston
Bostock Res.
Gordon
Mt. Cottrell 204
Exford
Millbrook
Truganina
ALTONA
Parwan Creek
Mt. Egerton
GEELONG
WATER
SUPPLY
East
Moorabool
Yaloak Ck.
Glenmore
Rowsley
Lal Lal Reservoir
Spring Ck.
Balliang East
18
R.A.A.F. Base
Laverton
Tarneit
Bungal
One Tree Hill
Lolly Pop Ck.
WERRIBEE
State Research Farm
Lal Lal
Mount Wallace
Mt. Wallace
Moorabool
Ballark
Point Cook
R.A.A.F. Base
Clarendon
Mount Doran
Twin Lakes
Beremboke
Balliang
LITTLE
Werribee South
Staughton Vale
Morrisons
Eclipse Ck.
Upr. Stony Ck. Res.
Durdidwarrah
Anakie Gorge
Lower Stony Ck. Res.
FORD Proving Ground
Manor
Elaine
M.M.B.W. Farm
BRISBANE RANGES NATIONAL PARK
Mt. Anakie 399
THE YOU YANGS
FOREST RESERVE
Flinders Peak
Little River
MIDLAND
Anakie Junction
Fairy Park
Cargerie
Meredith
Steiglitz
Anakie
Anakie East
Lake Borrie
Woodbourne
She Oaks
Kirk Pt.
LEIGH
To Shelford
Lara Lake
Lara
Avalon Airfield
PORTARLINGTON
Pt. Richards
Maude
Prohibited Area
Explosives Jetty
Pt. Wilson
Lethbridge
Sutherland's Creek
Corio
Pt. Lillias
Bellarine
HIGHWAY
MOORABOOL
Pt. Abeona
Mt. Bellarine
Clifton Springs
Moorabool
CORIO
Pt. Henry
Alcoa Works
Drysdale
To Shelford
Bannockburn
BAY
Gheringhap
Batesford
GEELONG
Curlewis
BELLARINE
Teesdale
Salt Beds
Mannerim
Moolap
BELLARINE
Leopold
HWY
Wallington
Marcus Hill
HAMILTON
HWY
PENINSULA
To Mortlake
RIVER
Inverleigh
Murgheboluc
BARWON
Ceres
Marshall
RIVER
Lake Connewarre
Point Lonsdale
OCEAN GROVE
Surf Beach
Barrabool
Waurn Ponds Ck.
Grovedale
BARWON HEADS
Gnarwarre
Waurn Ponds
Pt. Flinders
Surf Beach
Mt. Duneed
Mount Duneed
Connewarre
Mt. Moriac 256
HWY
Mt. Moriac
Pettavel
Mt. Pollock
Freshwater Creek
PRINCES
Breamlea
Bancoora Surf Beach
Moriac
170
MELBOU
Buckley
Lake Modewarre
Modewarre
Paraparap
Surf Beach
RIVER
Lake Gherang
TORQUAY
Pt. Danger
Bellbrae
Rocky Pt.
Jan Juc Surf Beach
WINCHELSEA
Thompsons
PRINCES

ENVIRONS
15
20 KILOMETRES
10
15 MILES
KINGLAKE
NATIONAL
PARK
Humevale
WHITTLESEA
Strathewen
Steel's Creek
Dixon's Creek
HEALESVILLE
Maroondah Reservoir
Mt. Juliet
Acheron Gap
Smith Hill
McMahon's Creek
O'Shannassy
Smoko Hill
Yan Yean Res.
Arthur's Creek
St. Andrews
Yarra Glen
HIGHWAY
Tarrawarra
Sanctuary
Panton Gap
Mt. Riddell
Mt. Donna Buang
Cement Creek
Turntable
WARBURTON
Warburton East
Big Pat's Creek
Mt. Toole-be-wong
Ben Cairn
Millgrove
Wesburn
Yan Yean
Doreen
Nutfield
Cottle's Bridge
Christmas Hills
Panton Hill
Yering
Gruyere
Mernda
HURSTBRIDGE
Yarrambat
Wattle Glen
PLENTY
MAROONDAH
Launching Place
Yarra Junction
Coldstream
Morang
Plenty
Diamond Ck.
Kangaroo Ground
WARBURTON
SEVILLE
Woori Yallock
Gladysdale
Powelltown
Three Bridges
Gilderoy
Hoddle's Creek
Mt. Thule
BLUE
RANGE
Mt. Beenak
LILYDALE
MOUNT EVELYN
ELTHAM
YARRA
RIVER
MOOROOLBARK
SILVAN
Silvan Res.
BUNYIP
Gentle Annie
Tomahawk Ck.
Shepherds
Nangana
TEMPLESTOWE
MAROONDAH
MONTROSE
Mt. Dandenong
Olinda
Monbulk
Macclesfield
Gilwell Park Scout Camp
HEIDELBERG
CROYDON
THE BASIN
DONCASTER
RINGWOOD
NORTHCOTE
Kallista
Gembrook
Tonimbuk
Mt. Tonimbuk
NUNAWADING
KEW
BOX HILL
BURWOOD
HWY
DANDENONG
BELGRAVE
Emerald
Cockatoo
UPR. FERNTREE GULLY
Mount Burnett
Cardinia Creek Reservoir
FITZROY
COLLINGWOOD
RICHMOND
HAWTHORN
CAMBERWELL
WAVERLEY
Dewhurst
Ararat
Pakenham Upper
Nar-Nar-Goon North
Maryknoll
Tynong Nth.
Lysterfield
Lysterfield Res.
PRAHRAN
MALVERN
CAULFIELD
SOUTH MELB.
PORT MELB.
HOBSONS BAY
ST. KILDA
Beaconsfield Upper
Narre Warren Nth.
Harkaway
SPRINGVALE
PRINCES
OAKLEIGH
PRINCES
HWY
Bunyip
Garfield
Tynong
Nar-Nar-Goon
Iona
Vervale
Hallam
BERWICK
Beaconsfield
Officer
Pakenham
Pakenham East
BRIGHTON
MOORABBIN
NEPEAN
DANDENONG
Narre Warren
SANDRINGHAM
Cora Lynn
MORDIALLOC
Cardinia
Pakenham South
Rythdale
Bayles
Koo-Wee-Rup North
Catani
Ricketts Pt.
CHELSEA
Patterson River
Eumemmerring Creek
CRANBOURNE
SOUTH
Clyde
Cardinia
Yallock
Yannathan
KOO-WEE-RUP
Monomeith
Devon Meadows
Five Ways
Tooradin
Dalmore
GIPPSLAND
Tooradin
Pelican Pt.
Lang Lang
LANG LANG
BASS
HWY
FRANKSTON
Pearcedale
Cannons Creek
Warneet
Quail Island
Adams Pt.
Watsons Inlet
Lang Lang Beach
G.M.H. Proving Ground
Davey Pt.
Mount Eliza
Baxter
Mt. Eliza
Somerville
Palmer Pt.
Stockyard Pt.
Sandy Pt. (Spit Pt.)
The Gurdies
Scrub Pt.
Blue Gum Pt.
PHILLIP
Schnapper Pt.
MORNINGTON
Tyabb
Mooroodue
River Pt.
Mt. Wellington
FRENCH
ISLAND
Penal Settlement
Freeman Pt.
Grantville
Long Island Pt.
HASTINGS
Sandstone Is.
Fairhaven
Tenby Pt.
Devilbend Res.
BAY
Mount Martha
Settlement Pt.
Corinella
Glen Forbes
Bittern
Crib Pt.
Crib Point
Stockyard Pt.
Red Bluff
Elizabeth Is.
Tankerton
Mt. Martha
MORNINGTON
Martha Pt.
Stony Pt.
Hanns Inlet
Long Pt.
Ram Is.
Tortoise Head
Peck Pt.
Cobb Bluff
BASS
Merricks North
Balnarring
Somers
Sandy Pt.
Reef Is.
Stony Pt.
Bass
Woolamai
Mud Islands
DROMANA
PENINSULA
Red Hill
WESTERN PORT BAY
Observation Pt.
Rhyll
Merricks
Cowes
Koala Sanctuaries
Church Hill Island
McCrae
Arthurs Seat
Red Hill Sth.
ROSEBUD
Point Leo
Pt. Leo
Newhaven
The Narrows
San Remo
Anderson
Kilcunda
PHILLIP ISLAND
Ventnor
Griffith Pt.
Davis Pt.
PORTSEA
SORRENTO
Blairgowrie
RYE
NEPEAN
Main Ridge
Shoreham
Woolamai Surf Beach
Mutton Birds
Red Pt.
Cape Woolamai
Boneo
Hyldberry Ck.
Flinders
West Head
CAT BAY
Penguin Parade
Pyramid Rock
Redcliff Head
The Nobbies
Grant Pt.
Seal Rocks
Cape Schanck
Cape Schanck
To Noojee
To Warragul
To Drouin
To Korumburra
To Wonthaggi

PHILLIP ISLAND

(Population 1 711)

Approximately 80 kilometres south-east of Melbourne (or 124 kilometres via Bass Highway), Phillip Island stands at the entrance to Westernport Bay. If is 23 kilometres long and 10 kilometres across at its widest and has an area ot about 10 300 hectares. The island has been almost entirely cleared of native bush except for some stands of manna and other gums at the eastern end and its land is used for grazing and chicory growing. Holiday and retirement homes have recently begun to mushroom over the landscape.

The island is reached by crossing a bridge from the fishing port of **San Remo** where fish can often be bought cheaply at a fishermen's co-operative store near the wharf.

The main settlement of **Cowes** (population 1 200) on the north coast is a popular summer resort. Its gentle beach is especially safe for children. It has facilities for golf, tennis, bowls, and water sports of all kinds and its motor racing circuit is one of the best known in Australia. Smaller settlements are at **Rhyll** and **Newhaven.** The scenery on the south coast is impressive.

HISTORY George Bass spent 13 days in Westernport Bay in 1798 and charted most of the island's coast with the exception of a few kilometres on the southern side. In 1801 Lieutenant Grant visited it in the *Lady Nelson* to report to Governor King on the suitability of Westernport as the site for a settlement. A year later Nicholas Baudin, the French navigator, examined the island and named it 'Ile des Anglais'. He was enthusiastic about its possibilities. By this time a number of sealers and whalers were using it as a base. They erected huts on the shore and even cultivated a few crops, but the first permanent settlers were the McHaffie brothers, who established themselves soon after the foundation of the Port Phillip colony.

Places of Interest

Koala Sanctuary on the road from San Remo bridge to Cowes. Seal colony at **Seal Rocks. Fairy Penguin colony** at **Cape Woolamai.** During the summer nesting season the birds come ashore after their day's fishing shortly after dark and parade to their burrows in the tussocks across Summerland beach; tourists from Melbourne make special excursions by bus to observe the parade. The **Nobbies** and **Pyramid Rock,** spectacular rock formations offshore, usually pounded by heavy seas. **Forrest Caves.**

Accommodation

One **hotel.** Nine **motels.** Recommended: Sunseeker Flag Motor Inn, Church Street, Cowes; Erehwon Point, Esplanade, Cowes. Three **camping and caravan parks,** all facilities. One **caravan park,** all facilities.

Transport

Rail to Dandenong, thence **bus** via San Remo bridge. **Road coach** from Melbourne or Dandenong to Stony Point, then **ferry. Boats** and **launches** for hire.

THE DANDENONG RANGES

The Dandenong Ranges, about 48 kilometres from the centre of Melbourne, are a natural asset of incalculable value to the city. They receive almost double the rainfall of the coastal plains, have a rich, light-textured volcanic soil which is easily cultivated, and carry a dense cover of native and exotic vegetation. The highest point in the ranges is Mount Dandenong (472 metres) from the summit of which superb panoramic views can be obtained.

The area is now fairly closely settled and is served by a network of good motor roads connecting a number of small settlements, most of which are unobtrusive in their bushland surroundings. Most of the residents of the district are assiduous gardeners and tree-lovers, and excursions through the hills are delightful at any time of the year—but particularly so in spring when fruit trees and ornamentals are in blossom and the numerous commercial flower and bulb farms are at their best. Autumn after the first frosts is also excitingly colourful.

Although European trees have been extensively used in the development of private gardens, there are carefully managed areas of native bush which delight nature-lovers. The most memorable of these is the Sherbrooke Forest Park through which the road from Belgrave to Kallista passes. Intelligent development and control of this forest has left it entirely unspoiled although it is used by tens of thousands of visitors every year. It has so far escaped damage in the the serious fires which have devastated parts of the ranges almost every summer for a number of years and it is a bird sanctuary in which numerous lyrebirds have established themselves and become almost tame. They may be observed in the Sherbrooke Forest at any time of the year, but the tourist hardy enough to walk quietly through the undergrowth just after dawn on winter mornings may be fortunate enough to see their elaborate mating dance and display.

Other specific attractions in the Dandenongs include the **tourist road** traversing the park areas from Ferntree Gully to the Maroondah Highway; **William Ricketts Sanctuary** near Mount Dandenong, administered by the Forest Commission, where the work of Ricketts, a noted sculptor of aboriginal themes, is displayed; **art galleries** at Emerald; **rhododendron** gardens just east of Olinda on the road to Monbulk; **tulip farms** on the Monbulk-Burleigh Road; **Silvan Reservoir** and picnic ground; and the narrow-gauge veteran train, **Puffing Billy,** which runs between Belgrave and Menzies Creek three times a day at weekends all the year with extra trips on public and school holidays (timetable from Victorian Government Tourist Bureau). The ride through bushland and flower farms is delightful. There is now an exellent **restaurant** near the summit lookout on **Mount Dandenong.**

Main Settlements in the Dandenongs

FERNTREE GULLY is virtually an outer suburb of Melbourne. It is the centre of a pastoral and agricultural district at the foot of the ranges, 35 kilometres from Melbourne. Ferntree Gully National Park, 375 hectares wooded with grey gums, messmate, peppermint and longleaf box eucalypts, is of interest; wildlife plentiful.

Accommodation. Three **hotels.**

Transport. **Electric train** service from Melbourne. **Bus** service to ranges settlements.

BELGRAVE and **BELGRAVE HEIGHTS** 40 kilometres from Melbourne. Bowling, tennis, swimming baths.

Accommodation. **Guest-houses.** **Caravan park,** all facilities.

EMERALD Lavender farms, residential golf club. Swimming at Emerald park. Nearby creeks of interest to gem fossickers.

Accommodation. One **private hotel. Guest-houses.** Two **Caravan and camping parks,** all facilities.

KALORAMA Forty five kilometres from Melbourne.

Accommodation. Guest-houses.

KALLISTA Near Sherbrooke Forest; many plant nurseries and bulb farms in neighbourhood.

Accommodation. Guest-houses. Caravan and camping ground (controlled by Forests Commission).

MONBULK ɜurteen kilometres from Ferntree Gully, 41 kilometres from Melbourne.

Accommodation. Two **guest-houses.**

OLINDA Public golf course.

Accommodation. One **hotel. Guest-houses. Holiday flats available.**

SHERBROOKE

Accommodation. Guest-houses.

YARRA VALLEY AND HILL RESORTS

LILYDALE

(Population 36 162)

Lilydale is an attractive semi-rural town built on the sides of a valley 39 kilometres east of Melbourne. The surrounding land is given over to dairy farming and orchards. The town has a light engineering works and cheese, plastic-cable and footwear factories.

Lilydale was one of the pioneer wine-growing areas of Victoria. The first vines were planted at nearby Yering in 1838 and over the next 30 years the area had increased to 1 200 hectares. The district produced distinguished white and red table wines for many years, until the vineyards were wiped out by phylloxera in the opening years of the century. Early frosts also made the vignerons' task difficult. The town was named (some say) after Lily, the wife of one of the first and most distinguished viticulturists, Paul de Castella. The less romantic claim that it was named after a popular song of the day.

Places of Interest. Coombe Cottage at Coldstream (5 kilometres from town), childhood home of Dame Nellie Melba, Australia's most famous opera singer (not open for inspection). **Clifford Park,** on the Yarra.

Sports. Tennis courts. Bowling and croquet greens. Swimming pool.

Accommodation. Three **hotels. Guest-houses.**

Transport. Electric train and **road** service from Melbourne.

HEALESVILLE

(Population 5 223)

Healesville is a pleasantly situated town 58 kilometres from Melbourne at the junction of Watts River and Graceburn Creek, tributaries of the Yarra River. The district embraces rich river flats used for dairying and mixed farming, hilly grazing country and heavily timbered mountains. The main industries are timber logging and milling, dairying, fruit farming and raising fat stock. The town is also a summer holiday resort and the base for excursions to Mount Donna Buang after snowfalls in winter and spring. Some of the most impressive forests in the Victorian mountains are within a short distance. The largest known tree in Victoria, a mountain ash 87 metres high and 19 metres in girth is on the Mount Monda track, 16 kilometres north-east of town.

The district was settled about 1860 and the original village named after Sir Richard Heales, Premier of Victoria. It was created a shire in 1887.

Places of Interest. Sir Colin Mackenzie Wild Life Sanctuary (5 kilometres from town) is a 32 hectare reserve on Badger Creek; extremely popular day's outing for Melbourne children; contains many tame native animals and Platypus Research Station where first platypus was bred in captivity in 1943. Named after eminent surgeon and scientist who was director of National Museum. **Maroondah Reservoir,** picturesque expanse of water in woodland setting. **Coranderrk,** former aboriginal reserve, with cemetery where 300 members of the extinct Yarra Yarra tribe are buried; contains grave of Barrah, the last of his people. Farther afield are **Stevenson Falls** (82 metres), 31 kilometres north-east, over Black's Spur (fine view from summit). **Myer's Creek Falls** and **Sylvia Falls** (due north). **Badger** and **Coranderrk Weir** (south-east, past Mackenzie Sanctuary). The whole district is splendid bush-walking country.

Sports. Two golf courses. Tennis, bowls and swimming at Queen's Park in town. Fair fishing in Upper Yarra and tributaries. Good shooting.

Accommodation. Three **hotels.** Recommended: Dennis, Harker Street. One **motel. Guest-houses.** Holiday **flats** and **cottages** available. Four **caravan and camping parks,** all facilities. Several unimproved **camping areas.**

Transport. **Electric train service** from Melbourne. Also direct **bus** service. Daily **road** services to surrounding towns.

MARYSVILLE (population 630). A small, attractive mountain town 90 kilometres north-east of Melbourne, was once largely dependent on the timber industry, but is gaining popularity as a summer holiday resort. There are numerous bush-walking tracks leading to beauty spots including **Keppel's Lookout** (one hour), **Mount Gardon** (1½ hours) and **Stevenson Falls** (2 hours). **Lake Eildon** and the **Cumberland Valley** forests are within easy driving distance.

Accommodation. One **hotel. Guest-house.**

WARBURTON (population 1583). The timber milling and tourist town of Warburton, 79 kilometres west of Melbourne on the Upper Yarra River in the foothills of the Great Dividing Range, is equally suited for a quiet holiday or as a base for sightseeing trips into the mountains. **Mount Donna Buang** (1 224 metres) is 7 kilometres north-west. Motor coach tours to **Upper Yarra Dam** (the main Melbourne water storage), **Maroondah Dam** and the **Acheron Way** (magnificent forest country) are available. Founded in 1864 after gold strikes in the area, the town was named after the district magistrate, Charles Warburton Carr. The original site was between Mount Little Joe and Mount Tugwell.

Sports. Tennis, bowls, croquet, nine-hole golf course. Fishing and shooting.

Accommodation. One **hotel.** One **motel.** One **motel-guest-house.** Eight **guest-houses.** One **camping park,** all facilities.

Transport. **Road** services from Melbourne.

MACEDON—MOUNT MACEDON (Population 915) A secluded residential township 61 kilometres north-north-west of Melbourne at an altitude of between 750 and 900 metres, Macedon is distinguished for its bracing climate and the beautiful gardens and plantations thriving in its rich soil. Mount Macedon itself is an extinct volcano, 1 013 metres high. It was sighted by Hume and Hovell in 1824 and named Mount Wentworth, but Mitchell, who climbed it in 1836, renamed it Macedon after Philip of Macedon (apparently because he could see Port Phillip from the summit). The area was first settled in 1837. The road from Macedon to Woodend through the Black Forest was a favourite haunt of bushrangers in the goldrush days. It was on the main coach route to Bendigo. There are many pleasant walks and drives in the district and some trout fishing in the streams.

Places of Interest. Include the **Memorial Cross** at the summit, erected in honour of those who died in the first world war; **Hanging Rock;** the **State Government Nurseries;** Headquarters of State **Civil Defence Training Organisation.**

Accommodation. Mount Macedon: One **hotel. Guest-houses.** One **caravan and camping park,** all facilities. Macedon: One **hotel.** One **guest-house.**

WESTERN DISTRICTS

Much of Victoria's pastoral wealth stems from the pastures established in the volcanic plains of the hinterland behind the coast west of the 144th degree of East longitude. This Western District—in reality the south-western corner of the State—carries about one-third of the sheep and beef cattle population although its area is only about one-sixth of the State total.

The south-western coast is extremely rugged and provides little shelter for shipping except at Portland Bay where an artifical harbour has now been built. That part of coast which extends from Cape Otway almost to the Bellarine Peninsula is backed by wooded mountain ranges. Scenically it is unusual and beautiful and is traversed by the Great Ocean Road from which a number of secondary roads lead north to connect with Princes Highway.

The plains inland are flat, monotonous country west of Lake Corangamite and have been cleared of most of the natural timber to permit cropping and pasture improvement.

GEELONG

(Population 115 047)

Victoria's largest provincial city and wool-selling centre for the State's Western District which produces about 10 per cent of Australia's clip, Geelong is 72 kilometres west of Melbourne on Corio Bay in Port Phillip Bay. It is expanding rapidly as an industrial centre and its port handles the fifth-largest cargo tonnage in the Commonwealth. Its principal trade is in crude and refined petroleum products, wheat, oats, barley, wool, skins, frozen meat, butter, phosphatic rock, sulphur, coal, steel, pig-iron and motor vehicles and parts. The port comprises 17 shipping berths, a bulk grain terminal, an oil wharf and large cool stores. It can accommodate vessels drawing up to 11 metres.

The city is pleasantly laid out, has a number of fine public and commercial buildings and is liberally provided with parks and gardens in which the community takes great pride. Several select independent (private) schools are established in the district including Geelong Grammar School, Geelong College (boys) and Morongo and The Hermitage (girls).

Wool research conducted by the Commonwealth Scientific and Industrial Research Organization in Geelong laboratories and experimental stations has been of great value to the wool industry and extremely important to the development of the Corriedale breed of sheep.

The city's secondary industries include nine major woollen mills, automotive works, an oil refinery and petrochemicals plant, engineering works, phosphatic fertilizers plant and factories for the production of carpets, furniture, home appliances, safety glass, rope and cordage, aerated waters, agricultural machinery, salt, butter and cement. There are additionally tanneries, a wire-drawing plant, timber mills, grain storage and shipment installations, meatworks, flour mills, food processing factories, a distillery and an aluminium refinery. Arrangements may be made to inspect many of these industries.

Geelong is a convenient base from which to visit the pleasant and picturesque seaside resorts of the **Bellarine Peninsula** and the really magnificent scenic areas of the south-west coast.

History. Corio Bay was discovered in 1802 by Lieutenant John Murray. In the same year Matthew Flinders climbed Station Peak, north of Corio Bay, and examined the surrounding countryside, but the first attempts to settle the area failed. From 1805 to 1835, William Buckley, a convict escaped from Van Diemen's Land, lived among aboriginal tribesmen in the area.

In 1835 and 1836 large areas of the district were surveyed by J.H. Wedge, a member of the Port Phillip Association of land seekers from Launceston, on whose behalf John Batman, one of the founders of Melbourne, claimed to have made extensive land purchases from the natives.

The first settlers were J. A. Cowie and David Stead who took up a property called Cowie's Creek. In the following year Dr Alexander Thomson settled on his property 'Kardinia', which included the present townsite. In August 1838, the town was surveyed, and proclaimed three months later.

In 1840 two pioneer women, Ann Drysdale and Caroline Newcombe, took up two separate sheep runs, one at South Corio and the other on the Bellarine Peninsula. By September 1841, the township boasted a post office, store, clerk of works' office, two watch-houses and a newspaper—the 'Geelong Advertiser', Australia's oldest morning newspaper. (It started publication in 1840.)

The 1840s was an era of steady growth. Flour mills, tanneries, a soap works, and a bridge across the Barwon were built. In the early years of the decade extensive vineyards were planted which were successful until wiped out by phylloxera in 1877. By 1849 Geelong became a municipality.

However, when gold was discovered in 1851, Geelong, like Melbourne, was rapidly depopulated as the townspeople flocked to the diggings. Despite this, progress continued. In 1852 Donaghy's rope works opened (thought to be the first in Australia) and in 1856 James Harrison developed in the town the world's first system of commercial refrigeration.

Flood destroyed the Barwon bridge in 1852 and it was not rebuilt until 1859 when an iron bridge was constructed. Two years earlier, though, the town had been linked to Melbourne by a railway. In the 1880s the McCann family started a cement works and in 1905 the Geelong Harbour Trust was constituted.

Geelong was site for an event of national economic importance when the Shell Company opened its sulphuric acid works in 1957 and launched Australia's petrochemicals industry.

Geelong was originally called Jillong which means 'the place of native companion'. In this case 'native companion' signifies a long-legged water bird. For a time the settlement was also known as Coraiya (meaning obscure) which was later corrupted to Corio.

Buildings of Historic Interest. Merchiston Hall, Gordon Street, East Geelong, an 8-roomed stone house built in 1856 for James Cowie, the first settler. **Christ Church,** Moorabool Street, with foundation stone laid in 1843. Built during 1845-7 and designed by a number of architects. **Customs**

Collins Street, Melbourne

Bourke Street, Melbourne

Exhibition Building, Melbourne

House, Brougham Place, built in 1855-6, probably to the modified design of E. Davidson. **The Hermitage** Church of England Girls' Grammar School, Pakington Street, built 1859-60 for George Armytage and designed by Edward Prowse of Geelong. **Lunan House,** Lunan Avenue, Drumcondra, built for J. F. Strachan and designed by Charles Laing, 1849-51.

Parks and Gardens. About 40 per cent of the city's area has been reserved for parks, gardens and sports grounds. They include: The **Botanical Gardens,** Eastern Park, overlooking Corio Bay. **Johnstone Park,** with **Art Gallery, War Memorial, Library** and **City Hall. Queens Park** (golf course, sports oval and swimming pool, with walks to Buckley's Falls). **Kardinia Park** (sports ovals, children's playgrounds etc). **Rippleside** and **St Helen's** parks.

Other Places of Interest. Brownill **Observation Tower,** Ceres, south-west of town. **Fairy Park** (behind You Yang Ranges), on summit of Mount Elephant, displays quaint miniature houses and scenes from fairy tales for the amusement of children. **You Yangs Wildlife Sanctuary** (in volcanic range north of city). **Twin Lakes** fauna sanctuary (19 kilometres from city), 486 hectares fauna sanctuary, a breeding place for kangaroos, emus, koalas and wildfowl, including the Cape Barron goose. **Gordon Institute of Technology,** Australia's leading textile college, Fenwick Street.

Entertainments. Plaza **Theatre.** GAMA (Geelong Association of Music and the Arts) **Theatre.** Two **cinemas.** Two **drive-ins. Palais Royal** (dancing).

Sports. Racecourse. Trotting and greyhound racing course. Yacht, rowing, rifle and gun clubs. Bowling and croquet greens. Lawn tennis court. Table tennis centre. Tenpin bowling alleys. Three first class golf courses. Boat ramps on Corio Bay beaches. River and bay fishing. Water skiing etc.

Accommodation. Fourteen residential **hotels.** Recommended: Carrington, Yarra Street; Carlton, Malop Street. Ten **motels.** Recommended: Travelodge, Myer Street; Hamilton Hume, Esplanade; Kingsway, Aberdeen Street. Two **guest-houses.** Three **caravan and camping parks,** all facilities.

Transport. Fast **rail** service to Melbourne. **Bus** and **road coach** services to nearby coastal resorts and country towns. **Car rentals, taxis** etc.

BELLARINE PENINSULA AND OTWAYS COAST

PORTARLINGTON. A popular seaside resort and fishing point, is 31 kilometres from Geelong on the north-eastern shore of the peninsula and inside Port Phillip Bay. It is enjoyed for its safe beach and good fishing.

Accommodation. One **hotel.** One **motel.** One **private hotel.** Three **caravan and camping parks,** all facilities.

INDENTED HEAD. Small, picturesquely sited beach and fishing resort, between Portarlington and St Leonards. One **motel.**

ST LEONARDS. 32 kilometres east of Geelong, beach resort. Good fishing. One **hotel. Holiday cottages** available. **Two caravan and camping parks,** all facilities.

QUEENSCLIFF-POINT LONSDALE. At the entrance to Port Phillip Bay on western headland, Queenscliff was established as a commercial fishing centre in the 1850s and a large fishing fleet is still based on its harbour. The town and its twin settlement, Point Lonsdale, have been extensively developed as a holiday and tourist resort. There are good swimming and surfing beaches in the vicinity and numerous parks and recreation reserves.

Sports. Excellent golf course at Swan Island. Bowling and croquet greens. Tennis courts.

Accommodation. One **hotel. Guest-houses. Motel holiday flats. Holiday flats** and **bungalows** available. One **camping and caravan park,** all facilities.

OCEAN GROVE. On southern shores of peninsula and on mouth of Barwon River. It is popular for its safe surfing beach and attractive situation.

Sports. Bowls, golf, tennis, fishing.

Accommodation. One **motel. Guest-houses.** One **children's guest-house.** Two **caravan and camping parks,** all facilities. One **caravan park.**

BARWON HEADS. Over bridge across Barwon River from Ocean Grove. Golf coures. Boatsheds.

Accommodation. One **hotel.** One **guest-house.** One foreshore **caravan and camping park.**

TORQUAY. Resort 93 kilometres from Melbourne. It has an excellent surfing beach at which interstate surf and lifesaving carnivals are held. The sea fishing is good. Tennis, bowls, golf course and shooting.

Accommodation. One **hotel.** One **motel. Guest-houses. Holiday flats** and **bungalows** available. Three **camping and caravan parks,** all facilities.

Transport to Bellarine Peninsula resorts is by **rail** from Melbourne to Geelong, thence by connecting **bus** or **road coach.** There are occasional week-end road coach services from Melbourne.

Note: The best beaches for surf-board riding in Victoria are found on this section of coast. They include **Thirteenth Beach, Bramlea, Bancoora, Jan Juc and Bell's Beach.**

ANGLESEA (Population 1 054). One of the most attractive of the south-west coast seaside towns near Melbourne, Anglesea is 109 kilometres from the capital on the Great Ocean Road. It has good swimming, surfing and boating and an interesting golf course. There are many delightful bush walks along the Anglesea River and in the nearby hills.

Accommodation. One **hotel.** One **motel. Holiday flats** available. Two **caravan and camping parks,** all facilities.

Transport. Daily **bus** service from Melbourne; or **rail** to Geelong, connecting with road service.

AIREY'S INLET, eleven kilometres farther west, has one **hotel,** and **guest-houses. Holiday flats** and **lodges** are available. There are two **caravan and camping parks** with all facilities and one foreshore **camping site.**

LORNE (Population 909)

At the foot of the Otway Ranges on Loutit Bay, 134 kilometres from Melbourne, Lorne is one of Victoria's most popular seaside resorts. It has a mild climate in both summer and winter, and its approaches on the Great Ocean Road are scenically superb. Unfortunately erosion has caused some damage to its beach in recent years, but there is still good swimming, surfing and skin-diving to be had. The mountains of the hinterland, although heavily exploited for their timber in bygone days and since repeatedly ravaged by fire, are still very beautiful.

History. The district was opened up by timber-getters in the 1850s, when it was called Loutit Bay after Captain Loutit who anchored there in 1841 while on his way to London with the first cargo of Western District wool. The village was established in 1871 as a seaside resort for the pastoralists and farmers inland and named Lorne after the town in Argyllshire, Scotland. The Great Ocean Road was opened in 1932, and thereafter Lorne and adjacent settlements gained great popularity with city holidaymakers.

Places of Interest. Teddy's Lookout. Kalimna, Phantom, Erskine, Straw's and Splitters' **Falls.** Erskine River **Rapids. Mount Defiance,** on road a few kilometres south-west.

Sports. Golf course, tennis courts, bowling greens etc.

Accommodation. Two **hotels.** Recommended: The Lorne. Two **motels.** Recommended: Kalimna. **Guest-houses.** Six **camping and caravan parks,** all facilities. **Holiday flats** available.

Transport. Daily **road** service from Melbourne or **rail** to Geelong, then connecting buses.

WYE RIVER. Tiny but charming holiday settlement 19 kilometres west of Lorne. Shooting, fishing, golf, tennis, surfing. One **hotel.** One **caravan park.**

APOLLO BAY (Population 822)

A fishing, dairying, timber-getting and tourist town, 189 kilometres from Melbourne and 116 kilometres south-west of Lorne on the Great Ocean Road, Apollo Bay is base for a fishing fleet and has the biggest fish-freezing plant in Victoria. The scenery in the wooded, mountainous hinterland is memorable. The district offers good sea and river fishing and excellent shooting.

History. The Henty family established a whaling station at Point Bunbury to the south-east of the present township in the 1830s, but the land was not permanently settled until 1856. The village was founded in 1860 and in 1919 Apollo Bay became part of the newly created shire of Otway. The rugged coast hereabouts was the scene of many shipwrecks in the days of sail.

Places of Interest. Submarine **cable terminus** three kilometres north of township. Inspection by arrangement. **Turton's Pass** and **Otway Forest** in back country. **Paradise picnic grounds** in valley of Barham River.

Sports. Golf course, bowling greens, tennis courts.

Accommodation. Two **hotels.** Recommended: Ocean Road. Two **motels.** Recommended: Greenacres, Wilson Street. **Guest-houses. Holiday flats** available. One **caravan park,** all facilities. Three **camping grounds,** some facilities.

Transport. Daily **road** service from Melbourne, and services from Geelong and Colac, connecting with **rail.**

PORT CAMPBELL (Population 323). The small seaside town of Port Campbell, 257 kilometres from Melbourne, is situated between Cape Otway and Warrnambool, within reach of some of the finest coastal scenery in Australia. Good rock and beach fishing. Swimming, golf and tennis.

Accommodation. One **hotel.** One **motel. Guest-houses. Caravan park. Camping reserve.**

FAR WESTERN COAST

WARRNAMBOOL

(Population 18 663)

A regional commercial centre for the Western District and for the rich dairy farming lands along the section of the Victorian coast between Cape Otway and Portland Bay, Warrnambool is 262 kilometres west-south-west of Melbourne on Lady Bay, a sheltered but shallow harbour no longer of any commercial importance. The city is attractively laid out and is a favourite holiday resort for residents of south-eastern South Australia and western Victoria. There are good beaches and impressive scenery in the neighbourhood. Facilities for sport are well developed and the standard of accommodation in the city is well above that of the average Victorian provincial centre. The citizens have marked civic pride and make efforts to welcome visitors.

History. The French navigator, Nicholas Baudin, entered Lady Bay in 1802 and sealers and whalers used the anchorage sporadically during the early years of the 19th century. The first permanent settlers did not arrive until 1839, but the village was founded in 1847 and from then on the rich hinterland assured rapid development. The municipality was proclaimed in 1855 and town status was achieved in 1883, seven years before the railway line to Melbourne was completed. Warrnambool was gazetted as a city in 1918. The name was originally spelt Warnimble, a corrupt version of an aboriginal word meaning 'plenty of water'.

Places of Interest. Museum, Art Gallery and **Public Library. Botanical Gardens. Albert and Victoria Parks. Lighthouse, cottage** and **store** built in 1859 by W. K. Paterson; classified as worthy of preservation by the National Trust. **Tower Hill** and lake, west of city, a volcanic cone overlooking one of the largest lava plains known to geologists. **Milk-processing factory** at Dennington, 5 kilometres west, is the largest in Australia.

Sports. Warrnambool is particularly proud of its 58 bowling rinks. A Seaside Bowling Carnival for visitors is held every year in February-March, lasts for two weeks, and attracts players from all over Australia. Racecourse—Warrnambool Cup meeting and Grand Annual Steeplechase in May is a major turf event in the State. Midget car racing at showgrounds. Hot-rod racing at specially built track at the racecourse. Good 18-hole golf course. Weekly greyhound races. Sailing and power-boat club (regatta in December). Surf lifesaving club stages a carnival in January.

A 'Florado Festival' of arts, education and sports is organized in March every year.

Accommodation. Seven **hotels.** Recommended: Lady Bay, Pertrobe Road; Commodore Western. Five **motels.** Recommended: Mid-City, Western Highway; Warrnambool Caravilla, Princes Highway. **Guest-houses.** Three **caravan and camping parks,** all facilities. One **camping park,** limited facilities.

Transport. Rail from Melbourne. **Road** services from Melbourne and to Ballarat. **Air** to Melbourne and Portland (daily except Thursday and Saturday).

Motor coach tours of district available.

PORT FAIRY (Population 2 404)

The second-oldest town in Victoria, Port Fairy was originally a whaling station. It is situated on the eastern headland of Portland Bay at the mouth of the Moyne River, 30 kilometres west of Warrnambool. It was named by Captain J. Wishart, when he took his cutter *The Fairy* across the bar to escape a violent storm in April, 1810. In 1835, James Atkinson, of Sydney, received a large grant of land in the locality and he named the settlement Belfast, but the original name was restored after later land sales. Today Port Fairy is the base of a large fishing fleet.

Places of Interest. Battery Hill, old fort and signal station site at the mouth of the river. **Captain John Mill's cottage** in Gipps Street, built in the early 1850s, has open ironwork posts of a type rarely seen in Australia. Anglican **Church of St John** and Roman Catholic **Church of St Patrick. Griffiths Island** (connected to the town by a causeway), lighthouse and mutton-bird rookeries. **Lady Julia Percy Island** (accessible in calm weather only), fur-seal rookeries.

Accommodation. Five **hotels.** Recommended: Star of the West, Sackville Street. One **private hotel.** One **guest-house.** Four **camping and caravan parks,** all facilities.

Transport. Rail from Melbourne. **Road** services to Hamilton and Mount Gambier, SA.

PORTLAND

(Population 8 212)

Portland, 363 kilometres west-south-west of Melbourne, is the only deepwater port between Melbourne and Adelaide and is an important industrial and commercial centre for western Victoria pastoral and agricultural areas. The first permanent settlement in Victoria, it was founded by the Henty brothers in 1834. It has several good beaches and numerous places of historic interest and has for many years been a popular summer holiday resort.

The country in the immediate vicinity of the town produces wheat, fruit and vegetables, wool, dairy produce, cut flowers, fat lambs and cattle. Fishing and stone quarrying are also important. Secondary industries include a large freezing works, a fish cannery, light engineering works, hypodermic needle factory and a ready-mix concrete plant. Agricultural lime is also made.

History. Portland Bay was discovered by Lieutenant James Grant in the *Lady Nelson* on the first passage through Bass Strait in 1800. He did not actually enter the bay but named it after the Duke of Portland. (It is possible that whalers knew of it even before this date, but the fact is not recorded.) In 1802, Captain Nicholas Baudin examined it in *Le Geographe* and named it Tourville Bay, by which name it was known to whalers and sealers later.

In 1828 William Dutton, a sealer, visited the area and the following year landed and built a house in which he lived for 12 months. However, Dutton's period of residence is not considered to constitute permanent settlement and credit for the establishment of the town goes to the Henty family who arrived in 1834 and began a sheep run and whaling station.

Thomas Mitchell visited the Henty homestead in 1836 and a year later Captain James Fawthorp brought 700 sheep to the settlement in the Henty's ship *Eagle.* By the following year, 34 whalers were operating out of the bay but the industry declined between 1840 and 1860. In 1839 the town was proclaimed and in 1855 the municipality was incorporated.

By 1894 the beef and mutton industry was established sufficiently to warrant the establishment of the Portland Freezing Works. The works were taken over in 1905 by Thomas Borthwick.

In 1950 the Portland Harbour Trust was established to develop a deepwater port. Work started in 1952 and the harbour was finished in 1961 at a total cost of $16 million.

Places of Interest. **Kurtze's Museum,** Burswood, the homestead built for Edward Henty in 1854. Designed by James Barrow of Adelaide. **Court House,** Cliff Street, built prior to 1842 when it was used for Anglican Church services. **Customs House,** Cliff Street, built in 1850 for the Public Works Department by contractors, John Hughes and Alexander Grant. **'Maretimo' homestead** on the Princes Highway near Portland, built about 1854 for James Norman McLeod. **Blowholes** at Cape Bridgewater, 21 kilometres south-west. **Mount Richmond National Park,** 45 kilometres north-west. Excellent for pink boronia and wild pea flowers in spring. **Forestry Commission's Kentbrack Plantations** containing one million pine seedlings.

Sports. Golf course. Tennis courts. Bowling and croquet greens. Motor speedway. Cycle and trotting tracks. Rifle club. Squash and badminton courts. Surfing, water-skiing, fishing and shooting.

Accommodation. Two **hotels.** Recommended: Mac's, Gawler Street. Three **motels.** Recommended: Siesta, Julia Street. **Guest-houses.** Four **caravan and camping parks,** all facilities.

Transport. **Rail** from Melbourne. **Road** services to Hamilton, Warrnambool, Mount Gambier, SA. **Air** to Warrnambool and Melbourne (daily except Tuesday and Saturday). **Air** charter flights available.

NELSON (Population 74). Tiny but charmingly situated hamlet at the mouth of the Glenelg River favoured as a seaside resort by the people of Mount Gambier. Nearby Princess Margret Rose Caves are interesting. River trips can be arranged. Good fishing.

Accommodation. One **hotel. Guest-houses.**

Transport. **Road** service from Mount Gambier, SA.

WESTERN HINTERLAND

HAMILTON

(Population 9 662)

The unofficial capital of a large grazing district which is one of the finest wool-producing areas in the world, Hamilton is 290 kilometres west of Melbourne on the north bank of the Grange Burn River. It is a pleasantly situated, prosperous city with well-designed public buildings and well-kept street plantations and parks. Secondary industries: Knitting mills, sawmills, butter and cheese factories, rabbit and poultry-freezing works and a plaster sheet factory.

History. When the explorer Major Mitchell passed through the district in 1836, the present townsite was an aboriginal corroboree ground. Mitchell named the river Grange Burn and the name was retained for his property by the first settler, Henry Wade, who arrived in 1838. The town was surveyed in 1850 but a few years later for some unrecorded reason the name was changed to Hamilton. The aboriginal name for the area had been *mulleraterong*. It became an important staging station for Cobb and Co coaches and was proclaimed a municipality in 1859. It achieved the status of a town in 1928 and became a city in 1949.

Places of Interest. **Lake Surprise,** in the crater of Mount Eccles an extinct volcano. **Wannon**

and **Nigretta Falls,** on the Wannon River, north-west of the city. **Mount Napier** (442 metres) 19 kilometres south, believed to have been Victoria's last active volcano. **Art Gallery. Botanical gardens. Zoo.**

Sports. Racecourse and trotting track. Bowling and croquet greens. Tennis courts. Golf course. Olympic swimming pool. Shooting.

Accommodation. Two **hotels.** Recommended: The George, Gray Street. Three **motels.** Recommended: Botanical, French and Thompson Streets. **Caravan and camping park,** all facilities.

Transport. Rail from Melbourne. **Road** services to Ballarat, Mount Gambier, SA and Naracoorte. Daily **air** service to Melbourne (except Saturday and Sunday).

CASTERTON (Population 2 175). On Glenelg River, 66 kilometres west of Hamilton, Casterton serves an agricultural and grazing district. Scenic launch trips can be taken to Nelson at the mouth of the river. Good sports facilities.

Accommodation. Two **hotels.** Recommended: Glenelg Inn, Henty Street. One **caravan and camping park.**

Transport. Rail from Melbourne. **Road** services from Hamilton, Ballarat, Melbourne, and to Mount Gambier.

COLERAINE (Population 1 386). In Wannon River valley, 35 kilometres west of Hamilton, Coleraine district has attractive river scenery. There are sports facilities.

Accommodation. One **hotel.** One **motel.**

Transport. Rail from Melbourne. **Road** service to Hamilton etc.

COLAC

(Population 10 418)

On the southern shores of Lake Colac, 164 kilometres south-west of Melbourne, Colac is the main centre of a prosperous, closely settled, very fertile agricultural district. It has an annual rainfall of more than 680 millimetres and is the largest onion-growing area in the State. Other primary products of importance are oats, rye, millet, linseed and flax, dairy produce, pigs, poultry, wool, fat lambs and beef cattle. Besides associated secondary industries, the town has sawmills, an agricultural implements and windmill factory, a brickworks and a cordial factory.

History. The area was settled by land-seekers from Tasmania in 1837. In 1839, the Buntingdale Mission for Aborigines was established by the Reverend F. Tuckfield—possibly the earliest mission to the natives in Victorian history. Surveys were made in 1844 and 1848, but it was not until 1859 that the town was officially founded. In 1864 it became a shire, and was gazetted as a city in 1960. Its name is thought to be derived from a corruption of Coladjin, the original tribe in the area.

Places of Interest. Memorial Square, two hectares of parkland and gardens in the centre of the city. **Botanic Gardens,** 18 hectares on the foreshores of the lake. Densely timbered. **Otway Ranges,** to south through which scenic roads run down to the coast.

Sports. Golf course. Tennis courts. Bowling and croquet lawns. Tenpin bowling. Rifle Club, Swimming pool. Rowing and yachting clubs. Racecourse.

Kanyana Festival is held annually in March—10 days of sporting events, agricultural competitions and exhibits, concerts etc. (*Kanyana* means 'a meeting of the people').

Accommodation. Two **hotels.** Recommended: Commodore Commercial, Murray Street. One **motel.** One **caravan and camping park,** all facilities. Two **guest-houses.**

Transport. Rail from Melbourne. **Road** services to neighbouring towns, Warrnambool, Ballarat, and south coast seaside resorts.

CAMPERDOWN (Population 3 416)

On Princes Highway, 195 kilometres from Melbourne, Camperdown is the centre of a pastoral district producing wool, fat lambs, and dairy produce. The Camperdown-Glenormiston Dairy Company is the largest co-operative factory of its kind in Victoria.

History. The district was pioneered by John and Peter Manifold in 1838 and the village was founded in 1850. It was named by Governor La Trobe after the Battle of Camperdown of 1797. It was gazetted a town in 1959 and a borough in 1962.

Places of Interest. Mount Leura, extinct volcano typical of area with lookout on the rim of the crater. There are 38 crater lakes in the vicinity. **Clock tower** erected by the Manifold family, and an **elm avenue** planted by schoolchildren in 1876. **Lake Bullen Merri** near the town has good trout and salmon-fishing and water sports.

Sports. Racecourse. Tennis court. Bowling green. Rifle club.

Accommodation. Two **hotels.** Recommended: Leura, Manifold Street. Two **motels.** Recommended: Yeilinda, Princes Highway. One **camping and caravan park,** some facitilies.

Transport. Rail service to Melbourne. **Road** services to surrounding towns.

TERANG (Population 2 235). Centre of a large soldier-settlement area in rich country which produces fine wool and dairy produce, Terang is well laid out and has good sports facilities—a racecourse, golf course, bowling and croquet lawns and a swimming pool.

Accommodation. One **hotel.** One **motel.**

Transport. Rail service from Melbourne. **Road** service to Ballarat and Warrnambool.

CENTRAL WEST AND WIMMERA

The Wimmera is the relatively flat, central-western part of Victoria where the bulk of its wheat and oats and other cereal crops is grown. With the exception of the Grampians mountains in the south-east corner of the district, the country is far less topographically varied than the eastern half of the State. It is far more typical of inland Australia, but it has appeal to the type of traveller whose interest is not confined solely to picturesque scenery. It contains a number of Victoria's largest national parks and wildlife sanctuaries and also offers great opportunities to keen fishermen and shooters on its many lakes. Considerable areas of the Wimmera are irrigated. The summer climate is hot.

ARARAT

(Population 8 317)

Ararat is 200 kilometres north-west of Melbourne near the Hopkins River and the south-eastern ridges of the Grampians mountain chain. It is the commercial centre of a district which produces wheat, wool, fat lambs, dairy produce and wine grapes. Secondary industries include textile and timber mills, light engineering and railways locomotive plants, butter, ice and cordials factories, a brickworks and a maintenance centre for the equipment of the Postmaster-General's Department.

It is a civically lively little city, which takes great pride in its parks and recreation grounds and organizes an annual Golden Gate Festival, a Highlands sports meeting at New Year and a chess tournament at Queen's Birthday weekend which attracts players from all over Australia.

History. Major Mitchell traversed the area during his expedition through the Western District in 1836. The first settler, Horatio S. Wills, arrived about 1841 and named Mt Ararat (606 metres) when he wrote in his journal, 'Mount Ararat, for like the Ark, we rested there'. The native name was *butingitch.*

Although the first-comers were much troubled by hostile natives, most of the available grazing land had been taken up by squatters in 1843.

In 1854, Joe Pollard, a prospector, and his mates discovered gold at Pinkey Point, but the pay dirt petered out and the rush was short-lived. Another short rush occurred the following year when an American negro, Black Harry, found gold on Blackman's Lead.

In May 1857, however, the big Ararat rush began. One of the richest alluvial deposits on the Victorian fields was found at Canton Lead. The shallow workings yielded 3 000 ounces of gold in three weeks. At the height of the Canton boom (which, like the previous ones, was short in duration), Ararat's population reached 20 000 and water cost sixpence a bucket.

The borough was proclaimed in 1858 but by the 1860s the gold was worked out and the district went back to sheep farming. This decade, however, saw the break-up of the large sheep runs and an increased emphasis on agricultural rather than pastoral production. There was a scramble for land around Ararat by free-selectors (and numbers of speculators) in the second half of the 1860s after the revision of the Land Act of 1860. However, although the population increased after the opening of the railway in 1875, close land settlement did not occur until after the depression of the 1890s.

Attempts at soldier settlement after the first world war were not very successful because the acreage allotted was too small, but those farmers established after the second war fared better.

The first vines in the district were planted in 1863 by two Frenchmen, Jean Pierre Trouette and Emile Blampied. The town was proclaimed in 1934 and the city in 1950.

Places of Interest. Alexandra Park and **Botanical Gardens,** noted for begonia hothouses. **Green Hill Park. Civic Square and War Memorial.** Bridal Hill **Wildflower Sanctuary. Great Western Vineyards** (established in 1865 by Joseph Best), 16 kilometres west; some of the finest dry red wines and champagne types produced in Australia come from Great Western estates. Tours of the cellars and winery may be arranged with the proprietors, Seppelt and Sons, who purchased some of the best vineyards in 1918 and have since developed them extensively.

Sports. Racecourse and trotting track. Cycling. Bowling greens. Tennis courts. Fishing. Olympic swimming pool. Archery.

Accommodation. Four **hotels.** Recommended: Rex, Barkly Street. Three **motels.** Recommended: Ararat Central, Barkly Street. One **caravan and camping park,** all facilities.

Transport. Rail from Melbourne. **Road** services; on Adelaide-Melbourne route.

THE GRAMPIANS

The Grampians, three stark and spectacular ridges of upthrust sandstone running north and south for 90 kilometres and rising in peaks to a height above 1 070 metres, are the western extremity of the Great Dividing Range.

In form and mood these mountains are very different from the south-eastern highlands—different, indeed, from any other mountains in Australia. Their sedimentary strata are tilted towards the west at an angle of about 30 degrees and sharply fractured, so that the ridges have long, sweeping slopes on one side and almost perpendicular cliffs on the other. Wind and water have eroded many of the rock faces into bizarre shapes.

The highest peak in the system is Mount William (1 167 metres). The higher tops carry only harsh, scrubby vegetation and heaths and the forests at lower levels have been repeatedly ravaged by bushfires, but the region is nevertheless rich in native fauna and flora. Of the 395 species of indigenous birds identified in Victoria more than 100 have been reported in the Grampians. In the Victoria and Wartook Valleys kangaroos range in mobs of up to 50 and several koala colonies have established themselves near Hall's Gap. Duck-billed platypuses still inhabit the streams. There are also some herds of acclimatized deer in the hills. However, it is for wildflowers that the Grampians are famous. In spring and summer thousands of hectares are clothed with brilliant heaths, flowering peas, wild fuchsias, boronia, thryptomene, ground orchids and wattle. More than 700 species of flowering plants have been catalogued in the area.

All sections of the Grampians offer fascinating bush walks for the nature lover—and some challenging country for rock climbers—but less energetic tourists are now catered for by a highway which traverses the mountains from Dunkeld and Victoria Valley in the south to roads from Stawell and Horsham in the north.

Hall's Gap is the tourist centre in the mountains—a small, beautifully sited settlement where **accommodation** can be obtained at **guest-houses** and three **motels.** Recommended: Grand Canyon, Grampians Road. **Holiday flats** are also available and **caravan and camping parks** are situated at Hall's Gap, Fyan's Lake, McKenzie Creek (22 kilometres on Horsham Road) and Wartook (permission to camp from Forests Officer).

Coach tours are available from nearby towns of Ararat, Stawell and Horsham—and from Hamilton. But the best of the mountains can be seen only by the walker or the private motorist with time to stop and explore.

The best time to visit the Grampians is late September to late October.

STAWELL

(Population 5 826)

An agricultural and manufacturing town to the east of the Grampians and Lake Lonsdale, Stawell is just off the Western Highway 233 kilometres west-north-west of Melbourne. It is only 25 kilometres from Hall's Gap. The surrounding district grows good wool, fat lambs, cereals, vines and poultry. The town's industries include woollen and timber mills, a butter factory, a flour mill, a brickworks and a factory producing components for prefabricated houses.

History. Major Mitchell traversed the area in 1836. Alluvial gold was discovered at Pleasant Creek in 1851 but the field was not exploited until 1853 when the rush led to the establishment of a makeshift town. It was first called Pleasant Creek (the aboriginal name was *kobram*) but it was officially named after Sir William Foster Stawell, Chief Justice of Victoria.

By 1857 the population numbered between 20 000 and 30 000. The shire was incorporated in 1864. Five years later the borough was severed from the shire. In 1957 Stawell was proclaimed as a town.

Places of Interest. Big Hill, landmark of Stawell and the place where gold was first discovered. **Bunyil's Cave,** 10 kilometres south of town in the Black Ranges, contains aboriginal cave paintings in ochre. **Cato Park,** lake and swimming pool. **Sister Rocks, Fyan's Lake** and **Bellfield. Tottington Woolshed,** 55 kilometres north-east on the road to Saint Arnaud—a rare example of traditional woolshed construction in the mid-19th century (classified by the National Trust). **Central Park** and **botanic reserve. Museum** and **Shell Collection,** Wimmera Street. **'Overdale'** sheep and cattle station, (inspections at 10 am, Tuesday and Thursday). Accommodation available.

Sports. Racecourse. Trotting track. Golf course. Bowling and croquet greens. Olympic swimming pool. Axemen's club. Tennis courts. Good swimming, boating and fishing on nearby lakes.

The Stawell Athletic Club holds an Easter Carnival every year during which Australia's best-known professional footrace, the Stawell Gift, is run over 120 metres. **Stawell Festival** is held late September —early October.

Accommodation. Seven **hotels.** Recommended: Brix, Barnes Street. Two **motels.** Recommended: London, Western Highway. **Guest-houses.** One **caravan and camping park,** all facilities.

HORSHAM

(Population 11 046)

Horsham, 301 kilometres north-west of Melbourne, is regarded as the capital of the Wimmera. It is an important stock-selling centre and the administrative seat of several State Government instrumentalities, including the Soldiers' Settlement Commission. It is on the junction of the Henty Highway, from Portland in the south-west to Mildura on the Murray, and the Western Highway which links Adelaide and Melbourne. Much agricultural land in the immediate vicinity of Horsham and Murtoa, 31 kilometres north-east, is under irrigation. The district produces fruit and vegetables, fat lambs and cattle, pigs, poultry and cereals. Secondary industries: Textile and flour mills, grain storages, plaster and brick works, light engineering shops, a foundry, an iceworks and butter factory.

History. The explorer Mitchell referred to the region as 'Australia Felix' in his 1836 journals. He saw it after rain. The first settler was James Monckton Darlot who selected the 'Brighton' homestead and the original township began on the property's borders during the 1840s. It was named after Darlot's home town in Sussex. The village gained official recognition when George Langlands set up a post office and store there in 1849. Five years later the town site was surveyed.

Burke and Wills passed through Horsham on their ill-fated expedition to Central Australia.

In 1870 the first flour mill was built but it was not until the land was opened up by free selection in the 1870s that real development began. In 1879 the town was connected by rail to Melbourne, and in 1882 was proclaimed a borough.

During the 1890s irrigation was begun. Despite this, the area was heavily hit by drought in 1897, and by floods eight years later.

Horsham was proclaimed a town in 1932 and a city in 1949. The native name for the district was *bongambilor*, meaning 'place of flowers'.

Places of Interest. Botanical Gardens. Pine Lake (24 kilometres south-east). **Lake Natimuk** (24 kilometres north-west). **Longerenong Agricultural College,** cereal research centre (13 kilometres north-east). Inspection by arrangement. **Art Gallery** and **Historical Museum.**

Sports. Racecourse; tennis courts; bowling and croquet greens; swimming, fishing and shooting at nearby lakes.

Accommodation. Three **hotels.** Recommended: White Hart, Firebrace Street. Seven **motels.** Recommended: Commodore, Western Highway.

Transport. Rail to Melbourne and Adelaide. **Road** services to Melbourne and Adelaide. Daily **air** services to Melbourne. **Aero club.** Charters available.

WARRACKNABEAL (Population 2 867)

The centre of the Wimmera wheatlands and a big wool-growing area, Warracknabeal is at the junction of the Borung and Henty Highways, 343 kilometres north-west of Melbourne. The town has flour mills, a clothing factory, a power-alcohol distillery and a light engineering works for farm machinery and implements.

History. The explorer Eyre made an expedition along the Wimmera River in 1844, and discovered Lake Hindmarsh about 48 kilometres west of the town. The following year the Scott brothers established the Warracknabeal run and by the end of the decade most of the nearby countryside had been taken up by sheepmen. Closer settlement began in the 1860s and 1870s, but the farmers had great trouble with rabbits and dingoes and were forced to build a rabbit and dog-proof fence along the 36th parallel to protect them from invasion by animals in the wild mallee country to the north. The first buildings in town were built in 1870 but it was not until 1890 that the municipality was proclaimed. From 1896 to 1902 the district suffered the most severe and prolonged drought in its history and the Wimmera-Mallee water supply project was evolved in an attempt to cope with the situation. It now comprises 10 000 kilometres of channelling. Warracknabeal's present water storage, Lake Whitton, was built in 1918.

Places of Interest. Lake Buloke, near the township of Donald, 56 kilometres east, is said to provide good fishing. **Lake Hindmarsh,** the largest natural fresh-water lake in Victoria, is about 48 kilometres west. The small town of **JEPARIT,** near the lake's south-eastern shore, is the centre of the State's best-known barley-growing district. It is the birthplace of the Australian statesman, Sir Robert Menzies. Thirty-two kilometres still farther north is a slightly larger town, **RAINBOW,** near Lake Albacutya, another large sheet of water where there are facilities for fishing and water sports. Again to the north lies Victoria's largest wildlife reserve, the **Wyperfield National Park,** 59 000 hectares of arid mallee country abounding with bird life and marsupials. For the serious naturalist it is one of the most rewarding areas in southern Australia.

Sports. Warracknabeal and the smaller towns of the district have the usual facilities for games and swimming.

Accommodation. One **hotel.** Two **motels.** Recommended: Warrack, Dimboola Road. **Caravan park,** all facilities.

Transport. **Rail** to Melbourne via Murtoa. Local **road** services. **Aero club** and flying school. Charters available.

DIMBOOLA (Population 1 696)

Dimboola is a small town on the Wimmera River, 337 kilometres north-west of Melbourne, 40 kilometres east of Warracknabeal. The name is from a Ceylonese word meaning 'land of figs'.

Places of Interest in the district include the **Lowan sanctuary** at Kiata, 24 kilometres west in the **Little Desert National Park** where the lowans, or Mallee fowl, may be seen working on their incubator nests at all times of the year. **Wimmera Forest Nursery,** at Wail, 11 kilometres south-east, specializes in cultivation of eucalypts and native plants for low-rainfall areas. **Salt Lake,** evaporation pans.

Sports. Facilities are good and the fishing and shooting in the district are excellent. Dimboola Regatta, held annually in November, attracts the State's best oarsmen.

Accommodation. Two **hotels.** Recommended: Dimboola. One recommended **motel. Caravan and camping park,** all facilities.

Transport. **Rail** from Melbourne via Ballarat. Local **road** services.

THE MALLEE

The Mallee district is the extreme north-western corner of Victoria, comprising mainly flat, semi-arid sand plains which were originally covered by a many-stemmed eucalyptus scrub called *mallee* by the natives. The soil, though very light, is fertile after rain and responds to irrigation. The scrub has been cleared from large areas which are now the State's second-largest grain-producing district. The countryside, although it can appear lush after rain, is monotonous and has appeal only to travellers with specialized interests in agriculture, angling and shooting, or Australian fauna and flora.

Technically the Victorian towns of the Murray irrigation area from Mildura to Swan Hill are included in the Mallee division, but for the purposes of this *Guide* they have been grouped under the heading 'Murray Valley'.

NHILL (Population 2 107)

A small, neat wheat town on the Western Highway, exactly halfway between Melbourne and Adelaide, Nhill claims to have the world's largest single-bin wheat silo with a capacity of 2 250 000 bushels. The town has the usual facilities for games and is within easy driving distance of the Kiata Mallee fowl sanctuary (see Dimboola) and large Lake Hindmarsh. The town was named by the first white men to establish themselves in the district, D. Macpherson and G. F. Belcher, who selected land in 1877. The aboriginal word *nyell* means 'a place of spirits' or 'white mist on the water'. Nhill was the first country town in Victoria to install an electric lighting plant. It was linked by rail with Melbourne in 1887.

Accommodation. Two **hotels,** no preference. Three **motels.** Recommended: Wimmera, Western Highway. **Caravan and camping park,** all facilities.

Transport. **Rail** and **road** services to Melbourne and Adelaide. **Aerodrome.**

SEA LAKE (Population 971). On the Calder Highway, three kilometres south of Lake Tyrrell and 364 kilometres north-west of Melbourne, Sea Lake services a large wheat and wool-growing district and irrigated areas carrying dairy cattle and fat lambs. It has sports facilities and a swimming pool.

Accommodation. Two **hotels.** One **motel.** Two **caravan parks,** all facilities. **Camping ground** at Green Lake, 11 kilometres south of town.

Transport. **Rail** to Melbourne. **Road** service to Bendigo.

OUYEN (Population 1 645). About 100 kilometres south of Mildura and 457 kilometres from Melbourne, Ouyen is on the Calder Highway and is a rail junction of lines serving Mildura and Pinaroo, over the South Australian border. The name from the aboriginal means 'wild duck'. The district produces wheat, barley, oats, fat lambs and wool. It was first settled in 1904. The town has a meat-freezing works. It has the usual sports facilities and a swimming pool.

Accommodation. One **hotel.** One **motel.** One **caravan park,** all facilities.

Transport. **Road** and **rail** services to Mildura and Melbourne.

GIPPSLAND

Gippsland is, broadly speaking, the south-eastern section of Victoria which lies between the high plateaux and ridges of the Great Dividing Range and Bass Strait and the Tasman Sea. The summer climate, particularly in East Gippsland, is equable and pleasant. The coastal plains are well watered, fertile and comprise the State's richest dairy lands. The mountains are heavily timbered and the base of important forest industries. They are also the catchment areas for rapidly growing industrial towns in the Latrobe Valley which have grown up about the enormous deposits of brown coal being mined by open-cut methods in the vicinity of Yallourn and Morwell. The Yallourn thermal electricity generating plants supply two-thirds of the power used by Victorian industry. The coal measures extend for 65 kilometres in a belt between 8 and 16 kilometres wide and are estimated to contain 17,880 million tonnes.

The economic importance of Gippsland has recently been increased by the discovery of large deposits of natural gas and oil off the coast. It has been estimated that the Bass Strait oil and gas fields, although they are as yet only partly explored and exploited, are now capable of supplying half the Commonwealth's annual consumption of petroleum crudes and, in addition, supplying Melbourne and Sydney with almost unlimited quantities of natural gas.

Gippsland is traversed from east to west by the Princes Highway, from which radiate a number of good sealed roads serving the rich coastal farming lands and the more important of the hill districts. Several roads lead north off the highway—from Sale, Lakes Entrance and Orbost. They cross the Great Dividing Range and its spurs and link with the highway networks of New South Wales in the Murray Valley and the far south coast. These traverse the most spectacular mountain and forest areas in Victoria but they are by no means first class. Their potential as tourist routes has not yet been fully developed, although the improved road through Omeo to the snowfields of Mount Hotham, and the Bonang Highway through Delegate and Bombala to the Monaro Highway are now carrying a good deal of traffic in summer and autumn.

The chain of large lakes behind the Ninety Mile Beach are popular holiday resorts for Victorians.

HISTORY Gippsland was first explored by Angus McMillan in 1839, although the colourful and publicity-conscious Polish explorer, Count Strzelecki who passed through the following year, is usually given the credit. McMillan named the district Caledonia Australis because it reminded him of his native Scotland, but the name given it by Strzelecki—in honour of Sir George Gipps, Governor of New South Wales (1838-46)—was officially adopted. Development was accelerated by the discovery of gold at Omeo, Dargo and Crooked River in the mid 1850s, but it was not until the railway from Melbourne was extended to Bairnsdale in 1887 that the pastoral and agricultural possibilities of the province were fully realized.

LATROBE VALLEY

MORWELL

(Population 22 403)

Morwell is an industrial town in the heart of the Latrobe Valley brown-coal fields 147 kilometres south-east of Melbourne. Its chief manufactures are briquettes, wood pulp and paper, textiles, clothing and shoes. Dairy and beef cattle and sheep are grazed on the surrounding countryside which is undulating with broken ranges of hills. Its satellite town of Churchill (formerly Hazlewood) was built by the Victorian Housing Commission and the Shire of Morwell. Power plants at Morwell, Churchill and Yallourn generate two-thirds of Victoria's electricity.

History. The village of Morwell was founded in 1861 and it became a shire in 1892. During the 1880s and 1890s it was a convenient stopping place for travellers making their way to the goldfields at Walhalla and Tanjil in the mountains to the north. In 1916 the Department of Mines began full-scale mining of brown coal in the area and in 1924 the newly created State Electricity Commission took over the operation. Development of the area was particularly rapid after the second world war. The 1947 census, for instance, showed that the shire population was only 3 000. Today it is more than 22 000. The briquette works started production in 1959.

Places of Interest. The **SEC mining projects, briquette works** and **power plants** are open daily for inspection.

Sports. Squash and tennis courts. Bowling and croquet greens. Swimming pool. Tenpin bowling alley.

Entertainments. One **cinema.** One **drive-in.**

Accommodation. Three **hotels.** Recommended: Morwell, Vincent Road. Three **motels.** Recommended: Latrobe Valley, Princes Highway. **Caravan and camping park,** all facilities.

Transport. **Electric train** services from Melbourne. **Road** services to surrounding towns.

MOE

(Population 15 605)

One hundred and thirty-four kilometres east of Melbourne, Moe is another of the Latrobe Valley towns which has grown phenomenally in the past 20 years from industrialization centred on the brown-coal fields. It produces milled timber, powdered milk and casein products, butter, concrete pipes, furniture, gloves and aerated waters and has large engineering, photographic processing and whole milk bottling plants and spinning mills.

The city contains some controversial low-cost housing estates built by the State Electricity Commission in the 1950s. It was proclaimed a borough in 1955 and a city in 1963. A fine scenic road leads north to **WALHALLA,** a gold mining ghost town in which interesting historic buildings and relics have been preserved, and through the mountains to **JAMIESON.**

Sports. Two good 18-hole golf courses. Racecourse. Bowling and croquet greens. Tennis courts. Olympic swimming pool. Fishing in Thompson River.

Accommodation. One **hotel.** One **motel. Caravan and camping park,** all facilities.

Transport. **Electric train** services from Melbourne. **Road** services to surrounding towns.

YALLOURN

The only town planned and built entirely by a public authority, the State Electricity Commission of Victoria, Yallourn is 144 kilometres east of Melbourne on a loop road off the Princes Highway, between Moe and Morwell. The commission owns all buildings except the post office, churches, schools, banks and associated residences. The model settlement has wide streets with lawns and tree plantations, well-designed public buildings and an attractive shopping area about the central square. The town will, however, be evacuated and demolished as the enormous brown-coal open-cut is extended. The power station and briquette works are open daily for guided inspections. The name Yallourn is the aboriginal word for 'yellow fire'.

Sports. Golf course. Rifle range. Swimming pool. Tennis and basketball courts.

Accommodation. Two **hotels.** Recommended: Yallourn, Railway Avenue. One **guest house. Caravan and camping park,** all facilities.

Transport. Co-ordinated **rail-road** service from Melbourne. Regular **bus services** to other Latrobe Valley towns.

TRARALGON

(Population 14 624)

Traralgon is an agricultural and industrial city in the Latrobe Valley, 166 kilometres east of Melbourne.

Primary industries are dairy and sheep farming, fruit growing and limestone quarrying. It is the centre of the paper-making industry in Victoria, drawing on native and exotic forest resources in the mountains to the north. It also produces cement, bricks, and small miscellaneous manufactures. It was created a borough in 1961 and a city in 1964. Traralgon is an aboriginal word for 'crane feeding on frogs'.

The Traralgon Chamber of Commerce runs an annual Industrial Exhibition and the annual agricultural show and eisteddfod create widespread interest.

Sports. Racecourse. Swimming pool. Tennis courts etc.

Accommodation. Four **hotels.** Recommended: Grand Junction. Four **motels.** Recommended: Trans Eastern, Princes Highway. **Camping ground,** limited facilities.

Transport. **Electric train** service from Melbourne (terminus). **Road** services to surrounding towns.

Smaller Towns in District

WARRAGUL (Population 7 103) is regional centre of West Gippsland's prosperous dairy farming country and a light, manufacturing town (metal fabrication, rope-making and linen) of increasing importance. Most of Melbourne's milk comes from the district. The Victorian State Dairying Festival is held every February. Good sports facilities include greyhound coursing track, racecourse, motorcycle and cycle velodrome, Olympic swimming pool, and excellent 18-hole golf course.

Accommodation. Four **hotels.** Recommended: Club, Queen Street. One **motel. Caravan and camping park,** all facilities.

DROUIN (Population 2 944), agricultural and pastoral town 96 kilometres from Melbourne, is in a scenically attractive area. The road north to Noojee and Warbuton is worth exploring.

Accommodation. Two **motels.** Recommended: Casa Blanca, Princes Highway. **Caravan and camping park,** all facilities.

TRAFALGAR (Population 1 826) is a dairying centre, conveniently situated for trips to the Upper Latrobe and Tanjil River valleys in the mountains. Good shooting and fishing. **Trafalgar South Lookout, Narracan Falls,** and **Henderson's Gully** are worth visiting.

Accommodation. One **hotel.**

EAST GIPPSLAND

SALE

(Population 10 404)

The administrative capital of Gippsland near Lake Wellington and the mouths of the Thompson and Latrobe Rivers, Sale is on Princes Highway, 276 kilometres east of Melbourne. It is the centre of a productive pastoral district and the city's secondary industries include a foundry and engineering works, a plastics plant, butter, bacon and cordials factories and joinery shops. It is the seat of Anglican and Roman Catholic bishoprics. A canal connects it with the Gippsland lakes.

The urban area itself is not particularly attractive, but it is a base from which many excursions to interesting country can be made. To the north and east lies the intensively cultivated country about the prosperous towns of **HEYFIELD, MAFFRA** and **STRATFORD,** the large **Glenmaggie Reservoir** favoured by speedboat enthusiasts, and the road across the Dargo High Plains to the alpine highway at Mount St Bernard, west of Hotham Heights. This part of the Victorian mountains is scenically exciting and as yet very little known. Only recently have the roads been improved enough to carry conventional motor traffic.

The Ninety Mile Beach resort, **SEASPRAY,** is 32 kilometres south of Sale on a good, sealed road. It provides good surfing and surf fishing.

HISTORY The first settler in the Sale district was Archibald McIntosh who established himself soon after Strzelecki passed through in 1840. His property was badly flooded soon after he arrived and he called it Flooding Creek—but when a village had been established in 1845, it was named in honour of Sir Robert (Fighting Bob) Sale, who was killed in India in 1845. The district progressed rapidly after the gold strike at Omeo in 1851. The borough of Sale was gazetted in 1863, the town in 1924, and the city in 1950. During the second world war, the RAAF base at East Sale was an important training centre for bomber pilots.

Places of Interest

Lake Guthridge **bird sanctuary.** Lake Wellington **wildlife sanctuary. Hazelwood Pondage** water sports resort.

Sports

Racecourse. Golf course. Tennis courts etc. Fishing.

Accommodation

Several residential **hotels.** Recommended: Wurruk Motor Hotel, Princes Highway. Five **motels.** Recommended: Commodore Hacienda. **Caravan and camping park,** all facilities.

Transport

Rail, road and **air** services from Melbourne.

BAIRNSDALE

(Population 8 549)

In the centre of Gippsland's sweeping coastline east of Wilson's Promontory, the southernmost tip of the Australian mainland, Bairnsdale is 285 kilometres east of Melbourne at the mouth of the Mitchell River. The town is the commercial centre of an important dairying, sheep-farming and timber-getting district, but derives at least some of its prosperity from the steadily increasing tourist traffic to the Gippsland Lakes (see Lakes Entrance). It supports a number of small secondary industries including butter, clothing and cordial factories and large timber mills.

History. The townsite was surveyed in 1860. Timber industries flourished from the earliest days, but initially some difficulty was experienced in establishing agriculture because the district was remote from markets. The importance of the town increased, however, as Lakes Entrance, 35 kilometres to the east, developed as a port for timber logged in the hills and the pastoral products of the Monaro Plains across the NSW border. Extension of the railway from Melbourne in 1887 assured the rapid development of the district thereafter.

Bairnsdale is believed to be a corruption of 'Bernisdale', the name given to the locality by an early settler from Scotland. The aboriginal name was *wyyung*, the meaning of which is obscure.

The terrain surrounding the town is flat and scenically uninteresting, but it is close to the lakes and the fascinating dune country behind the Ninety Mile Beach.

Places of Interest. Botanical Gardens. St Mary's Church, notable murals by Italian artist.

Sports. Golf course. Bowling and croquet greens. Racecourse. Rifle club. Swimming pool. Boating and fishing.

Accommodation. Eleven **hotels.** Recommended: Victoria, Main Street. Four **motels.** Recommended: Gateway Court, Princes Highway. Two **guest-houses.** One **caravan park,** all facilities. Two **camping grounds,** all facilities.

Transport. Rail and **road** services from Melbourne. **Bus** services to neighbouring centres. **Launch trips** on lakes.

Resorts in District

LAKES ENTRANCE (Population 2 581) is a well developed and popular seaside holiday resort and fishing town on the coast 37 kilometres east of Bairnsdale and marking the entrance to a chain of interconnecting lakes which stretch for 80 kilometres parallel to the Ninety Mile Beach fronting eastern Bass Strait. These scenically beautiful lagoons are separated from the sea by a narrow ridge of dunes and hummocks. The largest are Lake Wellington, Lake King, Lake Victoria and Lake Reeve. Lakes Entrance is the home port for many pleasure craft and a large fishing fleet which operates in Bass Strait. A bridge across North Arm gives access to **Ninety Mile Beach.**

Places of Interest. Shell Museum in Marine Road. **Kalimna Point. Jimmy's Point,** for panoramic views. **Lake Tyers,** for fishing and boating in sheltered water; also site of a large aboriginal settlement, (mainly of interest to sociologists). **Antique Car and Folk Museum** (open 8 am to 10 pm) on Princes Highway. **Festival Park** picnic playground.

Sports. Golf tennis, bowls etc. Fishing, sailing, swimming.

Accommodation. Three **hotels.** Recommended: Tambo River, Princes Highway, Swan Reach. Thirteen **motels.** Recommended: Sherwood Lodge, Esplanade; Glenara, Princes Highway; Bamboo, Princes Highway. Numerous **private hotels** and **guest-houses. Holiday flats** available. Nine **caravan and camping parks,** varying facilities.

Transport. Rail (to Bairnsdale) and **road** service from Melbourne. **Launch trips** on lakes. **Cabin cruisers** and **power boats** for hire.

BUCHAN (Population 221). A small town 93 kilometres north-east of Bairnsdale, set in fine mountain scenery, with picturesque river reaches and waterfalls. The fishing in the district is good. Buchan's main tourist attraction, however, is a series of **limestone caves,** now opened up and lit by electricity, which are undoubtedly the best in Victoria. Royal and Fairy are the most popular and best lit. There are conducted tours twice daily at 10.30 am and 2.30 pm with an extra inspection at 1.30 pm during Christmas and Easter holidays. The black marble used in the construction of Australia House, London, and the Shrine of Remembrance in Melbourne was quarried nearby. Motorists should note that the road north from Buchan to the Snowy Mountains towns in New South Wales can now be travelled without difficulty in good weather. It is scenically memorable.

Accommodation. One **hotel.** One **motel. Guest-house.** Excellent **caravan and camping park.**

Transport. Connecting **rail-road** service from Melbourne. **Tourist coaches** from Bairnsdale and Lakes Entrance.

LINDENOW (Population 521). In the Mitchell River valley, 19 kilometres west of Bairnsdale, Lindenow is close to the charming **Glenalandale National Park** which contains the Den of Nargun, a fascinating aboriginal ceremonial ground. Excellent for bush walking.

Accommodation. Two **hotels.**

PAYNESVILLE (Population 961). Eighteen kilometres south-east of Bairnsdale, Paynesville offers good surfing on the Ninety Mile Beach and safe swimming in sheltered water of Lake King. It is the headquarters of the Gippsland Lakes Yacht Club. Speedboat championships are held at Christmas and Easter. Fishing and shooting in the area are good.

Accommodation. One **motel hotel. Guest-houses. Holiday flats** and **cabins** available. Four **caravan and camping parks,** all facilities.

Transport. Road service from Bairnsdale.

EAGLE POINT (Population 186). Ten kilometres from Bairnsdale on road to Paynesville.

Accommodation. One **guest-house.** One large **caravan and camping park** (32 hectares).

ORBOST (Population 2 924)

Orbost is 377 kilometres from Melbourne on Princes Highway near the mouth of the Snowy River. The district carries large numbers of dairy and beef cattle, and grows maize, beans and other vegetables on the rich river flats. The town has timber mills and butter and vegetable-processing factories. It is also growing in importance as a tourist centre. The **Bonang Highway,** recommended as a scenic route, leads north through densely timbered mountains to join the Monaro Highway in NSW.

History. The first settler was a grazier, Peter Imlay, who arrived in 1842. The town was proclaimed in 1885 and incorporated in the shire in 1892. A rail link with Melbourne was established in 1915, but the terminus of the passenger service is still Bairnsdale. The town was named for Orbost in the Isle of Skye.

Sports. Good golf course. Tennis courts. Bowling and croquet greens. Olympic swimming pool. Fishing.

Accommodation. Two **hotels.** Recommended: Commonwealth, Nicholson Street. Two **motels.** Recommended: Amalgamated, Princes Highway. Two **caravan and camping parks,** all facilities.

Transport. Rail-road service from Melbourne. **Road** coach service on Princes Highway.

MARLO (Population 209). Sixteen kilometres from Orbost. Excellent fishing in Snowy and Broadribb Rivers. Good shooting on nearby lakes and lagoons.

Accommodation. One **hotel.** One **caravan and camping park.** One **camping park.**
Transport. **Road** service from Orbost.

BEMM RIVER (Population 105). Small fishing and boating settlement on Sydenham Inlet, 61 kilometres east of Orbost. Scenically dull, but excellent country for the enthusiastic angler.
Accommodation. One **hotel. Guest houses. Holiday cabins** available. One **camping ground,** limited facilities.
Transport. No public transport.

CANN RIVER (Population 335). Sixty-five kilometres east of Orbost at junction of Princes and King's Highways (the latter leading north to Bombala in NSW). A popular halfway stop for Sydney-Melbourne motorists using Princes Highway. The surrounding district produces maize and dairy produce. There is excellent fishing and bush walking in the rugged hinterland.
Accommodation. One **hotel.** One **motel.** One good **camping ground,** all facilities.
Transport. Through **road** services on Princes Highway.

MALLACOOTA (Population 215). Near the mouth of a deep inlet of the same name, Mallacoota is a tiny seaside holiday settlement much favoured by keen anglers and nature-lovers, set in a national park of about 5 000 hectares. It is 24 kilometres south-east of another small township, **GENOA,** on Princes Highway, 520 kilometres from Melbourne. The Cann River-Genoa section of the highway is rough, but it passes through very beautiful mountain and rainforest country. The **Winjan National Park** on Winjan Inlet and the **Lind-Alfred National Park,** through which the highway passes 23 kilometres east of Cann River, repay any time spent exploring them. Mallacoota itself provides some of the best fishing to be found on the Victorian coast. The town has a cinema and sports facilities. The inlet is a magnificent expanse of sheltered water. It was on this section of the coast that the explorer, George Bass, made a landing in December 1797.
Accommodation. Genoa: One **motor hotel. Camping ground,** limited facilities. Mallacoota: One **motor hotel. Guest house. Holiday flats** available. Two **caravan and camping parks,** all facilities. One **camping reserve.**
Transport. **Road** service from Bairnsdale. **Aerodrome.**

SOUTH GIPPSLAND

WONTHAGGI (Population 3 825)

A coalmining, industrial, pastoral and agricultural town 130 kilometres south-east of Melbourne, Wonthaggi is centre of the fertile Bass Valley and Glen Alvie dairying districts, but its chief importance over the years has rested on the coal it supplied the Victorian Railways before the switch-over to diesel-electric locomotives. Its secondary industries, on which more and more emphasis has been laid in recent years, include drop-forging and the manufacture of farm implements, automobile parts, clothing and cotton yarn.
History. Hume and Hovell discovered black coal deposits at nearby Cape Patterson in 1824 but early attempts to exploit the field were unsuccessful. The Victorian Railways after the 1870s were dependent on coal from the Newcastle fields of NSW and when a strike occurred there in 1909 the Victorian authorities became desperate. They hastily started to mine the Wonthaggi fields and a shanty town sprang up overnight. Thousands of miners lived under canvas until the town was laid out and partly built in late 1910. A railway to open up the town was pushed through in 1909. It was proclaimed a borough in 1911. The aboriginal word *wonthaggi* means 'to drag or pull along'.
Places of Interest. Nearby beach resorts of **INVERLOCH** (13 kilometres east on Anderson's Inlet); **WALKERVILLE,** on Waratah Bay; and **TARWIN LOWER.** They are off the beaten tourist track and offer good coastal scenery, swimming and fishing. Inverloch has a hotel and Walkerville has motel accommodation.
Sports. Golf course. Tennis courts etc.
Accommodation at Wonthaggi. Three **hotels.** Preferred: Miner's Rest, McKenzie Street. One **caravan park,** all facilities, near town, and **camping ground** at Cape Patterson.
Transport. **Rail** from Melbourne (via Nyora). **Road** services to surrounding towns.

KORUMBURRA (Population 2 916)

Market town of a district which produces butter, cheese, fat lambs, poultry, vegetables and fodder crops, Korumburra is 122 kilometres south-east of Melbourne in the centre of a high-rainfall area. Some bituminous coal and silica have been mined in the locality. which is very hilly. The giant Gippsland earthworms of interest to zoologists (and fishermen) are often found in the vicinity.
History. In the early days the Korumburra hills were densely wooded and the district was known

as Wild Cattle Run. Eventually the timber was cut out and pastures improved to carry dairy herds. The village was founded in 1880 and in 1891 it was gazetted as a shire and connected by rail with Melbourne, after which its development was steady. *Korumburra* is the aboriginal name for blowfly.

Sports. Usual facilities.

Accommodation. Three **hotels.** Recommended: Korumburra, Commercial Street. One **caravan and camping park.** One **camping ground.**

Transport. **Rail** service to Melbourne. Local **road** services.

LEONGATHA (Population 3 419)

Progressive agricultural and pastoral town 125 kilometres south-east of Melbourne, Leongatha is a base from which to make trips to **Wilson's Promontory National Park** and the seaside and fishing resorts at the south-western end of the Ninety Mile Beach.

Places of Interest in the district include **Moss Vale Park,** where there are impressive plantation of English trees.

Sports. Championship golf course at Leongatha South. Night bowling greens and tennis courts. Swimming pool.

Accommodation. Two **hotels.** Recommended: Otago. Two **motels.** Recommended: Leongatha, Turner Street. **Caravan and camping park** (Berry's Creek), some facilities.

Transport. **Rail** from Melbourne. Local **road** services.

Small Towns in District

FOSTER (Population 839). Forty-four kilometres south-east of Leongatha, Foster is a pleasant town in attractive country, and is within easy reach of Corner Inlet and Wilson's Promontory.

Accommodation. One **hotel. Camping and caravan park,** all facilities.

WELSHPOOL and **PORT WELSHPOOL** (Population 351) are a small dairying town and a one-time fishing port with romantic marine atmosphere. The port services the offshore oil rigs in Bass Strait. Excellent fishing and boating can be had by the enterprising.

Accommodation. One **hotel. Holiday flats.**

Transport. **Rail** from Melbourne.

PORT ALBERT (Population 231) was one of the earliest port settlements in Victoria (established before Melbourne for trade with Tasmania). Still an active fishing port. It is popular for fishing and shooting (some deer in back country).

Accommodation. One **hotel.** One **guest-house.** One **camping and caravan park,** all facilities, off South Gippsland Highway at McMillan's Bay. One **camping ground,** some facilities.

Transport. **Rail** to Alberton (request stop), thence bus. **Bus service** to Yarram twice weekly.

YARRAM (Population 2 028) is the centre of a dairy-farming district, 228 kilometres from Melbourne. Close to beauty spots in Strzelecki Ranges. **Tarra Valley** (with **caravan park**) and **Bulga National Parks** are both about 27 kilometres from town—and both more neglected by tourists than they should be.

Yarram is an excellent base for expeditions to Ninety Mile Beach, Wilson's Promontory and the foreshores of Corner Inlet and the Gippsland Lakes.

Sports. Golf, tennis, bowls etc. Fishing, swimming, boating and bush walking.

Accommodation. Two **hotels.** Recommended: Commercial, Main Street. Two **motels.** Recommended: Ship Inn, South Gippsland Highway. **Caravan park,** all facilities.

WILSON'S PROMONTORY

This wild, desolate headland with an area of roughly 42 000 hectares, projecting from the mainland into Bass Strait, has been closely reserved as a national park and sanctuary since 1908 and sustains much wildlife in spite of the many bushfires which have swept over it through the years. It is mountainous and heavily wooded—with tea tree and other xerophytic species on the western or windward side and with larger species on the east. Its coastal scenery is superb.

The highest point on the promontory is Mount Latrobe (743 metres) and the average annual rainfall is about 1 143 millimetres.

Walking tracks have been cleared from Tidal River, the tourist centre on Norman Bay, but the Prom, as it is popularly known, is country which will please only the genuine and fairly hardy nature-lover. For the skilled rock and beach angler, the fishing is good.

Accommodation. **Caravan and camping park,** some facilities. **Holiday lodges** and **cabins** must be booked through Government Tourist Bureau.

Pioneer settlement, Swan Hill

Lyrebird, Sherbrooke Forest

Stained glass ceiling, Victorian Arts Centre

NORTH AND NORTH-EASTERN VICTORIA

via Hume, Goulburn or Maroondah Highways

SEYMOUR (Population 5 761)

A commercial, industrial and agricultural town on the Hume Highway 98 kilometres north of Melbourne, Seymour marks the junction of the Hume and Goulburn Highways (beginning the Olympic Way deviation for north-bound travellers to Sydney). The district carries dairy cattle, sheep and stud stock, and produces cereals. Granite comes from the Trawool quarries, 11 kilometres south-east. Secondary industries include textile and knitting mills, timber mills, railway workshops, a tile factory, a gasworks and gravel pits.

History. The area was settled in 1837 and the town, surveyed in 1841, was named after Lord Seymour, son of the 11th Duke of Somerset. The district was proclaimed in 1863 and the shire in 1871. A severe earthquake, a phenomenon very rare in Australia, damaged the town in 1892. During a visit to Australia in 1909, Lord Kitchener recommended the area as particularly suitable for a military base. Nearby Puckapunyal became an important training extablishment for troops of the Second AIF in the second world war and is still used by the army. **Mangalore** aerodrome, 10 kilometres north, is an alternative landing place for Melbourne Airport in bad weather.

Place of Interest. Hume and Hovell **Memorial.**

Sports. Racecourse and usual facilities for games. River fishing.

Accommodation. One **hotel.** Three **motels.** Recommended: Wattle, Hume Highway.

Transport. **Rail** from Melbourne. On regular Sydney-Melbourne **road** coach route.

YEA (Population 1 055)

On the Yea River, a tributary of the Goulburn, and 103 kilometres north-north-east of Melbourne, Yea is a delightfully situated small town on the Goulburn Highway with a great deal to attract the sightseer and holidaymaker. The surrounding countryside is fairly closely settled pastoral and dairy-farming land which is scenically charming. There are some beautiful gorges and fern gullies close to the road between Yea and Tallarook, and to the east there is easy access to the magnificent mountain country south of Eildon Reservoir. Yea has been a winner in the Ideal Town competition.

History. The district was first settled in 1837 by overlanders from New South Wales—mostly bachelors whose rowdy behaviour on their occasional visits to town earned them the nickname 'the Goulburn Mob'. Gold was discovered in 1859, but the field was never very productive and the miners soon turned their attention to farming and timber-getting in the mountain forests to the south and east. The townsite was surveyed in 1856 and the shire proclaimed in 1873.

Places of Interest. **Kinglake National Park** to the south-south-west, with several beautiful waterfalls and **Ned Kelly's Lookout. King Parrot Creek. Mineral springs** at Dropmore, north, off the back road to Euroa. **Grotto,** at Caveat, off the same road to the east. The Snob's Creek **fish hatcheries** are easily accessible from Yea.

Sports. Racecourse (with golf course). Bowling greens. Tennis courts. Swimming pool. There is good fishing, shooting and bush-walking in the area.

Accommodation. Four **hotels. Guest-houses. Caravan and camping park,** all facilities.

Transport. **Rail** from Melbourne. Daily **road** service from Melbourne and services to neighbouring towns.

ALEXANDRA (Population 1 865). The farming town of Alexandra is situated 24 kilometres west of Lake Eildon, within easy reach of **Frazer National Park.** The National Billy Goat Derby is run at Easter every year on a specially made track.

Sports. Golf course. Lawn tennis courts. Bowling and croquet greens. Swimming pool. Picnic racecourse.

Accommodation. Four **hotels,** no preference. One **motel. Guest-houses.** Three **caravan parks,** all facilities.

Transport. **Road** service from Melbourne.

TAGGERTY (Population 208). Taggerty is in the Acheron Valley, 18 kilometres south of Alexandra on Maroondah Highway. **Rubicon Falls** is on a turnoff 11 kilometres along the Eildon Road to the west. Good trout fishing in the Acheron and Little Rivers.

Accommodation. **Guest-houses. Holiday flats** available.

Transport. **Rail** to Healesville, thence **road** service.

EILDON (Population 1 200)

The flourishing holiday town of Eildon, favoured for fishing and water sports, lies on the south-western shore of the reservoir of the same name, 142 kilometres from Melbourne. The storage for irrigation and hydro-electric power has an area of 13 000 hectares and a shoreline of 515 kilometres in times of normal rainfall. It is almost surrounded by the bush-clad foothills of the Victorian Alps and their offshoot ranges. The foreshores have been extensively developed for recreational purposes. There are two major boat harbours and launching ramps, picnic grounds and lookout points.

Places of Interest. **Frazer National Park** on the western shores. **Snob's Creek Fish Hatchery,** where two million brown and rainbow trout are bred every year; open from 10 am to 4 pm every day (except Christmas Day); pleasant park surroundings (one **motel**). Fisheries and Wildlife Department **fauna sanctuary** on road to hatchery. **Snob's Creek Falls** (107 metre cascade). **Morris Lookout,** views of township and lake. **Mount Pinniger** summit (543 metres), panorama of Mount Buller and the Alps.

The roads south from Eildon, to Marysville and Healesville, and to Warburton via the **Cumberland Falls** and the **Upper Yarra** and **O'Shannassy Dams** (Melbourne water storages) pass through some of the most spectacular mountain and forest country in Victoria. From Cumberland junction the road east to Matlock and thence south through Aberfeldy to Walhalla and Moe is also spectacular in clear weather. It commands magnificent panoramas of the high country.

Sports. Fishing; there is no closed season for trout in the lake, which is also stocked with Murray cod and Murray and English perch (redfin). Water skiing. Yachting and boating. Olympic swimming pool at Community Centre. Nine-hole golf course. Tennis and badminton courts.

Entertainments. One **cinema.**

Accommodation. One **motel.** One **guest-house.** **Holiday flats** available. Two **caravan and camping parks.**

Transport. **Road** service from Melbourne. **Launches and boats** for hire. **Ferry** trips and pleasure cruises.

JAMIESON (Population 142). Jamieson is an old mining town near the south shores of the lake and the junction of the Goulburn and Jamieson Rivers. One of the few mercury mines in the British Commonwealth is worked 26 kilometres east of the settlement. It can be reached by a bridle track skirting the gorges of the river.

Accommodation. One **hotel.** Two **motels.** No preference. **Holiday cabins** available.

Transport. **Road** services.

MANSFIELD (Population 2 021)

Nearest town to **Lake Eildon,** a reservoir formed by damming the Delatite and Goulburn Rivers Mansfield is becoming one of the most popular inland holiday resorts in Victoria. It is 198 kilometres by road from Melbourne.

Mansfield district produces wool, beef, dairy produce and timber. It was settled in the 1850s and named after Mansfield, England. The shire was proclaimed in 1866.

It is a sprawling, sleepy, prosperous town with an air of spaciousness and security, and is on the way to the popular Mount Buller snow resort. The road north-east over the mountains to **WHITFIELD** in the King River valley is scenically memorable.

Sports. Racecourse. Tennis courts. Golf course. Bowling greens. Swimming pool. There is good trout fishing and shooting in the area.

Accommodation. Three **hotels.** Recommended: Mansfield, Highett Street. One **motel.** One **caravan and camping park.**

Transport. **Rail** and **road** services from Melbourne.

EUROA (Population 2 680)

On the Hume Highway, 153 kilometres north-east of Melbourne, Euroa district produces wool, fat lambs, beef, dairy produce and cereals. It is said to have bred the first merino sheep in Victoria soon after its settlement. The village was founded in 1850 and 28 years later it became famous for the bank robbery in which the notorious Ned Kelly and his gang rounded up 50 people, locked them in the local police station and decamped with £2 200. Its name is an adaptation of the aboriginal *yera-o*, meaning 'joyful place'.

Euroa is a good base from which to explore the **Strathbogie Ranges** and tablelands, an off-beat, beautiful part of Victoria filled with atmosphere. The scenic drive to Polly McQuinn's **Gooram Falls** is also well worth while.

Every year in December, Euroa re-enacts the Kelly raid in costume. For those who enjoy that sort of thing it's great fun.

Sports. Good golf course, bowls, croquet, tennis etc.

Accommodation. Three **hotels.** Recommended: Euroa. Two **motels.** Recommended: Castle Creek, Hume Highway. One **caravan and camping park,** all facilities.

BENALLA

(Population 8 213)

A small provincial city, 198 kilometres north-east of Melbourne on the Broken River, Benalla serves a district which grows wool, fat lambs, mixed-farm and dairy produce, poultry, wheat, flax, oats, barley and potatoes. Its secondary industries are flour and timber mills, a chain factory, clothing, cordials and butter factories and railway workshops.

History. The explorer Thomas Mitchell crossed the Broken River close to the present townsite in 1836 and two years later a squatter parson, the Reverend Joseph Docker, took up a sheep run in the locality and called it 'Benalta'. The same year a party of 19, led by William Faithful, one of two brothers from the Hunter River district in New South Wales who had come south looking for land, was attacked by aborigines and 13 of the party were killed—one of the few occasions on which the natives struck successfully against the white invaders.

In 1846 a township was surveyed and named for an aboriginal word meaning 'crossing place'. The shire was incorporated in 1869. During the late 1870s and early 1880s it was the focal point for the operations of Ned Kelly's gang of bushrangers. Benalla was constituted a borough in 1948 and gazetted a city in 1965.

Sports. Racecourse, coursing track. Lawn tennis courts. Croquet and bowling greens. Two good golf courses. Gun club.

Accommodation. One **hotel.** Four **motels.** Recommended: Koala Motor Inn, Hume and Midland Highways. One **caravan and camping park,** all facilities.

Transport. Rail and **road** services.

SHEPPARTON

(Population 19 409)

Hub of the highly productive agricultural and fruit-growing area irrigated by the Yarrawonga and Eildon Reservoir schemes, Shepparton is on the junction of the Goulburn and Broken Rivers, 180 kilometres north-north-east of Melbourne. The surrounding land is largely flat to undulating with ridges marking courses of old streams, sandhills in the Cobram and Tatura areas and flood plains. The annual rainfall is about 500 millimetres.

Primary production: Fruit, vegetables, fodder and cereal crops, butter, cheese, milk, fat cattle and lambs, pigs and poultry and timber (from the Barmah red gum forests). Secondary industries: Canning and can-making, dairy produce factories, woollen mills, sawmills, winery, plaster, brick and tile works, light engineering plants.

It is estimated that there are 4 000 hectares of orchards within a 10-kilometre radius of the city and 4 000 hectares of market gardens along the river valley nearby. The district has many famous stud farms.

In 1958, Shepparton received an award for the best-planned city in Victoria and three years later was declared the winner of a premier town contest. It has a fine shopping centre surrounded by 68 hectares of parkland, an open-air music bowl, an art gallery and a public library.

History. The first settlers to overland cattle to the new colony in South Australia, Hawdon and Bonney passed through the district in 1838. It was then the tribal country of the Bangerang aborigines who called it *Kannygoopna*—'the river of big fish'. The first sheep run was Tallygaroopna which was granted to Edward Khull. However, he soon handed over to a young Irishman, Sherbourne Sheppard, who ran the property from 1843 to 1857.

In the 1850s a man named Macguire built an inn and established a punt across the Goulburn for the convenience of squatters, diggers and shepherds. For a time the spot was known as Macguire's Punt, although Shepparton was in use by the time the town was surveyed in 1855.

The Grant Land Acts (1869-71) opened up the district to closer settlement and by the end of the 1870s much of the land was taken up. Shepparton became a shire in its own right in 1879. It had previously been part of the Echuca Shire. During the late 1870s and 1880s industries based on the region's agriculture were started in the town. It was connected by rail to Melbourne in 1880. Between 1887 and 1910 irrigation resulted in even closer settlement, although at first dairy farming failed to prosper and attention was turned to fruit-growing. In 1927 the township was separated from the shire to become a borough and in 1959 it was declared a city.

Of Interest. Inspection of **canneries, fruit-packing plants** and **orchards** may be arranged —and tours to **outstanding farms** in the **TATURA, KYABRAM, TONGALA** and **MOOROOPNA** districts. **Radio Australia** transmitting station (6 kilometres); inspection can be arranged. **Lake Victoria,** beside highway, has magnificent swimming area and is surrounded by well-kept parklands. Tatura **Horticultural Research Station** (19 kilometres south-west, via Toolamba West). Dookie **State Agricultural College,** established in 1886, can be visited by appointment (34 kilometres east).

Sports. Good golf course. Bowling and croquet greens. Tennis courts. Race and trotting track. Olympic swimming pool (at Lake Victoria).

Accommodation. Six **hotels.** Recommended: Commodore, Wyndham Street. Six **motels.**

Recommended: Parklane, Wyndham Street. Two **guest-houses.** One **caravan and camping park,** all facilities.

Transport. Daily **rail** services from Melbourne. Weekly **road coach** service from Melbourne. Regular **bus** services from Bendigo, Benalla, Echuca and Griffith (NSW). **Aerodrome** 5 kilometres from town.

WANGARATTA

(Population 15 535)

At the junction of the Ovens and King Rivers, 238 kilometres north-east of Melbourne, Wangaratta is the gateway to some of the most beautiful and characterful upland and mountain country in Victoria. The Ovens Highway, which joins the Hume Highway near the town, leads south-east through the small towns of Myrtleford and Bright into the heart of the Victorian Alps.

Wangaratta is one of the best planned and most attractive provincial cities in Victoria. It has 122 hectares of parkland. The surrounding district produces wool, wheat, oats, wine and table grapes, dairy produce, tobacco, hops and flax. Urban industries include cheese, butter, bacon, cordials, tile and plaster factories, woollen, knitting, timber, rayon and flax mills, motor engineering works, gas and bulk petrol storages.

History. The district was traversed by the explorers Hume and Hovell in 1824 when they discovered and named the Ovens River and Major T. H. Mitchell examined it in 1836. The following year the first settler, George Faithfull, established a run. The spot became a stock and punt crossing and a village began to grow up near the homestead. It was gazetted as a township under the aboriginal name which means 'home of the cormorants' or, as others believe, 'a meeting of rivers'. The borough was constituted in 1863 and it reached city status in 1959.

Places of Interest. GLENROWAN, a small township 16 kilometres south-west, famous because it was the scene of the last stand made by the notorious bushranger, Ned Kelly, who was captured after a bloody gunfight in and about the local hotel, and subsequently condemned and hanged in Melbourne. The place of Kelly's capture and the site of the hotel, which was burned down, are close to the present settlement.

Sports. Racecourse. Motor-racing circuit at Tarrawingee (11 kilometres east). Golf course. Tennis courts (lawn). Coursing. Bowling greens. Olympic swimming pool. An Australia Day racing, sports and athletic carnival is held in January every year.

Accommodation. Two **hotels.** Recommended: Royal Victoria, Faithfull Street. Six **motels.** Recommended: Merriwa Park, Ryley Street. Wangaratta Motor Inn, Roy Street. One **caravan and camping park,** all facilities.

Transport. Good **rail** and **road** services from Melbourne and to nothern towns.

BEECHWORTH (Population 3 117)

A small town, magnificently sited on the edge of the Victorian Alps at an altitude of 550 metres, 272 kilometres from Melbourne and 39 kilometres from Albury, Beechworth has a temperate summer climate and is also pleasant in winter.

Its public buildings are of architectural merit and considerable historical interest. They have been carefully and intelligently preserved with the help of the National Trust which has classified 32 as historically important. The town's keen civic pride, expressed in plantations of exotic and native trees and well-tended gardens, has resulted in its twice winning the Victorian 'Ideal Town' award.

The primary industries of the district are fruit, hops and tobacco growing, some tin mining and forestry.

History. Hume and Hovell passed close to the present site of the town in 1824, but the first settler in the valley did not arrive until 1839. A shepherd employed by the original pioneer discovered the fabulously rich alluvial goldfield on Woolshed Creek in the 1850s. Three million ounces of gold were won in 14 years.

The original name of the mushroom town which sprang up to accommodate the diggers was Mayday Hills, but the Government surveyor renamed it Beechworth after his birthplace in England. It is claimed that a candidate for election to the Victorian Parliament, Daniel Cameron, campaigning to represent the Ovens Valley constituency, once rode through the township at the head of a procession of gorgeously clad miners on a horse shod with golden shoes. Sceptical researchers have since alleged that the shoes were merely gilded—but the story illustrates the spirit of times when Beechworth had a population of 8 000, 61 hotels, and a theatre in which international celebrities of the entertainment world performed. The town was officially gazetted in 1856.

Places of Interest. Post Office, rebuilt in 1867 after a serious fire. The tower clock was imported in 1859 and the only repair it has required since is replacement of its pendulum. **Powder Magazine,** built of local granite in 1859, restored and furnished as a museum. **Government Buildings,** Ford Street, still intact as a historical and architectural entity; built of local honey-coloured granite in the 1850s. **Robert O'Hara Burke Memorial Museum,** with carefully preserved relics of goldrush days. **Old gaol and cell** in which bushranger Ned Kelly was held after arrest. **Harness and Carriage Museum. Chinese funeral ovens,** at the Beechworth Cemetery. **Kelly's Lookout** overlooking Woolshed Creek. **Waterfalls** at Reid's Creek, Woolshed, and Clear Creek. **Beechworth Gorge.**

The Woolshed and other streams in the district, which is highly mineralized, are good fossicking grounds for gem prospectors. Small diamonds, sapphires, rubies and many kinds of semi-precious stones have been washed out of the sands.

Sports. Golf course. Grass and hardcourt tennis courts. Bowling greens. Angling at Lakes Kerford and Sambell. Olympic swimming pool.

Accommodation. Three **hotels.** Recommended: Commercial, Ford Street. One **motel.** Two **caravan and camping parks,** all facilities.

Transport. Road service from Wangaratta.

BRIGHT (Population 4 825)

On the Ovens River, 314 kilometres from Melbourne, Bright is situated in scenically beautiful country in the shadow of the Alps and is a popular base for winter sports enthusiasts in the season. It is on the road to some of Victoria's finest skiing grounds. The district produces mixed-farm produce, tobacco, apples and timber from native forests and pine plantations. It is excellent for trout fishing, walking and colour photography.

History. The first pastoral property in the area was owned by Thomas Buckland (or Bucklin) who ran sheep and cattle on 25 000 acres in the Ovens Valley in 1845. Alluvial gold mining began in the valley in 1853. Tensions between white and Chinese miners led to the notorious Buckland riots of 1857 in which the Chinese were driven from their claims with great brutality. The village of Bright itself was not founded until 1862. It was named after John Bright, English orator and statesman (1811-89) and was gazetted as a shire in 1866. Goldmining was revived in 1899 by the introduction of dredges, and profitable operations continued for many years. By 1913, 38 dredges were operating. The alluvial ground is now fully exploited.

Of Interest. An Autumn Festival of the Falling Leaves is held every year and has become a major tourist attraction. Good panoramic views can be had from **Mount Porepunkah, Clear Spot, Higgins Lookout** and **Tower Hill.**

Sports. Tennis court. Bowling and croquet greens.

Entertainment. One **cinema.**

Accommodation. Two **hotels.** Recommended: Pinewood, Gavan Street. Two **motels.** Recommended: Buffalo View, Porepunkah (six kilometres north-west). Five **guest-houses. Holiday cottages.** Three **caravan and camping parks,** all facilities.

Transport. Road service from Wangaratta.

MYRTLEFORD (Population 2 738)

Situated in the rich Ovens River valley 272 kilometres north-east of Melbourne, Myrtleford is the centre of a progressive agricultural district which produces tobacco, hops, timber, dairy produce, prime beef and walnuts—it boasts the largest walnut grove in the southern hemisphere. A tobacco and hops festival is held at Easter, an agricultural and pastoral show late in October, and a rodeo on Boxing Day. The town is a convenient base for tours of the Victorian snow resorts and the Kiewa Hydro Electric Scheme.

Sports. Tennis, bowls, golf etc. Swimming pool. Motor racing circuit. Excellent fishing in nearby streams.

Accommodation. Four **hotels.** Preferred: Myrtleford, Standish and Smith Streets. Two **motels.** Recommended: Myrtleford, Ovens Highway. **Caravan and camping park,** all facilities.

SNOW RESORTS OF THE NORTH-EAST

Victoria's seasonal snowfields—the first heavy falls usually occur towards the end of May or early June and ski runs remain in good condition until mid-October—cover an area greater than that of all Switzerland. The major resorts have been established at an altitude of about 1800 metres in terrain which provides a wide variety of runs and a maximum of shelter.

Skiing has become widely popular in Australia only since the second world war, after which alpine accommodation was vastly improved, well-engineered roads built on to the high plains, and refinements such as ski tows and chair lifts introduced. But oddly enough Australia was one of the first countries in the world to begin snow sports and competitions. The population of the gold-mining towns in the high mountains travelled on crude skis back in the 1860s and they amused themselves by organizing downhill races and contriving obstacle courses probably a good deal more difficult and dangerous than most modern slaloms.

Old photographs show Chinese miners on the high plains glissading down slopes astride poles with which they braked their descent when the speed became dangerous. As the mines were worked out, however, snow sports declined for many years, but skis, snowshoes and sleds had wide utilitarian use among pastoral workers on sheep and cattle runs in the mountains. Skiing was kept alive by a few enthusiasts who had acquired a taste for it overseas and who were hardy enough to make long, difficult and often dangerous journeys to the good runs on foot from base camps below the snowline.

Development of construction roads to various hydro-electric works and improvement of forestry and fire-control roads substantially contributed to the opening of the snow sports country. Within recent years access has been so improved that cars equipped with chains can get to within a short distance of most chalets and lodges in almost any weather and tracked snow vehicles can carry visitors over the remainder.

Accommodation at the commercial chalets is now very comfortable indeed, but Australia generally and Victoria in particular still lacks the luxury winter sports hotel which has become an institution in Europe, Canada, New Zealand or the United States. Concentration has been almost exclusively on straight skiing facilities. There are no great toboggan runs, skating rinks—or solariums for the indolent. The resorts are gay, highly informal and mainly for the young in years or heart.

Because of relatively moderate winter temperatures, Australian snow is a good deal 'wetter' than it is in Europe, and the best skiing is not to be had until it has compacted and formed a firm crust. In most years this does not happen until August or September. Then the running can be as fine as it is anywhere in the world.

Compared with alpine areas elsewhere in the world, the terrain is gentle—although you can get all the long, fast running you want—and there are few hazards from precipitous ravines or avalanches. As touring country the Australian Alps are unsurpassed.

HOTHAM HEIGHTS (1 832 metres)

Most reliable for snow, Mount Hotham is also the most difficult to reach of all the Victorian resorts. It is 373 kilometres from Melbourne by the shortest route. There are two approach roads—one through Harrietville via Wangaratta to the north-west, and one through Omeo via Bairnsdale in the south-east. The latter is undoubtedly the easier and safer under severe conditions.

There is a good variety of runs at Hotham and magnificent touring in Swindler's Valley, but the area is generally speaking more suited to the experienced skier than to the novice. The surroundings are extremely beautiful both in winter and summer, with fine panoramas of the 'roof' of Australia. Hotham Heights chalet is Australia's highest inhabited house. Ski facilities. Poma lift pole line. Rope tow. Chair lift.

Accommodation. **Hotham Heights Chalet. The Drift Chalet. White Crystal Chalet.** Ski club **lodges.** (Advance bookings absolutely necessary.)

Transport. Regular **road** services from Bright, Harrietville and Omeo, weather permitting.

MOUNT BEAUTY (Population 1 569). A model township created for construction workers on State Electricity Commission's **Bogong High Plains (Kiewa) hydro-electricity scheme,** now largely a holiday resort. A fine scenic road gives access to **Falls Creek** ski resort and **Rocky Valley Dam,** highest water storage in Australia, and plateau beyond. (Difficult travelling in winter.) One **motel.**

HARRIETVILLE (Population 310) is a starting place for alpine resorts. One **hotel.** One **camping ground,** some facilities (hot water, electricity).

OMEO (Population 417)

On Livingstone Creek, 413 kilometres by road north-east of Melbourne, Omeo is situated in the heart of the Victorian Alps at an altitude of 643 metres. It is a base for winter traffic approaching the snow resort at Mount Hotham from the south and for bush-walking and fishing expeditions to the Bogong High Plains in summer and autumn. There are many fine trout streams and interesting caves to explore in the district. Besides the alpine highway which leads into the Murray Valley road complex, a scenic road—narrow and difficult to negotiate in bad weather—leads north-north-east to Corryong near the NSW border. The high country carries a large number of cattle after the snows have melted and there is much valuable timber in the valleys. Motorists using the road to Corryong should be alert for timber transports and wandering stock.

History. The high plains around Omeo were opened up as early as 1835 when overlanders from the Monaro moved stock south on to the lush summer pastures. The first permanent settler was an employee of Angus McMillan, who penetrated the coastal plains of Gippsland in 1839 before Count Strzelecki crossed the mountains in 1840. In 1851 the Reverend W. B. Clarks discovered gold in the hills and a rush set in, but the field was never of much real importance. The shire of Omeo was incorporated in 1872.

The little settlement has several times suffered natural disasters. Earthquakes devastated it in 1885 and 1892 and it was destroyed by the Black Friday bushfires of 1939. Omeo is an aboriginal word for 'mountains'. Many old buildings in the district are of considerable historic interest.

Sports. Tennis courts and golf course.

Accommodation. Two **hotels.** Preferred: Golden Age, Day Avenue. One **motel. Caravan and camping park,** all facilities.

Transport. Road service from Bairnsdale.

MOUNT BULLER (1 570 metres)

Only 257 kilometres from Melbourne and 48 kilometres from Mansfield, Mount Buller is the most developed of the alpine tourist villages. In a normal year the snow is good from June to September. The runs do not provide quite the challenge and variety found on Hotham. There are seven T-Bars, 5 Poma lifts and one chair lift on the most popular slopes. The village has a ski hire and repair service and two ski schools.

Accommodation. Kooroora Chalet (heated swimming pool). **Ivor Whittaker Lodge. Arlberg House.** Privately owned **chalets** and **lodges.** (Inquire Government Tourist Bureau.)

Transport. Rail to Mansfield, then **road.** Special trains at weekends during the season. The journey from Melbourne takes approximately six hours. **Coach** service leaves Melbourne at 11.15 am Sunday.

FALLS CREEK SKI VILLAGE (1 500 to 1 800 metres)

Surrounded by some of the highest mountains in Victoria, Fall's Creek ski runs, 29 kilometres from Mount Beauty and 373 kilometres from Melbourne, are so protected that they can be used safely in almost any weather. The village is built in an area controlled by the State Electricity Commission and a permit must be obtained at either the Government Tourist Bureau in Melbourne or from the gate house at Mount Beauty before entering. No four-wheel drive vehicles are permitted in the vicinity of the village and access in the snow season is by way of tracked vehicles from the car park just beyond Mount Beauty. The runs are equipped with four T-Bars, one chair lift and two Poma lifts. There is a ski hire service and a ski school. Many skiers stay at Mount Beauty which is just below the snow line and travel to the runs daily.

Accommodation. Eleven **lodges** and **chalet.** (Details from Victorian Government Tourist Bureau).

MOUNT BUFFALO

Mount Buffalo is not purely a winter sports resort. It has many scenic attractions and in summer is popular for fishing and boating at **Lake Catani,** swimming, riding, bushwalking and tennis. The snow is somewhat unpredictable, but after good falls is satisfactory on the Cresta run, high on the mountain, and on gentler slopes at Dingo Dell. There is a ski school, one 500 metre chair lift, a Poma lift and a T-bar. There is skating on the lake after a heavy freeze.

The mountain was named by the explorers, Hume and Hovell, because its humped granite mass which rises to nearly 1 800 metres reminded them of a bison.

Accommodation. **The Chalet,** run by the Victorian Railways. **Tatra Motor Inn** (licensed). **Camping and caravan park** on the shores of Lake Catani, open December to May only.
Transport. **Rail** from Melbourne to Wangaratta (about five hours) thence **road** service to chalet.

CENTRAL VICTORIA

WESTERN SECTION (via Western Highway)

BACCHUS MARSH (Population 4 143). On the Werribee River and off the Western Highway 53 kilometres west-north-west of Melbourne, Bacchus Marsh serves a dairying, fruit-growing and brown coal-mining district. Secondary industrial products include condensed milk, firebricks, hardboard and plastics. Founded by Captain W. H. Bacchus in 1839, it was a staging post for Cobb and Co coaches to the goldfields and was gazetted a shire in 1856.
Places of Interest. **Captain Bacchus's house** in Manor Street. **Werribee Gorge National Park** and **Lerderderg Gorge** (of interest to lapidarists and bushwalkers).
Sports. Bowls, golf, swimming.
Accommodation. Two **hotels.** Recommended: Court House, Main Street. **Camping ground,** some facilities.
Transport. **Road** and **rail** services from Melbourne.

BALLAN (Population 620). A small township on the Werribee River, Ballan is noted for its mineral springs and serves a farming and potato-growing district. Good trout fishing in Pykes Creek reservoir 8 kilometres east on highway.
Accommodation. One **hotel.** One **camping park** on Spargo River.
Transport. **Rail.**

BALLARAT

(Population 58 434)

In Victoria's central highlands 112 kilometres west-north-west of Melbourne and at an altitude of 438 metres, Ballarat is Australia's largest inland city. It serves a productive pastoral and agricultural district growing wool, cereals, fruit and vegetables but it is also the centre of thriving secondary industry. More than 300 factories in the Greater Ballarat area employ some 9 000 workers producing wool and cotton goods, bricks, tiles and pipes, cement, furniture, foodstuffs, industrial chemicals, light machinery, paper, beer, paints, iron, steel and tinware. The main workshops of the Victorian Railways are the city's largest heavy industry, employing 1 250 men.

Ballarat preserves to a great extent the atmosphere of the 1860s and 1870s when many of its fine public buildings and churches were built. It also boasts more than 270 kilometres of tree-planted streets and avenues, many of which also have flower beds, lawns and statuary. Its public parks and gardens are beautifully kept and extremely colourful, particularly in autumn. Unfortunately the new suburbs have considerably less architectural and aesthetic merit than the old city itself.

The aboriginal word *ballaarat* means 'resting place'.

History. In August 1837, a Scot, Thomas Livingstone Learmonth, climbed Mount Bonan Yowang (Buninyong) and first looked down on the area where Ballarat was to be built. Several months later, in March 1838, Henry Anderson and William Cross Yuille selected a sheep run on the shores of Black Swamp (now Lake Wendouree). For the next decade the area developed slowly as a grazing district. Then, in July 1851, James Esmond found gold at Clunes, 33 kilometres to the north. On 3 August a nugget was grubbed out of the ground near Buninyong cemetery by Thomas Hiscock and in August rich strikes were also made at Golden Point. The Ballarat field had the richest deposit of alluvial gold ever found. Within one year of the first strike, the little pastoral community had been proclaimed a town. The population in 1853 was over 20 000.

The turmoil of the rush and the profound changes wrought in the Australian economy and social order led to the only serious attempt at revolution the country has ever known—and it wasn't a particularly dangerous attempt at that.

In 1854, angered by chaotic conditions on the field and inept administration, and by what they claimed to be a miscarriage of justice in a criminal case, a group of diggers led by J. B. Humffray, Timothy Hayes, Peter Lalor, Colonel Frederick Vern, Raffaello Carboni and George Black, demanded the abolition of miners' licences, manhood suffrage, payment of Members of Parliament and abolition of property qualifications for electors and members alike. On 29 November the miners burned their licences and swore allegiance to a new Australian flag. A stockade was built and fighting between the rebels and police and troops broke out on 3 December. Five soldiers and about 22 of the insurgents were killed and 128 taken prisoner.

At their trial the leaders of the 'Eureka Stockade' were found not guilty and in March 1855 a government commission recommended the granting of the miners' more urgent demands. The licence fee was replaced by an export fee on gold and a miner's right, which could be purchased for £1, permitted the miner to vote.

In 1858 the famous Welcome Nugget was found at a depth of 58 metres by a party of 24 prospectors at Bakery Hill. It weighed 2217 ounces and was sold for £10 500. When melted down in London it proved to have a pure gold content of 99.20 percent.

In 1863 Ballaarat was proclaimed a borough.

Five years later the peak of the boom was reached. Three hundred companies were operating in the district and the population was approximately 64 000. In 1870 the city was proclaimed, but the same year saw an unaccountable recession in population. Some 40 per cent of the population left, either for other goldfields or to invest their profits in agricultural land. In 1921 the city of Ballarat and East Ballarat were amalgamated.

Deep mining of gold-bearing reefs continued profitably for many years until production costs overtook the fixed price of gold. The city no longer depends on its mines, but nurtures hopes that changes in the future may one day resurrect them. The oldtimers declare there is as much gold left in the deep orebodies as ever came out.

Places of Interest. **Lake Wendouree,** a man-made lake on what was originally swamp land. It has an area of 243 hectares and has been developed for aquatic sports. The foreshores have been pleasantly landscaped. **Botanic Gardens,** about 41 hectares adjoining Lake Wendouree. They contain the famous Begonia House, centre of a **festival** held every year in March, which attracts flower-lovers and horticulturists from all over Australia and New Zealand. (A begonia is the city's floral emblem.) Fine statuary, including Benzoni's 'Flight from Pompeii', Ball's 'Wallace' and Summer's 'Susannah' is housed in the pavilion. **Victory Arch and Avenue of Honour,** 22 kilometres long on the Burrumbeet Road leading into the city, contains 391 trees, one for each man and woman who enlisted during the first world war. The planting took over two years. The Arch of Victory was opened by Edward Prince of Wales in June 1920. **Eureka Stockade Memorial,** at the site of the original stockade in East Ballarat. **Montrose Cottage** and **Eureka Military Museum.** **Sovereign Hill,** an authentic and notable replica of early gold mining town, with model 'mine' workings, shops, offices, bank etc. and restored vehicles of the period. **Lal Lal Falls,** on Moorabool River, south-east of city. **Flagstaff Hill Lookout,** Grenville, west of city. **Calembeen Park,** Creswick, 18 kilometres north. Wildlife and pool where Victorian State Diving Championships are held. **School of Forestry** and State Nursery at Creswick. **Old Curiosity Shop,** Queen Street South, with period furniture and pioneer relics built by a Cornish migrant who came to Australia in 1855. **Shell House,** Lindisfarne Crescent, remarkable examples of mosaic work. **Lake Burrumbeet,** 23 kilometres north-west, developed for speedboats and water skiing (excellent trout fishing). Fine **Art Gallery** (notable collection), **Historical Museum, Ballarat School of Mines and Industries,** city. **Adam Lindsay Gordon's Cottage,** Botanic Gardens. **Smeaton House,** Smeaton, north of Creswick, built for pioneer Captain Hepburn between 1844 and 1850. Fine examples of architecture of the times.

Annual Events. Begonia Festival, March. Royal South Street Eisteddfod. Competitions in music and dramatic arts held in September and October and lasting seven weeks. Held in the Royal South Street Memorial Theatre.

Sports. Ballarat has facilities for most popular modern sports, including three first class golf courses and a dog racing track.

Accommodation. Five **hotels.** Recommended: Begonia City, Western Highway. Seven **motels.** Recommended: Mid City, Doveton Street. **Guest-houses.** Two **caravan and camping parks,** all facilities.

Transport. **Rail** services to all parts of Victoria. **Road** services to nearby country towns and to NSW and South Australia. **Electric tram** and **bus** services within the city limits.

Note. To guide visiting motorists to points of major interest a scenic route starting at the City Hall has been signposted with the begonia emblem. There is an office of the Victorian Government Tourist Bureau at 34 Lydiard Street North.

BEAUFORT (Population 1 200). Midway between Ballarat and Ararat, 156 kilometres from Melbourne, Beaufort is a pastoral, mining and agricultural town in pleasant, open country. There is a fine scenic road, north of the highway, to Ararat via Mount Cole on the Dividing Range, with interesting **caves** nearby. There are sports facilities and a good swimming pool in town. Beaufort has a gliding club.

Accommodation. Three **hotels.** No information. One **camping park.**

Transport. **Rail** from Melbourne.

DAYLESFORD (Population 2 946). Spa resort 126 kilometres north-west of Melbourne, Daylesford is a quite town situated in picturesque hilly country. **HEPBURN SPRINGS,** 3 kilometres north, have waters reputed to possess high therapeutic value. The town was founded in goldrush days and a few relics still survive of architecture favoured by early Swiss-Italian miners and settlers.

Places of Interest. Botanic Gardens on Wombat Hill, **Jubilee Lake, The Blowhole, Break-neck Gorge, Sailors Falls, Loddon** and **Trentham Falls, Mount Franklin** 13 kilometres (north—extinct volcano).

Sports. Golf, tennis, bowls, swimming, fishing. A Highland gathering is held in November.

Accommodation. Several **hotels.** Recommended: Belvedere, Vincent Street. One **motel. Holiday flats and cottages** available. Four **camping and caravan parks,** limited facilities.

Transport. Rail motor service to Melbourne daily. Weekly **motor coach** service. Daily **bus** services from Ballarat and Bendigo. Frequent bus services to Hepburn Springs from town.

KYNETON (Population 3 472). On Calder Highway and Campaspe River 83 kilometres from Melbourne, Kyneton is noted for its magnificent street plantations and excellently preserved bluestone buildings, some of which pre-date the gold-rush of 1851. The town, situated in rich mixed farming country, is closely associated with the history of inland settlement in Victoria. The first stations in the district were carrying stock and the first croplands ploughed as early as 1841. The townsite was surveyed in 1849 after a visit by Superintendent La Trobe and named by the wife of a pioneer settler after her birthplace in Warwickshire. Kyneton farms prospered greatly from the gold rushes and supplied the diggings at Ballarat and Bendigo with large quantities of fresh food. The district is still one of the most productive agricultural and pastoral areas in Victoria.

Places of Interest. Historical Museum, Piper Street, in original Bank of New South Wales built in 1855, with a **drop-log cottage** built in 1840 re-erected in the grounds. (Open Monday to Friday, 1.30 pm to 4.30 pm; Saturday and Sunday, 10 am to noon). **Municipal Gardens** with more than 500 ancient trees on six hectares site above river. **Old Malt House** (splendid bluestone building). **Mechanic's Institute. Old Police Depot. La Trobe's country residence** (3 kilometres south). **St Paul's Anglican Church** (1855). **St Mary's Roman Catholic Church** (1861). **Methodist Church** (1855). **Lauriston** and **Malmsbury Reservoirs.**

Sports. Race and trotting tracks. Golf, tennis, bowls etc. Swimming, Fishing and shooting. Coursing. Hunt Club.

Accommodation. One **hotel.** One **motel. Caravan park,** all facilities.

Transport. Rail service.

HEATHCOTE. A small township on the McIvor Highway about 120 kilometres from Melbourne in charming countryside.

Places of Interest. McIvor Range Reserve with historic **Powder Magazine,** now being restored. **Viewing Rock** lookout. **Pink Cliffs** (eroded spoil from gold sluices with brilliant mineral staining). **Mount Ida Lookout. Stranger Rock,** a red granite boulder deposited by ancient glacier. **Heathcote Hospital,** sandstone building erected in 1859. **Lake Eppalock,** Victoria's fourth largest reservoir, developed for fishing and water sports.

BENDIGO

(Population 45 860)

The second 'golden city' of Victoria's central highlands, Bendigo is today an extremely prosperous commercial centre for the rich pastoral and agricultural district north of the Great Dividing Range between the Campaspe River valley and the Loddon River flats. It is 155 kilometres north of Melbourne on the Calder Highway to Mildura. It is the third-largest sheep market in Australia—after Homebush, Sydney, and Newmarket, Melbourne—more than one million head passing through the saleyards every year. Besides wool, the surrounding countryside produces wheat, apples, poultry, dairy and market-garden produce. Secondary industries include a railway engineering works, plaster, steel and tile works, brick kilns, pottery factories and a Commonwealth Ordnance Factory.

Bendigo is interesting architecturally in that it is probably the best-preserved example of Victorian building tastes left in Australia. In the ornate, neo-classical style of the mid-19th century, many of the public and commercial buildings in the city were solidly built in the flush days of the gold-rush and have been—so far at least—carefully preserved. Architecturally it is the most interesting and integrated provincial city in Australia. Many buildings have fine iron lace decoration.

History. The first sheep run in the district was taken up in 1840 by Charles Sherratt (or Sherrard) at Ravenswood. Among the shepherds employed in the valley was a local pugilist nicknamed 'Bendigo' after the then-famous British prizefighter, Abednego William Thompson. Although the little settlement that grew up about the outstation was first known as Castleton and then as Sandhurst, it was always colloquially referred to as 'Bendigo'.

In 1851, gold was discovered by a shepherd at the Rocks (now Golden Square). Eventually the field extended over an area of 3 600 hectares and during the first decade it produced over four million oz. The record year was 1856, when 661,715 oz was mined. About 25 million ounces came from the field before active mining was discontinued in 1955. Several large nuggets, including the Victoria (340 oz) and another of 573 oz, were found in the White Horse Gully field. In 1853 Cobb and Co opened a coach run from Sandhurst to Melbourne and in 1855 the area was proclaimed a municipal district. In 1863 it became a shire and in 1871 a city. Bendigo remained officially Sandhurst until 1891 when the name was changed after a plebiscite of district residents.

Places of Interest. **Botanic Gardens** at White Hill (3 kilometres, bus service). **Rosalind Park** and **Mall Gardens. Alexandra Fountain** at Charing Cross. **Post Office** (elaborate Renaissance style) and **Shamrock Hotel. State Public Offices** and **Capital Theatre. Bendigo Art Gallery,** with fine collection of Australian paintings and the Neptune Scott collection of French impressionists. **Statue of George Lansell,** Bendigo's most successful miner. **Lake Weeroona,** Echuca Road. **Eppalock Weir** (24 kilometres). **The Whipstick Reserve. Chinese Joss House,** Emu Point (restored and furnished with various curios and *objets d'art*).

Entertainments. The city organizes three annual carnivals—The **Easter Fair** (at which the Chinese community's elaborate dragon, Loong, is paraded); the **Fountain Carnival** in November (**Bendigo Cup** race meeting); **Bendigo Two Thousand** athletic meeting at Labour Day weekend in March (Australia's richest footrace for professional runners).

Sports. Facilities for all popular games. Racecourse. Trotting track at Junorton. Olympic pool. Dog racing at Eaglehawk.

Accommodation. Seventeen **hotels.** Recommended: Murray's Motor Hotel, High Street. Eight **motels.** Recommended: Commodore, View Street; Elm, High Street. Two **guest-houses.** Three **caravan and camping parks,** all facilities.

Transport. **Rail** services from Melbourne, northern Victoria etc. **Road** services from Melbourne, Ballarat and Echuca.

Smaller Towns (north on Calder Highway)

INGLEWOOD (Population 760). Historic goldmining town in district where 98 sizeable gold nuggets, the largest of which was the Welcome Stranger (2 280 oz), were found. Sites of the major finds have been signposted.

Of Interest. **Melville's Caves** (19 kilometres west) where the notorious bushranger Captain Melville had his hideout.

WEDDERBURN (Population 785). At this small settlement 29 kilometres north of Inglewood, a gold strike was made in the 1860s. Ninety years later nuggets worth $20 000 were found in the backyard of a local house.

Of Interest. **General Store Museum** and **Pottery** using local clay. **Wychitella Forest Reserve,** a wild life and lowan (Mallee fowl) sanctuary.

Accommodation. One **hotel.** One **motel. Camping and caravan park.**

CHARLTON (Population 1 395). Centre of a wheat and wool district, 182 kilometres north of Bendigo, Charlton excels in sports facilities.

Of Interest. **Wooroonook Lakes** for swimming and boating. Avoca River for fishing.

Accommodation. Two **hotels.** Preferred: Cricket Club. One **motel. Caravan and camping park.**

WYCHEPROOF (Population 1 000). Service centre of wheat growing area, 278 kilometres from Melbourne on margins of Mallee. The railway line to Mildura runs down the middle of the main street.

Of Interest. Sections of netting **Dog Fence,** built in 1885 from the South Australian border to the Murray River, have been preserved as historical curiosity (about 20 kilometres north of town).

Accommodation. Two **hotels.** No preference. **Camping and caravan park.**

ST ARNAUD (Population 3 755). Once a goldmining town, St Arnaud is now the centre of a prosperous agricultural area, 231 kilometres from Melbourne, on the junction of the North-Western and Wimmera highways. It is the seat of an Anglican bishopric, and has pleasant **Botanic Gardens** and fine sports facilities at **Pioneer Park,** overlooking town, as well as race and trotting tracks.

Accommodation. Two **hotels.** Recommended: St Arnaud, Melbourne Road. One **motel. Caravan and camping park.**

Transport. **Rail** from Melbourne. **Road** from Maryborough.

CASTLEMAINE

(Population 7 547)

Old goldmining town 119 kilometres north-west of Melbourne at junction of the Midland and Pyrenees highways, Castlemaine is centre of a pastoral, agricultural and timber-getting district. Wattle Gully mine near the town is still producing gold. One of the biggest engineering workshops in Victoria produces condensers, pumps and railway equipment. There are also brickworks, a woollen mill and bacon, cordial and sausage casing factories.

History. The locality was settled in 1836. In 1851 gold was discovered in Specimen Valley and the population of the original settlement, Forest Creek, soared. It was gazetted a borough in 1855 and named after Viscount Castlemaine; proclaimed a town in 1950 and a city in 1965.

Places of Interest. Town Market, built 1861 at a cost of £7 000. **Vaughan Mineral Springs** (13 kilometres south-west via Yapeen). **Mount Alexandra Koala Park** (13 kilometres. **Art Gallery** and **Museum.** Campsite of **Burke and Wills** expedition at Fryerstown (18 kilometres south-east).

Sports. Golf course. Tennis courts. Bowling and croquet greens. Olympic swimming pool.

Accommodation. Two **hotels.** One **motel. Guest-houses.** Excellent **caravan and camping park.**

Transport. Rail from Melbourne. Bendigo-Ballarat **bus** and **road** services to neighbouring towns.

MALDON (Population 938). An agricultural and mining town on the slopes of Mount Tarrangower, 125 kilometres from Melbourne and 18 kilometres north-west of Castlemaine, Maldon has the distinction of being the only town declared as notable in its entirety by the Victorian branch of the National Trust.

Gold was discovered at the foot of Mount Tarrangower in 1853 by a Polish prospector named Mechosk, who scored other almost uncanny successes in other parts of Victoria and retired on the proceeds of the rewards he won from the State Government. Maldon's alluvial fields lasted only a few years but the deep reef mines turned out to be among Victoria's richest and produced several million ounces of gold. At one stage there were 20 000 men on the Tarrangower diggings. The town, built mainly of local stone, grew rapidly, and most of its important buildings are still in a fair to good state of preservation. They include the **Maldon Hospital,** built in 1859; the **post office,** where the famous novelist **Henry Handel Richardson** lived as a child; **St Augustine's Church;** old **Council Offices,** now converted into a **Folk Museum** containing many fascinating relics; **'Dabb's General Store'** in the main shopping centre where the old store fronts have been faithfully restored.

The last of the big mines, some of which were worked to a depth of more than 457 metres, closed in 1926, but as late as 1930 a freak strike earned a syndicate £33 000 from a shaft only 27 metres deep. A dredge still operates in the district and fossickers are still active.

Maldon is of great interest to students of Australian history generally and of goldfields history in particular. It attracts some 15 000 tourists a year.

Sports. Golf course. Tennis courts. Bowling greens. Swimming pool.

Accommodation. Three **hotels.** Preferred: Kangaroo, High Street. One **caravan and camping park,** all facilities.

Transport. Rail from Melbourne to Castlemaine thence connecting **road** coach.

MARYBOROUGH

(Population 7 469)

On the Pyrenees Highway and the northern slopes of the Great Dividing Range, 166 kilometres north-west of Melbourne, Maryborough is a pleasant, well-planned little city in a district which produces large quantities of wheat, oats, barley and timber from nearby State forests. Secondary industries: Knitting mills, joinery, printing, steel-construction and welding plants, butter factory, wire works, cordial and hand-tools manufacturing plants.

History. In 1839 or 1840 three Scottish brothers named Simson started sheep farming in the area. At first the region was called Simson's or Charlotte Plains after one of the Simson wives. In 1854 rich gold was discovered and the rush began. In the first year development was speedy. The 'Maryborough Advertiser' (one of Australia's oldest newspapers) was published for the first time, the first church was established and the first hospital began work under canvas. A police camp was set up and the name of the township was changed to Maryborough after the Irish birthplace of Police Commissioner Daly. Two years later Maryborough was gazetted a borough.

In 1874 it was connected to Melbourne by rail via Castlemaine and the following year the rail link through Ballarat was opened. In 1959 the Tullaroop Dam which supplies both the town's water and electricity needs was completed. In 1961 it was proclaimed a city.

Places of Interest. Pioneer Memorial Tower on Bristol Hill has fine views of the surrounding countryside. **Princes Park,** 28 hectares, has good sports facilities. **Lake Victoria,** 7 hectares, boating and water skiing. **Botanic Gardens** and **Phillips Gardens. Simson Memorial Cairn,** Roscholler Park.

An annual Highland Society Festival is held on New Year's Day, a Golden Wattle Carnival in August, and the district agricultural and pastoral show in October.

Sports. Good golf course. Trotting meetings at Carisbrooke. Lawn tennis courts. Bowling and croquet greens. Water sports on Lake Victoria. Fishing and boating on Goldfields Reservoir.

Accommodation. Two **hotels.** Recommended: Albion, High Street. Two **motels.** Recommended

Maryborough, Sutton Road. One **camping and caravan park.** One **guest-house.**

Transport. **Rail** from Melbourne, via Castlemaine and Bendigo. **Road** services to St Arnaud, Donald, Charlton and Bendigo.

CLUNES (Population 934). Old mining township 155 kilometres from Melbourne on Mildura railway, Clunes has historical associations with goldfields days. It was here that the first discovery was made which touched off the rush of 1851.

Accommodation. Two **hotels.** One **camping ground.**

AVOCA (Population 1 962) was established in 1852 when gold was discovered 3 kilometres east of present townsite. It is now the centre of a pastoral and agricultural district about 170 kilometres from Melbourne and 70 kilometres north-west of Ballarat.

Of Interest. **Old bluestone buildings** and **powder magazine.** **Remy Martin** vineyards 6 kilometres west of town.

Accommodation. Three **hotels.** No preference. **Caravan and camping park.**

THE MURRAY VALLEY

Australia's greatest river, the Murray, rises in the Snowy Mountains of the alpine region in the south-eastern sector of the continent and flows west and finally south for more than 2 500 kilometres before joining the Southern Ocean at Lake Alexandrina in South Australia. It traverses an extraordinary diversity of terrain, through deep, heavily wooded gorges overtopped by snow-peaks, gently undulating foothills, marshlands, and vast red sandy plains which without irrigation support only sparse desert vegetation. Follow the course of the Murray from the highlands to the sea and you will cut a truly representative cross-section of temperate-zone Australia. From east to west, the following places are the main centres of population on the Victorian side of the river. (See also Southern Riverina, New South Wales; the Snowy Mountains and Upper Murray, South Australia).

WODONGA (see ALBURY-WODONGA)

RUTHERGLEN (Population 1 208) is about 40 kilometres west of Albury. It is the centre of an important wine growing and pastoral area. Vines were first planted in the district by Lindsay Brown in 1851. In 1899 the vine disease, phylloxera, wiped out most of the vineyards, but the establishment of resistant strains has again made Rutherglen one of the most important wine areas in the State. It produces full-bodied dry red table wines, many delicate white wines, and sherry, port and muscat type wines of great distinction. The wineries are open to the public on weekends and in some cases on Saturday morning. The cellars of the 'All Saints' Estate are classified as a building of historical importance by the National Trust. A Wine Festival is held in March, during vintage.

Places of Interest. **Viticultural Research Station,** near Rutherglen, is open to visitors with a genuine interest in viticulture. **Lake Moodemere,** 8 kilometres west, is a pleasant native fauna sanctuary with facilities for aquatic sports.

Accommodation. One **hotel. Caravan and camping park.**

YARRAWONGA (Population 3 115)

A small town on Lake Mulwala (Murray River storage behind Yarrawonga Weir), 262 kilometres from Melbourne, Yarrawonga concentrated on the development of tourist attractions. It has good sports facilities—bowls and croquet greens, tennis courts, an excellent golf course, and provision for aquatic sports and fishing on the lake, which has an area of 6 075 hectares with 43 kilometres of foreshore. Aquatic Festival held at Christmas.

Accommodation. Five **hotels.** Recommended: Royal Mail, Elmore Street. Four **motels.** Recommended: Yarrawonga Highway. One **boatel-motel** (highly recommended): Cypress Gardens, Mulwala Road (NSW). First class **camping and caravan park.**

Transport. **Rail** and **road** services (the latter recommended), **air** services to Corowa, connecting with inland and inter-capital services.

ECHUCA

(Population 7 510)

The aboriginal word *echuca* means 'meeting of the waters' and the Murray Valley town of that name is at the junction of the Murray, Campaspe and Goulburn Rivers. It is 205 kilometres from Melbourne and the centre of a district which produces fat cattle and lambs, fruit, vegetables, tobacco, cotton, timber, rice, linseed and butter. Much of the land is under irrigation. Secondary industries; Sawmills, flour mills, rice mill (established in 1953 to process rice grown in the Wakool-Tullakool irrigation area of New South Wales), chilling works, butter and cordial factories, ball-bearing factory (established by the Commonwealth Government during the second world war and subsequently sold to private industry).

History. The settlement had its origin in a punt service across the Murray established in 1847 by Isaac White but taken over later by a colourful figure of pioneering days named Henry Hopwood, who affected the eccentricity of always carrying an umbrella. During the 1850s Echuca, originally known as Hopwood's Ferry, grew into a roaring river port for the freighting of wool and timber. At one time its wharves handled 100 000 wool bales a year. For a time after 1864, when the railway from Melbourne was put through, the town's river trade was still further increased and it was created a borough in 1865. However, as other rail links to river towns were completed, paddle steamer traffic on the Murray declined. A bridge was built across the river in 1877-8 and created interstate tension because the NSW Government refused to honour an agreement to pay half the cost. Echuca was gazetted a city in 1965.

Of Interest. The paddle steamer **Adelaide** built in 1866 has been restored as a monument to the river trade. The modern paddle steamer **Canberra** operates daily excursions. **Historic iron bridge** linking Echuca with **Moama** across the river.

Sports. Racecourse, cycling track. Golf, tennis, bowls and croquet. Rifle and gun clubs. River and Olympic swimming pools.

The district offers good fishing for Murray cod and English and Murray perch and the nearby lagoons and swamps abound with duck and snipe.

Accommodation. Ten **hotels.** Recommended: Caledonian, Hare Street. Three **motels.** Recommended: Echuca, Murray Valley Highway and High Street. One excellent **camping and caravan park,** all facilities.

Transport. **Road** and **rail** services.

KYABRAM (Population 4 623) is 203 kilometres from Melbourne, centre of a productive fruit growing district in the valley of the Goulburn Riven near its junction with the Murray.

Sports. Golf, tennis, bowls, swimming, fishing and shooting.

Accommodation. Three **hotels.** No recommendation. One recommended **motel,** Ky, Allen Street.

Transport. **Rail** connection with Melbourne. **Road** services.

COBRAM (Population 2 833) is a fruit growing and dairying town 70 kilometres north of Shepparton. Community events include a Peaches and Cream Festival at Easter, and a popular sports meeting during the last weekend in March.

Sports. Golf, tennis, bowls, swimming, shooting and fishing.

Accommodation. Three **hotels.** No preference. One **motel.**

Transport. **Rail** connection with Melbourne and **road** services.

ROCHESTER (Population 2 117). On the Campaspe River and the Northern Highway 28 kilometres south of Echuca, Rochester claims the largest dairy factory in Australia processing 909 000 litres of milk a day.

Of Interest. **Corop Lakes** (14 kilometres) **Mt Camel Range** for scenery and gemstone fossicking. **Torrumbarry Weir** and **Kow Swamp** reservoir.

Sports. Golf, tennis, bowls, fishing, rifle club, duck and quail shooting in season.

Accommodation. One **hotel.** One **motel.**

Transport. **Rail** connection with Melbourne. Daily **road** service to Melbourne.

KERANG (Population 4 250)

On the Loddon River, at the junction of the Murray and Loddon highways, 299 kilometres north-west of Melbourne, Kerang serves a pastoral, fruit-growing and mixed-farming area established by intensive irrigation of an alluvial plain studded with low sandhills and lakes. The water is pumped from the Torrumbarry Weir.

The marshes of the district are of particular interest to bird-lovers. They are the home of enormous flocks of ibis and other waterfowl. During the nesting season it is estimated that there are more than 50 000 birds in the colonies among cumbungi reeds in the swamps. They are closely protected because of their value in controlling locusts and other insect pests. Ornithologists say that the Kerang ibis consume not less than five tonnes of insects a day.

The district produces wool, wheat, citrus fruits, dairy and mixed farm produce. The town has timber mills, flour mills, a butter factory, an agricultural implements works and a clothing factory.

The swamps and lakes in the locality provide some of the best duck shooting in Victoria. Thousands of shooters flock into the area for the opening of the season.

History. The Loddon was explored by Mitchell in 1836, but the first settler was Woodfull Patchell, a graduate of Trinity College, Dublin, who took up land near Kerang in 1857 and set up a pump on the river to irrigate his crops.

The shire was proclaimed in 1871. In 1888 the council built the Kerang-Koondrook 'tramway' (to the Victorian rail gauge) to carry the produce of the Riverina on the NSW side of the Murray to Kerang and Melbourne for sale—a rural enterprise not matched anywhere else in Australia. Kerang is an aboriginal word variously translated as 'cockatoo', 'parasite', or 'moon'.

Places of Interest. Kangaroo Lake. Lake Charm (about 24 kilometres north-west). **Apex Park. Reedy Lake,** for swimming, boating and fishing. **Second Reedy Lake,** bird sanctuary and ibis rookeries **Torrumbarry Weir and Lock.**

Sports. Racecourse. Golf, tennis, bowling and croquet. Olympic swimming pool, with deep diving pool. Shooting and fishing.

Accommodation. Two **hotels.** Recommended: Commercial, Victoria Street. Two **motels.** No preference. One **caravan and camping park,** all facilities.

Transport. Rail, road and **air** services. **Air charters** available.

SWAN HILL

(Population 7 693)

Swan Hill is a small city of pleasing appearance 357 kilometres north-west of Melbourne. It is a market centre for the Southern Riverina and the district produces stone and citrus fruit of fine quality, grapes, wheat, dairy produce, vegetables and fat lambs. Experiments with tobacco, cotton and peanuts have been encouraging, but the area, which receives an annual rainfall of only 305 millimetres, is only partly irrigated. Secondary industries include a co-operative dairy factory, flour mills, cordial factory, winery, plasterboard works, engineering shops. The climate resembles that of Mildura.

History. When the explorer Thomas Mitchell camped on a sand dune beside the Murray River near the present site of the town in 1836, he was kept awake all night by the noise of swans. He called the spot Swan Hill. The native name was *martiragnir.*

In 1846 the first settlers moved into the locality with flocks of sheep and some cattle. Seven years later, in 1853, Francis Cadell in his paddle steamer *Lady Augusta* navigated the Murray from its mouth in South Australia and reached Swan Hill, his farthest point upstream.

The township itself grew up around a punt at the river crossing and by the middle of the century had become a busy river port.

In 1862 the Road District of Swan Hill was proclaimed and in 1893 the area was incorporated as the Castle Donnington Shire. Eleven years later it was renamed the Swan Hill Shire. In 1939 a block of 3600 acres was separated from the rural area and proclaimed a borough.

During the second world war Lake Boga, 16 kilometres to the south, was used as a flying boat station. In 1965 Swan Hill was gazetted a city.

Places of Interest. Folk Museum, built about the old paddle steamer *Gem*, preserved as a relic of the days when such craft were the Murray Valley's main form of transport. The restoration of the old boat, the re-creation of buildings of the period, and the collection of horse-drawn vehicles, old locomotives etc, is possibly the most impressive project of its kind in Australia. Thousands of tourists visit Swan Hill to see the exhibits every year. **Lake Boga** (16 kilometres south) for water skiing, fishing and boating. Three well-tended **public parks. Art Gallery. Tyntyndyer,** historic homestead and museum of pioneer relics and aboriginal artifacts etc, 17 kilometres north on Murray Valley Highway.

A **Shakespearean play festival** has been held in Swan Hill annually in March since 1948.

Sports. Racecourse. Bowls, tennis, croquet, swimming etc.

Accommodation. Five **hotels.** Recommended: Oasis. Four **motels.** Recommended: Swan Hill, Campbell Street. One **camping and caravan park,** all facilities.

Transport. Road, rail and **air** services.

ROBINVALE (Population 2 800). The new, progressive township built to serve a mallee land development of about 10 000 hectares began as a soldier settlement project in 1947. The area about 80 kilometres south-east of Mildura produces cotton, dried fruits, olives (large plantation at Tol Tol 8 kilometres from town) and wine grapes.

Sports. Golf, tennis, bowls, swimming.

Accommodation. One **hotel.** One **motel.**

Transport. Rail connection to Melbourne. **Road** services to Albury, Mildura and Adelaide.

MILDURA

(Population 13 190)

On the Murray River 573 kilometres north-west of Melbourne, Mildura is the centre of one of the most prosperous irrigation areas in the Commonwealth. It is a small city with substantial buildings and wide, tree-lined streets, reflecting the prosperity of a district which contains some 19 000 hectares of citrus orchards, vineyards, olive groves and intensively cultivated farmlands. Now known as Sunraysia, it produces more than 93 per cent of Victoria's dried fruits, large quantities of high quality table and fortified wines, and fresh fruit and vegetables for southern Victorian markets. Its secondary industries include fruit processing and packing, a flour mill and plaster, brick and pipe factories.

The climate, dry the year round, and the rich, red soil make Sunraysia an ideal locality for the production of high quality citrus fruit and grapes under irrigation. Sunny, mild winters, a peaceful and picturesque location on the banks of southern Australia's greatest river and well developed recreational facilities attract many thousands of holidaymakers to the district every year. Tourism is estimated to bring about $A3 million into Sunraysia towns every season.

Mildura—the name means 'dry red earth'—may lack spectacular scenic attractions and sophisticated accomodation, but it is probably one of the most comfortable and pleasant inland towns in southern Australia in which to spend a restful holiday. There is abundant wildlife along the river and irrigation channels, including mallee fowl, numerous water birds, kangaroos and emus. Fishing for Murray cod, perch and bream is good for any angler who takes time to familiarize himself with local conditions.

History. The explorer, Charles Sturt, passed the town site of Mildura during his trip along the Murray in 1830. Six years later Major Mitchell went down the river as far as the Darling junction (Wentworth) about 32 kilometres downstream.

In 1846 Frank Jenkin took up a run in the locality but, because he was holding the land without Government consent, he was evicted by the agents of the Jamieson brothers of Murray Downs station who were seeking additional grazing. The Jamieson brothers maintained the run and named it Mildura During the 1850s and 1860s the station was well known to river traders who were always assured of receiving fresh fruit from the small orchard on the property.

But it was not until the 1880s that anyone thought to develop the district as a fruit-growing area. The statesman, Alfred Deakin, advocate of irrigation, visited California in 1885 to look over the model towns which had been created in the desert by the enterprise of two Canadian brothers, George and William Benjamin Chaffey. Deakin persuaded them that Australia would be of interest to irrigators. With the intention of making money in the young colony (this was their confessed aim) George Chaffey arrived in Victoria in 1886. William (W.B.) was to follow when the land had been selected and details finalized.

An area of about 101 000 hectares was selected at Mildura, but difficulties arose about transfer of land rights. Political pressure led the Victorian Government to reject the Chaffey brothers' plans. No sooner had George been rejected by the Victorians than the South Australian Government came forward with an offer of 100 000 hectares at Renmark. Within a few days the Victorians withdrew their opposition and the brothers were left with 200 000 hectares of arid semi-desert to turn into agricultural land.

By August 1887 the company of Chaffey Brothers Ltd had official title to the area and work started on the surveying of the town, orchard lots and the irrigation system. The land was advertised to small settlers at £20 an acre for orchard land, £20 for a town allotment and £100 for a residential site. The surveyor was E. W. Cross who laid out the town on the lines of model American rural settlements of the period.

Irrigation was carried out for a time by two makeshift pumps—one on an old paddle steamer—while pumps specially designed by George Chaffey (direct acting triple expansion engines to drive centrifugal pumps) were being made in Birmingham. They went into commission in 1891 and were successful despite engineering controversy about their design.

The settlement prospered in its early years. By 1892 it was well established and in 1893 the harvest was a record. But all was not well. Irrigation works had closed the river to its normal steamer and barge traffic and there was no way to transport the fruit to market. Heavy rain at harvest time ruined the 1895 crop and salt, drawn from the subsoil by the irrigation waters, was beginning to ruin the land.

The economic depression of the 1890s further added to the misfortunes of the little community. Gradually settlers left their land and went west to try their luck on the Kalgoorlie goldfields.

The Chaffey brothers' company went bankrupt and George returned to the United States broken by the long fight to save the district. But William stayed on. The brothers' task was taken up by the Mildura Irrigation Trust, constituted in 1895 to conduct and control the irrigation project. Improved techniques lessened the salt menace, and Federation in 1901, which eliminated many petty problems and Customs restrictions, put Mildura back on its feet. Stability of transport was assured by the opening of the long-awaited railway from Melbourne.

In 1910 a satellite settlement at Merbein was founded and in 1920 Redcliffs was opened up as a soldier settlement area. In the same year the borough of Mildura was proclaimed and in 1922 it

Twelve Apostles, south-west coast, Victoria

Goanna

Tiger snake

became a town with W. B. Chaffey as its first mayor. Locking of the Murray was fully completed in 1928 and in 1934 Mildura became a city.

During the second world war it was an RAAF base and when the war ended a second soldier settlement was opened up at Robinvale.

It is of interest to note that the Chaffey brothers were strong prohibitionists and that they asked the Victorian Government to exclude the issue of liquor licences from the Irrigation Act. This proved contrary to Australian sentiment and the difficulty was overcome by encouraging the formation of licensed clubs. There are now three clubs in the district to which practically every adult male belongs—and only four hotels, catering mainly for visitors. Their licenses are of comparative recent date.

Places of Interest. **Statue** of W. B. Chaffey, Deakin Avenue. **Art Gallery** and original irrigation pump at 'Rio Vista', the old Chaffey home. **Carnegie Library,** gift of Andrew Carnegie to the town in 1908; clock tower added in 1922 as war memorial. **Lock II** and **Lock Island.** Apex and Henderson **Parks.**

An annual agricultural and horticultural show and mardi gras is held in March.

Sports. Golf. Bowls (seven district greens). Tennis (lawn and hardcourts). Water skiing. Olympic swimming pool. Fishing.

Accommodation. Three **hotels.** Recommended: Grand. Fourteen **motels.** Recommended: Northaven Travelodge, Deakin Avenue; Commodore, Deakin Avenue and Seventh Street. **Guest-houses. Holiday apartments.** Four **camping and caravan parks,** all facilities.

Transports. **Road, rail** and **air** services from Sydney and Melbourne. **Air** service from Adelaide via Broken Hill. **Road** service from Adelaide via Renmark. **River cruises.**

REDCLIFFS (Population 2269), Fourteen kilometres from Mildura, has the largest co-operative dried fruits packing house in Australia. The town has attractive parks, tennis courts, bowling green and a swimming pool. The large pumping station, which delivers 540 million litres a day into the channels, is worth a visit.

Accommodation. One **hotel. Guest-houses.** One **caravan park,** all facilities.

Transport. **Road** service from Mildura.

IRYMPLE (Population 432). Ten kilometres from Mildura, is within the original settlement and the lands in the vicinity are irrigated under a franchise held by the First Mildura Irrigation Trust. Most of the citrus fruit in the irrigation area is grown about here.

Accommodation. One **hotel,** community owned—first of its kind in Australia.

MERBEIN (Population 1 519). Opened for settlement in 1910, 11 kilometres from Mildura, has a winery and distillery and a horticultural research station run by the Council for Scientific and Industrial Research. Lake Hawthorn, between Merbein and Mildura, is an outfall for the Mildura district's drainage system.

Accommodation. One **hotel.**

Queensland

Queensland, with an area of 173 million hectares, is the second largest State of the Commonwealth and slightly more than half of it is north of the Tropic of Capricorn. Its population at last official count was 1 860 000 and is estimated to be increasing by a little more than 2 per cent yearly. From Cape York in the far north to the New South Wales border is a distance of about 2 100 kilometres and from Sandy Cape, in the east, to the border of the Northern Territory, more than 1 450 kilometres.

Physically Queensland can be described as comprising four main regions which all run north and south—the coastal strip, somewhat wider overall than that in New South Wales and Victoria, the fairly complex mountain system of the Great Dividing Range, the 'tableland' country to the west of it, and the wide, semi-arid plains of the Great Artesian Basin.

The coastal strip receives good and fairly reliable rainfall. Its soils are fertile and it supports a number of prosperous and (by Australian standards) populous cities and towns which are ports of outlet for the produce of surrounding agricultural districts and the pastoral and mining industries of the interior.

Scenically Queensland is in all probability the most richly varied of all Australian States. It lacks only the snow-covered peaks of Tasmania and the south-east to run the full continental gamut.

The far north is classically tropical, particularly in the shadow of the tall mountain peaks of the Bellenden Ker Range where Mount Bartle Frere rises to 1 683 metres and rainfall exceeds 2 300 millimetres a year. The mountain forests are here typical jungle, superficially indistinguishable in coloration and form from the jungles of South-East Asia. The cultivated areas somewhat resemble West Java. There are more than 750 offshore islands and islets, most of which are in the waters protected by the Great Barrier Reef, although several of the largest, such as Stradbroke, Moreton and Frazer Islands, lie south of Capricorn.

The mountain belt is most rugged and spectacular at its northern and southern extremities, where the peaks are closest to the sea. The tablelands to the west, mainly in the 500-750 millimetres rainfall belt, are rolling and lightly timbered with slow-flowing, gum-fringed rivers. Two areas—the Atherton Tableland comprising 3 100 000 hectares of volcanic soil in the north and the Darling Downs, nearly 1 500 000 hectares of black soil in the south—are particularly fertile and productive.

Still farther west are the plains which comprise more than half the area of the State—a vast ocean of grass after rain and a bare, parched desert of stones, clay and sand after prolonged drought. Permanent settlement of this region has been made possible only by tapping the waters of the Great Artesian Basin through bores. The bore water varies in quality and temperature when it reaches the surface, but it is usually suitable for stock and, when distributed through channels to watering points, permits sheep to be carried on large areas of grassland that, lacking natural surface water catchments, could not otherwise be put to use.

The climates of Queensland are as complicated as its topography. The western plains are, of course, typical of the arid and semi-arid centre of the continent. The heat of summer is fierce, daily maxima often rising above 38°C, and winters are sunny and mild by day and cool to cold by night. Frosts are not uncommon in the south, both on the plains and tablelands.

On the coast, readings above 38°C are rare—much rarer than in the southern States. This is due to the monsoon which brings heavy summer rain to the coast as far south as the northern rivers district of New South Wales. Humidity tempers the extremes of heat, but for unacclimatized people the discomfort level is fairly high between November and early April. More winter rain falls on the coast than inland, but wet spells are not often accompanied by strong winds and chilliness. For upwards of seven months of the year the Queensland weather is notably pleasant. During the rest of the year, heat and humidity on the coast are somewhat offset by sea breezes which blow almost every day. Considering the fact that so much of it lies within the tropics, Queensland is singularly free of tropical diseases. In the north there a is slight incidence of dengue fever and similar mosquito-borne infections. Cases of hookworm occasionally occur, but malaria is extremely rare and other tropical killers such as cholera, yellow fever, amoebic dysentery and rickettsia are unknown. This is no doubt a prime reason why European settlement of the far northern coast has been remarkably successful.

ECONOMY Of all the Australian States, Queensland is perhaps the most richly endowed with natural resources. Its development has, in relation to its potential, hardly begun, but it already produces an extraordinary diversity of foodstuffs and raw materials—food grains, wool, beef and mutton, sugar, tropical and temperate zone fruits of all kinds, dairy produce, cotton, peanuts (or ground nuts), fish, tobacco and timber; copper, coal, lead, zinc, silver, gold, bauxite, mineral sands, natural oil and gas, manganese, salt and phosphate.

Queensland has shared in the mining revival which has had so profound an influence on the Australian economy in the past 15 years. The famous Mount Isa mines in the far west now produce 112 000 tonnes of copper, lead and zinc ores a week, but expansion is most marked in coal and bauxite mining.

For many years the existence of vast coalfields has been known in Central Queensland, but distance from markets and lack of transport have held back exploitation. The rapid growth of heavy industry within Australia itself and the emergence of Japan as a major industrial power in the Far East have altered the situation. The fields are now being vigorously exploited for export to Japan.

Bauxite is another mineral of increasing importance. The output of the Weipa field near the tip of Cape York peninsula has now passed 2 540 000 tonnes a year. The crude material is exported to the United States and Japan, but it is also supplying Australian alumina refineries in New South Wales and Tasmania and a large plant established at a cost of $A350 million at Gladstone, about 483 kilometres north of Brisbane.

Oil and gasfields have been discovered and are in production in the south-east. Exploitation of large phosphate deposits recently discovered in the north will also considerably increase the State's prosperity.

In recent years manufacturing industries have developed rapidly. Factory production is now worth more than $A7 600 000 million a year and increasing at an extraordinary rate.

HISTORY The settlement of that part of Australia which is now the State of Queensland was rapidly accelerated by the strong sentiment against the continued transportation of convicts to New South Wales which grew up in Sydney during the second and third decades of the 19th century. The British Colonial Office attempted to meet the objections of free settlers by establishing penal settlements in more remote parts of the continent and transferring to them the more intractable felons—especially those who had committed further offences after having been transported to Australia.

When Sir Thomas Brisbane became Governor of New South Wales in 1821 he sent the Surveyor-General, John Oxley, to reconnoitre the virtually unknown country to the north of Liverpool Plains for suitable prison camp sites. Oxley recommended Moreton Bay and in 1824 Brisbane sent a detachment of troops and convicts to Redcliffe. The hostility of the natives, however, caused them to move to the present site of Brisbane. In the beginning free settlers were excluded from the new country thus opened up, but they slowly infiltrated the Darling Downs. In 1839, the Moreton Bay penal settlement was abandoned. The rich pastoral potential of the hinterland was soon realized by the squatters and the population of both Moreton Bay and the Darling Downs increased rapidly.

By 1850 a strong movement had developed among the northern settlers for separation from New South Wales. They were impatient of the administrative delays inherent in being governed from a distance and by officials who did not understand the nature of their problems. The separationists received influential support in Sydney, notably from the Reverend John Dunmore Lang, a fiery Presbyterian cleric who had helped Victoria win its independence.

Eventually the British Government agreed that the tropical part of New South Wales should be made a separate colony and, after prolonged haggling, a boundary was drawn along the 29th parallel and the State of Queensland proclaimed on 10 December 1859. The population of the new State was then 23 520.

The colony was at first completely without financial resources, but fortunately it was so rich in pastoral and agricultural land that it soon established itself on a firm footing. Wool and beef grown on the western plains and tablelands were its economic mainstay, but sugar grown on the rich alluvial river flats all the way from the Clarence River in New South Wales to Mossman in the far north soon assumed great importance. The pioneer of the industry was the Honourable Louis Hope, who established plantations and built beautiful Ormiston House on Redland Bay, south-east of the capital.

Acute labour shortage plagued the industries of Queensland from the beginning and, since convicts were no longer available, the sugar planters imported kanakas from the Pacific islands to do the field work. The system of recruiting the natives was open to such abuses that the labourers were, to all intents and purposes, slaves. A curious parallel to the quarrel between the southern and northern states of America developed in Queensland when the northern planters, bitterly resisting the abolition of 'blackbirding', as the recruitment of kanaka labour was called, agitated for a further partition of Queensland to evade the reforms urged by the Government in Brisbane and by liberal elements in other States.

By 1881 sugar lands in Queensland totalled nearly 100 000 hectares and it and it was not until 1904 that indentured labour was banned altogether and

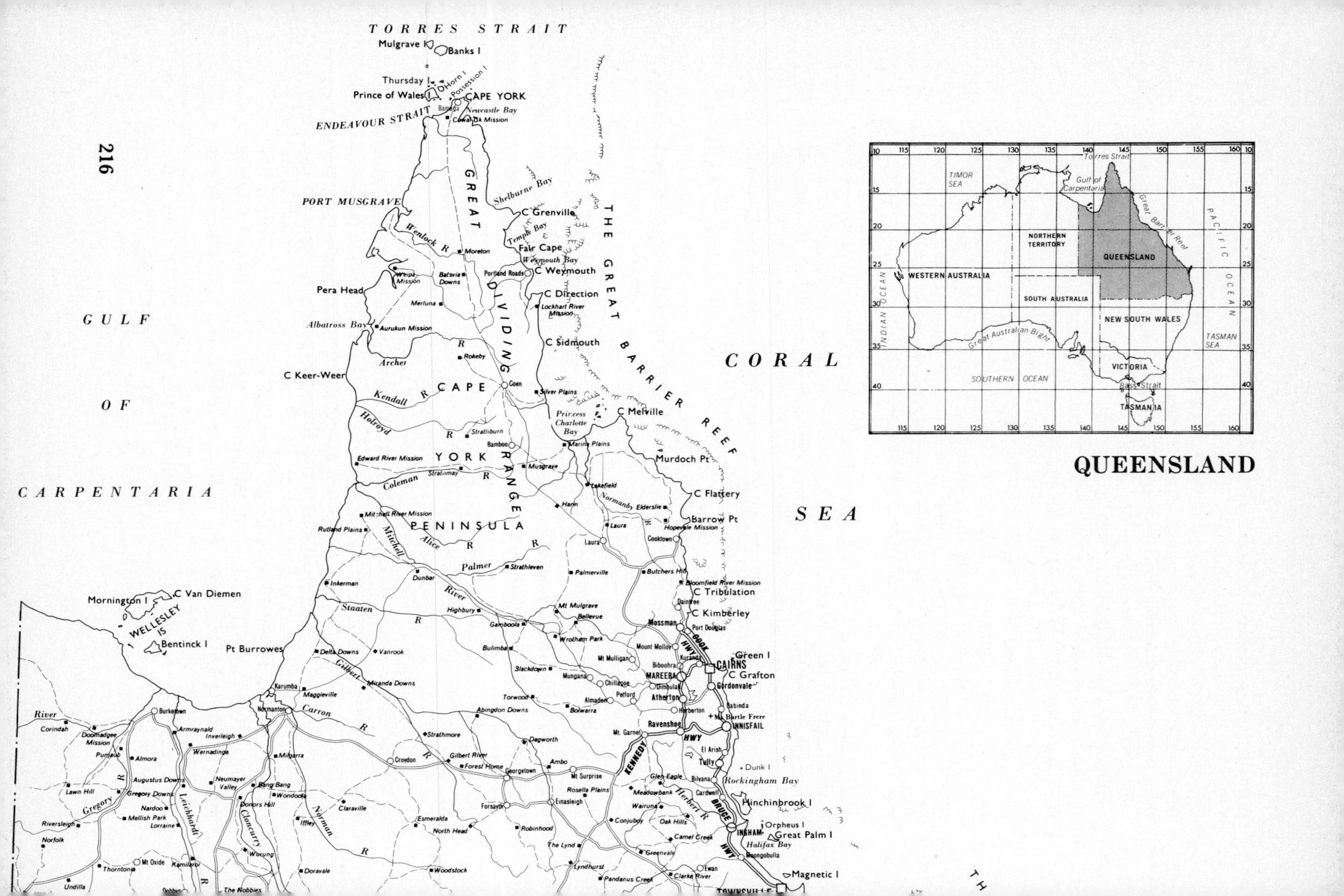
QUEENSLAND
TORRES STRAIT
ENDEAVOUR STRAIT
CAPE YORK
GULF
OF
CARPENTARIA
CORAL
SEA
THE GREAT BARRIER REEF
GREAT DIVIDING RANGE
CAPE YORK PENINSULA
PORT MUSGRAVE
WELLESLEY IS
Mornington I
C Van Diemen
Bentinck I
Pt Burrowes
C Keer-Weer
Pera Head
Albatross Bay
C Grenville
Fair Cape
C Weymouth
C Direction
C Sidmouth
C Melville
Murdoch Pt
C Flattery
Barrow Pt
C Tribulation
C Kimberley
Green I
C Grafton
Rockingham Bay
Hinchinbrook I
Orpheus I
Great Palm I
Halifax Bay
Magnetic I
CAIRNS
MAREEBA
INNISFAIL
INGHAM
Cooktown
Mossman
Atherton
Ravenshoe
Gordonvale
Tully
Coen
Normanton
Burketown
Croydon
Georgetown
Karumba
COOK HWY
KENNEDY HWY
BRUCE HWY
PACIFIC OCEAN
INDIAN OCEAN
SOUTHERN OCEAN
TIMOR SEA
TASMAN SEA
Torres Strait
Gulf of Carpentaria
Great Barrier Reef
Great Australian Bight
Bass Strait
WESTERN AUSTRALIA
NORTHERN TERRITORY
SOUTH AUSTRALIA
QUEENSLAND
NEW SOUTH WALES
VICTORIA
TASMANIA

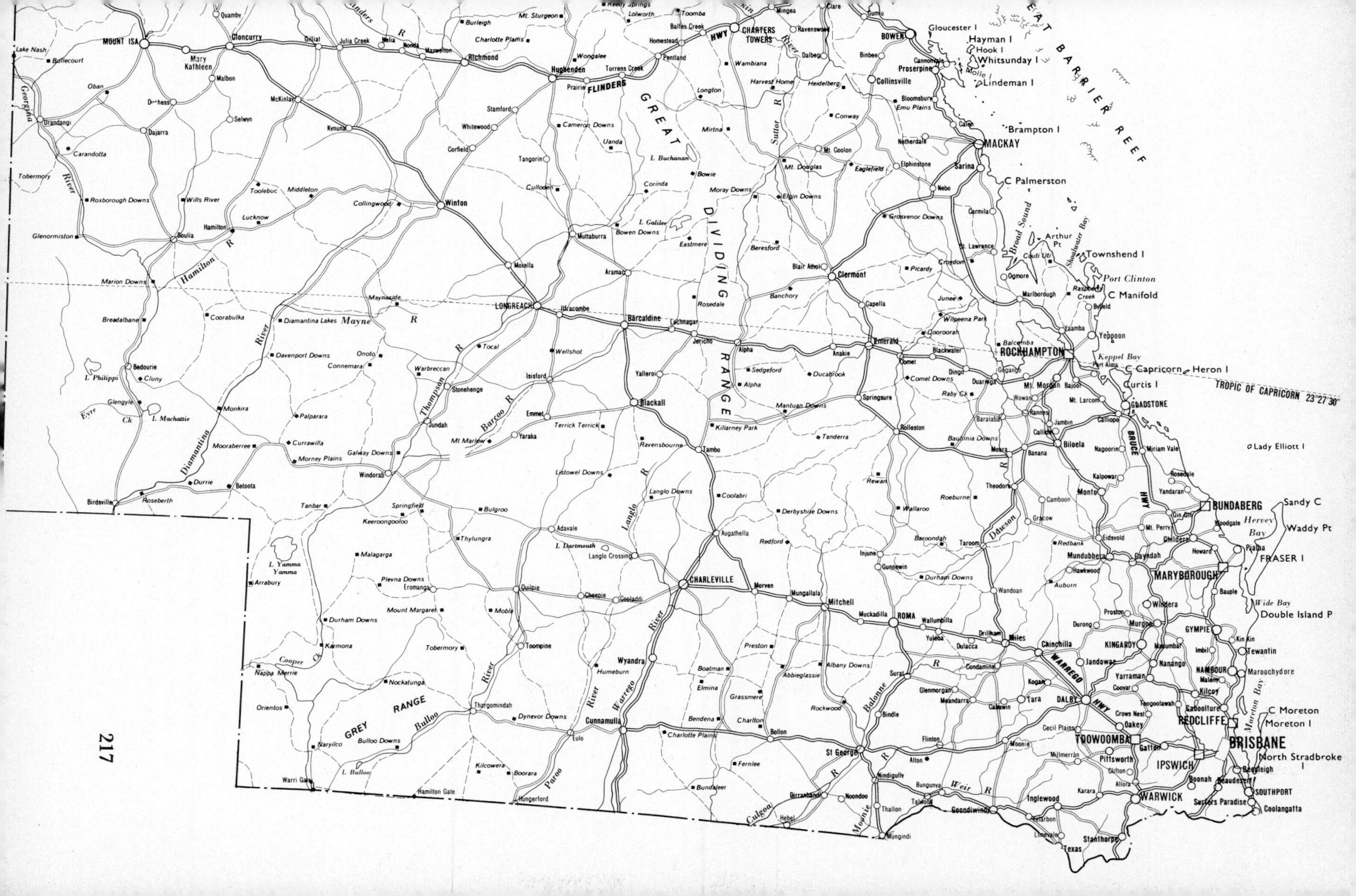

GREAT BARRIER REEF
GREAT DIVIDING RANGE
GREY RANGE
TROPIC OF CAPRICORN 23°27'30"
Gloucester I
Hayman I
Hook I
Whitsunday I
Lindeman I
Brampton I
C Palmerston
Arthur Pt
Townshend I
Port Clinton
C Manifold
Keppel Bay
C Capricorn
Heron I
Curtis I
Lady Elliott I
Sandy C
Hervey Bay
Waddy Pt
FRASER I
Wide Bay
Double Island P
Moreton Bay
C Moreton
Moreton I
North Stradbroke I
Broad Sound
Shoalwater Bay
MOUNT ISA
Cloncurry
Richmond
Hughenden
FLINDERS
HWY
CHARTERS TOWERS
BOWEN
Proserpine
Collinsville
MACKAY
Sarina
Clermont
Emerald
ROCKHAMPTON
GLADSTONE
Biloela
BRUCE HWY
BUNDABERG
MARYBOROUGH
GYMPIE
NAMBOUR
KINGAROY
REDCLIFFE
BRISBANE
IPSWICH
TOOWOOMBA
DALBY
WARREGO HWY
WARWICK
SOUTHPORT
Coolangatta
Winton
LONGREACH
Barcaldine
Blackall
Tambo
CHARLEVILLE
Mitchell
ROMA
Miles
Chinchilla
St George
Cunnamulla
Quilpie
Windorah
Boulia
Bedourie
Birdsville
Thargomindah
Hamilton R
Diamantina River
Mayne R
Thompson R
Barcoo R
Cooper Ck
Bulloo
Paroo
Warrego River
Langlo R
Dawson R
Balonne R
Weir R
Culgoa
Moonie R
Georgina River
Eyre Ck
Suttor R

the industry set about adapting itself to the use of costly white labour—with the help of protection and heavy subsidies which have been continued up to the present.

Mining has also had decisive economic and social effects on the development of Queensland. Gold was discovered at Canoona on the Fitzroy River in 1858, before separation. In 1867 the strike at Widgee Station near Gympie got the State Government out of serious financial difficulties. In 1872 the rich Charters Towers field was opened up. The same year the rush to the Palmer River from Cooktown began a colourful and brutally violent chapter in the history of the north. The Myall aborigines of the district waged ceaseless war on the invading army of diggers and killed and ate many of them. The blacks paid particular attention to the Chinese immigrants who joined in the rush. They are reported to have said that they preferred Chinese flesh to European because 'it was less salty and was equal to the finest bandicoot'. Sporadic warfare also raged between the Chinese and the whites and between the tong factions among the Chinese themselves. The maps of the day are studded with such names as 'Hell's Gates', 'Murdering Gully', 'Cannibal Creek' etc.

The great Mount Morgan field was opened in 1882, when the first assay showed an incredible return of 5 700 ounces to the ton.

Copper was discovered at Peak Downs in 1863, at Mount Perry in the Burnett River district in 1873 and subsequently at Cloncurry and Chillagoe.

Tin, silver and lead were mined at Stanthorpe and Herberton in the 1880s and the immense Mount Isa field, which also produces most of Queensland's copper today, came into production 1931-32.

The enormous coal deposits of central Queensland at Callide, Blair Athol, Moura and elsewhere are only now being significantly exploited as transportation and handling methods are being improved. The original coal discovery at Ipswich near Brisbane was of incalculable economic benefit to the State in its early days. Bauxite, phosphates, uranium ores and rutile-zircon sands have also assumed significance during the last decade.

TOURING IN QUEENSLAND Queensland's mild, sunny winter climate and the variety and beauty of its mountains and reef-fringed tropical coast have attracted holidaymakers for many years, but with the improvement of transport and roads from vigorous industrial development tourism has now become a factor of major importance to the regional economy. It is estimated that tourists spend at least $A140 million a year in the State.

The Gold Coast south of Brisbane, for long promoted as Australia's premier playground, and the Great Barrier Reef, known throughout the world as a natural wonder of the first magnitude, still attract between them the majority of visitors; but as time goes on new pleasure resorts are being developed which cater for the tastes of those who do not demand conventional attractions and amenities on vacation.

Many of these new tourist districts are centred on the State's national parks, which now total about one million hectares of the country with scenic, scientific or recreational resources. Fauna sanctuaries have been declared over an additional 5 600 000 hectares.

The Queensland Government has followed an enlightened policy in this aspect of conservation and reserves are maintained as nearly as possible in their natural condition. Controlled by the State Forestry Department, they are preserved against commercial timber-getting and the destruction of flora and fauna. Mining operations are restricted. Road-building projects are carefully evaluated before being approved and defacement of the landscape by advertising signs and hoardings is prohibited.

The national parks exhibit a wide range of vegetation native to the region, much of which has elsewhere been destroyed by unsound pastoral methods or the destructive logging of native forests in the early days of settlement.

The rainforest reserves contain a great variety of trees which are becoming scarce elsewhere in Australia—kauri, hoop and bunya pine, Queensland cedar, brush box, native tamarind, Queensland maple and silkwood. In the north botanically interesting species which have been preserved from complete extinction include the giant stinging tree (*laportea*), the large, velvety leaves of which can inflict a sting much more severe than that of the nettle, and the strangler fig, a parasite of the ficus family. Among the more spectacular flowering natives are the flame tree and the firewheel tree. More than 8 000 species of smaller flowering plants and ferns have been listed within the boundaries of the State.

Queensland fauna is of great interest to naturalists and wild life abounds in the great national parks. There are more than 400 species of birds. Among the more uncommon are the cassowaries of the northern rainforests, the regent and golden bower birds, the brush turkey, the jabiru, the brolga or native companion, and birds of paradise elsewhere found only in New Guinea. Marsupials native to Queensland but not to other parts of Australia include the cuscuses, several distinctive varieties of possum, pigmy gliders and the rabbit bandicoots of the far south-western desert which look like rabbits but carry their young in pouches.

Most of the common continental kinds of marsupials and monotremes—kangaroos and wallabies, echidnas, platypuses and koala bears—are, of course, represented in the wide range of environment found in the State.

Queensland's highways and main roads have been vastly improved in the past 20 years and they are being improved still further to cope with inland mining and beef cattle development and the increasing tourist traffic to central and north Queensland. However, beyond the well-populated south-east of the State and the immediate vicinity of the larger northern towns and cities, they cannot by any stretch of the imagination be described as first class. Where sealed they tend to be narrow and poorly graded. Where not sealed they can be atrocious both in very dry weather and after rain. Only motorists accustomed to driving in 'frontier' conditions can feel relaxed and comfortable on the State's inland highways.

RECOMMENDED AREAS For overseas visitors with a limited amount of time to spend in the State, the **Whitsunday Passage** area of the Great Barrier Reef accessible from Mackay and Proserpine is a 'must'. If the budget permits, it could be combined with a visit to the **Atherton Tableland** and a round trip by air with Ansett-ANA to the **Gulf Country** stations and settlements.

Those intending to spend some time in or around the capital, Brisbane, should make a point of visiting the dramatic **Lamington Plateau,** travelling via the **Gold Coast.** A round trip to the **Channel Country** settlements from Brisbane with TAA will provide at least a nodding acquaintance with inland Australia, a far different and more austere world than that of the coast.

Interstate visitors who want to sample the best of Queensland by way of scenery and accommodation for a short sojourn could follow the above recommendation. If, however, they are interested in a gay holiday, they may be better advised to choose between the Gold Coast, the more-developed Barrier Reef resorts and the Cairns region.

Tourists with a predominant interest in various aspects of natural history and the outdoors should consider spending some time at one of the less-developed Barrier Reef islands, the Lamington Plateau or the Carnarvons. Those who hanker for the Outback should consider the merits of Mount Isa and Longreach as travel bases. Fishing and aquatic sports enthusiasts should be able to enjoy themselves thoroughly on the Sunshine Coast.

June to October are the best travel months in Queensland. Tourism promoters are assiduously trying to 'extend the season', but resist their blandishments unless you enjoy or are acclimatized to tropical conditions.

Bush flies—the ineradicable curse of the Australian country side—and mosquitoes and sandflies can be annoying almost anywhere in Queensland during the warmer, damper months. Young children can often be greatly troubled. Remember that fairly efficient repellents are available in stores and pharmacies.

Surfers and swimmers should remember that tropical seas have their perils anywhere in the world. Make a point of exercising extreme caution in unfrequented areas. Bathing or skin-diving in estuaries or tidal rivers in North Queensland is **not** to be recommended. Shark and crocodile attacks are rare, but by no means unknown and between October and May the deadly sea wasp (a species of jellyfish) is a hazard in inshore waters. Seek local advice from a reliable source such as the police if in any doubt about the suitability of an area for swimming.

ORGANIZED TOURS The Queensland Government Tourist Bureau in 1973 listed 12 organized regional tours lasting from two to 16 days for which it accepted bookings at a flat rate for local transportation and accommodation. Fares to points of departure were not included. The airlines, TAA and Ansett, also offer a number of attractive and inexpensive tours of the State's most popular resorts. Short aerial tours run by charter companies are available from the Gold Coast, Brisbane, Hervey Bay, Rockhampton, Mackay, Townsville, Cairns, Mt Isa and Roma.

ACCOMMODATION The standard of accommodation in Queensland cities and the more developed tourist resorts is on the whole good in the more expensive hotels, motels and tourist establishments—and, after all, with a few exceptions they are not **very** expensive. However, air-conditioning is by no means general and only very recently has it been accepted as standard practice to provide guests with private bathing and toilet facilities. The motels, most of them of recent vintage, are more predictable by tariff than are hotels and guest houses. They are also more expensive and impersonal.

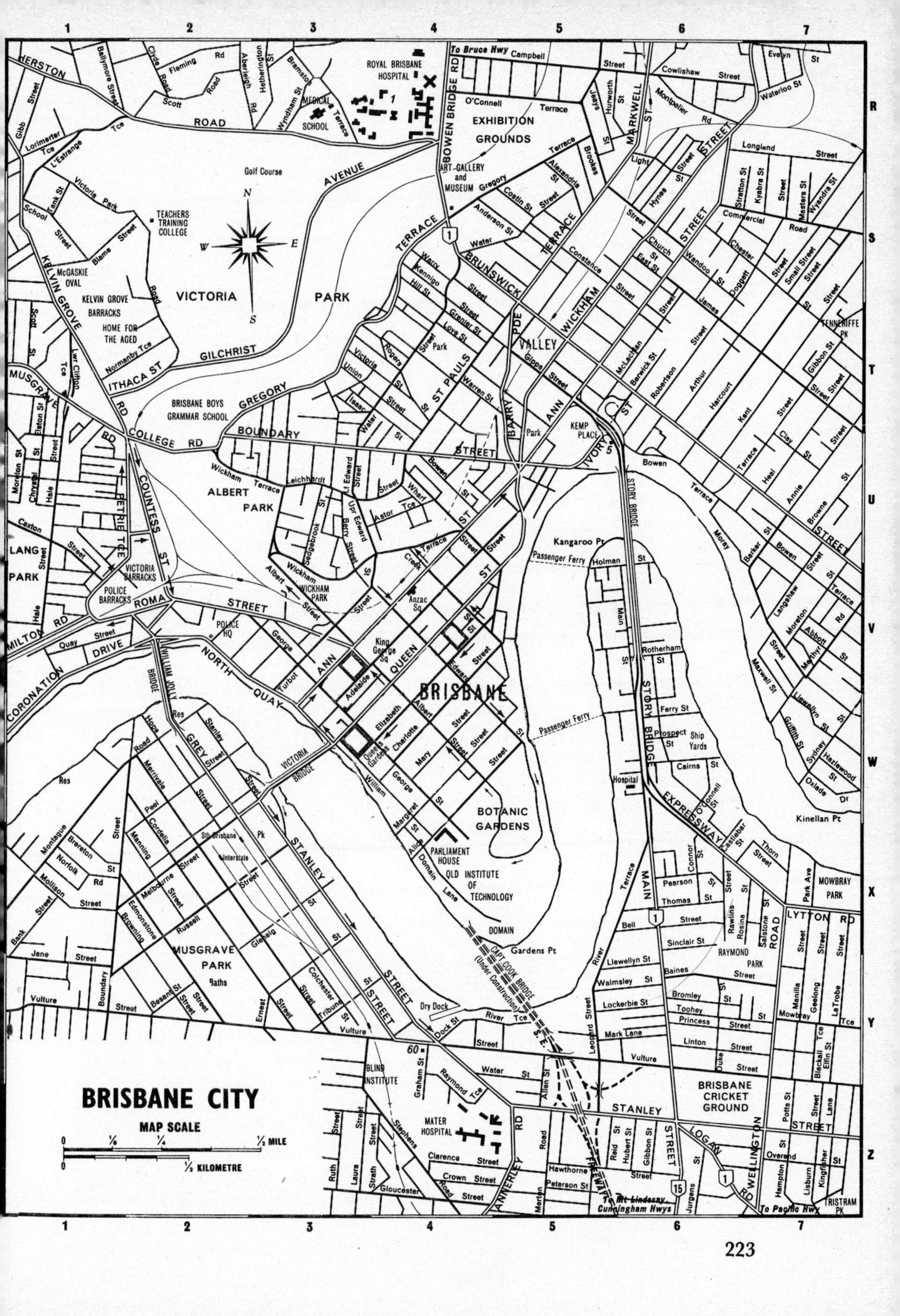

BRISBANE CITY
MAP SCALE
0
1/8
1/4
1/2 MILE
0
1/2 KILOMETRE
1
2
3
4
5
6
7
R
S
T
U
V
W
X
Y
Z
HERSTON
Ballymore Street
Clyde Road
Fleming Rd
Scott Road
Aberleigh Rd
Hetherington St
Bramston
Wyndham St
MEDICAL SCHOOL
Terrace
ROYAL BRISBANE HOSPITAL
To Bruce Hwy
Campbell Street
Cowlishaw Street
Evelyn St
Waterloo St
BOWEN BRIDGE RD
O'Connell Terrace
EXHIBITION GROUNDS
Jeays St
Hurworth St
MARKWELL ST
Montpelier Rd
ROAD
Gibb Street
Lorimer Tce
L'Estrange Tce
Tank St
Victoria Park
School Street
Golf Course
AVENUE
ART GALLERY and MUSEUM
Gregory Terrace
Alexandria St
Brookes St
Light St
Hynes St
Longland Street
Stratton St
Kyabra St
Masters St
Wyandra St
Commercial Road
TEACHERS TRAINING COLLEGE
N
W
E
S
Blame Street
KELVIN GROVE
McGASKIE OVAL
KELVIN GROVE BARRACKS
HOME FOR THE AGED
Normanby Tce
VICTORIA
PARK
Road
Anderson St
Costin St
Water St
TERRACE
BRUNSWICK
Constance
Church St
East St
Wandoo St
James St
Doggett
Chester
Small Street
Warry
Kennigo
Hill St
Grenier St
Love St
Park
Rogers
Victoria
Union
ST PAULS
VALLEY
Gipps Street
WICKHAM
McLachlan
Berwick St
Robertson
Arthur
Harcourt
Kent
TENNERIFFE PK
Gibbon St
Scott St
Lwr Clifton Tce
MUSGRAVE
ITHACA ST
GILCHRIST
GREGORY
BRISBANE BOYS GRAMMAR SCHOOL
BOUNDARY
COLLEGE RD
Isaac
Water
Warren St
BARRY PDE
ANN
Park
KEMP PLACE
IVORY ST
Bowen
Terrace
Clay St
Heal
Annie
Browne
Elston St
Moreton St
Chrystal
Hale
Street
PETRIE TCE
COUNTESS ST
Wickham Terrace
ALBERT PARK
Leichhardt
Upr Edward Street
Berry Street
Astor Tce
Wharf
STREET
STORY BRIDGE
Caxton
LANG PARK
Sedgebrook St
Wickham Terrace
WICKHAM PARK
Albert Street
Creek
Anzac Sq
Kangaroo Pt
Passenger Ferry
Holman St
Moray
Barker St
Bowen St
Langshaw
Terrace
VICTORIA BARRACKS
POLICE BARRACKS
ROMA
STREET
MILTON RD
Hale
Quay Street
DRIVE
CORONATION
POLICE HQ
George
Turbot
King George Sq
ANN
QUEEN
Edward
BRISBANE
Main St
Rotherham St
Moreton
Abbott
Merthyr
Maxwell St
NORTH QUAY
WILLIAM JOLLY BRIDGE
Res
Stanley Street
Hope
Road
GREY
Adelaide
Elizabeth
Charlotte
Albert
Mary
Queens Gardens
Street
Passenger Ferry
Ferry St
Prospect St
Ship Yards
Llewellyn St
Griffith St
Sydney
Hazlewood
Oxlade Dr
Res
Merrivale
Peel
Cordelia
VICTORIA BRIDGE
William
George
Margaret
Alice
St
Cairns St
Hospital
O'Connell St
EXPRESSWAY
Castlebar St
Thorn Street
Kinellan Pt
Montague
Brereton
Norfolk
Rd
Manning
Sth Brisbane
Interstate
Pk
STANLEY
BOTANIC GARDENS
PARLIAMENT HOUSE
Domain Lane
OLD INSTITUTE OF TECHNOLOGY
Terrace
MAIN
Connor St
Pearson St
Thomas St
Rawlins
Rosina
Salstone St
Park Ave
MOWBRAY PARK
Mollison
Street
Melbourne Street
Edmonstone
Browning
Russell
MUSGRAVE PARK
Glenelg
Colchester Street
DOMAIN
Gardens Pt
Bell Street
Sinclair St
RAYMOND PARK
LYTTON RD
ROAD
Bank Street
Jane Street
Boundary
Vulture Street
Besant St
Baths
Ernest
Tribune
STREET
CAPT. COOK BRIDGE (Under Construction)
River
Llewellyn St
Walmsley St
Baines
Bromley St
Manilla
Geelong
LaTrobe
Dry Dock
Dock St
River Tce
S.E.
Leopard Street
Lockerbie St
Toohey
Princess Street
Mowbray
Tce
Vulture
Mark Lane
Linton Street
Blackall Tce
Elfin St
60
BLIND INSTITUTE
Graham St
Raymond Tce
Water St
Allen St
Vulture
Duke Street
BRISBANE CRICKET GROUND
Potts St
Lane
MATER HOSPITAL
ANNERLEY RD
Road
STANLEY
STREET
LOGAN
WELLINGTON
STREET
Ruth
Laura
Strath
Stephens
Gloucester
Clarence Street
Crown Street
Road Street
Merton
Hawthorne
Peterson St
Reid St
Hubert St
Gibbon St
Jurgens
15
1
FREEWAY
To Mt Lindesay, Cunningham Hwys
Hampton St
Overend
Lisburn
Kingfisher St
To Pacific Hwy
TRISTRAM PK

HISTORY The Brisbane River was discovered in 1823 by two escaped convicts who had been shipwrecked on an island in Moreton Bay. The following year it was explored by the Surveyor-General of NSW, John Oxley, who reported that the Moreton Bay region generally was suitable for a penal colony. A settlement was established at Redcliffe, 35 kilometres north-east of the present site of the capital, but it was soon abandoned because of the hostility of the local natives and Brisbane was chosen as a more defensible locality.

Brisbane was named after Governor Brisbane of NSW (1821-25) and was gazetted in 1834 as a town—or, more accurately, as a prison, because free settlement was forbidden within a radius of 81 kilometres of the site. Even before the abolition of transportation in 1840, however, free settlers had defied the ban and established themselves in the district. In 1842 it was officially opened for settlement and a considerable influx of population occurred. Almost immediately a quarrel broke out between the Government in Sydney and the newly arrived squatters who contended that the Sydney administration was so preoccupied with problems closer to home that it had neither time nor inclination to concern itself with the welfare of the northern part of the colony. Agitation began for separation and the establishment of an independently governed colony.

For some years an acrimonious debate continued between the squatters and Sydney as to whether Brisbane or Cleveland, a small settlement on Moreton Bay to the south-east, should be developed as the major port of shipment for the produce of the area. The pastoralists favoured Cleveland, but Governor Sir George Gipps favoured the river port. The matter was resolved in 1854 when a disastrous fire destroyed the wharf installations at Cleveland and shipments of wool had to be made from Brisbane.

The 1840s and early 1850s were lean times for the Moreton Bay settlers, drought and disease having seriously depleted their flocks and herds during a period in which all the Australian colonies were suffering first from economic depression and then from the labour upheavals caused by the gold discoveries in Victoria and New South Wales. Their troubles were considerably exacerbated by inefficient local administration and by bickering between rival settlements.

In 1859, however, Queensland (so called in honour of Queen Victoria and at her own suggestion) was separated from New South Wales. Brisbane was declared its capital. Sir George Bowen was appointed as Governor and his house, now the official residence of the Dean of Brisbane, still stands on a high cliff overlooking Adelaide Street in the heart of the city.

In 1864 a great fire destroyed most of the old buildings in the area between Queen, George, Elizabeth and Albert Streets.

In 1861 telegraphic communication was established with Sydney and in 1865 the first section of railway in Queensland was laid between Ipswich and Grandchester. Ten years later the line had been extended to Brisbane. In 1887 the narrow Queensland gauge line was extended to Wallangarra to which the NSW Government had built standard gauge track. Brisbane was now for the first time connected by rail with southern State capitals. Previous communication had been mainly by sea. In 1930 the first step towards uniform-gauge communication between the cities was effected when a standard-gauge line between Grafton on the North Coast of New South Wales and Brisbane was

Coral gardens, Great Barrier Reef

Mustering sheep, western Queensland

Underwater observation port, Green Island, Qu eensland

Mustering cattle, western Queensland

completed. This service is operated by the NSW Department of Railways.

In 1885 10 kilometres of horse-drawn tram track was opened in the town. The system was electrified in 1897 and by 1962 had been extended to 193 kilometres of track serving the major suburbs.

Until 1864 the town's water supply was drawn from wells in the wedge of land bounded by Roma, Ann and George Streets and was sold to residents by licensed water carriers. In that year, however, work was begun on the Enoggera Reservoir. In 1907 a metropolitan water supply and sewerage board was established to organize and control storage and reticulation projects to meet the requirements of a community which was by now growing rapidly, and had reached city status five years before.

In 1925 the City of Greater Brisbane was established, amalgamating the old town and the newer settlement of South Brisbane which had been proclaimed a town in 1888. The first Lord Mayor was William Alfred Jolly, after whom one of the city's three major bridges was named.

Places of Interest

City Hall, overlooking King George Square, built in Italian Renaissance style of Queensland freestone marble, granite and native timbers. Circular auditorium seating 2 000. Observation platform on clock tower offers panoramic views of city and surrounding countryside. Open 9 am-4.30 pm Monday to Friday, 9 am-12 noon Saturday.

The Observatory, Wickham Terrace, built by convict labour in 1829. Used originally as a windmill and later as a punishment treadmill to grind hominy. A Quaker mission in 1836 complained of the cruelty of a system which required prisoners to work 14-hour shifts on the mill without rest periods. The building was used as a fire lookout station and meteorological observatory after the abolition of the convict settlement. The first experimental television transmission in Australia was made from here in 1934.

Parliament House, built in 1868, in style of French Renaissance. Opposite Botanic Gardens at corner of George and Alice Streets in picturesque setting of tropical trees and shrubs.

State Public Library, William Street, including John Oxley Memorial Library. Open week days 10 am to 9.30 pm; Sundays 1.30 to 5.30 pm. Closed public holidays.

Old Government Stores. One of the first permanent buildings erected in Brisbane. The lower floors comprised the commissariat of Captain Patrick Logan, officer-in-charge of the Moreton Bay Penal Settlement. The top floor was added later.

Government House, Bardon Heights, west of city. Originally the residence of J. C. Huessler, MLC. Purchased by Government as official vice-regal seat in 1910.

Treasury Building, in style of French Renaissance, Queen Street, near Victoria Bridge.

University of Queensland, St Lucia, modern buildings in unusually beautiful riverside setting.

Queensland National Art Gallery and Museum, Gregory Terrace and Bowen Bridge Road. Monday to Saturday 10 am to 5 pm, Sunday 2 pm to 5 pm.

'Miegunyah', memorial to pioneer women, Jordan Terrace, Bowen Hills, Historic house and folk museum. Open Tuesday, Saturday and Sunday 10.30 am to 3.30 pm.

Royal Historical Society of Queensland Museum, Newstead House, Newstead Park (Ascot or Clayfield bus). Oldest historic residence in Brisbane. Monday to Friday 12 noon to 3.30 pm, Sunday 2 pm to 4.30 pm.

Queensland Aboriginal Creations Gallery, 135-137 George Street, displays examples of modern and ancient native art. Monday to Friday 9 am to 4.30 pm.

John Oxley Memorial, North Quay, marking spot where Oxley first landed on banks of river.

Old Court House, Cleveland (32 kilometres southeast), built 1853, now restored.

Ormiston House, Wellington Street, Ormiston (32 kilometres southeast), historic homestead built on site of first commercial sugar plantation in Queensland (1853). Carmelite Order has built monastery in grounds. Open Sundays and public holidays.

Wolston House, Wacol. First property acquired by National Trust of Queensland. Built 1852 of handmade bricks and freestone. Restored. Open Sunday 1.30 to 5 pm.

OUTER SUBURBS of General Interest

MOUNT GRAVATT (9 kilometres), with views of Glasshouse Mountains and southern ranges.

Bamboo Factory, Pacific Highway, Slack's Creek (21 kilometres).

Steam Locomotive Museum, Redbank (28 kilometres west).
African Lion Park, near Beenleigh (37 kilometres south).
Mount Coot-tha Park and Lookout (8 kilometres), with vistas of city and Moreton Bay.

Parks and Gardens

The Brisbane metropolitan area contains about 3 250 hectares of public parks, gardens and recreation reserves. Most are well maintained and contain a wide variety of tropical trees and shrubs including the spectacular poinciana, bird of paradise tree, jacaranda and frangipani. The most popular are:

Botanic Gardens, Alice Street, on the point of a bend in the river, adjoining the main city area, covering an area of about 20 hectares.

Queen's Gardens, George and William Streets, developed on the site of St John's Pro-Cathedral which was demolished in 1904.

New Farm Park, of 17 hectares on river bank east of main city, contains a magnificent collection of 12 000 rose bushes which bloom from September to November.

Newstead Park, containing Lyndon B. Johnson Place and the USA Memorial.

Centenary Park, corner of Ann and Wickham Streets, the city's public forum, lively on Sunday afternoons.

Albert and Wickham Parks, noted for tropical plants and views of the city.

Mount Coot-tha Park, also provides fine panoramas.

Anzac Park, Ann Street, containing impressive war memorial.

Oasis Tourist Garden, Sunnybank (14.5 kilometres). About three hectares of landscaped garden with three swimming pools and a small zoo of native animals. Open daily. Dining room and kiosk.

Acacia Tourist Gardens, Sunnybank. Similar to above.

The Plantation, Gumdale (19 kilometres south east). About seven hectares of landscaped parkland with animal sanctuary, swimming pools etc. Open daily.

Bunya Park, Albany Creek (19 kilometres north). About six hectares of native bush surrounding artificial lake. Native animals.

Children's Adventureland, via Samford (22 kilometers north). Adventure playground.

Principal Churches

St John's Cathedral (C. of E.), Ann Street, near Petrie Bight.
St Stephen's Cathedral, (R.C.), Elizabeth Street, behind G.P.O.
St Andrew's Presbyterian Church, corner Ann and Creek Streets.
Albert Street Methodist Church, corner Albert and Ann Streets.
St Andrew's Lutheran Church, Wickham Terrace.
City Baptist Tabernacle, Wickham Terrace.
City Congregational Church, Ann Street.
First Church of Christ, Scientist, North Quay.
Salvation Army Temple, Ann Street.
Jewish Synagogue, Margaret Street.
Greek Orthodox Church of St George, Edmondstone Street.
City Church of Christ, Ann Street.

Sports and Recreation

Many public sports facilities are concentrated in the **Victoria Park** reserve, north of city. They include the **Municipal Golf Links** and the elaborate **Centenary Swimming Pool** (with glass-walled restaurant) on a site opposite the park's western boundary in Gregory Terrace. Most Brisbane sports clubs offer hospitality and facilities to visiting members of interstate and overseas clubs and associations.

Brisbane Cricket Ground at Woolloongabba is venue for Test and Shield cricket matches and major tennis fixtures are played at the QLTA's courts at Milton.

Three **racecourses** are at Eagle Farm, Doomben and Albion Park, all to the north of the river and the city.

Aquatic sports are mainly centred on various seaside resorts on the shores of Moreton Bay. The headquarters of the Royal Queensland Yacht Club is at 45 Kemp Place, City.

Notable Annual Events

Winter **Racing** and **Trotting** Carnivals in June and July.
Royal Brisbane Show in August.
Warana Festival in September.

Entertainment

Theatres. Her Majesty's Theatre, Queen Street (fully professional); **Arts Theatre,** Petrie Crescent; **Twelfth Night,** Wickham Terrace; **La Boite Repertory,** Hale Street, Milton; **Rialto,** West End. **Theatre Restaurant: The Living Room,** Everard Street.

Cinemas: Hoyt's Town, Wickham Street; Forum, Albert and Elizabeth Streets; Hoyt's Paris, Albert Street; Odeon, Queen Street; Wintergarden, Queen Street; George, George Street; Metro, Albert Street; Regent, Queen Street. Six suburban and outer-suburban **drive-ins.**

Restaurants

Recommended: **Rainbow Room,** Lennons Hotel; **Polynesian Room,** Travelodge Motel, Kangaroo Point; **Cordon Bleu,** Leichardt Street; **Room at the Top,** at Tower Mill Motel, Wickham Terrace; **Two Seasons,** Queen Street; **Chez Tessa,** Wickham Terrace; **Little Tokyo,** Charlotte Street (Japanese dishes); **Burleigh Marrs,** Russell Street, South Brisbane (excellent for seafoods); **Top of the State** (revolving restaurant, 24th floor S.G.I.O. Building, Albert and Turbot Streets; **Leo's,** Edward Street; **The Wine Cellar,** Queen Street; **Gold Fish Bowl,** Crest Hotel, King George Square; **Angus Steak House,** National Hotel, Queen Street.

Accommodation

Ten residential **hotels** are directly listed in the Brisbane city area. Recommended: **Crest International,** King George Square; **Lennons,** George Street (suites available); **Criterion,** George Street; **National,** Queen Street. There are 13 **motels** in the city. Recommended: **Gateway Inn,** North Quay; **Park Royal,** Alice and Albert Streets; **Terrace Motor Hotel,** Wickham Terrace; **Zebra,** George Street; **Noah's Tower,** Wickham Terrace; **Metropolitan,** Edward and Leichardt Streets; **Albert Park,** Wickham Terrace.

Among **suburban motels** of high standard are: **Queensland,** Main Street; **Story Bridge,** Main Street; **Travelodge,** Main Street (all at Kangaroo Point); **Bel Air,** Oxlade Drive (at New Farm); **Coronation,** Coronation Drive (at Milton).

There are three **caravan and camping parks** within eight kilometres of the city—at Newmarket Gardens, Ashgrove; City Caravan Park, Hawthorne; and Amaroo Gardens, Holland Park. Sixteen are listed in the Greater Brisbane area.

Main Department Stores

David Jones, Queen Street, City; The Valley.
Myer, Queen Street, City; Cooparoo; Chermside; The Valley.
Barry and Roberts, Queen Street, City.

Business Hours

Banks, 10 am to 3 pm Monday to Thursday, 10 am to 5 pm Friday.

Shops, 8.15 am to 4.40 pm Monday to Friday, 8.35 am to 11.30 am Saturday.

Post Office, Queen Street, open 24 hours a day for cable, telegram, telephone, stamps.

Transport

The city and suburbs are served by diesel **buses** which run at frequent intervals. Cross-river **ferry** services link West End bus terminus and St Lucia; West End and Toowong; Edward Street and Kangaroo Point; New Farm Park and Norman Park; Hamilton and Bulimba; Customs House and East Brisbane. There are **vehicular ferries** from Colmslie to Meeandah and at Moggill. **Taxis** are metered with tariff rates displayed in each registered car.

Tours. Brisbane is the starting point of numerous day and half-day coach tours of Moreton Bay resorts, the Gold Coast, the Darling Downs and the city's environs. Inquiries from Queensland Government Tourist Bureau, 208 Adelaide Street.

Rail. Travellers should note that the interstate terminal is in Melbourne Street, South Brisbane. Queensland Railways terminals at Roma Street, city, and Central Station.

Emergency Telephone numbers

Fire, Police, Ambulance—Dial 000

BRISBANE'S ENVIRONS

Moreton Bay, into which the Brisbane River flows 19 kilometres east of the city, has an area of roughly 190 000 hectares and is sheltered from the Pacific Ocean by three large offshore islands, Stradbroke, Moreton, and Bribie. Many smaller islands are dotted through the enclosed waters of the bay, which is ringed with small, prosperous holiday resorts and service settlements for a rich fruitgrowing and market gardening region. Tropical, citrus and berry fruits grown here over the winter months are exported to profitable southern markets. The fishing, boating and swimming facilities are excellent.

BRIBIE ISLAND

At the northern end of Moreton Bay and 63 kilometres north-east of Brisbane, Bribie Island has been a popular holiday resort with Brisbane people for many years. It is 31 kilometres long, from two to eight kilometres wide, and has an area of about 14 600 hectares. The island is a wildlife sanctuary and has a sizeable population of native animals and birds, but it is now being developed as a residential area and is subject to a town-planning scheme. A large oil refinery has been built on reclaimed land in the north, where the pipeline from the Moonie oilfield, about 320 kilometres inland, terminates at Bulwer Island.

Bribie is connected with the mainland by a concrete toll bridge between Toorbul Point and Bellara, settlements on either side of the entrance to Pumicestone Passage. It is reached by turning right on a well-formed bitumen road off the Bruce Highway just south of the town of Caboolture. The bitumen continues around the south point of the island to the settlements of Bongaree and Woorim.

Bribie Island is noted for its wildflowers, notably boronia. The flowering season is from August to December.

History. Matthew Flinders landed at the southern tip of the island in 1799 and named it Skirmish Point because his party was attacked there by a band of warlike aborigines. The Bribie Island tribe (see Caboolture) was for long noted for its savagery and cannibalism and was greatly feared by the mainlanders. It was on Bribie that John Oxley met the shipwrecked convict, Pamphlett, who guided him to the entrance of the Brisbane River.

Sports. Crabbing and fishing are to be had in Pumicestone Passage and boats may be hired for reef and game-fishing excursions. Ocean Beach usually has good surf. There are two bowling clubs with first-class greens where carnivals are conducted at Christmas and Easter. An 18-hole golf course was recently laid down.

Accommodation. One **hotel** at Ocean Beach. Two **motels.** Recommended: Koolamarra, Boyd Street. Two **caravan and camping parks,** all facilities. Holiday **cottages** and **flats** available. Further information from Queensland Tourist Bureau.

Transport. Daily **motor coach** service to Brisbane. **Four-wheel drive vehicles** available for inland travel. **Launches** for charter.

TANGALOOMA (MORETON ISLAND)

Moreton Island is about 32 kilometres east of the mouth of the Brisbane River. It has an area of 16 700 hectares and it is 39 kilometres long. The island's sand dunes are claimed to be the highest in the world—Mount Tempest 279 metres and Storm Mountain 267 metres.

Recreations available to visitors include surfing at Ocean Beach, swimming in a shark-proof enclosure, riding, walking, sandhill tobogganning, fishing and spear fishing, game-fishing and table tennis at the community centre.

History. The island was named by Matthew Flinders in 1799 although Moreton Bay had been discovered and named by James Cook nine years previously. In 1857 Queensland's first lighthouse was erected on Cape Moreton. A whaling station was established at Tangalooma in 1952 but subsequently abandoned.

Accommodation. The Tangalooma resort centre accommodates 80 in self-contained family **cottages** and **suites** or single and twin rooms in **lodges.** There is a store, a community lounge, dining room, writing room and sports room.

Transport. MV *Tambo Lady* ferries between the Hamilton Game Fishing Wharf off Kingsford Smith Drive, Brisbane, and Tangalooma four times weekly, with additional trips over Easter. The voyage takes approximately two and a half hours. (The island is connected with the mainland by radio telephone.)

STRADBROKE ISLAND

Named after the Earl of Stradbroke after its discovery in 1823, Stradbroke Island, immediately south of Moreton Island (see above) is a tourist resort and the centre of a beach sands mining industry developed by Consolidated Zinc Ltd. The rare minerals, rutile, zircon and titanium are extracted from

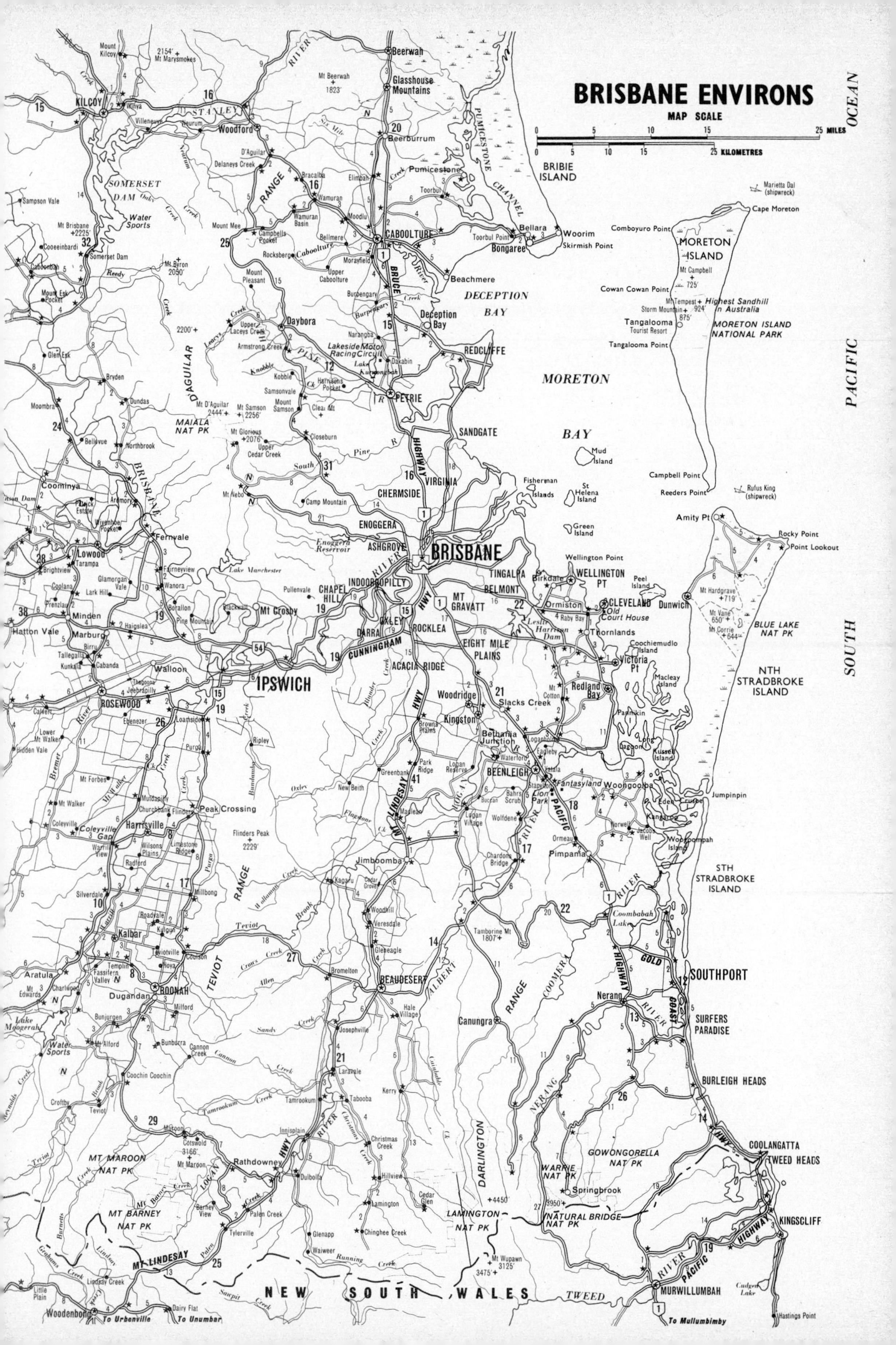
BRISBANE ENVIRONS
MAP SCALE
0 5 10 15 25 MILES
0 5 10 15 25 KILOMETRES
OCEAN
PACIFIC
SOUTH
BRIBIE ISLAND
PUMICESTONE CHANNEL
Marietta Dal (shipwreck)
Cape Moreton
Comboyuro Point
MORETON ISLAND
Mt Campbell 725'
Cowan Cowan Point
Mt Tempest 924' Highest Sandhill in Australia
Storm Mountain 875'
Tangalooma Tourist Resort
MORETON ISLAND NATIONAL PARK
Tangalooma Point
MORETON
BAY
Mud Island
Campbell Point
Reeders Point
Rufus King (shipwreck)
Fisherman Islands
St Helena Island
Green Island
Amity Pt
Rocky Point
Point Lookout
Wellington Point
WELLINGTON PT
Peel Island
Dunwich
Mt Hardgrave 719'
Mt Vane 650'
Mt Corrie 644'
BLUE LAKE NAT PK
CLEVELAND
Old Court House
Thornlands
Coochiemudlo Island
Victoria Pt
Macleay Island
NTH STRADBROKE ISLAND
Redland Bay
Russell Island
Jumpinpin
Woongoolba
Jacobs Well
Woogoompah Island
STH STRADBROKE ISLAND
Beerwah
Glasshouse Mountains
Mt Beerwah 1823'
Beerburrum
Pumicestone
Toorbul
Bellara
Woorim
Bongaree
Skirmish Point
Toorbul Point
CABOOLTURE
Beachmere
DECEPTION BAY
Deception Bay
REDCLIFFE
PETRIE
SANDGATE
VIRGINIA
CHERMSIDE
ENOGGERA
ASHGROVE
BRISBANE
INDOOROOPILLY
CHAPEL HILL
MT GRAVATT
TINGALPA
BELMONT
Birkdale
Ormiston
Raby Bay
OXLEY
DARRA
ROCKLEA
EIGHT MILE PLAINS
ACACIA RIDGE
CUNNINGHAM
IPSWICH
Woodridge
Kingston
Slacks Creek
Bethania Junction
Loganholme
Eagleby
Waterford
BEENLEIGH
Yatala
Fantasyland
Lion Park
Ormeau
Pimpama
Coombabah Lake
SOUTHPORT
SURFERS PARADISE
Nerang
BURLEIGH HEADS
COOLANGATTA
TWEED HEADS
KINGSCLIFF
Cudgen Lake
Hastings Point
MURWILLUMBAH
To Mullumbimby
TWEED
NEW SOUTH WALES
GOWONGORELLA NAT PK
WARRIE NAT PK
Springbrook
NATURAL BRIDGE NAT PK
LAMINGTON NAT PK
Mt Wupawn 3125'
Canungra
Tamborine Mt 1807'
BEAUDESERT
Jimboomba
Logan Village
Park Ridge
Greenbank
Browns Plains
Hale Village
Josephville
Laravale
Tabooba
Kerry
Christmas Creek
Hillview
Lamington
Cedar Glen
Chinghee Creek
Rathdowney
Innisplain
Dulbolla
Palen Creek
Tylerville
Glenapp
Waiweer
MT LINDESAY
MT BARNEY NAT PK
MT MAROON NAT PK
Mt Maroon
Cotswold 3166'
Maroon
Woodenbong
To Urbenville
To Unumbar
Dairy Flat
Lindsay Creek
Little Plain
Croftby
Teviot
Coochin Coochin
Bunburra
Cannon Creek
Mt Alford
Bunjurgen
Lake Moogerah
Water Sports
Milford
BOONAH
Dugandan
Fassifern Valley
Templin
Charlwood
Aratula
Mt Edwards
Kalbar
Teviotville
Coulson
Hoya
Roadvale
Silverdale
Millbong
Harrisville
Peak Crossing
Flinders Peak 2229'
Coleyville
Mt Walker
Mt Forbes
Hidden Vale
Lower Mt Walker
Calvert
ROSEWOOD
Ebenezer
Loamside
Purga
Ripley
Walloon
Marburg
Minden
Hatton Vale
Lowood
Fernvale
Wanora
Pine Mountain
Mt Crosby
Pullenvale
Lake Manchester
Enoggera Reservoir
Camp Mountain
Mt Nebo
Mt Glorious 2076'
MAIALA NAT PK
Mt D'Aguilar 2444'
Mt Samson 2256'
Samsonvale
Kobble
Closeburn
Dayboro
Armstrong Creek
Laceys Creek
Lakeside Motor Racing Circuit
Lake Kurwongbah
Dakabin
Narangba
Burpengary
Morayfield
Upper Caboolture
Rocksberg
Bellmere
Moodlu
Wamuran
Wamuran Basin
Bracalba
Elimbah
Mount Mee
Campbells Pocket
Mount Pleasant
Mt Byron 2050'
Delaneys Creek
D'Aguilar
Woodford
Neurum
Villeneuve
Winya
KILCOY
Mount Kilcoy
2154' Mt Marysmokes
SOMERSET DAM
Water Sports
Sampson Vale
Mt Brisbane 2225'
Cooeeinbardi
Somerset Dam
Mount Esk Pocket
Glen Esk
Bryden
Dundas
Moombra
Bellevue
Northbrook
Coominya
Wivenhoe Pocket
Brightview
Glamorgan Vale
Lark Hill
Coolana
Prenzlau
Haigslea
Tallegalla
Kunkala
Cabanda
D'AGUILAR RANGE
BRISBANE RIVER
STANLEY RIVER
BRUCE HIGHWAY
PACIFIC HWY
MT LINDESAY HWY
GOLD COAST HIGHWAY
TEVIOT RANGE
DARLINGTON RANGE
LOGAN RIVER
ALBERT RIVER
COOMERA RANGE
NERANG RIVER

the sand and sold for use in welding and the manufacture of pigments, alloys and refractories. There is a considerable export trade to USA and the UK.

The island is also a popular and fairly well-developed tourist resort, with small holiday settlements at Dunwich, Amity Point and Point Lookout. Its beaches offer good surfing and fishing and its wooded interior is rewarding to bush walkers and naturalists. Wildflowers, including ground orchids, wild iris and wedding bush, flourish in the sandy soil. There is a small national park and wildlife sanctuary surrounding Lake Karboora, one of several large lagoons in the centre of the island, which is 61 kilometres long and divided into two segments, North and South Stradbrooke, by a channel (Jumpinpin) cut by the sea after a cyclonic storm in 1896. There are several high features in the centre of the island, including Mount Hardgrave, 219 metres above sea level.

Accommodation. One **hotel. Guest-houses.** Two and four-unit **holiday cabins. Caravan and camping reserve,** Dunwich, all facilities; and at Point Lookout.

Transport. **Launch service** daily from North Quay, Brisbane, to Amity Point and Dunwich, connecting with bus for Point Lookout; **vehicular ferry** from Redland Bay; **passenger ferry** from Cleveland to Dunwich and Amity Point. **Bus tours,** via vehicular ferry, may be booked with Greyhound Coaches, South Brisbane.

REDCLIFFE
(Population 26 000)

An attractive and well-developed residential town and tourist resort 36 kilometres north-east of Brisbane which has in recent years become almost a suburb of the city. It is situated on a peninsula known as Humptybong, a corruption of an aboriginal term meaning 'dead houses'. (The hostility of savage local tribes had forced the abandonment of the first settlement in 1824.)

Nearby are 19 kilometres of safe bathing beaches fronting Moreton Bay. The best known are at the adjoining settlements of Scarborough and Margate. Amusement facilities on the peninsula include playgrounds, cinemas, fun-fairs and foreshore picnic areas.

Sports. Golf, 18-hole Clontarf course (Royal Queensland Golf Club), open to visitors; public tennis courts; croquet and bowling lawns; squash courts; Lakeside Motor Racing Circuit; Redcliffe Raceway (trotting, Saturdays and public holidays); water skiing, Lake Kurwongbah; Humptybong Yacht Club. Fishing in the area is good. A fleet of prawn trawlers operates from Scarborough boat harbour. Cod, snapper, groper and jewfish are caught in offshore waters, whiting, bream and flathead from beaches and jetties. There is also good spearfishing off headlands and reefs. Motor boats and dinghies can be hired at Scarborough and Hay's Inlet. Larger craft can be chartered for game-fishing off Cape Moreton.

Accommodation. Two **hotels.** Preferred: Seabrae. Three **motels.** Recommended: Waltzing Matilda, Margate Parade. Holiday **cabins, apartments** and **houses** for rent. One council and four privately owned **camping and caravan parks,** all amenities.

Transport. Co-ordinated **rail** and **bus** services link the Peninsula with Brisbane.

Tours. The Redcliffe area is a convenient point of departure for motor-coach tours north to Sunshine Coast resorts, the D'Aguilar Ranges and State forests, and Bribie Island (by MV *Miramar* Sundays and holidays).

REDLAND BAY RESORTS. Publicized as Brisbane's 'Salad Bowl', the Redland Bay district is about 39 kilometres south-east of the city. It grows 50 per cent of Queensland's famous strawberries for export to the southern States. Main settlements are **Redland Bay** township itself, **Cleveland, Victoria Point** and **Wellington Point. Manly** and **Wynnum,** prosperous bayside suburbs of the capital, are on Waterloo Bay to the north.

THE GOLD COAST

The Gold Coast is the most intensively developed and highly publicized tourist resort in Australia. It comprises about 34 kilometres of foreshore land extending northwards from the border of New South Wales and Queensland and 18 communities have now been incorporated for administrative and promotional purposes as the City of the Gold Coast.

The region is favoured with the pleasant, equable climate common to the sea-level regions of southern Queensland, has an average maximum temperature of 24°C and an average minimum of 15°C. The average rainfall is about 1 350 millimetres. Its popularity was originally based on a number of fine ocean beaches with broad stretches of golden sand and a regular, rolling surf.

The natural environment of the coast has been destroyed by high density building but the Coast still offers its visitors an enormous variety of man-contrived diversions and it is close to some of the most beautiful mountain and forest country in the Commonwealth—the McPherson Ranges which mark the border between the States.

SOUTHPORT, the administrative centre of the local government area, is south of Brisbane on the Pacific Highway. Other major centres, now almost fused by intensive strip development, include **SURFERS PARADISE, BURLEIGH HEADS, PALM BEACH** and **COOLANGATTA-TWEED HEADS.**

Tourism, which has attracted multi-million dollar investment in holiday accommodation of all kinds from luxury hotels and apartment blocks to economical holiday units and inexpensive guest-houses, dominates the economy of the district. The great boom on the Coast during the late 1950s and early 1960s created a highly competitive situation within the industry. At one time it was regarded as something of a millionaires' playground, but it is now possible to find surprisingly inexpensive and satisfactory accommodation, particularly before and after the peak of the winter season from June to August.

Gold Coast development has tended to follow American models. Emphasis is on organized entertainment and social diversions.

History. The first settlers in the district are believed to have been timber-getters, E. Harper and W. Duncan, who logged the dense stands of Queensland cedar in the foothills of the mountains. They established rafting grounds at the mouth of Tallebudgera Creek and built Harper's Wharf at Burleigh Heads.

Early in the 1850s William Duckett White established Beaudesert Station in the area now traversed by the Mount Lindsay Highway, but soon afterwards small selectors moved in and grew cotton until the boom burst, after which they turned to sugar. In the 1880s a Royal Mail coach service was established between Nerang, Southport and Tweed Heads, but the district remained a rural backwater until it began to gain popularity as a seaside holiday resort after the dawn of the motor age. Intensive exploitation did not begin until wartime building restrictions were lifted in 1952.

Places of Interest. Ski Land of Australia, The Spit, Southport. Water Ski shows at 11 am and 3 pm daily. **Chairlift, Mermaid Beach,** 5 kilometres south of Surfers Paradise, to restaurant with panoramic views of the McPherson Ranges. **House of Shells,** Burleigh Heads, fine collection of shells and marine specimens. **Pet Porpoise Pool,** Tweed Heads. Trained dolphins and seals perform at 10.30 am and 2.30 pm. Aquarium containing sharks, gropers, turtles etc. **Marineland of Australia,** Southport. Trained dolphins, whales etc. Divers feeding sharks etc. Four performances daily. **Natureland Zoo,** one kilometre north of Coolangatta. **Currumbin Bird Sanctuary,** between Coolangatta and Burleigh Heads. Flocks of wild birds, including honeyeaters, lorrikeets, soldier birds, spangled drongos and kookaburras fly in from forest to be fed at 8 am and 4 pm. **Giltrap's Auto Museum,** Coolangatta. A fascinating collection of ancient cars authentically restored. **Fleays Fauna Reserve,** Burleigh Heads. One of the finest collection of native animals, birds and reptiles in Australia. Specimens of kangaroos, koalas, golden possums, dingoes, Flinders Island wombats, native cats (Tasmanian devils,) cuscuses, echidnas, Australian crocodiles and snakes, including the (taipan). David Fleay, who runs the reserve, is a noted zoologist and world authority on Australian wildlife. **Burleigh Heads National Park,** home of many native animals, has fine stands of rain forest on southern slopes. There are several well-graded walking paths from Tallebudgera Creek. **Traintasia Miniature Railway,** Nobby's Beach. **Barrier Reef Aquarium,** Surfers Paradise. **Waxworks and Poineer Museums,** Surfers Paradise. **Captain Cook Memorial and Lighthouse,** Point Danger.

Sports. Gold Coast Race Club, 20 weekday meetings during the year. Trotting, Saturday afternoon meetings at Southport. Tennis, Surfers Paradise courts. Squash, Beach Road Courts, Surfers Paradise; Blue Skies Courts, Leonard Avenue. Bowls, 18 clubs, all resorts. Ten-Pin Bowling, Chevron Building, Surfers Paradise. Croquet Lawns at Broadbeach, Southport, Burleigh Heads, Coolangatta. Golf, 18-hole courses at Southport, Burleigh Heads, Tweed Heads-Coolangatta, Surfers Paradise; 9-hole course at Terranora Country Club, Tweed Heads. Roller Skating, rinks at Burleigh Heads, Coolangatta and Southport. Yachting, Southport Yacht Club. Fishing and Game-fishing. Boats and gear may be hired at Southport, Surfers Paradise, Tallebudgera Creek, Landsend, Labrador, Tweed Heads, The Spit, Angler's Paradise, Hollywell and Coombabah. Car Racing, International circuit, Nerang River. Archery, Gold Coast Company of Archers, Southport.

Evening entertainment. Larger hotels and motels employ dance bands and variety artists to entertain restaurant patrons and guests. Four amateur theatrical groups give occasional performances at Surfers Paradise and Coolangatta-Tweed Heads.

Accommodation

Bilinga. Four **motels.** Recommended: Shipmates, Gold Coast Highway.

Broadbeach. One **hotel.** Eight **motels.** Preferred: Whitehall Motor Inn, Elizabeth Street.

Burleigh Heads. Two **hotels.** Preferred: Burleigh Heads, Esplanade. Six **motels.** Preferred: Fifth Avenue, Fifth Avenue and Gold Coast Highway.

Coolangatta. Three **hotels.** No recommendation. Four **motels.** Recommended: Beachcomber Motor Lodge, Griffith Street.

Currumbin. One **hotel.** Five **motels.** Recommended: Golden Moon, The Esplanade.

Labrador. One **hotel.** Five **motels.** Preferred: Seacrest, Brisbane Road.

Main Beach. One **motel,** recommended.

Mermaid Beach. Eight **motels.** Preferred: Caravilla, Gold Coast Highway.

Miami. One **hotel.** Four **motels.** No recommendation.

Palm Beach. One **hotel.** Four **motels.** Recommended: Tropic Sands, Gold Coast Highway.

Southport. Three **hotels.** Preferred: Queens, Davenport and Nerang Streets. Three **motels.** Recommended: Imperial, Marine Parade.

Surfers Paradise One **hotel,** recommended. Fifty **motels.** Highly recommended: Apollo, The Esplanade; Iluka, The Esplanade; Courtesy Inn Sands and Courtesy Inn Shore, The Esplanade; Recommended: Travelodge, Beach Road.

Tugun. One **hotel.** Three **motels.** Preferred: Binalong, McLean Street.

There is a wide choice of serviced and unserviced **holiday houses** and **apartments.** Advice from tourist bureau or travel agencies.

Caravan and camping parks at Broadbeach, Burleigh Heads, Kirra Beach Park, Currumbin, Surfers Paradise, Tugun, Palm Beach, Miami, Northcliffe and Southport—all amenities.

Transport. Direct **air services** to Coolangatta Airport from Sydney, Melbourne and Adelaide. **Charter flights** in light aircraft may be arranged at Coolangatta Airport. Express **coach services** run between Surfers Paradise and Sydney, Melbourne and Adelaide. There are co-ordinated **rail and bus** services from southern capitals. Regular **bus and coach** services between all resorts and Brisbane. **Rental cars** available.

Tours. Both major domestic **airlines** offer package deal routs of the Coast from all State capitals Pioneer **coaches** run tours from Adelaide, Melbourne, Sydney and Canberra. **Motor** and **motor-coach tours** run from beach resorts to hinterland resorts daily. **Launch cruises** for Stradbroke Island leave Southport daily.

GOLD COAST HINTERLAND

The mountainous hinterland of the Gold Coast is undoubtedly the region's most precious natural asset. The traveller who concludes that the Coast's natural beach attractions have been over-promoted may well be compensated by the magnificent scenery and amazingly diverse fauna and flora to be found in the McPherson Ranges and the Lamington and Roberts Plateaux. Accommodation in the hills is neither as lush nor as sophisticated as it is on the beach, but the motorist these days can enjoy the best of two worlds since the most interesting of the accessible mountain country is no more than an hour's drive from the Pacific Highway.

LAMINGTON NATIONAL PARK

Queensland's best-known national park, the Lamington Plateau, is about 112 kilometres south of Brisbane and 32 kilometres inland from the coast road. It about 600 metres above sea level, receives heavy rainfall, and much of its soil is of volcanic origin. As a consequence its vegetation is dense and lush and the streams draining it clear and rapid. Several peaks on the southern and western margins of the reserve have altitudes above 900 metres. In the main range the high features rise well above 1 200 metres, at which level stands of Antarctic beech occur. These remarkable trees, which also occur in New Zealand and Terra del Fuego, are considered by some authorities to be evidence that a great southern continent once extended northwards from Antarctica to the Australian mainland. Some of the larger specimens are estimated to be 3 000 years old.

The rain forests of Lamington are rich in epiphytic orchids, elkhorns, staghorns and ferns. There are more than 20 species of prominent rock and tree orchids ranging in colour from pure white to deep mauve. In the lower-level forests many brilliantly coloured flowering trees grow, including flame, firewheel, waratah and Moreton Bay chestnuts.

Rare native birds and animals which can be observed in the area include brush turkeys, the rufous scrub bird (*atrichornis*), olive whistlers, eastern bristle birds, satin and regent bower birds, purple-breasted pigeons, albert lyrebirds, green catbirds and dormouse possums.

The park is well provided with graded walking tracks to the best stands of forest and to spectacular waterfalls and lookout points with panoramic views of the ranges and coastal plains.

There are two main access routes to Lamington proper—via Canungra to **O'Reilly's Guest House** in the heart of the reserve, or via Nerang and Beechmont to **Binnaburra Lodge** near the north-eastern boundary. The accommodation provided is simple and comfortable, designed to meet the taste of physically active nature lovers. Forward booking is advisable at both resorts during holiday periods.

The climate is, on the whole, mild the year round but even summer evenings can be chilly and visitors should include warm clothing, waterproofs and stout walking boots or shoes in their luggage. February, March and early April is the wet season.

Places of Interest. Glow Worm Cave; Ballanjui Cascades; Talangai Caves; Booboora Falls; Natural Arch picnic area; **Twin Falls; Springbrook; Billborrough's Lookout.**

Entertainments and sports include riding, bush walking, organized camping trips, table tennis etc.

Tours by motor coach leave Binnaburra Lodge for Springbrook Plateau, Tamborine and Gold Coast resorts.

TAMBORINE MOUNTAIN

An outlying scarp of the McPherson Ranges, eight miles long and up to four miles wide, Tamborine Mountain has an elevation of 564 metres. It is due north of Lamington and, although much of the district has been exploited by timber-getters, considerable areas have been reserved as national parks. They have many of the same physical characteristics as the Lamington Plateau but are less secluded and extensive.

The name Tamborine is derived from the aboriginal *dumberin*, meaning 'a place where yams grow'. The western slopes of the mountain are noted for their prolific stands of macrozamia palms, a cycad plant species of great antiquity, which has changed little since carboniferous times. Some of the specimens at Tamborine have been calculated to be 1 000 years old. Another remarkable tree which grows prolifically in the rain forests here is the carrabeeb, with deeply buttressed roots covered with moss and creeping ferns.

Two main roads give access from Brisbane to Tamborine's reserves—the Beaudesert Road with a signposted turnoff about three kilometres past the Maclean Bridge over the Logan River and another road turning off the Pacific Highway at Beenleigh. Motorists based on Gold Coast beach resorts can travel north from Southport on the Pacific Highway and turn west at Oxenford for Eagle Heights and Tamborine village.

Places of Interest. Macrozamia Park Reserve; Macdonald Park; Cameron Falls; Witches' Falls Park; Western Cliff Road lookouts; **Cedar Creek Falls; Advancetown,** pioneer slab house (authentically restored and furnished); **Jasper Farm** (fossicking for gemstones); **Upper Coomera Tulip Farm** (in spring); **Boomerang Factory,** Springbrook Road.

Accommodation. At Gold Coast resorts and St Bernard's, Mt Tamborine.

SUNSHINE COAST AND HINTERLAND

The long string of beach and fishing resorts stretching north from Bribie Island to Tin Can Bay, east of Gympie, has in recent years been promoted as 'The Sunshine Coast' and the district is steadily gaining popularity with tourists and holidaymakers who are not particularly attracted by the intensely commercial atmosphere of the Gold Coast.

The coast north of Brisbane is, in fact, much more scenically interesting than the coast to the south. It has more variety of form and colour and its beaches offer better surfing. The resorts themselves have preserved an air of leisure and serene isolation from the electronic age.

However, it is true that the hinterland of the Sunshine Coast has nothing to equal the breathtaking and exotic splendour of Lamington and the McPherson Range. The Glasshouse Mountains and the Blackall Range are fascinating and offer many panoramic views of ocean, forest and plain, but they lack the stature of the great national parks 200 kilometres to the south. Except in the luxury bracket, accommodation tariffs are slightly higher than on the Gold Coast. The choice is not nearly so wide.

The major Sunshine Coast settlements are:

CABOOLTURE (Population 3 420)

On the northern railway and the Bruce Highway 55 kilometres north of Brisbane, Caboolture is the centre of a closely settled and productive agricultural area which supports large herds of dairy and stud beef cattle and grows citrus and tropical fruits, sugar, tobacco and vegetables. The name derives from the aboriginal word *cabul-tur* meaning carpet snake.

History. The district is closely associated with nearby Bribie Island and was originally opened up for grazing. In 1860 J. Corseldine purchased part of the original Caboolture station and set up a company to grow cotton which was fairly extensively cultivated in Queensland when world shortages resulted from the American Civil War. When the market slumped most plantations turned to sugar. The first sugar crop in the district was harvested in 1865. In the early days of the Pacific War of 1944-45, Caboolture was the secret headquarters of the Allied High Command.

Places of Interest. Aboriginal **Bora Ground at Toorbul Point** near the Bribie Island toll bridge. The large ring and sunken tract of ground once used by the natives for religious dances and ceremonies is well preserved. **Halmakuta Memorial,** near the road to Bribie Island, was erected in memory of Arima Halmakuta, the last surviving member of the Joondoburri tribe, who died in 1897. She is reputed to have been an expert boatwoman and swimmer. The tribe originally numbered about 600, but its numbers diminished to 300 by 1870, less than 40 years after the arrival of the first white settlers. Halmakuta is buried under the ancient Morton Bay fig tree near the monument. **Ninghi Creek,** about a hundred metres north of the road, is famed for an old oyster house standing on stilts in the water. The Ninghininghi tribe were fierce warriors and cannibals. The oyster house is said to stand on the spot where a hero of the Nooghies tribe of Moreton Island rescued his wife Kinterribah after she had been kidnapped by Ninghis. An attractive picnic spot.

Sports. Good 18-hole golf course; bowling greens; boating and fishing in sheltered Pumicestone Passage. Boats and launching ramps at Toorbul, Deception Bay, Beachmere, and Donnybrook.

Accommodation. See Bribie Island.

NAMBOUR (Population 6 744)

A prosperous sugar town about 124 kilometres north of Brisbane, Nambour is regarded as the 'capital' of the Sunshine Coast. It is the centre of a network of roads leading to the various beach resorts and mountains and possesses a rich volcanic soil on which pineapples, bananas, strawberries, ginger and macadamia nuts are grown as well as cane. The town is a good base for exploration of the Blackall Ranges and the Glasshouse Mountains to the south.

History. Nambour was first settled in the 1860s, largely by prospectors who had been disappointed in the Gympie gold rush. *Nambur* is the native name for a variety of red-flowering tea tree which grows prolifically in the district. Sugar was first established as a major commercial crop in the 1890's when the Moreton Central Sugar Mill was first established. Deposits of asbestos and manganese have been discovered in the area, but they have never been exploited commercially.

Sports. Usual facilities.

Accommodation. One **hotel,** recommended. One **motel.** One **caravan and camping park** (one and a half kilometres south of town) with overnight cabins and all facilities.

Transport. Rail and coach services on northern railway and Bruce Highway.

Of Interest Nearby: Kondalilla National Park, on crest of Blackall Ranges. A small area of virgin rainforest containing the spectacular Kondalilla Falls (90 metres) and rock pools where lung fish may be observed.

GLASSHOUSE MOUNTAINS

Named by Captain Cook in 1770 because of their resemblance to the glass furnaces of his native Yorkshire, the Glasshouse Mountains, lying about 24 kilometres north of Caboolture, are a series of steep, massive pillars of trachyte. There are 11 principal peaks, the three highest being Beerwah (aboriginal meaning 'up in the sky') 556.6 metres, Crookneck or Coonawrin 376 metres and Beerburrum 'the noise of parrots' wings' 276 metres.

Although they carry some sparse vegetation they present climbers with considerable difficulties. However, all have been scaled.

Beach Resorts in District

CALOUNDRA, at the northern end of Pumicestone Passage, has 13 kilometres of first rate surfing beaches, two of which (King's and Dicky) are regularly patrolled by surf lifesaving clubs; has good fishing for whiting, flathead and bream; there are many attractive picnic grounds.

Accommodation. Two **hotels.** Recommended: Caloundra, Bulcock Street. Nine **motels.** Recommended: Rolling Surf, King's Beach. Nine **caravan and camping parks,** most with all facilities. Motor-coach **tours** available.

MOOLOOLABA. Alexandra Headland, well-known fishing resort at mouth of the Mooloolaba River. Name derives from the aboriginal word meaning 'the place of the snapper'. Good surf beaches on either side of the estuary. Charter boats for deep-sea fishing are available.

MAROOCHYDORE. Excellent surf beach. Good surf and river fishing. Water-skiing. Maroochy River has large flocks of pelicans and black swans. Boats for hire.

Accommodation. One **hotel.** Thirteen **motels.** Recommended: Sixth Avenue, 6th Avenue; Surfront Motor Inn, Kingsford Smith Parade; Lanham Lodge, Aerodrome Road. **Camping and caravan park,** all facilities.

COOLUM. Excellent surf beach. Surrounding country is hilly and there are many lookout points with panoramic views of coast and hinterland.

Accommodation. Two **motels.** Recommended: Clansman. One **caravan and camping park,** some facilities. **Holiday lodges** available at moderate rent.

NOOSA HEADS AND NOOSAVILLE. Noted for exceptionally fine coastal scenery—Witches' Cauldron, Hell's Gates, Devil's Kitchen, Paradise Caves etc. Sunshine Beach has attracted international surf board champions. Five kilometres from Noosa is the 334 hectare Noosa National Park containing a chain of lakes densely populated with waterfowl of all kinds. Exploration by boat is fascinating. Park area has been intelligently and unobtrusively developed.

Accommodation. One **hotel.** Eleven **motels.** Recommended: Los Nidos, Hastings Street. **Chalet** and two **caravan and camping parks,** all facilities (Pine Trees and Noosaville); two others with limited facilities.

TEWANTIN, on Noosa River, centre of the extensive Noosa Lakes area and base for professional fishermen. Attractions include Mary Valley, Boreen Point on Lake Cootharaba, Double Island Point and the famous **Teewah** multi-coloured sands in a 250 metre cliff face. (Organized tours by coach and launch from other resorts).

Accommodation. One **motel.**

BUDERIM, a few kilometres inland from Mooloolaba but close to beach resorts. Good golf course. Tours of ginger factory. Seal park and koala sanctuary.

Accommodation. Three **motels.** Recommended: Mountain Maid, King Street. One **caravan and camping park,** all facilities.

WARWICK

(Population 9 356)

On the Condamine River, 160 kilometres south-west of Brisbane, Warwick is the centre of a prosperous dairying, mixed farming and grain-growing area. Its agricultural lands produce wheat, maize, barley, oats, millet, sorghum and oil seeds. There are also a number of famous stud farms (horses, cattle and sheep) in the district. Secondary industries include bacon, butter and cheese factories, flour mills, sawmills, engineering works and a stockfood processing plant.

Warwick is a noted educational centre, with six primary and seven secondary schools.

History. Patrick Leslie, a prominent figure in the early political life of Queensland, and his brothers brought flocks from New South Wales into the Darling Downs in 1840 and established a sheep station at Canning Downs. In 1854 Gilbert and Walter Davidson bought the property and attempted to acclimatize Peruvian llamas as the price of mohair was then very high and the price of wool low. The llamas, however, could not adapt to the climate and pastures of Queensland and died without having produced mohair or progeny.

The actual town site of Warwick was settled in 1848 when the Walker family established the first store in the district. The town and municipality was incorporated in 1861 and became a city in 1936.

An incident at Warwick in 1917 led to the formation of the Commonwealth Police Force. The then Prime Minister, William Morris Hughes, was struck by an egg thrown by a man in a crowd he was addressing on the issue of military conscription. Hughes ordered a State policeman to arrest the egg thrower. The policeman refused to obey the order—hence the establishment of a Commonwealth force.

Places of Interest. **Leslie Park,** in the main street, popular for its arbours, ornamental trees and colourful borders. **Queen Mary Falls,** 31 kilometres east, centre of a reserve of well-managed hardwood and hoop pine forests, noted for bird life and a dense population of rock wallabies. **Blackfellows' Knob National Park, Leslie Dam,** 11 kilometres west, covering an area of 800 hectares, has facilities for aquatic sports. **Leichhardt's Tree,** near Rosenthal Homestead, bears marks made by the explorer, Ludwig Leichhardt, when he passed through the district in 1844 on his way to Port Essington (Darwin). **Historic Station Homesteads.** South Toolburra, Canning Downs, Risdon.

Annual Events. Warwick **Rodeo and Gold Cup Campdraft,** held late in October, is one of the finest in Australia. **Boxing Day** is celebrated with a Highland dancing and pipe band contest and **St Patrick's Day** with street processions and a sports meeting.

Sports. Good 18-hole golf course. Boating, sailing and water-skiing on Leslie Dam. Gliding at Warwick aerodrome—the State championships are held here. Olympic swimming pool in town.

Accommodation. Four **hotels.** Recommended: Horse and Jockey. Three **motels.** Recommended: Travelodge. **Caravan and camping park,** all amenities.

Transport. **Road** and **rail** connections with Brisbane, south-west Queensland towns and New South Wales.

THE DARLING DOWNS

The blacksoil plains of the Darling Downs, covering an area of some 7 000 000 hectares, are one of Australia's richest and most productive agricultural and pastoral areas. They produce more than 90 per cent of the State's wheat, nearly half its maize, between 80 and 90 per cent of its oil seeds, two-thirds of its fruit and one-third of its tobacco. The district is also famous for its bloodstock studs.

The population of the division now exceeds 150 000. Its towns are well-ordered, cheerful communities which reflect general prosperity and a good deal of civic pride expressed in the vigorous development of public amenities of all kinds.

On the Downs the visitor sees rural Australia at its best. The region enjoys an equable climate with adequate and usually reliable rainfall and it is scenically attractive because of its proximity to a well-watered and fertile segment of the Great Dividing Range. There are many carefully preserved national parks and wildlife sanctuaries near the major centres of population.

TOOWOOMBA

(Population 57 543)

The largest inland city of Queensland, Toowoomba is 135 kilometres west of Brisbane. Situated at an elevation of 610 metres on the rim of the Great Dividing Range, it has a notably fine, healthy climate. It is the chief commercial centre of an almost incredibly rich agricultural and pastoral district and supports industries associated with agricultural production—meat processing, butter and cheese factories, flour mills, tanneries, sawmills, yeast and malt factories and a large brewery. Other industries include engineering and railway workshops, an iron foundry, established in 1871 and claimed to be one of the largest in the southern hemisphere, and clothing and footwear factories.

The city is on the New England Highway and is an important road and rail junction in the transportation complex serving the pastoral areas of south-western Queensland, the Moonie oilfields and the Roma gasfields as well as rapidly developing agricultural areas to the north. Toowoomba is noted for its wide, tree-lined streets and the beauty of its public parks, gardens and sports grounds. In September every year its Carnival of Flowers attracts visitors from many parts of eastern Australia.

History. The origin of the name is obscure. Some authorities hold that it derives from the natives' attempt to say 'swamp'; others that it comes from the native word *chowoom*, meaning a place where melons grow. The village from which the city spread was first known as The Swamps. It was founded in 1849 near the present suburb of Drayton and became an important staging-point for teamsters and other travellers between the northern and central Downs and Brisbane. The town was incorporated in 1860 and in 1904 was gazetted a city.

Places of Interest. Ravensbourne **National Park,** 45 kilometres north-east of the city, is noted for its bird life; the **Botanic Gardens;** the **Art Gallery,** housing the notable Gould collection and incorporating the **Lionel Lindsay Memorial Gallery,** opened in 1957; **Helidon Crystal Spa,** with water-ski pool; **Lookouts** at Picnic Point, Webb Park, Mt Lofty and Mt Kynoch. Toowoomba is also a convenient base for expeditions to **Bunya National Park.** (See below.)

Sports. Usual facilities for tennis, bowls, golf etc.

Accommodation. Six **hotels.** Recommended: Lennons, Ruthven Street. Twelve **motels.** Recommended: Travelodge, Margaret Street; Picnic Point Inn, Long Street. Three **caravan and camping parks,** all facilities.

Transport. Rail, road and **air services** (TAA) link Toowoomba with Brisbane and major towns of Western Queensland. The airport is at Oakey on the Warrego Highway, north-west of the city.

DALBY

(Population 8 890)

On the northern Darling Downs, about 80 kilometres north-west of Toowoomba, Dalby is a well planned, pleasant country town typical of the more prosperous grain-growing and pastoral districts of southern Queensland. It is the centre of the State's most productive wheat-growing area. Timber and linseed are also important to the town's economy.

History. Established in 1842 and named after the Isle of Man town, Dalby was proclaimed a municipality in 1863. From nearby Jimbour House, Leichhardt set out in 1848 to cross Australia from east to west—the expedition from which he never returned.

Sports. Golf links, bowling greens, tennis courts, racecourse, Olympic swimming pool.

Accommodation. Three **hotels.** Recommended: Commercial. Two **motels.** Recommended: Windsor, Condamine Street.

Transport. Road and **rail** services to Brisbane and Charleville.

BUNYA MOUNTAINS NATIONAL PARK

The area of Bunya Mountains National Park, 48 kilometres north-east of Dalby on the road to Kingaroy, is just over 9 700 hectares. It is one of the most picturesque reserves on this section of the Great Dividing Range. Main peaks in the region are Mount Kiangarow (1 134 metres), Mount Mowbullan (1 100 metres) and Mount Haly (1 116 metres). The mountain slopes are densely timbered with bunya pines (*Araucaria bidwillii*), a tall, coniferous tree endemic in south-east Queensland. The bunya is ornamental, having an immense, dome-shaped crown. It yields a valuable timber—pale, easily worked and suitable for joinery, cabinet work and plywood. The large, sweetish nuts were once an important food for the aborigines of the Darling Downs, who ate them roasted. Every third year the crop was plentiful and feasts were held. During these long celebrations all laws on tribal land boundaries were suspended and traditionally hostile groups observed a truce. Relics of these ancient feasts are still to be found in the park.

Other unusual species of vegetation in the reserve include backhausia scrub, yellow stringybark, bottle trees, native cypress and grass trees of great antiquity. Twenty four kilometres of graded walking track have been formed in the park, giving access to its most spectacular lookouts and waterfalls.

Accommodation. One **guest-house.**

Transport. Information from Queensland Government Tourist Bureau.

SOUTH EASTERN HINTERLAND

IPSWICH

(Population 56 000)

Thirty nine kilometres south-west of Brisbane on the Bremer River, Ipswich is the centre of Queensland's most important coalfield. Its mines are vital sources of fuel for thermal power-generation stations in the south. The coal deposits cover an area of more than 23 000 hectares.

The town's industries include railway workshops, light and heavy engineering plants, foundries, woollen mills, clothing factories, brick, pipe and other earthernware works (based on the clay deposits at nearby Dinmore), sawmills, abattoirs, fertilizer works and hardboard factories. The surrounding district of West Moreton produces dairy products, maize, lucerne, potatoes and beef cattle.

Of Interest. Queen's Park and **Cunningham Knoll.**

Sports. Horse racing, tennis, bowls etc; boating, cycling, water-skiing. Olympic pool.

History. In 1827 a convict settlement was established to work limestone deposits in the nearby hills. Burned lime and quarried stone were transported downriver to Brisbane in convict-manned whaleboats. Coal was discovered in the same year, but the mines were not developed until some years later. In 1828 the explorer Cunningham used Limestone Hills, as the settlement was then known, as the starting point for his exploration of the Darling Downs. The first free settlers arrived in the district 10 years later.

In 1842 the village was renamed after Ipswich, Suffolk, and it began to grow rapidly. In the 1850s it had become the main river port for the shipment of produce between the Darling Downs and Brisbane and was at one time seriously considered as a possible capital for the new State when separation was achieved. Cobb and Co established a coach service from Brisbane to Ipswich, but it was not until the railway went through to Brisbane in 1876 that the river trade declined. By the turn of the century the coalmining industry was well established and in 1904 Ipswich was gazetted a city.

Accommodation. Two **hotels.** Preferred: Prince Alfred, Brisbane Road. Three **motels.** Preferred: Tulmur Park, Warwick Road.

Transport. Rail and **road** service from Brisbane and to south.

BOONAH (Population 1 922)

Principal town of the Fassifern Plains district, about 88 kilometres south-west of Brisbane. The name is derived from an aboriginal word for the bloodwood tree. The shire which now has a population of more than 6 000, is one of the principal potato-growing areas in the State. Other primary industries in the area include dairying and the growing of lucerne, maize and other fodder crops under irrigation. Light engineering works in the town manufacture agricultural machinery and implements. Timber logged in the nearby ranges supports two large sawmills.

The Fassifern district celebrates an annual potato Festival beginning on the first Saturday in September with parades, concerts, a play festival, a ball, and ring events in the showground at **Kalbar,** a small town to the west near the Cunningham Highway, which closely follows the route of the explorer Alan Cunningham when in 1828 he discovered the gap in the Great Dividing Range—a discovery which made possible land communication between the southern settlements and the Moreton Bay district. Boonah became an important staging place for bullock teams on the Sydney-Moreton Bay route in the 1850s.

Places of Interest. Cunningham's Gap **National Park,** with fine panoramic views, areas of rain forest, waterfalls etc, traversed by scenic roads, off the Cunningham Highway from Ipswich and connecting with New England Highway at Warwick. **Mount Mitchell** and **Spicer's Gap,** with pioneers' cemetery, Governor's Chair Lookout, Moss's Well and Bell Bird area (with length of stone-paved road believed to have been constructed by convicts). **'Coochin-Coochin'** homestead, south of town on road to Rathdowney and Kyogle, a historic property on which visiting royalty has been entertained. **Lake Moogerah** (aboriginal word for 'place of thunderstorms'), a large reservoir built to supply water to surrounding towns and irrigated farmlands; it has facilities for boating, water-skiing and ski jumping. **Mount Maroon, Wilson's Peak** and **White Swamp,** vantage points near road south.

Sports. Golf course, bowling greens, public playing fields, swimming pool.

Accommodation. Information from Government Tourist Bureau.

Transport. Daily **motor-coach** service to Ipswich and Brisbane.

STANTHORPE (Population 3 500)

Stanthorpe is the chief town of an important fruit-growing district 225 kilometres south-west of Brisbane and close to the NSW border. It is noted for its apple and pear orchards and for high-quality stone fruit. Located in the Granite Belt, it is popular as a tourist resort because of its spectacular and unusual rock formations and the variety of wildflowers which bloom in the nearby mountains during July and August. More than 50 species of wattle and 60 species of orchids have been identified and a number of boronias, tea trees, insect-catching trigger-plants, lilies and rock roses are unique to the district. The area is also popular with prospectors for precious and semi-precious gemstones. Rubies and sapphires as well as various types of rock crystal, garnets and topaz have been found in the creeks. The whole district is highly mineralized. Tin mining has recently been resumed. Gold, wolfram and molybdenite also occur alluvially.

History. The town was founded after tin had been discovered at Quartpot Creek in 1872. In 1880 silver and lead strikes were made, but the deposits were small and difficult to work and the mining industry slowly died. Stanthorpe Shire was proclaimed in 1902, by which time the fruit-growing industry had been established.

Places of Interest. Wyberba and Bald Rock Creek **National Parks,** noted for rock formations, waterfalls and wildflowers. **Storm King Dam,** with facilities for aquatic sports. Undercliffe, Boonoo Boonoo, Severn River and Jolly's Falls **waterfalls. Red Rock Gorge,** with its precipitous granite cliffs over 152 metres high. An annual Apple Blossom Festival is held in October, when tours of the orchards are made and evening entertainments and an aquatic carnival organized.

Accommodation. Two **hotels.** Recommended: Country Club. Three **motels.** Recommended: Granite Court, Wallangerra Road. **Caravan and camping park,** all facilities.

Transport. Rail to Brisbane and Wallangarra (connecting NSW system). Motor **coach** services on New England Highway.

BEAUDESERT (Population 3 500)

Centre of a dairy farming, agricultural and grazing district on the Mount Lindsay Highway, 66 kilometres south of Brisbane. Noted for its race club which organizes some of the most successful provincial meetings in southern Queensland. Tourism is becoming more important in the district's economy. Beaudesert Agricultural Show, in September, is of considerable interset.

Accommodation. One **hotel.** One **motel.** One **camping and caravan park.**

CENTRAL COAST AND HINTERLAND

The central coast of Queensland and its hinterland comprise a region of enormous but as yet only partially exploited agricultural, mineral and marine resources. Its towns and cities already enjoy a large measure of prosperity, and the prospect of rapid growth as modern industry establishes itself and attracts investment and population.

The climate is warm, moist and amazingly equable, varying little in temperature between winter and summer, but because of the rainfall distribution May to October is the best time of the year for holiday makers.

GYMPIE

(Population 11 131)

On the Mary River, 198 kilometres north of Brisbane, Gympie is the centre of an important dairy farming, tropical fruit and vegetable-growing area. The district also produces high-quality beef cattle. There are very large pine plantations in the nearby Toolara State Forests which support a milling and joinery industry in the town. In the surrounding countryside are several butter factories and a condensed-milk factory.

History. Gympie began as a goldmining town in 1867. A prospector, James Nash, found rich gold in a dry creekbed at the base of Caledonian Hill. A rush began and the gold won from the Gympie diggings did much to tide Queensland over the financial difficulties it experienced in the early days of statehood. By 1909, 51 mining companies were operating in the district. The largest mine, the Scottish Gympie, had more than 48 kilometres of underground workings. Over 4 million ounces of gold were won including the famous Curtis nugget before the mines declined in the 1920s. The settlement was originally named Nashville, but this was changed in 1868 to Gympie after the aboriginal *gimpi-gimpi*, meaning 'stinging tree'.

Gympie is a conventional base from which to tour the northern Sunshine Coast resorts and the Blackall Ranges and wide Bay resorts.

Of Interest. Gympie and district **Historical Museum. Spring Valley Brahman Cattle Stud.**

Accommodation. Three **hotels.** Preferred: Empire, Mary Street. Four **motels.** Recommended: Gympie, Bruce Highway. Two **caravan parks,** all facilities.

Transport. Gympie is on the Bruce Highway and the main northern railway between Brisbane and Cairns. It has good **rail** and **motor coach** services to other coastal cities. **Air** services to nearby Maroochy Airport.

MARYBOROUGH

(Population 19 962)

The city of Maryborough is the administrative and commercial hub of the Hervey Bay, Wide Bay and Burnett River districts. It is 298 kilometres north of Brisbane, on the Bruce Highway and the main northern railway line, close to the mouth of the Mary River. The main primary products of the area are sugar, fish, coal, timber, dairy produce, maize, sorghum, oats and fruit and vegetables. The secondary industries of the city are sawmilling, the manufacture of heavy machinery, ship-building and factories or mills making bricks, bacon, flour, pipes, joinery and butter.

The climate of Maryborough is warm and moist, temperatures varying little between summer and winter. The city's parks and gardens have beautiful tropical trees and flowering shrubs.

History. The Mary River was discovered in 1842 by A. Petrie and Henry Russell. The following year a village was established and grew rapidly as a convenient point of shipment for the wool produced in the rich pastoral hinterland. In 1859 it was gazetted a port of entry and in 1861 the municipality was proclaimed. In the 1860s cotton was grown extensively, but after 1865 was replaced by sugar after the Maryborough Sugar Company established 1 000 acres of cane successfully in the Tinana River region. About the same time extensive coal deposits were discovered near the Burrum River and coal has been a significant factor in the district's economy ever since. Timber, from natural stands of red cedar and eucalypt hardwoods and from acclimatized slash and loblolly pine, is also important among regional resources.

Places of Interest. **Queen's** and **Elizabeth Parks. Musical Box Museum. Teddington's Weir.** Hervey and Wide Bay **beach resorts. Frazer Island.**

Sports. Usual facilities.

Accommodation. Five **hotels.** Recommended: Granville. Six **motels.** Recommended: Arkana South, Caravilla. Two **caravan and camping parks.**

Transport. **Rail, road** and **air** services to Brisbane and to northern centres.

HERVEY BAY

Several seaside settlements on the foreshores of Hervey Bay have been developed as holiday resorts for the people of Bundaberg and Maryborough districts. They include Gataker's Bay, Point Vernon, Burrum Head, Pialba, Scarness, Torquay and Urangan. Swimming, fishing and boating are the main recreations, but there are bowling greens at Scarness and Pialba, an 18 hole golf course at Pialba, tennis courts at Torquay and Scarness, croquet lawns at Urangan and Pialba and a skating rink at Scarness. A yachting regatta is held at Scarness over Easter and a water-skiing area has been reserved at Torquay. Hervey Bay Shell Museum at Urangan is well worth a visit. Urangan is now assuming commercial significance as a deep water port for overseas and coastal ships.

Accommodation. Three **hotels** (Pialba, Scarness and Torquay). Recommended: Torquay. Five **motels.** Recommended: Reef, Torquay. One **guest-house,** Scarness. Twelve **caravan and camping parks.** Recommended: Dayman Point. Holiday **cottages** and **cabins** available.

Transport. **Road** services between Bay resorts and Maryborough. Local **bus** services.

FRAZER ISLAND

The largest island off the Queensland coast, Frazer Island is 144 kilometres long and roughly 14 kilometres wide. It is now being developed as a fishing and beach resort by private enterprise. Its interior is heavily wooded, teeming with wildlife, and fishermen report large catches from its beaches and rocky headlands.

A tourist village planned on 'Polynesian' lines has been established at Orchid Beach at the north-eastern extremity of the island.

Provisions may be ordered in advance and are flown from the mainland. Hire-drive vehicles suitable for traversing the rugged interior and the beaches are available. The services of a professional fishing guide may also be obtained.

Launch and **air** services connect the island with Hervey Bay and Maryborough. The island is connected to the mainland by radio-telephone and has a 240-volt electric lighting and power plant.

Less developed settlements on the island include Woongoolba, Boogimbah (with air strips) and Ungowa. The Forestry Commission also maintains an air strip at Lake Coomboo, one of several fresh-water lagoons in the interior.

BUNDABERG

(Population 26 570)

Located 14 kilometres from the mouth of the Burnett River and 417 kilometres north of Brisbane, Bundaberg is an important commercial and shipping centre for a large area of rich coastal and river-flat country producing sugar, tobacco, pineapples and other tropical fruit, peanuts and winter vegetables and dairy produce. About $A27 million worth of sugar is produced annually at seven mills operating in the district.

The Burnett River now has an artificial harbour which gives anchorage to ships up to 8 000 tonnes and has facilities for bulk-sugar loading. Other secondary industries include a rum distillery, plants for the manufacture of agricultural machinery and furniture, a large butter factory and shipbuilding yards.

Bundaberg is renowned for tropical plant nurseries. It is a city of wide, tree-lined streets where the bauhinias and poincianas make a brilliant display in the spring.

History. Settlement of the district dates back to 1866 when John and Gavin Steuart selected 130 hectares and planted coffee and sugar. Two years later the first mill was established and between 1872 and 1882 kanaka labour was imported to work the plantations. The town and municipality were proclaimed in 1881 and the Millaquin Sugar Refinery established by John and Robert Cran in 1882. The district continued to depend almost entirely on cane-farming until 1897 when the dairy industry was established. Bundaberg was proclaimed a city in 1913. The first peanut crop was harvested in 1947.

Places of Interest. Famous surf beaches at **Bargara** (14 kilometres), **Moore Park** (23 kilometres).

Aquatic sports resorts at **Elliot** and **Burnett Heads. Turtle breeding ground** near Nielson Park, 14 kilometres from city. **Alexander Park and Zoo. Anzac Park.** Bauer's and Lanbecker's **plant nurseries. Rum distillery** (total production of 6 042 500 litres of rectified spirit and rum a year). **The Hummock** (110 metres), the only high feature in the area with views of surrounding canefields and fruit farms. **Memorial to Squadron Leader H. J. L. Hinkler,** Buss Park, (first solo flight from UK, 1928).

Annual Sugar Festival, early October. Sports and race carnivals, mardi gras, street procession. Industrial and trade exhibitions.

Entertainments. Three **cinemas.**

Sports. Golf courses; tennis courts; bowls and croquet greens; Olympic swimming pool; polocross field; racecourse; motor and cycle-racing circuit; squash courts; archery, rowing, sailing, rifle and water-skiing clubs.

Accommodation. Three directory listed **hotels.** Recommended: Royal, Bourbong Street. Ten **motels.** Recommended: Motelodge, Takalvan Street; Park Lane, Bourbong Street. Six **caravan and camping parks,** all facilities.

Transport. Frequent **rail, road** and **air** services to Brisbane and northern centres.

KINGAROY (Population 5 000)

Main town in the South Burnett district, north of the Darling Downs and inland from Gympie and Bundaberg, Kingaroy is famous for the peanuts (groundnuts) produced from its fertile red soil. About 30 000 hectares are cultivated each year. Giant silos and cool stores for kernals are located in the town, which is 233 kilometres north-west of Brisbane.

Other products of the district include maize, barley, oats, wheat, sorghum, soy and navy beans, honey, dairy produce, pigs and beef cattle. Corkwood trees flourish in the area and the drug hyacin, used in the relief of nausea, is extracted from their crushed leaves.

The town has progressed rapidly as a manufacturing centre for specialized agricultural machinery. Its architecture is modern and its public buildings include a well-designed civic centre, district court house, library and child welfare centre. There is a number of public parks and recreation grounds. **Bunya Mountains National Park** is 51 kilometres south-west.

History. The Kingaroy district was pioneered by H. S. Russell in 1843, but agriculture was not established until 1886 when Arthur Youngman settled Kingaroy Paddock. (The name is derived from an aboriginal word meaning 'red ant'.) By 1924 peanuts had been proved a profitable crop and the Queensland Peanut Marketing Board established its headquarters in the town.

Sports. Tennis, basketball, 18-hole golf course, two bowling greens, squash, croquet, gun club, aero and gliding club, water-skiing on Gordonbrook Dam, west of town, Olympic swimming pool, indoor bowling alley, football and cricket grounds. Annual events include the Kingaroy Show, usually held in late March or early April. The Wooroolin Sports and Highland Gathering (noted for axemen's competitions) is held in October.

Accommodation. Three **hotels.** Preferred: Kingaroy. Three **motels.** Recommended: Holliday, Youngman Street. One **caravan and camping park,** all facilities.

Transport. Daily **rail, motor-coach** and **air** service to Brisbane.

ROCKHAMPTON

(Population 48 188)

Rockhampton and the nearby Port Alma (51 kilometres south-east) at the mouth of the Fitzroy River serve a vast area of Central Queensland rich in mineral resources and pastoral and agricultural land. The city is on the Tropic of Capricorn 797 kilometres north-west of Brisbane. It serves as the centre of a web of main roads, railways and air routes to the grain lands and cattle and sheep pastures of the west—and to the great coal measures of the hinterland as yet only partly exploited. Mount Morgan gold and copper mine, a huge open-cut which has produced some eight million ounces of gold and more than quarter of a million tons of copper, is 38 kilometres south-west of the city. Other mineral products of importance include limestone, coking coal, pyrites and salt.

Rockhampton lies between the river and the heavily wooded Berserker Range. It is a city of considerable architectural charm, with many fine stone public buildings and churches dating back to 1890s. Yellow flowering peltophorum, bauhinia, bird of paradise trees and brilliant bougainvilleas brighten the city's plantations and gardens from June to September.

The most important secondary industry is the meat-processing works, where large quantities of beef, veal, pork and mutton are chilled, frozen or canned for export. The city also has large engineering works and railway workshops, butter factories, a fruit cannery, a cotton gin, soap, chemicals, fertilizer and cement works.

Its economy is expected to expand extensively as further developments occur in the hinterland coalfields and treatment with trace elements and modern chemical fertilizers opens to agriculture and intensive grazing millions of hectares of relatively unproductive 'brigalow country' to the west.

History. In 1853, Charles and William Archer discovered and named the Fitzroy River (after Governor Charles Fitzroy) while travelling northwards from the Burnett district to investigate Leichardt's theory that a large river would be discovered in the area. In 1855 they established Gracemere Station where Rockhampton now stands. Two years later, however, the settlement was renamed Rockhampton after a chain of rocky outcrops in the river and Hampton, the birthplace of Land Commissioner Wiseman.

A Cornish prospector named Chapple made a gold strike at Canoona, 55 kilometres north-west of the town, and a rush ensued. Actually the new field produced very little gold and many disappointed diggers remained to establish farms and businesses. It was recognized that the locality was an excellent centre in which to establish supply and export bases for the pastoral back country.

In 1860 the municipality was proclaimed and the following year the young settlement received an economic boost by the discovery of tin and copper at Peak Downs, some 320 kilometres inland. The year 1868 saw the first beef exports from the little river port, but the industry did not really flourish until the introduction of refrigerated ships in the late 1880s.

The Mount Morgan copper and gold deposits were discovered in 1882, but technical difficulties in the treatment of the low-grade ores slowed progress, and the great drought at the turn of the century also set the district back. The City of Greater Rockhampton was proclaimed in 1919.

Places of Interest. Botanic Gardens, one of the finest tropical gardens in Australia, is on Athelstane Range 1.6 kilometres from city. Lookouts. **Queensland Art Gallery** (Rockhampton Branch) City Hall. Open Monday to Friday 10.30 am to 4 pm. **Central Park** with illimunated rainbow fountain. **The Barrage,** 1.6 kilometres from city on Fitzroy River. Picnic grounds, water sports, fishing. **Mt Archer Lookout** (14 kilometres) on summit of Berserker Range at an altitude of 600 metres, reached by scenic road. **St Christopher's Chapel,** Nerimbera, (11 kilometres on Emu Point Road) built by American troops stationed in area during second world war. **Cammoo Caves** (26 kilometres) and **Olsen's Caves** (31 kilometres), limestone caverns in tropical forest area. Four or five guided inspections daily. **Salt Works,** Port Alma. **Gracemere Cattle Sale Yards** (11 kilometres) Monday auctions.

Sports. Usual facilities. Weekly race meetings.

Annual Events. Central Queensland Drama Festival, Little Theatre. Eisteddfod. Round-up and Rodeo.

Accommodation. Ten **hotels.** Recommended: Leichardt, Bolsover Street. Thirteen **motels.** Recommended: Caravilla, Musgrave Street. Two **caravan parks,** all facilities.

Transport. Rail, road and **air** services. **Charter launches** available. **Tours.**

MOUNT MORGAN (Population 3 733)

The crater of the open-cut mine at Mount Morgan, 38 kilometres south of Rockhampton, is more than 800 metres in diameter, 250 metres deep and 1.4 kilometres in circumference. It is one of the largest mining excavations in the world—larger than the Kimberley diamond mine in South Africa.

Guided Tours of the surface workings are conducted twice daily at 9.30 am and 1.30 pm. **Mt Morgan Museum,** East Street, contains interesting relics and displays.

History. Traces of gold were discovered in the area by stockmen as early as 1870, but no payable strike was made until 1882, when Edward Morgan and his family discovered promising 'colour' on their property 'Calliungul', which contained roughly half the area of Mount Morgan itself. In 1886 the Mount Morgan Gold Mining Company was formed, but although mining continued for more than 30 years, many difficulties were experienced with excavation methods and treatment of the ore. The company went into liquidation in 1927, but two years later a new company, Mount Morgan Ltd, was formed and new and more successful techniques were adopted. In 1967 Mt Morgan Ltd and Peko Wallsend, a holding company with diversified mining and industrial interests, merged. Mount Morgan operations include the mining of limestone, coal, pyrites, and ironstone in various localities.

Transport. Road service from Rockhampton.

KEPPEL BAY

Several small towns and settlements on Keppel Bay to the north of the Fitzroy River delta 32 kilometres east of Rockhampton have been developed as seaside holiday resorts. Beaches are sheltered and fishing in the bay is good.

YEPPOON (32 kilometres), is the largest centre and serves an important fruit growing district. It celebrates a Pineapple Festival during the first week-end in August. To the north are large areas of State softwood and pine forests. The extremely rare Byfield fern is found in the surviving stands of native bush. Scallop and prawning fleets are based in the area and the bay is the headquarters of the Capricornia Game Fishing Club. A scenic highway connects Yeppoon with **Emu Park,** 18 kilometres south. A settlement for tourists has recently been developed on **Great Keppel Island,** 48 kilometres from Rockhampton and east of Emu Park. The island is linked with Yeppoon by daily launch service, and Barrier Reef launch cruises can be booked at Rosslyn Bay boat harbour. Charter craft for fishing etc. are available.

Sports. Golf course, tennis courts, bowling greens, water-skiing on Causeway Lake, basketball courts, rifle club, spearfishing. Ramps for trailer boats are provided at convenient points on the foreshore.

Accommodation. Two **hotels.** Recommended: Pine Beach, Emu Park. Four **motels.** Recommended: Surfside, Yeppoon. Six **caravan and camping parks.** Holiday **flats and cottages** avaliable.

Transport. **Rail** service from Rockhampton. **Motor-coach** service. Charter **launches** available.

GLADSTONE

(Population 15 365)

Since the establishment of a great alumina refinery to treat bauxite mined at Weipa on Cape York Peninsula and the development of the coalfields inland at Callide, Kianga, Moura and elsewhere, Gladstone has become one of Australia's most important interstate and export-cargo ports and has trebled its population in a decade. The town is situated on Port Curtis, a magnificent natural harbour 528 kilometres by rail north of Brisbane and 130 kilometres from Rockhampton.

Gladstone is one of the busiest ports in the Commonwealth. It exports millions of tonnes of coal (mainly to Japan) every year, receives anything up to four million tonnes of bauxite and dispatches two million tonnes of alumina. Additionally the wharves, which can accommodate vessels up to 70 000 tonnes, handle cargoes of pyrites, copper concentrates, grain, frozen and chilled meat, butter, fish, petroleum products and industrial chemicals.

An Australian-American-Japanese consortium (Thiess-Peabody-Mitsui) is responsible for the coal developments, and the alumina project is jointly owned by the Kaiser Aluminium and Chemical Corporation of the United States, Aluminium Ltd of Canada, Pecheney Company of France and Conzinc Riotinto of Australia.

Gladstone is, like Rockhampton, a point of departure for expeditions to the southern islands of the Barrier Reef. Port Curtis itself is a maze of small, beautiful islands in a sea alive with marine creatures. A Harbour Festival, centred on the annual Brisbane-Gladstone ocean yacht race, is held at Easter.

History. Matthew Flinders discovered Port Curtis in 1802. However, no attempt was made to settle the district until 1847 when, at the instigation of the Secretary of State for Colonies, William Gladstone, an attempt was made to establish a penal colony. It was abandoned after a short time because of isolation and the rigours of the tropical climate. One convict wrote: 'We have three evils to contend with here—excessive heat, heavy rains and mosquitoes in millions. . . .'

The rich soil, nevertheless, had attracted squatters to the district by 1853 and surveys were made. In 1859, the NSW Government suggested Port Curtis as the capital of the new State of Queensland, but Brisbane interests prevailed. In 1863 the municipality was proclaimed. A meatworks was built in the town in 1893.

Places of Interest. Open-cut **coal mines** at Callide, Kianga and Moura in the hinterland. Seaside resorts at **Tannum Sands** and **Barney's Point.** Natural aquarium at **Panorama Point.** Calliope **Hereford Stud,** where some of the finest beef cattle in Queensland are bred. **Rodd's Bay Experimental Farm. Quoin Island** tourist resort.

Sports. Usual facilities. Excellent game-fishing in offshore waters. Yachting.

Accommodation. Four **hotels.** Preferred: Club, Tank Street. Seven **motels.** Recommended: Arkana, Agnes Street.Two **camping and caravan parks,** all facilities.

Transport. **Rail** and **road** services. Regular **air** service to Brisbane and main coastal centres north and south. **Launch** cruises and **aerial tours** of reef and islands.

MACKAY

(Population 25 000)

The centre of Australia's largest sugar-growing district, Mackay is 1 141 kilometres north-west of Brisbane at the mouth of the Pioneer River. It is a progressive, attractive city with wide streets planted with royal palms and pipul trees introduced from Ceylon and isleted with small, well-kept tropical flower gardens. Seven sugar mills in the area produce about two million tonnes a year—nearly one-third of the State's total. Besides sugar, the Mackay district produces beef, dairy produce, pigs and poultry, timber, tropical fruit, coal and power alcohol.

The port of Mackay is one of the largest and most ingeniously contrived artificial harbours in Australia. Its bulk-sugar loading terminal is the largest in the world.

Tourism has been important to Mackay for many years. Its accommodation generally is above average in standard. It is the point of departure for a number of Barrier Reef cruises and for air and launch services to Hook, Brampton, Lindeman and Whitsunday Islands.

History. The Pioneer River was discovered by Captain John Mackay in 1862 and soon afterwards the first land surveys were made and selections taken up. A small settlement was established near the present site of the city. In 1865 the first cane was grown by John Spiller and a mill set up. Four years later the town and municipality were proclaimed. City status was reached in 1918. In 1939, the port —in the shelter of a long, man-made breakwater—was opened to shipping. Previously ships had anchored under the lee of Flat Top Island off the coast and lightered passengers and cargo to and from the shore. A national sugar-research institute was established at Mackay in 1953.

Places of Interest. Bayersville **Aquarium** and **Zoo; Queen's Park** and **Orchid House; Rosewyn cane farm** (7 kilometres from city), open for guided inspection Wednesday, Friday and Sunday. Pleystowe **Sugar Mill,** conducted tours from July until end of December. **Cape Hillsborough National Park** (56 kilometres from city), fishing, swimming, caves, bush walking. **Eungella Range National Park** (80 kilometres west). **Mount Basset Lookout,** overlooking harbour. **Rotary Lookout,** North Mackay.

Sports. Golf course; bowling green; tennis courts; squash courts; Olympic swimming pool.

Accommodation. Eight **hotels.** Recommended: Whitsunday, Macalister Street. Fourteen **motels.** Recommended: Caravilla, Macalister Street. Five **caravan and camping parks,** all facilities.

Transport. Frequent **rail, road** and **air** services to Brisbane and other coastal cities. Departure point of Barrier Reef **cruises** on launches and sailing craft. **Air tours** available.

PROSERPINE (Population 2 955)

Centre of 12 000 hectares of highly productive cane farms, Proserpine is also an important point of trans-shipment for visitors bound to and from the islands of the Whitsunday Passage. It is 132 kilometres north-west of Mackay and 35 kilometres from Shute Harbour.

Accommodation. One **hotel.** Three **motels.** Recommended: Proserpine Motor Lodge, Bruce Highway. Two **caravan and camping parks,** all facilities.

Transport. Rail, road and **air** services.

SHUTE HARBOUR

Thirty-five kilometres east of Proserpine, Shute Harbour fronts the spectacularly beautiful Whitsunday Passage and Barrier Reef islands of Hayman, Hook, South Molle, Long, Daydream and Lindeman. Several superbly sited holiday resorts have been developed on or close to the coast, including Airlie, Cannonvale and Conway. The entire peninsula from Muddy Bay to Cape Conway has been declared a national park and has not been much spoiled by tourist development. The trip by road from Proserpine to Shute Harbour itself, or to Conway Beach on Repulse Bay, reveals some of the most charming and colourful scenery on the entire Queensland coast.

Accommodation. Airlie Beach. One **hotel,** recommended. Four **motels.** Recommended: Shingle Beach Lodge. Shute Harbour. One **motel.**

Transport. Air service from Mackay. **Bus** from Proserpine.

EUNGELLA NATIONAL PARK

Eighty kilometres west of Mackay, Eungella, 48 600 hectares of mountain bush and jungle, is Queensland's largest national park if one excepts the huge sections of the Simpson Desert in the far west. Although not as developed for tourism as the Lamington Plateau parks, Eungella has nevertheless many of the same attractions—magnificent stands of rain forest with interesting tropical trees, ferns and flowers, some fine lookout points and spectacular waterfalls, and prolific bird and animal life. The aboriginal word *eungella* means 'land of the clouds'.

A section of the Clarke Range reserve, it lies at an altitude of 600 to 900 metres, but some peaks, notably Mount William, Mount David and Mount Dalrymple, are in the 1 200 metre class. The park is approached by way of a first class scenic road along the Pioneer River valley in which some of the district's richest cane and fruit farms are located and is traversed by well graded walking tracks. Notable vantage points are Bevan's Lookout, the Sky Window Walk, and Pease's Lookout.

Accommodation is available at the Eungella Hotel.

Transport. Tours from Mackay.

NORTH COAST AND HINTERLAND

Queensland's north coast and hinterland contain some of the State's most memorable and unusual scenery—and some of its most valuable natural resources, most of which have as yet been only partially exploited. The mountains and the narrow lowland strip between them and the sea receive heavy monsoonal rainfall, but the area is somewhat less prone to severe cyclonic storms than the north-western seaboard of the continent in the same latitudes.

Nevertheless the climate between October and March is hot and humid on the lowlands and the most reliably pleasant weather occurs between June and September.

Townsville is the northern 'capital', but Cairns is probably the most convenient base for travellers who wish to explore the region's natural beauties—the lush sugarlands, the jungle-clad mountains lowering over them, the harsh, desolate wilds of Cape York Peninsula, and the fascinating lagoons and islands of that part of the Great Barrier Reef not yet developed for tourism.

TOWNSVILLE

(Population 68 000)

Queensland's second city, Townsville, is on Cleveland Bay at the mouth of the Ross River, 1 584 kilometres by road north-north-west of Brisbane. It is the outlet port for a vast hinterland including the cattle country of the Gulf of Carpentaria, the far western sheep country, the highly productive agricultural lands of the Atherton Tableland to the north, the sugar of the Lower Burdekin River canefields to the south and the minerals produced in the Mount Isa-Mary Kathleen-Cloncurry fields, 800 kilometres to the west. Secondary industry is developing rapidly and the population growing as a result of the minerals and beef boom of the 1960s and early 1970s.

Townsville is probably the most sophisticated of Australia's tropical settlements. It has a number of excellently designed public buildings, a vigorous commercial life, a number of secondary schools and a university. The climate is tropical—pleasantly mild in winter months, unpleasantly oppressive to the unacclimatized from late October until April. February is the hottest month when the thermometer occasionally reaches 38°C with fairly high humidity.

The port is an artificial harbour contained by two breakwaters and is difficult to maintain because of siltation. Constant dredging is required to keep it open to large ships, but development and reclamation work is being tackled energetically. There are two bulk-sugar loading terminals and facilities for the loading and storing of metal concentrates.

Secondary industries include two of Australia's largest meatworks at Ross River and Alligator Creek, a copper refinery for Mount Isa ore, steel, cement and paint works, sawmills, boat-building yards, sugar factories, a can-making plant and railway workshops. Tourism is becoming increasingly important as Barrier Reef and tableland resorts are developed.

History. The city was named after Robert Towns, a pioneer of industrial and commercial development in Queensland. Born in Northumberland, he emigrated to Australia and established himself as a successful merchant and shipowner in Sydney. South Seas trade turned his attention to the north and he became the first man to grow cotton on a commercial scale in Australia. He converted his plantations to sugar after the American Civil War and dispatched an agent, John Melton Black, to search for land and a site for a suitable settlement north of the Mackay-Bowen area. In 1864, Black began a settlement on Cleveland Bay and built a wharf and wool store. Later, when the little port was established as an outlet for the hinterland cattle and sheep stations, he built a large boiling-down works for the production of tallow and meat extract. In 1865 Townsville was named and gazetted and it grew into an important centre for trade with the Pacific Islands and the post of entry for thousands of kanakas recruited or 'blackbirded' as sugar-plantation labour.

Until 1870, when the first breakwater was built, ships anchored under the lee of Magnetic Island and used lighters to load and land cargo. The gold-rush to Charters Towers after 1872 boosted the city's population as well as its economy. By 1895 a large meatworks was well established and a cannery in operation. The harbour works were extended.

Townsville was declared a city in 1903. During the second world war it became a strategic base for Allied forces operating in the South-West Pacific and its airfield at Garbutt was used for operation of land-based aircraft in the Battle of the Coral Sea.

Places of Interest. **Mount Spec, Hidden Valley** and **Paluma Dam,** off the Bruce Highway, 85 kilometres north-west of the city (one of the most popular tourist excursions). The 19 kilometre climb to the summit of the Paluma Range provides many fine panoramic views of the coast and offshore islands, and of the canefields of the Ingham district. There are a number of walking tracks and picnic spots beside streams through the bush and rain forest. Paluma Dam is the main source of the city's water supply. Hidden Valley has a number of interesting aboriginal rock paintings. **Townsville Zoo,** 8 kilometres from the city, is sited beside a large lily-covered lagoon on which numerous water fowl converge for feeding. The area is a sanctuary and the zoo contains many native animals and reptiles living under natural conditions. The crocodiles are of particular interest. Some specimens are up to 7 metres long. Some exotic animals are also on display in the zoo. **Castle Hill Lookout.** Castle Hill (Mount Cutheringa), 305 metres high, dominates the city. Its summit of 28.3 hectares can be reached by car. **Copper Refinery.** Guided tours may be arranged. **Queens Gardens,** noted for orchids and tropical plants. **Palm Island** Aboriginal Settlement, 51 kilometres north of Townsville. Launch and air tours can be arranged. The island, controlled by the Department of Aboriginal and Island Affairs, provides industrial training, general education, health and recreational facilities for natives. Its interior is mountainous and well wooded. The settlement is built from timber felled and milled locally. One of the chief occupations of the aborigines is boat-building. **Magnetic Island** (see Barrier Reef). **Tobruk Baths,** Olympic swimming pool used to train Australia's champion swimmers.

Sports. Usual sports facilities for a small Australian city—racecourse, golf courses, tennis courts, aquatic sports, clubs etc.

Accommodation. Eleven **hotels** (directory listed). Recommended: Lowth's, Flinders and Stanley Streets. One **motor hotel.** Twelve **motels.** Recommended: Robert Towns, Stanley Street; and Beachouse, The Strand. One **caravan park,** all facilities.

Transport. **Rail** services to Brisbane and Cairns, and to Charters Towers, Hughenden, Cloncurry and Mount Isa, with loop to Winton. **Road** services on highways north, south and west to Tennant Creek, connecting with services to Darwin and Adelaide. **Air** services to all major coastal and inland towns and to Papua-New Guinea. Numerous **launch, air** and **motor-coach** tours and charters to Barrier Reef islands, the Gulf Country, Cape York Peninsula and the far west are available. Details from Queensland Government Tourist Bureau.

BOWEN

(Population 5 792)

The port for an extensive pastoral and agricultural region, Bowen is 193 kilometres south-east of Townsville. The district grows large quantities of sugar, tropical fruit and vegetables. The harbour on Port Denison is being deepened to handle increasing exports from the meatworks at Merinda and from the coalmines at Collinsville, 98 kilometres south, and an open-cut at Scottville.

Secondary industries include a coke works and a solar evaporation plant for the production of salt. Tourism is not well developed, but the district is of considerable interest to travellers who are not tour-minded.

History. The town was named after Sir George Ferguson Bowen, first Governor of Queensland, who was influential in encouraging development of the north. He strongly supported the importation of kanaka labour. Port Denison was discovered by Captain H. Sinclair in the schooner *Santa Barbara.* He had been dispatched by the NSW Government on offer of a £2 000 reward to find a suitable port for the newly opened up Kennedy district. But while he was away, Queensland was separated from New South Wales and his discovery was not followed up until 186[illegible], when the first settlement was founded and the shire incorporated. Bowen became an important port for a time, but was overshadowed by the rapid development of Townsville and Mackay. An obelisk on the beach now marks the spot where Sinclair landed.

Accommodation. Three listed **hotels.** Recommended: Queen's Beach. One **motel.** Two **caravan and camping parks,** all facilities.

Transport. **Rail** and **road** services to centres north and south and to Collinsville. **Air** services to Proserpine with **bus** connections. **Rental cars** available.

AYR—HOME HILL

(Population 8 272)

On the delta of the Burdekin River, 80 kilometres south-east of Townsville, Ayr and its twin town of Home Hill are the centre of the Lower Burdekin sugar-producing district. The canefields are intensively irrigated by underground waters from the Burdekin system and are highly productive. Extensive experiments are now being carried out with beef production from irrigated, improved pastures and with rice and sorghum growing. The Lower Burdekin region is regarded as having an extremely high potential for development with dry-season irrigation.

History. The district was first penetrated by the explorers Wickham and Leichhardt during the 1840s. In 1846, James Morrill, sole survivor of the wreck of the ship *Peruvian* at Cape Cleveland, joined local aboriginal tribes and lived with them for 17 years, suffering appalling mistreatment and privations. The first settlers, R. W. Graham and A. C. Macmillan, arrived in the 1870s and in 1879 merged their properties to form the Burdekin Delta Sugar Company. In 1881, the town was surveyed and proclaimed. Three years later the Queensland condensed-milk industry began at Dyrnie sugar mill near the town. The shire was incorporated in 1903. In 1959 a severe cyclone did extensive damage to the town and district.

Places of Interest. **Didgeri Doo Zoo** (19 kilometres south). Ayr **Regional Experimental Station,** of particular interest to people concerned with tropical agriculture. **Alva Beach** near the town. **Two sugar mills,** the Burdekin River Bridge and Kalamia, may be inspected during crushing season.

Accommodation. Two **hotels.** Recommended: Ayr. Three **motels.** Recommended: Sugar Mill Inn, Edward Street. One **caravan and camping park,** all facilities.

Transport. **Rail** and **road** services to towns north and south.

INGHAM

(Population 5 797)

Picturesquely sited a few kilometres from the sea near the mouth of the Herbert River, 113 kilometres north-west of Townsville, and in the heart of the northern cane belt, Ingham is one of the most attractive and prosperous small towns along the Queensland coast. In addition to cane the surrounding country-side produces tobacco and large quantities of beef and timber. The Colonial Sugar Refining Company's Victoria Estate mill, one of two in the town, is the largest in the southern hemisphere. The production of the Herbert Valley cane farms averages two million tonnes a year.

Ingham's port at Lucinda Point is the point of departure for launch cruises through **Hinchinbrook Channel,** second only to the Whitsunday Passage in scenic beauty.

History. The first settlers came to the area in 1864, but it was not until the 1870s that William Ingham, after whom the town is named, established the first successful sugar plantation in the district. In 1879 the shire was proclaimed and in 1881 CSR established the Victoria Estate mill.

Places of Interest. **Rotary Park,** fine tropical gardens in town. **Wallaman Falls,** with 300 metres sheer drop. **Forrest and Lucinda Beaches. Orpheus Island,** in Palm Group. **Taylor Beach. Jourama Falls. Mt Fox** (dormant volcano).

Sports. Golf courses; bowling greens; tennis courts; Olympic swimming pool; water-skiing at Dungeness Boat Harbour.

Accommodation. Four **hotels.** Recommended: Lees, Lannercost Street. Two **motels.** Recommended: Ingham, Townsville Road. Two **camping and caravan parks.**

Transport. **Rail, road** and **air services** to main centres north and south. **Launch charters** and cruises available at Lucinda Point.

CARDWELL and **TULLY** are small towns on the Bruce Highway north of Ingham which serve a productive sugar, timber and fruit growing district which receives Australia's highest rainfall—an average of more than 500 centimetres a year. Tea and beef cattle are in the hinterland.

Of Interest. **Tully Falls** (7 kilometres north-west of Tully). **Kareeya Power Station. King Ranch** (cattle) 48 kilometres west. **Reptile Farm,** on northern outskirts of Cardwell. Seaside resorts of **Bingil Bay, Mission Beach** and **Clump Point.** (Launch service to Orpheus Island from Clump Point. Hinchinbrook cruises.)

Accommodation. **Hotel** at Tully. **Hotel** and two **motels** at Cardwell. Preferred: Cardwell, Bruce Highway. Two **motels** and **caravan park** at Mission Beach.

CHARTERS TOWERS

(Population 7 529)

Charters Towers, 128 kilometres south-west of Townsville on the road and railway line to Mount Isa and Cloncurry, is nowadays a quiet pastoral town serving the upper Burdekin Valley. Its altitude is 305 metres and it has an invigorating climate which in part accounts for the number of secondary schools established in the district, many of which cater for boarders. Citrus fruit and grapes grow well in the area. The name is a corruption of Charters Tors in Dartmoor, England.

Between 1872 and 1916 Charters Towers was the centre of Queensland's most famous goldfield which produced more than £25 million of ore from its mines. Silver, lead and zinc were also mined at Mount Leyshon and Liontown nearby.

The town is now a flying doctor base for the Gulf country and has a seismological observatory of international status located on an old mine shaft at Towers Hill. Many of its old neo-classical buildings have been preserved and are admired for their ornamental iron lacework. Good views of the nearby ranges and the Burdekin Valley can be obtained from Buckland's Hill lookout.

Of Interest. The **Weir picnic grounds. Great Basalt Wall. Red** and **White Falls,** and **Powlathanga Lake** (off Flinders Highway west of town). **Old Stock Exchange** historical museum. **Ravenswood ghost town** (east, off Burdekin Highway).

History. An aboriginal boy, Jupiter Mosman (often spelt Mossman), made the first gold strike while seeking horses stampeded by a thunderstorm in 1872. The boy was employed by Hugh Mosman, son of a well-known Sydney merchant and shipowner (after whom the Sydney suburb of Mosman was named), who had gone north to seek his own fortune in 1860. Hugh received £1 000 reward for the gold discovery and himself worked a number of claims successfully. He adopted Jupiter and educated him. The native became a respected figure in the booming gold town. At the peak of the rush more than 30 000 people were in Charters Towers. The municipality was proclaimed in 1877 and in 1909 it became a city. The desperate labour shortage created by the first world war caused the last of the mines to close. The minerals boom of the 1960s has renewed interest in prospecting the highly mineralized country in the nearby hills.

Accommodation. Four **hotels.** Recommended: Rix, Mossman Street. One **motel.** One **caravan and camping park.**

Transport. **Rail** services to Townsville and far western towns. **Road** services. **Air** services to Townsville and Mount Isa, via Hughenden, Richmond, Julia Creek and Cloncurry.

CAIRNS

(Population 32 570)

The most northerly city in Queensland, situated on Trinity Bay, 1 678 kilometres north-north-west of Brisbane, Cairns is a popular tourist resort in winter and is the port and commercial centre of a rich hinterland which produces sugar, tobacco, peanuts, maize, timber, tropical fruit, dairy produce and minerals. It is remarkable for its broad, tree-lined streets and colourful median garden plots and for the variety of scenery along the nearby coasts and in the nearby countryside. The climate is uncomfortably hot from November to March.

Cairns is the terminal of the State's northern railway and, for all practical purposes, of the coastal highways system—although in recent years a bitumen road known as the Cook Highway has been extended to Mossman and Port Douglas about 64 kilometres north and it is possible to drive during the dry season on a gravel road, inland via Mareeba, to Cooktown. Air services extend to Thursday Island, off the tip of Cape York Peninsula, to Gulf country settlements and stations, and to Port Moresby, the capital of Papua-New Guinea.

Tourism is well established in Cairns and the standard of accommodation and transport service is high.

History. The first white settler of the Cairns district arrived there in 1873. Three years later gold was discovered on the Palmer River and, three years after that, a rich tin field was found at Herberton on the Atherton Tableland. The Government established a Customs collection output on Trinity Bay and gradually a settlement grew up around it to serve the inland mining towns. It was named after William Wellington Cairns, Governor of Queensland from 1875 to 1877. For a few years the new port had rivals in Port Douglas and Smithfield, a wild American-type frontier town long since vanished, but when the sugar era dawned in the 1880s and a railway was built to Herberton, Cairns gained supremacy over its rivals. At the same time it began to serve grazing properties in the Atherton area. The settlement was proclaimed a town in 1903 and a city in 1923. During the second world war it was a base for Catalina flying boats operating over the Coral Sea.

Places of Interest. **Oceanarium. House of 10 000 shells,** Shields Street, displays a fine collection of shells from the Barrier Reef and other parts of the world. **Limberlost Nursery,** Freshwater. Open from 8.30 am daily. **City Council Gardens,** Edge Hill. Open daily 8.30 am to 5 pm. **Poinsettia and Birds Garden,** via Redlynch (13 kilometres from city). **Crystal Cascades,** via Redlynch (22 kilometres). **District Timber mills,** inspection by arrangement. **Bulk Sugar Loading Terminal,** Smith's Creek. **North Australia Brewery,** inspection Wednesday, 2.30 pm. **Hambledon Sugar Mill, Edmonton** (14 kilometres south). **Kuranda Railway and Barron Falls and Gorge** (half or full day trips). **Lake Placid** (Barron River). **Hartley's Creek Jungle Reserve,** Cook Highway. **Ellis Beach** (27 kilometres) Cook Highway.

Launch trips are available to **Green Island** (see Barrier Reef); **Port Douglas** (fishing and shelling); **Koombul Park** (aboriginal rock paintings and native animals); **Yarrabah Aboriginal Community; Fitzroy Island** and **Michaelmas Cay** (nesting birds); **Mulgrave and Russell Rivers** (49 kilometres south).

Sports. Bowling greens, tennis courts, golf courses, swimming pool etc.

Accommodation. Four **hotels** (directory listed). Recommended: Great Northern, Abbott Street; Hides, Lake and Shield Streets. Twenty two **motels.** Recommended: Trade Winds, Florence and Abbott Streets; Lyons, Abbott Street. Numerous **private hotels** and **guest-houses.** Six **caravan and camping parks.**

Transport. **Rail** and **road** terminal for services from south. **Air** services from south to and from Gulf country, Thursday Island and Papua-New Guinea. **Charter launches** for cruising and fishing available. Air coach, taxi and launch **tours** of district. **Package air, road** and **rail tours** from southern cities are popular.

PORT DOUGLAS (Population 377)

Situated on the Cook Highway, 68 kilometres north of Cairns, Port Douglas is gaining popularity as a tourist resort, partly because it evokes memory of the wild years when thousands of diggers rushed the Palmer goldfields and partly because it is situated in terrain of lush tropical beauty with many picturesque road and seaside picnic and camping spots along the highway from Cairns. There are some excellent

Table Top Hill, north-western Australia

The Olgas, central Australia

TRANSPORT IN

AUSTRALIA

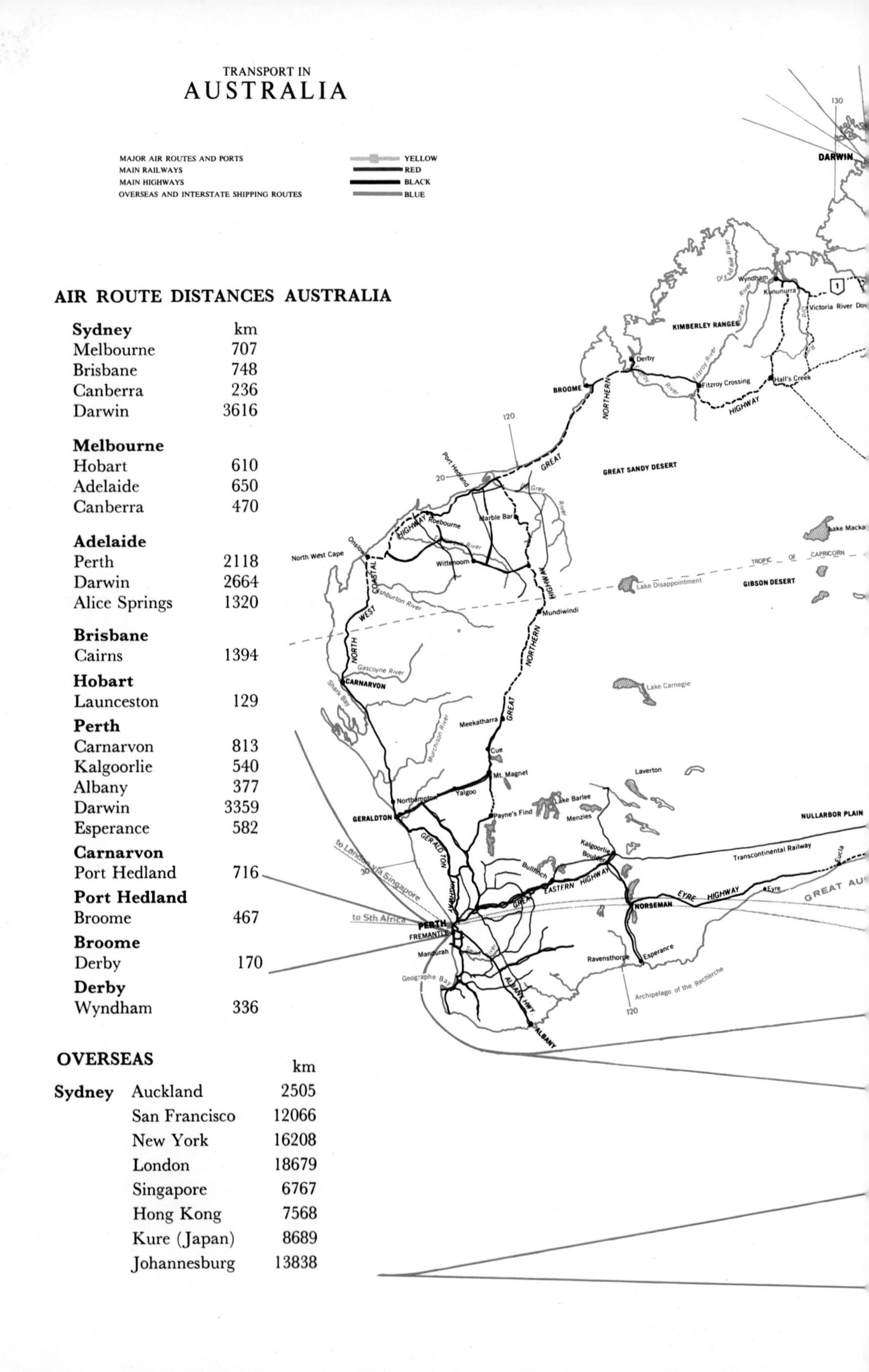

AIR ROUTE DISTANCES AUSTRALIA

	km
Sydney	
Melbourne	707
Brisbane	748
Canberra	236
Darwin	3616
Melbourne	
Hobart	610
Adelaide	650
Canberra	470
Adelaide	
Perth	2118
Darwin	2664
Alice Springs	1320
Brisbane	
Cairns	1394
Hobart	
Launceston	129
Perth	
Carnarvon	813
Kalgoorlie	540
Albany	377
Darwin	3359
Esperance	582
Carnarvon	
Port Hedland	716
Port Hedland	
Broome	467
Broome	
Derby	170
Derby	
Wyndham	336

OVERSEAS

		km
Sydney	Auckland	2505
	San Francisco	12066
	New York	16208
	London	18679
	Singapore	6767
	Hong Kong	7568
	Kure (Japan)	8689
	Johannesburg	13838

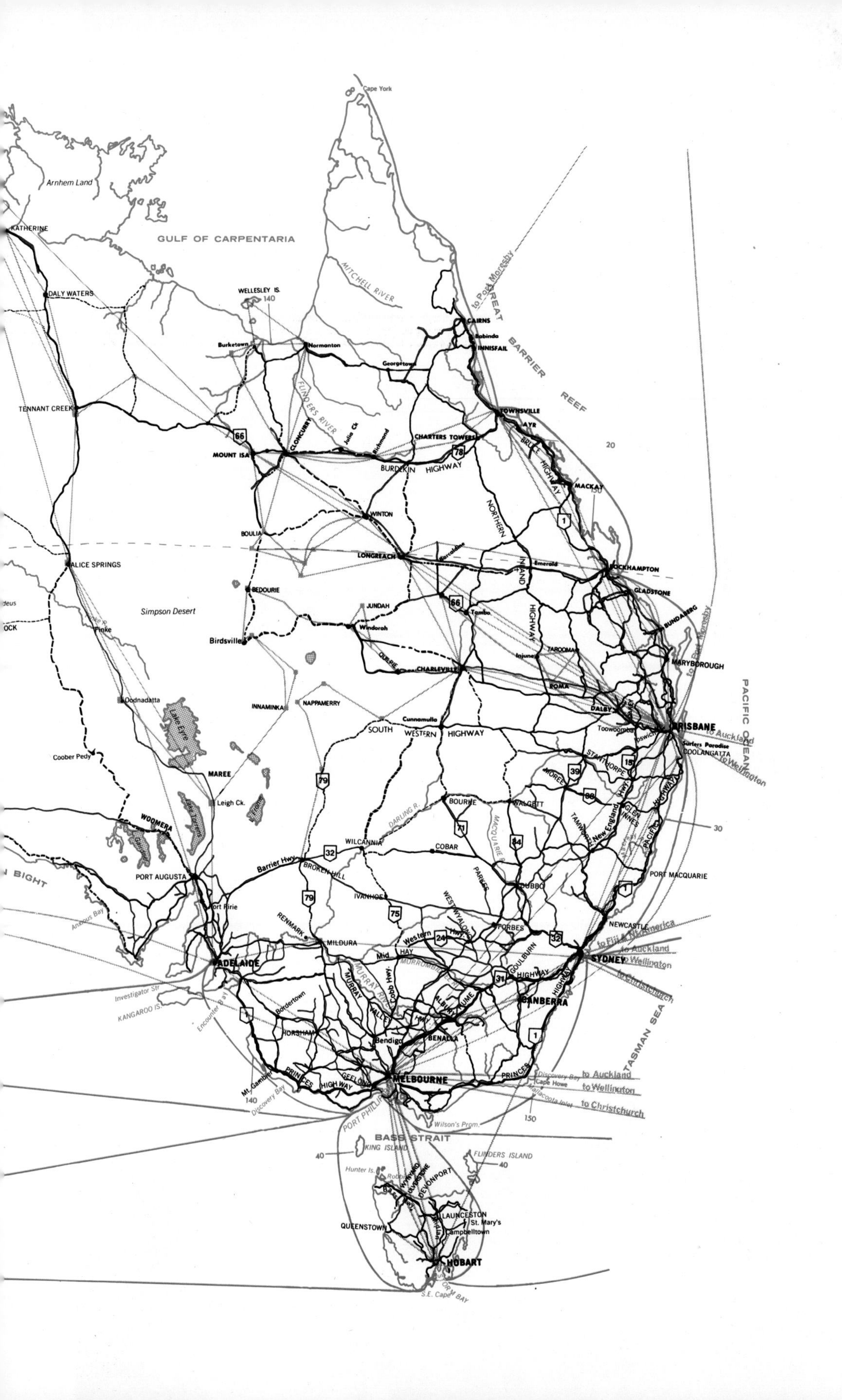

Cape York
Arnhem Land
KATHERINE
GULF OF CARPENTARIA
MITCHELL RIVER
to Port Moresby
REAT
BARRIER
REEF
WELLESLEY IS.
140
DALY WATERS
CAIRNS
Babinda
INNISFAIL
Burketown
Normanton
Georgetown
TENNANT CREEK
TOWNSVILLE
AYR
FLINDERS RIVER
Julia Ck
Richmond
CHARTERS TOWERS
66
CLONCURRY
MOUNT ISA
78
BURDEKIN HIGHWAY
BRUCE HIGHWAY
MACKAY
20
150
NORTHERN
WINTON
1
BOULIA
ALICE SPRINGS
LONGREACH
Barcaldine
INLAND
Emerald
HIGHWAY
ROCKHAMPTON
GLADSTONE
BEDOURIE
JUNDAH
66
Tambo
Simpson Desert
BUNDABERG
Finke
Windorah
Birdsville
QUILPIE
TAROOM
Injune
CHARLEVILLE
to Port Moresby
MARYBOROUGH
PACIFIC OCEAN
ROMA
Oodnadatta
Lake Eyre
INNAMINKA
NAPPAMERRY
DALBY
BRISBANE
Toowoomba
Ipswich
to Auckland
Surfers Paradise
COOLANGATTA
to Wellington
Cunnamulla
SOUTH WESTERN HIGHWAY
STANTHORPE
15
39
Coober Pedy
MAREE
79
MOREE
88
Leigh Ck.
BOURKE
WALGETT
Lake Torrens
DARLING R.
GLEN INNES
New England Hwy
TAMWORTH
PACIFIC HIGHWAY
30
WOOMERA
71
MACQUARIE R.
64
WILCANNIA
COBAR
Barrier Hwy
32
BROKEN HILL
PORT AUGUSTA
BIGHT
PARKES
DUBBO
PORT MACQUARIE
Port Pirie
79
IVANHOE
75
WEST WYALONG
1
NEWCASTLE
Anxious Bay
RENMARK
MILDURA
FORBES
Western Hwy
24
Mid
HAY
32
to Fiji & N. America
to Auckland
SYDNEY
to Wellington
GOULBURN
to Christchurch
ADELAIDE
MURRUMBIDGEE
Investigator Str
KANGAROO IS.
Encounter Bay
Cobb Hwy
31
HIGHWAY
CANBERRA
TASMAN SEA
MURRAY VALLEY
HUME
ALBURY
Bordertown
HORSHAM
BENALLA
Bendigo
1
PRINCES
MELBOURNE
GEELONG
PRINCES HIGHWAY
Discovery Bay
Cape Howe
Mallacoota Inlet
to Auckland
to Wellington
to Christchurch
Mt. Gambier
140
Discovery Bay
150
PORT PHILLIP
COBAR
Wilson's Prom.
BASS STRAIT
KING ISLAND
40
FLINDERS ISLAND
40
Hunter Is.
DEVONPORT
LAUNCESTON
St. Mary's
Campbelltown
QUEENSTOWN
HOBART
S.E. Cape
STORM BAY

Baobab trees, near Derby (W.A.)

Geikie Gorge, east Kimberleys

shell collections to be seen in the town, which is the centre of the Australian shell-jewellery trade. Six kilometres of hard, clean beach near town offers good swimming.

Of Interest. Four wheel drive tours to rainforests and superb coastal scenery at **Cape Tribulation,** north of town. **Barrier Reef Shell Display. Randall's Antique Bottle Collection.**

Accommodation. Two **hotels.** One good **motel.** One **camping and caravan park** with all facilities. **Guest-houses** and holiday **flats** and **cottages.**

Launches are available for shelling and fishing trips to the Barrier Reef.

MOSSMAN, 75 kilometres from Cairns, and inland from Port Douglas, is the centre of a small sugar growing district and the administrative centre of the Douglas Shire. Nearby Mount Demi and Good Shepherd Rock are geologically interesting. Mossman Gorge, 5 kilometres out of town, has a series of small, charming waterfalls.

Accommodation. One **hotel.** One **caravan and camping park** at Newell, 6.4 kilometres out of town. Some facilities.

COOKTOWN (Population 589)

On the Endeavour River 338 kilometres north of Cairns, Cooktown is also sharing to some extent the benefits of booming tourism in the north. The surrounding district has considerable agricultural potential and grows some sugar, tobacco, citrus fruit and beef, but it is still largely undeveloped.

In 1874, Cooktown was a roaring, cosmopolitan port second only to Brisbane, with a population of 30 000, main street two miles long and 94 hotels. Its Chinatown had a population of 2 500 and from time to time it was the scene of wild race riots. But the Palmer field declined after producing more than £5 million worth of gold in 10 years and in the 1890s its port had become a ghost town. In 1907 a cyclone flattened most of the remaining buildings and nobody bothered officially to report the damage.

Today only three hotels remain. There is no trace of Chinatown except a joss-house bell, a gong, carved screens and other relics preserved in the town museum.

Places of Interest. Cooktown **Museum,** with relics of goldfield days; **Hopevale Aboriginal Mission; Coral Sea Industries** souvenir shop; **Black Mountains** scenic drive; **Chinese shrine** at cemetery; Rossville **tin mine; Grassy Hill** lookout.

Accommodation. Three **hotels.** Recommended: Sovereign, Charlotte Street. One **motel.** One **private hotel.**

Transport. Twice-weekly **motor-coach** service and weekly **launch** from Cairns. Ansett runs a **air** service four days weekly from Cairns to Cooktown and thence via Coen, Iron Range to Weipa. Twice a week the flight continues to Thursday Island, returning via Croydon and Normanton in the Gulf Country. This circuit by air is of exceptional interest.

INNISFAIL

(Population 7 475)

Ninety three kilometres south of Cairns, Innisfail, with an average annual rainfall of 380 centimetres is one of the wettest towns on the Australian mainland. It is, however, the centre of a highly productive district which produces large crops of sugar cane and tropical fruit and mills considerable quantities of timber logged in the nearby mountains—black walnut, Queensland maple, red cedar and silky oak. Dairying and cattle raising are also important primary industries. Australia's only tea plantation is at Nerada, 34 kilometres west on Palmerston Highway. Secondary industries include a plywood mill, foundries and an engineering works.

Innisfail is an excellent base from which to explore the less-frequented lagoons and islands of the Barrier Reef and a good all-weather road connects it with the Atherton Tableland. The coast north and south of Johnstone River, on which the town is situated, is scenically memorable. A detour road has been built to serve the Mission Beach and Bingal Bay tourist area.

History. The Johnstone River district was discovered by George Elphinstone Dalrymple in 1873, but not settled until the early 1880s when Thomas Fitzgerald established a sugar plantation near Mourilyan Harbour to the south of the Johnstone estuary. In 1885 the Colonial Sugar Refinery built a mill and planted the Goondi estate. Innisfail was known as Geraldton until 1911, when it was decided to change the name to Innisfail after Fitzgerald's pioneer property, 'Innisfallen' (Gaelic for Isle of Destiny). Confusion had been caused by the existence of another Geraldton in Western Australia. After the second world war the region was closely settled by Italian immigrants who made very successful cane farmers.

Places of Interest. Bureau of Tropical Agriculture, South Johnstone (inspection by arrangement). **Joint Tropical Research Unit,** 8 kilometres along Palmerston Highway. **Chinese Joss House,** Owen Street. **Flying Fish Point,** swimming beach and camping reserve. **Mourilyan Harbour,** bulk-sugar terminal and fine coastal scenery. **Sugar mills,** Mourilyan and Goondi (inspections June-December). **Mount Bartle Frere** (1 608 metres), highest mountain in Queensland to north-west with a hiking track to the summit. **Paronella Park,** scenic reserve, curio museum, waterfall etc (19 kilometres south, on Silkwood Road, off Bruce Highway). **The Boulders,** Babinda, scenic reserve (34 kilometres north). **Pioneers' Monument,** Fitzgerald Esplanade.

Sports. Golf courses; racecourse; tennis and squash courts; bowling greens; water-skiing; big-game fishing off outer reef; gun club.

Accommodation. Eleven **hotels.** Recommended: Grand Central and Exchange, Edith Street. Two **motels.** Recommended: Walkabout, McGowan Drive. Two **camping and caravan parks,** all facilities (one at Paronella).

Transport. **Rail, road** and **air services** to and from Cairns and southern centres. **Boats** and **launches** for hire or charter at Flying Fish Point and Kurrimine.

ATHERTON TABLELAND

The Atherton and Evylyn tablelands comprise a triangular area of extremely rich, volcanic land on a plateau of the Great Dividing Range between the Palmer and Burdekin River headwaters, west and south of Cairns. With an average altitude of between 600 and 900 metres, the climate is temperate the year round and in summer maximum temperatures rarely rise above 27°C. Chief products are dairy produce, maize, peanuts and tobacco. Surrounding mountains carry heavy tropical forests and, although logging is these days strictly controlled to regenerate areas over-exploited in the past, considerable quantities of valuable timbers such as kauri, cedar, Queensland maple and walnut are still being produced.

The area is known for its prolific plant and animal life, for the high mineralization of its rocky hills and for its superb scenery. The winter climate can be chilly. Visitors at this season should carry warm clothing.

The tableland was first settled in 1877 by John Atherton after whom it was named. Gold had been discovered in the Palmer River region in 1873. In 1879 this was followed by rich tin discoveries near Herberton and by the end of the next decade more than 300 mines were operating in the district. After the turn of the century, however, the mines declined and attention turned to agriculture. Growth was slow for many years until modern roads were built through the rugged mountains which surround the highly fertile areas about the towns of Mareeba and Atherton. During the second world war American Flying Fortress bombers operated from a secret base on the plateau and the area was a training and staging base for land forces bound for New Guinea. Tableland centres of interest include:

KURANDA. A small township near the great falls of the Barron River, 29 kilometres from Cairns. The river has been harnessed to produce hydro-electric power and the falls are now really spectacular only when water is released after heavy rain, but Kuranda is still a great tourist attraction because of the beauty of its railway station gardens and because it is close to a section of railway which is regarded as one of the most difficult feats of engineering ever achieved in Queensland. The track climbs 305 metres in 19 kilometres to traverse the Barron Gorge and incorporates a hair-raising viaduct along the side of a 244 metres precipice. The line was built to serve the Herberton mines in the early 1880s. The work took four years and cost the lives of 20 construction workers. It is recorded that the annual rainfall in the locality while the line was being built was more than 400 centimetres.

Accommodation. Two **hotels.**

Transport. **Rail** and **road** tours from Cairns.

ATHERTON (Population 3 081)

On Kennedy Highway to Hughendon and Winton, 100 kilometres south-west of Cairns, Atherton is traditionally the commercial centre of the tablelands. Maize-drying, peanut-processing and storage silos are located in the town.

Places of Interest. **Lake Eacham** and **Lake Barrine** off the Yungaburra Road, fascinating crater lakes of tremendously deep, crystal-clear water, which are the subject of many aboriginal legends. They are surrounded by dense tropical forest and are developed for water sports. The area abounds with wild life and is carefully managed to preserve the ecology as far as possible. Giant red cedars have been preserved near Lake Eacham.

Accommodation. Three **hotels.** Preferred: Barron Valley. One **motel.** Three **caravan and camping parks,** all facilities. There is a **lodge** and small **motel** at Lake Barrine.

TINNABURRA is a small settlement on the great artificial lake created by Tinaroo Falls Dam, a water conservation and irrigation project on the headwaters of the Barron River east of Atherton. More than one thousand tobacco and mixed farms are supplied. The foreshores of the lake traversed by a good motor road have been imaginatively landscaped and planted with hoop pines and other trees. A pleasantly designed tourist settlement has been developed which attracts more than 100 000 visitors every year.

Of Interest nearby. **Orchid nursery** (at settlement). An ancient **curtain fig tree** on the road between Malanda and Youngaburra. **Malanda Falls** and swimming pool. **Malanda Jungle. Lamond's Hill Lookout** (west of Malanda). **Hypipamee Crater,** an eerie spectacular volcanic vent now containing a pool at least 100 metres deep and surrounded by virgin bush (off Atherton-Ravenshoe Road). **Millaa Millaa Falls** and others, off the scenic Palmerstone Highway to Innisfail.

Accommodation is available at one small **motel** (forward booking essential) and there is a well appointed **caravan and camping park.** The lake, beautifully situated in open, rolling country, is being developed for fishing and water sports.

MAREEBA (Population 5 169)

Main town of Tablelands tobacco country where production of leaf fluctuates but has approached one million kilograms in a good season. The district now greatly benefits from Tinaroo Dam and irrigation project. It also produces beef, bacon and timber. One of the biggest rodeos in North Queensland is held in July each year. Mareeba district itself is not particularly attractive scenically but beyond the tobacco town of **Dimbulah,** 50 kilometres to the west, a gravel road runs to the old mining town of **Chillagoe,** near which are located some of the finest **limestone caves** in Queensland. There are guided tours of the caves every day at 9 am and 1.30 pm. The drive over the Great Dividing Range through old gold and tin mining centres is particularly interesting.

Accomodation. Mareeba. Two **hotels.** Recommended: Masterson's. One **camping ground,** limited facilities. Chillagoe. One **hotel.** One **camping ground.**

Transport. Road service. (Note that road from Dimbulah is often closed between January and and March.)

RAVENSHOE. Small town at the junction of Palmerstone and Kennedy Highways, 24 kilometres from Atherston.

Places of Interest. Tully Falls, 24 kilometres from town. Once the most spectacular falls in Queensland, but flow of water is now limited. **Millstream Falls,** 6 kilometres from town. **Koomboo-loomba Dam,** on Tully River, is 34 kilometres south.

HERBERTON (Population 974) is 16 kilometres south-west of Atherton. This is an old mining town of great historical interest. It was the centre of a highly productive tin-mining area from 1879 until well after the turn of the century. Copper, silver, lead and wolfram have also been mined in the district. The Herbert River valley was the stronghold of many large aboriginal tribes in the old days and contains interesting and unusual plant and animal species. The Norwegian scientist, Carl Lumholtz, discovered the tree kangaroo in the locality in 1883. The district now produces a little tin from ore crushed at the Government battery in town, timber and mixed farm produce.

Accommodation. Two **hotels.**

Motorists should note that the Alberton-Herberton Road is often impassable in the wet season.

MILLAA MILLAA is a small dairying town, 66 kilometres west of Innisfail, with average **hotel accommodation** and a good **caravan and camping park** with all facilities. Nearby Millaa Millaa, Zillie and Elinjaa Falls are worth a visit. There are many interesting bush walking tracks and panoramic lookouts in the district.

WEIPA

A small, model mining town on the estuary of the Embley and Mission Rivers in the Gulf of Carpentaria and on the west coast of Cape York Peninsula. It exists to exploit, mainly by mechanized means, one of the largest deposits of high-grade bauxite in the world. The reserves of ore are estimated to exceed 2 000 million tonnes. The bauxite is mined by open-cut methods and conveyed to ore carriers which can berth in the deep waters of Albatross Bay. It is shipped to Gladstone, Queensland, and to Bell Bay, Tasmania, for treatment at alumina refineries. The company operating the mine, Comalco, associated with Conzinc Riotinto of Australia, has long-term contracts to supply buyers in Japan, Germany and France.

The town was planned by D. Fulton, who co-planned the model uranium mining town of Mary Kathleen. Its amenities include a swimming pool, bowling greens, tennis courts and a sports oval.

Accommodation. For company employees or guests only.

Transport. Ansett-ANA **air** service from Cairns and Thursday Island only.

THURSDAY ISLAND

(Population 2 218)

Thirty nine kilometres north-east of Cape York and 2 200 kilometres by air from Brisbane, Thursday Island is a small island (364 hectares) in the Prince of Wales Group, administered by the Government of Queensland. The origin of the name is obscure. There is also a Wednesday and a Tuesday Island in the group.

The settlement is officially called Port Kennedy, but the name is rarely used. It is the principal port and the Customs and quarantine station for the Torres Strait area and has a cosmopolitan population of Europeans, Torres Strait islanders, aborigines, Chinese, Japanese and people of mixed blood. It is the headquarters of the Torres Strait pilots' service.

Traditionally, Thursday Island is associated with pearl diving, an industry which has greatly declined since the techniques of cultivating pearls by artificial means was perfected by the Japanese in the 1930s and since plastics have largely replaced mother-of-pearl as a material for button-making. However, some pearling vessels still operate from Thursday Island and employ divers to obtain young oysters suitable for pearl culture. Several pearl culture farms have been established in nearby waters. Most are run by Japanese and Australians in partnership. The majority of luggers still in commission are these days owned and operated by Torres Strait Islanders, a mixed ethnic group outstanding for its energy and seafaring talents.

Thursday Island is off the beaten tourist track, but it is a colourful, unusual place with a magnificent winter climate. The island itself is not as scenically beautiful as many others of the group, but it has both charm and distinction. Many of its shops sell shells and shell ornaments at reasonable prices. Swimming, skin-diving and shell-gathering in the locality are extremely good. Expeditions to the mainland to hunt crocodiles and wild pigs can be arranged.

History. Somerset, on the mainland about 11 kilometres south of Cape York, was established as the administrative centre of the area in 1863, but its unsatisfactory anchorage caused a transfer to Thursday Island in 1877. After a few years the pearling industry began to boom and scores of luggers were based in its sheltered waters. Most were owned by Europeans who employed New Guineans, islanders, Filipinos and Japanese as divers and crewmen. The industry was notorious for the appalling conditions under which its employees worked and for its diving casualty rate. From time to time cyclonic storms also caused heavy loss of life but in this respect the dangers of pearling off Thursday Island were less marked than at Cossack and Broome on the coast of Western Australia.

Soon after its establishment Port Kennedy became a coaling station for warships and steamers plying between the East Indies and Australian ports. Fortifications were built and naval guns emplaced in concrete bunkers at the island's highest point to dominate the narrow reef passages which all vessels passing between New Guinea and the Australian mainland must negotiate. A military garrison was maintained on the island until 1933 when it was withdrawn. During the second world war, the airstrip at nearby Horn Island (which is nowadays the civil aerodrome) was an important fighter base for the American and Australian forces. It was repeatedly and heavily bombed by the Japanese.

Places of Interest. Quetta Memorial Cathedral, built to commemorate the wreck of the steamer *Quetta* in the 1890s. Many lives were lost. Some of the church's furnishings are made from timber from the ship. The *Quetta's* bell was also used in the cathedral belfry until it had to be replaced in the 1950s. **Quetta Memorial Museum,** attached to the cathedral. **Culture pearl farms** (tours can be arranged). **Old fortifications** on the peak (fine panorama of the island and surrounding waters). European and Asian **pearlers' cemeteries.**

Accommodation. Three **hotels.** No recommendation. The standard is not elaborate but it is adequate.

Transport. Twice-weekly **air service** from Cairns to Horn Island, thence by launch. Several **taxis** operate on the island. **Launches** and **boats** can be chartered.

GREAT BARRIER REEF

The Great Barrier Reef extends from the mouth of the Fly River in western Papua to Breaksea Spit east of Gladstone on the Central Queensland coast—a distance of 2 012 kilometres. It is the largest coral reef in the world, with an area of 21 million hectares, approximately the same as that of England, Wales and Ireland. Its seaward margin is accepted as the official eastern boundary of Queensland.

The greater part of the reef is at all times submerged, but large areas of crest, mostly encrusted with the red algae *lithothamnion*, are at low water of the spring tides often exposed to a depth of between 61 and 152.5 centimetres. The reef is studded with innumerable cays and continental islands, the larger of which support a dense tropical vegetation. Some of these have been developed as tourist holiday resorts.

In the far north the reef is only 16 to 19 kilometres wide, but south of Cairns the submarine slope of the coral flattens, the formations are more scattered and less linear and regular in form. They thrust out as far as 320 kilometres to sea. The depth of the water in the lagoon between the reef and the mainland is usually less than 60 metres. Inner reefs rise from it—many of them horseshoe-shaped and pointing south-east as the result of the tendency of wind-whipped currents from that direction to pile up debris.

Patch or platform reefs also occur—broad and oval or irregular in outline—which are sometimes partially covered by mangroves. Often these inner reefs form cays of fine sand and coarse coral which become stabilized and thus make a bed for vegetation.

The depth of the reef, tested in several places by drilling, is more than 122 metres. Three hundred and forty varieties of coral have been identified on it of which the commonest are: *Acropora* (staghorn coral), *symphillial* (brain coral), *porites* (rounded masses up to 510 millimetres in diameter), *fungia* (mushroom coral) and *alcyonarians* (organ pipe and blue coral).

The reef waters support a tremendous range of marine life, shellfish of all kinds from giant clams weighing several hundredweight to tiny cowries and marine snails; fish, including red emperor, coral cod, Spanish mackerel and brilliantly coloured sunfish, sharks, reef-eels, pearl-oysters, bêche-de-mer; green turtles which come ashore between October and February to lay their eggs; and dugong. Seabirds of many kinds and in multitudes nest on numbers of islands during the spring and summer.

Vegetation on the islands and cays is, of course, of continental origin, seed having been carried on to them by wind, tide and birds. The commonest varieties of trees are casuarinas and pisonias, pandanus and coconut palms and tournefortia. Goatsfoot convolvulus and creeping leguminous plants also flourish. Many varieties of mangrove are established on the lower cays.

The islands of the Great Barrier Reef with accommodation for tourists are divided into four groups, according to their position relative to the nearest mainland departure point.

Group 1: Cairns—Green Island and nearby cays.

Group 2: Townsville— Bedarra, Dunk, Hinchinbrook, Magnetic, Orpheus and Palm Islands.

Group 3: Mackay-Proserpine—Brampton, Hayman, Lindeman, Long, South Molle and Daydream.

Group 4: Rockhampton-Gladstone—Heron, Quoin, and Great Keppel.

There are **light aircraft services** from Cairns and Townsville to Dunk Island, and from Mackay-Proserpine to Lindeman and Brampton Islands.

Helicopter service operates between Proserpine and Hayman Island, and Gladstone and Heron Island. Otherwise access is by **launch**.

A wide range of accommodation is available at reef resorts—from luxury hotel suites to simply furnished beach cottages and lodges. Small motor ships and auxiliary sailing vessels make three to seven-day cruises from Mackay, Shute Harbour and Townsville. Every resort has its own fleet of launches for fishing and reef excursions.

The most spectacularly beautiful and scenically varied section of the reef is off Proserpine in the vicinity of the famous Whitsunday Passage, where six of the most popular resorts are located. However, the accessible islands to the north and south of this focal point are also very beautiful and have the advantage of being less commercialized.

'Package tours', including air, road or coach fares from the capital cities, are an inexpensive way of having a holiday on the reef. If economy is not important, a base on the mainland and private air and launch charter is the ideal combination.

Hints for Reef Visitors December to early April is the cyclone season and, in spite of what the travel brochures say, this is **not** a good time for people unacclimatized to the tropics to visit the reef. Insect pests are at their worst and the incidence of dangerous marine creatures such as sea-wasps, stonefish and Portuguese men-o'-war is higher than at other times of the year.

Very low tides are necessary for the best coral viewing. Daylight low tides coincide with the new and full moon phases. The best viewing of all is to be had at low water with the spring tides. Shell collectors should note that desirable specimens are much more numerous at the northern end of the reef than at the southern. Shell collecting is prohibited in some areas. Turtles and seabirds come in to the reef islands from mid-October to December.

Personal equipment should include light leather or canvas boots with a fairly stout sole for walking on coral. Light slacks and long-sleeved shirts offer some protection against coral cuts and grazes which can occur as the result of an accidental fall. Such injuries are painful and infect easily. Gloves should be worn by shell collectors. Some kinds of conus shellfish and octopi are extremely poisonous.

Exploration of a coral bank should be made while the tide is going out. Always turn back before the tide does. Beware of sunburn—particularly on slightly overcast days and carry sunglasses as a protection against glare.

Always replace any rock you overturn while looking for shells. Damage to many forms of marine life is thus reduced. More than 300 000 people visit reef resorts every year, so obviously observance of this rule is important.

Dress at tourist centres is casual—beach wear or swim suits during the day, with a change to light tropical clothing during the evening. A light woollen pullover or a cardigan and light raincoat are useful items. Tropical showers can be sudden and chilly.

Group One - Access from Cairns

GREEN ISLAND

A true coral cay, 13 hectares in area, 30 kilometres north-east of **Cairns.** The interior is heavily wooded. The surrounding reef waters teem with tropical marine life. Green Island is an excellent resort for visitors whose interest is primarily to observe forms of life in the coral, but it has suffered in recent years from the depredations of the Crown of Thorns starfish. It is a national park sanctuary and spear-fishing is prohibited.

An **underwater observatory** has been built to allow visitors to see the coral gardens and their population of brilliantly coloured and patterned fish.

Glass-bottomed boats tour spectacular areas of reef.

Great Barrier Reef Theatre screens films and slides of reef life. Regular sessions.

Marineland features aquarium tanks, a turtle pool and a crocodile nursery.

Accommodation. Up to 86 guests can be accommodated at the Coral Cay **Hotel,** in lodges and suites. Some have private showers and toilets. Evening entertainment includes indoor games, dancing and badminton.

Transport. Daily **launch** services run from Cairns except during the cyclone season when traffic is curtailed. Package tours available.

Group Two - Access from Townsville

MAGNETIC ISLAND

A mountainous and thickly wooded island in Halifax Bay, 8 kilometres from **Townsville,** Magnetic Island has an area of 4 900 hectares and is roughly 19 kilometres long and 5 kilometres wide. Papaws are grown commercially on its relatively small area of fertile soil. It is a national park and bird sanctuary and a koala colony has been established there since 1930.

Magnetic is the most easily accessible of the reef islands but, although its bird and animal life is varied and prolific and its coast and bushland picturesque, it lacks the atmosphere of the more remote resorts because it has in recent years become virtually a suburb of Townsville from which water and electricity are reticulated. There are about 40 kilometres of sealed road on the island and a number of bushwalking tracks. The eastern beaches are shaded by fine stands of casuarinas, poincianas and banyans.

History. The island was discovered by Captain James Cook in 1770 and so named because the navigator believed that deposits of iron ore in the area affected the accuracy of his compasses. The phenomenon has not been observed since. The area has been a popular playground for the people of Townsville almost since the foundation of the city.

Places of Interest: Sphinx Lookout (altitude 332 metres); **Picnic Bay Beach; Mount Cook** (513 metres, highest point on island). **Marine Gardens** aquarium, displaying forms of marine life, including giant clams, giant sea anemones, butterfly cod, stonefish etc. **Koala Sanctuary,** Horseshoe Bay.

Sports. Tennis courts; bowling green; golf course; water-skiing; spear-fishing. An annual swimming race is held between Townsville and the island.

Entertainments. One cinema; open-air dance floor, cabarets.

Accommodation. Two **hotels.** Recommended: Hotel Magnetic, Picnic Bay. **Guest-houses and lodges.** Holiday **flats. Youth hostel.**

Transport. Frequent **launch service** and **vehicular ferry** from Townsville. **Bus, taxis, rental cars** and **mini-mokes** available on the island.

ORPHEUS ISLAND is 80 kilometres north of Townsville beyond the notably beautiful Hinchinbrook Passage and in a maze of colourful reefs, cays and small continental islands. It is about 11 kilometres long and 1 600 metres wide, is heavily timbered and noted for its prolific birdlife. The fishing is particularly good.

Accommodation is in **lodges** and **cabins** with private facilities.

Transport. Launch from Ingham (Lucinda Point). **Reef cruises** available.

DUNK ISLAND

Five kilometres off the coast and opposite the town of **Tully,** Dunk Island is one of the least spoiled and most attractive of the Barrier Reef resorts. It is 120 kilometres south of Cairns and 160 kilometres north of Townsville. It has an area of about 1 550 hectares and carries dense vegetation. The tourist settlement of suites and cabins adjacent to a central office and amenities block is at Bramma Bay on the west coast. The resort is supplied from its own farm and tropical orchards and has its own oyster beds. Facilities for tennis, golf, water-skiing etc.

There are some caves with aboriginal wall painting in the interior. The island is noted for its fine palms, golden beaches and exquisite coral gardens. During the season October to December it is visited by large numbers of turtles. Ninety-four species of birds have been identified in its forests. Excellent fishing, swimming and bush walking.

History. Dunk Island was discovered by Captain Cook and named for Montagu Dunk, the Earl of Halifax. Its native name is Coonangalbah. It originally carried a heavy aboriginal population. As late as 1858, 400 natives were reported to be living on the island. Between 1897 and 1923, it was the home of the famed Australian writer 'Beachcomber' (E. J. Banfield).

Accommodation. One **hotel** with accommodation for 124 in suites and family units.

Transport. Daily **flights** from Innisfail, Tully, Townsville and Cairns. **Launch** from Clump Point (Tully) Sunday, Tuesday, Wednesday and Saturday. Cruises and fishing trips by **launch** may be arranged.

BEDARRA ISLAND

Bedarra is an islet about 1 600 metres long and 800 metres wide, near Dunk Island and about six kilometres from the mouth of the **Hull River.** The interior is covered with heavy jungle.

Accommodation is available for 10 in twin bedded **cottages** with private showers and toilets. Fresh running water and continuous electricity. Radio-telephone.

Transport. **Air services** from Innisfail, Tully, Townsville and Cairns to Dunk Island, thence **launch** to Bedarra. **Taxi-launch** service between Bedarra and Tully, or Hull River landing. **Launch cruises** etc. available.

Group Three - Access from Mackay-Proserpine and Shute Harbour

LINDEMAN ISLAND

One of the Cumberland Group, 64 kilometers north of **Mackay,** Lindeman is a mountainous island at the southern entrance to Whitsunday Passage. Its area is about 810 hectares and its highest point is Mount Oldfield (212 metres) from which more than 70 other islands in the area are visible.

Lindeman is a national park. It was settled by the Nicholson family, pioneers of tourism on the Barrier Reef, in 1923, when 10 guests were accommodated in grass cabins built by Torres Strait islanders. Springs supply the island with unlimited quantities of fresh water.

Accommodation. In four blocks containing single, double, twin and family rooms, each with private shower and toilet. The moderate tariff includes local cruising, coral viewing and aquaplaning. Launches for long cruising or big-game fishing trips are available at extra charge.

Transport. Feeder **air** service from Mackay daily.

BRAMPTON ISLAND

Also in the Cumberland Group, Brampton Island has an area of about five square kilometres. It is 39 kilometres north of **Mackay.** The island is a national park and wildlife sanctuary. Its forest contains specimens of the cycad palm and megapode birds which hatch their eggs in heat generated by mounds of fermenting grass and leaves. The usual reef amusements are available. The resort is well developed. There are tennis courts, a well-stocked shop, a scenic railway along the coast, a bank and a dry-cleaning service. Speedboats and catamarans may be hired. A glass-bottomed boat is also available for reef viewing.

Accommodation. One **hotel** with lodge units, all with private showers and toilets. Hot and cold water. Evening entertainments are organized. Short cruising is included in the tariff. Telephone to mainland.

Transport. **Air service** from Mackay. Frequent **launch services.**

LONG ISLAND (HAPPY BAY)

Long Island resort, Happy Bay, is one hour by launch from Shute Harbour on the landward side of Long Island Sound. It offers visitors the usual reef diversions—sunbathing, shell-gathering, reef exploration, fishing and bush walking. The interior is heavily wooded.

Accommodation. Twenty-three **suites,** also single and double **cabins.** Private showers and toilets. Tennis, water-skiing. Fishing trips and cruises by specially equipped diesel launches. Three free cruises each week. Telephone, postal service etc.

Transport. **Rail, road** and **air** services to Proserpine; **bus** to Shute Harbour; **launch** to Long Island. Package tours available.

SOUTH MOLLE

A sparsely timbered island due east of Shute Harbour, South Molle is four kilometres long and about two kilometres wide. It has about 13 kilometres of coral and sand foreshore. Highest point, Mount Jeffrey (198 metres). The island is a national park.

Accommodation. Good grouped **cabin and bungalow units** of varying price and with varying amenities. Short golf course; tennis courts; bowling green; indoor bowls; fresh-water pool. Coral House Shell Museum. Store. Glass-bottomed boat. Telephone and post office. Bank facilities. **Group camping sites** have recently been developed. Consult Queensland Government Tourist Bureau.

The tourist centre runs a vegetable and fruit farm to supply the dining room. Launch available for charter and speedboats for hire for water-skiing etc. Daily cruises.

Transport. **Rail** and **road** services to Proserpine, connecting by **bus** to Shute Harbour; thence by **launch. Air** service from Mackay to Shute Harbour, connecting with launch. **Helicopter** service from Proserpine. Package tours available.

DAYDREAM ISLAND (WEST MOLLE)

A tiny island about two kilometres long and only a few hundred metres wide, Daydream Island was originally developed as a resort by the Ansett tourist interests. It lies close inshore north-east of Shute Harbour and north-west of South Molle. Water shortage and other difficulties caused Ansett to transfer to Hayman Island some years ago, but Daydream has since been taken over and redeveloped. A luxury **hotel,** opened in 1968 for about 200 guests, is almost entirely surrounded by a swimming pool and features a bar on an island. Fresh water is supplied by a desalination plant. Cabaret entertainment, water sports and cruising.

Transport. **Launch** from Shute Harbour.

HAYMAN ISLAND

Possibly the best publicized of the reef resorts, Hayman Island is the most northerly of the Whitsunday Group. The island is about three kilometres long and two kilometres wide and has an area of 348 hectares. It has been intensively developed. Hayman was proclaimed a national park in 1941 and since the early 1950s has had luxury accommodation for tourists.

The life of the island centres round the **Royal Hayman Hotel** which can accommodate more than 350 guests in self-contained lodges, a proportion of which have private showers and toilets. A la carte meals are available. Amenities include an illuminated swimming pool, a store, a post office, banking facilities, a hairdressing salon, a TAB betting-agency, cabaret entertainment in the evening and a baby-sitting service.

Sports. Tennis courts; badminton; deck tennis; bowling green; game-fishing for black marlin, black kingfish, Spanish mackerel, sailfish, tuna and oceanic bonito; catamaran sailing.

Regular day and half-day **cruises** for fishing and coral viewing are organized—to Lindeman, Dent, Hook and South Molle Islands or, in suitable weather, to the outer reef.

Transport. Twin-engined 26-seater **helicopter** service operates between Proserpine and Mackay and the island.

Launch services co-ordinate with **buses** from Proserpine, ply from Shute Harbour daily.

Package tours available.

HOOK ISLAND

A large island directly south of Hayman and north of Whitsunday Island on the southern extremity of which an underwater observatory has been developed. Most Whitsunday tours include the observatory in their schedule. Refreshments are available.

NEWRY ISLAND. Forty-eight kilometres north of Mackay and five kilometres offshore—embarkation point at Springcliffe (Seaforth) with lock-up garage for guests' cars. Launches leave Saturday, Sunday, Wednesday at 11 am. Newry is a lushly wooded, hilly island on which wild life abounds and on which there are three good bathing beaches. Visitors are **accommodated** in **self-contained units** for up to five people, or may opt for full board. Good fishing and oystering.

HERON ISLAND

Just south of the Tropic of Capricorn and 77 kilometres from **Gladstone,** Heron Island is a true coral cay of about 16 hectares in a lagoon of 4 000 hectares. It is distinguished by the tremendous variety of marine life in its waters. From the viewpoint of the naturalist, Heron's attractions are unmatched. The Marine Biological Station and Aquarium run by the Great Barrier Reef Committee on the island has classified more than 1 150 varieties of fish and 200 varieties of coral in the lagoon. It also attracts large numbers of turtles and sea birds (including noddy terns, mutton birds and sea eagles) in the breeding season, October-December.

The island is a wildlife sanctuary and spear-fishing is prohibited on its reefs. The annual convention of Australian skindivers' clubs is held at the hotel each November.

Accommodation is comfortable but possibly less luxurious than at most other reef resorts. Fresh water is from rain catchment tanks only and must occasionally be rationed for bathing. Amenities include shop, post office, radio-telephone, bank and glass-bottomed boat. There is a good tennis court on the island.

Transport. **Helicopter** service from Gladstone, Saturday, Monday and Tuesday. **Launch** from Gladstone (five hour trip) Tuesday and Saturday, connecting with **rail** and **air** services. Launches may be chartered for cruising, fishing and water-skiing. Package tours are available.

QUOIN ISLAND

The most southerly of the Great Barrier Reef resorts, Quoin Island is four kilometres north-east of Gladstone. It has an area of 35 hectares and is about five kilometres long. The terrain is extremely rugged and heavily wooded and provides cover for a large variety of native animals and birds, including koalas and many colourful parrots. Fishing and shelling are reported to be good in the area.

Accommodation. Twenty-eight guests can be accommodated in eight **self-contained units.**

Transport. Two scheduled **launch** trips between Gladstone and the island each week.

GREAT KEPPEL ISLAND. Though not strictly a Great Barrier Reef island, Great Keppel (about 1 400 hectares) has many of the advantages of more frequented and expensive resorts further north. It has 18 kilometres of good beaches and **accommodation** of high standard in **motel-type units** with all amenities and a central restaurant.

Transport. **Air** service from Rochkampton or **launch** (twice daily) from Emu Park.

WESTERN QUEENSLAND

Western Queensland is a vast area of sparsely populated plain drained mostly by rivers which flow westward and lose themselves in the salt pans of the central deserts. It stretches from the Gulf of Carpentaria in the north to the borders of north-eastern South Australia and north-western New South Wales. Except for the low-lying Gulf Country which receives monsoonal rain, most of Western Queensland is semi-arid but supports a large pastoral industry because its artesian and sub-artesian water has been tapped by deep bores for stock and domestic supply.

There are important mineral deposits in the vicinity of Mount Isa in the north and natural gas and oil have been located in the south. A few low mountain ranges occur, but only one of any particular interest or significance—the unique Carnarvons, accessible from Roma and Rockhampton via Emerald.

Main centres of population from south to north are Roma, Charleville, Longreach, Winton, Cloncurry and Mount Isa.

ROMA

(Population 5 860)

The principal town of the Maranoa district, Roma is 504 kilometres west of Brisbane on the Warrego Highway to Charleville. It is a progressive commercial centre serving an extensive wool and wheat-growing area which also produces citrus fruit, grapes, dairy produce and beef. Its secondary industries include abattoirs, a flour mill, a butter factory, and sawmills.

During the past decade oil-prospecting companies in the area have discovered large reservoirs of natural gas which is being used to generate the town's electricity supply and is conveyed by pipeline to Brisbane. The search for oil in commercial quantities continues vigorously, encouraged by numerous small 'shows'.

History. The district was first settled in 1847. Ten years later Mount Abundance cattle station was established and soon became an important depot for supplies to outlying properties dispatched from Ipswich. In 1862 the town site was selected and surveyed and the municipality was proclaimed in 1867. Vines had already been established in the locality by S. S. Bassett, who made the first commercial wine grown and sold in Queensland. Bore sinkers discovered shows of gas and oil near the town in the early 1900s. Pastoral and agricultural land in this part of Queensland was badly affected by prickly pear, a noxious weed of the cactus family, in the early years of this century, but the pest was brought under control by the introduction of a biological control agent, the cactoblastis beetle, in 1928-30. In Queensland and New South Wales more than 10 million hectares of land was reclaimed.

Of Interest. **Campbell Park** (east) with natural gas barbecues in picnic area.

Sports. Golf course, tennis courts, bowling greens, swimming pool etc.

Accommodation. One directory listed **hotel.** Three **motels.** Recommended: Carnarvon, Northern Road. **Camping and caravan park,** all facilities; **motel-type units** available.

Transport. **Rail, road** and **air** services to Brisbane, Cunnamulla and Quilpie.

CARNARVON RANGES NATIONAL PARK

One of the most unusual and spectacular scenic reserves in inland Australia, the Carnarvon Ranges National Park is 720 kilometres by road north-west of Brisbane. The best surface approach is through Roma via the Warrego Highway, turning north on the Carnarvon Highway through the town of Injune, terminus of a branch railway from Roma.

The reserve has an area of about 27 000 hectares and is in the heart of the Great Dividing Range, which here curves back to a distance of more than 480 kilometres from the coast.

The Carnarvons are now being vigorously developed as a tourist resort by the Queensland Government and private enterprise. The terrain is extremely rough and broken, with deep, narrow sandstone gorges, overhanging cliffs and numerous caves. Many of these caves contain aboriginal rock paintings and engravings in a good state of preservation. They are conceivably the finest 'gallery' of primitive art in the Commonwealth. Cathedral Cave, 61 metres high, 82 metres long and 21 metres wide, is particularly rich in decoration.

The ranges were once densely populated by aborigines who found an abundance of food there, but the last of the tribesmen died about 80 years ago. Many of the gorge caves are burial grounds and the inspiration of innumerable legends.

The beauty and interest of the region, which is entirely different in coloration and mood from the other mountainous areas of the Outback, attract thousands of visitors, amateur explorers and naturalists every year. In spring the growth of wildflowers is prolific and brilliant. Ancient macrozamia palms flourish in the soil and climate.

The gorges, some of which are flanked by white precipices 180 metres deep, carry small, ice-cold streams and have many cascades and waterfalls.

Motorists touring Queensland who make the long journey to the ranges from Brisbane—well worth it for people who appreciate the unusual and as yet unspoiled—can return to the coast by continuing north to the Capricorn Highway at Emerald, turning east and following the sealed road to rejoin the Bruce Highway at Rockhampton.

Accommodation. **Tourist lodge** with cabin type units, dining room, shop etc. Electricity, water. **Forestry camping area,** some facilities.

LONGREACH

(Population 3 453)

Longreach township is one of the most prosperous and progressive in western Queensland. It has been considerably redeveloped during the past decade and is now provided with a modern civic centre, sealed streets, sewerage and improved recreational facilities which include a racecourse, golf links, swimming pool etc. It is 689 kilometres by rail west of Rockhampton, on the Thomson River. The name derives from a long reach of the river near the town. Almost exactly on the Tropic of Capricorn, it has long, hot, dry summers and short, cold winters.

Wool and, to a lesser extent, beef-growing are the main industries in the district which is estimated to pasture more than 600 000 head of sheep and about 22 000 head of cattle. Oil-prospecting companies are active in the district.

History. The town began as a camping ground for teamsters hauling wool and tallow from the back country to the coast or returning with loads of stores. The township was gazetted in 1887 and the shire in 1900, but long before that the district was producing large quantities of wool and beef cattle.

In 1870 Bowen Downs station, 128 kilometres north-east of the settlement on Long Reach, grazed more than 300 000 sheep and many thousands of cattle. In March of that year, Harry Redford (otherwise known as Captain Starlight) and four associates carried out one of the greatest stock thefts in Australian history. They rounded up 1 000 head of mixed cattle on the Mount Cornish outstation and drove them 2 400 kilometres down the Thomson, Barcoo, Cooper and Strzelecki Rivers through country rarely penetrated by white men to Adelaide, where Redford sold them on the open market under the noses of the police. He was arrested for the theft and tried at Roma, but the jury would not convict him and he was acquitted. He died in 1901. An account of the great 'lift' is given by Rolf Boldrewood in the novel 'Robbery Under Arms'. The town was connected by rail and telephone with Rockhampton in 1892.

QANTAS had its headquarters at Longreach in the early days of the company, and the town also has the distinction of having had the first aircraft-production factory in Australia. The first machine, a DH50, was assembled in August 1926 and five more machines were subsequently built. The workshop and hangars may still be seen at the airport, which was a US bomber base in the second world war.

In 1958 the world's first flying surgeon service was begun at Longreach. The service covers an area of 10 million hectares with a population of 80 000.

Places of Interest. **Community Centre. Historic buildings** at airport. **Longreach Pastoral College.** Sheep and cattle **stud farms** of district. (Visits can usually be arranged for interested travellers.)

Accommodation. Two directory listed **hotels.** Recommended: Commercial. One **motel.**

Transport. **Rail** service to Rockhampton. **Air** services by TAA and Ansett-ANA to Brisbane, other western towns and settlements. **Road** services by Pioneer to Brisbane and Alice Springs via Mount Isa.

CHARLEVILLE

(Population 3 939)

Charleville is the centre of an enormous pastoral district in central south-west Queensland. It is 778 kilometres west-south-west of Brisbane on the Warrego River at a height of nearly 300 metres above sea level.

From the town a road network serves the Cunnamulla and Thargomindah districts to the south and south-west, the Channel Country which is so productive after rain, and the Barcoo River plains south and west of Barcaldine and Longreach. Its airport, now a flying doctor base, is historically associated with the development of civil aviation in Australia. It was here that Ross and Keith Smith landed in 1919 on the first flight from England to Australia, and where the first commercial air service in the Commonwealth was started in 1922 by Queensland and Northern Territory Air Services (QANTAS). Charleville was its southern terminal.

History. Edward Kennedy, the explorer, followed the course of the Warrego River in 1847. Soon afterwards the first squatters moved into the plains he discovered. An area of 677 000 hectares was selected by the Honourable Edward Flood of Sydney and named Gowrie Station. By 1865 a village had started to grow up on the property but its existence was not officially recognized for three years until a townsite was surveyed by a government agent, William A. Tully, who named it after Charleville in Ireland, his boyhood home. The municipality was not proclaimed until 1894.

In 1902 the first rain-making experiments in Australia were conducted on the Gowrie property by the Queensland meteorologist, Clement Wragge. Wragge emplaced makeshift cannon and attempted unsuccessfully to induce a fall of rain by detonating explosive charges in the atmosphere. Wragge's 'guns' can still be seen today.

Sports. Golf course, tennis courts, bowling greens etc.

Accommodation. Two **hotels.** Recommended: Victoria, Alfred Street. Two **motels.** Recommended: Charleville, King and Wills Streets.

Transport. **Rail** service to and from Brisbane and Cunnamulla. **Air** service by TAA on Channel Country station runs. **Road** services to Brisbane and Darwin by Pioneer.

WINTON

(Population 1 309)

Some of the best merino wool grown in Australia comes from the Winton district, where the predominantly hot, dry climate suits the breed of sheep. Because of its geographical position, 626 kilometres south-west of Townsville, the town is also one of the natural trucking centres for cattle raised in the Channel Country and is served by a 'beef road' from Boulia 371 kilometres west. Its meatworks processes beef and mutton for the export trade. Normal production of wool is about 28 000 bales a year and the turnoff of cattle about 25 000 head.

The town and district, which have an annual rainfall of less than 381 millimetres, are largely dependent on artesian and sub-artesian water tapped by deep bores. The two bores which supply Winton itself deliver about 3 600 000 litres a day which come to the surface at a temperature of 70°C—from a depth of 1 200 metres. Castle Hill bore, west of the town delivers its water at a temperature only one degree below boiling point.

History. The first white men, the explorer McKinlay and his party, reached the Winton district in 1862. The first land was taken up in 1873 by W. Forsyth, F. Barry and the Nesbitt brothers. The town was proclaimed in 1879 and named by its postmaster, Robert Allen, after his birthplace, a suburb of Bournemouth, England. In the early days, the region was notorious for the harsh punitive action taken against aborigines who attacked white men invading their country. Skull Hole, to the south of the settlement, was the scene of a massacre by black troopers stationed on the Diamantina under Inspector Murray of the Queensland police force. The only evidence of native occupation of the country which today remains is cave paintings near the river's waterholes.

In 1895, A. B. (Banjo) Paterson composed the famous song 'Waltzing Matilda' at Combo Hole on the road to Cloncurry, a few kilometres out of town. There is a statue commemorating the event in the grounds of the Memorial Swimming Pool.

QANTAS airlines was founded in Winton in 1920, but moved to Longreach, because it was more centrally situated, before the first service was begun.

Places of Interest. **Artesian bores** and **cooling dam** for town water supply. **Combo Hole,** on the Diamantina River. **Opalton,** 97 kilometres south, scene of an opal mining rush at the turn of the century; some stone is still mined from time to time.

Sports. Golf course, tennis courts, bowling green, War Memorial swimming pool, rifle club.

Accommodation. Five **hotels.** Recommended: North Gregory. One **motel.** A nearby **Sheep Station,** 'Colston', has accommodation for 12-14 guests.

Transport. **Rail** services to Townsville and Rockhampton. **Air** service by TAA to Brisbane, Mount Isa and Tennant Creek. **Road** service to Brisbane and Darwin by Pioneer. Air charters available.

CLONCURRY

(Population 2 190)

On the Cloncurry River, 788 kilometres west of Townsville and 2 113 kilometres from Brisbane, Cloncurry is primarily a mining town although sheep and beef cattle are grazed in the area and the native pasture lands of the Gulf of Carpentaria are now being further developed by the beef roads programme of the Commonwealth Government. Mines in the district have produced gold and copper —sporadically and with varying economic success—ever since the first settler, Ernest Henry, found a rich copper ore outcrop in 1867. A railway built from Townsville to serve the field was opened in 1908. Nearby Black Mountain (officially Mount Leviathan) has rich deposits of iron ore still unexploited.

The Cloncurry aerodrome is a flying doctor base and an important link in the chain of outback air services.

Accommodation. Several **hotels.** No recommendation. One **motel** (air conditioned).

Transport. **Air** service by TAA to Brisbane and Tennant Creek. **Rail** service to Mount Isa and Townsville. **Road** service to Townsville and Tennant Creek-Darwin by Redline.

MOUNT ISA

(Population 25 240)

On the banks of the Leichhardt River and in the Selwyn Ranges 121 kilometres west of Cloncurry, Mount Isa is by far the most important industrial, commercial and administrative town in north-western Queensland. Its mines are Australia's largest copper field and second largest lead field. They are now operated by Mount Isa Mines Ltd, a company financed largely by British and American capital. It has built a model town for its employees on the west bank of the river and provided modern amenities of all kinds to compensate them for the discomforts of a fiercely hot climate throughout most of the year and the monotony and isolation of life in the spinifex country south of the Gulf of Carpentaria. Moreover, the Leichhardt River (19 kilometres north) has been dammed to create Lake Moondarra, a 1 550 hectare expanse of water from which the town's supply is drawn and which is used for aquatic sports.

Mount Isa has many well-stocked shops, eight churches and 12 schools, including a technical college and a centre for sub-normal children. The district is beginning to attract winter tourists interested in seeing something of the 'real Australia' behind the coastal plains and mountains.

At midwinter every year the town's Rotary Club sponsors a two-day rodeo which brings rough-riders from all over Queensland and almost doubles the population for the period of the festivities, which include a mardi gras procession through decorated streets, dancing and sports meetings.

History. In 1923 John Campbell Miles, a wandering bushman and prospector, discovered a rich deposit of silver lead ore near the site of the present town. Miles named the area after his sister, Isabella.

Owing to the remoteness of the area and the violent fluctuations in metal prices which had plagued the Cloncurry copper mines since their discovery, some time was to elapse before Miles's discovery was adequately exploited. However, in 1931 Mount Isa Mines Ltd was incorporated and deep mining of sulphide ores commenced.

In 1942, copper was discovered, mined and milled because of the acute wartime shortage of that metal. Production ceased in the slump immediately after the war but was resumed in 1953. A refinery was built in Townsville in 1959 to treat ingot copper smelted on the field. In 1963 diamond drilling revealed new ore bodies of great size and shafts to a depth of 1 150 metres are now planned to extract the material. An open-cut mine at Black Rock, now producing about 15 per cent of the field's copper, is to be worked to a depth of 122 metres. Large quantities of zinc also are being produced.

Places of Interest. **Lake Moondarra. Black Rock Open Cut**—spectacular by night. Tours of **surface mining installations** and the **mills and smelters** are conducted at 8.15 am and 1.15 pm Monday to Friday. **Memorial Swimming Pool,** elaborately developed. **Campbell Miles Memorial Clock Tower.**

Sports. Golf course, tennis courts, squash courts, seven bowling greens (floodlit for night play), air-conditioned tenpin bowling alley, velodrome, archery, judo club, water-skiing, sailing etc.

Accommodation. Two **hotels.** Recommended: Barkly, Barkly Highway. Seven **motels.** Recommended: Verona, Marion Street.

Transport. **Rail** service to Townsville. **Road** service to Townsville and Tennant Creek-Darwin. Frequent **air** services to Sydney, Brisbane, Townsville, Darwin, Alice Springs and to Channel and Gulf Country centres.

MARY KATHLEEN

A $A4 million dollar town built to accommodate uranium miners and their families in the late 1950s. Mary Kathleen with its rich ore is being held 'in mothballs' by the operating company. Only 30 families and a security guard now reside in it. It is 61 kilometres west of Cloncurry on the highway to Mount Isa.

Uranium was discovered in the district by two prospectors, Clem Watson and Norman McConachie, in 1954. They formed a syndicate to exploit the deposits. The mine and treatment plant, operated by Conzinc Riotinto and Mary Kathleen Uranium Ltd, was opened in 1958 to supply uranium to the UK Atomic Energy Authority under contract. The installations were closed down and the town evacuated in 1963 when the contract had been fulfilled.

KARUMBA is a prawning and fishing port on the Gulf of Carpentaria at the mouth of the Norman River, near the declining frontier mining and cattle towns of Normanton, Bourketown and Croydon. The country provides excitement for gemstone fossickers.

Accommodation. Residential **hotels** at Normanton and Karumba.

Tasmania

Tasmania, the smallest of the Australian States, has an area of about 68 million hectares—roughly the same size as Scotland. Its greatest length from north to south is 291 kilometres and from east to west 305 kilometres. Its population at the 1971 census was 396 000.

The island is separated from the Australian mainland by Bass Strait, a shallow and often turbulent strip of water which covers what was a land bridge between 25 and 40 million years ago. The terrain is mountainous and dominated by the great Central Plateau which rises to an altitude of nearly 1200 metres, with several of its peaks rising above 1 500 metres. The surface of the plateau is broken by river valleys and ridges and increases in ruggedness from east to west.

Although Europeans colonized the coastal plains of the south-east and the north at the beginning of the 19th century and in population density Tasmania is second only to Victoria in terms of land occupation, some millions of hectares of mountainous country in the west and south-west have yet to be explored on the ground. The unpopulated area is covered by impenetrable forests and scrub and webbed by precipitous ravines carrying torrential rivers.

Tasmania's rainfall is the highest of any Australian State. On the West Coast the annual average is from 127 to 152 centimetres, rising to 213 centimetres at Lake Margaret in the mountains behind Queenstown. In the far north-east the average varies from 76 centimetres on the coast to 125 centimetres in the high country. In rain shadow areas of the midlands, under the lee of the Central Plateau, the yearly average drops as low as 48 centimetres. In general terms the climate can be described as mild in summer and cool in winter at altitudes below 900 metres. In the mountains it is cold for five or six months of the year with heavy snowfalls on the peaks.

February is the hottest month. The mean maximum temperature in Hobart the capital, on the estuary of the Derwent River, is then 21.5°C. July is the coldest month, with a mean maximum of 11.5°C in Hobart.

Except in areas where fertile and relatively flat country has been cleared for agriculture, most of Tasmania is covered by dense vegetation. It is estimated that more than 47 per cent of the land area is covered by forests of potential commercial value.

Large areas of the south-west are covered by the dreaded 'horizontal' (*anodopetalum*), which grows so densely that explorers can penetrate it only by hacking out a path through it with an axe. Flowering heaths and shrubs, including brilliant waratahs, banksias, grevilleas and blandfordia, flourish in the more open country, and innumerable species of ferns are found in the deep, moist valleys.

The Tasmanian landscape is physically and atmospherically very different from that of the mainland. It is far more green and lush and nowhere on the island is one out of sight of blue ranges or hills or distant mountain peaks.

In the hollow of the Central Plateau there is an extensive area of freshwater lakes and lagoons, many of which are the headwaters of the streams which in the past 50 years or so have been harnessed to generate hydro-electric power.

The Tasmanian bush is fascinating to naturalists. There are about 220 species of birds, 14 of which are peculiar to Tasmania, and numerous unique varieties of plants. Native animals, while in the main representative of Australian types, include creatures of great antiquity which are extinct elsewhere on earth.

Notable among these are the Tasmanian devil (*sarcophilis*) and the Tasmanian tiger (*thylacine*), maybe the rarest and shyest animal in the world. It is in reality a marsupial wolf with a brown pelt marked across the hindquarters with darker brown or black stripes. It is a lone, nocturnal hunter and frequents the more inaccessible scrublands. Its young are born in litters of four and carried for several months in a pouch which opens backwards.

The coast of the island is indented at many points and its scenery has a quality of grandeur, particularly in the south and south-east. Fish of numerous species abound in estuarine waters and in the shallows above the continental shelf. Lakes, rivers and creeks are well stocked with native fish and acclimatized rainbow and brown trout and English perch.

ECONOMY Although the value of factory production in Tasmania has exceeded that of primary industry since 1953-4, the State's economy relies heavily on agriculture and associated pursuits. About 12 per cent of the work-force is in rural employment and the net value of primary production is now approximately $A200 million a year. The principal crops are apples and pears for export, potatoes and other vegetables, hops and some cereals. Sheepraising is carried on mainly in the midlands and dairying in the north and north-west. Mining of zinc, lead, silver, tin and iron-ore is confined mainly to the West Coast and the north-east, and King Island in Bass Strait produces scheelite, the ore of tungsten.

The State's manufacturing industries are now producing goods to a value of well over $A200 million yearly. The most important items are industrial metals and machines, paper, timber and processed foods and beverages. One of the world's largest electrolytic zinc plants is at Risdon, near Hobart, and the largest aluminium refinery in the Southern Hemisphere operates at Bell Bay, north of Launceston. High carbon ferro-manganese is produced for the Australian steel industry at another plant in the same locality. An iron-ore pelletizing plant has been established at Port Latta on the north-west coast which produces $A20 million worth of material every year for export to Japan.

HYDRO-ELECTRIC POWER Tasmanian hydro-electric stations now generate one-eighth of Australia's total electricity. Although much less publicized, their output is greater than that of the Snowy Mountains scheme in New South Wales. The largest development so far is at Great Lake where the total installed generating capacity is 300 000 kilowatts. Twenty major power stations are now in commission and three others were under construction at the begining of 1973.

DISCOVERY AND SETTLEMENT The first European to sight Tasmania was the Dutch navigator, Tasman, who made landfall on the West Coast in November 1642, on a voyage of exploration in the ships *Zeehan* and *Heemskirk* out of Batavia. Tasman named the island Van Diemen's Land after the Dutch Governor of the Indies who had authorized his expedition. Bad weather prevented several attempts to land from the ships' boats, but eventually a crewman swam ashore at Blackman's Bay, a desolate spot on the East Coast, and planted the Dutch flag. The sailor reported seeing notches cut in the trunk of a tree ('so far apart that surely only a giant could use them to help him climb') and animal tracks that looked like those of a tiger. Tasman seems to have had no regrets sailing away. An obelisk now marks the spot where he is thought to have landed.

It was 1772 before the island was again seen by a European, this time by a French captain, Marion du Fresne. Five years later Captain Cook landed at Adventure Bay on Bruny Island, but it was not until 1802 that Van Diemen's Land was formally annexed by Great Britain. In February 1804 a settlement was established at the present site of Hobart and a few months later another at the mouth of the Tamar River, north of Launceston.

For nearly 50 years Van Diemen's Land was a penal colony and most of its early developmental work was done by convict labour under military supervision. Relics of those grim, brutal days are to be seen all over the island. The savagery with which the unfortunate prisoners were treated was matched only by the cruelty with which the authorities mobilized their forces to exterminate the Tasmanian aborigines who resisted the seizure of their tribal lands. After a long war of extermination, the few survivors of the race were settled on Flinders Island in Bass Strait, where the last one, a woman known as Queen Truganini, died in 1876.

Transportation of convicts ceased in 1852, by which time agriculture and forest and marine industries had been firmly established. Political separation from New South Wales had been achieved in 1825. Between 1871 and 1886 important discoveries were made on the West Coast and mining started to play an important part in the colony's economy.

TOURING IN TASMANIA More than 200 000 tourists visit Tasmania every year and facilities for the holidaymaker are being steadily improved. There are few parts of the island which are not scenically attractive and which do not provide excellent opportunities for a variety of outdoor recreations. The temperate summer climate makes the island especially attractive to visitors from the hotter areas of the mainland.

While basically Australian in character, the Tasmanian countryside is refreshingly different from that of even the southern parts of New South Wales and Victoria.

Roads are good, but in the mountains are narrow and winding and unsuitable for fast cruising, particularly when wet.

The establishment of many modern motels on the highways and scenic roads has greatly improved the standard of accommodation in recent years. They are fully the equal of similar establishments in other parts of the Commonwealth.

With the exception of the Wrest Point Gaming Casino and Hotel in Hobart, the first-class hotels in Hobart and Launceston do not yet equal those in mainland capitals but in country towns they are in general somewhat better than in centres of comparable population elsewhere in Australia. They do not provide luxury, but they are essentially comfortable. The standard of personal service is, like the cuisine, rather unpredictable.

Again with the exception of Wrest Point tariffs in motels and hotels are somewhat cheaper than on the mainland.

Undoubtedly the most satisfactory way of seeing the whole of the island is

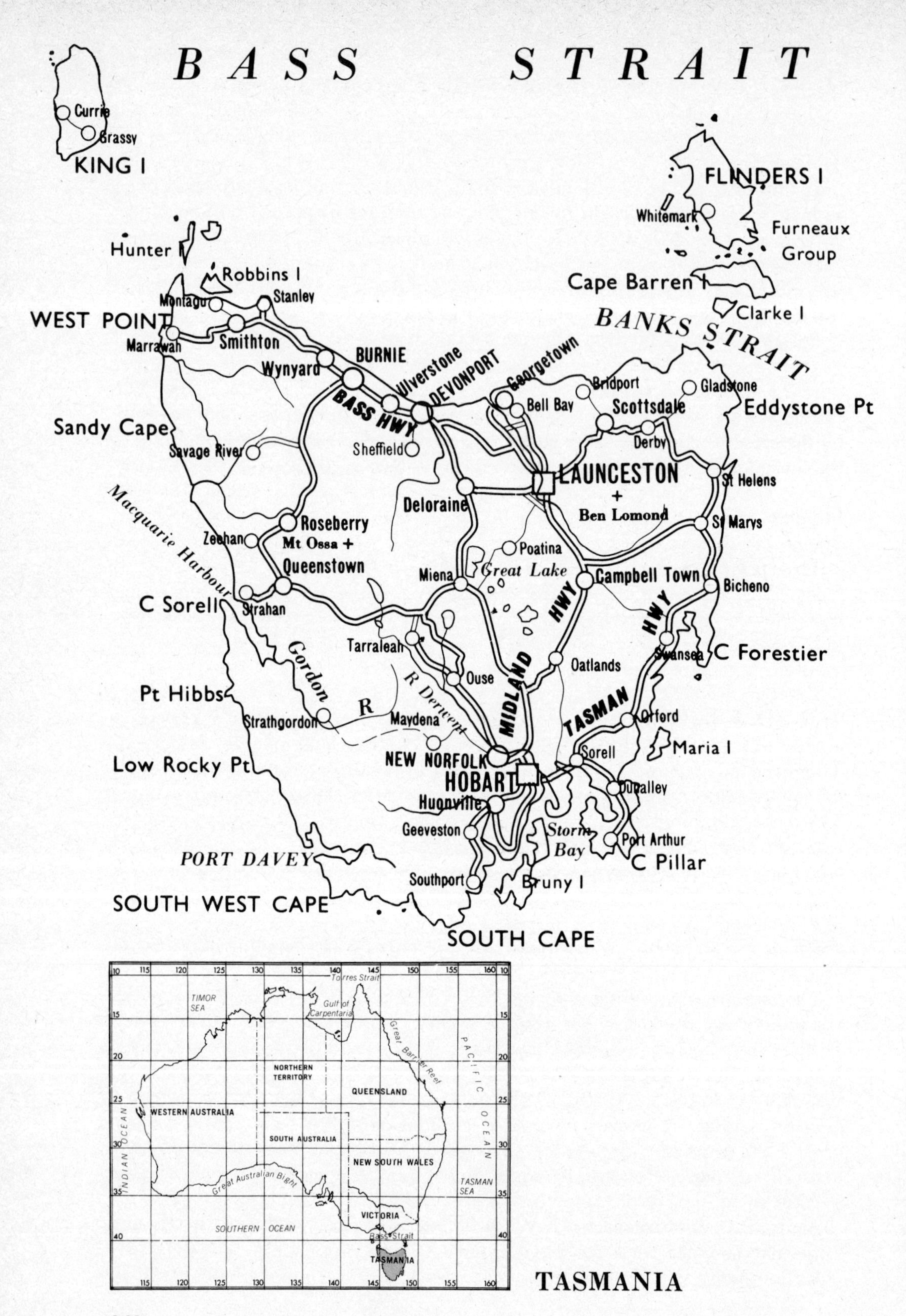
BASS STRAIT
KING I
Currie
Grassy
FLINDERS I
Whitemark
Furneaux Group
Cape Barren I
Clarke I
BANKS STRAIT
Hunter I
Robbins I
Stanley
Montagu
WEST POINT
Smithton
Marrawah
BURNIE
Wynyard
Ulverstone
DEVONPORT
BASS HWY
Georgetown
Bell Bay
Bridport
Gladstone
Scottsdale
Eddystone Pt
Sandy Cape
Savage River
Sheffield
Derby
LAUNCESTON
Ben Lomond
St Helens
St Marys
Macquarie Harbour
Deloraine
Roseberry
Mt Ossa
Zeehan
Queenstown
Poatina
Great Lake
Miena
Campbell Town
Bicheno
C Sorell
Strahan
HWY
MIDLAND
Gordon
Tarraleah
Oatlands
Swansea
C Forestier
Pt Hibbs
Ouse
R Derwent
R
TASMAN
Strathgordon
Maydena
Orford
Maria I
NEW NORFOLK
Sorell
Low Rocky Pt
HOBART
Dunalley
Huonville
Geeveston
Storm Bay
Port Arthur
C Pillar
PORT DAVEY
Southport
Bruny I
SOUTH WEST CAPE
SOUTH CAPE
Torres Strait
TIMOR SEA
Gulf of Carpentaria
Great Barrier Reef
NORTHERN TERRITORY
QUEENSLAND
PACIFIC OCEAN
WESTERN AUSTRALIA
INDIAN OCEAN
SOUTH AUSTRALIA
NEW SOUTH WALES
Great Australian Bight
TASMAN SEA
VICTORIA
SOUTHERN OCEAN
Bass Strait
TASMANIA

TASMANIA

to travel by motor car and, possibly, charter a light aircraft to see spectacular parts of the mountains and coastline not yet served by motor roads. (The cost of light aircraft charters is not prohibitive for parties of from two to six.)

Motorists planning to bring private cars from the mainland by vehicular ferry should, however, remember that bookings are exceptionally heavy between December and April and that during the Christmas holiday period passages can be obtained only by booking many months ahead. This has the disadvantage of inflexibility. It is not much more expensive, all factors considered, to rent a car for a stay of not more than three weeks or a month.

Organized coach tours are, of course, the cheapest, and simplest way of seeing the sights, but they too have the disadvantage of inflexibility—and of over-full itineraries.

The great tourist rush to Tasmania occurs between mid-December and late January. This is a convenient time for most mainlanders to take their annual vacation. If precise timing is not important, however, intending visitors should consider the advantage of making the trip in late spring or autumn when the weather is as reliable as it is in midsummer and the countryside colourful with apple and pear blossom or with autumn leaves.

There is good skiing in the high country of Tasmania from as early as June to as late as October, but winter sports accommodation and facilities are not yet well developed. Ski tows have been installed at Mt Mawson (Mt Field National Park) and Ben Lomond. They operate at weekends and during school holidays in the season.

TOUR SUGGESTIONS For the visitor primarily interested in sightseeing and with *not less* than 14 days to spend in the State, a complete circuit of the island with occasional detours from the main highways is rewarding. Route: Hobart - New Norfolk (deviation to Mt Field National Park and Gordon River hydro-electric scheme via Maydena and new HEC road and return if weather is clear) - Bothwell - Miena (via Lake Highway) - Derwent Bridge - Queenstown (via Lyell and Marlborough Highways) - Strahan - Zeehan - Rosebery - Waratah - Wynyard (deviation to Stanley and return) - Burnie - Devonport (deviation via new HEC roads through Mersey-Forth projects) - Deloraine (via Mole Creek) - Launceston (deviation Georgetown or Beauty Point and return) - Scottsdale (via Lilydale and Bridport) - St Helens - Swansea - Triabunna - Sorell (deviation to Port Arthur and return) - Richmond - Hobart and, time permitting, overnight trip to Huonville or Cygnet, returning via the Channel Highway.

The East Coast resorts can be recommended for beach, boating and sea fishing enthusiasts, the northern and central streams and lakes for trout fishermen, and the national parks at Cradle Mountain, Frenchman's Cap, Mt Field and Ben Lomond for keen naturalists, walkers and mountaineers.

FISHING Anglers are required to take out licences which are available at most sports stores and hobby shops. *Fees:* Full season, male over 17 years, $A6.00; women, children, 10-17 years, $A2.00. Two-week licence, $A2.00. *Trout season:* Saturday nearest to first day in August until Sunday nearest thirteenth day of April following for most areas, including estuarine waters, for brown trout. For rainbow trout in lakes and lagoons, last Saturday in October until the Sunday nearest 31 May following. *Game fishing:* Fishing for shark, yellowtail, southern bluefin and albacore tuna is centred mainly on Eaglehawk Neck and Fortesque Bay on the Tasman Peninsula. There are good waters for *skin diving and spear fishing* near the East Coast resorts and Bruny Island in the south. West Coast waters are too rough for these sports.

PUBLIC TRANSPORT **Sea.** Two vehicular-passenger ferries link Tasmania with the mainland. *Empress of Australia* makes three round trips a week between Melbourne and Devonport and *Australian Trader* makes three round trips a fortnight between Sydney and Hobart, Bell Bay and Burnie.

Air. The two major airlines in Australia, Trans-Australia Airlines and Ansett Airways of Australia, maintain frequent daily air services between Melbourne and the airports at Hobart, Launceston, Wynyard, Devonport and Smithton. Less frequent services connect Melbourne and Launceston by way of King Island and Flinders Island.

Interstate Coach Tours. The airlines and several mainland tourist coach companies run regular package deal tours of Tasmania from Sydney, Melbourne, Brisbane and Adelaide, using the same sea and/or air links. Details from the Tasmanian Government Tourist Bureau or any travel agency on the mainland.

Intrastate Rail. There are 946 kilometres of railway in Tasmania, of which 804 kilometres are operated by the State Government and 142 kilometres by the Emu Bay Company. The main line is between Hobart and Launceston (316 kilometres) with branch lines from Bridgewater Junction to Kallista in the Derwent Valley (72 kilometres) and from Conara Junction to St Marys on the East Coast (76 kilometres). From Launceston the Western Line runs to Stanley (270 kilometres) and the North-Eastern Line to Herrick (137 kilometres). The Emu Bay Company's line connects Zeehan and Burnie. All rail passenger services are operated by diesel electric locomotives.

The Tasman Limited Express runs between Hobart, Launceston and Wynyard daily, except Sunday. It is a well-appointed train with comfortable seating and a cafeteria car. Branch line services must be classed as strictly utilitarian. The Emu Bay Company runs a daily service, Sundays excepted.

Road. The State highways network of 1900 kilometres services all regions of the island except the extremely rugged south-west.

The Tasmanian Transport Commission runs efficient and comfortable **motor coach** services on daily schedules between Hobart, Launceston, Devonport, Burnie and Queenstown. Private operators supplement these and provide regular communication between the major and most minor centres of population.

Public **bus services** in the cities of Hobart, Launceston and Burnie are controlled by the Metropolitan Transport Trust and most of the larger towns have internal bus services.

All cities and larger towns have **taxi** and **hire car** services.

Nine firms operate **car rental** services. Cars may be rented on both King and Flinders Island.

Air Charters. Light aircraft may be chartered at Hobart, Launceston and Devonport.

HOBART

(Population 148 000)

Australia's second oldest and most southerly city, Hobart is the most attractively sited of all the State capitals and, in spite of its rapidly industrial expansion which has caused considerable redevelopment and replacement of historic buildings, it retains much of its original architectural character and 19th-century atmosphere.

The city proper is on the west bank of the Derwent estuary and its high land commands splendid marine views. Behind the city Mount Wellington (1 250 metres), with forest-clad slopes and snow-capped for many months of the year, dominates the landscape.

Hobart's waterfront, not yet completely transformed by modernization, has rich historical associations and unique, picturesque charm. The commercial heart of the city is still pleasantly provincial and, despite the vigorous growth of tourism and the industrial prosperity of the community, relatively unsophisticated. The pressures of urban living in the mid-20th century have not yet greatly affected the population. The city's parks, gardens and public squares are carefully maintained.

Suburban development, mainly on the west bank of the Derwent now spanned by the Tasman Bridge and along the highways leading to the north and west, is fast increasing the area of the metropolis. The standard of planning and architecture is functionally sound in the newly built-up areas which retain a semi-rural character.

COMMERCE AND INDUSTRY The largest single industrial enterprise in the vicinity of Hobart is the plant of Electrolytic Zinc Company of Australia, at Risdon. It supplies zinc and zinc alloys to the Australian market and for export. By-products include sulphuric acid, cadmium, superphosphate, sulphate of ammonia and aluminium sulphate. Established in 1916, the Risdon works now employ more than 3 000 people.

At Electrona, a few kilometres south of the city at the entrance to D'Entrecasteaux Channel between Bruny Island and the mainland, the Australian Commonwealth Carbide Company produces the only calcium carbide manufactured in Australia. The works and Ida Bay limestone quarries employ more than 200.

Other important industries in or near the city are the Cadbury-Fry-Pascall factory at Claremont on the west bank of the river, the largest cocoa and chocolate factory in Australia; the Stanley-Titan tool factory; the Silk and Textile Printers plant for the weaving, dying, printing and finishing of silk, nylon, rayon and cotton piecegoods; and fruit processing plants.

HISTORY The establishment of the first two settlements in Van Diemen's Land, on the Derwent and Tamar, was due to fears held by Governor Philip Gidley King, the third Governor of New South Wales, that the French would attempt to annex regions of Australia not under direct British control. On 31 October 1803 he dispatched Lieutenant Bowen to found a village at Risdon

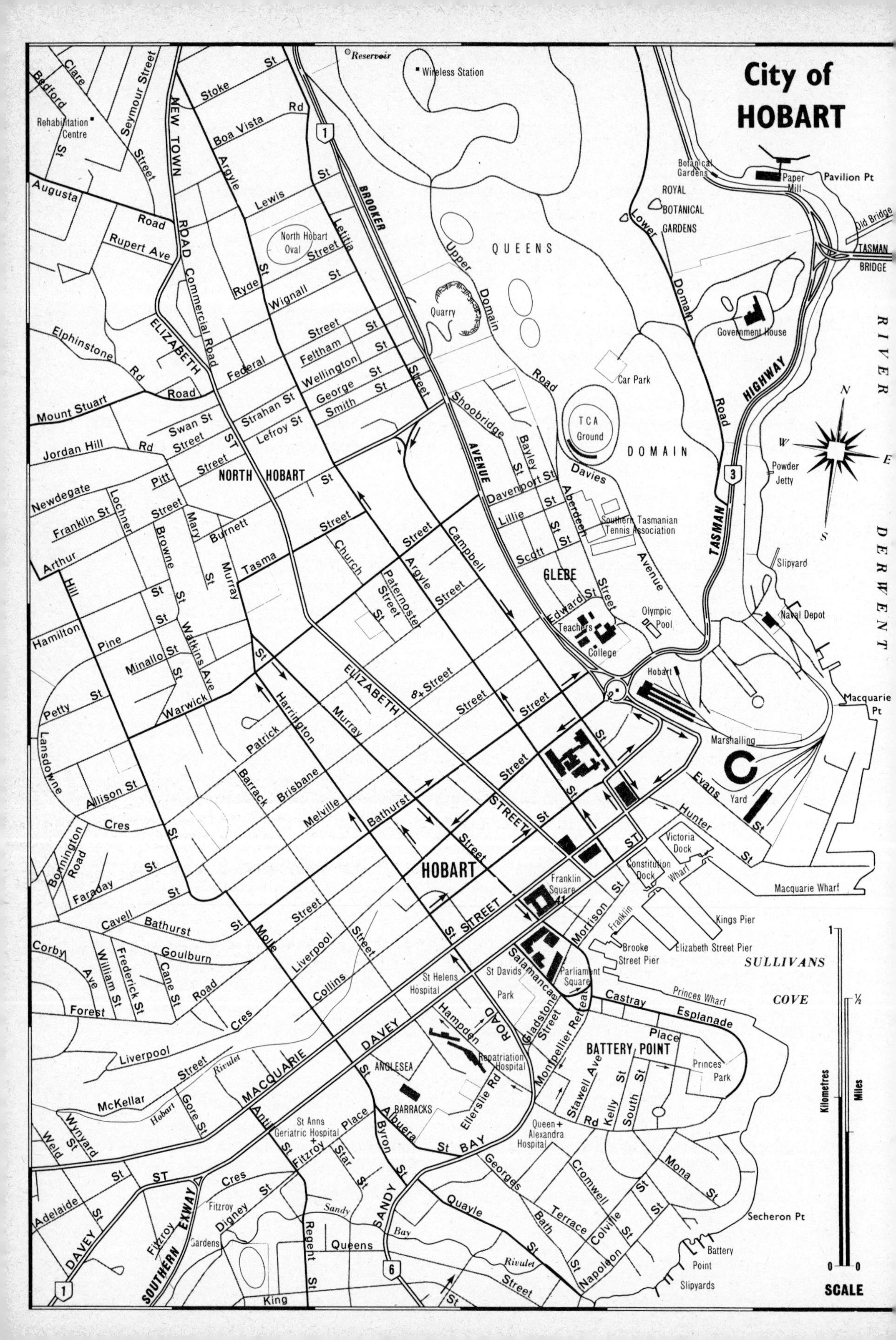

City of
HOBART
Reservoir
Wireless Station
Clare
Bedford
Seymour Street
Rehabilitation Centre
St
Stoke
St
Rd
Boa Vista
NEW TOWN ROAD
Argyle
Street
Augusta Road
Lewis
St
BROOKER
Letitia
Rupert Ave
North Hobart Oval
Street
St
Ryde
Wignall
St
Commercial Road
ELIZABETH
Elphinstone Rd
Upper Domain Road
Quarry
QUEENS
DOMAIN
Street
St
Feltham
St
Federal
Wellington
George
St
Smith
St
Street
Mount Stuart Road
Strahan St
Lefroy St
Swan St
Jordan Hill Rd
Street
ST
Street
NORTH HOBART
Shoobridge
Bayley St
AVENUE
Davenport St
TCA Ground
Car Park
Davies Avenue
Aberdeen Street
Lillie
St
Newdegate
Pitt Street
Lochner
Franklin St
Mary
Browne St
Burnett
St
Street
Church
Arthur
Hill
Tasma
Murray
St
Paternoster Street
Argyle Street
Campbell Street
Scott
St
St
GLEBE
Edward St
Teachers College
Olympic Pool
Southern Tasmanian Tennis Association
Botanical Gardens
ROYAL BOTANICAL GARDENS
Lower Domain Road
Paper Mill
Pavilion Pt
Old Bridge
TASMAN BRIDGE
Government House
HIGHWAY
TASMAN
1
3
N
W
E
S
Powder Jetty
RIVER DERWENT
Slipyard
Naval Depot
Hamilton
Pine
St
St
Minallo St
Watkins Ave
St
Warwick
Petty St
Lansdowne
St
Harrington
ELIZABETH
Murray
8½ Street
Street
Street
Hobart
Marshalling Yard
Evans St
Macquarie Pt
Patrick
Barrack
Brisbane
Allison St
Cres
Bathurst
Melville
Street
STREET
St
St
Hunter St
Victoria Dock
Constitution Dock
Wharf
Macquarie Wharf
Bonnington Road
St
Faraday
St
HOBART
Street
Franklin Square
Cavell
Bathurst
St
Molle
Street
STREET
Morrison St
Franklin
Kings Pier
Brooke Street Pier
Elizabeth Street Pier
Corby Ave
William St
Frederick St
Goulburn
Cane St
Liverpool
Collins
St
St Helens Hospital
St Davids Park
Salamanca Square
Parliament Square
SULLIVANS
COVE
Forest
Road
Cres
DAVEY
Hampden
ROAD
Castray Esplanade
Princes Wharf
Gladstone Street
Montpellier Retreat
Place
BATTERY POINT
Liverpool
MACQUARIE
St
ANGLESEA
Repatriation Hospital
Ellerslie Rd
Stawell Ave
St
St
Princes Park
McKellar
Street
Rivulet
Hobart
Gore St
BARRACKS
Antill St
St Anns Geriatric Hospital
Fitzroy
Place
Star St
Byron St
Albuera St
BAY
Queen Alexandra Hospital
Rd
Kelly
South
Wynyard St
Weld
St
ST
Cres
Georges
Cromwell
Mona St
St
St
Adelaide
St
Fitzroy Gardens
Digney
SOUTHERN EXWAY
Fitzroy
Sandy
SANDY BAY
Quayle
Bath
Terrace
Colville St
Secheron Pt
Battery Point Slipyards
DAVEY
Queens
Regent St
6
Rivulet
St
Napoleon
Street
King
St
1
Kilometres
Miles
½
0
0
SCALE

Cove, a site on the Derwent estuary highly praised by Bass after his voyage of exploration a few years previously.

At the same time, King also sent Captain Collins who had been Judge Advocate of New South Wales under Governor Phillip to occupy a suitable site on Port Phillip Bay on the south coast of the mainland. Collins landed his company of settlers on barren land near the entrance to the bay and accepted the verdict of one of his junior officers who carried out a perfunctory exploration of the foreshores that the land was unsuitable for permanent settlement. Collins reported this to his superior and was given permission to transfer to Van Diemen's Land.

In February 1804 Collins took over from Bowen at Risdon and a few days later moved camp to the present site of Hobart which was named after Robert Hobart, Fourth Earl of Buckinghamshire, then Secretary of State for the Colonies.

In the early days the colonists experienced lean times, but the soil was fertile and the little community was firmly established within a few years.

In 1831 Launceston and Hobart were placed under the charge of Lieutenant-Governor Davey, an army officer who did much to encourage commerce and agriculture. The island was soon able to export wheat and other produce to the mainland, and Hobart became an important watering and victualling port for whaling ships operating in the Southern Ocean.

Escaped convicts turned bushrangers, who lived by robbing travellers and lonely farmers, were a serious problem for many years. Davey took vigorous action against them, but fell out with Governor Macquarie, King's successor, and was recalled.

Lieutenant-Colonel William Sorell, who followed Davey, began a reform of the penal system which depended on segregation of the more refractory convicts. In 1821 he founded the notorious maximum-security settlement at Macquarie Harbour on the remote west coast. Eleven years later it was abandoned for a more accessible penal establishment at Port Arthur on Tasman Peninsula.

In spite of its convict troubles, the colony flourished and became almost as prosperous and well populated as New South Wales. In December 1825 it was separated from New South Wales. Hobart was by now a solid, well-to-do town hardly less important than Sydney.

After the 1830s, however, the rate of progress steadied down. Reserves of easily arable land were not practically limitless as they were on the mainland. The island's economy remained largely dependent on small-holding agriculture, forest and marine industries. Manufacturing industries were not firmly established until the second and third decade of the present century. Many were based on the cheap power available from hydro-electric stations.

Places of Interest

Battery Point area. First residential buildings in Hobart, of great historic interest (listed individually below).

Cat and Fiddle Arcade. Opens on to Cat and Fiddle Square where animated mural enacts nursery rhymes hourly.

Tasmanian Museum and Art Gallery, 5 Argyle Street. Emphasis on early colonial and aboriginal exhibits. Opens daily.

State Library of Tasmania, cnr Murray and Bathursts Streets. Houses reference, lending and children's libraries and State archives. Visitors may borrow. Interstate newspapers available.

Model Tudor Village, 827 Sandy Bay Road, Lower Sandy Bay. Created by J. Palotta.

Mt Stuart Lookout—high-level reservoir. Dale Crescent bus from outside Tasmanian Government Insurance Office in Argyle Street to Mt Stuart terminus.

Shot Tower, Channel Highway beyond Taroona. Of historical interest, and provides good views of Derwent Estuary.

Salamanca Place and Art Gallery. Finest row of early merchant warehouses in Australia. Most date from the 1840s. (Market on Staurday mornings.)

Lands and Surveys Department building, cnr Davey Street and Salamanca Place. Formerly St Mary's Hospital. Designed by W. P. Kay and begun in 1847.

Public Buildings, Franklin Square. Built between 1884 and 1887. Probably the work of the Government architect, W. W. Eldridge.

Scots Church, Bathurst Street—formerly St Andrew's Church. Built 1834-36. Lengthened in 1860. Architect of the addition J. E. Addison.

Scots Church Hall, Bathurst Street. Oldest Presbyterian Church building in Tasmania. Begun in 1823 and open for worship in September 1824. Possibly designed by William Wilson.

Arthur Circus on Battery Point, is a quaint reminder of the Georgian style of town-planning in which houses were built around a circular green.

Cottages, Napoleon Street, Battery Point. Probably date from 1846 and said to have been built to house workers from the nearby shipyards.

Van Diemen's Land Memorial Folk Museum, Narryna, 103 Hampden Road, Battery Point. Pioneer exhibits.

St George's Anglican Church, Battery Point. Designed by J. Lee Archer and built between 1836 and 1838. The design of the tower which was not completed till 1847 is by James Blackburn. Portico not added till much later date.

Gaol, Anglesea Barracks, Battery Point. Built around 1846 and possibly designed by Lieutenant-Colonel J. C. Victor.

Custom House Hotel, cnr Morrison and Murray Streets, Hobart—licensed 1846 as the 'Custom House Tavern and Chop House'. Apart from the removal of the rounded corner doors, the Custom House is typical of Hobart hotels of the period.

Runnymede, Newtown (5 kilometres) built by Robert Pitcairn, a prominent lawyer, in 1844. Acquired and furnished in period by National Trust.

St Matthew's Anglican Church—designed by James Blackburn and begun in 1840. The Reverend Robert 'Bobby' Knopwood, first Anglican chaplain in Van Dieman's Land, is buried in the churchyard.

Memorial Congregational Church, cnr Elizabeth and Brisbane Streets. Built in 1870-2, the design of this pink and white stone building was influenced by the French style. Francis Butler was the architect.

St John's Presbyterian Church, Macquarie Street. Built in 1841-3, St John's shows the influence of the Greek revival. The former manse 'Bellkirk' (in Davey Street) was built in 1849.

Public Buildings, Murray Street. The central block was designed by J. Lee Archer in 1837 and building begun in 1840. The portico, added in 1842, was designed by James Blackburn.

St Michael's Collegiate School, Macquarie Street. A Regency building of the mid-1830s. One-time residence of Alfred Stephen, Attorney-General of Van Diemen's Land. The columns and balustrades are wooden and the original facade is unspoiled.

Town Hall, Macquarie Street. A competition for the design was won in 1861 by Henry Hunter. Italianate style. Built 1864-6. The ceiling of the main reception room upstairs is worthy of note.

Parliament House, Murray Street. Originally the Customs House. Built 1835-41. Designed by J. Lee Archer. The cellars have vaulted ceilings of bricks marked with convict broad arrows. The Legislative Council Chamber is a good example of mid-Victoriana.

Queen Mary Club, Macquarie Street. Originally the Bank of Australasia. Built in 1843 and designed by James Blackburn.

Synagogue, Argyle Street. Believed to be the first place of Jewish worship in Australia. Designed by J. A. Thompson and built between 1843 and 1845. The unusual Egyptian style is one of the few known examples.

Old Hutchins School, Macquarie Street. Designed by William Archer. Built between 1847 and 1849 at a cost of £2367/7/5.

The Priory, Davey Street. Believed to have been built by Hugh Ross in the late 1830s. Red brick building with a portico which was added later.

Eardley-Wilmot Tomb, St David's Park. Elaborate Gothic monument to Sir John Eardley-Wilmot, Lieutenant-Governor in 1840s. Designed by W. P. Kay and built in 1850.

Criminal Court, Brisbane and Campbell Streets. Designed by John Lee Archer. Originally the Trinity Church. Mellowed brick tower, one of the building's finest features, was added by Archer in 1833-4. In 1860 the nave became the criminal court although one transept was still used as a chapel.

Government House, Queen's Domain. Completed 1853.

University of Tasmania, Sandy Bay (guided tours by arrangement).

War Memorial, Queen's Domain.

Note. Excellent brochures on Hobart's historic buildings are available from the Government Tourist Bureau.

Public Gardens and Parks

Botanical Gardens and Conservatory, Queen's Domain; **Franklin Square,** Macquarie and Elizabeth Streets; **St David's Park,** Davey Street; **Fitzroy Gardens,** Fitzroy Place; **Parliament Square,** Morrison Street; **Princes Park,** Costray Esplanade.

Entertainment

Four **cinemas,** one **newsreel theatrette,** two **drive-ins.** Two **theatres—Royal,** Campbell Street; **Playhouse,** (Australia's oldest theatre), Bathurst Street. Several hotel cabarets and **Gaming Casino** (Australia's first) at Wrest Point.

Restaurants

Ball and Chain Tavern, Salamanca Place; **Room at the Top** (Four Seasons Downtowner), Bathurst Street; **Hobart Town House,** Macquarie Street; **The Gaslighter,** Elizabeth Street; **Astoria,** Macquarie Street; **Wrest Point Riveria,** Sandy Bay Road.

Sports and Recreation

Grounds: Tasmanian Cricket Association, Queen's Domain; North Hobart Recreation Ground, Argyle and Ryde Streets; Queenborough Recreation Ground, Sandy Bay; King George V Oval, Glenorchy; New Town Sports Ground, Clare Street; South Hobart and West Hobart Recreation Grounds; Elwick Racecourse, Glenorchy; Elwick Showgrounds, Glenorchy (trotting). **Golf.** Public course, Rosny Park; four club links open to visitors; nine-hole course, Berriedale. **Bowls.** Seven clubs open to visitors. **Squash.** Public courts, Sandy Bay and New Town. **Royal Tennis.** Court at 45 Davey Street (one of two Royal Tennis Clubs in Australia. Built 1875.) **Tennis.** Public courts at most recreation grounds. **Swimming.** Olympic pools at Hobart, Glenorchy and Clarence. River and ocean beaches.

Annual Events

Royal Hobart Regatta, early February. Sydney-Hobart Yacht Race terminating at Constitution Dock.

Accommodation

Twenty-nine **hotels.** Recommended: **Wrest Point Riviera,** Sandy Bay Road; **Beach House,** Beach Road; **Hadley's Orient,** Murray Street; **Shoreline,** Rokeby Road, Howrah; **Beltana,** East Risdon Road; **Brisbane,** Brisbane Street. Nine **motels.** Recommended: **Travelodge,** Park Street; **Four Seasons,** Sandy Bay Road; **Marquis of Hastings,** Hill Street; **Jason,** Lindisfarne; **Blue Hills,** Sandy Bay. **Guest-houses. Caravan and camping parks.** Hobart City Council, Peel Street, South Hobart, all amenities; Elwick, off main highway six kilometres from city, all amenities; Berriedale, off Midland Highway, all amenities.

Department Stores

Myers, Murray and Liverpool Streets; **Fitzgeralds,** Collins Street; **Soundy's,** Liverpool and Elizabeth Streets.

Transport

Metropolitan Transport Trust **buses** serve all suburbs. **Taxis.** Rate of fares is clearly displayed in each metered cab.

Coach and car tours (half-day) to summit of Mount Wellington, Richmond, Kingston Beach, New Norfolk and to Cadbury and Silk and Textiles factories leave the Government Tourist Bureau, cnr Macquarie and Murray Streets, twice daily in season. Day tours available include Port Arthur and Eaglehawk Neck, Hastings Cave and Thermal Pool, Bruny Island, hydro-electric undertakings, Mount Field National Park, Huon Valley and D'Entrecasteaux Channel. **River, harbour** and **Bruny Island cruises** by ferry and launch are run during the summer months; inquiries from Tourist Bureau.

Business Hours

Banks, Monday to Friday 10 am to 3 pm. **Post Offices,** Monday to Friday 9 am to 5 pm; Saturday 9 am to 11.30 am. **Shops,** Monday to Friday 9 am to 6 pm, some supermarkets to 9 pm, (no Saturday trading).

Miscellaneous

Motorists should check one-way traffic streets on maps of Hobart. Note that use of horn is forbidden except in emergencies. **Emergency Telephone numbers** dial 000.

HOBART'S ENVIRONS

TASMAN AND FORESTIER PENINSULAS

The Tasman and Forestier Peninsulas which extend east and south of Hobart and screen Pitt Water and the Derwent estuary from the Tasman Sea comprise what is probably the most popular sightseeing and tourist district in the State. The whole area is scenically magnificent and rich in historical associations and relics. There are rolling pasture lands, heavily timbered hills, a seaward coastline of towering cliffs and capes weathered into strange shapes by the ocean, and a multitude of sheltered bays and beaches where excellent fishing, boating and bathing can be had. There are numerous secondary roads and walking tracks giving access to secluded beauty spots in the hills and along the coast.

PORT ARTHUR, 151 kilometres south-east of Hobart, is the focal point of interest for visitors. The ruins of one of the most infamous penal establishments in Tasmania have been preserved and in part restored.

The prison at Port Arthur was established in 1830 by Governor Arthur when it was decided to centralize the numerous scattered penal establishments in Van Diemen's Land. It was not abandoned until 1877 although transportation itself had ceased in 1853.

During the 47 years of its existence over 30 000 convicts passed through Port Arthur and only a small number managed to escape and remain at liberty. The settlement included a boys' reformatory for 800 at Puer Point which was abandoned earlier than the main prison, in 1849.

Port Arthur is the site of the first 'railway' in Tasmania. It was built during the 1830s and ran between Taranna and Deep Bay. Convicts pulled the trucks about 8 kilometres along timber rails.

In August 1878 all the buildings except the church and penitentiary were put up for public auction. Many of them were bought by contractors and demolished. However, the church, penitentiary, lunatic asylum, hospital and model prison were left standing. These buildings were badly damaged by a bushfire which swept through the peninsula in 1897.

The ruins now standing include:

The Church, said to have been designed by the convict James Blackburn (later City Surveyor in Melbourne) and built between 1836 and 1841. It was undenominational and never consecrated. Originally there were 13 spires representing Christ and the Apostles. It seated a total congregation of 1 140, of whom 1 036 were convicts.

The Model Prison, which followed the design of Pentonville, England. It was wheel-shaped so that one warder standing in the centre could see every cell. There was a solitary confinement system for punishment of refractory prisoners and dumb and dark cells for persistent offenders. (Their rations were a half-pound of bread and one quart, a little over one litre, of water every 24 hours.) Even in the chapel, solitary confinement prisoners were prevented from seeing their fellow-inmates by being seated in separate compartments.

The Exile Cottage. This was the home of William Smith O'Brien, Irish rebel transported in 1848. He attempted escape from Maria Island and was sent to Port Arthur for greater security. The cottage was originally a military hospital.

Two notable buildings which escaped destruction were the **Lunatic Asylum** (now used as the Tasman Council Chambers) and the **Commandant's Residence** (now privately owned).

Subsidiary convict establishments of which relics still remain include the Coal Mines settlement at Slopen Main, the Saltwater Creek agricultural centre, and the timber mills at Predmaydena and Koonya on the shores of Norfolk Bay.

In the middle of Port Arthur Bay east of Puer Point stands the Isle of the Dead where 1 646 graves are recorded. Of these only 180, those of prison staff and military personnel, are marked.

Accommodation. One **motor hotel. Caravan and camping ground,** all facilities, at Port Arthur. **Stewart's Bay** camping ground, toilets only.

EAGLEHAWK NECK, 19 kilometres north of Port Arthur, is a small but well-developed resort on the isthmus between Tasman and Forestier Peninsulas. In the days of the penal colony, hounds were tethered in a line across the Neck to prevent escapes. A semaphore system gave warning of attempted escapes. The line was continually patrolled by soldiers and police and guard posts were established in the nearby hills. No prisoner ever pierced the barrier. Those few who escaped did so by swimming.

Within three or four kilometres of Eaglehawk Neck are four coastal features of particular interest—**Tasman's Arch, Devil's Kitchen, The Blowhole,** and the **Tesselated Pavement.**

The Neck jetty serves a professional tuna-fishing fleet and the craft of the Tasmanian Tuna Fishing Club.

Accommodation. One **hotel.** One **private hotel. Caravan and camping park,** all facilities, boats for hire. Dining room available.

Transport. There is a daily **motor coach** service between Hobart and Port Arthur via Eaglehawk Neck, and frequent car and coach tours in season. Details from Government Tourist Bureau.

DERWENT VALLEY AND ESTUARY

NEW NORFOLK (Population 5 590)

The centre of the Tasmanian hop-growing industry, New Norfolk is on the Derwent River 34 kilometres north-west of Hobart. The surrounding countryside is scenically very beautiful and rich in associations with the early history of the colony. Picturesque oasthouses, or hop-drying kilns with conical roofs, are a feature of the landscape which is brilliantly colourful in autumn when the willows, poplars and other European trees planted by early settlers are losing their leaves.

Although the New Norfolk district produces some 80 per cent of the hops used by Australian brewers, the chief industry today is paper manufacture. Australian Newsprint Mills at Boyer, five kilometres down-river, produce the only newsprint made in Australia. Production began in 1941 and has risen to more than 160 000 tonnes a year. Eucalypt hardwoods are cut from a 150 000 hectare forest concession in the Florentine, Styx and Plenty River valleys, pulped, mixed with long fibre kraft imported from New Zealand, manufactured into newsprint, and transported by barge to Hobart for export to the mainland. (Tours of the mills may be arranged; inquiries, Tourist Bureau.)

History. The New Norfolk district, first known as 'The Hills', was explored in 1805. It was not settled until three years later, when settlers who had been transferred from Norfolk Island arrived in Van Diemen's Land. They were granted 10 acres of land for every one that they held on Norfolk Island and were guaranteed free rations for a year.

In 1811 the site of the town was chosen by Governor Macquarie and named Elizabeth in honour of his wife. By 1825 the little settlement had progressed so rapidly that the Executive Council of the Van Dieman's Land colony definitely recommended that Elizabeth Town should become the site of a new capital. However, the expense of shifting major establishments from Hobart caused the plan to be dropped.

In 1827 the name of the town was changed to New Norfolk. The area was proclaimed a shire in 1863.

Places of Interest. The Bush Inn Hotel, claimed to be the oldest licensed public house in Tasmania. It was built in 1824 and the license given to Mrs Ann Bridger in September 1825. It has been considerably extended and altered from the original—and not for the better.

St Matthew's Church of England, which was consecrated in 1825. It is the oldest church still standing in Tasmania.

Old Colony Inn. An old hostelry restored and furnished with period pieces. Walnut tree 170 years old in grounds.

Plenty Salmon Ponds (11 kilometres west). The first fish hatchery in the Southern Hemisphere. Ova of brown and rainbow trout were imported from England in 1864. The hatchery has stocked rivers in Australia and New Zealand. Piscatorial museum.

Accommodation. Two **hotels.** Recommended: New Norfolk. One **motel. Youth Hostel. Caravan and camping park,** Esplanade, limited facilities.

RICHMOND (Population 557)

This small settlement, 26 kilometres north-east of Hobart in open grazing, dairying and mixed farming country at the head of Pitt Water, is of great historical interest.

In 1803 Lieutenant John Bowen, while on an exploratory expedition, discovered deposits of coal outcropping on the banks of a small stream. The district was named Coal River but settlement did not begin until 1815 when Governor Macquarie granted 3 000 acres of land to Lieutenant-Governor Thomas Davey. 'Carrington Estate', as it was known, was the largest free land grant made in Tasmania and was later owned by two Governors, Sorell and Arthur.

Also in 1815, Robert Nash built Tasmania's first flour mill in the district which proved suitable for wheat growing. The settlement apparently made lively progress. In 1823 Governor Sorell directed that a bridge be built across the river to give access to the East Coast and the Tasman Peninsula. The following year Sorell purchased 90 acres of David Long's estate 'Richmond Park' to provide a town site. By 1825 the gaol and courthouse had been built.

It was during the 1830s however that Richmond became the 'granary' of the Van Diemen's Land colony and ranked among the six largest towns on the island. Many of the buildings erected during that decade are still standing.

By 1861 Richmond had reached municipal status and a year later in 1862 the population had reached

1 608. However, in the '70s the causeways across Pitt Water at Sorell had been finished and Richmond declined in importance.

Places of Interest. Richmond Bridge. Designed by David Lambe and built by convicts in 1823, the freestone bridge is the oldest still in use in Australia. It was built from local stone quarried at Butcher's Hill and cost £20 000. **Richmond Goal** pre-dates Port Arthur as a penal settlement. It was built in 1825. The walls are one metre thick and the gaol features solitary-confinement cells and a square and gaoler's house which were built by John Lee Archer between 1834 and 1836. **St Luke's Church of England.** Built between 1834 and 1836 and designed by Archer. It was consecrated in 1838 by Australia's first Anglican Bishop, Bishop Broughton. Noted for ceiling and gallery. **St John's Roman Catholic Church.** Built between 1836 and 1837, St John's is the oldest Roman Catholic Church in Australia.

Other historic buildings include the original **Courthouse** of 1825 (now the Council Chambers), the **Schoolhouse** (1834), the **Rectory** (built by James Gordon 1831), **Bridal Cottage** (1830), the former **Richmond Hotel** and stables (circa 1830), the **Granary** and **General Store** (circa 1830), **'Fernville'** (built by first Anglican rector and later used as a school), and the converted steam **Flour Mill** (built by George Burn in 1855).

Accommodation. One **hotel.**

SORELL (Population 779)

Centre of a rich and well-developed pastoral and agricultural area, Sorell is 26 kilometres north-east of Hobart on Pitt Water. Its industries also include timber getting and fishing.

History. In 1850 Lieutenant-Governor Collins named Pitt Water in honour of the Chancellor of the Exchequer. By 1808 settlers had shown interest in the area but marauding gangs of bushrangers made settlement dangerous. In 1816, Governor Davey strongly urged his superior, Macquarie, to forbid the establishment of a township there. Macquarie overrode Davey's judgment when, in 1821, he visited the district, approved the townsite and renamed it Sorell after Lieutenant-Governor William Sorell.

The bushranger danger had not been overrated for in 1824 the notorious Matthew Brady captured the entire town and imprisoned the garrison soldiers and citizens for a short time.

By the time the town had been established the country about Sorell was becoming an important grain-growing area. It was, however, hampered by difficulties in marketing. Governor Sir William Denison proposed causeways across Pitt Water in 1854 and these were eventually built and opened to traffic in 1872.

Places of Interest. Dunalley, a small fishing village on the road from Sorell to Port Arthur, is the site of the Tasman Monument, erected to commemorate the first landing by a European in 1642. **Denison Canal,** built at the beginning of the century, is 2 200 metres long and links Blackman's Bay and Norfolk Bay near the village.

Accommodation. Two **hotels.** No preference. **Caravan park,** all facilities.

THE SOUTH WEST

BRUNY ISLAND

Named after Admiral Bruni D'Entrecasteaux who surveyed the channel between the island and the mainland of Tasmania in 1793, Bruny is a long, irregular land mass (really two islands connected by a narrow isthmus) south of Hobart sheltering the estuary of the Huon River. It was first discovered by Tobias Furneaux, second-in-command on Cook's second voyage in 1773. Cook himself landed there in 1777. It is said that the first apple trees in Tasmania were planted at Adventure Bay by Robert Brown, a botanist with William Bligh's expedition in 1788. By 1804 whalers were using the bay to flense whales taken off the coast.

The island, which is mountainous in the south, well wooded and picturesque, has an area of 10 300 hectares and is now sparsely settled. It grows fruit, mixed farm produce and flowers and has a small dairying industry.

The scenery is good. Forests and fern glade cover the hilly sections and the east coast is rugged with bold headlands jutting into the sea. There are many enclosed bays which offer safe anchorage to small craft.

At **Adventure Bay** the Bligh Museum of Pacific Exploration contains many interesting relics of the island's early days. The building is constructed of hand-made bricks originally intended for the church of St Peter's. The museum is open daily (except Wednesday) from 1.30 to 3 pm. Nearby a memorial has been erected to the early navigators. It consists of five plaques surmounted by the model of a square-rigged ship.

The scenic reserve at **Waterfall Creek** is administered by the Scenery Preservation Board. **'Lenanville'** at Barnes Bay is a privately owned timber house built in 1838 and an excellent example of early colonial architecture.

Accommodation. One **hotel** and one **motel** at Alonnah, South Bruny. One **motel,** Adventure Bay. Reservation advisable. Two **camping and caravan areas,** Adventure Bay, with all facilities. **Caravan park** at Dennes Point.

Transport. A **vehicular ferry** runs between Kettering, 37 kilometres south of Hobart on the Channel Highway, and Barnes Bay. It makes several trips daily on summer and winter schedules.

HUON DISTRICT

The Huon River valley and the Huon Peninsula just south of Hobart is the most famous apple-growing district in Australia. Many of its magnificent orchards are more than a century old. Shipments of fruit to British and European markets have been made since 1864, but it was not until the introduction of fast refrigerated cargo ships that the export side of the industry assumed much economic significance. Main settlements are Huonville, Cygnet, Dover and Geeveston.

The orchard country is now, of course, highly cultivated, but it was once swamp and densely wooded. The terrain was so difficult that the first settlement was not established until 1845 although it was only 37 kilometres south of Hobart. Before this, however, timber getters had exploited the forest and it is recorded that 200 tonnes of Huon pine had been exported to London as early as 1829.

The river and peninsula were named by Admiral D'Entrecasteaux for his second-in-command when he surveyed the channel between the mainland and Bruny Island in 1792.

Lady Franklin, wife of Sir John Franklin, Governor of Tasmania from 1837 to 1843, is credited with having first encouraged apple-growing in the district when she purchased a farm at Franklin on the western shores of the estuary, although an apple orchard had been planted at Garden Island Creek on the tip of the peninsula some time previously.

The district is now traversed by the Huon Highway with a branch road serving the peninsula and linking with the Channel Highway to the east. The country is beautiful and attracts many tourists from Hobart, particularly during the apple harvest festival at **Cygnet,** a small town on the left bank of the river.

At **Huonville,** where a deepwater port has been developed to service fruit and timber ships, APM Ltd has established a wood pulp mill which produces about 75 000 tonnes a year.

HARTZ MOUNTAINS NATIONAL PARK

An area of 9 300 hectares of rugged bushland, dominated by a central peak 1 235 metres high, the Hartz Mountains National Park rates a place in any travel itinerary for southern Tasmania. The peaks are snow-capped for most of the year and their lower slopes are clad with magnificent rain forests. There are several high-altitude lakes of great beauty in the reserve, the largest being Hartz Lake. Below the pinnacle, fine panoramic views of the surrounding mountains and distant coast can be obtained.

Access to the park is through **Geeveston,** a small dairy farming and sawmilling town 82 kilometres south-west of Hobart on the Huon Highway. Twenty four kilometres of scenic road has been constructed from the highway to the eastern boundary of the reserve and a second road, about 11 kilometres from the terminus, leads north along the banks of the Arve River and then turns west to a point near the junction of the Huon and Picton Rivers. A suspension bridge across the Picton serves the bushwalkers' track to Mount Picton, the Arthur Range and the famous Federation Peak (1 203 metres) in the heart of the island's roughest country.

The country south of the Hartz Mountains reserve lies outside the usual tourist circuit, but it has much to commend it to travellers who like to get off the beaten track.

Dover, a fishing port 23 kilometres south of Geeveston on the highway, is on the shores of Port Esperance under the shadow of Adamson's Peak (1 206 metres) which fanciful travellers have likened to Fujiyama because of its snow-clad symmetry in winter. A further 23 kilometres south is **Southport** and **Hastings,** a pleasant little seaside settlement about 8 kilometres from **Hastings Caves.** The largest, **Newdigate Cave,** is illuminated and open for inspection daily. Hourly guided tours in season. Nearby is a small, thermal swimming pool, unusual in that its heat (28°C to 30°C) is derived not from volcanic action but from radiation from the earth's magma because of the depth from which its source water is derived.

Accommodation. Huonville. One **hotel.** Cygnet: Three **hotels.** Recommended: Commercial. **Caravan and camping park,** all facilities: Geeveston. One **hotel. Camping ground,** moderate facilities. Dover: One **hotel.**

MOUNT FIELD NATIONAL PARK—GORDON RIVER ROAD

The second-largest scenic and wildlife reserve in Tasmania with an area of 16 200 hectares, Mount Field is about 40 kilometres north and slightly west of New Norfolk, the largest town in the Derwent

Valley. The highest peak in the park is Mount Field West (1 420 metres) and the whole region receives heavy snowfalls from July to October. There are several ski club huts and a ski-tow operates near Mount Mawson.

Scenic attractions include **Russell Falls** (near the park entrance), a symmetrical and beautiful series of cascades dropping 50 metres into a gorge of rain forest and tree ferns; **Barron Falls; Lake Dobson** (1 330 metres above sea level); **Lake Fenton;** and a complex of smaller lakes and waterfalls on the lower slopes of the range.

The road to Mount Field passes through some of the most charming parts of the Derwent Valley. It continues past the National Park turn-off to Maydena and the new **Gordon River** road to Strathgordon township which in clear weather is probably the most spectacular mountain highway in Australia. With an eye to growing tourist use, the Hydro-Electric Commission—which built the road with funds from a Commonwealth development grant—has provided drive-off areas at scenic vantage points.

Intelligently unobtrusive signposts indicate topographical features and identify geological formations in the cuttings, and various tree species.

The whole district is of particular interest to naturalists. The deciduous beech occurs in the forests. Streams and lakes abound in 'mountain shrimps' (*Anaspides tasmaniae*) and there is a thriving population of native animals and birds in the unspoiled bush. Even the shy Tasmanian devil is occasionally sighted in the walking tracks.

High rainfall, however, is a disadvantage from the tourists' point of view. Travellers restricted by time limitations should be prepared to cancel visits to the Mount Field and Gordon River road sectors on heavily overcast days.

Accommodation. One **hotel,** National Park. **Caravan and camping park,** South National Park, all facilities. Park board **hut** near Lake Dobson.

NORTHERN TASMANIA

The narrow and irregular strip of coastal plain between the island's central mountains and Bass Strait is roughly 306 kilometres long. It is the richest agricultural land in the State and the most densely settled. A number of short, fast-flowing rivers drain the high, heavily wooded country to the south. In normal years rainfall exceeds 760 millimetres, summer temperatures are mild, and the farms, orchards and pastures are green in all seasons.

Travellers often remark that this countryside reminds them of rural England, but the resemblance, if it exists at all, is tenuous and due more to the fact that the early settlers introduced English trees and hedge plants than to the coloration and configuration of the land.

West of the city of Launceston, at the head of the deep tidal estuary known as the Tamar River, the coastal plain is served by the Bass Highway and a railway which terminates at Wynyard. A web of secondary roads, most of them sealed and maintained in good condition, extends southward into the mountain and lake country.

The coastline fronting Bass Strait west of the mouth of Franklin River and Port Sorell may fairly be described as interesting but by no means spectacular. The shore is flat, rocky and, with the exception of the stretch between Wynyard and Circular Head where several austerely impressive headlands thrust into the sea, rather featureless. Beaches which would be regarded as good by Australian standards are few and far between. The charm of the region lies in its gentle pastoral landscapes, its vistas of distant, often snow-clad, peaks and ranges, the multitude of small, clear streams which cross it, and its pleasant and relatively reliable climate.

Any of the larger towns along the Bass Highway, most of which are sited on river mouths, provide a convenient base from which to explore both the lowlands and the magnificent mountain country which can be reached in an hour's leisurely driving from the coast road.

Two areas are of particular interest to lovers of mountain scenery—the Cradle Mountain-Lake St Clair National Park and the Great Western Tiers region about 64 kilometres south of Devonport.

The country west of Wynyard, where the Waratah Highway and its extension the Murchison Highway joins the Bass Highway, is often neglected by tourists; but it is well worth a day or two to explore the coast between Table Cape and Circular Head and to extend a motor tour to the termination of the Bass Highway at Marrawah and beyond, to the tiny settlement of holiday shacks and cable ferry at the mouth of Arthur River, which is navigable for about 28 kilometres from its mouth. A launch trip up the river, which cuts a deep gorge through typical West Coast 'tiger country', repays the effort of making inquiries and arrangements at Smithton. Sea and river anglers should note that some of the most rewarding water in Tasmania can be found by the sportsman with the time to familiarize himself with the area. It is still unspoiled.

The north-eastern sector is most conveniently explored from a base in Launceston. The wide Tamar estuary, flanked by two first-class highways serving the newly developed heavy industrial districts and port at the mouth of the river, is picturesque and full of interest. The valley is the second most important fruit-growing district in the State. Spring, when the trees are in blossom, is an excellent time to see it.

The East Tamar Highway, linking Georgetown with Launceston, is one of the oldest roads in Tasmania. It was surveyed and built with convict labour in the late 1820s. Twenty kilometres from Launceston, travellers can make a short detour to visit the historic church of St Mathias on the banks of the river. The church was built by Dr Mathias Gaunt in 1842 and stands amid fine groves of English oaks and elms. Thirteen kilometres farther north, at Mount Direction, are the remains of three convict-built semaphore stations used to send messages between Georgetown and Launceston until the electric telegraph was installed in 1857. The highway terminates at Low Head, four kilometres north of Georgetown.

Places of interest on the West Tamar Highway which serves the deepwater port at Beauty Point include Notley Fern Gorge, a charming nature reserve administered by the Scenery Preservation Board, reached by turning west at Exeter; Sidmouth, where early Presbyterian settlers built the 'Auld Kirk' in 1845; the Trevallyn dam and power station and Beaconsfield, six kilometres south of Beauty Point, a prosperous goldmining centre at the turn of the century, where the ruins of the big pithead buildings of the famous Tasmania Gold Mine are still standing.

There are many fine fishing reaches all along the Tamar and some good beaches in the vicinity of the heads. From Beauty Point, tourists can arrange a return launch trip to Georgetown and Bell Bay.

The Tasman Highway, which connects Launceston with Hobart via the East Coast, cuts through rich dairying and mixed farming country about Scottsdale and the old tin-mining town of Derby. There is a fine variety of scenery all along the route as far as St Helens, but the motorist with the time and inclination to deviate a little from the usual circuit will find it rewarding to take the northern loop road through Lilydale and Bridport, and rejoin the highway at Scottsdale. Bridport is a secluded, pleasant little seaside resort on Anderson Bay. Lilydale is distinguished for its charming setting in a valley between rolling hills and its commercial lavender farms.

West and south of Scottsdale the main road passes through some of the finest stands of myrtle forest in Tasmania. The area is also highly mineralized and fascinating to amateur prospectors and collectors of lapidary material.

LAUNCESTON

(Population 62 181)

The largest centre of population in Northern Tasmania, Launceston is situated 64 kilometres from the northern coast on the junction of the North Esk, South Esk and Tamar Rivers. It is a small, rather sleepy provincial city in pleasant, hilly countryside and an excellent base for tourists who wish to explore the rich and scenically attractive coastal plain, the Tamar Valley, and the more accessible mountain country to the north of the lakeland area in the island's central plateau.

Although it contains many buildings of considerable historic interest to Australians, the city's architecture is generally without distinction, but its parks and private gardens must be classed as among the best in Australia. European trees, particularly oaks and elms, and flowering shrubs flourish in the mild, moist climate.

Launceston has direct air links with Melbourne and Hobart and a bus and rail connection from the mainland ferry terminal at Devonport. It is the junction of highways serving the rich coastal farm lands to east and west, the pastoral country of the midlands and the picturesque East Coast.

History. In 1798 George Bass and Matthew Flinders first circumnavigated Tasmania in the vessel *Norfolk*. During the voyage they discovered and named Port Dalrymple and ventured up the Tamar River as far as Shoal Point. Six years later Lieutenant-Colonel Paterson established a settlement at the mouth of the Tamar River and called it Georgetown. He took formal possession of the land on 11 November 1804.

Although the merits of transferring to the site of present-day Launceston were advocated for many years, final decision was not reached until 1824 when the township was officially proclaimed and named for the Cornish birthplace of Governor King.

The settlement grew rapidly. Agriculture flourished and in the 1830s the town became an important base for whalers and sealers operating in the Southern Ocean. In the 1870s rich strikes of gold and tin were made in the Tasmanian mountains and communications were rapidly improved. The rail link with Hobart was established in 1871.

Launceston was proclaimed a city in 1888. In recent years secondary industry has become important in the community economy with the establishment of heavy-engineering, machine-making and textile plants. Its river port handles about one million tonnes of shipping a year.

Places of Interest. Cataract Gorge. A few minutes' drive from the centre of the city. The South Esk River has cut a deep canyon through the hills near its junction with the Tamar and its rapids are particularly spectacular when heavy rain has fallen in the highlands. A pathway on the north side of the gorge leads to Cataract Cliff Grounds Park, where European trees and shrubs have been established with the native flora. The South Esk is here crossed by a suspension bridge which leads to a picnic area, an Olympic swimming pool and a children's paddling pool. There is now a chair lift across the gorge. Kiosk and dressing rooms.

Trevallyn Dam and Hydro-electric Power Station. Three kilometres north-west of city on the South Esk River. Four turbines each of 28 000 hp and four alternators each of 20 000 kW. Water for generation is conserved in a dam 23 metres high. The station is close to the site of Australia's first, and one of the world's earliest, hydro-electric projects. In 1895, the Launceston City Council built a power station at nearby Duck Reach. The plant was in continuous operation for 60 years and supplied the city with electricity. The original buildings, flying-fox conveyor and suspension bridge across the river are still standing. Picnic grounds open daily until 5 pm.

Wildlife Sanctuary. South of city on Punchbowl Road. Native animals, birds and reptiles in natural surroundings. Kiosk.

Queen Victoria Museum and Art Gallery. Exhibits of historical interest; native flora, fauna and minerals; early china and glassware; 19th-century and contemporary art. Situated in Royal Park, overlooking Tamar River. Radio guide system.

Franklin House. Six kilometres south of city. Built in 1838 for an early settler by convict labour. Bought in 1842 by William Keeler Hawkes who used it as a school. It was regarded as one of Tasmania's foremost educational establishments until Hawkes's death in 1882. Renamed 'The Hollies' when bought in 1888. In 1960 it was bought by the National Trust and furnished with appropriate period pieces. Renamed Franklin House after the nearby village.

Entally House. Thirteen kilometres south of city at Hadspen. Built in 1820, and an excellent example of early colonial style. Specimens of early horse-drawn vehicles are on display in the outhouses. Maintained by the Tasmanian Scenery Preservation Board. Light refreshments are available.

City Park. Five hectares containing a small children's zoo and the John Hart Conservatory. Hothouses give fine displays of begonias and cyclamens in season. **The Albert Hall** adjoins the park (seating for 2 500).

Princes Square, City. Features a baroque fountain brought from Paris in 1859.

Royal Park. A formal civic park fronting the South Esk River, with adjoining sports and recreation reserve.

Other buildings of historical or architectural interest include: St John's Church (Elizabeth and St John's Streets), built of clay bricks by convicts labour 1824-30—Melbourne, founders John Batman and John Fawkner were both married in this church; Town Hall (St John's Street), built 1864; Public Library (St John's Street), built for £8 000 in 1857-60 as Launceston Mechanics Institute.

Sports. Golf: Three 18-hole golf courses. Tennis and squash: Northern Tasmanian Lawn Tennis Association welcomes visiting players (seven all-weather courts, two squash courts). Bowls: Eight clubs make rinks available to visitors. Croquet: Lawns at Royal Park and Windmill Hill (Adelaide and High Streets). Dog racing: White City Course, Invermay Road. Horse racing: Mowbray Racecourse, Georgetown Road. Fishing: Angling licences available from Government Tourist Bureau (Cameron Street).

Entertainments. Two **theatres** (Princes and Little). Two **cinemas.**

Accommodation. Twenty four **hotels.** Recommended: Cornwall; Launceston Town; St George; St James. Six **motels.** Recommended: Commodore; Travelodge. **Caravan and Camping park,** Glen Dhee Street.

Rail services. Monday to Saturday daily service west to Devonport, Burnie and Wynyard, south to Hobart. Monday to Friday and Sunday evening service to Hobart. Monday to Friday daily service to Herrick, and Saturday service to Scottsdale.

Motor Coach services. Run to Hobart and to Queenstown via North West Coast.

Taxis, hire and **rental cars** available.

Tours. A number of half-day, full-day and extended (two to three-day) tours by car or car and coach can be booked in Launceston. Consult Government Tourist Bureau.

DEVONPORT

(Population 18 150)

Devonport is a busy industrial town and agricultural export centre 105 kilometres west and north of Launceston, at the mouth of the Mersey River. Its industries include paper manufacture, textiles, carpet manufacture, can-making, shipbuilding and food processing, sawmilling. Devonport is the terminal of the ferry service from Melbourne.

History. The municipality first comprised the towns of Torquay (now East Devonport) and Formby. Torquay was surveyed in 1851 and Formby in 1853. Agriculture developed rapidly in the district and in the 1880s extensive reclamation and other work was done in the harbour area. The two towns voted to amalgamate in 1890 and in 1893 Devonport was proclaimed. Industrialization began in 1942 when a food-processing factory was established.

Places of Interest. Braddon's Lookout, west on the highway near the small township of Forth, gives a good panoramic view of the coastline. **Mersey Bluff,** parkland and beach resort (aboriginal rock carvings). **Latrobe,** 11 kilometres south, founded in 1850 and noted for Bell's Parade, a beautiful riverside reserve on the banks of the Mersey; two good hotels in the township. **Railton,** about 22 kilometres south, site of Goliath-Portland Cement works (tours can be arranged). **Port Sorell,** 20 kilometres north-east on Rubicon River estuary, with wildlife reserve and 12 hectares of foreshore reserves for camping and picnicking; sheltered beaches; good fishing; four caravan parks and holiday cottages available.

Sports facilities. Woodrising and Spreyton golf courses. Bowling greens and tennis courts. Croquet rink. Night trotting. Greyhound racing. Swimming at Mersey Bluff Beach, Coles Beach and East Devonport. Yachting.

Entertainments etc. One **cinema,** one **drive-in.** Agricultural show in early December; Dahlia Festival, February; Apex Regatta in March; Mersey Valley Apple Festival, in March; Eisteddfod, three weeks in August-September.

Accommodation. Five **hotels.** Recommended: Formby, Formby Road. Two **motels.** Recommended: Gateway, Fewton Street. Three **caravan and camping parks,** Terminal (near Ferry), Coles Beach, Mersey Bluff.

Car rentals. Six firms operate.

Tours. Short, half-day and full-day coach tours along coast and to mountains available. Information, Government Tourist Bureau, 41 Stewart Street.

Air services. Scheduled flights daily by both airlines to mainland. Charter flights by light aircraft available at airport.

ULVERSTONE

(Population 8 005)

Centre of agricultural, pastoral and timber getting district, 144 kilometres east of Launceston. There are vegetable-processing and furniture-making factories in the town which is at the mouth of the Leven River.

History. The area around Ulverstone was first settled in 1848 by paling splitters. Exploration of the Leven valley revealed rich land and by 1855 the town was surveyed and named after Ulverston in the Lake District of England. By 1872 a road had been built through the valley and the population of the district increased rapidly. In 1890 the railway connected it with Launceston and in 1908 it was proclaimed a municipality.

Places of Interest. **West Ulverstone Lookout,** 5 kilometres west. **Turner's Beach,** 6 kilometres east. **Lobster Creek,** in river valley south of town. **Goat Island,** a rocky outcrop off the coast which can be reached on foot at low tide. **Gunns Plains Caves** (guided tours by arrangement) and **Leven Canyon. Nietta eucalypt forests** about 32 kilometres south.

Sports. Nine-hole golf course. Tennis courts. Bowling and croquet greens. River and sea angling. Headquarters of North West Coast Walking Club. Yachting.

Accommodation. Three **hotels.** Recommended: Stones, Victoria Street. Two **motels.** Recommended, Beachway, Heathcote Street. Three **caravan parks,** Beach Road and Picnic Point, all facilities; Turner's Beach, limited facilities.

Car rentals. One firm operates.

Tours. Coach tours along coast and to limestone caves areas and mountains to the south are available.

PENGUIN (Population 2 287)

A small coastal town 124 kilometres west and north of Launceston, centre of a pastoral, dairying and market gardening district, largely settled by Dutch migrants since the second world war.

History. The village was founded in 1858 and the town proclaimed in 1888. The area provided pit props for Victorian goldmines during the 1850s. The town was so named because a number of small penguins frequented the nearby creek mouth and coast.

Places of Interest. **Ferndene Gorge,** south of town, administered by the Scenery Preservation Board.

Sports. Tennis courts. Bowling green. Fishing in river and from foreshores. There is a boat ramp at West Penguin.

Accommodation. Two **hotels.** Recommended: Neptune Grand Hotel.

BURNIE

(Population 20 028)

Tasmania's third-largest municipality, 148 kilometres west of Launceston, on Emu Bay at the mouth of Emu River, Burnie is the port of a rich agricultural and forest-products region in which there has been considerable secondary industrial development in recent years. The town has grown rapidly since the establishment of one of the State's largest industrial enterprises, Associated Pulp and Paper Mills Ltd and its subsidiaries which produce writing and printing papers, wrappings, building hardboard and particle board from eucalyptus wood pulp. Other important factories in the area include plants for the manufacture of sulphuric acid, titanium oxide pigments and dried milk and chocolate products. The port of Burnie, developed for the handling of containerized cargo, handles 17 per cent of the State's sea trade. It is the outlet for several of the West Coast mining centres, notably Rosebery and Mount Cleveland.

History. The Van Diemen's Land Company purchased 50 000 acres of land in the vicinity of Emu Bay in 1826. A year later the colony's Chief Surveyor, Henry Hellyer, made extensive exploration in the north-west and in 1829 a village was founded at the mouth of the river. The name of the Emu Bay settlement was later changed to Burnie in honour of William Burnie, then a director of the company. Although the town was proclaimed in 1866, its progress was slow until the enormously rich tin mine at Mount Bischoff, near Waratah, came into production in the early 1870s. Burnie became the port which supplied the mine workings and from which the tin concentrates were shipped. A horse-drawn tramway linked the town with the mine until 1884 when the Emu Bay railway was built. The State rail system was extended to the town in 1901 and in 1908 it was incorporated as a municipality. The first paper mill was established in 1938.

Places of Interest. **Folk Museum,** High Street. **Round Hill,** five kilometres from town and 244 metres above sea level, offers panoramic views of the district. **Ridgley,** 13 kilometres south, has well-tended picnic grounds and views of five waterfalls, the largest of which is the **Guide Falls. Fern Glade,** 5 kilometres south, has fine bushland scenery.

Sports. Sports ovals for cycling, football, cricket and hockey. Two 18-hole golf courses, tennis courts, two bowling greens, croquet club, gun club.

The Burnie New Year's Day Sports Carnival is one of the largest meetings of its kind in Australia.

Entertainments. One **cinema** and a **drive-in** at Somerset, 8 kilometres west on highway.

Accommodation. Five **hotels.** Recommended: Beach Motor Hotel. Three **motels.** Recommended: Burnie Motor Lodge, Queen Street. **Caravan park,** Wivenhoe, east of town on beach.

Car rentals. Four firms operate at Burnie.

Tours. Half-day and full-day **coach** tours available. Information, Government Tourist Bureau, Wilson Street, Burnie.

Air services. Serviced by Wynyard airport, 19 kilometres west. A coach service connects with flights.

WYNYARD (Population 4 013)

Centre of a productive dairying, vegetable growing and mixed farming district, and a small fishing port, at the mouth of the Inglis River, 162 kilometres west of Launceston, Wynyard's industries include a pea cannery, modern cheese, butter and bacon factories and a large sawmill. The coast to the westward is interesting and the countryside attractive. The Waratah Highway, linking the Murchison and Lyell Highways serving the West Coast, joins the Bass Highway near the town.

History. Table Cape (116 metres above sea level) was sighted and named by Bass and Flinders in 1798, but the first settlers did not arrive in the district until the early 1840s. By 1856 the population had grown to several hundred and a municipality, first called Table Cape or Ramsay, was proclaimed. In 1861 the town was officially named after Major-General E. B. Wynyard, one time commander-in-chief of British forces in New South Wales, Van Diemen's Land and New Zealand.

Places of Interest. Table Cape and **Lighthouse,** north of town. **Fossil Bluff,** near Wynyard Golf Links. **Boat Harbour,** 11 kilometres west (one of the most picturesque seaside resorts on the coast). **Rocky Cape aboriginal caves,** about 32 kilometres west, north of highway.

Sports. One good 18-hole golf course, one nine-hole course. River and beach swimming. Bowling and tennis clubs open to visitors. River fishing for trout, blackfish, salmon and lobster. Rock fishing for cod, bluehead, parrot fish, perch and crayfish. Sea fishing for salmon, flathead, barracouta, shark, pike and crayfish.

Entertainments. Cinema and **drive-in.**

Accommodation. Wynyard: Three **hotels.** Recommended: Commercial, the Esplanade. One **motel. Caravan and holiday cottage park.** Boat Harbour: Two **motels.** Recommended: Inglis View, the Esplanade. **Holiday cottages, flats** to let. **Two caravan and camping parks,** cabins and stationary caravans available.

Car rentals. Three firms operate at Wynyard.

Air services. Daily flights to and from Melbourne and regular connections with other Tasmanian airports.

SMITHTON and STANLEY (Population (3 917)

The Circular Head district is about 240 kilometres west of Launceston. It is one of the most productive dairying and potato-growing areas in Tasmania. Smithton has the largest butter factory in the State and is an important timber-milling centre. The town is attractively sited in low-lying, undulating, rich country and possesses a well-equipped port. Stanley, 20 kilometres to the north-east, is a picturesque little settlement with an artificial harbour from which cray and shark-fishing fleets operate.

History. Bass and Flinders sighted the extraordinary rock formation known as The Nut in 1798 and named it Circular Head. It is 152 metres high. In 1825 the colonial Government granted the Van Diemen's Land Company land totalling 422 000 acres in six separate localities of north-western Tasmania for a farthing an acre annual rental (£468 a year in all). The company established its headquarters at Highfield, an estate near Stanley. The first settlers arrived in 1826. Exploitation of the district's magnificent beech and hardwood forests began in 1884 and in 1902 copper was discovered nearby Balfour. The aboriginal name for the district was Martula, but Smithton was named after Peter Smith, an early settler.

Places of Interest. Original buildings of **Highfield Estate,** homestead near Stanley built of locally hewn stone and lime mortar from shells gathered on the beaches and burned. **Shell collection,** signposted at entrance to Stanley, reputed to be one of the finest in Australia. **Ruins** of original convict settlement above town. **Dip Falls,** a 150 metre cascade on the Dip River off the highway south-east of Stanley. **Arthur River,** about 64 kilometres south-west of Smithton, where excellent fishing and duck-shooting are to be had. (Hotel accommodation at Marrawah, 14 kilometres from river mouth.)

Accommodation. Stanley: One **hotel.** One **caravan park,** near Tatlow Beach. Smithton: One **hotel.** One **motel.**

Car rentals. One firm operates.

Motor coach service daily to Burnie.

CENTRAL HIGHLANDS

CRADLE MOUNTAIN-LAKE ST CLAIR NATIONAL PARK. The Cradle Mountain-Lake St Clair National Park covers an area of 135 400 hectares and is the largest wildlife sanctuary and scenic reserve in Tasmania. The first part of it was gazetted in 1927. Roads to the north and south give access to the bush walking track which links Waldheim Chalet in the north with Lake St Clair. The northern access is from Devonport through Sheffield and Wilmot to Waldheim and the southern access is through Derwent Bridge on the Lyell Highway about 160 kilometres from Hobart.

The main bushwalking track between Waldheim and Cynthia Bay on Lake St Clair is approximately 97 kilometres. Tracks are well marked and huts are located at one day's walk from another. Average hikers complete the trip in five days.

Lake St Clair itself lies at an altitude of 665 metres and has an area of 5 160 hectares. It is the head-waters of the western arm of the Derwent River and the storage for the hydro-electric power station at Tarraleah. There is some doubt about who discovered the lake. Although the Surveyor-General, W. S. Sharland, claimed to have discovered it in 1832, it is thought that Jorgen Jorgensen, one-time ruler of Iceland, found it in 1826. It was named by Surveyor-General George Frankland in 1835 in honour of the St Clair family of Loch Lomond, Scotland. Its aboriginal name was Leeawulena.

The Lake St Clair area is the home of the Bennett's and rufous wallabies, both unique Tasmanian varieties.

The park contains many notable peaks. Cradle Mountain itself stands at the northern extremity and is 1 520 metres high. It was first climbed by the Austrian alpinists, Franz and Julius Malcher.

Other mountains include Mt Ossa (1 591 metres), Pelion West (1 530 metres), Mt Gould (1 506 metres), Barn Bluff (1 533 metres), Falling Mountain and Massif Mountain (both 1 500 metres). Some of the mountains (notably Mt Rufus) are eroded into fantastic shapes. Scientists believe that the plateau of the Western Tiers region is the remnant of a great land mass which stretched from present-day Antarctica across the Pacific to South America.

At the Waldheim Chalet there is a natural history museum which has exhibits of native flora and fauna and geology of the region.

Travelling conditions. The plateau is subject to heavy rain and snowfall and changes of temperature can occur rapidly. Sudden blizzards can blow up, even in summer months. Hikers should carry adequate warm clothing, waterproof jackets, and a light plastic raincoat and wear stout, protective leather footwear and suitable headgear. Women are advised to wear slacks. A complete change of clothing should be carried. Provisions can **not** be purchased along the track. All gear and rations should be carried in a rucksack to leave both hands free. Inclusion of a small first-aid kit and sunglasses is recommended. Walkers and climbers should always consult the Park Ranger before setting out on long trips. He will advise about tracks and weather and equipment required.

Accommodation. Waldheim **Chalet. Cabins.** Lake St Clair West **camping and caravan park,** chalet and cabin accommodation.

Note: Lake St Clair is easily accessible by car from the Lyell Highway near Derwent Bridge. A tourist launch runs on the lake in summer.

GREAT LAKE AND CENTRAL LAKES AREA. The central lakes area is the main hydro-electric power region of Tasmania and its scenery is superb. Northern access is through Devonport or Launceston and Deloraine; southern access via Marlborough Highway, off Lyell Highway east of Derwent Bridge.

The Hydro-Electricity Commission maintains power stations at Waddamana, Tarraleah, Butler's Gorge, Tungatinah, Wayatinah, Liapootah, Catagunya and Poatina. Principal dams are the Clark, Miena, Pine Tier, Liapootah and Catagunya. The lake storages include Great Lake, Lake Augusta, Lake King William (south of Lake St Clair and serving the Butler's Gorge station). Lake St Clair (serving Tarraleah), Lake Echo and Arthurs Lake.

Viewing galleries for the public are situated at Tungatinah, Tarraleah, Liapootah and Trewallyn power stations. Tours (day trips or longer) to these and other stations can be made through the Tasmanian Tourist Bureau.

Accommodation in HEC **chalets** at Bronte Park, Tarraleah and Poatina, the **hotel** at Great Lake, the **guest-house** at Waddamana and **camping sites** at Lake St Clair, Wayatinah and Tarraleah.

Great Lake itself is 16 kilometres long and is 1 016 metres above sea level. Attempts were made to stock it with trout in 1842 and 1852 but were unsuccessful. However, with the establishment of the hatchery at Plenty in 1864, acclimatization was achieved.

The first hydro-electric dam was built at Great Lake in 1911 by the Hydro-electric Power and Metallurgical Company and the water was conveyed to Waddamana. The State Government took over the company's assets in 1914.

MERSEY-FORTH POWER STATIONS.

Seven new hydro-electric power stations have recently been completed in the valleys of the Mersey and Forth Rivers north of the Great Lake and Lake St Clair area. The scheme, the largest project yet undertaken by the HEC, cost more than $A104 million. Headquarters of the project are at Gowrie Park, about 16 kilometres from Sheffield on the main road south of Devonport. The commission's newly constructed road through the mountains from Gowrie Park to Liena, west of Mole Creek, is now open to motorists.

DELORAINE (Population 1 816)

Picturesque Deloraine is under the shadow of the Great Western Tiers, 48 kilometres west and south of Launceston. It is the centre of a fertile red-soil dairying and mixed farming district and an important highway junction. It is a convenient base for visits to the lakes area to the south, the Mersey-Forth hydro-electric power stations, dams and scenic service roads, and a number of interesting limestone caves.

History. The first land grants in the Deloraine district were made to individual settlers in 1825 and to the Van Dieman's Land Company in 1826. In 1831 the area was surveyed by Thomas Scott, a relative of Sir Walter Scott, who named it after Deloraine in his kinsman's 'Lay of the Last Minstrel'. The town was founded in the 1840s and was proclaimed a municipality in 1863. It was connected with Launceston by rail in 1871.

Places of Interest. St Mark's Church of England, built 1857, on hill overlooking town. **Roman Catholic Church of the Holy Redeemer. Holy Trinity Church of Rome,** Westbury, 16 kilometres east on Bass Highway; one of the State's largest country churches, consecrated in 1874. **Westbury Zoo,** containing a Tasmanian devil. **Folk Museum,** Emu Bay Road. **Devil's Gullet Lookout** (via Lake McKenzie Road). **King Solomon and Marapooka** limestone caves, **Mole Creek,** about 24 kilometres west (open daily 10 am-4 pm). **Liffey and Meander waterfalls** within 30 minutes drive. **Alum cliffs.**

Sports. Golf course. Tennis courts. Bowling green. Turf club which runs the Tasmanian Grand National, over live brush hurdles, and Deloraine Cup race, every Easter Monday. Fishing in Great Lake and adjacent streams and lagoons 44 to 48 kilometres south, for rainbow and brown trout, blackfish, perch and tench. (Inquiries from Deloraine Fisheries Association.)

Accommodation. One **hotel.** One **motel. Caravan park** on Meander River, north of town. All amenities.

THE MIDLANDS

The most direct route between Hobart and Launceston is by way of the Midland Highway, 199 kilometres of first-class road which traverses rich pastoral and agricultural country between the lake country of the Great Plateau and the ranges of the north-east and east. The terrain is gentle and the vistas broad. The early settlers replaced the native forests they cleared with European oaks, willows, poplars and elms and planted hedgerows of briar and hawthorn. The countryside is brilliantly colourful in autumn.

The northern part of the district is drained by the South Esk River which has its source in the highlands about Ben Lomond (1 503 metres) and Legge's Tor (1 548 metres). The Esk Highway connects the Midland and Tasman Highways and serves an area of pastoral country between high ranges which is not usually penetrated by tourists.

Midlands farms and pastures were developed early in the island's history and the little towns of the region are rich in architectural relics and associations with pioneering days.

LONGFORD (Population 1 712)

A quiet country town, one of the earliest settlements in northern Tasmania, Longford, is best known as the venue of one of Australia's major motor race meetings. Its road circuit tested the nerve and skill of some of the world's best speed drivers but the meetings have been discontinued.

The town is situated about 6 kilometres west of Perth on the Tasman Highway and 24 kilometres south of Launceston. It was first settled in 1813 when former residents of Norfolk Island were granted land in the district by Governor Macquarie and was originally known as Norfolk Plains, later as Latour.

Places of Interest. Christ Church. The foundation stone was laid by Sir John Franklin in 1839 and the building consecrated in 1884. The west window, designed by Thomas Archer, is regarded as one of the most beautiful church windows in Australia. The square tower, not completed until 1961, houses a large bell and a clock believed to have been given the local administration by King William IV. **Cressy Research Farm,** about 16 kilometres south on the Lake Highway, run by the State Department of Agriculture.

Accommodation. Three **hotels.** Recommended: Country Club, Main Road. **Caravan and camping park,** North Longford, all amenities.

CAMPBELL TOWN (Population 1 040)

Sixty-six kilometres south of Launceston, Campbell Town is the centre of a district noted for merino wool production since the early 19th century. The settlement was established in 1811 by Governor Macquarie and named after his second wife, Elizabeth Campbell. The first high-grade wool from the district was exported in 1822 and brought 7d a lb on the London market. The following year the district produced more than 1 000 bales. The municipality was incorporated in 1866.

Places of Interest. Convict built bridge of red brick (1836). **St Luke's Church** (1839). **Campbell Town Inn** (1840). **Powell's Hotel** (1834). **Harold Gatty Memorial** (the famous aviator was born in Campbell Town). **Shearers' cottages** on View Point estate. They are of simple design, built in 1860 by Robert Gatenby, and feature delicate bargeboarding on the gables. **The Grange.** Owned by the National Trust. An interesting brick house with a bluestone wing. Designed by James Blackburn and completed in 1849. **Old Methodist Chapel,** built about 1839. The chapel shows a marked resemblance to the Methodist chapels of Cornwall.

Accommodation. Two **hotels.** Recommended: Powell's Motor Hotel.

OATLANDS (Population 548)

Highest point on the Midland Highway, Oatlands is 84 kilometres north of Hobart on the shore of Lake Dulverton, a popular fishing spot. The district was a notorious haunt of bushrangers in the early days. In 1826 a party of soldiers and convicts was dispatched from Hobart to establish a military post close to the present townsite.

Places of Interest. Callington Mill. Built by John Vincent and finished in 1837. **St Luke's Presbyterian Church** and the **Manse,** built in 1860 by pioneer settler, George Wilson, as a gift for his daughter who married the minister. **Catholic Church of St Paul,** built in 1850 and designed by English architect, A. W. Pugh. **St Peter's Church of England,** designed by John Lee Archer in 1837. **Lake Sorell,** approximately 48 kilometres to the north-west. **Lake Crescent,** adjoining Lake Sorell, the headwaters of the Clyde River. (Both lakes are stocked with trout.) **Table Mountain,** to the south-west of Lake Crescent (1 091 metres). **Lemon Springs,** a few kilometres south of Oatlands, the scene of various raids by the notorious bushranger, Richard Lemon. **Plantation of trees** on the road to Antill (north) trimmed by topiarists to resemble animals etc.

Accommodation. Two **hotels.** Preferred: Kentish, High Street.

BOTHWELL (Population 389)

A popular fishing resort on Lake Highway, about 72 kilometres north north-west of Hobart, Bothwell was originally known as Fat Doe River and was settled in 1817. It was named for Bothwell, Scotland, by Governor Macquarie. It has two particular distinctions. The Town Council claims for it the Australian record for rate collection. Between 1862 and 1963, there was only one defaulting ratepayer who still owes the council 10/- ($A1.00). And the Young Ireland Party political exiles, Mitchel and Martin, lived in nearby Nant Cottage during the 1850s.

Places of Interest. St Luke's Presbyterian Church (1830). **Wentworth House** (1833). **Nant Mill,** a massive rough-masonry mill built in 1857. Privately owned. **Clifton Priory,** on Barrack Hill overlooking the township. It was built between 1847 and 1848 by the Reverend Robert Wilson, an early Anglican chaplain. **Anglican Chapel of St James,** Montacute, a nearby hamlet. Built by Captain William Langdon in 1857, it is one of the few surviving private 'Estate' chapels.

Accommodation. One **hotel** (historic building).

ROSS (Population 288)

On the banks of the Macquarie River and on the Midland Highway 119 kilometres north of Hobart, Ross and its district are famous for high-quality merino wool—particularly the clip of the Mount Morrison Estate. It was established in 1812 as a military post for the protection of travellers. It was named after the Scottish seat of H. M. Buchanan, a friend of Governor Macquarie. The historic homestead 'Mona Vale' was used as a training centre for the Light Horse Division of the 1st AIF and in the second world war it was requisitioned as a military training camp.

At one time, Ross was an important stone-quarrying area. Many of the buildings are made of the local freestone.

Tasman Bridge, Hobart

Derwent River, Tasmania

Dove Lake, Tasmania

Westbury House, Tasmania

Places of Interest. State School, Ross, typical of Tasmanian schools of the 1860s to 1880s. Made of local freestone with Huon pine bargeboards and finials. Design throughout the country was similar and only building materials differed. **Ross Bridge,** designed by John Lee Archer and built between 1830 and 1836. Considered to be the finest of the period still extant in Australia. Convict-built of local sandstone. **'Mona Vale',** Ross, designed by William Archer for his brother-in-law and built between 1865 and 1869. 'Mona Vale' is one of the largest and most tasteful of Victorian Italianate mansions. Privately owned—365 windows, 52 rooms, 12 chimneys, seven entrances to symbolize units of time. **St John's Anglican Church,** designed by Henry Hunter and opened in 1869. Made of local stone and featuring unusual tower treatment. **Scotch Thistle Inn** and **Art Gallery. Wool and Craft Centre** (in building restored by National Trust). **Tooms Lake Dam,** built early last century. Stocked with trout. **Long Marsh Dam,** commenced with convict labour in 1840 but when transportation ceased in 1853, work ceased. It was never completed.

Accommodation. One **hotel. Caravan park,** all facilities.

EAST COAST

The east coast of Tasmania, traversed by the Tasman Highway, enjoys the advantage of a mild and equable climate throughout most of the year and its seaside resorts are popular with Tasmanian holiday-makers. Most are on sheltered inlets but within easy reach of good surf beaches and fishing grounds.

The scenery is not on the whole as spectacular or distinctive as it is throughout the rest of the island, but it has variety to offer for the traveller with leisure to stop over and explore the hinterland and the less obviously accessible stretches of coastline.

Pastoral industries, mixed agriculture, timber getting, crayfishing, fishing and fish processing are the basis of the region's economy but tourism is increasing in importance as roads and transport are improved.

SCOTTSDALE (Population 1 800)

Largest town in the relatively undeveloped north-east corner of the State. The district industries are dairying and mixed farming, seed growing, market gardening, timber getting and tin-mining. The town has a butter factory, a large vegetable dehydration plant, cannery, sawmills, and furniture and joinery works.

History. The first settler arrived in the region in 1842, but the town area was not surveyed until 1855. It was named Scottsdale after the first surveyor and selector in 1893 and incorporated as a municipality in 1906. Alluvial tin was discovered in the district towards the turn of the century and the fields have been worked on and off ever since, mainly by small companies or individual miners.

Places of Interest. Bridport, seaside village 23 kilometres north; **'Bowood'** homestead (privately owned) is a fine example of the type of colonial country house built in early-Victorian Tasmania. **Weldborough Pass,** on highway to St Helens, traverses magnificent mountain forest.

Accommodation. Two **hotels.** Recommended: Scottsdale Motor Hotel. **Caravan park,** with swimming pool.

ST HELENS (Population 824)

At the western extremity of George Bay, where the Tasman Highway turns south towards Hobart, St Helens is probably the best-known and best-endowed resort on the East Coast proper. It is 256 kilometres north-north-east of Hobart. The bay has about 13 000 hectares of sheltered water for fishing, boating and aquatic sports. Good surf beaches on the open coast are within easy reach and the forest country in the mountains to the north and west is very beautiful. There is excellent trout fishing in the streams.

Three freezing works in or near the main settlement handle the catch of the crayfishing fleet based on the bay.

History. The first settlers came to George Bay in 1834. St Helens Point to the north-east has barracks which once housed convicts. Poor communications, however, retarded the development of the district until the tin strikes were made at Weldborough and elsewhere in the north-east of the island towards the end of the 19th century. St Helens then became the main port of shipment for concentrates.

Places of Interest. Binnalong Bay (10 kilometres) a small anchorage for crayfishing boats and a favourite fishing spot. **Sloop Rock** (offshore reef shaped like a small ship in sail); **'The Gardens',** a privately owned farm settled more than a century ago and named by Lady Franklin (wife of Sir John Franklin, Governor of Tasmania and famous polar explorer) because of the profusion of wildflowers in the area. **St Helens Point,** an elevated headland from which magnificent views of the coast can be obtained in fine weather. **Museum. Gould's Country** and **Weldborough Pass,** fine forest areas to the north-west on the road to Scottsdale. **St Columba's Falls,** a 122 metre cascade on the headwaters of the George River, reached by turning south off the main highway at Pyengana, 26 kilometres west of St Helens township.

Sports facilities. Golf course; tennis courts; bowling green available to visitors; fishing boats for hire.

Accommodation. Two **hotels.** Recommended: St Helens Hotel. One **motel.** Three **caravan and camping parks**—Parkside and King's Park, all facilities; Binnalong Bay, limited facilities. Holiday **apartments, cottages** and **cabins** available.

Restaurant. St Helens Hotel specializes in locally caught crayfish and seafood dishes.

SCAMANDER (Population 71)

Nineteen kilometres south of St Helens, with good fishing water and beaches.

Accommodation. One recommended **hotel.** One **motel,** five kilometres north of settlement on highway. **Youth Hostel** (1 kilometre north). Holiday **apartments.**

ST MARYS (Population 745)

A small town at the junction of the Tasman and Esk Highways, centre of a dairying, pastoral and timber district, but largely dependent on coalmining in the nearby St Nicholas Range.

Places of Interest. St Marys Pass Reserve, north of town, administered by the Scenery Preservation Board. **Elephant Pass,** on highway to Bicheno.

Accommodation. Two **hotels.** Recommended: St Marys Hotel.

BICHENO (Population 250)

A fishing port 173 kilometres south-east of Launceston which has in recent years gained popularity with holidaymakers. It is believed to be the first whaling station established on the Tasmanian mainland. The climate is unusually mild and nearby beaches are suitable for surfng and surf fishing. Tennis courts and a bowling green are open to visitors. Deepwater fishing trips can be arranged with local crayfishermen.

History. Whalers and sealers used Peggy Point as a base from 1803 until the industry declined in mid-century. James Kelly landed there on his circumnavigation of the island in a small boat in 1816. Permanent settlement began in 1849 after coal was discovered at Douglas River to the north and a mine established. Two years later the village was named in honour of James Ebenezer Bicheno, Colonial Secretary from 1843 to 1851. Another coalmine was opened at Denison River in 1854, but the industry declined when most miners emigrated to Victoria during the gold rush. It was not until the 1930s that Bicheno was revived as a crayfishing and tourist centre.

Places of Interest. Old whaling station buildings at Peggy Point. **Grave of Wauba Debar,** an aboriginal woman after whom the original settlement was named. She died in 1832.

Accommodation. One **motor hotel.** Two **motels. Caravan park,** all facilities. **Camping area. Youth Hostel.**

COLES BAY (Population 37) and **FREYNICET NATIONAL PARK**

Thirty nine kilometres south of Bicheno on a secondary road off the Tasman Highway, Coles Bay is the accommodation centre for visitors to Freynicet National Park, a 6 500 hectare reserve and wildlife sanctuary proclaimed in 1916. The peninsula was discovered by Nicholas Baudin in 1802 and named after one of his party. Its backbone is a red-granite mountain range known as The Hazards, with peaks between 300 and 600 metres above sea level. The region is of great interest to botanists and ornithologists. More than 60 varieties of ground orchids have been identified in the unspoiled bush in which bird life is prolific.

Accommodation. Private motel. Camping ground, limited facilities. Holiday **apartments. Youth Hostel.**

SWANSEA (Population 370)

A small town of historical interest, 137 kilometres from Hobart on the shores of Oyster Bay. There is excellent deep sea and river fishing in the district, which is the venue of the Tasmanian annual angling championships in November. Prizes are valued at more than $A10 000. There is an open gold championship in June and an athletic and water-sports carnival at Christmas.

History. The first land grant in the district was made to a Lieutenant George Meredith in 1821, but it was not until 1827 that the town area was settled and a military establishment set up at Waterloo Point to accommodate units of the 88th Regiment. Like many east coast towns, Swansea was a whaling station in the early part of the 19th century. The rural municipality, Glamorgan, is the oldest in Tasmania. It was proclaimed in 1860.

Places of Interest. **Historical museum** with relics of early settlement; District **War Memorial Institute; Public Library** (built 1862); **Morris' Store** (built 1838); **Spiky Bridge,** believed to have been built by convicts at the nearby Rocky Hills Probation Station, in the early 1840s. Eyle family's **Log Cabin** (1826), **Schouten House** (circa 1850).

Accommodation. One **motor hotel.** Two **caravan and camping parks,** all amenities. **Apartments** and **stationary caravans** available. Boats for hire.

TRIABUNNA (Population 591)

A prosperous fishing port on the shores of Spring Bay, from which the municipality takes its name. It is 51 kilometres south of Swansea. A sizable fishing fleet is based on the bay. It was once a garrison town when convicts were imprisoned on Maria Island and was a whaling base in the 1830s. Triabunna is the aboriginal word for native hen.

Accommodation. One **hotel. Caravan park,** all amenities.

ORFORD (Population 311)

Eight kilometres south of Triabunna, Orford is the centre of a pastoral and mixed farming area. Melbourne Law Courts and several other public buildings were built of sandstone obtained from quarries in the locality at the end of the 19th century. There are good beaches and fishing waters nearby.

Accommodation. One **motor hotel.** One **motel. Caravan park,** limited facilities.

BUCKLAND (Population 179)

The Buckland district, 64 kilometres north-east of Hobart on the Prosser River, was opened up in 1829. The town was once an important staging place on the coast road from Hobart.

Places of Interest. **St John the Baptist Church,** built in 1846 and noted for its stained-glass window, said to date from the 14th century. It was given to Dean Cox, first rector of Buckland, by his friend, Lord Robert Cecil, then Secretary of State for the Colonies.

It was reputedly designed for Battle Abbey on the site of the Battle of Hastings and was severely damaged by fighting in Cromwell's time. It has been clumsily restored, but is still of great beauty. **Maria Island,** at the entrance to Prosser Bay, was discovered and named by Tasman in 1642. It was a convict settlement from 1825 to about 1850. Mount Maria in the centre of the island is 692 metres above sea level. Several unsuccessful attempts have been made to develop the island. In 1884 an imaginative Italian, Diego Bernacci, tried to establish a wine and silk industry but failed. A large cement works was built there in 1924, but it, too, failed during the great depression.

Accommodation. One **hotel.**

WEST COAST

The lonely, sparsely populated West Coast of Tasmania is without doubt the most unusual and fascinating part of the island. Its mountain scenery can only be described as superb and its character as unique. There could be no greater contrast of regional atmosphere than that existing between the gentle calm of the rich river valleys in the south-east and the savage magnificence of Frenchman's Cap National Park or the bare, stark hills of Queenstown.

The whole of the area is highly mineralized and over the years immense fortunes have been made from mining gold, silver, copper, lead, zinc and osmiridium in the hills and gorges. But until 1932, when a road was pushed through the tangle of mountains between Queenstown and Hobart, the mining towns' only connection with the outside world was provided by small ships which could negotiate the difficult entrances to Macquarie and Trial Harbours. Not until recent years was the road link with Hobart improved enough to encourage its use by any but the hardiest travellers.

Modern road-making machinery and modern prospecting and mining techniques have now completely altered the situation of the Coast. Mineral deposits which could not have been economically exploited a couple of decades ago have suddenly become payable propositions and the entire region, from which the 'cream had been skimmed' under heartbreaking conditions by the old-timers, is in process of resurrection. Its towns are now linked with the Bass Highway in the north by the Zeehan, Murchison and Waratah Highways and the original road to Hobart, the Lyell Highway, has been substantially re-engineered and improved. Only relatively short stretches of the Zeehan and Lyell Highways remain unsealed. Any ordinarily competent motorist can negotiate them without difficulty.

A trip on the West Coast road circuit, which traverses mountain and forest country of unsurpassed grandeur, is unforgettable. There is only one catch—like the south-west the area is subject to exceptionally heavy rainfall, even in summer and autumn, and the chance to enjoy the best of the scenery is to some extent a matter of luck.

QUEENSTOWN

(Population 4 984)

By far the largest settlement on the coast, Queenstown is 254 kilometres north-west of Hobart. It is a rather pleasant but nondescript town of considerable prosperity, overshadowed by its fantastic environment of brightly stained, naked hills. Originally these hills were covered by forest and dense undergrowth, but when smelters were installed towards the turn of the century to treat the copper ore from the nearby Mount Lyell mine, the big timber was cut for fuel and sulphur fumes from the treatment plant completely denuded the slopes of the remaining vegetation. The heavy rain washed away the topsoil and the skeletal rocks were stained in hues of chrome yellow, purple, grey and pink. Since 1922 when the ore concentration process was changed and the fumes eliminated there has been a slow regeneration of plant cover.

Since 1896 the Lyell mines have produced more than half a million tons of copper, 16 million ounces of silver and 600 000 ounces of gold. Modern prospecting methods recently established the existence of large reserves of low grade copper ore in close proximity to the ore bodies already worked by open cut. These discoveries and advanced mining and treatment techniques have almost indefinitely prolonged the life of the mines which would otherwise have been closed before 1980.

The great open cut at West Lyell is nearly 12 000 metres long, 6 000 metres wide and 185 metres deep.

Average rainfall in the district exceeds 300 centimetres a year.

History. Although the coastal area around Macquarie Harbour, 29 kilometres away, had been used as a penal settlement from 1823 to 1834 and the prospectors, Conrad Lynch and Thomas Currie, had discovered payable gold in Lynch Creek in 1881, the Queenstown mineral field was not discovered till 1883. In that year, William and Michael McDonaugh pegged out a gold claim in the area. They waited two years before they made a strike on the outcrop of the original Mt Lyell mine. They worked the mine only for gold until 1891 when the existence of copper pyrites was recognized. A syndicate comprising the Karlson brothers, James Crotty, William Dixon and F. O. Murphy formed the Mount Lyell Mining and Railway Company in Melbourne and in 1896 production of blister copper started. In 1897 the township was proclaimed and named after Queen Victoria.

By 1901 Queenstown was the third-largest town in the State with a population of 5 051. Two years later the assets of the Mount Lyell Mining Company amalgamated with its rival the North Mount Lyell Company.

Places of Interest. **Stricht Library.** Built in 1924 and named in honour of R. C. Stricht, one of the early managers of the company. **Linda.** Ghost township on the Lyell Highway. Originally the thriving headquarters of the Lyell Mining Company, a railway connected the township with Kelly's Basin on Macquarie Harbour and continued to haul timber until 1925. **Frenchman's Cap National Park**—between Derwent Bridge and Queenstown, off Lyell Highway. 10 200 hectares dominated by the mountain (1 430 metres) with an unusual white rock formation on its crest which gives rise to the name.

Accommodation. Five **hotels.** Recommended: Four Seasons Motor Hotel; Empire Hotel. Two **motels. Caravan park,** Preston Street Reserve, all facilities.

Transport. Scheduled **air** service to aerodrome. **Car rentals:** One firm. **Taxis.**

STRAHAN (Population 426)

The only developed port on the West Coast, Strahan is 44 kilometres from Queenstown at the northern extremity of Macquarie Harbour. The use of the port facilities is limited to ships of shallow draught because of the formidable bar at the mouth of the harbour. The entrance, known as Hell's Gates, is extremely difficult to negotiate in rough weather. The Strahan wharves handle freight to and from Queenstown mines and occasional shipments of timber. A few crayfishing boats also use the port as a base.

The little town is used as a seaside resort by West Coasters, for there is a large ocean beach to the west, good fishing is to be had in the inlet itself and **launch trips** can be made for a considerable distance up the **Gordon River** which cuts through spectacular mountain country covered by rain forest.

History. The first recorded entry into the landlocked Macquarie Harbour was made in 1815 by explorer James Kelly after whom Kelly Bay is named. In 1821 Governor Sorell decided to establish a penal settlement on the West Coast and dispatched two ships with 74 convicts later the same year. Sarah Island, which had been named by Kelly (later it became Settlement Island) was chosen as the prison site. The settlement, however, lasted barely more than a decade. It was too difficult to supply. In 1834 it was abandoned and the convicts transferred to Port Arthur. In January the brig *Frederick* sailed out of the harbour with the last load of convicts. The convicts seized the ship and sailed her to South America, but were later retaken and condemned to death.

Macquarie Harbour was deserted for more than 40 years until the prospector, Conrad Lynch, prospected the King River and discovered gold. Timber getters also moved in and a village was established at Strahan. It became a loading point for ships carrying Huon pine logged in the Gordon River forests.

The copper boom at the Mt Lyell mine greatly accelerated Strahan's development. When the Strahan-Zeehan railway was opened in 1892, the village became a busy port. It was named after Major Sir George Strahan (Governor of Tasmania, 1881-6). It was proclaimed a town in the same year.

Seven years later, in 1899, the Mt Lyell rack railway forged the link between the port and the mine. In two years, 1900 and 1901, the value of cargo which passed through Strahan exceeded that handled by any other Australian port. In 1908 the municipality of Strahan was proclaimed.

Places of Interest. Settlement Island, ruins of penal establishment, maintained by Scenery Preservation Board. **Isle of Condemned. Marble Cliffs,** 32 kilometres from mouth of Gordon River, reached by launch. **Ocean Beach,** six kilometres from township, 40 kilometres of surf. **Port and post offices,** stone buildings built during the copper boom.

Accommodation. Three **hotels.** Recommended: Hamer's. Three **camping and caravan areas,** no facilities except water and fireplaces.

ZEEHAN (Population 1 476)

Until the late 1960s, when the interest of mining companies was aroused by encouraging prospects made in the district by modern methods and the big tin mine at Renison Bell was reopened, Zeehan was a ghost town. Seventy years ago, however, the settlement was the third-largest in Tasmania with a population of more than 10 000. New life has now been infused into the municipality by a housing project to accommodate workers at **Renison Bell,** 17 kilometres north, and by the hope that the new highway connecting the district with the Bass Highway to the north will stimulate agriculture in a fertile tract of country between the town and Granville Harbour to the west, and revitalize a declining timber industry. Zeehan is 38 kilometres north-west of Queenstown and 7 kilometres west of the Murchison Highway.

History. In 1882 rich silver-lead ore was discovered by prospectors hoping to find another Mount Bischoff. Within six years the Zeehan-Dundas area was inundated with miners and the boom had begun.

In 1890 the small exposed port of Trial Harbour was considered inadequate to handle mine traffic and a railway was built to connect Zeehan with the port at Strahan. The following year there were 159 companies or syndicates working in the area.

The great depression of the early 1890s curtailed many operations but the setback was temporary. By 1898 a smelting plant had been installed and was processing over 20 000 tons of ore annually.

However, by 1908, the mines began to decline. Payable ore was not discovered below 180 metres and the smelters were closed down just before the beginning of the first world war.

Places of Interest. Gaiety Theatre (now dark!) In the boom years the largest legitimate theatre in Australia. Nellie Melba and many other famous opera stars sang from its stage. **West Coast Pioneers' Memorial Museum.** Excellent small collection of mineral specimens from the Tasmanian mines and from overseas. **Trial Harbour,** 19 kilometres west on tertiary road, offers good sea fishing.

Accommodation. Two **hotels.** Preferred: Cecil.

ROSEBERY (Population 2 381)

Rosebery, lying on the Pieman River 29 kilometres north-east of Zeehan, is dependent on the Electrolytic Zinc Company's working of ore bodies from which zinc, lead and smaller quantities of silver, gold and cadmium are extracted. Eight kilometres south-west at Williamsford starts a spectacular system of aerial bucket conveyors which feed the ore from the mine into the refinery. Five kilometres west, reached by a passable bush track, are the **Montezuma Falls,** the highest waterfall in the State. The township is dominated by Mount Murchison (1 256 metres) to the east.

History. Ore was discovered at Mount Read in 1894, but the high zinc content prevented successful lead smelting until metallurgical problems were solved. The mines were not worked profitably until they were reopened by the Electrolytic Zinc Company in 1936.

Accommodation. One **hotel.**

WARATAH (Population 216)

About seven kilometres from the junction of the Murchison and Waratah Highways, Waratah was the site of the first mining bonanza in Tasmania. Today it is a lonely, bleak little settlement in mountain heathland, but in 1900 it had a population of 2 000, most of them dependent on the workings at Mount Bischoff, then the richest tin mine in the world.

The Bischoff deposits were discovered in 1872 by James 'Philosopher' Smith, one of the most colourful characters on the coast in the old days. Mount Bischoff Tin Mining Company was formed in 1873 and issued 12 000 £5 shares (of which only £1 was ever called up). Ten years later the shares were quoted at £92 on the London Stock Exchange. By the time the mines were closed in 1935, dividends totalled £200 for every £1 of original investment.

In 1878 a wooden tramway drawn by horses carried ore concentrates to Burnie, but six years later it was replaced by a steam railway.

During the tin famine of the second world war the workings were reopened but abandoned again when the price of tin dropped.

The area is again being intensively prospected for tin and other minerals. A rich tin lode has been discovered at **Mount Cleveland,** several kilometres to the south-east and a model township built to accommodate mine workers at **Luina.** The Cleveland mine came into production at the beginning of 1968.

A new, excellently engineered and sealed road now connects the Waratah Highway with Luina and the open-cut iron mines at **Savage River,** about 40 kilometres from Waratah township.

The Savage River ore deposits were discovered in 1877, but the ore is of relatively low grade and extraction and shipment was uneconomic because of the extremely rugged terrain. In 1965, however, a consortium of American, Japanese and Australian companies conducted a survey and decided that the ore could be profitably treated and shipped to Japanese markets by a revolutionary method. The crude material is quarried, crushed to a fine powder, mixed with water and pumped by a pipeline 86 kilometres to Port Latta, east of Stanley on the north coast. There it is settled, magnetically treated to separate the waste from the iron, which is then made into high-grade pellets for use in blast furnaces.

The development of the project cost about $A72 million. It is estimated that it will contribute about $A400 million to Tasmanian export earnings over 20 years. The first shipments of pellets from the port began in 1968. Berthing for ships of 65 000 tonnes has been provided.

A model town to accommodate 1 500 has been built near the mine site. The new road continues beyond it to **Corinna,** a small settlement on the spectacularly wild and beautiful Pieman River not far from its mouth to which a daily launch service runs. Corinna was once the centre of alluvial mining for osmiridium.

The route from Waratah to Corinna passes through a variety of magnificent scenery, but again high rainfall is a disadvantage to sightseers with schedules to observe.

Accommodation. At Waratah, one **hotel.** At Savage River, one **motel.** At Corinna, several holiday **cabins.**

South Australia

Of all the Australian States, South Australia is the least bountifully endowed by nature. Its area is just under 100 000 000 hectares and of this about two-thirds, above 32° South latitude, is desert or near desert which receives low and erratic rainfall.

The terrain is generally of low relief, half the land surface lying less than 160 metres above sea level. The northern plains are either sandy or covered by gibber (small, weathered rocks), with large areas of salt lake pans containing water only when exceptional rains have fallen in their catchment areas to the north and east. The biggest is Lake Eyre, 11 metres below sea level, fed intermittently by the Finke, Diamantina and Cooper Rivers, one of the largest inland drainage areas in the world.

The major mountain system includes the Mount Lofty and Flinders Ranges extending from Kangaroo Island (a part of the system) and the tip of the Yorke Peninsula 800 kilometres northward to the northern end of Lake Torrens. The highest peak in the Mount Lofty Ranges, Mount Lofty is 707 metres and Mount Mary's Peak in the Flinders Ranges is just under 1 200 metres. The slope of the mountains is gentle on the east and fairly steep on the west. They have pronounced effect on rainfall.

In the western half of the State there is a series of low ranges, running more or less parallel with the Northern Territory border, of which the most prominent are the Warburtons and the Musgraves. Mount Woodroffe, 1 496 metres, is the highest point here and in the entire State. There are large iron ore deposits in the hill country behind Whyalla, and the Eyre Peninsula to the south receives sufficient rainfall for good crops of wheat and barley.

A few isolated volcanic peaks occur in the extreme south-east, where pockets of highly fertile land are exceptional and the general configuration of terrain prevents agriculture and encourages pastoral use.

The Murray is South Australia's only major river. It flows on the eastern side of the Mount Lofty-Flinders mountain chain and discharges into shallow, heavily silted Lake Alexandrina and Lake Albert. The coastline is deeply indented by St Vincent's and Spencer Gulfs which in effect separate the eastern third of productive land in the State from the western two thirds.

ECONOMY In spite of the high industrialization of the metropolitan area of Adelaide and the heavy industrial development at Port Pirie and Whyalla, South Australia's economy remains basically agrarian. Only about 4 850 000 hectares of 61 million hectares of rural holdings are devoted to cropping or to permanent improved pastures. There is an important irrigated area on the Murray near Renmark, used mainly for horticulture and growing of grapes and fruit. Eighty per cent of the cropped area of the State grows wheat, barley and oats, and five per cent produces fodder crops. The remainder is devoted to orchards, vineyards and market gardens.

South Australia has 43 per cent of the Commonwealth's vineyards. It is famous for its quality wines and its irrigation areas produce almost all Australia's dried apricots, peaches, pears, nectarines and figs.

So far the State provides a high percentage of the Commonwealth's requirements in industrial salt. Gypsum is also an important mineral export.

The opal fields of Coober Pedy and Andamooka account for almost all current production of this gemstone which is growing in value and popularity, particularly in Asia.

The entire South Australian coastline is fished commercially, but not yet either scientifically or intensively.

The climate of coastal regions is temperate in the south and south-east, warm to hot in the south-west and extremely hot during the summer months in the north.

DISCOVERY AND SETTLEMENT The first Englishman to examine the shores of St Vincent Gulf was Matthew Flinders who made a survey of the whole South Australian coast in 1801 and 1802. Charles Sturt made his great journey down the Murray River in 1829 and 1830, news of which reached England towards the end of 1830. The following year Captain Collet Barker followed up the primary explorations, examined Port Adelaide inlet, climbed Mount Lofty and confirmed that there was good land along the western shore of the Gulf as well as at the mouth of the river.

Meanwhile the Australian colonies were provoking vigorous debate in London. Among those who became intensely interested in their prospects and problems was Edward Gibbon Wakefield, an economic philosopher who, despite the questionable nature of his private life, exercised considerable influence on the thinking of powerful people in Britain.

After a prolonged study (made while in Newgate Goal) of the colonial records to that date, Wakefield developed the theory that the difficulties being experienced by New South Wales and Van Diemen's Land were attributable to the ease with which land could be obtained by emancipists (ex-convicts) and new settlers. This, he argued, created a labour shortage which prevented the proper exploitation of the country's resources and made it unattractive for capital investment. The Australian colonies would never succeed while they were simply communities of small, struggling, peasant farmers. Furthermore, convict labour was proving just as wasteful and inefficient as slave labour, so that nothing would be solved by simply increasing the transportation of convicts.

Wakefield urged that land should be made available only to men with capital. He suggested that the Government should charge about £2 an acre instead of making free grants. This would ensure that both emancipists and free labourers who emigrated would have to remain as employees for a number of years before they could save enough to set up farms of their own. Such a system would be an incentive to capitalists and the revenues generated by land sales could be used both for public developmental works and to provide financial assistance for labourers and tradesmen who wished to emigrate.

The theory gained a good deal of support among influential men, but it was apparent that it could be tried out fairly only in a completely new Australian colony, unencumbered by the disadvantages of the old system.

The discoveries of Flinders, Sturt and Barker indicated that a suitable area to test Wakefield's ideas existed on St Vincent Gulf. The Colonial Office was by no means happy with the project, but after prolonged negotiation the South Australian Company was formed, sufficient capital raised, and a beginning made with the novel enterprise. Administrative control of the new colony was vested in a Board of Commissioners in London who were to be responsible for the sale of land and the expenditure of the money raised. Wakefield himself was not satisfied with this adaptation of his scheme, but his objections did not prevail.

Lieutenant-Colonel William Light was appointed Surveyor-General and dispatched from England with two surveying vessels in May 1836, charged with the task of selecting a site for the capital.

Light was an unusually capable man. He made a rapid, efficient reconnaissance, chose the site of Adelaide and began the work of laying out the town. Unhappily others associated with the venture were of less calibre. The Surveyor-General finished his town survey by March 1837, but his staff was completely inadequate to carry out the farm surveys necessary before sales of agricultural and pastoral land could be conducted. Hundreds of settlers were arriving who could find neither land nor employment.

Light appealed to the Board of Commissioners for help but, like so many bureaucrats, they had no conception of the problems faced by the men in the field and they accused Light of inefficiency. He and his staff promptly resigned —but not before they had set out a plan for a truly model town.

One of Light's bitterest enemies was Governor Hindmarsh who arrived in the colony after the site for the capital had been chosen. He wished to remove to Encounter Bay. The representative of the Board, Resident Commissioner Fisher, sided with Light and the entire establishment of officials and colonists took sides. So many scandalous threats were made and so many violent public quarrels occurred that both Hindmarsh and Fisher were recalled and George Gawler was appointed both Governor and Resident Commissioner.

Gawler attacked the practical problems vigorously, instituted a system of relief work in town for the unemployed and speeded up rural surveys. Lack of basic organization had, however, done the damage and by August 1840 the Wakefield colony was bankrupt.

The British Government could not let the colonists starve. It decided to take over South Australia and run it in exactly the same way as New South Wales, Van Diemen's Land or Western Australia. A new Governor, George Grey, who had had West Australian experience, was appointed. He proved an admirable if unpopular Governor, ruthlessly increasing hours of work, slashing expenditures and increasing taxes. In spite of furious demonstrations against him, the British Government backed Grey and at last his tough policy succeeded. By firmly forcing down the price of labour, he gave the farmers a chance to establish themselves. By 1843 the area of cultivated land had increased from 2 500 acres to 30 000 acres and the value of exports had risen from £15 600 to £66 000. Unemployment was beaten by the end of 1842 and by 1845 the economy of the new colony was on a sound basis, with wheat and sheep farming established and mineral resources on the verge of profitable exploitation.

Pastoralists controlling large areas of land were much less influential in South Australia than elsewhere in Australia so that much more arable land was readily available for cereal cropping. By 1880 nearly half the farming land in all Australia was in South Australia.

Of course attempts were made to farm semi-arid land which was suitable, in the long run, only for grazing. Drought ruined many over-confident farmers in the last half of the 19th century and the beginning of the 20th century (although agricultural science has now perfected methods of farming semi-arid areas which 50 years ago were fit only for light grazing). Even so, without

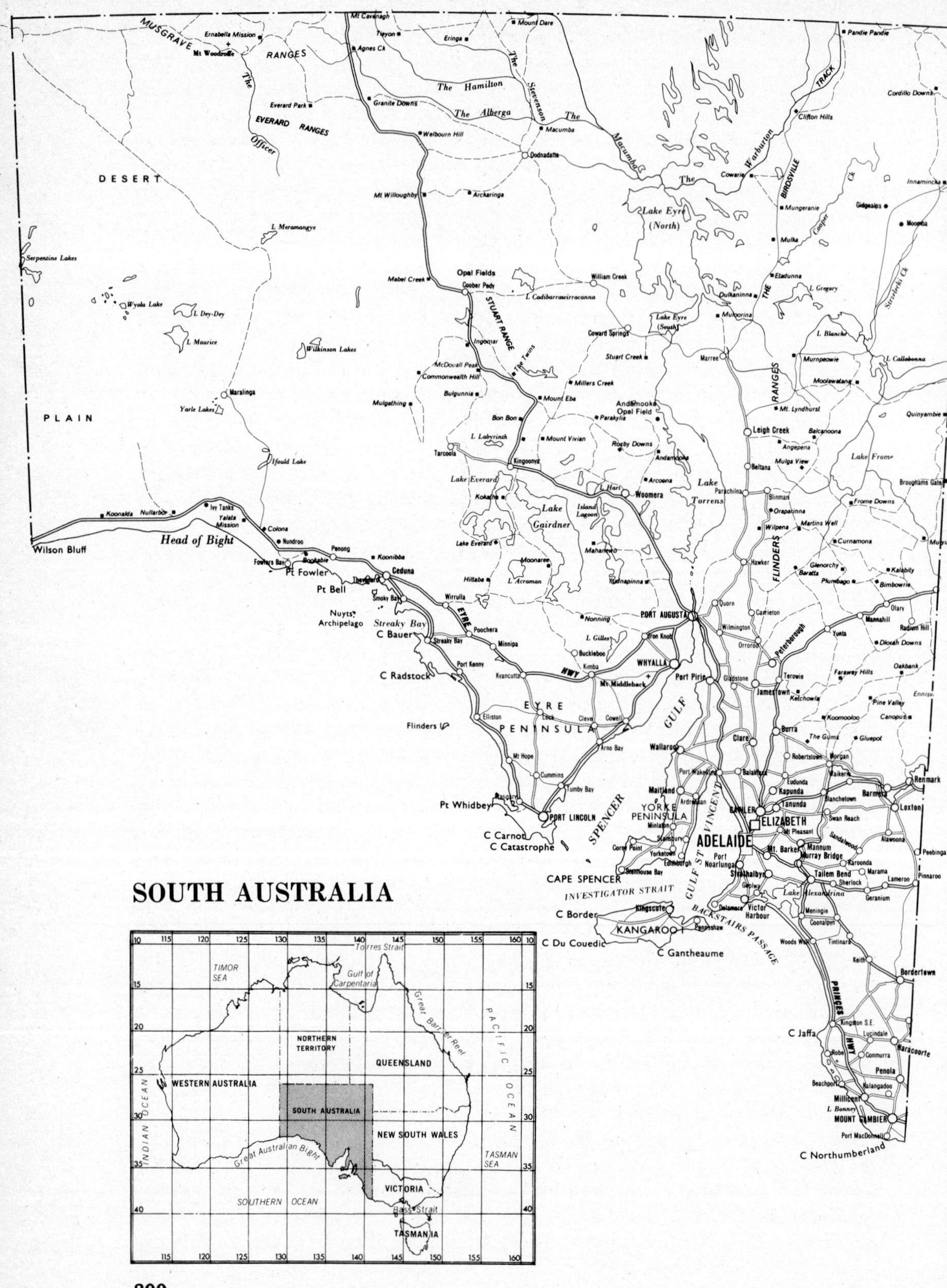
MUSGRAVE RANGES
Ernabella Mission
Mt Woodroffe
Mt Cavenagh
Mount Dare
Agnes Ck
Eringa
Pandie Pandie
The Officer
EVERARD RANGES
Everard Park
Granite Downs
The Hamilton
The Alberga
The Stevenson
The Macumba
Macumba
Welbourn Hill
Oodnadatta
Cordillo Downs
Clifton Hills
THE BIRDSVILLE TRACK
The Warburton
Cowarie
Innamincka
DESERT
Mt Willoughby
Arckaringa
Lake Eyre (North)
Mungeranie
Cooper Ck
Gidgealpa
Moomba
L Meramangye
Mulka
Serpentine Lakes
Mabel Creek
Opal Fields
Coober Pedy
William Creek
Etadunna
Wyola Lake
L Dey-Dey
L Maurice
Wilkinson Lakes
STUART RANGE
L Cadibarrawirracanna
Lake Eyre (South)
Dulkaninna
Mulorina
L Gregory
Strzelecki Ck
Ingomar
Coward Springs
L Blanche
McDouall Peak
Commonwealth Hill
The Twins
Stuart Creek
Marree
Murnpeowie
L Callabonna
Maralinga
Yarle Lakes
Bulgunnia
Millers Creek
Moolawatana
Mulgathing
Mount Eba
Andamooka Opal Field
Mt. Lyndhurst
PLAIN
Bon Bon
Parakylia
Quinyambie
L Labyrinth
Mount Vivian
Roxby Downs
Leigh Creek
Balcanoona
Tarcoola
Angepena
Ifould Lake
Kingoonya
Andamooka
Beltana
Mulga View
Lake Frome
Lake Everard
Arcoona
Lake Torrens
Kokatha
L Hart
Woomera
Parachilna
Blinman
Broughams Gate
Koonalda
Nullarbor
Ivy Tanks
Yalata Mission
Lake Gairdner
Island Lagoon
Oraparinna
Frome Downs
Colona
Wilpena
Martins Well
Head of Bight
Nundroo
Lake Everard
Mahanewo
Curnamona
Wilson Bluff
Penong
Koonibba
Moonaree
Hawker
FLINDERS RANGES
Glenorchy
Baratta
Kalabity
Fowlers Bay
Bookabie
Pt Fowler
Ceduna
Thevenard
Hiltaba
L Acraman
Yudnapinna
Plumbago
Bimbowrie
Pt Bell
Smoky Bay
Wirrulla
Quorn
Olary
Nuyts Archipelago
Streaky Bay
Poochera
Nonning
PORT AUGUSTA
Wilmington
Carrieton
Mannahill
Radium Hill
C Bauer
EYRE HWY
Minnipa
L Gilles
Iron Knob
Orroroo
Peterborough
Yunta
Dlorah Downs
Streaky Bay
Buckleboo
Port Kenny
Kimba
WHYALLA
Port Pirie
Terowie
Faraway Hills
Oakbank
C Radstock
Kyancutta
Mt Middleback
Gladstone
Jamestown
Ketchowla
Pine Valley
EYRE PENINSULA
Elliston
Lock
Cleve
Cowell
GULF
Koomooloo
Canopus
Flinders I
Arno Bay
Burra
The Gums
Gluepot
Wallaroo
Clare
Mt Hope
Robertstown
Morgan
Cummins
Port Wakefield
Balaklava
Eudunda
Waikerie
Renmark
Tumby Bay
SPENCER
Maitland
Kapunda
Blanchetown
Barmera
Pt Whidbey
Coulta
PORT LINCOLN
YORKE PENINSULA
ST VINCENT
Ardrossan
GAWLER
Tanunda
Loxton
Minlaton
ELIZABETH
Swan Reach
C Carnot
C Catastrophe
Stansbury
Mt Pleasant
ADELAIDE
Sandalwood
Alawoona
Corny Point
Yorketown
Edithburgh
Port Noarlunga
Mt. Barker
Mannum
Murray Bridge
Karoonda
Peebinga
Stenhouse Bay
Strathalbyn
Tailem Bend
Marama
Pinnaroo
CAPE SPENCER
Goolwa
Lake Alexandrina
Sherlock
Lameroo
INVESTIGATOR STRAIT
GULF ST VINCENT
Victor Harbour
Geranium
SOUTH AUSTRALIA
C Border
Kingscote
Delamere
BACKSTAIRS PASSAGE
Meningie
KANGAROO I
Penneshaw
Coonalpyn
C Du Couedic
C Gantheaume
Woods Well
Tintinara
Keith
Bordertown
PRINCES HWY
C Jaffa
Kingston S.E.
Lucindale
Naracoorte
Robe
Coonawarra
Penola
Beachport
Kalangadoo
Millicent
L Bonney
MOUNT GAMBIER
Port MacDonnell
C Northumberland
Torres Strait
TIMOR SEA
Gulf of Carpentaria
Great Barrier Reef
PACIFIC OCEAN
NORTHERN TERRITORY
QUEENSLAND
WESTERN AUSTRALIA
INDIAN OCEAN
SOUTH AUSTRALIA
NEW SOUTH WALES
Great Australian Bight
TASMAN SEA
VICTORIA
SOUTHERN OCEAN
Bass Strait
TASMANIA
10
15
20
25
30
35
40
115
120
125
130
135
140
145
150
155
160

the benefit of today's specialized knowledge, by 1900 South Australia led Australia in agriculture and was at the same time a substantial wool producer.

TOURING IN SOUTH AUSTRALIA In the south and south-east of the States roads are, on the whole, well engineered and maintained. In the north and the extreme west they are very bad and traversed only by motorists itching for adventure or on urgent business. The Eyre Highway to Western Australia beyond Ceduna is being improved but the roads north of Marree and Port Augusta to Alice Springs in the Northern Territory are still very rough. They are clearly defined, graded, but little more can be said in their favour.

The range of attractions for tourists in South Australia itself is not as great as in other States but scenery in the Flinders Ranges has a quality of grandeur and individuality quite different from that of other inland mountain systems of Australia. The Barossa Valley near Adelaide is scenically charming, as are many other localities in the Mount Lofty Ranges, and the south-west contains some extremely beautiful river, lake and forest country. Lovers of the sea will be well satisfied by time spent on the southern coast of Eyre Peninsula and on the western end of Kangaroo Island, and big game fishermen who take the the sport seriously should investigate the potential of the waters offshore from Port Lincoln to Ceduna—the home of giant white sharks and large tuna. Less ambitious fishermen will also find the sport good.

The most rewarding time to visit South Australia is in spring and early summer when the countryside is at its best.

PUBLIC TRANSPORT **Air.** Trans Australia Airlines and Ansett Airlines of Australia operate frequent daily flights to and from eastern State capitals, and from Perth. Ansett Airlines of South Australia runs scheduled daily services from Adelaide to Port Lincoln, Kangaroo Island, Whyalla; to Broken Hill on Tuesday, Thursday, Friday and Sunday; to Ceduna via Port Lincoln on Monday and Thursday. Charter flights run to Woomera, Monday to Friday inclusive.

Road. Pioneer, Greyhound and Panther coaches run daily services between Adelaide and Melbourne. Panther and Pioneer together provide a daily service between Adelaide and Mildura and Adelaide and Mount Gambier. Australian-Pacific Coaches run tours to Perth across the Nullarbor Plain on the Eyre Highway, and Pioneer to Alice Springs on the Stuart Highway.

Rail. The **Overlander** overnight express runs daily to Melbourne and the **Transcontinental** on Monday, Wednesday, Thursday and Saturday to Perth. On Tuesday and Friday, connections may be made with the **Indian-Pacific** (Sydney-Perth) at Port Augusta or Port Pirie. **The Ghan** express to Alice Springs runs twice a week.

Sea. Two small **motor ships,** the *Troubridge* and the *Philanderer*, operate a ferry service for passengers, vehicles and freight between Port Adelaide and Kangaroo Island twice a week in winter and three times a week in summer.

ADELAIDE

(Population 842 611)

Adelaide, South Australia's capital, is situated on the Torrens River, between the Mount Lofty Ranges and the Gulf of St Vincent. Despite its rapid growth during 30 years, it retains an atmosphere of spacious, unhurried living and the social character of a large, prosperous country town—often quaintly parochial, stratified and orientated to provincial rather than urban standards. Nevertheless the community is vigorous and industrially enterprising and has a strong civic pride which is reflected in the excellence of its parks and gardens and the care with which public and commercial buildings are maintained.

The soil of the coastal plain on which the city is sited is good, but the average annual rainfall, slightly over 5 centimetres, is lower than that of any other Australian capital. The climate generally is conducive to comfortable living, although severe heatwaves are occasionally experienced in the height of summer when temperatures above 38°C are recorded for several consecutive days. The mean for February, the hottest month, is 23°C and for July, the coldest, about 12°C.

The nearby ranges, which rise abruptly from the flat land, are wooded on their steeper slopes but cultivated or planted with a variety of European trees in the valleys. Adelaide's hills, like Melbourne's Dandenong Ranges, are well populated without having become urbanized. They are scenically delightful at all seasons, but particularly so in early spring and late autumn.

For many years Adelaide had the reputation of being a city which had virtually no night life and became entirely comatose at the weekends. During the 1960s there was a pleasantly surprising transformation, caused largely by the abolition of puritanical licencing laws affecting the service of wines and and other alcoholic beverages in restaurants and places of public entertainment. As in other Australian cities, European migration also has had an enlivening effect. Adelaide has made a resounding success of the 'festival' idea. Every second year (the years of even numbers) it organizes a festival of concert, opera, ballet, drama, art, literature and light entertainment which brings thousands of visitors from other States and even from overseas.

Another highly successful public celebration in Adelaide is the John Martin Christmas Pageant, held on the morning of the first or second Saturday in November—a street parade of floats depicting nursery book characters and carrying bands and clowns to hail the arrival of Santa Claus.

Apart from the entertainment and diversion the city itself has to offer, Adelaide is, of course, a convenient starting place for tours of Central Australia, the fascinating Flinders Ranges, and the lower Murray Valley.

COMMERCE AND INDUSTRY For the first century of its life Adelaide was, apart from its administrative function, primarily the commercial and service centre of grain, wool, fruit and wine growing regions. Its industrialization has occurred very rapidly over the last quarter century since the establishment of large automobile manufacturing plants and vehicle body-making works. These and associated specialist industries manufacturing electrical equipment,

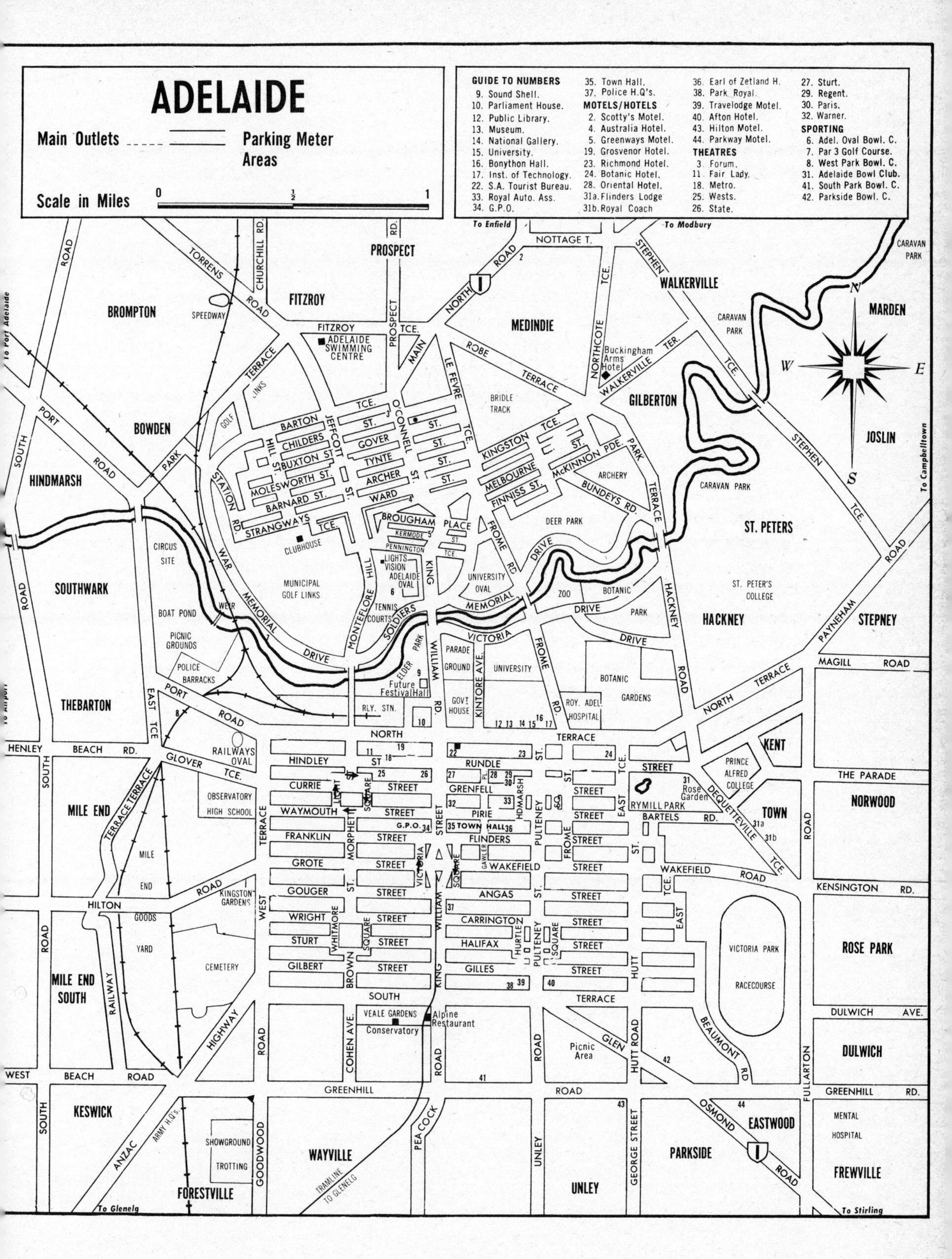
ADELAIDE
Main Outlets
Parking Meter Areas
Scale in Miles
0
½
1
GUIDE TO NUMBERS
9. Sound Shell.
10. Parliament House.
12. Public Library.
13. Museum.
14. National Gallery.
15. University.
16. Bonython Hall.
17. Inst. of Technology.
22. S.A. Tourist Bureau.
33. Royal Auto. Ass.
34. G.P.O.
35. Town Hall.
37. Police H.Q's.
MOTELS/HOTELS
2. Scotty's Motel.
4. Australia Hotel.
5. Greenways Motel.
19. Grosvenor Hotel.
23. Richmond Hotel.
24. Botanic Hotel.
28. Oriental Hotel.
31a. Flinders Lodge
31b. Royal Coach
36. Earl of Zetland H.
38. Park Royal.
39. Travelodge Motel.
40. Afton Hotel.
43. Hilton Motel.
44. Parkway Motel.
THEATRES
3. Forum.
11. Fair Lady.
18. Metro.
25. Wests.
26. State.
27. Sturt.
29. Regent.
30. Paris.
32. Warner.
SPORTING
6. Adel. Oval Bowl. C.
7. Par 3 Golf Course.
8. West Park Bowl. C.
31. Adelaide Bowl Club.
41. South Park Bowl. C.
42. Parkside Bowl. C.
To Enfield
To Modbury
To Port Adelaide
To Campbelltown
To Airport
To Glenelg
To Stirling
PROSPECT
FITZROY
BROMPTON
MEDINDIE
WALKERVILLE
GILBERTON
MARDEN
BOWDEN
HINDMARSH
JOSLIN
ST. PETERS
SOUTHWARK
HACKNEY
STEPNEY
THEBARTON
KENT
TOWN
NORWOOD
MILE END
ROSE PARK
MILE END SOUTH
DULWICH
KESWICK
WAYVILLE
UNLEY
PARKSIDE
EASTWOOD
FREWVILLE
FORESTVILLE
NOTTAGE T.
NORTH ROAD
TORRENS ROAD
CHURCHILL RD.
PROSPECT RD.
FITZROY TCE.
MAIN
LE FEVRE TCE.
ROBE TERRACE
NORTHCOTE TCE.
STEPHEN TCE.
WALKERVILLE TER.
Buckingham Arms Hotel
ADELAIDE SWIMMING CENTRE
SPEEDWAY
GOLF LINKS
BARTON
CHILDERS
BUXTON ST.
MOLESWORTH ST.
BARNARD ST.
STRANGWAYS TCE.
HILL ST.
JEFFCOTT ST.
GOVER ST.
TYNTE ST.
ARCHER ST.
WARD ST.
O'CONNELL ST.
BROUGHAM PLACE
KERMODE
PENNINGTON
KINGSTON TCE.
MELBOURNE ST.
FINNISS ST.
McKINNON PDE.
BUNDEYS RD.
PARK TERRACE
ARCHERY
BRIDLE TRACK
DEER PARK
CARAVAN PARK
PORT ROAD
PARK TCE.
STATION RD.
CLUBHOUSE
MUNICIPAL GOLF LINKS
LIGHTS VISION
ADELAIDE OVAL
TENNIS COURTS
MONTEFIORE HILL
KING WILLIAM RD.
UNIVERSITY OVAL
FROME RD.
ZOO
BOTANIC PARK
BOTANIC DRIVE
HACKNEY ROAD
ST. PETER'S COLLEGE
PAYNEHAM ROAD
MAGILL ROAD
CIRCUS SITE
WAR MEMORIAL DRIVE
WEIR
BOAT POND
PICNIC GROUNDS
POLICE BARRACKS
SOLDIERS MEMORIAL
ELDER PARK
Future Festival Hall
VICTORIA DRIVE
PARADE GROUND
UNIVERSITY
KINTORE AVE.
GOVT HOUSE
BOTANIC GARDENS
ROY. ADEL. HOSPITAL
RLY. STN.
NORTH TERRACE
EAST TCE.
RAILWAYS OVAL
HENLEY BEACH RD.
GLOVER TCE.
HINDLEY ST
RUNDLE STREET
CURRIE STREET
GRENFELL STREET
WAYMOUTH STREET
PIRIE STREET
FRANKLIN STREET
FLINDERS STREET
GROTE STREET
WAKEFIELD STREET
GOUGER STREET
ANGAS STREET
WRIGHT STREET
CARRINGTON STREET
STURT STREET
HALIFAX STREET
GILBERT STREET
GILLES STREET
SOUTH TERRACE
WEST TERRACE
LIGHT SQUARE
MORPHETT ST.
VICTORIA SQUARE
HINDMARSH SQUARE
HURTLE SQUARE
WHITMORE SQUARE
PULTENEY ST.
FROME ST.
HUTT ST.
TOWN HALL
G.P.O.
RYMILL PARK
BARTELS RD.
Rose Garden
PRINCE ALFRED COLLEGE
DEQUETTEVILLE TCE.
THE PARADE
WAKEFIELD ROAD
KENSINGTON RD.
VICTORIA PARK RACECOURSE
OBSERVATORY HIGH SCHOOL
KINGSTON GARDENS
HILTON
GOODS YARD
CEMETERY
RAILWAY
TERRACE
ANZAC HIGHWAY
VEALE GARDENS
Conservatory
Alpine Restaurant
COHEN AVE.
Picnic Area
GLEN OSMOND ROAD
HUTT ROAD
BEAUMONT RD.
FULLARTON ROAD
DULWICH AVE.
WEST BEACH ROAD
GREENHILL ROAD
GREENHILL RD.
SOUTH ROAD
GOODWOOD ROAD
ARMY H.Q's.
SHOWGROUND
TROTTING
PEACOCK ROAD
UNLEY ROAD
GEORGE STREET
TRAMLINE TO GLENELG
MENTAL HOSPITAL
N
S
E
W

parts and accessories, sheet metal, etc. provide employment for many thousands. Other manufactures include industrial chemicals, salt, plastics, agricultural equipment, textiles, clothing and footwear, pipes and tubes etc.

Port Adelaide on Largs Bay, 14 kilometres north-west of the city proper, accommodates vessels to about 10 000 tonnes. Industry is largely concentrated in the intervening area, the appearance of which is in startling contrast to the studied order and grace of the commercial quarter.

HISTORY The history of Adelaide is inextricably linked with the history of South Australia itself, a brief account of which has been given above. The city was named after Queen Adelaide, wife of King William IV. It is the oldest municipality in Australia, having been incorporated in 1840. Although its development has closely paralleled the development of pastoral and agricultural industries in the State, the discovery of the rich copper mines of Kapunda and the Yorke Peninsula in the mid-19th century proved a strong economic stimulus —as did the later exploitation of the great silver-lead-zinc deposits of Broken Hill. The economic affinity of Broken Hill and Adelaide is, because of geography, much closer than that of Broken Hill and Sydney so that Adelaide has benefited a great deal from the fabulous wealth of the outback mines.

The South Australian capital has some interesting Australian 'firsts'. Its Chamber of Commerce, founded in 1839, and its Chamber of Manufactures, established in 1869, were the first institutions of their kind in the colonies. In 1856 the first State-owned steam railway in the British Empire was opened between Adelaide and Port Adelaide. Adelaide was also the first Australian city to have a complete system of horsedrawn tramcars and, with completion of the overland telegraph to Darwin in 1872, was the first major Australian settlement to have a telegraph-cable link with London.

Adelaide was gazetted a city in 1919, when the population of the State was less than half a million.

Places of Interest

Festival Theatre, King William Street, ingeniously designed centre for the performing arts. First stage in March 1974. The whole complex, still being developed,will accommodate about 5 000.

All the following buildings are situated on North Terrace in the centre of the city:

Government House, in an expanse of gardens and lawns.

State War Memorial, bronze group by G. Rayner Hoff, set against marble.

Art Gallery of South Australia, with distinguished collection of paintings, ceramics, sculpture, coins etc. Open Monday to Saturday, 10 am to 5 pm. Sundays and holidays 2 pm to 5 pm.

State Library, housing about 200 000 volumes. Open Monday to Saturday, 9.30 am to 9.30 pm. Sunday 2 pm to 5.30 pm.

Museum of Natural History, with notable collection of Australian fauna and ethnological section. Open Monday to Saturday, 10 am to 5 pm, Sundays and public holidays, 2 pm to 5 pm.

National Gallery, art exhibits and Australia's best coin collection.

University of Adelaide, on landscaped 12 hectare site, with **Bonython Hall,** the great hall of the University named after its donor, Sir Langdon Bonython. Open to the public.

Parliament House, built of marble from Kapunda and grey granite from Victor Harbour. A plaque commemorates Edward Gibbon Wakefield.

Holy Trinity Church of England, built in 1838, the oldest church in South Australia. The town clock was made by the clock-maker to King William IV.

The following are in Pennington Terrace, North Adelaide:

St Peter's Anglican Cathedral, built of South Australian freestone. Fine peal of eight bells. Verger welcomes visitors, Monday, Tuesday, Thursday, Friday, 9 am to noon.

Light's Vision, on south side of Pennington Terrace, has statue of city's planner, Colonel William Light, and panoramic views of city.

Outback homestead

Shearers at work

Parks and Gardens

Central Adelaide, an area of 258 hectares, is surrounded by 688 hectares of parks, lakes, formal gardens and playing areas which are tended with great care. **Torrens Lake,** created by a weir across the Torrens River, divides the city proper from North Adelaide which has been built on high ground. It is surrounded by many charming reserves and is flanked along the river by a particularly beautiful boulevard, the **War Memorial Drive.**

Pinky Flat, a formal garden overlooking the lake.

Cresswell Gardens, on the approaches to Adelaide Oval, with a statue of the pioneer aviator, Sir Ross Smith.

Elder Park, on the slopes of the lake's southern banks, with a sound shell and bandstand for open air concerts. (Motor launches provide 20-minute cruises).

Pioneer Women's Memorial Gardens, with **Cross of Sacrifice,** a first world war memorial established by the women of South Australia.

Zoological Gardens, a good collection of animals in parkland setting. Open Monday to Saturday, 9.30 am to 5 pm, Sundays 10 am to 5 pm.

Botanic Garden and Botanic Park. The garden covers 16 hectares and has three large lakes inhabited by waterfowl; excellent collection of water lilies and lotus, other aquatics, cacti etc; rose garden, glasshouses. The park is planted as an arboretum. **Museum of Economic Botany,** in the garden, houses exhibits of plants and plant products from all over the world.

Rymill Park, east of Rundle and Grenfell Streets, contains boating lake, barbecue and picnic areas.

Veale Gardens, South Terrace, alpine type garden with small weirs and fountains and a fine conservatory.

Sports and Recreation

Adelaide's main public sports facilities are concentrated in the parklands north of Lake Torrens. There are two 18-hole public **golf courses** and a Par 3 chip-and-putt course (lighted at night) on Memorial Drive, north-west of the central city. There are several other club courses close to the city. The Memorial Drive **tennis courts** and stadium have been the venue of Davis Cup matches. They adjoin **Adelaide Oval,** where Sheffield Shield and Test **cricket** is played. Night **baseball** and **soccer,** and night or day **football** and **cricket** are played at Norwood Oval. There are **racecourses** at Morphetville (Glenelg tram), Cheltenham (train or bus) and Victoria Park, East Parklands. The **Olympic Sports Field** is at Kensington. **Night trotting** is held at Wayville Showgrounds. **Motor races** are held at Mallala (57 kilometres), Brompton (5 kilometres) and Virginia Speedway (29 kilometres). **Swimming.** At Adelaide Swimming Club, North Adelaide. **Sailing.** Eight clubs welcome visiting yachtsmen. Night **basketball** is played at Apollo Stadium, Richmond.

Entertainment

Five **theatres: Arts, Her Majesty's, Scott, Union** and **Q theatre.** One **theatre restaurant—Olde King's Music Hall.** Six **cinemas—My Fair Lady, Paris, Regent, State, Sturt, West's.**

Restaurants

Recommended: **Hotel Australia,** Brougham Place; **Asio's,** King William Street; **El Matador's,** Rundle Street; **The Copper Grill,** Parkroyal Motor Inn; **Arkaba Steak Cellar,** Gilbert Place; **Claridges,** Glen Osmond Road.

Accommodation

Seventeen residential **hotels** are listed in the Adelaide and North Adelaide city areas. Recommended: **Australia,** North Adelaide; **Regal Park,** Benton Terrace. There are seven listed **motels** in the city. Highly recommended: **Park Royal,** South Terrace; **Travelodge,** South Terrace.

There are many hotels and motels in the suburbs. Recommended suburban **hotels: St Leonard's Inn,** Glenelg; **Arkaba,** Glen Osmond Road, Fullarton; **Rex,** West Beach Road, Richmond; **Tonsley,** Clovelly Park. Recommended **motels: Commodore,** Glen Osmond; **Hilton,** Parkside. Main **caravan and camping parks:** Payneham Road, Glenbrook; West Beach (3 kilometres west of Adelaide Airport); Windsor Gardens, North East Road.

Department Stores

David Jones, Rundle Street; **Myer Emporium,** Rundle Street; **Big W,** Rundle Street.

Business Hours

Banks, 10 am to 3 pm Monday to Thursday; 10 am to 5 pm Friday.

Harvesting grapes, Barossa Valley, S.A.

Shops. 9 am to 5 pm Monday to Friday; 9 am to 11.30 am Saturday.
Time. South Australia is 30 minutes behind Eastern standard Time.

Miscellaneous

Travel Information. South Austrlian Tourist Bureau, 18 King William Street, Tel. 51-3281. **Royal Automobile Club of South Australia,** headquarters in Hindmarsh Square.
Emergencies. Police, tel. 8-0333; fire, tel. 23-3000; ambulance, tel. 46-1616.

Adelaide Suburbs

Places of Interest. Inner Western Suburbs: Bonython Park, West Parklands, with boating lakes, picnic ground. **Southwark Brewery Gardens.** Port Adelaide **Nautical Museum,** Vincent Street. **Snowdon's Beach,** west side of Port River, for speedboat racing. **Marineland of South Australia,** West Beach (performing seals, dolphins etc). **Largs Bay** and **Semaphore,** bathing beaches. **Fort Glanville,** South Australia's first fortification, built 1880, once a position for four heavy cannon commanding the Gulf, now surrounded by a caravan and camping park. **Captain Sturt's Cottage,** 'Grange', at Grange, a small seaside resort, built 1840, restored and now open during afternoons Wednesday to Sunday and public holidays. **Beach resorts** of Henley, West Beach Reserve (good sports facilities), Glenelg (landing place of Governor Hindmarsh and first colonists in 1836, marked by commemorative obelisk), Brighton and Seacliff. **Kingston Park,** with kiosk which is the old homestead of Sir George Kingston who arrived in South Australia in 1836. Built about 1840 and one of the oldest surviving buildings in the State. **Flinders University,** South Road, Bedford Park, opened 1966. **Inner Eastern and Southern Suburbs: Windy Point,** 9 kilometres south of the city with spectacular views, particularly at night. **Waterfall Gully,** Burnside. **Morialta Falls Reserve,** a beautiful gorge with graded walking tracks. **Waite Agricultural Research Institute,** Fullarton. **Penfold Vineyards** and Winery, beyond Kensington; inspection Monday to Thursday 2.30 pm. **Stonyfell Winery,** Stonyfell, inspection Wednesday 11 am. **Horsedrawn Vehicles Museum,** Magill Road, Maylands, opens Sunday 2 pm to 5 pm. **Electrical Transport Museum,** St Kilda, open Sunday 2 pm to 5 pm. **Aldersgate Village Community** for aged people, open to public.

ELIZABETH

(Population 50 000)

Elizabeth is a satellite town of Adelaide, designed on modern town planning principles, which was proclaimed in 1955 and named after Queen Elizabeth II. Although it is 28 kilometres north of the city it has been incorporated in the metropolitan area. It covers an area of about 2 580 hectares and has 566 hectares of parkland, including a common of 26 hectares. It has a large number of English and European migrants and is the fastest growing urban area in South Australia.

Secondary industries: Weapons research establishment, car assembly plant, factories making sewing machines, clothing and aluminium utensils, salt production works, bitumen works. The district beyond the built-up area has numerous market gardens and poultry farms and also produces wheat, wool, fat lambs, fodder crops and dairy produce.

Sports. Excellent facilities for all sports.

Accommodation. Four **hotels.** Recommended: Kariwara, Peachey Road. One recommended **motel.**

Transport. Rail and **road** services.

MOUNT LOFTY RANGES

Adelaide Hills. There are many delightful little towns and hamlets in the picturesque hill country north, south and east of Adelaide. Settlement dates back 130 years and there are many buildings of historic significance. Most convenient access is by the Main North East and Lower North East Roads, but there are many charming secondary roads into the gentle, wooded valleys which are at their scenic best in spring and late autumn.

Places of Interest. Mount Lofty summit (707 metres), highest point in the ranges, overlooking Piccadilly Valley, one of the finest lookouts in the State. **Old Toll House,** Glen Osmond, where Princes Highway enters the hills; tolls were collected between 1841 and 1846 to finance the construction of a road to Mount Barker. **Belair National Park,** 1 580 hectares of bush parkland, with picnic grounds, sports facilities etc; containing old Government House built as summer residence and occupied from 1860 to 1880; restored and contains museum of Victorian period household and workshop tools and horsedrawn vehicles. Open for inspection Wednesdays to Sunday and public holidays 1 pm to 4.30 pm (access by continuation of Unley Road). **Torrens Gorge Wildlife Park,** tame animals and birds, snake collection; access by scenic road passing Millbrook Reservoir. **Athelstone Wildflower Garden,** with displays of South African as well as Australian wildflowers, and some tame animals.

Open Sunday to Thursday. **Mount Bold and South Para Reservoirs,** Adelaide's largest water storages. **Para-Wirra National Park,** about 1 250 hectares of bush with lake, kiosk and picnic grounds, 40 kilometres from city via Modbury. Adjoining the park is **Humbug Scrub,** wildlife sanctuary.

Southern Vales district begins at O'Hallorhan Hill, 19 kilometres south of Adelaide and extends 20 kilometres through the Fleurieu Peninsula hinterland to Willimga. It is noted for its vineyards and the excellent red wines made at various wineries in or near the settlements of Reynella, Morphett Vale, McLaren Vale and McLaren Flat.

NORTHERN ENVIRONS

GAWLER

(Population 6 953)

Gawler is a prosperous and progressive town 40 kilometres north-north-east of Adelaide at the junction of the North and South Para Ranges, where they become the Gawler Range. The primary products of the surrounding district are wheat, fruit, wine grapes, wool, fat lambs, poultry, pigs and dairy produce. Secondary industries in town: Flour mill, agricultural machinery factory, clothing factory, iron foundries, dairy factories, winery, egg pulp plant and cement and clay brick works.

History. The area was examined by Colonel Light in 1837, and in 1839 land was allotted to a number of settlers. The township was surveyed and named after George Gawler, Governor and Resident Commissioner in South Australia from 1838 to 1841. It was proclaimed a municipality in 1857.The first locomotive made in South Australia was built in Gawler in 1890.

Places of Interest. **Roseworthy Agricultural College,** 11 kilometres north, one of the most respected agricultural schools in Australia. **Memorial** to explorer, John McKinlay.

Sports. Racecourse. Trotting track. Golf, tennis, bowls etc.

Accommodation. Two **hotels.** Recommended: Kingsford, Murray Street. **Caravan and camping park,** some facilities.

Transport. **Rail** and **road** services.

KAPUNDA (Population 1 301)

In the Mount Lofty Ranges north of the Barossa Valley, Kapunda is a small, attractively situated town 80 kilometres north of Adelaide. It serves a grain-growing and pastoral district and rock phosphate is mined nearby. Francis Dutton discovered copper ore in the locality in 1842 (the first copper strike in Australia), and a town grew up about the mines rapidly. It was proclaimed in 1848 and reached municipal status 20 years later. By 1886 water seeping into the lower levels of the mines became uncontrollable and they were closed. Agriculture was by then well established. The name Kapunda is derived from an aboriginal word meaning 'spring' or 'source of water'.

Accommodation. Two **hotels.** Recommended: Sir John Franklin. **Caravan and camping park,** all facilities.

Transport. **Road** and **rail** services.

BALAKLAVA (Population 1 111)

Balaklava is 90 kilometres north of Adelaide near the Wakefield River. The area grows grain and supports dairy cattle. There is a butter factory in town, which was founded originally near a ford over the river. Low-grade coal deposits have been discovered in the district but never mined. The town was proclaimed in 1877 and named for the Battle of Balaklava in the Crimean War.

Place of Interest. **The Rocks Reserve,** with a natural waterhole set between towering cliffs.

Accommodation. One **hotel.**

Transport. **Rail** and **road** services.

THE BAROSSA VALLEY

The Barossa Valley, one of the most important wine growing areas in Australia, begins about 48 kilometres north-east of Adelaide and extends for about 50 kilometres. Its average width is about 8 kilometres. It was named after the Barossa district of Andalusia, Spain. It is a gently beautiful area of vineyards, olive groves and orchards, charming at any time of year but especially so in spring when the vines are coming into leaf or the vintage time, from mid-

Feburary to the end of April, when thousands of colourfully clad grape pickers are at work with the harvest.

Twenty-five wineries in the valley and overlooking hills produce almost one-third of Australia's light table wines. The three principal towns, Tanunda, Angaston and Nuriootpa, as well as many smaller settlements such as Lyndoch and Rowland Flat, are built mainly in stone, have long-established plantations in their streets, and generally a much greater air of solid permanence than most Australian rural settlements. A majority of the early settlers were German immigrants who formed their communities around a Lutheran church of traditional design with square tower and belfry. Many of the wineries are also built in a style reminiscent of schloss architecture.

A Barossa Valley Wine Festival, featuring parades, concerts, traditional dances and historical re-enactments, is celebrated during vintage every second year (the years with odd numbers). It is possibly the most spontaneous and uncontrived of all such gatherings in Australia. The communities are noted for their social coherence and civic pride.

Coach tours of the Barossa Valley are run from Adelaide.

ANGASTON (Population 1 816)

Angaston is 78 kilometres north-east of Adelaide, just off the Sturt Highway. Besides wine-making and distilling, its industries include stone fruit canneries, flour mills, sawmills, a dried fruits packaging plant and a cement works. Fine marble is quarried in the hills nearby.

History. The Angaston district was visited by Colonel Light in 1837. Four years later it was selected by George Fife Angas, a pioneer colonist of the State, as suitable for settlement by German Lutheran migrants who had fled religious persecution in their own country. Angas provided financial help to the first immigrant group from Prussia and Silesia led by Pastor Augustus Kavel. In 1846 copper was found in the neighbourhood, but the ore bodies were mined for only a short period. Angas himself came in 1850 to live in the town named for him. The land was at first used for fruit growing and mixed farming, but a geologist, Johann Menge, pointed out that the soil was eminently suited for viticulture and the first vineyard was planted in 1847. Within 20 years production of wine grapes had become the main industry of the countryside. The town was first known as German Pass.

Place of Interest. The **Yalumba Wineries** are open for inspection from Monday to Friday at 11 am and 3 pm.

Accommodation. Two **hotels.** Preferred: Angaston. One recommended **motel.**

Transport. **Road** services, from Adelaide and local.

NURIOOTPA (Population 2 467)

On the North Para River and the Sturt Highway 72 kilometres from Adelaide, Nuriootpa is noted for the fact that the town is run largely on co-operative lines. A hotel, a department store and one of its large wineries are community-owned. The first vineyard in the vicinity was planted by Joseph Seppelt in 1851. It has now grown into the magnificent **Seppeltsfield estate,** with one of the largest family-owned wineries in the world. Two other great Australian vigneron families, the Penfolds and the Hardys, also have holdings in the area. The township was laid out in 1854 by William Couthard. The name is from the aboriginal word for 'meeting place'.

Places of Interest. **Barossa Co-operative Winery** (Kaiser Stuhl wines) open for inspection Monday to Friday (excepting public holidays) 10 am to 2.45 pm. **Penfold's Winery,** open for inspection Monday to Thursday 2.30 pm.

Sports. Golf course, Olympic swimming pool.

Accommodation. Two **hotels.** Recommended: Vine Inn. One recommended **motel. Caravan and camping park,** all facilities.

Transport. **Road** services.

TANUNDA (Population 1 936)

Tanunda is 66 kilometres from Adelaide, the oldest of the Barossa settlements. The district grows olives and some wool and the secondary industries of the town include fruit canning, an agricultural implement factory and several tanneries, but viticulture is its mainstay. There are nine wineries within a five kilometre radius. The first vines were planted at Rowland Flat, about three kilometres west, in

1847 by Johann Samuel Hoffman and Johann Gramp. Tanunda is the aboriginal name for 'water birds on a creek'.

Places of Interest. The **Langmeil** and the **Tabor,** the two oldest Lutheran churches in the valley. **Tanunda Historical Museum** open 1 pm to 3.30 pm, Sunday 2 pm to 4.30 pm. **Gramp's Orlando Cellars,** Rowland Flat, open Monday to Friday, 9.30 am, 11 am, 2 pm and 3.30 pm. **Chateau Yaldara,** Lyndoch (beyond Rowland Flat), open Monday to Friday, 10 am to 3 pm.

Brass band competitions are held every year in November.

Sports. Golf links near Rowland Flat.

Accommodation. Two **hotels.** Preferred: Tanunda, Murray Street.

Transport. **Road** services.

SOUTH COAST

The district south of Adelaide where the Mount Lofty Ranges run down to the sea is thoroughly interesting and varied country. There are good surf beaches on the coast, impressive coastal scenery, and fascinating tracts of lake and fenland with a tremendous population of waterfowl towards the mouth of the Murray. The region contrasts strongly with the northern and western parts of the State. It is a green, friendly land with few reminders that a vast, thirsty country begins just over the horizon. The south coast has been a favourite holiday place for South Australians for many years. It is now being actively developed for tourism, particularly in the Port Victor-Goolwa area.

Towns of the area include:

VICTOR HARBOUR (Population 3 533)

The largest and probably the most popular seaside resort on the coast, Victor Harbour is 84 kilometres south of Adelaide. It is bounded by the Hindmarsh and Inman Rivers and protected on the seaward side by Granite Island and The Bluff. It was in Encounter Bay that the British and French explorers, Matthew Flinders and Nicholas Baudin, met in 1802. In 1839 the town was named after HMS *Victor* by Captain Crozier, who later died on an expedition in search of the North West Passage from the Atlantic to the Pacific.

Places of Interest. **Museum of Historical Art,** Porter's Hill. **Cornhill Museum and Art Gallery,** Cornhill Road. **Hindmarsh Falls** off the road from Victor Harbour to Myponga via the Hindmarsh Valley. **Granite Island,** joined to the mainland by a causeway. (A tractor train takes visitors to and from the island from November to May.) There is a chair lift on the island itself. **Whalers Haven,** at Rosetta Bay, with a private collection of relics from the early days, special emphasis being laid on the whaling industry. **Glacier Rock** (13 kilometres north-east) exemplifying glacial erosion. **Cape Jervis,** overlooking Backstairs Passage between Kangaroo Island and the mainland, terminates the coast road. **Port Elliot,** a few kilometres north-east, the first port on Encounter Bay, with sheltered beach and scenic drive. An art pottery workshop is open for inspection.

Sports. Golf course, foreshore bowling greens and tennis courts. Aquatic sports.

Accommodation. Three **hotels.** Recommended: Victor, Albert Place. Two **motels.** Recommended: Bayview Victor, Hindmarsh Road. Four **caravan and camping parks,** all facilities.

Transport. **Road** and **rail** services from Adelaide.

GOOLWA (Population 680)

Goolwa is a little township on the shores of Lake Alexandrina about 11 kilometres from the mouth of the Murray River. The area is now being subdivided and developed as a tourist resort on a large scale. Goolwa is close to surf and still water swimming beaches, lake waters suitable for yachting and cruising and excellent fishing grounds. An appreciable proportion of the developmental capital is being spent on foreshore beautification, tree planting and gardening.

Goolwa was favoured as a site for the capital of South Australia by Governor Hindmarsh when he examined the coast towards the end of 1836, but the Surveyor-General, Colonel Light, preferred Adelaide. Hindmarsh, however, was so impressed with Goolwa that he immediately built a hunting lodge there. The building still stands and, with several other houses built in the same period, has been classified for preservation by the National Trust. In the early days it was marked on maps as Port Pullen, but by the time it had become the terminal port of the Murray River steamboats and was called 'the New Orleans of Australia' it was known by its aboriginal name. The first railway passenger carriage used in South Australia is preserved and exhibited in the town.

Sports. South Lakes golf course (3 kilometres). Fishing trips by beach buggy to Murray Mouth and by boat to the mouth of The Coorong. (See Kingston S.E.)

Accommodation. One recommended **motel. Camping and caravan park,** all facilities.

Transport. Road and **rail** services from Adelaide and Victor Harbour. **Vehicular ferry** to Hindmarsh Island where a view of the mouth of the Murray may be obtained. **Lake cruises** to Murray mouth, Port Sturt and Loveday Bay.

STRATHALBYN (Population 1 547)

The largest inland town of the south coast district, 58 kilometres from Adelaide, Strathalbyn is the market centre of a substantial area of mixed farms and vineyards in the valley of the Angus River. It is noted for several beautiful riverside parks and for stately St Andrew's Presbyterian Church, built more than a century ago.

Langhorne Creek, a famous wine growing district, is 13 kilometers south-east.

Accommodation. Two **hotels,** no preference. **Caravan and camping park** near town, all facilities. **Camping area** at Doctor's Creek (8 kilometres).

Transport. Rail and **road** services from Adelaide.

PORT NOARLUNGA (Population 384)

A well known seaside village, 32 kilometres south of Adelaide, with protected swimming in the Gulf and some fishing, Port Noarlunga is a pleasant base from which to visit the **Southern Vales vineyards.** Many almond orchards are now established in the district.

Accommodation. One **hotel.** One **motel. Caravan and camping area.**

Transport. Road and **rail** services.

KANGAROO ISLAND

Kangaroo Island, which lies across the mouth of Spencer Gulf 113 kilometres south of Adelaide, is about 90 kilometres long and 40 kilometres wide at its widest. Its coastline is extremely rugged and beautiful, particularly at the western end of the island. The waters surrounding it teem with fish. It has become a popular holiday place for South Australians, speecially since a regular air service linked Adelaide with **Kingscote,** its main settlement on Nepean Bay west of Cape Jervis on the mainland.

Most of the interior was formerly covered by low eucalyptus scrub and *xanthorrea* grasstrees and was regarded as infertile until the soil was discovered to be deficient in copper and zinc. The use of phosphatic fertilizers with added trace elements has transformed the appearance and productivity of the island. It now grows good oats, barley, wheat and wool in areas which were previously almost useless. There is a flourishing soldier settlement surrounding **Parndana,** about 28 kilometres west of Kingscote.

The deficiencies of the soil in its original state did not, however, extend to the extreme west of the island which is heavily wooded and has been reserved as a native animal and bird sanctuary. The coastal scenery here and for some distance along the north-western coast is really magnificent. There are several koala colonies in the forest and platypuses still live in the streams.

The climate is mild, appreciably cooler than the mainland in summer and much warmer in winter.

History. Flinders landed from *Investigator* in 1802 and named the island for the large herds of kangaroos he saw there. Next year Nicholas Baudin surveyed the south coast. In the years that followed Kangaroo Island became the haunt of sealers and kangaroo hunters. Adelaide's first Surveyor-General, Colonel Light, landed near the site of Kingscote in 1836, but scarcity of water in the locality caused him to move on to the mainland.

The township of Kingscote was founded in 1838 and named after Henry Kingscote, a director of the South Australian Company. To curb smuggling it was at the same time declared an official port. Despite this official establishment the island continued for many years to be the home of riffraff and deserters from ships. In 1849 a lighthouse was built on Cape Willoughby (and later at Cape St Albans) to mark the approaches to Backstairs Passage. The treacherous waters surrounding the island are the graveyard of no fewer than 22 ships, most of which were wrecked during the last half of the 19th century.

Unusual industries which have been carried on from time to time include the gathering of *xanthorrea* resin for use in lacquers and varnishes, and tourmaline mining. A pure strain of Ligurian bees exist on the island, of great interest to apiarists.

Places of Interest. Flinders Chase, a 54 950 hectare fauna and flora reserve on the western tip of the land, 101 kilometres from Kingscote. The Chase is a fascinating area, rich in wild life of all kinds and Australian plant species. The coastal scenery is majestic. Access is by the Thomas Playford Highway which is sealed as far as the soldier settlement of Parndana.

On south coast: **Seal Bay,** a breeding ground for sea lions. Some beaches are open to observers, others (clearly marked) are out of bounds. **Little Sahara,** an area of spectacular white sand dunes west of the Seal Bay Road. **Vivinne Bay** crayfishing port and natural swimming pool at the mouth of the Harriet River. **Kelly Hill Caves,** limestone caverns some of which are open for inspection. There is a pleasant picnic ground and kiosk nearby. **Hanson Bay,** a breeding ground for fairy penguins. **Remarkable Rocks,** Kirkpatrick Point, a collection of huge boulders on a granite dome 80 metres above sea level.

On north coast: **Bay of Shoals,** with bird sanctuary, **Reeves Point,** site of South Australia's first post office. **Stokes Bay** for beach fishing and swimming. **Snelling's Beach,** reservoir and picnic area. **Cape Borda Lighthouse** and meteorological station (fine views east to Cape Torrens).

On Dudley Peninsula: **Penneshaw** holiday resort, with **National Trust Museum. Antechamber Bay,** with good beach and fishing grounds and stands of ancient Yacca trees (*Xanthorrhoea Tateana*). **Chapman River** for bream fishing. **Cape Willoughby Lighthouse,** overlooking rugged coastline with perpetual heavy surf.

Accommodation. Kingscote: One recommended **hotel.** One **hotel-motel.** Two **motels.** No preference. **Flats, lodges** and **cabins** for rent. American River: Two **motels.** Penneshaw: One **hotel.** Most establishments have a minimum charge at Easter.

Transport. By sea, MV *Troubridge*, a vehicular ferry, operates a service between Kingscote and Port Adelaide thrice weekly in summer and twice weekly in winter. Daily **air** services between Adelaide and Kingscote, with a **bus** connecting for other resorts. **Rental cars** and **launches** are available. **Bus tours** of island's beauty spots are made from hotels and guest-houses.

SOUTH EAST AND LOWER MURRAY

The South-East district of South Australia extends from the Murray River about 80 kilometres east of Adelaide to the border of Victoria east of Mount Gambier. Its northern limit is set by the Adelaide-Melbourne railway line and its southern limit by the ocean. It is traversed by the Princes, Duke's and Ouyen Highways.

Wildlife abounds in the lakes and lagoons at the mouth of the Murray and there is excellent fishing and seasonal duck shooting. The largest acclimatized pine forests in Australia have been established in the Mount Gambier and Penola areas. The district generally has interesting historical associations.

MOUNT GAMBIER

(Population 17 867)

The largest commercial centre of South Australia's productive south-eastern districts, Mount Gambier is on Princes Highway, 468 kilometres from Adelaide. The mountain from which the town takes its name is an extinct volcano on which there are four deep and very beautiful crater lakes. The town's institutions and its well-tended parks and public reserves reflect a keen civic pride. The nearby countryside is picturesque and has a number of features interesting to visitors.

The district's wealth derives from farmlands which produce fine wool, wheat and other cereals, fat lambs and cattle, pigs, potatoes and onions and dairy produce. The largest plantations of radiata pine in Australia are steadily increasing the importance of the timber industry. Coralline limestone (the white Mount Gambier stone is a splendid and widely used building material), dolomite and diatomite are quarried in the area. Secondary industries include many cheese and butter factories, a meatworks, a flour mill, timber mills, a woollen mill, a bacon-curing plant and factories for the production of cellulose. Power for the town is generated at a plant which uses timber waste as fuel.

History. In 1800 Lieutenant James Grant in the *Lady Nelson* sighted Mount Gambier (190 metres) and named it after Admiral Lord Gambier. It has the distinction of being the first part of South Australia to be discovered and named. In 1839 Stephen G. Henty of Portland, Victoria, and two companions climbed the mountain. Henty established a station nearby. In 1841 the first dwelling in the area was built to house Henty's men. Three years later it was discovered that Henty's claim to the land was not valid. The boundaries of the States had been set and Mount Gambier was part of South Australia—not, as Henty had believed, in NSW. (Victoria had not at this time been separated from the parent colony). Nevertheless, the settlers trickling into the district were much more orientated to Melbourne than to Adelaide. The crossing to Adelaide over the Ninety Mile Desert was far more difficult than travel on the routes in Victoria.

In 1847 Mount Gambier's first hotel was opened by an American negro, John Byng, and by 1850 the settlement was large enough to warrant a weekly postal service from Adelaide. In 1854 the town was founded as a private venture by Hastings Cunningham. It was surveyed by William Murray and Cunningham called it Gambier Town, but the old name of Mount Gambier persisted. It was during the years 1853 to 1855 that the poet Adam Lindsay Gordon served in the district as a mounted police trooper and made his famous horse jump beside the Blue Lake.

In 1876 Mount Gambier was constituted a municipality and after three years was connected by rail to Adelaide. In 1886 the first *pinus radiata* trees were planted in the district, although the plantations were not a commercial proposition until after the first world war. By 1920 the South Australian Woods and Forest Department had established several large forests in the area. Mills were opened at Mount Burr, Nangwarry and Mount Gambier itself.

Places of Interest. **The Blue Lake,** which provides Mount Gambier with its water supply, has an area of 71 hectares and is more than 180 metres deep. Its limestone bowl has walls 93 metres high. The waters of the lake have the strange and unexplained property of changing colour with the seasons. From March to November they are slate grey and from December to March a bright blue. An obelisk at the Lake marks the site of Adam Lindsay Gordon's spectacular jump on his horse, Red Lancer. **Leg-of-Mutton Lake, Browne Lake** and the green **Valley Lake,** also in craters, are nearby. The whole area has been most attractively developed as parkland. **Cave Garden Reserve,** a terraced garden about a natural cave in the hillside just behind the Town Hall, is illuminated at night. **Mount Gambier State Sawmill** is open for inspection on Tuesday afternoons; **Nangwarry mill** (28 kilometres north) is open for inspection from Monday to Thursday. **Black's Museum** and **Model Railway Exhibition,** open daily and every evening. **Cafpirco Quarries,** 11 kilometres west of town, produce the famous coralline limestone which is so soft immediately after quarrying that it can be cut into blocks with a carpenter's saw. The material later hardens on exposure to the air. The quarries are open for inspection daily.

Sports. Excellent golf course. Racecourse. Bowling clubs, tennis courts. Night trotting (fortnightly meetings in summer). Oldest gun club in Australia. Swimming in Valley Lake and Olympic pool. A popular sports carnival is held at Vansittart Park every New Year's Day.

Accommodation. Nine **hotels.** Recommended: Jens Town Hall. Ten **motels.** Recommended: Commodore, Jubilee Highway and Penola Road; Travelodge, Jubilee Highway. Three **caravan parks,** all facilities; **stationary vans** for hire.

Transport. Daily **road** and **air** services from Melbourne and Adelaide. **Rail** service via Portland.

MURRAY BRIDGE

(Population 6 650)

On the Murray River about 112 kilometres from its mouth at Lake Alexandrina, Murray Bridge is a busy commercial and industrial town on the Duke's Highway 84 kilometres south-south-east of Adelaide. The district's primary produce includes wheat, fruit, vegetables, fat lambs, poultry and dairy produce. In the urban area there are factories making butter, bacon, condensed milk and cheese, a flour mill, and plants manufacturing ice and ice-cream, aerated waters and cordials, electrical switch gear and fibrous plaster.

History. In the early 1850s the first settler, R. Edwards, established himself on the river bank and the locality became known as Edwards Crossing or The Turnoff, because it marked the turnoff point for drivers bound for Adelaide with stock from the inland grazing areas. In 1860 the Hundred of Mobilong was proclaimed and the township became the main port of the lower Murray. In 1873 work was started here on a bridge across the river, resulting in a political controversy which lasted for nine years. The name Murray Bridge came into general usage, but was not officially recognized until 1924. The bridge was opened to road traffic in 1879 and the railway crossing was completed in 1886. In the early years of the 20th century large-scale reclamation of swampland along the river considerably added to the agricultural and pastoral potential of the district.

Places of Interest. **Sturt Reserve,** a recreation area of about 20 hectares on the river bank with a wharf at which the paddle steamer *Coonawarra* berths. Five-day cruises upriver to Morgan and return are available. The vessel is a 255-tonne three-decker and accommodates 44 passengers. **Native Vegetation Reserve,** 3 kilometres west with specimens of rare wattle *A. Retinocarpa.* **Avoca Dell,** 5 kilometres upstream on the eastern riverbank, with boat launching ramps. **Folk Museum,** Thomas Street.

Sports. Usual facilities for tennis, bowls etc. Water-skiing. River fishing. Olympic pool.

Accommodation. Two **hotels.** Preferred: Bridgeport, Bridge Street. Four **motels.** Highly recommended: Murray Bridge, Princes Highway. Four **camping and caravan parks,** all facilities. Catamaran **houseboats,** sleeping 8-10, are available.
Transport. **Rail** service from Adelaide. River cruise **launches** for hire.

Smaller Towns in District

WELLINGTON (34 kilometres south) with punt service across river; an excellent base for fishermen and field naturalists. One **hotel.**

TAILEM BEND, a railway workshops town, 107 kilometres from Adelaide on the banks of the river. One **hotel.** One **motel.**

MENINGIE, a sleepy little rural town astride the Princes Highway on the eastern shore of Lake Albert and near northern end of the Coorong lagoons. Also an excellent base for fishermen and field naturalists. One **hotel.** One **motel.** **Caravan and camping park,** all facilities.
Transport. **Road** service from Adelaide, Mount Gambier etc.

MANNUM (Population 3 000)

An historic settlement on the banks of the Murray, 84 kilometres east of Adelaide, Mannum is now a small market and manufacturing town serving a district which produces cereals, wool and beef. Mannum stands at the head of the Mannum-Adelaide pipeline, completed in 1962 at the cost of $A22 million to supplement Adelaide's water supply.

In mid-Victorian days Mannum was the headquarters of W. R. Randell and his brothers who launched the first Murray River paddle steamer, the *Mary Ann.* The town was surveyed in 1868 and the district council formed in 1877. In 1900 the first steam automobile was built in Mannum by the firm of David Shearer which now makes the Shearer header for grain harvesting.

Places of Interest. **Marion Paddlewheel Museum,** anchored at a permanent dock on the river and accommodating a museum of relics from early days on the Murray. Replica of **Sturt's whaleboat** in which the explorer made his famous journey down the continent's longest waterway. **Replica** of the *Mary Ann* and her boiler at the river reserve. **Halidon Bird Sanctuary,** mainly inhabited by ducks, waterfowl, geese and pelicans.
Accommodation. Two **hotels.** No preference. **Camping and caravan park,** all facilities.
Transport. **Road** service to Adelaide.

KINGSTON S.E. (Population 1 173)

A crayfishing port on Lacepede Bay, Kingston S.E. is 305 kilometres south-east of Adelaide. A large factory run by Safcol, the South Australian Fishermen's Co-operative, processes for export crayfish caught by the fleet based on the port. The district produces wool and fat lambs.

Kingston is on the southern approaches to The Coorong, an extraordinary series of claypans and shallow, salt lagoons divided from the sea by sandhills and extending for about 145 kilometres south-east of Lake Alexandrina at the mouth of the Murray River. The whole area is covered with low scrub and sparse heath. It swarms with wildlife, especially waterfowl of all kinds which breed and feed in the lakes and marshes. The Coorong can be fascinating even to the casual tourist with the time and enterprise to investigate it, and it is a paradise for bird watchers and field naturalists. The duck shooting (in season) and the fishing are excellent. Unfortunately for the type of traveller who expects to make his explorations of Australia from a base provided with all modern conveniences, the wayside accommodation between Kingston and Meningie to the north is fairly primitive.

History. Lacepede Bay was discovered and named by Nicholas Baudin in 1802. The district was known for a time as Maria Creek after a brigantine wrecked offshore in 1840 and later Port Caroline after another vessel which took shelter in the harbour from a violent storm. In the same year as the *Maria* was wrecked the Governor of South Australia, Sir George Strickland Kingston, built a house within the bounds of the town which was officially established 18 years later. The Governor's house is now the kiosk in Kingston Park. In 1926, a canal near Kingston was dug across the sandhills of The Coorong to permit its waters a second exit into Lacepede Bay.

Accommodation. Two **hotels.** Preferred: Royal Mail. Two **motels.** Recommended: Lobster, Princes Highway. **Camping and caravan park,** all facilities.
Transport. **Road** services.
Note: Motorists travelling south on Princes Highway to Mount Gambier and Melbourne should consider deviating west on a good road through Robe which rejoins the highway at Clay Wells, north-west of Millicent.

ROBE (Population 440)

A crayfishing port and holiday resort 336 kilometres south-east of Adelaide on Guichen Bay, Robe is one of the oldest settlements in South Australia. It is a bleakly beautiful little town on a rugged windy coast indented with numerous secluded beaches. There are also many interesting lagoons and salt lakes in the district, including Lake Eliza, Lake St Clair and Lake George. The countryside produces wheat, wool, beef cattle and potatoes, but the most important industry is crayfishing. A local factory processes cray tails for export to the United States.

History. Nicholas Baudin named Guichen Bay in 1802, but land exploration did not begin until Charles Bonney overlanded stock along the coastal route from Port Phillip to Adelaide in 1839. In 1846 the Governor, Lieutenant-Colonel F. H. Robe, reached Guichen Bay in the government schooner *Lapwing* and selected the townsite. By the 1850s Robe had become a wool port of some importance, and later was used as a point of disembarkation for Chinese immigrants bound for the Victorian goldfields but trying to evade the Victorian poll tax of £10. It has been estimated that more than 17 000 Chinese entered Australia by this route. With the improvement of overland communications towards the end of the century the traffic of the port dwindled.

Places of Interest. **Karatta House** beside Lake Butler, former Governor's summer residence. Ruins of **old gaol.** Original **customs house,** now council offices. **Lake Fellmongery,** remarkable for the high mineral content of its water which causes the patterns formed by skiers to remain a long time on the lake's surface. Cliff-top **scenic drive.**

Sports. Golf course. Bowls, croquet, tennis etc. Yachting, spear fishing, swimming and lake and sea fishing.

Accommodation. One **hotel.** Five **motels.** Recommended: Harbour View. Three **camping and caravan parks.**

Transport. **Road** services to Mount Gambier and Kingston.

MILLICENT (Population 5 075)

Millicent is a prosperous commercial and industrial town 408 kilometres south-east of Adelaide. The primary produce of the district includes wool, wheat, barley, chicory, fat lambs, cattle, limestone, crayfish and timber from extensive pine forests. There are large Cellulose and Apcel paper mills west of the town on the road to Kangaldoo.

History. The township was named after the wife of one of the first settlers, George Glen, who arrived in 1846. It was not, however, founded until 1871. A district council was inaugurated in 1888 and in 1955 a broad gauge railway was extended from Mount Gambier.

Places of Interest. **Millicent Art Gallery** featuring exhibits by South Australian artists. **Lake Butler,** fishing fleet anchorage. **Crayfish Processing Factory** (visitors welcome). **Tantanoola,** a small township about 16 kilometres east of Millicent (on a three-kilometre detour from highway) became famous during the 1890s because it was terrorized by a mysterious animal known as 'the Tantanoola Tiger', about which extraordinary tales were told. The beast was eventually shot and identified as a Syrian wolf, but how it came to be loose in the district has never been explained. The 'tiger' was stuffed and mounted and may now be seen in the bar of the local hotel. **Tantanoola Limestone Cave,** near the main road, is open to the public. **Cellulose and paper mills,** 10 kilometres west, may also be inspected.

Sports. Excellent golf course. Tennis, bowls etc. Fishing and boating at Lake Bonney, 13 kilometres south.

Accommodation. Two **hotels.** Preferred: Somerset. Two **motels.** Recommended: Radiata. Two **caravan and camping parks,** all facilities.

Transport. **Road** and **rail** services to Mount Gambier.

PORT MACDONNELL (Population 584)

A small fishing port on the western shores of Discovery Bay, 28 kilometres south of Mount Gambier, Port MacDonnell in the 1860s and 1870s was a bustling town through which practically all the agricultural and pastoral produce of the south-east passed. It had two breweries, a wool-scouring plant, a flour mill and half a dozen hotels. Then it was by-passed by the roads and railway line linking Melbourne and Adelaide and thereafter steadily lost importance. Today its rugged coastal scenery and good fishing attract holidaymakers who like to get off the beaten track.

Places of Interest. **Dingley Dell,** home of the poet and legendary horseman, Adam Lindsay Gordon, between 1864 and 1866. He purchased the stone cottage two years after his marriage to Maggie Park, of Robe, in 1862, and wrote some of his best loved verses there. Gordon represented the South-East in the South Australian Parliament in 1865 and 1866, but resigned, left the district and went to live in Ballarat. He suffered from melancholia attributed to financial worries and injuries received in falls from horses and in 1870 took his own life at Brighton, Victoria, at the age of 37. Dingley Dell was purchased by the South Australian Government in 1922. The room Gordon used as a study is now a museum housing a collection of relics of his life and times. It is open for inspection. Visitors may picnic in the garden. **Cape Northumberland Lighthouse** on the wild and beautiful headland to the west of the township.

Accommodation. One **hotel.** One **motel.**

Transport. **Road** service to Mount Gambier.

PENOLA (Population 4 800)

Situated 51 kilometres north of Mount Gambier, Penola is the centre of extensive pine forests and a district which produces wool, fat lambs and cattle, dairy produce, fruit and wine grapes. The famous Coonawarra table wines, among the most distinctive and delicate in Australia, are produced at wineries about 10 kilometres north of the town.

The district was first settled by Alexander Cameron who overlanded cattle from Portland in 1840. The town was proclaimed in 1902. The name is derived from an aboriginal word meaning 'big swamp.'

The **Coonawarra Estate winery** is open for inspection in the mornings only. **Lindeman's winery** is open Monday to Friday 10 am to 11 am and 2 pm to 4 pm.

Accommodation. One **hotel.** One **motel.**

Transport. **Road** services to Mount Gambier and Adelaide.

NARACOORTE (Population 4 399)

Naracoorte is the market town for a wool, wheat and dairy farming district about 350 kilometres south-east of Adelaide. The frequent use of local stone as building material gives it an air of quiet solidarity which is also characteristic of several other towns about the limestone country.

History. When it was first settled in the early 1840s the district was known as Mosquito Plains. In 1845 a private town named Kincraig was founded and achieved importance in the 1850s when gold escorts and large numbers of Chinese immigrants were on the roads to and from the Victorian diggings. In 1859 it was proclaimed a government town, but a little later another private settlement, Skyetown, was established nearby. In 1869 all names except Naracoorte, which means 'running water', were dropped. Naracoorte was gazetted as a municipality in 1924.

Places of Interest. **Naracoorte Caves,** classified as a national pleasure resort, are 11 kilometres south of the township. There are 10 caves in the group, but only three, **Alexandra, Victoria** and **Blanche Caves,** are open to the public. The recently discovered **Fossil Cave,** leading off Victoria Cave, contains one of the most important deposits of extinct marsupial remains in Australia. Several inspections are made daily from Monday to Saturday and on Sunday afternoons. The caves are closed on Christmas Day and Good Friday. Every evening thousands of bats emerge from Bat Cave, about 17 metres off the Naracoorte Road. Other places worth visiting include the **Bool Lagoon Game Reserve,** the new **swimming lake and golf course** and the town's collection of **historic locomotives.**

Sports. Usual facilities. Night trotting.

Accommodation. Three **hotels.** Preferred: Kincraig. Three **motels.** Recommended: Naracoorte. One **guest-house. Camping and caravan park,** all facilities.

Transport. **Road** services to Mount Gambier and Adelaide.

BORDERTOWN (Population 1 977)

Bordertown is a small town on the Duke's Highway (continuation of Victoria's Western Highway) and the main Adelaide-Melbourne railway line, 290 kilometres south-east of Adelaide. The district's main industries are wool, wheat and dairy farming. The town has a cheese factory.

Although the district was populated and a settlement established before the 1850s, the main stimulus to growth came from the discovery of gold in western Victoria. In 1852 it was surveyed as a gold escort depot and became a major staging point for supplies to the fields.

These days it is often an overnight stop for westbound motorists.

Accommodation. Two **hotels.** Recommended: Woolshed Inn. Two **motels.** Recommended: Bordertown, Duke's Highway. **Caravan and camping park,** all facilities.

Transport. **Rail** service to Adelaide and Melbourne. **Road** service to Mount Gambier etc.

KEITH (Population 1 211)

In the heart of a district once known as the Ninety Mile Desert and now renamed Coonalpyn Downs, Keith is the growing centre of a rich farming district which owes its prosperity to the ingenuity of modern soil chemists and agronomists. It is on the Duke's Highway, 241 kilometres south-east of Adelaide.

History. Explorer pastoralists traversed the district in 1845 and the following year a Swedish farmer built a small homestead and began running a few sheep. The first real settlers, James Allen and Patrick Kelly, took up their land in 1851 around a red granite hill called Monster Mount. Soon afterwards travellers on their way to Bordertown and the Victorian goldfields made Monster Mount an overnight stopping place. It was not, however, until 1885 that the town was surveyed as a siding village in anticipation of the railway from Adelaide being pushed through to Bordertown. The surrounding countryside, though it received adequate rainfall in most years, was notoriously infertile and its low, scrubby pastures were infested by dingoes and rabbits. Only the most stubborn settlers persisted with their heartbreak holdings.

In 1933, when the effects of trace-element deficiencies on plant nutrition were first discovered, the Commonwealth Scientific and Industrial Research Organization made a series of soil surveys. Ten years later a team of experimenters conducted field tests with superphosphate to which minute quantities of zinc, copper and molybdenum had been added. The effect was dramatic, particularly where subterranean clover was sown to build up the nitrogen content of the soil.

In 1949 the Australian Mutual Provident Society, a large insurance organization, developed 200 000 hectares of land for closer settlement by using the CSIRO methods. This is now the productive and prosperous 'Brecon' area.

Similar techniques have been successful in other large areas of the South-East, on Kangaroo Island, and at Esperance in Western Australia.

Accommodation. One **hotel. Camping and caravan park,** all facilities.

UPPER MURRAY DISTRICT (SA)

The attractions of the Upper Murray River district in South Australia include fine river scenery, river cruising and fishing, and wildlife reserves with many water birds. Inspections can be made of wineries, distilleries, fruit packing plants, orchards and irrigated farmlands.

RENMARK

(Population 3 277)

Renmark is the principal town of a rich irrigation area on the Murray River 259 kilometres north-east of Adelaide and about 28 kilometres from the Victorian border. The total area under irrigation is 4 050 hectares. The district produces citrus and stone fruit, wine and table grapes, olives, vegetables, wheat, timber, sheep and whole milk. The town has large fruit packing and canning plants, wineries and light engineering works.

History. Sturt passed the site of Renmark on his journey down the Murray in 1830. The only industry in the district was wool-growing. Then, in February 1887, the Premier of South Australia, Sir John Downer, agreed to grant 250 000 acres of land to the Californian irrigation experts, George and William Chaffey, for development. The offer to make the grant came immediately after the Victorian Government had refused the Chaffey company's application for a grant near Mildura. When the Victorians heard of the South Australian Government's action, they withdrew their objections and the Chaffeys proceeded with both schemes.

However, just as Renmark was the first irrigation area in Australia so was it the first to set up an independent irrigation authority. In 1893 the Chaffey rights were transferred to the Renmark Irrigation Trust by Act of Parliament. Until 1960 the Trust acted as a local governing body but since then has been responsible for irrigation matters only.

The liquor prohibition clause in the Chaffey scheme of town development was a source of continual unrest, as it also was in Mildura. Renmark solved the problem by establishing a community hotel in 1897. It was the first community-run hotel in the British Commonwealth and profits were used to improve the town's amenities.

In 1904 the town was proclaimed and in 1910 Angoves opened a winery in Renmark. In 1916 the Renmark Grower's Distillery took over the Chateau Tanunda distillery which had been opened as a private concern the previous year.

After the first world war a war service land settlement scheme on 364 hectares was inaugurated at Chaffey near the town. A larger settlement of 486 hectares at Cooltong was started after the second war.

The name Renmark means 'red mud'.

Places of Interest. Riverside Gardens and **Memorial** to the explorer Sturt. **Lookout Tower,** 6 kilometres north of town. **Reptile Park** in Ral Ral Avenue. **Goat Island,** a National Trust sanctuary with a koala colony. Old **wine press,** on display in Renmark Avenue. **Chaffey irrigation pumps** of controversial design, displayed outside office of Irrigation Trust. **National Trust Museum,** Soldiers' Memorial Hall. **Fruit packing sheds,** open for inspection during season. **Renmark Growers' Distillery,** open for inspection Monday to Friday 10 am to 11 am and 2 pm to 3 pm. **Angoves Winery,** open for inspection by prior arrangement with the sales manager. **Chowilla Dam** site, 28 kilometres north-east. When constructed the dam will be the biggest body of fresh water on the

Australian continent.) **'Olivewood',** former residence of Charles Chaffey. **Picnic grounds** at Plush's Bend Beach and Lock Five. **Woolenock Bend,** game and forest reserve. **Ruston's Rose Garden. Paddle Steamer** *Industry* moored at main wharf.

Sports. Good golf course. Usual facilities for tennis, bowls etc. Water-skiing, boating and fishing. Circuit for motor car and cycle racing.

Accommodation. One **hotel.** Two **motels.** Recommended: Fountain, Renmark Avenue. Two **caravan and camping parks.** Liba Liba and catamaran **houseboats** for hire.

Transport. Road and **rail** services to Adelaide, Mildura etc.

BERRI (Population 2 712)

Community centre of a well-established fruit and grape-growing district 21 kilometres south-west oi Renmark, 227 kilometres from Adelaide, Berri grew up on the side of a wood pile established on the banks of the river to supply fuel for the Murray River paddle steamers. In 1906 the trade was declining and the owner of the depot began growing onions and fruit to supplement his income. The success of his orchard and garden indicated the district's possibilities under irrigation. By 1917 most of the land was taken up and a soldier settlement district was established in 1920 at nearby Monash. Berri was incorporated as a municipality in 1922 and the railway reached the town in 1928. Today 3 238 hectares are under irrigation.

Places of Interest. Tourist Lookout, Fielder Street. **Pumping Station,** west of town. **Berri Experimental Orchard.** Fruit and fruit juice **canneries** and **packing sheds.** Berri Co-operative **Winery and Distillery.** Inspection Monday to Friday 10 am to 11 am and 2 pm to 4 pm.

Sports. Racecourse. Usual facilities for golf, bowls, tennis etc. Fishing. Olympic pool.

Note: Swimming in the river here is dangerous.

A Bushman's Carnival or rodeo is held every year.

Accommodation. One **hotel.** One **motel. Camping and caravan park,** all facilities. **Stationary caravans** and **catamaran houseboats** (sleep 8-10) for rent.

Transport. Rail and **road** services to Renmark etc. **Road** services to Adelaide.

BARMERA (Population 1 683)

Like most of the Murray Valley irrigation towns, Barmera, 227 kilometres north-east of Adelaide, is communally orientated. Seventy-five per cent of the district's economy is based on co-operative enterprise. The district grows grapes, citrus fruit, peaches and apricots, wheat and wool. There are wineries, distilleries and fruit packing and drying plants in the town, which is situated on the shores of Lake Bonney, connected with the river by Chambers Creek.

History. Several squatters established holdings in the area during the 1840s. They were consolidated in 1867 into one huge run, 'Cobdogla', run by John Chambers. In 1911, the South Australian Government surveyed the land for irrigation and in 1922 the first soldier settlement lots were ready for occupation. In 1929 Barmera was proclaimed a town. During the second world war an internment and prisoner of war camp was situated at Loveday, 6 kilometres south-west. Barmera is derived from an aboriginal word meaning 'watering place'.

Places of Interest. Overland Corner, 19 kilometres north-west, was once a staging point on the overland stock route from the north-east to Adelaide and the starting point of the mail coach run to the capital. The Overland Corner Hotel is preserved by the National Trust as a museum. **Nappers Accommodation House,** at the mouth of Chambers Creek, was built in 1850 and was the first hotel in the area. It is now a ruin, but is preserved by the National Trust. **Captain Sturt Memorial** Clock Tower. **National Trust Gallery and Museum,** Lake Avenue. **Pumping plants** at Cobdogla and Loveday.

Sports. Racecourse and trotting track. Swimming. Golf, tennis, bowls etc. Aquatic sports on lake (Easter sailing regatta is popular).

Accommodation. One **hotel.** One **motel. Caravan and camping park,** all facilities.

Transport. Rail and **road** services to Renmark. **Road** service to Adelaide.

LOXTON (Population 2 658)

Centre of the largest war service settlement scheme in South Australia, Loxton is 251 kilometres north-east of Adelaide. Irrigated holdings of about 10 hectares are held by some 270 settlers and produce stone and citrus fruits and grapes. The non-irrigated lands of the district grow good wool, wheat and beef cattle. The town has fruit packing sheds, wineries, a distillery, a flour mill, pipe works and a cannery. It is civically progressive and the profits of the community-owned hotel-motel are devoted to improvement of public amenities. The area was first settled in the 1890s. The village was founded in 1907 and named after a boundary rider on the original station property, 'Bookpunong'.

Places of Interest. Sturt Memorial Obelisk. Yatco Lagoon, noted for bird life. **Old Pepper Tree** and **Loxton Hut. Billiat** and **Katarapko National Parks.** Department of Agriculture **Research Centre.**

Sports. Golf course, swimming pool etc.
Accommodation. One **hotel-motel. Caravan and camping park,** all facilities.
Transport. **Road** services to Adelaide and Renmark etc.

WAIKERIE (Population 4 000)

A typical Murray Valley irrigation town 48 kilometres west of Barmera, Waikerie is almost entirely surrounded by orchards and vineyards. Wild life on the river is prolific and the name is believed to have derived from an aboriginal word meaning 'Many Wings'. Waikerie has the most active gliding club in Australia and was chosen as venue of the World Gliding Championships in 1974.

Places of Interest. **Harts Lagoon Bird Sanctuary. Koala Sanctuary. Fruit packing sheds. Riverfront park** with fine stands of gums. **Glider hangars** at airport.

Accommodation. One **hotel.** One **motel. Camping and caravan parks,** all facilities.

Smaller Towns in Area

MORGAN, one of the oldest towns on the Murray and once Australia's busiest river port. Water for the industrial town of Whyalla on Eyre Peninsula is pumped from the river nearby.

Of Interest. **Old wharves. Customs house. Court house. Fossils** in quarry face south of town.

BLANCHE TOWN is an attractive village built on a row of small hills beside the first of the Murray's 26 locks. The nearby **Moorunde National Trust Reserve** was established to save the hairy-nosed wombat from extinction.

SWAN REACH, on the eastern bank of the river, a sleepy little settlement reflecting pioneer days, is gaining popularity as a holiday resort. The river scenery is picturesque and the fishing excellent.

Accommodation. One **hotel. Camping and caravan park.**

YORKE PENINSULA

Yorke Peninsula lies between St Vincent Gulf on the east and Spencer Gulf on the west. About 190 kilometres long and with an average width of 32 kilometres, it is gently undulating country with light soil suitable for grain farming. Barley is the main crop. Gypsum is quarried in the south-west.

During the last half of the 19th century rich deposits of copper were mined in the north-west. The southern section of the peninsula is sparsely settled and still contains virgin scrubland. There are numerous small seaside resorts on both the east and west coasts.

The tourist attractions of the peninsula are its dry, sunny climate, the impressive coastal scenery of the south, and good fishing off the coast.

WALLAROO-MOONTA-KADINA

(Population 7 000)

The three towns collectively known in South Australia as Little Cornwall are between 150 and 170 kilometres north-north-west of Adelaide. Their combined population is about 7 000 and the district produces barley and wheat, wool, fat lambs and cattle, poultry and some dairy produce. A small fishing fleet is based on Moonta's Port Hughes. Wallaroo is an important grain shipping port. Its huge silos (32 cells) dominate the skyline and its deepwater port installations also handle rock phosphate for treatment at the town's two fertilizer plants. Kadina, eight kilometres to the east, is the chief shopping and commercial centre of the district.

History. The history of the three townships is closely interrelated. During the 1850s the district was pastoral and the main station was Wallawaroo, owned by a Welsh pastoralist, Walter W. Hughes. Hughes had dabbled in mining and as early as 1851 made an unsuccessful application for a mineral lease in the area. His judgement was vindicated in 1859 when James Boor found specimens of rich copper ore near Wallaroo. This time Hughes obtained his lease and founded Wallaroo Mines Consolidated. In 1861 another rich strike was made at Moonta, by a shepherd named Ryan who was employed by Hughes. Again the shrewd Welshman scored when his friend, William Horn, registered his claim in Adelaide ahead of rivals after a wild and exhausting ride on horseback. In the same year a smelter was installed at Wallaroo and the township of Kadina was surveyed. Moonta was laid out in 1863 and received its name from the Governor, Sir Dominick Daly, who used a corruption of the aboriginal word *moonterra*, meaning 'a place of impenetrable scrub'.

The copper mines boomed and by 1890 the population of the district had risen to about 30 000. Most of the mine workers were Cornish and the three towns became known as Little Cornwall. The ore was so rich that the mines survived even the depression prices received for copper during the late 1880s and 1890s, but in the first two decades of the 20th century the rising costs of coal and labour combined with declining grades spelt the death of the industry. In the 60 years of its existence it had produced copper to the value of nearly £21 million.

Places of Interest. Wallaroo: **Cairn** marking the site of the old copper smelters. Moonta: **Old mine buildings. National Trust Museum** in the Town Hall containing exhibits of the early days. Moonta Mines **Methodist Church.** Museum in **Cornish-type cottage** maintained by National Trust. Kadina: **National Trust Museum** at Matta House.

Sports. Racecourse. Trotting track. Bowling, croquet and tennis clubs. Winter golf courses. At Wallaroo: Swimming and sea, rock and jetty fishing.

Accommodation. Four **hotels.** Preferred: Wallaroo. One **motel** at Wallaroo (recommended). **Camping and caravan parks,** most facilities, at Wallaroo, Moonta and Port Hughes.

Transport. **Rail** service to Adelaide. **Road** service to Port Pirie and peninsula resorts.

MAITLAND (Population 1 020)

Maitland is a small town in the centre of Yorke Peninsula serving a district which has a number of well known stud farms and grows wool, beef cattle, wheat and barley. It is 168 kilometres north-west of Adelaide, and 24 kilometres due west of the port of **Ardrossan** (two hotels), from which dolomite quarried nearby for the Broken Hill Proprietary Company is shipped. The smaller towns of **Port Vincent** (one hotel) and **Port Victoria** (one hotel) lie to the south-west and south-east respectively.

Accommodation. Two **hotels.** Preferred: Maitland. There is a **hotel** and a **caravan and camping park** with some facilities at **Edithburgh,** a small resort on the south-eastern tip of the peninsula, 259 kilometres from Adelaide.

Other Centres. **Coobowie** (one **hotel**), **Yorketown, Stenhouse Bay** (gypsum port) and **Foul Bay** (**camping area,** good fishing). Holiday **flats** and **cottages** are available at most Yorke Peninsula seaside villages.

CENTRAL AND NORTHERN DISTRICTS

BURRA (Population 2 550)

An old copper mining settlement in the Mount Lofty Ranges 157 kilometres north of Adelaide, Burra is now a market town for a district producing stud sheep, wool and mixed farm produce. The copper was discovered by a teamster named Picket in 1845 and two townships, Redruth and Kooringa, were founded near the mines—Redruth by a mining company and Kooringa by the Government. In time they became known collectively as The Burra—an aboriginal word for 'wait' or 'danger'. Although the Victorian goldrush lured many of the miners away and several mines flooded, the strike at The Burra was a rich one. It produced £5 million worth of copper in about 20 years and paid investors £800 000 in dividends.

Accommodation. Four **hotels.** Preferred: Kooringa. **Caravan and camping park,** some facilities.

Transport. **Rail** and **road** services.

CLARE (Population 2 105)

The commercial centre of a sound agricultural and pastoral area, Clare is 134 kilometres north of Adelaide. The gently undulating land produces wheat, barley, stone and other soft fruits, grapes, honey and beeswax, stud sheep, wool, beef and slate. Its wineries make more than four and a half million litres of table and fortified wines every year. The town also has a plant for milk products and packing sheds for dried fruit.

History. The explorer Eyre passed through the Clare district twice, in 1839 and 1840. Later in 1840, J. A. Horrocks made a detailed exploration and the first settlers, E. B. Gleeson and John Maynard, took up land. In 1851 Jesuit fathers set up a community, built a church and school and planted a vineyard. A district council was formed in 1853 and the town was named after County Clare, Ireland. It was proclaimed a municipality in 1868.

Places of Interest. **Old Casualty Hospital,** built in 1850 as a police station, is now closed but preserved. **Sevenhill College** and **Church of St Aloysius,** built 1856 and 1864 respectively, surrounded by vineyards which supply the winery which produces altar wine for all Australia. **Martindale Hall,** 21 kilometres south-east, built by Edward Bowman in 1879 and given, with 280 hectares of surrounding land, to the Waite Agricultural Research Institute in 1965. **St Mark's Church of England,**

Penwortham, built 1850. The churchyard contains the grave of the explorer Horrocks, who died of a gunshot wound while investigating country near Lake Amadeus in the far north-west of the State, now the Northern Territory. **Pioneer Memorial Park,** with a giant red gum to which is affixed a plaque detailing the arrival of the bodies of the ill-fated explorers, Burke and Wills, at Clare in 1862. **Nagles Rock Reserve,** a 73 hectare wildlife sanctuary, 5 kilometres west of town. **Red Stringy Bark Reserve,** some kilometres south, containing one of the only two stands of the rarest eucalypts in the world. **Mintaro State Quarries,** south-east of town, reached after a pleasant drive.

Sports. Racecourse. Golf course. Lawn and hard tennis courts. Bowling and croquet greens. Swimming pool.

Accommodation. Three **hotels.** Preferred: Bentley's. Two **caravan and camping parks,** all facilities.

Transport. **Road** services.

JAMESTOWN (Population 1 392)

A small but growing town 205 kilometres north of Adelaide and 70 kilometres east of Port Pirie on the Port Pirie-Broken Hill railway. There are several well known sheep and cattle studs in the region which also produces cereals, dairy produce and timber. There are differing views among authorities concerning the origin of the town's name. Some hold that it was named after James Ferguson, an early settler, and others that it was named after Sir James Fergusson, the Governor of South Australia from 1869 to 1873. The village was proclaimed in 1878, the year that the railway from Adelaide reached it.

Accommodation. One **hotel.**

Transport. **Rail** and **road** services.

PETERBOROUGH (Population 3 109)

Centre of a large grain-growing and pastoral district about 250 kilometres north of Adelaide, Peterborough is the main town on the Port Pirie-Broken Hill railway line at its junction with the line from Adelaide to Quorn, Port Augusta, Hawker, Leigh Creek and Marree. It was originally named Petersburg after Peter Doecke, but this was anglicised during the patriotic fervour which swept South Australia during the first world war.

Sports. Swimming pool and usual facilities.

Accommodation. Three **hotels.** Preferred: Peterborough. **Caravan and camping park,** all facilities. **Camping area.**

Transport. **Road** and **rail** services.

PORT PIRIE

(Population 15 506)

A thriving industrial and commercial city on Spencer Gulf 230 kilometres north of Adelaide, Port Pirie is of great importance to the South Australian economy. It has the largest lead smelters in the world to treat concentrates railed from the Barrier mines at Broken Hill, 322 kilometres east. Other Broken Hill products shipped from the port include zinc concentrates, copper-lead alloys, silver, gold, cadmium and antimony by-products and sulphuric acid. Treatment plants for uranium ores, rare earth oxides and beach sand minerals are operating again after a close-down of some years during which the Commonwealth Government banned the export of uranium oxide.

Port Pirie is the rail terminal for services from Adelaide, Perth and the Barrier and its bulk grain installations handle the wheat and barley crop of the mid-north. The city's water supply comes from the Murray River via the Mannum-Whyalla pipeline.

History. The first settler arrived about 1845 when the schooner *John Pirie* navigated the creek from Spencer Gulf as far as the present townsite. Three years later a small village had grown up around the homestead, but it was not until 1871 that the town was surveyed and the first land sales held. The northern wheatlands were by now coming into production and work to improve the port was begun. The municipality was incorporated in 1876. In 1897 the BHP Company decided to build smelters near the town and lead production began two years later. In 1953 the Commonwealth Government built a uranium treatment plant to obtain oxide from the deposits at Radium Hill to the north-east. The same year Port Pirie was gazetted as a city.

Places of Interest. The Broken Hill Associated **smelters** are open at 2 pm Monday to Friday for conducted tours. The south-western spurs of the **Flinders Rangers** are within 24 kilometres of the city. **Telowie Gorge,** 24 kilometres north-east, is a favoured picnic spot.

Sport. Usual facilities for golf, bowls, tennis etc.

Accommodation. Four **hotels.** Recommended: International, Ellen Street. Two **motels.** Recommended: Flinders Range Motor Inn.

Transport. **Rail, road** and **air** services.

LEIGH CREEK (Population 943)

The little town of Leigh Creek, 563 kilometres north of Adelaide and 966 kilometres south-east of Alice Springs, is surprisingly attractive considering its forbidding surroundings. The arid saltbush country carries stock. Magnesite, gypsum, ochre and pigment clays are quarried in the area, but it is chiefly important for its extensive sub-bituminous coal deposits which are mined by open cut and railed to Port Augusta where the Thomas Playford Power Station generates 70 per cent of the State's electricity. Production is now in the order of two million tonnes a year.

History. The first settlers arrived as early as 1841 but no run was really consolidated until the arrival of a pioneer named Harry Leigh in 1856. Coal was discovered in 1888—native legend had given indication of combustible material in the area long before this—but the deposits were not exploited in any consistent way until a serious coal shortage threatened to cripple the State's industries during the second world war. Exploratory drilling began in 1941 and by 1944 coal was being produced in commercial quantities. The forced investment in the days of emergency is now paying the State handsome dividends.

Places of Interest. Aroona Waters, 13 kilometres south of town, source of the settlement's water supply. **Open cut workings** may be inspected on weekdays between 9 am and 4 pm and on Saturday, Sunday and holidays from 10 am to 2.30 pm. **Sliding Rock Bore** at the site of an abandoned copper mine near Copley, south of the town.

Accommodation. One **hotel.**

Transport. Rail, road and **air** services.

MARREE (Population 342)

Marree, 645 kilometres north of Adelaide and 106 kilometres beyond Leigh Creek, stands on the Central Australian Railway. It marks the road junction of the notorious Birdsville Track and the fairly well defined but rough vehicular track through William Creek to Oodnadatta and the Kingoonya-Alice Springs road (also rough). It is in flat, dry, saltbush country which, although it can be only sparsely stocked, produces good wool.

History. In the old days, Marree had considerable importance. It was a depot for the Afghan camel trains which carried provisions to scores of outback stations and the numbers of stock driven down the 510 kilometres of almost waterless country from Birdsville in Queensland to Marree were very much greater than they are now. The explorer, John McDouall Stuart, passed through Marree on his first expedition in 1859 and named it Hergott Springs after the Bavarian artist and naturalist in his party. Later it was a main depot for parties working on the overland telegraph line from Adelaide to Port Essington (Darwin) between 1871 and 1883, when it was proclaimed a town. Its aboriginal name, meaning 'a place for possums', did not come into common usage until 1918.

Accommodation. One **hotel.**

Transport. Rail service to Alice Springs and Adelaide. (The railway here changes gauge.)

OODNADATTA (Population 234)

Site of the Australian Inland Mission and a siding with stock trucking yards, Oodnadatta is 1 146 kilometres north of Adelaide. The tiny township is often supplied with water brought in by rail tankers. It was a busy depot in the 1870s, when the overland telegraph line was being built, and retained some importance until 1930 when the railway was put through to Alice Springs. After that it declined. Most of the surrounding countryside is too poor and arid to support stock. The name is the aboriginal word for 'flower of the mulga'.

Accommodation. One **hotel.**

Transport. Rail and **air** services to Alice Springs and Adelaide.

COOBER PEDY (Population 1 391)

Coober Pedy is a famous opal-mining centre near the Stuart's Range 952 kilometres north of Adelaide on the rough route between Kingoonya and Alice Springs. With the boom in Central Australian travel and the beginning of air tours from Adelaide, the extraordinary little settlement is becoming something of a tourist centre. For three or four months of the year the daily maximum temperature considerably exceeds 38°C and sometimes exceeds 50°C, so most of the population lives underground in dugouts. Water is imported in tankers.

Stuart was in the area in 1858 but it was not until 1911 that opal was discovered. By 1920 about 400 miners were on the field, living in appalling conditions. The field has suffered many vicissitudes, but mining has been stepped up since the second world war when opals regained popularity and prices rose. In 1956 the Olympic Australis stone was found in a Coober Pedy mine. It is probably the largest opal in the world. Many of the miners now on the field are European immigrants. Conditions have greatly improved since early days.

Tourists are welcome to 'noodle' for opal in the waste from the hundreds of shafts which pit the area. They sometimes make interesting if not particularly valuable finds. They are also shown how opal is cut and polished. Specimens and polished stones may be bought—but prices are somewhat higher than in city jewellers' shops.

Accommodation. One **hotel-motel.**

Transport. **Road** coach and **air** tours.

FLINDERS RANGES

The Flinders Ranges are part of a mountain chain which extends from Cape Jervis at the south-eastern extremity of St Vincent Gulf for 800 kilometres to a point about 160 kilometres east of the outback town of Marree on the railway line to Alice Springs. They begin west of the town of Peterborough, roughly 250 kilometres north of Adelaide, but the most colourful and spectacular of their peaks and valleys are in two areas—the first north-east of Port Augusta and the second north of Hawker, where several mountains rise to altitudes of between 1000 and 1200 metres.

Geologically the range is very old. The ranges themselves were thrust up after a shattering of the earth's crust about 60 million years ago in Tertiary times, but the rocks exposed by this gargantuan movement have been identified as deposits of the Proterozoic and Cambrian periods, from 500 million to more than 600 million years old. They are quartzites, enormous masses of sandstone hardened by heat and pressure, which have resisted the agents of erosion levelling the surrounding plains.

Scenically the Flinders Ranges have some similarity to other mountain systems of inland Australia, but in coloration and atmosphere they are highly individual. At Wilpena Pound, 53 kilometres north of Hawker, the great cliffs enclosing the hidden valley are white at their tops, reddish brown at their bases and set on a foundation of purple shale.

Unlike most of the desert ranges, the Flinders in parts carry a good deal of vegetation—huge river red gums in the creek beds, casuarinas and native pines, and many species of wattle. In spring after rain the display of brilliant wild-flowers is breath-taking. The play of light on rocky spurs, towers, gorges and valley floors makes this country a never-ending delight for landscape artists and colour photographers. Much of its rhythm and form and chromatic delicacy was captured by the eminent Australian artist, Sir Hans Heysen.

Passable motor roads, some sealed, serve the Flinders. The driver who goes north-east from Port Augusta over Pichi Richi Pass to Hawker and from there follows the loop road through Parachilna and Blinman, making a complete circuit of the Wilpena Pound area, will enjoy much magnificent scenery. But to see the range at its best, make a base at the Wilpena Pound chalet or at Arkaroola tourist resort, further north, and explore the mountains in a four-wheel drive vehicle, on horseback or on foot. There are many miles of signposted walking tracks, but visitors unfamiliar with the Australian bush should exercise great caution. Walking in the Flinders Ranges does not these days require exceptional bushcraft, but it is easy to lose the way. It is not good country in which to get lost. Reliable maps of the area are obtainable at the South Australian Government Tourist Bureau in Adelaide.

Secondary roads in the ranges are primitive and can be treacherous after rain. Before leaving main routes it is advisable to obtain local advice about conditions.

Needless to say, travelling in the northern part of South Australia can be highly uncomfortable in summer. Late autumn, winter and early spring are the best seasons.

Places of Interest

Southern Section: **Beetaloo Reservoir, Germein Gorge, Alligator Gorge, Mount Remarkable,** accessible from the road between Crystal Brook and Wilmington. **Hancock's Lookout,** south-west of the road from Wilmington to Port Augusta. **Pichi Richi Pass,** between Port Augusta and Quorn. **Devil's Peak,** a bare crag overlooking Quorn from the south.

Central Section: **Warren Gorge,** 23 kilometres north of Quorn on a side road, where 'Bitter Springs' was filmed. **Buckaringa Gorge,** 11 kilometres north of Warren Gorge. **Yourambulla Cave,** reached by side track 10 kilometres south of Hawker. It contains well preserved aboriginal drawings protected by a metal screen. **Hills of Arkaba,** on left side of the road from Hawker to Wilpena (take right fork of circuit road), the most beautiful spur of the middle Flinders, often called the Valley of a Thousand Hills. **Rawnsley's Bluff** (975 metres), a flat-topped mountain forming the southern wall of **Wilpena Pound,** a basin surrounded by jagged, vividly coloured peaks and precipices. Wilpena Chalet is at the entrance of the gorge which gives access to the Pound. **St Mary's Peak** (1 089 metres), north wall of the Pound.

Northern Section: **Bunyeroo Gorge,** north of Wilpena, accessible only by rugged and steep track. Much of the film 'Robbery Under Arms' was made here. **Willow Springs Lookout,** 1.6 kilometers east of road. **Great Wall of China,** a long rocky escarpment which can be seen from the road south of Blinman where the circuit road turns west. North of Blinman is **Hannigan's Gap. Mount Chambers** and **Chambers Gorge** are 67 kilometres east on a track passable only by four-wheeled drive vehicles. **Parachilna Gorge,** traversed by the road back to the highway from Hawker to Marree; **Mount Painter Sanctuary** and **Parlama Hot Springs.**

Accommodation

At Wilpena Pound: One recommended **motel. Cabins. Caravan and camping parks,** all facilities. **Horses** for hire. Guided bush tours available.
At Arkaroola: One highly recommended **motel.** Guided tours by four wheel drive vehicles available.
At Hawker: One **hotel.** One **motel.** One **caravan and camping park,** all facilities.
At Blinman: One **hotel.**
At Quorn: Three **hotels.** Prefered: Austral Railway Terrace. One recommended **motel.**

Transport

Many **road coach tours** of the Flinders Ranges lasting from three to seven days are available from Adelaide. **Air** services to Wilpena and Arkaroola.

Important Note: *Motorists and caravaners should never camp in a dry creek bed.* The area is particularly susceptible to flash floods.

It is forbidden by South Australian law to take Alsatian dogs north of Quorn.

EYRE PENINSULA

The Eyre Peninsula, between the eastern curve of the Great Australian Bight and the deep indentation of Spencer Gulf, is an important wheat growing district which has been settled for many years. Large iron ore deposits in the northern sector supply Whyalla, Australia's third iron and steel producing city. The climate of the peninsula in the north is fiercely hot in summer, but in the south is mild for most of the year. The countryside is dry and flat generally, but the coast is rugged and beautiful, appealing to holidaymakers who prefer the seclusion of small communities.

Attractions include aquatic sports, angling and big game fishing, and inspection of big industrial plants, shipyards, etc, at Whyalla.

PORT AUGUSTA

(Population 12 095)

A service town for a large area of the South Australian Outback, Port Augusta is 328 kilometres north-north-east of Adelaide at the head of Spencer Gulf. The primary industry of the area is wool growing on enormous holdings of semi-arid land to the north and west. The town has a large power plant, open for inspection daily, which is fuelled by coal from the Leigh Creek mines, 386 kilometres north, and supplies about 70 per cent of the electricity needs of the State. It also has works for refining salt, magnesite and barytes. The water supply comes from Morgan on the Murray, 193 kilometres south-east.

History. Matthew Flinders anchored *Investigator* a little south of Port Augusta in 1802 and John Eyre passed through the district in 1839, but the harbour was not discovered until 1852 by A. L. Elder and John Grainger in the *Yatala*. They named it after the wife of the Governor, Sir Henry Fox Young. A village was founded the same year and the first wool from the inland stations was shipped out in 1853. The town was proclaimed in 1875. In 1937 the standard gauge rail link with Port Pirie was completed. During the 1950s Port Augusta achieved transient fame as the site of the film locations for 'Bitter Springs', 'Kangaroo', 'Robbery Under Arms' and 'The Sundowners'.

A Poinsettia Festival is held yearly.

Accommodation. Eight **hotels.** Preferred: Flinders, Commercial Road. Five **motels.** Recommended: Augusta, Loudon Road. **Caravan and camping park,** all facilities.

Transport. Rail, road and **air** services.

WHYALLA

(Population 32 085)

Whyalla is an important and expanding industrial city 395 kilometres north-north-east of Adelaide on the western shore of Spencer Gulf, with iron and steel mills, ship-building yards, heavy engineering works and solar evaporation beds for the harvesting of salt. Despite its isolation and extremely hot summer climate, civic amenities have been developed energetically. Annual rainfall in the area is less than 250 millimetres.

History. The Broken Hill Proprietary Company, formed in 1885 to exploit the silver-lead ores of Broken Hill, began within a decade to diversify its mining interests. In 1900 it took out leases on the iron ore deposits of Iron Knob and Iron Monarch on the Eyre Peninsula and built a tramway to transport the ore to the small port of Hummock Hill, from which it was shipped to Port Pirie across the Gulf as a flux for the lead smelters.

In 1911 the company announced its intention of entering the steel industry and Hummock Hill became the port which supplied the furnaces at Newcastle, NSW. Actual production began in 1915 and thereafter the little township grew rapidly. In 1920 it changed its name to Whyalla, meaning 'a place with deep water'.

During the 1930s, BHP decided to create a deepwater port at Whyalla and to establish a shipyard. It was felt that Newcastle on the eastern seaboard was too exposed to be the sole shipbuilding centre in Australia if another war broke out. Whyalla had the advantage of being strategically protected but not entirely isolated. In 1940, a year after the construction of the yards began, they were sufficiently advanced to start building two corvettes for the Royal Australian Navy and ore carriers for the company. Work on the first blast furnace had begun in 1937 and by 1941 it was completed. For some years this furnace supplied most of the needs of Australian iron foundries and a considerable tonnage for export.

These activities rapidly increased the town's population, which grew from 1 400 in 1938 to more than 5 000 in 1946. The water main from Morgan, 360 kilometres away, was extended from Port Pirie and duplicated and relaid.

In 1945 the Whyalla Town Commission was constituted by special Act of Parliament. Previously it had been entirely a company town but henceforward administration was the responsibility of three elected representatives of the population, three company men and one Government nominee.

In 1951 BHP expanded its activities to salt harvesting. The high salinity of the Spencer Gulf waters (23 percent higher than average sea water), the hot, dry climate and an impervious clay subsoil made it a profitable venture. Salt from the Whyalla beds is used in the production of sodium sulphate, ammonium chloride and chlorine.

In 1958 the company announced plans to make Whyalla Australia's third steel manufacturing centre and in 1965 No 1 blast furnace produced the first steel. Two furnaces are now in operation with an output of about one million ingot tonnes a year. Whyalla was proclaimed a city in 1961.

Places of Interest. Steelworks and **shipyards.** Daily tours conducted (steelworks 9.30 am, shipyards 2 pm). Iron Monarch **iron ore** quarries, inspections Monday to Friday (inquiries from BHP offices first). Iron ore **Pelletizing Plant. Solar evaporation salt beds. Special dairy farm,** where 200 head of cattle are carefully managed in the difficult climate to supply the town with fresh milk. **Wyndyalla Art Gallery,** Farrell Street.

Sports. Race and trotting course. Golf course. Tennis, bowls etc. Yachting and swimming.

Accommodation. Six **hotels.** Recommended: Sundowner, Lincoln Highway. Three **motels.** Recommended; Whyalla Foreshore. **Caravan and camping park,** all facilities.

Transport. Regular **coach** and **rail** services to Adelaide. **Through coach** service to Adelaide once a week. Daily **coach** service to Port Lincoln. Frequent **air** services.

PORT LINCOLN

(Population 9 158)

On the eastern shores of Eyre Peninsula, 246 kilometres by air (806 kilometres by road) west of Adelaide, Port Lincoln is one of Australia's largest fishing ports and an important wheat export centre. Its bulk loading installations handle almost the entire crop of the productive peninsula grainlands. It is attractively sited on a deeply indented coastline traversed by good roads and enjoys a mild, Mediterranean-type climate. Since the establishment of commercial air services it is gaining popularity as a holiday resort.

The large fishing fleets based on the town take considerable quantities of tuna, whiting and other scale fish which are frozen or canned at local works. The town also has railway workshops, timber mills, abattoirs, butter and bacon factories.

History. Sealers based themselves on Port Lincoln as early as 1 800, but they did not settle there permanently. Flinders investigated and named the harbour in 1802. It was suggested in 1836 as the site for the capital of South Australia, but Governor Light rejected it because of the scarcity of water and the apparently barren nature of the land in the immediate vicinity. It was, however, surveyed in 1839-40 and in 1847 proclaimed a port. Its prosperity has been built on the development of quick-maturing wheat types suitable for light soils.

Places of Interest. Pioneer's Mill Museum, Dorset Place, built as a mill in 1847; open Wednesdays and weekends from 2 pm to 5 pm. Outside steps lead to the roof of the mill and these are open at all times. **Tumby Bay,** a small resort in picturesque scenery and with good beaches, 48 kilometres north. Talc is mined in the hills to the north-west. **Poonindie Aboriginal Training School,** off Tumby Bay Road, has church of unusual design with two chimneys. The school was founded by Archdeacon Matthew Blagden Hall. **Lincoln National Park,** a few kilometres south of town. **Coffin Bay** about 50 kilometres west of Port Lincoln, off Flinders Highway, is a fishing village set in a remote and particularly interesting wildlife reserve. It has an oyster farm and a number of small jetties of eccentric design. Coastal scenery hereabouts is spectacular.

Port Lincoln celebrates a 'Tunarama' Festival in January when the tuna fishing season opens. The Matthew Flinders Challenge Race for ocean-going yachts is sailed during Christmas week from Queenscliff in Port Phillip Bay in Victoria, 966 kilometres away. The event was first organized in 1964.

Sports. Racecourse. Golf course, swimming and surfing. Yachting. Excellent big game fishing.

Accommodation. Five **hotels.** Recommended: Tasman, Tasman Terrace. Five **motels.** Recommended: Hilton, King Street. **Caravan and camping park,** all facilities.

Transport. Daily **road** service from Adelaide and Whyalla, via Tumby Bay, Port Neill, Arno Bay and Cowell; also local services to peninsula settlements. Daily **air** services to Adelaide. **Rail** services to Minnipa, Ceduna, Kimba and Buckleboo. **Charter flights** and **launches** available. Local sightseeing **tours** by road coach. MV *Troubridge* runs a **ferry** service between Adelaide and the port.

STREAKY BAY (Population 2 050)

Streaky Bay, 727 kilometres north-west of Adelaide, is a fishing port, holiday resort and service town for a productive cereal-growing area. It has a charming aspect and improved road access is fast boosting its popularity.

History. It was at Streaky Bay that the Dutch navigators, Pieter Nuyts and Thijssen, of the *Gulden Zeepaard* decided to turn back from their exploration of the Australian coast in 1627. Two hundred years later Matthew Flinders sailed into the bay and named it for its unusual bands of discoloured water. The first overland exploration of the area was made in 1839 by Eyre and Baxter. Eyre also traversed the district the following year. In 1863 William Campbell set up a store and in three years a small settlement had started to grow around it. It was placed under local government administration in 1888.

Places of Interest. Nuyts Beacon, erected to commemorate the tercentenary of the Dutch voyage. **Point Labatt,** 37 kilometres south, the only permanent fur seal colony on the Australian mainland. (The access road is fairly rough and the surrounding countryside rugged.) Scenic walk to **Back Beach** (8 kilometres). **Scenic drives** to Yanaby (23 kilometres), Smooth Pool (26 kilometres), Granite Rock (28 kilometres), High Cliff (29 kilometres) and Sceale Bay (25 kilometres).

Sport. Swimming in sharkproof enclosure. Water-skiing, not shark protected. Fishing.

Accommodation. One **hotel-motel. Camping and caravan park,** all facilities.

Transport. Road service from Adelaide six days weekly, and from Port Lincoln three times weekly. **Air** service to Ceduna twice weekly.

CEDUNA (Population 2 056)

A small town near Port Thevenard on the shores of Denial Bay, 806 kilometres north-west of Adelaide, Ceduna is the centre of a district which produces wool, cereals, gypsum and fish. Its shallow offshore waters are said to yield the bulk of whiting—Australia's most prized scale fish—marketed in Adelaide and Melbourne. The South Australian Fishermens' Co-operative has a freezing works and depot at the port. The fleet is run mainly by Greek-born fishermen.

Ceduna is the last town on the Eyre Highway before the Nullarbor Desert. It is the base of the C of E Bush Church Aid Society's Flying Medical Service and the SA Government's School of the Air.

History. There was a whaling station on St Peter's Island off Cape Thevenard as early as 1850 but the village was not founded until 1896. It was proclaimed a town five years later under the name of Murat Bay which Baudin had given it in 1802. In 1915 this was changed to Ceduna from the aboriginal word *chedoona,* meaning 'a resting place'.

Accommodation. One **hotel.** Four **motels.** Recommended: Flag Motor Inn.

Transport. **Road** and **air** services to Adelaide.

Northern Territory

The Northern Territory comprises roughly one sixth of the Australian continent. It has an area of 135 million hectares—six times that of Great Britain—and its total population of white Australians and aborigines is now about 50 000.

With the exception of a strip of 290 kilometres wide along the South Australian border, the Territory lies north of the Tropic of Capricorn in the torrid zone. The terrain is of three main types—low-lying, heavily wooded coastal plains along the northern coasts washed by the Arafura and Timor Seas; broken, deeply eroded scarps and mountain ranges in the north-eastern and southern sectors; and wide, almost featureless plains sparsely covered by low eucalypt and acacia scrub or hardy semi-desert grasses.

The lowlands of the centre and south are semi-arid to arid. The coastal region receives heavy monsoonal rainfall between November and April, and the effect of the monsoon is also felt in the high country of the south, although the amount of rain is unpredictable. Good and bad seasons appear to occur cyclically. From May to October significant falls are rare in any part of the Territory. The climate in the dry season is warm and pleasant. In the wet season it is humid and unpleasant in the north and extremely hot in the south. Insect pests such as sandflies and mosquitoes are troublesome in the north during the wet.

The economy of the Northern Territory is predominantly pastoral, beef cattle being raised mainly on the open range system on huge landholdings up to 400 000 hectares. Recently mining for gold, copper, iron ore and other minerals has been revived and there are indications that modern methods and greatly improved communications will result in sound establishment of mining industries which have hitherto existed only precariously because of the region's isolation from major centres of population. Major fields are being opened up around Tennant Creek, and in the vicinity of Arthur River on the east coast fronting the Gulf of Carpentaria where important silver-lead-zinc discoveries have been made. Manganese deposits on Groote Eylandt off the east coast of Arnhem Land are being worked by BHP and have great bearing on the Australian steel industry.

So far, however, the greatest single revenue earner in the Northern Territory is tourism. This activity has developed enormously over the last 10 years. The chief drawcards are the spectacular mountain ranges in the vicinity of Alice Springs, where vivid colouring and amazing rock formations are a delight to lovers of unusual scenery.

The 'Top End' near Darwin is also gaining popularity because it, with the possible exception of the North Queensland coast between Townsville and Cooktown, is the most typically 'tropical' part of Australia. The coast is mangrove and palm-fringed, deeply indented by the estuaries of large rivers. The flora is predominantly Australian, but has a strong admixture of colourful South East Asian and Oceanic species.

Darwin and its environs particularly appeal to sportsmen with rod and gun. The Top End, and the much less accessible country of the northern Kimberley of Western Australia and Cape Yorke Peninsula north of Cairns, are the best shooting and fishing territory in the Commonwealth.

HISTORY The first close examination of the coast of the Northern

Territory east of Darwin was made by Matthew Flinders in 1802, and the first attempt at permanent settlement of the mainland in 1838. Ludwig Leichhardt traversed the coast of the Gulf of Carpentaria and crossed Arnhem Land to Port Essington not far from Darwin in 1844-45. About the same time Charles Sturt penetrated the south-eastern desert of what is now the Northern Territory, but it was not until John McDouall Stuart made his three epic journeys northward from Adelaide between 1860 and 1862 that anything was definitely known about the interior.

Pastoralists in search of new land soon followed in the footsteps of the explorer and mineral discoveries were made which encouraged speculative efforts at permanent settlement. The harsh nature of the country defeated all but the toughest and most adaptable of cattlemen and miners. Endeavours to establish tropical agriculture in the well-watered north were also defeated by the climate, the nature of which was totally misjudged by early colonists.

The Territory was a part of New South Wales from 1827 onwards until 1863 when the Imperial Government transferred responsibility for its administration to South Australia. The repeated defeat of developmental enterprises gravely embarrassed the State and in 1911 the Commonwealth Government took over. An overland telegraph line had by then been built between Adelaide and Darwin (1870-72) and railways had been built from Darwin to Pine Creek in the north and from Adelaide to Oodnadatta. The southern line was extended from Oodnadatta to Alice Springs in 1929 and from Pine Creek to Larrimah (Birdum) in 1929. The Darwin-Larrimah line does not now carry passengers.

The shaky economy of the Northern Territory received a boost during the second world war when garrisons and air force establishments were maintained there and more than 1 600 kilometres of the Stuart Highway from Darwin to Alice Springs were sealed to maintain supply by motor transport. After the war there was a brief uranium mining boom and further unsuccessful efforts were made to establish agriculture on a signficant scale. The Territory now depends largely on tourist revenues and Commonwealth governmental expenditure to maintain Darwin as a strategic and administrative settlement, improve road communication with mines and large cattle stations and introduce scientific methods of pasture improvement. Private interests backed by American capital are also attempting to grow sorghum on a large scale on Tipperary Station and to develop the beef cattle industry.

TOURING IN THE NORTHERN TERRITORY The Stuart Highway is the backbone of surface communications north of Alice Springs. Except where essential maintenance work is in progress the surface is good but, owing to the material which must be used in construction, will not take high speed cruising without excessive tyre wear. The 'feeder' Barkly Highway from Queensland which joins the Stuart Highway north of Tennant Creek is also a good road for many hundreds of kilometres, but motorists planning to drive either to Darwin or Alice Springs via the Landsborough or Flinders Highways from the Queensland coast should bear in mind that there are many stretches of appallingly bad road east of Cloncurry, although motor coaches regularly traverse the route.

The 'beef roads' programme has recently improved access from Wyndham

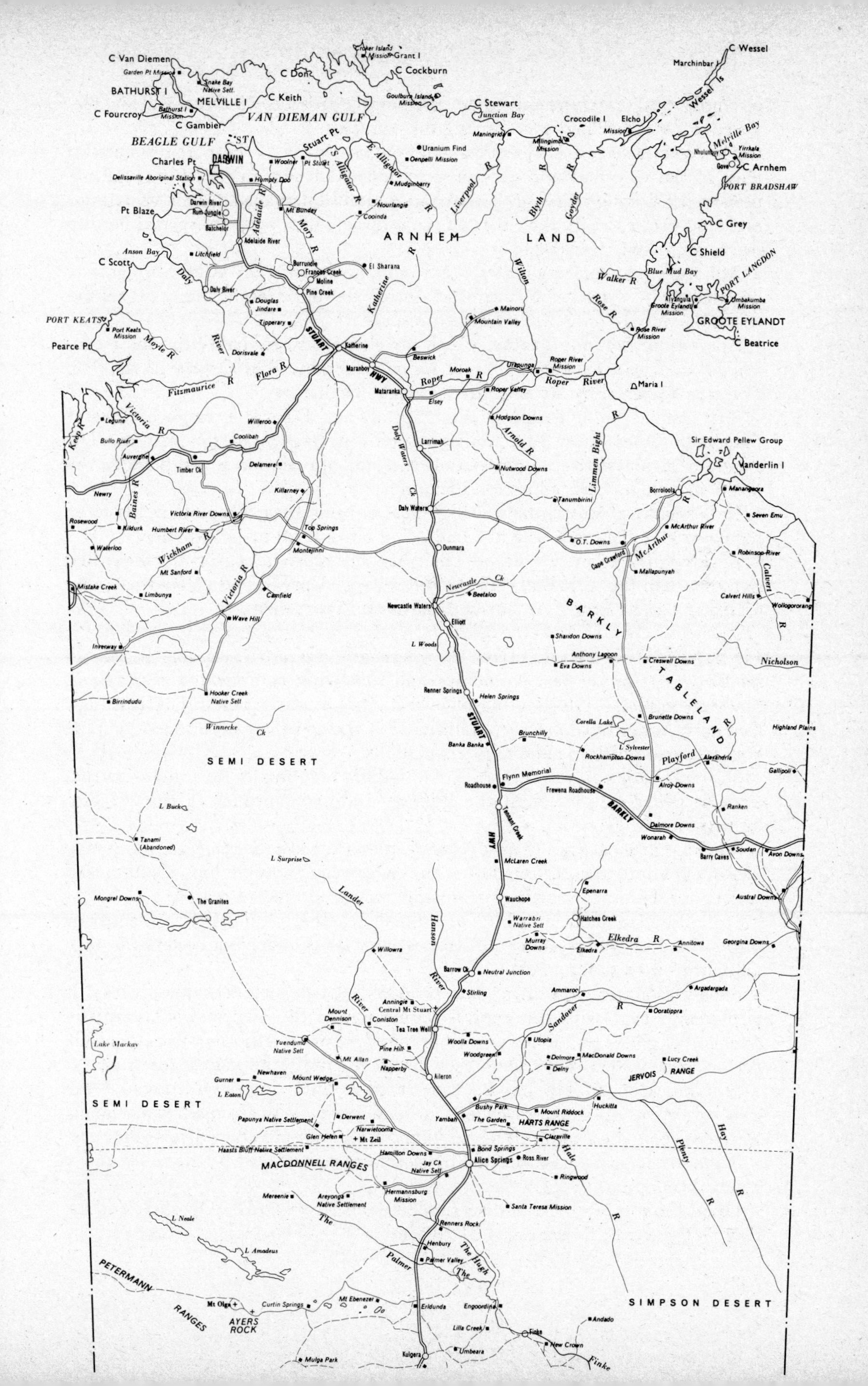

C Van Diemen
Garden Pt Mission
Snake Bay Native Sett.
BATHURST I
MELVILLE I
C Fourcroy
Bathurst I Mission
C Gambier
C Don
C Keith
Croker Island Mission
Grant I
C Cockburn
Goulburn Island Mission
VAN DIEMAN GULF
BEAGLE GULF
Charles Pt
DARWIN
Delissaville Aboriginal Station
Pt Blaze
Darwin River
Rum Jungle
Batchelor
Adelaide River
Humpty Doo
Woolner
Pt Stuart
Stuart Pt
S Alligator R
E Alligator R
Uranium Find
Oenpelli Mission
Mudginbarry
Nourlangie
Cooinda
Mt Bundey
Mary R
C Stewart
Junction Bay
Maningrida
Milingimbi Mission
Crocodile I
Elcho I
Mission
C Wessel
Marchinbar I
Wessel Is
Melville Bay
Yirrkala Mission
Nhulunbuy
Gove
C Arnhem
PORT BRADSHAW
Liverpool R
Blyth R
Goyder R
ARNHEM LAND
C Grey
C Shield
Blue Mud Bay
Walker R
PORT LANGDON
Angurugu
Groote Eylandt Mission
Umbakumba Mission
GROOTE EYLANDT
C Beatrice
Anson Bay
C Scott
Litchfield
Daly R
Daly River
Burrundie
Frances Creek
Moline
El Sharana
Pine Creek
Douglas
Jindare
Tipperary
Katherine R
Wilton
Rose R
Rose River Mission
PORT KEATS
Port Keats Mission
Pearce Pt
Moyle R
River
Dorisvale
Katherine
STUART HWY
Mainoru
Mountain Valley
Beswick
Maranboy
Mataranka
Roper R
Moroak
Urapunga
Roper River Mission
Roper River
Roper Valley
Elsey
Maria I
Flora R
Fitzmaurice R
Victoria R
Keep R
Legune
Bullo River
Auvergne
Timber Ck
Coolibah
Willeroo
Delamere
Hodgson Downs
Arnold R
Larrimah
Daly Waters Ck
Nutwood Downs
Limmen Bight R
Sir Edward Pellew Group
Vanderlin I
Newry
Baines R
Killarney
Daly Waters
Tanumbirini
Borroloola
Manangoora
Seven Emu
McArthur River
Rosewood
Kildurk
Humbert River
Victoria River Downs
Top Springs
Montejinni
Waterloo
Wickham R
Dunmara
O.T. Downs
Cape Crawford
McArthur R
Robinson River
Mallapunyah
Calvert R
Mt Sanford
Limbunya
Mistake Creek
Victoria R
Camfield
Newcastle Ck
Beetaloo
Newcastle Waters
Elliott
Calvert Hills
Wollogorang
Wave Hill
Inverway
L Woods
BARKLY TABLELAND
Shandon Downs
Anthony Lagoon
Eva Downs
Creswell Downs
Nicholson
Hooker Creek Native Sett
Birrindudu
Renner Springs
Helen Springs
Winnecke Ck
Corella Lake
Brunette Downs
Highland Plains
SEMI DESERT
Banka Banka
Brunchilly
L Sylvester
Rockhampton Downs
Playford R
Alexandria
Flynn Memorial Roadhouse
Frewena Roadhouse
Alroy Downs
Gallipoli
L Buck
Tennant Creek
BARKLY HWY
Ranken
Dalmore Downs
Wonarah
Tanami (Abandoned)
Barry Caves
Soudan
Avon Downs
L Surprise
McLaren Creek
Lander
Mongrel Downs
The Granites
Epenarra
Austral Downs
Wauchope
Hanson
Warrabri Native Sett
Hatches Creek
Murray Downs
Elkedra R
Elkedra
Annitowa
Georgina Downs
Willowra
Barrow Ck
Neutral Junction
River
Stirling
Ammaroo
Argadargada
Sandover R
Ooratippra
Anningie
Central Mt Stuart
Mount Dennison
Coniston
Tea Tree Well
Woolla Downs
Utopia
Lake Mackay
Yuendumu Native Sett
Pine Hill
Mt Allan
Napperby
Woodgreen
Dolmore
MacDonald Downs
Delny
Lucy Creek
JERVOIS RANGE
Gurner
Newhaven
Mount Wedge
Aileron
L Eaton
Bushy Park
Mount Riddock
Huckitta
Papunya Native Settlement
Derwent
Yambah
The Garden
HARTS RANGE
Glen Helen
Narwietooma
Mt Zeil
Claraville
Haasts Bluff Native Settlement
Hamilton Downs
Bond Springs
Ross River
Hale
Plenty R
Hay R
MACDONNELL RANGES
Jay Ck Native Sett
Alice Springs
Ringwood
Mereenie
Areyonga Native Settlement
Hermannsburg Mission
Santa Teresa Mission
The
L Neale
Renners Rock
Henbury
L Amadeus
Palmer
The Hugh
Palmer Valley
The
PETERMANN RANGES
Mt Olga
Curtin Springs
Mt Ebenezer
Erldunda
Engoordina
SIMPSON DESERT
AYERS ROCK
Andado
Lilla Creek
Finke
New Crown
Kulgera
Umbeara
Mulga Park
Finke

in North West Australia but some years may elapse before there is a reliable, sealed, all-weather highway circling the continent

The roads between Alice Springs and either Marree or Port Augusta are for most of the way bad and all but determined adventurers, with enough experience of driving in rough country to minimise damage to their vehicles or accident, prefer to ship their cars on the railway which provides special flat-top trucks for vehicle transport.

Although many places of interest around both Darwin and Alice Springs may be reached by conventional vehicles during the dry season, many others are accessible only by four-wheel drive transport.

Apart from organized tours, which are numerous, probably the most convenient and least expensive way of seeing either the Red Centre or the Top End is to travel in by air and hire a vehicle locally.

First class accommodation at Alice Springs and Darwin is somewhat dearer than most other Australian tourist resorts—in Darwin particularly so. The standard of physical accommodation is good, but service is indifferent even in the most highly priced establishments.

In the bush, of course, the traveller must be something of a philosopher to be happy to take the good with the bad—and chalk it all up to experience.

All in all, the country around 'The Alice' has more to engross the dedicated sightseer than the Top End. On the other hand, Darwin and its environs offer a greater variety of activity for naturalists and sportsmen.

FISHING AND SHOOTING There are no restrictions on fishing in inland waters or the sea. Numerous and somewhat complicated restrictions, however, apply to the shooting of birds, animals and reptiles. The Northern Territory Administration is committed to a policy of conservation of wildlife and acts vigorously to enforce its regulations.

Visitors wishing to hunt in the Territory should inquire for up-to-date instructions at police stations or at the Primary Industries Branch of the NT Administration in Darwin.

The importation and use of high powered firearms is virtually prohibited. They may be brought into the region only if the owner can show he has 'a substantial reason' for so doing. Sporting use does not constitute such a reason.

It is illegal to shoot any bird or animal, whether or not it is protected or unprotected elsewhere, in a wildlife sanctuary. It is, indeed, an offence to take a firearm into a sanctuary.

Shooting of any kind on private property (which includes station areas) is forbidden except with the express permission of the owner, who is usually reluctant to give it unless he knows that the applicant is a thoroughly responsible person. Heavy stock losses have been caused by indiscriminate shooters.

A number of animals has been declared vermin or pests throughout the Territory. The list includes rabbits, wild donkeys, pigs, camels, foxes, goats, cats, dingoes, snakes and fruit bats or flying foxes and introduced rats and mice.

Some species are part-protected by closed seasons or may be shot only under special licence and in special areas.

Open season for ducks and geese is between 1 July and 31 October; and for magpie geese from 1 August to 31 December.

Heavy penalties for breach of the game laws are imposed, and overseas visitors keen on shooting would be well advised to make arrangements to stay at one of a number of safari camps under the control of experienced Territorian bushmen. Details are available at the Tourist Bureaux in Alice Springs and Darwin.

DARWIN

(Population 35 281)

Capital of the Northern Territory and principal port of entry for passengers and freight on airlines plying between Europe, Asia and Australia, Darwin is a small, modern city centrally situated on the north coast of the continent. It has strategic and administrative significance and is the service centre of a large but as yet underdeveloped pastoral and mining area. Up to the present neither large nor small-scale attempts to establish tropical agriculture in the region have been very successful, owing largely to the extremes of the wet and dry seasons, difficult soils and the prevalence of insect and animal pests.

The winter—or, more accurately, dry season—climate is, however, delightful and tourism is fast becoming a big source of revenue. The Top End of the Northern Territory is an unusual fascinating part of Australia—possibly not the scenic paradise its promoters claim it to be, but nevertheless of inexhaustible appeal to the type of traveller interested in unusual forms of wildlife and the distinctive exotica of the Australian tropics.

Darwin proper is built on a peninsula on the eastern shores of Port Darwin, a deep inlet of Clarence Strait between Bathurst and Melville Island and the mainland. Both commercial and residential areas are well planned, with attractive public gardens, recreation parks and street plantations. They have been completely redeveloped since the second world war when the settlement was devastated by repeated Japanese bombing. Reconstruction was long delayed and the city, proclaimed in 1959, acquired its ordered and progressive appearance only in the last few years.

The standard of accommodation in the best hotels and motels is high but expensive although increasing popularity is now creating a number of less luxurious but still basically comfortable tourist establishments.

Darwin is an excellent base from which to explore the attractions of an enormous tract of varied and often picturesque country—from the 8 million hectares of aboriginal reserve of Arnhem Land in the west (permit to enter is required) to the Western Australian border on Joseph Bonaparte Gulf in the east, and as far south as Mataranka, 515 kilometres down the Stuart Highway to Alice Springs.

During the season there are numerous motor coach and hire car tours from the city to areas of interest. Guided 'safari' tours for buffalo and crocodile shooting, fishing and off-the-beaten-track sightseeing are available. Most are efficiently run.

Darwin's climate is equable. The average maximum for July, the coolest month, is 30°C and the minimum 22°C. In November, the hottest month, the figures are 34°C and 26°C. Relative humidity is high in the wet season and those unaccustomed to an equatorial climate find the conditions trying.

Northern Territorians have evolved sensible conventions of dress. Men wear shorts, open necked shirts and long socks during the day, and women choose light cotton frocks and light shoes or sandals. 'Darwin rig' for the informal occasions in the evening is white shirt, tie and dark slacks and shoes for men and slightly more elaborate cotton frocks or cocktail dress for women. 'Darwin

Central Australian landscape

Main street, Alice Springs

Asian tropical trees and flowering plants, and sound shell for outdoor concerts. **Government House,** dating from 1870. **Roman Catholic Cathedral,** with painting of 'Black Madonna'. **Supreme Court** buildings. **Mindil, Vestey's** and **Casuarina Beaches. Howard Springs Wildlife Reserve** (24 kilometres). **Humpty Doo Station** and **experimental farms** (36 kilometres east of Stuart Highway turnoff). Darwin environs: **Manton Dam** (city's water supply) and **lagoon** (71 kilometres south). **Tumbling Waters** near **Southport** (historic ruins), about 84 kilometres south and west. **Knuckey's Lagoons** (12 kilometres south). **Fog Dam Bird Sanctuary** on Humpty Doo road. Buffalo can be seen on surrounding plains. **Cemetery Plains,** magnetic anthills (termite hills) of greyish colour, up to 3 metres high, very thin and invariably running north and south (20 kilometres). **Yarrawonga Park Zoo,** containing specimens of most local animals, buffalo, crocodiles etc in natural setting. **Note:** Buffaloes, though appearing tame, should not be approached closely on foot. **Berry Springs** pools (64 kilometres) for excellent swimming and bush walks. **Robin Falls** (131 kilometres).

Most of these places are clearly signposted from the Stuart Highway.

Sports

Darwin is proud of the excellence and variety of its facilities for sports and games. They include a racecourse, tennis and squash courts, a golf course, motor car and cycling race circuits, rifle, pistol and archery ranges, bowling greens (turf and bitumenized rubber), fishing and water sports of all kinds. Numerous indoor games can also be played.

Note: It is highly dangerous to bathe in the open sea during the wet season and the months immediately before and after it. Sea wasps are prevalent.

Annual events which draw crowds include the Darwin Eisteddfod, an NT Walkabout Day when a 26 kilometre walking race is held and the town turns the occasion into a holiday; an agricultural, pastoral and industrial show; and The City of Darwin Festival which includes sports carnivals, street processions, and corroboree exhibitions by aborigines. The date of these celebrations varies from year to year, but most are held in June, July and August.

Accommodation

Nine **hotels** and licenced **hotel-motels** in city and suburbs. Recommended: Fannie Bay, East Point Road; Don, Cavanagh Street; Darwin, Hobart Street; Koala, Mitchell and Daly Street. Ten **motels.** Recommended: Darwin Motor Inn. Several **guest-houses** and **private hotels** in suburbs. **Camping and caravan park** (off Stuart Highway 13 kilometres south), all facilities.

Transport

Road services from centres on Stuart Highway. **Shipping** services by coastal passenger-freighters. **Air** services from all Australian States and northern inland settlements and between Bacau, Portuguese Timor, and Darwin. **Air charters** are available. Occasional **aerial tours** of aboriginal missions on Melville and Bathurst Islands are arranged by the Northern Territory Tourist Board. City **buses.** The town is served by a fleet of radio **taxis** which are not metered but operate on an area charge system. **Drive-yourself** and **hire cars** are available.

Stuart Highway Settlements

ADELAIDE RIVER (Population 200)

This small settlement in attractive country 116 kilometres south of Darwin is a good base for expeditions to **Rum Jungle** uranium mining area, **Batchelor** experimental farms, **Daly River** district and **Tipperary** sorghum project.

Accommodation. One **hotel.** Various **camping sites.**

PINE CREEK (Population 500)

An historic mining and station service centre 135 kilometres south-east of Adelaide River, near a new iron ore mining project, Pine Creek is about 1½ kilometres off Stuart Highway. There is unusually interesting country on the road to **Oenpelli, Waterfall Creek** and **Muirella Park** in the north-east.

Accommodation. One **hotel.**

KATHERINE (Population 2 520)

Katherine is a prosperous small town in some of the most promising agricultural and grazing country in the Territory. It is 354 kilometres from Darwin and a major centre for the northern cattle stations. The road from Wyndham, West Australia, now sealed, joins the Stuart Highway north-west of the town.

Katherine was an important military base during the Pacific war. Work now being done by the

Aboriginal bark painting

CSIRO research station and experimental farms on Townsville lucerne (leguminous tropical pasture plant) and other species is extremely significant for the northern grazing industry.

Katherine Gorge, 35 kilometres north-east of the town, is possibly the most colourful and grandly proportioned river canyon in inland Australia. The great cliffs through which the river flows are brilliantly tinted and are seen at their best in the early morning and late afternoon. Tours to the gorge are run from town. Guides and flat-bottomed aluminium boats may be hired for excursions upriver. **Katherine Caves** are 26 kilometres south.

Accommodation. Two **hotels.** Preferred: Commercial. Two **motels.** Recommended: Corroboree. **Camping and caravan park,** all facilities, near town. **Camping area,** limited facilities, near gorge.

MATARANKA

Mataranka cattle station, with accommodation for tourists, is 103 kilometres south-east of Katherine, 8 kilometres north-east of highway. Warm springs and picturesque palm forest are near homestead. The attractiveness of the area is somewhat spoiled by litter left by tourists. There is one small **hotel** on the highway near the turnoff. The **Elsey Memorial Cemetery** containing the graves of pioneers mentioned in Mrs Aeneas Gunn's famous book, 'We of the Never Never', is about 18 kilometres south off the highway. The road to Roper River joins the highway just south of the Mataranka turnoff.

LARRIMAH

A small settlement at the terminus of the railway from Darwin, 63 kilometres south of Mataranka. One **hotel.**

TENNANT CREEK (Population 1 797)

Tennant Creek is a small but growing town 26 kilometres south of the junction of the Stuart and Barkly Highways 503 kilometres north of Alice Springs. It has a number of well stocked shops and is the commercial centre of a district in which several profitable gold, bismuth and copper mines are being worked.

A **memorial** to the famous missionary of the Outback, John Flynn, stands at the junction of the highways. A collection of gigantic boulders, the **Devil's Marbles,** are about 96 kilometres south. **Tennant Creek Homestead,** 11 kilometres north-north-east, incorporates the old stone Telegraph repeater station built in 1871.

Accommodation. Two **hotels.** Preferred: Tennant Creek. One **motel. Camping ground.**

Transport. Coach services to Alice Springs, Adelaide, Darwin and Townsville. **Air** services.

ALICE SPRINGS

(Population 11 118)

Alice Springs, 1 688 kilometres by road north of Adelaide, has become the tourist capital of Central Australia during the last 10 or 15 years. A modern, well maintained town in the heart of the spectacular Macdonnell Ranges, it attracts tens of thousands of visitors every year between the months of May and September when the weather is superbly cloudless in any normal season and temperatures are moderate. However, freak rains do occasionally occur in the dry season and the town may have road and rail communications cut by severe flooding of the Todd River, which runs through the town, and of watercourses which are ordinarily either dry or sparsely dotted with pools. Even though the settlement is at an altitude of 610 metres, summer months are intensely hot and severe dust storms are not uncommon.

The country in the immediate vicinity of Alice Springs is not particularly interesting but there is spectacular mountain and desert scenery of great variety within a day's journey.

The region produces beef cattle on big runs and there is a minor dairying and fruit growing industry in pockets of land where irrigation is possible. Besides tourism, which has become a multi-million dollar business, some secondary industries such as joinery, cabinet making, cordial manufacture and sheet metal fabrication are established. The ranges of the Centre are highly mineralized and many small mines are worked within a 300 to 500 kilometre radius.

History. The first white man to traverse the Macdonnell Ranges was James McDouall Stuart who passed about 51 kilometres west of Alice Springs in 1860. Eleven years later, in 1871, John Ross passed near the present site of the town and chose Heavitree Gap as part of the route across the ranges for the overland telegraph line to Darwin. The Springs themselves (a waterhole in the Todd) were discovered and named soon afterwards in honour of Lady Alice Todd, wife of Sir Charles Todd who was responsible for the construction of the line.

The present town was surveyed in 1888 and called Stuart. The telegraph repeater station itself continued to be known as Alice Springs, but when it was abandoned and the installation moved into the town, its name was transferred with it and became official in 1933. The old station continued for some time as an aboriginal settlement known as The Bungalow, but it too was eventually abandoned.

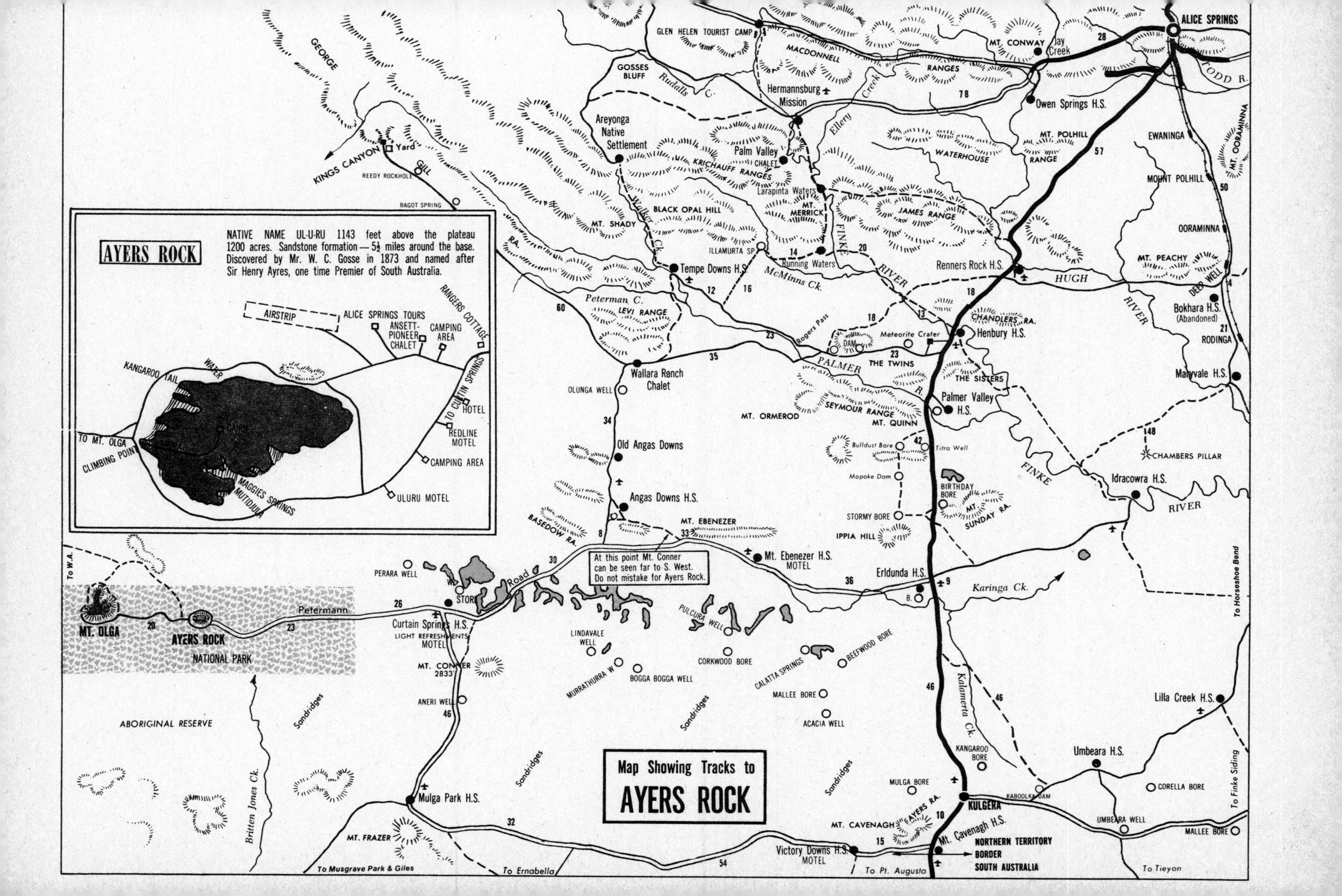
Map Showing Tracks to
AYERS ROCK
AYERS ROCK
NATIVE NAME UL-U-RU 1143 feet above the plateau 1200 acres. Sandstone formation — 5½ miles around the base. Discovered by Mr. W. C. Gosse in 1873 and named after Sir Henry Ayres, one time Premier of South Australia.
AIRSTRIP
ALICE SPRINGS TOURS
ANSETT-PIONEER CHALET
CAMPING AREA
RANGERS COTTAGE
KANGAROO TAIL
WATER
TO CURTIN SPRINGS
HOTEL
REDLINE MOTEL
CAMPING AREA
ULURU MOTEL
TO MT. OLGA
CLIMBING POINT
MAGGIES SPRINGS
MUTIDJULA
At this point Mt. Conner can be seen far to S. West. Do not mistake for Ayers Rock.
ALICE SPRINGS
MT. CONWAY
Jay Creek
TODD R.
MT. OORAMINNA
EWANINGA
MOUNT POLHILL
OORAMINNA
MT. PEACHY
DEEP WELL
Bokhara H.S. (Abandoned)
RODINGA
Maryvale H.S.
CHAMBERS PILLAR
Idracowra H.S.
FINKE RIVER
HUGH RIVER
Owen Springs H.S.
MT. POLHILL RANGE
WATERHOUSE
MACDONNELL RANGES
GLEN HELEN TOURIST CAMP
GOSSES BLUFF
Rudalls C.
Hermannsburg Mission
Ellery Creek
Areyonga Native Settlement
Palm Valley CHALET
KRICHAUFF RANGES
Larapinta Waters
MT. MERRICK
JAMES RANGE
Renners Rock H.S.
BLACK OPAL HILL
MT. SHADY
Walker Ck.
ILLAMURTA SP.
Running Waters
McMinns Ck.
Tempe Downs H.S.
GEORGE GILL RA.
KINGS CANYON
Yard
REEDY ROCKHOLE
BAGOT SPRING
Peterman C.
LEVI RANGE
Rogers Pass
Meteorite Crater
DAM
CHANDLERS RA.
Henbury H.S.
THE TWINS
PALMER R.
THE SISTERS
Palmer Valley H.S.
Wallara Ranch Chalet
OLUNGA WELL
SEYMOUR RANGE
MT. ORMEROD
MT. QUINN
Bulldust Bore
Titra Well
Old Angas Downs
Mopoke Dam
BIRTHDAY BORE
MT. SUNDAY RA.
Angas Downs H.S.
STORMY BORE
IPPIA HILL
BASEDOW RA.
MT. EBENEZER
Mt. Ebenezer H.S. MOTEL
Erldunda H.S.
Karinga Ck.
To Horseshoe Bend
PERARA WELL
Road
STORE
Curtain Springs H.S.
LIGHT REFRESHMENTS
MOTEL
Petermann
MT. OLGA
AYERS ROCK
NATIONAL PARK
To W.A.
LINDAVALE WELL
PULCURA WELL
CORKWOOD BORE
BEEFWOOD BORE
CALATTA SPRINGS
MURRATHURRA W
BOGGA BOGGA WELL
MT. CONNER 2833'
ANERI WELL
MALLEE BORE
ACACIA WELL
Kalamerta Ck.
Lilla Creek H.S.
ABORIGINAL RESERVE
Sandridges
KANGAROO BORE
Umbeara H.S.
CORELLA BORE
To Finke Siding
Britten Jones Ck.
Mulga Park H.S.
MULGA BORE
KULGERA
KABOOLKA DAM
AYERS RA.
UMBEARA WELL
MALLEE BORE
MT. FRAZER
MT. CAVENAGH
Mt. Cavenagh H.S.
NORTHERN TERRITORY
BORDER
SOUTH AUSTRALIA
Victory Downs H.S. MOTEL
To Musgrave Park & Giles
To Ernabella
To Pt. Augusta
To Tieyon
28
57
50
4
21
148
78
14
20
18
12
16
60
13
18
23
35
23
34
42
8
33
30
36
9
26
20
23
46
46
46
32
54
15
10

Between 1926 and 1931 Central Australia was administered as a separate Territory of the Commonwealth, and Alice Springs was the headquarters of government.

In 1927 the white population was only 27 but the town began to grow rapidly after the completion of the railway from Oodnadatta in 1929. In 1932 a short-lived and disastrous goldrush to the Granites 540 kilometres to the north-west, further swelled the population of The Alice, as the town is colloquially called.

During the second world war the permanent formation and sealing of the Stuart Highway to Darwin was undertaken as a strategic project and The Alice was an important supply base for the work, which cost about A $6 million.

In recent years Alice Springs has become a base for the Flying Doctor Service and the radio School of the Air.

Places of Interest. In or near town: **Anzac** and **Billy Goat Hills,** for views of town. **John Flynn Memorial Church. Tmara-Mara Art Gallery** with examples of landscape painting by aboriginal artists. **Pitchi-Richi Museum** and **Bird Sanctuary;** exhibits include opal collection. **Old telegraph station** buildings. **John Flynn's grave. Flying Doctor Base. School of the Air.**

Out of town: **Standley Chasm** (69 kilometres west), cliffs 75 metres high, only four to six metres apart and brilliantly coloured. **Simpson's Gap** (23 kilometres west), permanent waterhole and unusual scenery in Chewing Range. **Glen Helen Gorge** (121 kilometres west), with remarkable, vividly coloured rock formations. **Ormiston Gorge** (116 kilometres west), one of the most spectacular canyons, with red walls and purple floor. **Ellery Creek** and **Serpentine Gorge** (80 kilometres west). **Palm Valley** (120 kilometres west-south-west and south of famous **Hermannsberg Aboriginal Mission),** a natural oasis with many beautiful waterholes and much wildlife. It is a sanctuary and the habitat of the unique *Livistona Mariae* palm, which grows nowhere else, though related to the cabbage palm of eastern Australia. The valley was discovered in 1872. **Lodge accommodation** is available there. **Ross River Tourist Resort** and **Trephina Gorge. King's Canyon** (384 kilometres west)the largest and most spectacular gorge in Central Australia.

Annual events at Alice Springs include a show in June, a drama festival in July and in early spring a 'Henley on the Todd' carnival organized by the Rotary Club to raise funds for an outback children's holiday camp at the seaside. The river is usually dry at this time of the year and the events of a regatta are ingeniously mimed by local amateur comedians.

Sports. Golf, tennis, swimming etc.

Accommodation. Four **hotels** and **hotel-motels.** Recommended: Zdena, Khalic Street. Five **motels.** Recommended: Elkira Court, Bath Street. Numerous **guest-houses. Cabins** for rent. Four **caravan and camping parks,** all facilities.

Transport. Road services from Adelaide and Darwin. Twice weekly **rail** service from Adelaide. Regular **air** services from Darwin and Adelaide. **Taxis, hire cars, rental cars** and **four-wheel drive** vehicles are available. Numerous **coach** and **air tours** are conducted.

AYERS ROCK

A gigantic sandstone monolith rising from the desert 478 kilometres south-west of Alice Springs, Ayers Rock has become a major tourist attraction in Central Australia over the last decade. It is most easily accessible from Alice Springs.

The rock is 9 kilometres in circumference and rises 348 metres above the plain. During the day the great mass stores heat and during the night releases it so that mighty up and down draughts occur above the formation. After rain its cliffs are veiled in superb waterfalls which appear and vanish with magical rapidity.

The base of Ayers Rock supports relatively lush vegetation. It is undercut with strangely eroded caves in which the aboriginals have left galleries of rock paintings in charcoal and ochres. On the southern side there is a permanent waterhole known as Maggie Springs. The coloration of the cliff faces changes suddenly according to light conditions and reflection from the surface determined by the factor of moisture. About 32 kilometres west of Ayers Rock is **Mount Olga,** a series of rounded, massive rocks rising from the spinifex plain and also vividly coloured.

The road from Alice Springs is now clearly defined and as well maintained as difficult conditions permit. It does, however, become impassable after rain and a sign at the turnoff from the Stuart Highway advises if it is open. Motorists should on no account leave the graded formation and attempt to travel on the temptingly smooth surface of the salt lakes through which the road passes south-west of Angas Downs. The entire area in which Ayers Rock and Mount Olga are situated is a national park and wildlife sanctuary. Firearms are not permitted.

Accommodation. One **hotel** (recommended). Four **motels.** Recommended: Inland. **Caravan and camping reserve,** essential facilities. (Forward bookings essential.)

Transport. Frequent **road coach** services from Alice Springs during the season. **Air** service from Alice Springs. Combined **air-coach tours** may be arranged.

Western Australia

Western Australia, with an area of 246 million hectares, covers roughly one third of the Australian continent. Its extreme length from north-east to south-west is nearly 2 500 kilometres and its breadth from east to west is 1 600 kilometres. Topographically the State has three regions—the Great Plateau which comprises some 90 per cent of the land surface; the coastal plains; and the scarplands in between them.

The plateau rises to elevations of about 1 200 metres in the far north-west, but mostly it is from 300 to 450 metres above sea level and imperceptibly sloped. Here and there hills, peaks and ranges, remnants of ancient erosion, rise above the general surface.

The scarp to the east of Perth, known as the Darling Ranges, rises in points to an altitude of 600 metres and has a pronounced effect on rainfall which varies on the coastal plain between 500 and 1 300 millimetres a year. Annual precipitation rapidly diminishes east of this region until, 480 kilometres from the Indian Ocean, it drops to below 250 millimetres.

Thus vast stretches of inland Western Australia are extremely hot in summer, arid or semi-arid, and unsuited for agriculture or pasturage. In latter years it has been discovered that the rocks underlying these deserts are highly mineralized. Concerted, large-scale efforts to discover and exploit their wealth have only recently been made. Active prospecting for oil, natural gas, coal, metal ores and rare earths is now accelerating, and the discoveries made over the last decade are already big enough to have made a profound effect on the economy of the entire Commonwealth. Notable developments have been the establishment of nickel mining near the old Kalgoorlie goldfields, the exploitation of commercial oilfields off the north-western coast, natural gas strikes in the interior, and the even more significant exploitation of some of the world's greatest iron ore deposits in the Pilbara district, where operations have warranted the construction of new deepwater ports, small towns and many hundreds of miles of railways.

Even so, Western Australia remains sparsely populated by one million inhabitants. Despite the fact that closer settlement may—even in an age of technological miracles—prove impracticable in a high percentage of Western Australian land, huge tracts in the temperate south-west which receives adequate and reliable rainfall are suitable for farming and grazing since means have been discovered to correct chemical deficiencies in the soil. An average of 400 000 hectares of previously unproductive land in this part of the State has been brought under cultivation yearly for the last decade.

More than 1 600 kilometres north, in the East Kimberley, which receives heavy monsoonal rains but is drought stricken between April and November, water conservation projects have been undertaken in an attempt to encourage tropical agriculture on rich river flats which were formerly used only to graze beef cattle. A small farming industry has already been successfully established on the Ord River.

Apart from output of recently established heavy industries near Perth and the production from traditional goldmining and new iron and nickel mines, the Western Australian economy is predominantly rural. The State produces about one quarter of Australia's wheat, more than 11 per cent of its wool and more than 13 per cent of its timber. Under the current vigorous policy of land development in the temperate south-west, these percentages are rising. The fishing industry

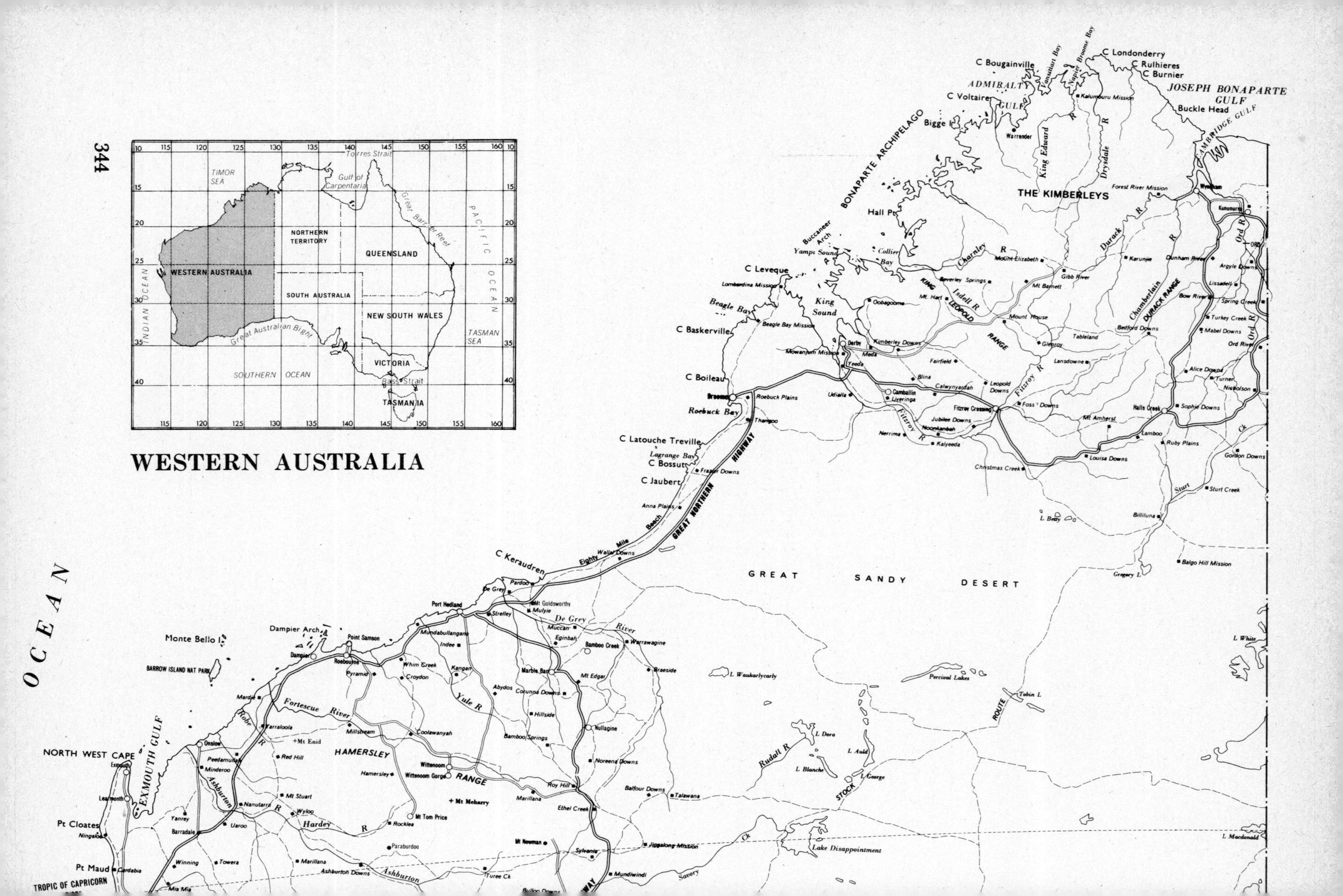

WESTERN AUSTRALIA
TIMOR SEA
NORTHERN TERRITORY
QUEENSLAND
SOUTH AUSTRALIA
NEW SOUTH WALES
VICTORIA
TASMANIA
Torres Strait
Gulf of Carpentaria
Great Barrier Reef
PACIFIC OCEAN
TASMAN SEA
INDIAN OCEAN
Great Australian Bight
SOUTHERN OCEAN
Bass Strait
OCEAN
C Londonderry
C Rulhieres
C Burnier
JOSEPH BONAPARTE GULF
Buckle Head
CAMBRIDGE GULF
C Bougainville
ADMIRALTY GULF
C Voltaire
Bigge I
BONAPARTE ARCHIPELAGO
THE KIMBERLEYS
Hall Pt
Buccaneer Arch
Yampi Sound
Collier Bay
C Leveque
King Sound
Beagle Bay
C Baskerville
C Boileau
Broome
Roebuck Bay
C Latouche Treville
Lagrange Bay
C Bossut
C Jaubert
Eighty Mile Beach
GREAT NORTHERN HIGHWAY
C Keraudren
GREAT SANDY DESERT
Port Hedland
Dampier Arch
Monte Bello Is
BARROW ISLAND NAT PARK
Point Samson
Dampier
Roebourne
Fortescue River
HAMERSLEY RANGE
NORTH WEST CAPE
EXMOUTH GULF
Pt Cloates
Pt Maud
TROPIC OF CAPRICORN
Wyndham
Kununurra
Ord R
Drysdale R
King Edward R
Durack R
Chamberlain R
DURACK RANGE
KING LEOPOLD RANGE
Fitzroy R
Derby
Fitzroy Crossing
Halls Creek
De Grey River
Yule R
Ashburton R
Robe R
Hardey R
Onslow
Marble Bar
Nullagine
Wittenoom
Mt Tom Price
Mt Newman
STOCK ROUTE
Lake Disappointment
L Dora
Percival Lakes

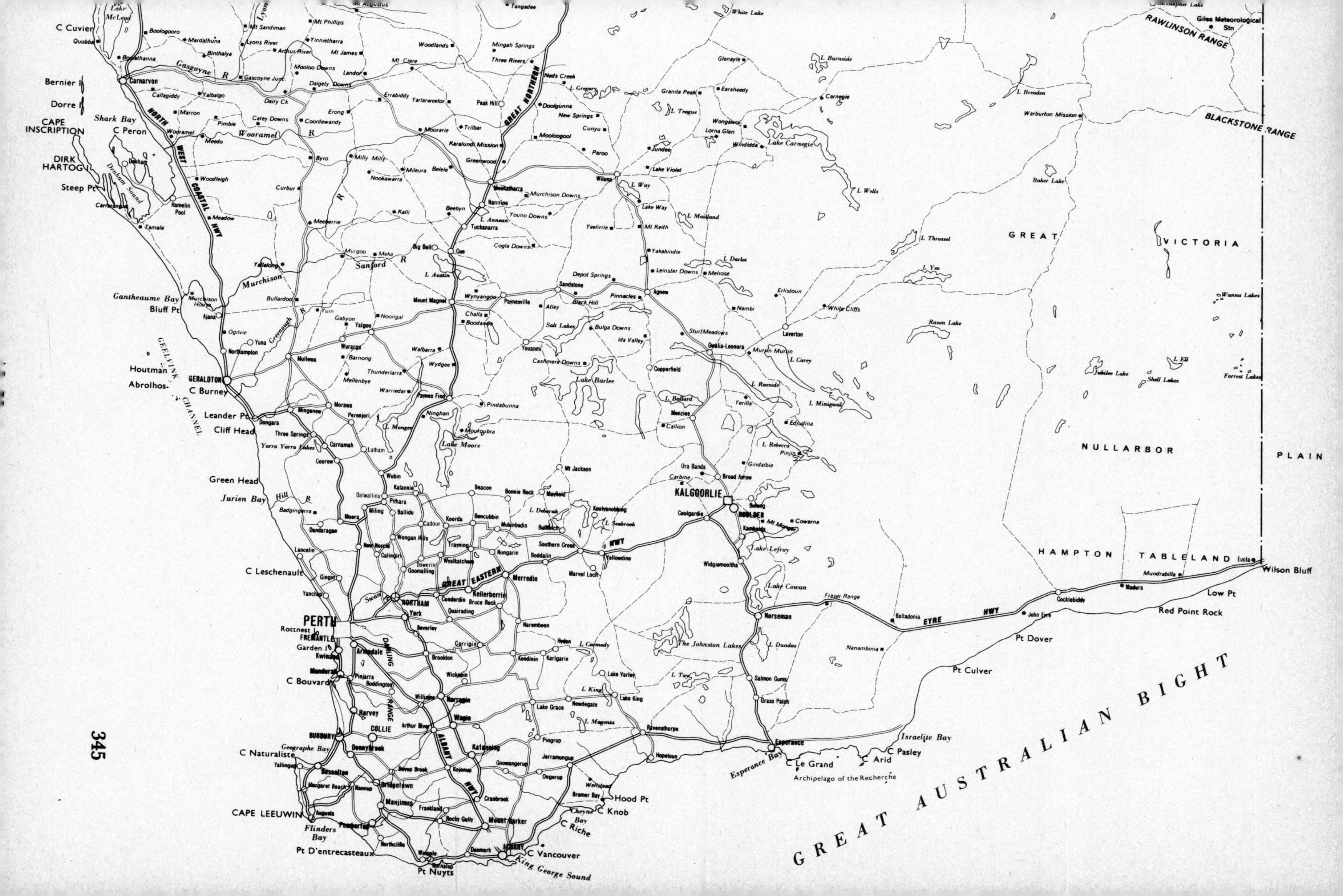

GREAT AUSTRALIAN BIGHT
GREAT VICTORIA
NULLARBOR PLAIN
HAMPTON TABLELAND
RAWLINSON RANGE
BLACKSTONE RANGE
Giles Meteorological Stn
Warburton Mission
Wilson Bluff
Eucla
Low Pt
Red Point Rock
Madura
Cocklebiddy
John Eyre
Pt Dover
EYRE HWY
Pt Culver
Balladonia
Israelite Bay
C Pasley
Arid
Archipelago of the Recherche
C Le Grand
Esperance
Esperance Bay
Norseman
Fraser Range
Salmon Gums
Grass Patch
Ravensthorpe
Hopetoun
Hood Pt
C Knob
C Riche
C Vancouver
King George Sound
ALBANY
Mount Barker
Denmark
Walpole
Pt Nuyts
Pt D'entrecasteaux
Flinders Bay
CAPE LEEUWIN
C Naturaliste
Geographe Bay
BUNBURY
COLLIE
DARLING RANGE
C Bouvard
Garden I
Rottnest I
FREMANTLE
PERTH
C Leschenault
Jurien Bay
Green Head
Cliff Head
Leander Pt
C Burney
GERALDTON
GEELVINK CHANNEL
Houtman Abrolhos
Bluff Pt
Gantheaume Bay
Murchison
NORTH WEST COASTAL HWY
GREAT NORTHERN
GREAT EASTERN HWY
ALBANY HWY
Shark Bay
C Peron
Denham
Denham Sound
Steep Pt
DIRK HARTOG
CAPE INSCRIPTION
Dorre
Bernier
C Cuvier
Carnarvon
Gascoyne R
Wooramel R
KALGOORLIE
BOULDER
Coolgardie
Southern Cross
Merredin
Kellerberrin
NORTHAM
York
Menzies
Gwalia-Leonora
Laverton
Lake Carnegie
L Wells
Wiluna
Meekatharra
Cue
Mount Magnet
Paynesville
Sandstone
Lake Moore
Lake Barlee
Lake Lefroy
Lake Cowan
L Dundas
The Johnston Lakes

is also flourishing and the value of prawns, crayfish and scale fish already considerably surpasses the value of production in any other State.

HISTORY An outline of the early exploration of the Western Australian coast by Dutch and English navigators has been given in the general section on Australia. In 1696 Commander Willem de Vlamingh in the *Geelvinck* discovered Rottnest Island off the mouth of the Swan River while looking for a vessel missing from his fleet. Shortly afterwards he discovered and named the Swan River and examined the land nearby. His report was unfavourable and this section of the coastline was thereafter virtually ignored for more than a century until the British Government became alarmed by the activity of French and American ships in the Southern Ocean. It decided to found settlements in the south and west which would justify annexation of the whole continent. In 1826 expeditions were dispatched from Sydney by Governor Darling to set up military posts at Westernport (Victoria) and Albany (West Australia). Westernport was found to be unsuitable and the expedition was withdrawn, but Major Lockyer with a party of 44 convicts and soldiers landed at Albany and formally took possession of Western Australia.

The tiny port overcame formidable establishment difficulties. The natives, who had been mistreated by sealers, were hostile and the land in the immediate vicinity was unsuited to agriculture, but it was maintained because of the strategic significance of Albany harbour.

In 1827, Captain James Stirling, RN, also dispatched by Darling, explored the Swan River, selected a town site and wrote enthusiastically about the potential of the land and the possibility that a port could be developed for trade with the Far East. The British Government was at first reluctant to sponsor a new colony on the Swan, but withdrew its objections when a group of capitalists led by Thomas Peel (a second cousin of Sir Robert Peel) undertook to finance the settlement of 10 000 emigrants.

It was decided to go ahead with the project in December 1828 and Captain Charles Fremantle (after whom the port of Fremantle was named) was sent ahead to take possession of the place. This he did on 2 May 1829. Stirling was appointed Governor and proclaimed the colony on 18 June.

As in the later case of South Australia, poor organization of the whole enterprise caused great hardship to the early settlers. Thomas Peel himself was incompetent and was unable even to provide employment for the 300 emigrants he had brought with him. Soon hundreds of others arrived to increase the difficulties of orderly land allocation and productive farming. As the settlers dispersed through the bush, trouble was experienced with the natives who naturally enough resented the sudden intrusion of the whites.

Trial-and-error alteration of the system of land distribution at last resulted in stabilization, but the colony was to remain poor and isolated until the great gold strikes of the early 1890s gave it the chance to make an economic breakthrough.

In the 1870s and 1880s the pearling industry established itself on the far north-western coast, gold was discovered at Hall's Creek in the East Kimberley, and pastoralists pushed out through the wilderness to found vast but insecure 'empires' on tropical pastures. Some for a time flourished, but the land deteriorated under persistent mismanagement and both sheep and cattle industries in the far north began to decline soon after the turn of the century. Only today is a concerted effort being made to reverse the trend and repair the damage by introducing scientific methods of pasture regeneration and stock management.

Western Australia did not receive full self-government from Great Britain until 1890, eleven years before Federation of the Australian States.

TRANSPORT **Rail.** The Western Australian Government operates nearly 7 000 kilometres of railways within the State and a direct standard gauge service connecting with the eastern States. Passenger services in the southern sector are, with the exception of those to Kalgoorlie and Bunbury, of indifferent standard. The northern half of the State has no rail link with the southern half. The new standard gauge railways built from the mines to the iron ore ports of Port Hedland and Dampier are company controlled and do not carry passenger traffic.

Road. There are about 175 000 kilometres of road open for general traffic in Western Australia. The principal highways are the Great Eastern, the North West Coastal to Geraldton, Carnarvon and Port Hedland, the Great Northern to Wyndham, the South Western to Albany via Bridgetown and Nornalup and the Great Southern to Albany via York and Katanning. To Kalgoorlie and in the south-west, major roads are sealed and of fair to good standard. The North West Coastal Highway is sealed to a point beyond Carnarvon, and the Great Eastern Highway is now sealed to the South Australian border on the Nullarbor Plain. Otherwise the highways are only partly stabilized though clearly defined. They are often badly corrugated, rough and treacherous after rain or sand and dust storms. Major centres of population throughout the State are served by railway buses beyond the effective passenger railhead and by motor coaches.

Air. Perth Airport is the terminal for frequent interstate and overseas jet services and centre of an intrastate network operated by Mac.Robertson Miller Airlines, covering the main towns of the south-west and virtually all important centres of population in the east, the north, the North West and the Kimberley. The company extends its service from the north-western towns to Darwin in the Northern Territory.

TOURING IN WESTERN AUSTRALIA Western Australia is the largest, least populated and least developed of the Australian States. Only a few kilometres from Perth, the traveller gets an entirely justified impression that he is in frontier country—huge, empty, harsh and hostile. Only in the Swan Valley and along the narrow plain north and south of the capital, or in the wooded Darling Ranges which hug the coastline for 350 kilometres northward from Albany, does the terrain give the impression of gentleness and fertility. Even the great wheatlands to the east of the scarp seem to have their winter green neutralized by the predominant red-ochre tints of the Great Plateau. The karri and jarrah forests of the south-west are sombre glades where the sound of running water is seldom heard and bright colours are seen only in spring when the wildflowers break into brilliant riot.

The voyager in the west must be prepared to take sightseeing in homeric doses, to travel hundreds of kilometres through a monotony of dreary mulga, saltbush or spinifex to experience the delight of discovering some scenic oasis—perhaps a deep, green waterhole in a dried-up river bed ringed with a pandanus jungle and teeming with bird and animal life, or a procession of peaks or table-topped mountains fantastically weathered and brightly stained by oxidised minerals.

Those who have neither the taste nor the time for such manner of exploration can these days skim the scenic cream from the air, but it is doubtful that they will come close to the spirit of the country. This reveals itself only to the patient, and admittedly hardy, surface traveller. The inland roads are mainly bad, distances between inhabited places daunting, heat, dust and flies often trying in all but the most favourable season, and accommodation—except in the vicinity of the cities and the new 'project' towns—primitive.

The most impressive scenery in Western Australia is in the far south-west and the far North West—along the surf battered cliffs of Leeuwin or among the stark, vivid gorges of the Hamersley Ranges or the sounds of the East Kimberley coast. The south-west can be reached easily by road from Perth. Half a day's driving will bring the tourist to the best of the forest country, the incomparable surf beaches, the caves and the clifftop panoramas. The North West is a different proposition. It is 1 500 kilometres or more from what the city dweller would describe as civilization. Its largest settlements are little more than villages and its biggest mines appear as inconsiderable pock marks on the face of the desert.

Air travel brings at least some of the fascinating features of this country within a few hours of Perth. By road the journey takes many days and, for the car driver, a good deal of skill and stamina.

The most practicable way for a time-limited traveller to see the North West and the Kimberley is to fly to Wittenoom, Roebourne, Derby and Kununurra on the scheduled air services after first making arrangements with the Government Tourist Bureau or a travel agency to reserve hire car or charter flight facilities for local sightseeing.

Package deal air-and-road and road coach tours of the North West and Kimberley can be booked in Perth. They are probably the simplest and cheapest way of seeing the country, but they have the disadvantage of running on fairly tight and inflexible schedules with stopover time rarely sufficient for the traveller to pursue his personal tastes and interests. They are, nevertheless, good value for money.

Accommodation of city standard can now be obtained at the iron ore mining towns and ports in the North West and at Derby and Kununurra in the Kimberley. Elsewhere in the northern half of the State, hotels are third rate although many of them, particularly in the more remote areas, can be fun for the easy-going traveller with a sense of humour.

Spring and early summer are the best seasons to tour in the south. Winter and early spring are the only seasons to tour in the north—at least if pleasure is a prime consideration. Claims by those wishing to promote off-season tourism in tropical Australia should be treated with the greatest reserve by all visitors unaccustomed to a hot, wet and often turbulent climate.

Tariffs in the few first-class hotels or motels in the north are approximately the same as those charged in first-class city establishments, or even a little more expensive. Rates in bush hotels, related to the standard of service given, are appreciably higher than in the eastern States. In the south-west charges are about the same.

PERTH

(Population 500 246)

The capital of Western Australia, Perth, is situated on the Swan River 19 kilometres from its mouth and the port of Fremantle. The metropolitan area is generally held to extend north and south for a distance of about 56 kilometres and east and west for about 40 kilometres. It lies over three parallel land strips—a heavily eroded coastal reef and dune region about 6 kilometres wide, a coastal plain about 15 kilometres wide made up of consolidated dunes, low sandhills and swamps, and the lower slopes of the Darling scarp with fertile clay and loam soils.

Perth enjoys the best climate of any Australian capital with a mean temperature of 24°C in the hottest month, February, and a mean of 13°C in the coldest month, July. Despite an annual rainfall average of 914 millimetres, there is a pronounced dry season from November to March and throughout the year the city has an average of eight hours sunshine daily. During occasional heat waves in summer, the thermometer climbs above 38°C.

Although, like all Australian towns and cities, Perth is an odd mixture of derivative architectural styles, it has the appearance of cohesive good order. The heavy industrial development of the last 20 years has occurred mainly in areas to the south and west and there is as yet no problem of air pollution. Multi-storey redevelopment is beginning in the heart of the city but it is still not far advanced.

One of the most attractive features of Perth is the river foreshore south of the commercial quarter which has been reserved as park and recreational land, carefully improved over the years. The city's founders are reputed to have been influenced by considerations of natural beauty in selecting a site and their descendants can claim with justifiable pride that they have made an effective attempt to preserve the advantages they inherited.

The tempo of life in Perth has speeded up since the mineral boom began in the early 1960s, but it is still leisurely by the standards of the eastern capitals. Tourism is an industry which West Australians are just beginning to evaluate as a result of enormously improved communications with the eastern States. Standards of accommodation and service are now excellent. Because of its delightful and mainly reliable climate, the scenic quality of the nearby Darling Ranges and the opportunity it presents for outdoor recreation of all kinds, Perth comes close to being an ideal holiday city.

The city stages a Festival of Arts every year between late January and early March.

COMMERCE AND INDUSTRY Only recently has Perth become an industrial city of importance. For well over 100 years it was only the administrative, commercial and cultural centre of a thinly populated rural 'province' covering the isolated western third of the continent. Light industries, such as paint and plaster factories, print shops and food canning and processing works, have long been established in the inner city and there are sheet metal and cement works, rubber factories, tractor assembly plants and railway workshops in the northern and eastern suburbs. But the last 15 years has seen a mushrooming of major industrial enterprises in the Fremantle-Kwinana area on Cockburn Sound to the east and south.

Twenty-four years ago Kwinana was an expanse of barren sandhills. Today it is the hub of a great work complex destined one day to rival such centres as Newcastle and Wollongong in New South Wales. It began in 1951 when British Petroleum decided to set up a $A80 million oil refinery in Western Australia and to promote, in conjunction with the State Government, oil port facilities on Cockburn Sound. Four years later the refinery came on stream. In the meanwhile Broken Hill Pty Company decided to develop an integrated iron and steel industry in the same area provided the Government would agree to construct a standard gauge railway between Kwinana and the company's iron ore deposits at Koolyanobbing near Southern Cross, 400 kilometres to the east. This railway was completed in 1968 and the Australian Iron and Steel Company (a subsidiary of BHP) opened a $A40 million blast furnace, the first phase of a long-term plan to install steel rolling mills.

While these developments were occurring, the discovery of large bauxite deposits in the Darling Ranges led Alcoa of Australia to build an alumina refinery nearby.

Western Mining Corporation, discoverer of Australia's first commercial nickel field at Kambalda, near Kalgoorlie, built a $A45 million refinery at Kwinana with capacity to produce at least 15 000 tonnes of metal a year.

The West Australian Government also has in hand a $A150 million model housing project near the seaside resort of Rockingham which will accommodate a population of at least 35 000. A revolutionary aspect of the town plan is the construction of underground pedestrian walks linking recreational and living areas.

Major industries now established in the vicinity of Fremantle, Perth's fast growing port, include the manufacture of superphosphate fertilizer, furniture, refined sugar, scoured wool, tanned leather and timber products. Exports include crude and refined oils, bulk grain, flour, wool, mineral concentrates, chilled and frozen meat and fish. A prosperous cray-fishing industry is based on the port.

Perth is now connected by standard gauge railway with Broken Hill and Sydney.

HISTORY Events leading to the establishment of the settlements on the Swan River have been outlined in the section on the colonization of Western Australia.

When Captain James Stirling had selected the site of the future city, he named it for Perth, Scotland, the birthplace of Sir George Murray, then Secretary of State for War and the Colonies.

Owing to its isolation, the Swan River colony made extremely slow progress. Some 300 settlers established themselves at Perth and Fremantle in the first year, 1829, but by 1848 the population of Perth was only 1 148 and that of the surrounding countryside approximately 1 400. When the city was gazetted in 1856 its population was less than 3 000. By 1871 this had increased only to 5 000, although by then the first bridge had been built across the Swan River and a steamer service to and from Fremantle provided.

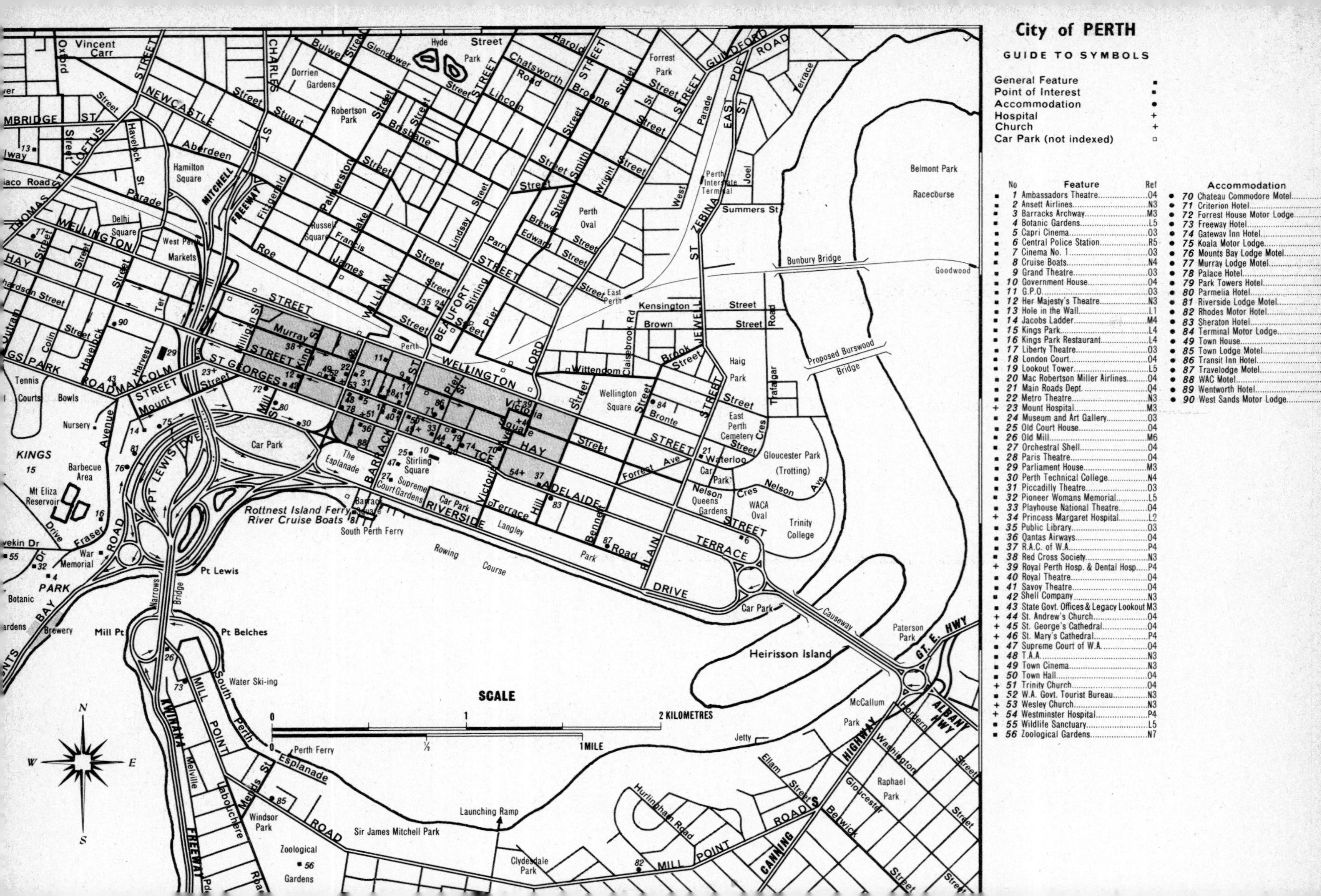
City of PERTH
GUIDE TO SYMBOLS
General Feature ▪
Point of Interest ▪
Accommodation ●
Hospital +
Church +
Car Park (not indexed) ▫
No Feature Ref
1 Ambassadors Theatre O4
2 Ansett Airlines N3
3 Barracks Archway M3
4 Botanic Gardens L5
5 Capri Cinema O3
6 Central Police Station R5
7 Cinema No. 1 O3
8 Cruise Boats N4
9 Grand Theatre O3
10 Government House O4
11 G.P.O. O3
12 Her Majesty's Theatre N3
13 Hole in the Wall L1
14 Jacobs Ladder M4
15 Kings Park L4
16 Kings Park Restaurant L4
17 Liberty Theatre O3
18 London Court O4
19 Lookout Tower L5
20 Mac Robertson Miller Airlines O4
21 Main Roads Dept. Q4
22 Metro Theatre N3
23 Mount Hospital M3
24 Museum and Art Gallery O3
25 Old Court House O4
26 Old Mill M6
27 Orchestral Shell O4
28 Paris Theatre O4
29 Parliament House M3
30 Perth Technical College N4
31 Piccadilly Theatre O3
32 Pioneer Womans Memorial L5
33 Playhouse National Theatre O4
34 Princess Margaret Hospital L2
35 Public Library O3
36 Qantas Airways O4
37 R.A.C. of W.A. P4
38 Red Cross Society N3
39 Royal Perth Hosp. & Dental Hosp. P4
40 Royal Theatre O4
41 Savoy Theatre O4
42 Shell Company N3
43 State Govt. Offices & Legacy Lookout M3
44 St. Andrew's Church O4
45 St. George's Cathedral O4
46 St. Mary's Cathedral P4
47 Supreme Court of W.A. O4
48 T.A.A. N3
49 Town Cinema N3
50 Town Hall O4
51 Trinity Church O4
52 W.A. Govt. Tourist Bureau N3
53 Wesley Church N3
54 Westminster Hospital P4
55 Wildlife Sanctuary L5
56 Zoological Gardens N7
Accommodation
70 Chateau Commodore Motel P4
71 Criterion Hotel O4
72 Forrest House Motor Lodge N3
73 Freeway Hotel M6
74 Gateway Inn Hotel O4
75 Koala Motor Lodge M4
76 Mounts Bay Lodge Motel M4
77 Murray Lodge Motel L2
78 Palace Hotel N4
79 Park Towers Hotel O4
80 Parmelia Hotel N4
81 Riverside Lodge Motel M4
82 Rhodes Motor Hotel O7
83 Sheraton Hotel P4
84 Terminal Motor Lodge Q4
49 Town House N3
85 Town Lodge Motel N7
86 Transit Inn Hotel O4
87 Travelodge Motel O5
88 WAC Motel N4
89 Wentworth Hotel N3
90 West Sands Motor Lodge M3
SCALE
0 1 2 KILOMETRES
0 ½ 1 MILE
N E S W
Heirisson Island
Belmont Park Racecourse
Bunbury Bridge
Proposed Burswood Bridge
Causeway
Kings Park
Rottnest Island Ferry
River Cruise Boats
South Perth Ferry
Rowing Course
Sir James Mitchell Park
Launching Ramp
Water Ski-ing
Narrows Bridge
Kwinana Freeway
Mitchell Freeway
Riverside Drive
St Georges Terrace
Wellington Street
Hay Street
Murray Street
Adelaide Terrace
Gloucester Park (Trotting)
WACA Oval
Trinity College
Perth Oval
Wellington Square
Stirling Square
Supreme Court Gardens
The Esplanade
Queens Gardens
East Perth Cemetery
Zoological Gardens
Mt Eliza Reservoir
Pt Lewis
Pt Belches
Mill Pt
Perth Interstate Terminal
Hyde Park
Forrest Park
Robertson Park
Dorrien Gardens
Hamilton Square
Delhi Square
Russell Square
Haig Park
Paterson Park
McCallum Park
Raphael Park
Clydesdale Park
Windsor Park

City of Perth from King's Park

Iron ore train, Pilbara, W.A.

The rate of development, however, began to accelerate after the telegraph line to Adelaide was built in 1875-77, and the 1880s saw the gradual development of local railways.

The discovery of gold at Coolgardie-Kalgoorlie in 1892-93 had an even more galvanic effect on Perth than gold strikes had had on the eastern capitals, Sydney and Melbourne, in the early 1850s. By 1901 the population had risen to 27 558 and many major public works were under way. At Fremantle major harbour improvements had been made, a rocky bar at the mouth of the river removed, channels dredged and breakwaters and wharves built. The State's agricultural and mineral production quickly increased under the stimulus of improved communications and transport, and the growth of the capital city kept pace. Construction of the transcontinental railway began in 1912 and was completed in 1915.

Notable Historic Buildings

Old Court House, Stirling Gardens, built in 1836, is the oldest surviving building in the city. Primitive Georgian style. Now used as Industrial Court.

Old Mill, South Perth, at southern end of Narrows Bridge, was built in 1835 and has been restored to its original appearance. It houses a number of relics of pioneering days. Open for inspection Monday, Wednesday, Thursday, 1 pm to 5 pm, Saturday 1 pm to 4 pm, Sunday 1 pm to 5 pm.

Barracks Archway, at western end of St George's Terrace. The original building was erected between 1863 and 1867 as a headquarters of soldier settlers of the Enrolled Pensioner Forces. It was of Tudor style and in brick. For many years it was the main office of the State Public Works and Water Supply Department and was demolished in 1966 to make way for the Mitchell Freeway. The archway has been left as a memorial to the early colonists.

Old Perth Boy's School, now an annexe of the Technical College, St George's Terrace. Rough stone construction in Gothic style. Built in 1854 to house Government Boys' School, it was the second oldest establishment of its kind in the Australian colonies.

The Cloisters, St George's Terrace. Built in 1858 by first Anglican Bishop Hale, as boys' sceondary school. The decorative brickwork is typical of early Perth architecture.

Government House, built in 1859-64 in romantic Gothic style, and set in formal gardens. (Not open for inspection.)

Old Town Hall, Barrack Street, built 1867-70 and designed by R. R. Jewell, Colonial Clerk of Works, who was responsible for the architecture of many of the city's early brick buildings. Nearby is a memorial tablet set in the pavement to mark the spot on which the founding of Perth was announced on 12 August, 1829.

Old Gaol and Court House, Beaufort Street, built in 1856, now part of the Perth Museum and Art Gallery. One of the few stone buildings in Perth designed by R. R. Jewell. (External inspection only.)

Treasury Building, built 1874, in Colonial style. Now houses Government departments.

St Mary's Cathedral, Victoria Square.

St George's Cathedral, Cathedral Avenue.

St Andrew's Presbyterian Church, St George's Terrace and Pier Street.

Places of Interest

Art Gallery and Museum, Beaufort Street, containing traditional and contemporary Australian paintings, prints, drawings, ceramics etc, some sculpture and a small collection of aboriginal bark paintings. Among other interesting exhibits are relics of early Dutch shipwrecks along the Western Australian coast. Open Monday to Friday 10.30 am to 5 pm, Saturdays and public holidays 9.30 am to 5 pm, Sunday 2 pm to 5 pm. Art gallery only open Wednesday and Friday 7.30 pm to 10 pm during period of special exhibitions.

State Library, James Street. Open Monday to Saturday 9 am to 9.45 pm, Sunday 2 pm to 5 pm. The **Battye Library** houses a good collection of archives in the same building.

Stirling House Museum and Library, Broadway, Nedlands. Administered by the Western Australian Historical Society. Contains relics and literature of State's early history. Open Monday to Thursday 2 pm to 4 pm, and one Sunday afternoon a month.

The Council House, contemporary skyscraper housing city administration, St George's Terrace.

Perry Lakes Stadium, west of city off Underwood Avenue. Built by Perth City Council for British Empire and Commonwealth Games, 1962. Seating for 38 000.

Cotton harvesting, Kimberley

Legacy Lookout, on 14th floor of State Government Building, King's Park Road; views of city.

London Court, 18th century style arcade between Hay Street and St George's Terrace.

University and St George's College, Crawley. Impressive buildings in setting of parks and gardens developed on 1 618 hectares of endowed land beside the Swan River. Sunken garden sometimes used for outdoor dramatic performances is notable.

Vintage Car Museum, Wembley. Collection of vintage and veteran cars all in perfect mechanical condition. Open Saturday and Sunday 2 pm to 5 pm.

Parliament House, Harvest Terrace. Visitors 10 am to 12 noon and 2 pm to 4 pm, when House is in recess, 10 am to 12 noon when House is sitting (usually August to December).

City of Perth Aquatic Centre, North Perth.

Parks and Gardens

King's Park. Approximately 405 hectares of bushland, most of it in natural state, covering the summit of Mount Eliza from which magnificent panoramic views of the city may be obtained. Reservation of the area for the public was first suggested by the Governor, Sir Frederick Weld, in 1871. Good motorways run through the park, which is without doubt one of the most beautiful recreation areas in Australia. The display of wildflowers in spring is superb. The park contains a restaurant and a **Botanic Garden** of 10 hectares of native plants which features a **Pioneer Women's Memorial Fountain** and a display of Western Australian wildflowers in cultivation. The State **War Memorial** is located at the highest point of King's Park. First known as Perth Park, its name was changed in 1901 to commemorate the accession of King Edward VII.

Queen's Garden's, at the eastern end of Hay Street, contain several miniature lagoons and a replica of the Peter Pan statue in Kensington Gardens, London. Cleverly landscaped.

Stirling Gardens, at the corner of Barrack Street and St George's Terrace, has shade and ornamental trees, well kept lawns and flower beds.

Supreme Court Gardens, south of Stirling Gardens, contain an orchestral shell and command fine waterfront views.

Hyde Park, 1.6 kilometres north of city. Fifteen hectares of lawns with mainly deciduous trees. Ornamental lake and island which attracts many wildfowl. Very colourful in autumn.

Zoological Gardens, South Perth. A small zoo, which can be reached either by river ferry from the foot of Barrack Street or by bus. Well planned and well kept, it has a restaurant in the grounds.

Sports

Perth is liberally provided with sports facilities of all kinds, many of which are concentrated centrally on the shores of Perth Water, the broad reach of the Swan River east of Barrack Square at the foot of Barrack Street.

Main **racecourses** are at Ascot, Belmont Park and Helena Vale. **Night trotting** is held at Gloucester Park, an elaborately equipped ground close to Queen's Gardens and the WA Cricket Association ground. **Motor races** are held at the Caversham Circuit off the Great Northern Highway, north-east of the city.

There are eight public **golf courses** within a short distance of the centre of the city. The location of numerous **bowling** and **croquet** greens, **tennis** and **squash** courts etc may be found by consulting the classified telephone directory or the WA Tourist Bureau.

The Swan River provides excellent water for swimming, boating, yachting, water skiing and all aquatic sports.

Main Beaches

River: Crawley, Nedlands, Como, Canning Bridge, Applecross, Point Walter, Peppermint Grove and Mosman Bay.

Ocean: Cottesloe (with Oceanarium open 8.30 am to 10 pm), City, Trigg, North, Waterman, Sorrento, Floreat and Scarborough.

Entertainment

Theatres. His Majesty's, Hay Street; **Playhouse,** Pier Street; **Hole in the Wall,** Stirling Street; **Grand,** Murray Street.

Cinemas. Ambassadors; Capri; Grand; Liberty; Mayfair (Theatrette); Metro; Paris; Piccadilly; Town. There are also numerous inner suburban **cinemas** and **drive-ins.**

Restaurants. Recommended: **Hofbrauhaus,** Bayview Terrace; **Park Towers,** Bayview Terrace; **Pumphouse,** Bayview Terrace; **Gateway Inn,** Irwin Street; **La Perouse,** Forrest Street; **Embers Room** at Travelodge Motel, Terrace Road.

Accommodation

City. Twenty two **hotels** are directory listed in the city of Perth. Recommended: **Parmelia,** Mill Street (de luxe); **Riverside Lodge,** Mounts Bay Road (de luxe); **Palace,** St George's Terrace. There are seven **motels.** Recommended: **Travelodge,** Terrace Drive; **Transit Inn,** Pier Street.

There are numerous **private hotels** and **guest-houses. Caravan and camping parks** are mostly near riverside and ocean beach resorts.

Transport

The city and most suburbs are served by **buses.** Suburban **trains** run from Central Railway Station, Wellington Street, to main western, north-eastern and south-eastern centres. **Ferry** service from Barrack Street Jetty to South Perth.

Taxis are metered and indicate flag fall and kilometre charges. **Hire and rental cars** are available and numerous half day and day **coach tours** of the city and its environs are available. (Inquire Tourist Bureau.)

Perth Airport on the Great Eastern Highway north-east of the city handles all international, interstate and most intrastate air traffic. There is a secondary airport at **Jandakot,** south-east of Fremantle.

Department Stores

Ahern's, Hay to Murray Streets; **Boans,** Murray to Wellington Streets; **David Jones,** St George's Terrace; **Big W,** Hay Street; **Myer,** Murray to Wellington Streets.

Banking and Business Hours

Banking hours are normally 10 am to 3 pm Monday to Thursday and 10 am to 5 pm Friday. Banks do not open on Saturday.

Shops in the city and suburbs are open from 8.35 am to 5.30 pm Monday to Friday and from 8.35 am to noon on Saturday. **Hotel** trading is from 10 am to 10 pm Monday to Saturday, 11 am to 1 pm and 4.30 to 6.30 pm Sunday. **Petrol** stations trade from 7 am to 7 pm Monday to Friday and 7 am to 1 pm on Saturday.

Time. Western Australia is two hours behind Eastern Standard Time.

Miscellaneous

Information. The **Western Australian Tourist Development Authority** is located at 772 Hay Street. **Royal Automobile Club** headquarters are at 228 Adelaide Terrace.

Emergencies. Dial 000 for police, fire, ambulance.

PERTH ENVIRONS

There are many small towns, scenic reserves and places of historic or general interest in the Darling Ranges or along the coast near Perth. The Ranges are particularly colourful in spring when an almost incredible variety of wildflowers come into bloom. The coast and the offshore islands are at their best in early autumn when the weather is perfect for aquatic sports of all kinds.

ROTTNEST ISLAND

A very popular summer holiday resort, particularly for the people of Perth, Rottnest Island is 19 kilometres north-north-west of Fremantle opposite the mouth of the Swan River. It is a low-lying sandy island with dunes rising to a height of 21 metres, 11 kilometres long and 5 kilometres wide at its widest. It has an area of 1 913 hectares.

Rottnest was declared a permanent public reserve and wildlife sanctuary in 1917 and is controlled by an island board which plans and supervises its development as a pleasure resort. Its attractions are simple—sand, sun, sea and a rich marine and terrestrial fauna including the quaint, rare marsupial known as the quokka. The Dutch seamen who first landed on the island named it 'Rats' Nest' because they thought the myriads of quokkas which inhabited it were giant rats. It was also called 'Island of the Mist' because of the mist-mirage which often occurs in calm, sunny weather.

The island was first settled in 1839 by Henry Vincent. In 1850 it became a penal settlement for native prisoners and between 1882 and 1906 was used as a reformatory for juvenile offenders. In 1954 the Commonwealth Scientific and Industrial Research Organization established an observatory for a population study of the quokkas.

Accommodation. One **hotel.** One **hostel.** Numerous furnished **cottages, lodges and flats.** All premises are sewered and have water and electricity supply. **Campsites** with essential facilities.

Transport. **Launch** services from Fremantle. **Air** service from Perth Airport. **Tours** to scenic points and fishing grounds are conducted on the island.

YANCHEP PARK

An attractive holiday and picnic resort on a reserve of 283 hectares, 52 kilometres north of Perth, Yanchep Park is famous for its koala and native animal park, its spring wildflowers, and three charming limestone caves which are open for inspection by scheduled bus tourists, and from 11.10 am to 5 pm on Sundays and holidays for casual visitors. Launch trips are available daily on nearby Loch McNess.

Sports. Golf course. Tennis courts. Playing field. Swimming pool. Surfing and fishing at beach (6 kilometres west).

Accommodation. One **hotel.** One **lodge** (with swimming pool). **Caravan and camping park,** some facilities, at beach.

MUNDARING WEIR

Mundaring Weir, 40 kilometres north-east of Perth, a storage dam with a capacity of more than 20 000 million litres completed in 1902, is the source of the eastern goldfields water supply. Reached by a good sealed road, it is situated in beautiful, wooded mountain country and is a popular summer picnicking spot. A disused pumping station, replaced by a modern electric installation in 1955, has been converted into a historical museum named for C. Y. O'Connor, the engineer of the water supply scheme which was in its day the most ambitious and ingenious project of its kind in Australia. The O'Connor Museum is open Monday, Wednesday, Friday and weekends.

Most coach tours from Perth include a visit to Mundaring and to the major Perth water storages, the **Canning** and **Serpentine Dams,** in their itineraries. The **John Forrest National Park,** a major State flora and fauna reserve, is situated 26 kilometres north-east of Perth.

ARMADALE (Population 2 000)

Now regarded as a residential outer suburb of Perth, Armadale is a non-municipal town 32 kilometres south-east of the city in dairying, market gardening, fruit growing and pastoral country. It is near the popular Darling Range resort of **Kalamunda,** where fine views of Perth can be obtained, and the Canning and Churchman Brook reservoirs which supply the metropolitan area.

A hotel, 'Ye Olde Narrogin Inne', still in business, was built in 1856 and was well patronized by travellers on the road south, but it was not until the Perth-Bunbury railway was opened in 1893 that the town was founded and the agricultural potential of the area realized.

Accommodation. One **hotel.**

Transport. **Rail** service from Perth.

NORTHAM

(Population 7 109)

Situated in the Avon Valley 107 kilometres north-east of Perth, Northam is an attractive rural town which serves a large area of the eastern wheat belt. Besides grain the district produces fodder crops, wool, beef cattle, fat lambs, pigs and timber. Town industries include flour and timber mills, iron and steel fabricating works, a plasterboard factory, brick and charcoal kilns and cold storage and iceworks. It is the site of Western Australia's main military camp and a depot for the Goldfields and Agricultural Water Supply service.

History. The town was founded in 1830 and named by Governor Stirling after Northam in Devonshire. The first settlers were colonists led by Ensign Robert Dale. The town was connected with Perth by telegraph in 1872 and in 1879 it was declared a municipality. When the Yilgarn, Eastern and Dundas (Norseman) goldfields were discovered in the 1890s it became a bustling base for thousands of diggers preparing to push out into the desert.

Sports. Golf course. Tennis courts. Bowling greens. Swimming pool.

Accommodation. Four **hotels.** Recommended: Commercial, Fitzgerald Street. One recommended **motel. Caravan and camping park,** all facilities.

Transport. **Rail** and **road** services.

YORK (Population 1 716)

In the Avon Valley and Darling Ranges 97 kilometres east of Perth, York is one of the oldest rural settlements in West Australia. It was explored by Robert Dale in 1830 and the townsite was surveyed and proclaimed the following year. It was named after York, England, because the pioneers saw in the terrain some resemblance to the downs of Yorkshire. It reached municipal status in 1871.

The York district today produces grain, wool, fruit and vegetables, fat lambs and cattle and fodder crops. There are flour mills and fruit preserving factories in the town. An excellent view of the river valley and the town can be obtained from Mount Bakewell (322 metres) and Mount Brown (336 metres), two high features in the nearby ranges.

Sports. Racecourse. Tennis courts. Bowling and croquet greens. Swimming in natural pool in river.

Accommodation. Three **hotels.** Preferred: Palace, Avon Terrace. Three **caravan and camping parks,** all facilities.

Transport. **Road** and **rail** services from Perth.

ROCKINGHAM

(Population 11 990)

Rockingham for many years a popular, quiet seaside resort 45 kilometres south of Perth at the southern end of Cockburn Sound, has now been developed as a model dormitory suburb for workers in the Kwinana industrial complex. Its stretch of broad, protected beach sheltered from heavy weather by Garden, Green and Penguin Islands is suitable for aquatic sports. The annual Rockingham Silver Sands Carnival is held in March and the Cockburn Yacht Regatta early in January.

The locality was first settled in 1829-30 to develop land granted to Thomas Peel, but the venture failed largely through lack of capital. In 1840 a whaling and fishing settlement was founded at nearby Warnboro Sound but it was abandoned when the port of Fremantle was opened in 1897.

Places of Interest. **Garden and Penguin Islands** (a boat service operates to Garden Island). **Serpentine Dam and Falls. Point Peron,** for panoramic views of coast.

Sports. Golf course. Tennis courts. Bowling greens. Yachting. Swimming. Game fishing and spear fishing off the islands. Surfboard riding at Point Peron. Skydiving Club.

Accommodation. Two **hotels.** Recommended: Rockingham, Kent Street. Four **caravan parks,** all facilities. **Camping** at Palm Beach park only, and at reserves on Garden and Penguin Islands. (At Garden Island firearms and dogs are banned, and spear fishing is permitted only at the northern end.) Semi-furnished holiday **cottages** are for rent on both islands.

Transport. Frequent **road** services from Perth.

MANDURAH

(Population 5 039)

Mandurah is one of the most popular seaside resorts on the coast south of Perth. It is about 80 kilometres from the city on the entrance to Peel Inlet, where the waters of the Murray, Serpentine and Harvey Rivers all enter the sea. Although tourism is its main industry, the town is also the commercial centre of a dairying, market gardening and fruit growing district. There are many excellent swimming and surfing beaches in the locality and the river valley country is attractive.

Mandurah was on the original Peel land grant but the town was not founded until 1895. It was incorporated as a shire in 1949. The name is derived from an aboriginal word *mandjar*, meaning 'trading place'.

Sports. Usual facilities for games and aquatic sports. Good sea, inlet and river fishing. Crabbing and crayfishing.

Accommodation. Three **hotels.** Preferred: Mandurah. Three **caravan and camping parks,** all facilities. Holiday **cottages** and **flats** for rent.

Transport. Direct **road** service from Fremantle. **Rail** service to Pinjarra, then connecting bus.

PINJARRA (Population 1 176)

One of the oldest rural settlements in Western Australia, Pinjarra is 88 kilometres south of Perth, west of the Darling Ranges and on the banks of the Murray River. Its primary industries are dairying and market gardening.

The district was settled in 1833, and in 1834 was the scene of a bloody fracas between soldiers and hostile aborigines in which 12 natives were killed. One white officer, Captain Ellis, later died of spear wounds. Disastrous bushfires swept through heavy bush near Pinjarra in 1961 and destroyed the nearby timber town of **Dwellingup.**

Accommodation Two **hotels.** No information on facilities.

Transport. **Rail** service from Perth.

SOUTH-WESTERN DISTRICTS

The south-western segment of Western Australia differs from most other natural divisions of the State in that it receives liberal, fairly evenly distributed rainfall, and enjoys a temperate Mediterranean climate. Large areas are covered by hardwood forests of great economic value which are at last being more efficiently managed and conserved than was the case for many years.

The two most prized species in the forests of the south-west are karri and jarrah, both of which produce extremely tough, durable and handsome timbers. Karri (*eucalyptus diversicolor*) is the more spectacular tree. Trees up to 88 metres in height with girths of 7.3 metres have been measured, and some shorter trees have girths up to 10 metres. The crown of a big karri will have a spread of anything up to 18 metres and its trunk will shoot straight upwards for 79 metres without branching.

Karri forests are mainly confined to the acid soils behind the southern coast where the annual rainfall exceeds 1000 millimetres. Jarrah is found more to the north and west of the district.

Besides timber, the south-western region produces much fruit, mixed farm crops, beef, fat lambs and wool. Hitherto infertile land at the eastern extremity of the liberal rainfall area is being brought into production by the use of trace elements, superphosphate and nitrogenous pasture plants (see Esperance).

From the point of view of the tourist, the south-west has special delights. The forests are, unlike the big timber country in the east, easily accessible because of their relatively sparse undergrowth, the spring wildflower display is undoubtedly the most colourful in Australia, and the beaches of the coast between Yallingup and Augusta provide incomparable surfboard riding. Those interested in limestone caves will be well satisfied.

BUNBURY

(Population 17 762)

Western Australia's third largest town, Bunbury, is 189 kilometres south-east of Perth on the junction of the Collie and Preston Rivers on Leschenault Estuary. It is a progressive centre with a rapidly increasing population. The district produces butter, cheese, beef cattle, fruit, vegetables, wool and fish, and rutile-zircon from beach sands. Secondary industries include power generation, superphosphate and plasterboard works and woollen and timber mills. The port is protected by a breakwater 1.5 kilometres long.

History. Leschenault Estuary was sighted by Captain Freycinet in the ship *Geographe* in 1803 and named after the expedition's botanist. In 1829 a military post was established after exploration by an expedition dispatched by Governor Stirling. No further development occurred until 1836 when Lieutenant Pierre-Bunbury, after whom the town is named, surveyed the area for rural settlement. The first settlers were the Scott family who arrived in 1838. The townsite was fixed in 1841 and declared two years later.

Nearby Koombana Bay, though dangerous when westerly and south-westerly gales were blowing, was used for many years by American whalers, but when a wharfage charge was imposed they transferred to Busselton, leaving Bunbury farmers without a profitable market for their produce. Thereafter progress was slow until the 1890s when a railway was pushed through from Perth. In 1903 the great breakwater works began and improvements to the artificial harbour have since continued.

The introduction of superphosphate fertilizer and the nitrogenous pasture plant, subterranean clover, in recent years has revolutionised land productivity in the district. Its progress has been further stimulated by beach sand mining which began in 1956. In that year the State Government approved the establishment of works to produce titanium oxide and allied chemicals. Actual production began in 1964.

Bunbury's power house, fuelled by Collie coal, is one of Western Australia's largest generating plants.

Places of Interest. Boulter's Heights, Apex Lookout for panoramic views of town. **Centenary Gardens,** with various memorials. **Withers Park,** developed by the Chamber of Commerce and

Bunbury Historical Society. It will eventually contain an historical museum. **Art Gallery** at Municipal Centre. **St Paul's Cathedral. Shell Collection** at 108 Mangles Street. **Old Picton Church,** built 1842. (Picton itself was the home of Lord Forrest, one-time Premier of West Australia.) **Australind township** (10 kilometres north on inlet) has one of the smallest churches in Australia. It was originally built as a workman's cottage but converted in 1848 by John Allnutt. The locality is scenically attractive and the fishing is good. **Bird Farm** at Boyanup, 40 kilometres south-east, has a large collection of birds and a few native animals. **Wellington** and **Harvey Weirs,** to the north-west and north. **Springhill Homestead** (26 kilometres, off Old Coast Road), built about 1855 and still occupied.

Sports. Racecourse. Trotting track. Golf course (8 kilometres). Tennis courts. Squash courts. Bowling greens. Rowing. Yachting. Archery range. Fishing. Surfing.

The Western Australian yachting classic, the Fremantle-Bunbury race, is held annually.

Accommodation. Five **hotels.** Recommended: Bussel, Bussel Highway. Five **motels.** Recommended: Ocean Drive, Ocean Drive. **Holiday cottages** for rent. Three **camping and caravan parks,** all facilities.

Transport. Rail services from Perth. Local **road** services.

COLLIE

(Population 6 802)

Collie is a coal mining town 207 kilometres south of Perth on the Collie River. Its mines are West Australia's only source of coal, of which most is used at Bunbury and for the generation of electricity. Most colliery towns are unattractive, but Collie is set in the midst of splendid forest country and cleared farmlands which produce wool, beef, butter, oats and fruit. The town has many well designed public and commercial buildings.

History. The Collie River was discovered by Dr Alexander Collie, Albany's first Resident, who explored the region in 1829. Coal was discovered on the river in 1883, but little notice was taken of the find for some years. In 1896 Collie was proclaimed a district and two years later commercial mining of the low grade, sub-bituminous seams was commenced. The municipality was incorporated in 1901.

Places of Interest. Muja open-cut Mines. Old Anglican Church. Nearby **jarrah forests. Wellington Weir. Minninup Pool.**

Sports. Usual facilities.

Accommodation. Four **hotels.** Preferred: Collie Fields, Throssell Street. One **motel. Caravan park,** all facilities.

Transport. Bus connection with **rail** services to Brunswick Junction.

BUSSELTON

(Population 5 020)

Busselton is on the shores of Geographe Bay, 238 kilometres south of Perth, and is the centre of a rich agricultural and timber-getting district which produces butter, high quality potatoes, fat lambs, pigs and lumber. Ilmenite is mined from the beach sands at Wonnerup, a few kilometres north-east. Secondary industries are boat building and furniture manufacture.

The town is also one of the most popular holiday resorts in Western Australia. Its summer climate is pleasantly mild and it lies near good ocean beaches, with excellent fishing and crabbing in season. The country inland although fairly flat is full of interest. Much is heavily wooded and rugged and there are delightful areas for picnicking and camping.

History. Nicholas Baudin visited the coast near Busselton in 1801. One of his crew members named Vasse lost his life in the surf (or was possibly killed by natives) and the River Vasse which enters the sea nearby was named for him. In 1832 the Bussell family, headed by John Garret Bussell, moved flocks and herds up from Augusta on Flinders Bay to the south-east and established a run called 'Cattle Chosen' because the animals themselves had found good pasture. A village grew up round the Bussell homestead and the town was proclaimed in 1837.

In 1854 the first timber mill in Western Australia was established at Quindalup, about 24 kilometres west, and in 1871 the WA Timber Company built 19 kilometres of private railway to transport timber to the port. This railway used the first steam locomotive in the State. Busselton again made news when the first butter factory in the west was opened there in 1893. Despite the progressive spirit of the community rapid development did not take place until after 1921 when the group settlement policy of Sir Thomas Mitchell, then Premier of Western Australia, was successfully tried out.

Places of Interest. Church of St Mary's, built in 1843, the oldest stone church in WA. **Bussell's 'Cattle Chosen'** homestead. **Old flour mill.** Busselton **Museum,** in Prospect Villa, built 1855 (also containing Busselton Tourist Bureau). **Timber mills** and **forestry areas** (inspections can be arranged). Wonnerup **ilmenite mine** (inspection can be arranged). **Yallingup Caves,** 32 kilometres south west (see South West Caves). **Cape Naturaliste.**

Sports. Golf course. Tennis courts. Bowling greens (very good). Sailing and water-skiing. Fishing and crabbing.

Accommodation. Four **hotels.** Preferred: Vasse, Queen Street. Six **motels.** Recommended: Geographe Bay Motor Inn. One **private hotel.** Furnished **cottages** and **flats** for rent. Four **caravan and camping parks,** all facilities.

Transport. Railway **bus** connecting with **rail** services to Bunbury. **Road** services. Scenic **coach** tours available.

Small Towns in District

DUNSBOROUGH (Population 100), with its fine beaches, is a popular camping area. **Cottages** for rent.

YALLINGUP (Population 199) for cave expeditions (see below). Good beaches and coastal scenery. One **hotel.**

MARGARET RIVER (Population 180), close to Mammoth and Lake Cave and coast and bush scenery. One **hotel.**

AUGUSTA is one of the oldest settlements in the State, near the mouth of the Blackwood River and about 8 kilometres from Cape Leeuwin lighthouse. Jewel Cave is nearby. One **hotel.** Furnished **flats and cottages. Caravan and camping park.**

SOUTH-WEST CAVES

The 100 kilometre stretch of country between Cape Naturaliste and Cape Leeuwin at the extreme south-western tip of the Australian continent contains more than 120 limestone caves, the majority of which have been only partly explored despite the great beauty and delicate coloration of the calcium carbonate, calcite and argonite formations within them. Only four have been developed for public inspection, but the work has been done with skill and imagination and the lighting is excellent. Times of inspection vary with the seasons. Inquiries should be made from the WA Tourist Bureau.

The formation of the South West Caves is geologically unusual. Limestones were formed over basic granite along the coast. Then a great subsidence occurred, leaving only the highest peaks above sea level. Drainage from the hinterland mountains was forced underground, gradually eroding channels and caverns in the more porous strata which in time became encrusted with deposits tinted by iron and manganese oxides.

The four caves are:

Yallingup, at the northern end of the series, 269 kilometres from Perth, which was discovered by accident in 1900 by a settler looking for a strayed horse. The cave contains many chambers with stalactite, stalagmite, shawl and column formations of intriguing delicacy and subtle colouring.

Mammoth Cave, 23 kilometres south of Margaret River, was discovered in 1894. It has immense vaulted chambers and subterranean canyons. A large number of fossilized marsupial bones has been discovered on the floors, including the skeletons of species now extinct on the mainland, such as a Tasmanian tiger and diprotodon which lived probably a million years ago. The skeletons of koalas, long extinct in the West, are also to be found.

Lake Cave, south of Mammoth, is approached through a deep, circular hollow apparently caused by a subsidence of the roof. The floor of the hollow is covered by luxuriant karri forest with fern undergrowth. The cave itself is an almost perfect dome, its ceiling and walls scintillating with myriads of multi-colored stalactites which are reflected in the still waters of its deep lake.

Augusta Jewel Cave, 6.5 kilometres off the Bussel Highway to Augusta, was known to exist as early as 1880 but was explored fully only in 1958. The main cavern is 83 metres long and 48 metres wide with a ceiling 29 metres high. Like the Lake Cave it has a number of beautiful, clear pools, and the variety of formations is excitingly wide. Of the series, the Augusta Jewel Cave is the most elaborately and effectively lit.

ALBANY

(Population 13 055)

Albany, 406 kilometres south of Perth, is the main port for the south coastal area of West Australia. It is superbly situated on a deep, protected inlet comprising three arms—King George III Sound, Princess Royal Harbour and Oyster Harbour.

Primary industries of the district are whaling and fishing, dairy farming, wheat growing and timber-getting. Baby beef, fat lambs, fruit and potatoes are also produced. The town's secondary industries are woollen mills, fish canneries, meat processing plants and brick, tile and superphosphate works.

This section of the West Australian coast is very beautiful, with many lookouts commanding views of the rockbound shore, fertile valleys and the Stirling and Porongurup Ranges in the hinterland. More than 3 500 varieties of wildflowers have been listed within a 50 kilometre radius of Albany. The climate of the entire region is temperate in summer, but rather bleak in winter.

History. King George Sound was discovered, charted and named in 1792 by Captain George Vancouver, who had served with Cook. He made a second voyage later, and sent ashore a party which climbed Mount Clarence and sighted Princess Royal Harbour to the north.

The first settlement was made by Major Edmund Lockyer and a party of 44 soldiers and convicts dispatched by Governor Darling to forestall any French attempt to colonize the coast. Lockyer's party arrived in the brig *Amity* on 26 December, 1826. He was unaware of Vancouver's previous visit and named the village Frederickstown in honour of Frederick, Duke of Albany. The name was never popular and instead Albany was used after 1832. The surrounding district received the name of Plantagenet County in 1830 and was surveyed the following year.

Growth was slow. By 1839 there were only 60 dwellings in the little town and 139 residents. But during the 1840s, when the Town Trust was set up, Albany was an important whaling centre. Then, from 1852 onwards, it became a coaling station for warships in the Indian Ocean and mail steamers on the Australian run. After Fremantle was completed in 1900, Albany's role as a port declined with the loss of the bunkering industry. It was proclaimed a municipality in 1871 and incorporated as a town in 1961.

Places of Interest. Mount Clarence (186 metres) and its twin peak, **Mount Melville** dominate the town and the view from the summit is well worth the climb. **Marine Drive,** which circles the little mountains, is an attractive route to **Middleton Beach. Emu Point,** 453 hectares of recreation parkland with a 46 hectare boronia reserve. **Old Farm,** Strawberry Hill, is the oldest dwelling place and the oldest station building in West Australia. It was developed as a Government farm from 1827 to 1830 and then bought by the Resident, Sir Richard Spencer, for £15/3/2. The building itself was erected in 1834 and has been partially destroyed by fire. **St John Evangelist Church,** one of the oldest existing churches in West Australia, was consecrated by Bishop Short of Adelaide in 1848. **Old Post Office. The Gap, Rock Bridge** and **The Blowholes,** impressive rock formations on the coast. **The Gorge. Frenchman's Bay Whaling Station.**

Many **scenic drives** of great interest may be made from Albany—to the magnificent karri forests of the Mount Barker area, to the Porongurup Ranges with their strangely sculpted rocks and to the Stirling Ranges, which are breathtakingly lovely in spring when the countryside is clothed in masses of the wildflowers which grow only in West Australia. September and October are by far the best months for a visit to this part of the State.

Sports. Golf courses. Bowling greens. Tennis courts. Surfing. Yachting and other aquatic sports. River fishing. Beach and boat fishing inshore. **Big game fishing** for tuna and marlin especially. Shooting.

Accommodation. Seven **hotels.** Recommended: Esplanade. Six **motels.** Recommended: Ace, Albany Highway. Holiday **flats** available. Three **camping and caravan parks.**

Transport. Rail services from Perth etc. (terminus of Great Southern Railway).

Small South Coast Towns

DENMARK (Population 1 159), on Denmark River and Wilson's Inlet, has good boating, swimming and fishing. It is near karri forest country and there is a good road through the most densely timbered part of the State to Bunbury. One **motel. Holiday cottages and flats.**

NORNALUP (Population 139) is an unusually beautiful little resort near Walpole Inlet. Excellent boating and fishing. Bush walking. One **guest-house. Holiday cottages.**

WALPOLE (Population 248) is a resort village surrounded by the 13 365 hectare Nornalup National Park.

Places of Interest include **Valley of the Giants, Knoll Drive, Giant Tingle Tree** (girth at breast height 20 metres, 300 to 500 years old), **Mount Frankland, Circular Pool, Coalmine Beach.** First class surfing and boating. One **hotel** (good). One **guest-house. Caravan and camping park,** all facilities.

MOUNT BARKER (Population 1 595)

An historic settlement 228 kilometres south-east of Perth and 50 kilometres north of Albany, Mount Barker is the market town of a district which produces beef, fat lambs, wool, apples, oats and barley, and vegetables. It has fruit packing sheds, an abattoir, a butter factory and a plant for the manufacture of concrete pipes.

History. Mount Barker was discovered by Surgeon T. B. Wilson, RN, in 1829 and named after Captain Collett Barker, the last military commandant at Albany. Settlers began to move into the district in the 1830s, among them Sir Richard Spencer, who established a very successful sheep farm west of Narrikup (16 kilometres south). Another successful early settler was John Hassell, of Kendenup, who used Chinese labour on his run. Kendenup was, incidentally, the site of West Australia's first goldmine. It was a commercial failure but its battery, near the old Hassell homestead, is still preserved.

Mount Barker was proclaimed a town in 1899. A private scheme to establish an irrigation area on the lines of Mildura and Renmark failed in the early years of this century.

Places of Interest. **St Werburgh's Farm,** a pioneer homestead with a unique chapel which may be visited by arrangement. **Kendenup Homestead** which has been carefully preserved. **Old gaol,** restored and used as a museum. **Rocky Gully,** centre of a disastrous project in relief works during the great depression of the early 1930s, is now centre of a thriving land settlement scheme (one hotel). **Lake Poorarecup,** for swimming and water-skiing.

Mount Barker is, naturally, a convenient base for excursions into the Stirling Ranges and the Porongurups. The town holds an Easter festival of sports and agricultural exhibits.

Sports. Golf course. Bowling greens. Tennis courts. Badminton and basketball courts. Polocrosse. Rifle range. Racecourse. Hot rod club.

Accommodation. One **hotel. Caravan and camping park,** limited facilities.

Transport. **Rail** services (on Great Southern Railway to Albany).

MANJIMUP (Population 3 523)

Manjimup, 309 kilometres south of Perth, centre of West Australia's largest apple growing district, also produces butter, fat lambs and beef, some tobacco and a great deal of jarrah timber. There are meatworks, timber mills, a paper pulp plant and food processing factories in the town. Two historic homesteads, Deeside House, built in 1856, and Manjimup House, built in 1856, repay inspection.

Sports. Golf course. Swimming pool etc.

Accommodation. One **hotel.** Two **motels.** Preferred: Manjimup. **Caravan and camping park,** all facilities.

Transport. **Bus** connects with **rail** services at Bunbury.

PEMBERTON (Population 818)

A scattered township in the heart of dense karri forest, Pemberton is 340 kilometres south of Perth and 34 kilometres south of Manjimup. Warren National Park is adjacent to the settlement. Cleared land in the area is used for dairy farming and raising fat stock, and for stone fruits, potatoes and hops. One of the biggest sawmills in Australia is located near the town.

Pemberton is named after its first settler, Pemberton Walcott. It was proclaimed a town in 1912, and in 1927 was the scene of a dramatic train robbery in which bandits got away with the mill workers' payroll of £1 000. In 1928 the World Forestry Commission judged Pemberton karri timber as second only to Californian redwood.

Places of Interest. **Carey Park** (18 kilometres) with trees up to 76 metres high. The undergrowth consists only of bracken. The **Gloucester Tree** (61 metres high), containing Forestry Department fire lookout. **Beedelup Falls,** two cascades with total drop of 107 metres. **Warren House,** built 1872. **Fonty's Pool** on road to Manjimup (well worth visiting).

Sports. Golf course. Tennis courts. Bowling green. Swimming pool. Trout fishing in streams recently stocked from local hatchery.

Accommodation. One **hotel.** One **holiday cottage** for rent.

Transport. Railway **bus** connects with **rail** services to Bunbury.

BRIDGETOWN (Population 1 531)

Situated in charming fruit growing and farming country along the Blackwood River, Bridgetown is 272 kilometres south of Perth. The district is known for its fine apples, dairy produce, beef and fat lambs. Secondary industries are sawmilling and fruit processing.

The village was founded about 1860, but not gazetted until 1868. The origin of the name is uncertain. Some claim it derived from a bridge over the Blackwood, but others hold that the settlement was called after the first ship to land cargo at Bunbury.

Of Interest. **Mill Stream Dam. Varied soil colours** of cultivated land in the area.

Sports. Usual facilities.

Accommodation. One **hotel. Caravan and camping park,** all facilities.

Transport. **Bus** connection with **rail** services to Bunbury.

NARROGIN (Population 4 843)

Narrogin is a major rail junction and market town 206 kilometres south-east of Perth on the main route to Albany. It serves a district which produces wool, beef, pigs, wheat, oats and fodder crops. There are also large plantations of mallet trees, the bark of which contains a high percentage of tannin, in demand for all tanning processes.

Narrogin land was held under pastoral lease by William Shaddick in the early 1860s, but the first resident settler was John Stephens. When the rail link between Perth and Albany was established in the 1880s a settlement developed around a trackside hotel, and after the Government took over the line a town was founded in 1895 and proclaimed a municipality in 1906. The name is from the aboriginal word *gnargajin*, meaning 'waterhole'.

Sports. Facilities are concentrated at the municipal sports ground which has playing fields, tennis courts, bowling greens and a swimming pool.

Accommodation. Two **hotels.** Preferred: Hordem, Federal Street. One **motel.** One **caravan and camping park,** all facilities.

Transport. **Rail** services.

KATANNING (Population 3 603)

Katanning is the centre of a highly productive grain growing and pastoral district 363 kilometres south of Perth and 106 kilometres south of Narrogin. The area is noted for the quality of its merino wool, and the Great Southern Sheepbreeders' Association holds its annual stud sales there. The town is well planned and has many attractive buildings. It was laid out in 1898. The meaning of the name is obscure, possibly derived from the aboriginal word *kartannin*, meaning 'big meeting place'.

Sports. Usual facilities, including a modern swimming pool.

Accommodation. Two **hotels.** Recommended: Katanning Unit, Austral Terrace. One **motel.**

Transport. **Rail** services to Perth and Albany.

Small Towns in Region

KOJANUP (Population 1 520) is one of the older established towns of the south-west. It was founded in 1840 as a coaching centre. The CSIRO has a research station in the district.

Accommodation. One **hotel.**

Transport. **Road** service.

WAGIN (Population 1 680) is the centre of a cereal growing, fat lambs and citrus fruit district. Nearby Lake Wagin is used for water sports.

Accommodation. Three **hotels.** Recommended: Federal.

Transport. **Road** service.

ESPERANCE

(Population 4 860)

Esperance is the small but fast-growing service centre for about 1 215 000 hectares of pastoral and agricultural land on the south coast of Western Australia, an area now in process of development by scientific methods of soil and pasture improvement. The town is 596 kilometres by air—or about 950 kilometres by road via Coolgardie—from Perth.

The countryside in its natural state is unattractive, consisting mainly of flat heathland with little or no groundwater, but its appearance is being gradually transformed by cultivation, tree planting and water conservation. Rainfall over most of the area avareges between 400 and 500 millimetres a year. On the coast is as high as 760 millimetres.

However, monotonous though the Esperance Plains may be, the coast is scenically delightful, splendid beaches alternating with bold, rocky headlands thrusting out into the usually turbulent Southern Ocean. For more than 50 years Esperance has been a summer holiday resort for the people of Kalgoorlie, but it is at last achieving economic importance as the port for a highly productive farming province and for the new nickel mines which have overshadowed the goldfields on the western margin of the Great Victoria Desert.

Of the millions of hectares of light land on the plains, about one third of the area is now in process of improvement by much the same methods as those used to improve tracts of mineral deficient country on Kangaroo Island in South Australia and the Ninety Mile Desert along the border of Victoria and South Australia. The Esperance 'miracle' has received much more publicity because of the involvement of American capital and the interest of Art Linkletter, the American television personality, the film stars Anne Baxter, Robert Cummings and Rhonda Fleming, and the financier, Davis Rockefeller. Nevertheless, the success of methods pioneered by soil and pasture scientists of the Government Research Station at Esperance Downs has been spectacular. Land that was only 15 years ago entirely useless for agriculture and almost useless for pasture is now producing prolific cereal crops or carrying up to 10 or 15 sheep to the hectare.

History. A member of Admiral D'Entrecasteaux's squadron, Huon de Kermandec, visited the bay in the frigate *l'Esperance* in 1792 while surveying the coastline of southern Australia. The first land explorer to traverse the region was John Eyre in 1841. Seven years later J. S. Roe overlanded sheep through Esperance on his way to Frazer Range on the western edge of the Nullarbor Plain, but the first permanent settler was Andrew Dempster who obtained a lease of 100 000 acres in 1866. The town and port of Esperance did not come into being until 1893 when the great rush to the goldfields of Murchison, Coolgardie and Dundas (Norseman) began. Its population rose to more than 1 200 by 1897, but in that year the railway from Perth to Kalgoorlie was completed and the town's new-found prosperity began to wane.

In the late 1920s ill-fated projects to grow wheat on the dry mallee country to the north brought Esperance into prominence. The port was improved and a railway was put through from Norseman. In its peak year Esperance shipped nearly 200 000 bags of wheat. Then the depression struck and the wheat farmers were driven off their land. Again the town became only a seaside resort for miners and their families.

A few stubborn men, however, retained their faith in the potential of the district and experimented with superphosphate and nitrogenous plants with encouraging results, but conclusive success was not achieved until after the establishment of the research station in 1949. Copper and zinc deficiencies were traced and remedial treatment devised.

An American investor, Allen Chase, was granted rights to develop about 600 000 hectares in the area in 1954, but his project failed largely because he tried to speed up the developmental procedures recommended by the scientists. The Chase Syndicate was followed by the American-run Esperance Land Development Company, which succeeded. The company develops the land one-third of the way to production and then is required to sell half the area, but it may retain the other half under management. It has been estimated that about $A30 000 capital is needed to develop a released 810 hectare block to its full productive capacity. More than 600 farms are now established in the Esperance area and it is expected that 900 more will be going concerns within the next 10 or 15 years.

Places of Interest near town: Scenic drive to **Cape le Grande, Frenchman's Peak** and the chain of lakes to the north. The **Pink Lake,** a deposit of 98 per cent pure salt which is harvested and exported. **Orleans Farms** and **Australian Art Collection** of David Rockefeller and Bemio Schmidt.

Sports. Usual facilities for games. Surfing and swimming. Good fishing.

Accommodation. Three **hotels.** Recommended: Pier, The Esplanade. One **motel. Holiday cottages** for rent. Two **caravan and camping parks,** all facilities.

Transport. Rail, road and **air** services from Perth.

MURCHISON COAST AND HINTERLAND

The coastal plain north of Perth contains some of the most productive agricultural and pastoral land in Western Australia, and its hinterland has yielded a wide range of minerals to exploiters of the past with their hit-or-miss methods. Like the Gascoyne and Pilbara regions to the north, it is now being carefully reassessed both by prospectors for oil and base metals and also agronomists who foresee the possibility of repeating the type of development which has already occurred in the mineral deficient heathlands of the south-west. The coast has strong appeal for the enterprising fisherman and surfboard rider—particularly in the vicinity of Jurien Bay, west of the small town of **Moora** on the Geraldton Highway 173 kilometres north of Perth, and at **Kalbarri** townsite, a tourist resort 166 kilometres north of Geraldton on Gantheaume Bay and the mouth of the Murchison River. There are good lookouts over the Murchison Gorge at Graham and Hawk, and lookouts on the road from the highway turnoff near **Ajana** to Kalbarri.

There is one **hotel** and one **motel** at Moora. Furnished **flats, cottages** and stationary **caravans** may be rented at Kalbarri, which also has a well-appointed **caravan camping park.**

GERALDTON

(Population 15 330)

West Australia's second seaport, Geraldton, is 503 kilometres north of Perth on Champion Bay. It is a highly prosperous, well designed town serving a community of extremely diversified industrial interests. The Perth-Geraldton Highway runs through some of the best farming country in the west and produces excellent wheat, wool, fruit and vegetables, wine grapes and dairy products. Tobacco, some cotton and peanuts have also been grown commercially.

Crayfishing, now a multi-million dollar earner in West Australia, has great economic importance for the town. The State's largest crayfishing fleet is based on the port, which also dispatches the prawn harvest taken from waters farther to the north.

Metal exports have also played a part in building Geraldton's prosperity—copper and then lead from Northampton (49 kilometres) in the early days, gold from the Murchison and Wiluna fields, and later iron ore from Koolanooka, manganese and natural gas from the Dongara field, now piped to

Perth and Kwinana. Secondary industries include a superphosphate works, iron foundries and flour mills.

The district enjoys a magnificent winter climate and Geraldton has become a much favoured holiday town because of this advantage. It also boasts excellent beaches and pleasant coastal scenery. Fishing is good, particularly off the Abrolhos Islands where most of the crayfishing boats operate.

History. The Abrolhos Islands, 64 kilometres west, were charted and named by the Portuguese early in the 16th century. Lieutenant (later Sir George) Grey examined the region in 1839. In 1848 lead was discovered in the Murchison River just north of Ajana by a party under A. C. Gregory. Further prospecting disclosed the Northampton mines which are still producing.

The townsite of Geraldton was surveyed and named for Governor Charles Fitzgerald in 1850, and the 99th Regiment was stationed there for the protection of settlers from hostile natives. The municipality was proclaimed in 1871. In 1879 the first Government railway line in the State was built from the town to the Northampton lead mines. The first regular airmail service in the State began flying from Geraldton to Derby in 1921. During the second world war the harbour was an American flying boat base.

Of Interest. **Kalbarri National Park.** Launch excursions to the **Abrolhos Islands** may be arranged (hostel accommodation available). Good view from heights above **Waggrakine Cutting.** Excellent **Shell Museum** on North West Coastal Highway near town.

Sports. Golf course. Tennis courts. Bowls and croquet. Yachting. Fishing. Shooting. Swimming.

Accommodation. Nine **hotels.** Recommended: Marquis Swan, Northwest Highway, Queen's, Durlacher Street. Three **motels.** Prefered: Highway, Queen Street. Holiday **cottages, flats** and **lodges** for rent. Three **caravan and camping parks,** all facilities.

Transport. **Road, rail** and **air** services from Perth.

NEW NORCIA

New Norcia, 132 kilometres north of Perth, is a mission station established by the Benedictine Order in 1846 to help Australian aborigines. It was the only mission surviving out of three founded by Bishop J. Brady, first Catholic Bishop of Perth, and it has a fascinating record. The original station was built by Dom J. B. Serra and Dom Rosenda Salvado at Batgi Batgi, 8 kilometres from the present site. The early days were particularly difficult and at one stage Dom Salvado, who was an accomplished musician, walked to Perth to give a fund raising concert.

In time, however, the industry of the monks made the mission self-supporting and in 1859 it was separated from the Perth diocese and became directly responsible to Rome. Ten years later it attained diocesan status in its own right and took care of aborigines within the 4 200 hectares under its control. In 1900 the diocese was extended to include about 7 740 000 hectares. Later still the famous Drysdale Mission (Kalumburu) in the North Kimberley was founded by missionaries from New Norcia.

Today the 9 000 hectare settlement in the secluded Maura Maura valley grows wheat, wool, wine and practically every foodstuff needed to support a permanent population of 250 which rises to about 600 during the school year. Aboriginal children and orphans from all over West Australia are educated at St Gertrude's College, which was founded by the missionaries in 1908.

Most of New Norcia's missionaries are of Spanish origin and Spanish architectural style predominates in the community buildings. The monastery possesses a valuable collection of paintings and rare manuscripts.

Male visitors are welcome to call at the establishment.

MEEKATHARRA (Population 921)

An old gold and copper mining town 764 kilometres north-east of Perth, Meekatharra was once an important railhead for cattle which had been overlanded down the Canning Stock Route across the Gibson Desert from the Northern Territory and the East Kimberley or down another stock route, known as 'the Madman's Track', from north-western stations. Gold was discovered in the district in 1896 and the town boomed until the outbreak of the first world war, after which it rapidly declined. Intensive prospecting for minerals, particularly nickel, is now going on in the region. The first regular School of the Air programmes for outback children were broadcast from Meekatharra Flying Doctor Base in 1959.

Accommodation. Three **hotels.** Preferred: Meekatharra, Main Street. **Caravan and camping park,** some facilities.

Transport. **Air** services.

MOUNT MAGNET (Population 632)

Mount Magnet, 468 kilometres from Perth along the Great Northern Highway, is a convenient overnight stop for motorists bound from Perth to Port Hedland on the inland route. It was once a flourishing mining town, but now mainly serves a scattered pastoral district.

Accommodation. Two **hotels.**

Transport. **Air** services.

WILUNA (Population 140)

Wiluna was once the centre of a rich goldfield and supported a population of more than 7 000 in the late 1920s and early 1930s. Today it is a ghost town in which only a few of the more solid public and commercial buildings are left standing. Although the annual rainfall approximates a mere 200 millimetres, plentiful water can be obtained from shallow bores and the soil is very productive under irrigation. Excellent quality citrus and other fruit is grown at the nearby **Ground Water Research Station,** which also produces pasture grass seed and conducts arid-zone agricultural research.

Wiluna is one of the few towns in West Australia from which sandalwood-getters still operate. It is, or was, the official terminal of the now disused Canning Stock Route.

Accommodation. One **hotel.**

Transport. **Mail car** service from Meekatharra.

EASTERN DISTRICTS

With the exception of the sparsely populated tropical Kimberley region in the far north, Western Australia is virtually uninhabited desert beyond any point east of Kalgoorlie. A few fettlers' camps are strung out along the transcontinental railway line and a few motels have been built on the Eyre Highway across the southern section of the Nullarbor Plain, but generally speaking the country can be penetrated only by travellers such as oil and mineral prospectors who are specially equipped for desert conditions.

The district known as the Eastern Goldfields, therefore, is really in the western half of the State. The goldfields, and the wheatlands which are gradually pushing out towards them as dryland farming techniques improve, are of interest only to travellers with specific objectives—or to the curious or adventurous.

KALGOORLIE-BOULDER

(Population 20 784)

One of the longest lived and most prosperous goldmining centres in the Commonwealth, Kalgoorlie is 597 kilometres east of Perth on the western margins of the Nullarbor Plain and the Great Victoria Desert. After more than 70 years' working the mines of the region still produce more than 70 per cent of the gold won in Australia, but their importance to the West Australian economy has been overshadowed recently by the discovery of rich nickel deposits at Kambalda, 55 kilometres south-south-east of the town, and elsewhere in the district. An upsurge of prospecting activity and increased employment provided directly and indirectly by nickel mining has enlivened Kalgoorlie which, because of the depressed state of the goldmining industry in Australia, might well have become a ghost town if the new discoveries had not been made.

The town itself, despite its age, remains an odd mixture of the permanent and the makeshift. Its broad streets have been planted with drought resistant trees and it has some solidly handsome public buildings and excellent civic amenities and recreation facilities, yet it still retains something of the atmosphere of a desert mining camp. The surrounding countryside, denuded of vegetation by the old-time miners, is forbiddingly ugly. The summer climate is extremely hot.

History. Gold was first discovered in Kalgoorlie by three Irish prospectors, Patrick Hannan, Thomas Flanagan and Dan Shea in June 1893. They had pushed east through dry country from the booming diggings at Coolgardie 40 kilometres away, where rich alluvial strikes had been made in September the year before by Arthur Bayley and William Ford. The three men did not even have to dig for their fortunes. Within two or three days they had collected 200 ounces of small nuggets which lay glittering on the surface of the red sand in the gullies.

The Coolgardie strike had been hardly less sensational and a tremendous rush of prospectors from all over the world ensued. The conditions under which the diggers lived and worked were at first appalling. Heat, drought and epidemic diseases exacted a heavy toll of lives, and although a rail link with Perth in 1896 made a great difference to life in the mining camps it was not until the Goldfields Water Supply Scheme was completed in 1903 that the situation was really alleviated. Under this scheme, designed by C. Y. O'Connor who also planned Fremantle harbour, water was piped 553 kilometres from Mundaring Weir in the Darling Ranges to the thirsty towns which had been established on a permanent basis in the face of all difficulties. By 1905 the population of the goldfields was 200 000, but as the alluvial gold was worked out and deep mining took over, this rapidly diminished.

Kalgoorlie, at first known as East Coolgardie, soon surpassed the parent town in importance—particularly as the pattern of lode formations was revealed by deep mining and metallurgical problems associated with the treatment of the ore were solved. The mines have produced more than 36 million ounces of gold.

Three local government authorities share administration of the urban area and its immediate environs—the Town of Kalgoorlie, the Shire of Kalgoorlie and the Town of Boulder.

Pastoral industry is also well established in the goldfields district. The sheep population is now about half a million with an annual clip of about 15 000 bales.

Places of Interest. School of Mines and Museum. Paddy Hannan's Tree, marking the spot where Hannan first found gold. **Paddy Hannan's Statue. Mount Charlotte Reservoir** at the end of the pipeline. **Golden Mile Museum** and collection of local gemstones. Kurrawang **Aboriginal Mission. Forestry Department Arboretum of drought resistant trees and shrubs. British Arms Museum. Boulder Town Hall.** Surface workings of the **Golden Mile mines** (inspections can be arranged). **Kambalda** model township (55 kilometres south on bitumen road) built by Western Mining Corporation to accommodate workers at Australia's first commercial nickel mines, and nearby **Lake Lefroy,** where mirages may be seen at sunset. High grade salt is harvested from the lake's surface.

Prospecting and fossicking expeditions can be arranged by contacting the Amalgamated Prospectors' Association, Maritana Street, Kalgoorlie. The region provides great opportunities for amateur lapidarists.

Sports. Racecourse and trotting track. Golf course. Bowling and croquet greens. Tennis and squash courts. Gliding Club. Clay pigeon club. Pistol shooting and archery ranges. Speedway. Olympic swimming pool.

Accommodation. Twenty two **hotels.** Recommended: Tower, Hannan Street; Palace, Hannan Street. Two **motels.** Recommended: Highway, Hannan Street. **Caravan and camping park,** some facilities.

Transport. Rail-road and **air** services. **Taxi tours** of town and district can be arranged.

COOLGARDIE (Population 622)

Probably Australia's most famous 'ghost town', Coolgardie is 40 kilometres west of Kalgoorlie. A few fine old stone buildings are all that remain to remind the traveller that it was once a roaring city with a population of more than 20 000 and that its mines on the Golden Mile alone yielded more than 34 million ounces of gold—not including the 1 135 ounces Golden Eagle nugget found in 1931 and the Eldorado nugget of 2 000 ounces found in 1951.

Of Interest. Collection of goldfields relics displayed by a garage proprietor in the main street.

Accommodation. Two **hotels.** Preferred: Denver City. One **motel.** Two **caravan and camping areas.** No information on facilities.

Transport. Rail and **road** services to Perth, Kalgoorlie and Esperance etc.

NORSEMAN (Population 1 757)

A gold and iron pyrites mining town on Lake Cowan and the Great Eastern Highway, Norseman is 741 kilometres from Perth and 201 kilometres south of Kalgoorlie. Motorists on the transcontinental route often use it as an overnight stopping place. The region is highly mineralized and is rewarding country for amateur prospectors and specimen collectors. Gold was first discovered there in 1892-3 when it was known as the Dundas field.

Accommodation. Two **hotels.** Preferred: Norseman, Robert Street. One **motel. Caravan and camping park,** all facilities.

Transport. Rail and **road** services to Esperance, Coolgardie etc. **Air** service to Kalgoorlie, Esperance and Perth.

SOUTHERN CROSS (Population 876)

The service centre of a large wheatland and pastoral area, Southern Cross is a tidy, prosperous little town 378 kilometres east of Perth. It was once a goldrush settlement after the proclamation of the Yilgarn fields in 1887, but although a number of profitable mines were established it was soon overshadowed by the bonanza at Coolgardie in 1892. Some mining is still carried on in the locality. Wheat has become an important crop only since the development of quick maturing strains and light land farming techniques.

Southern Cross is about 56 kilometres from the iron ore deposits of **Koolyanobbing,** which are being mined by Broken Hill Proprietary Ltd for the blast furnaces at Kwinana. A small, beautifully designed model town among gumtrees has been developed at the mine site for the workforce. The ore from the open cut is automatically crushed, screened and loaded for dispatch to the coast on a loop of the new standard gauge railway between Perth and Kalgoorlie.

Accommodation. Three **hotels.** Preferred: Southern Cross, Canopus Street.

Transport. Rail and **road** services to Perth and Kalgoorlie.

MERREDIN (Population 3 596)

Merredin is the market town of a wheat and wool growing district on the plains 261 kilometres east of Perth. The locality was examined by J. S. Row in 1839 but he was not impressed by its potential for settlement and it was not explored thoroughly until 1864 by C. C. Hunt. Sandalwood cutters were active in the area for many years. During the goldrush a shanty town grew up around a waterhole where miners camped on their way to the fields. Then, when the Kalgoorlie railway went through about 3 kilometres from the little settlement in 1893, it transferred to a trackside site, was surveyed and proclaimed a town. Early in the 20th century the wheatlands were pushed out into the dry country and the Nangeenan Experimental Farm, which later became the Merredin Agricultural Research Station, was founded in 1909. The Shire Council pioneered sewage water treatment for irrigation of public parks and recreation reserves in the arid areas.

Places of Interest. Merredin National Forest, 121 hectares of plantation 3 kilometres east of the town. **Harling Memorial Library.**

Merredin's agricultural show in September is a major event for West Australian farmers.

Sports. Trotting track. Bowls, tennis, golf. Olympic swimming pool.

Accommodation. Two **hotels.** Recommended: Merredin Oasis, Great Eastern Highway. One **motel. Caravan and camping park,** all facilities.

Transport. Rail and **road** services from Perth.

HYDEN (Population 100)

A small town in the eastern wheatlands, 351 kilometres from Perth on the sealed road through Corrigin and Kondinin about 124 kilometres south of the Great Eastern Highway, Hyden is remarkable only for an extraordinary formation of overhanging granite, known as **Wave Rock,** about 3 kilometres from the settlement.

Wave Rock, which is part of a larger formation known as Hyden Rock, has the appearance of a breaking wave, sculpted in stone. The overhang is more than 15 metres high and several hundred metres long and the surface of the granite is vertically streaked with water stains varying in colour from deep grey through ochres and reds to a pale, sandy tint. The granite is calculated to have been crystallized 2 700 million years ago.

The formation is so peculiar and spectacular that, although the surrounding country is semi-arid and monotonous, many hundreds of motorists detour from the Great Eastern and Southern Highways to view it.

Several other interesting rock formations in the district include **Bates Cave,** containing aboriginal rock paintings (hand imprints), **Hippo's Yawn, the Humps,** the **Gnamma Hole** and **King Rocks.** All can be seen on a 80 kilometre road circuit from Hyden.

Accommodation. One **hotel. Caravan and camp areas,** few facilities.

Transport. Road service.

THE NORTH WEST

The region generally known in Western Australia as 'the North West' is bounded on the south by the 26th parallel, on the north and west by the Indian Ocean and on the east by the Northern Territory. Its area is roughly 152 000 square kilometres and its permanent population, despite the exploitation of enormous iron ore deposits begun in the region since 1962, is still considerably less than 30 000.

Some two-thirds of this vast province must be regarded for all practical purposes as desert with an annual rainfall of less than 200 millimetres, its occurrence unpredictable. Parts of the remaining one-third, however, receive copious monsoonal rainfall of up to 13 centimetres. It has been calculated that the runoff of the large rivers in the Kimberley district equal or exceed the total runoff of the Murrumbidgee-Murray-Darling system in the south-east of the continent.

The problems associated with developing and populating the rich and well-watered country in the North West have for years engaged the attention of the West Australian Government and, indeed, of the Commonwealth Government.

Both have been committed to a policy which favours European immigration to Australia. So far, the inducements offered to encourage European settlement of this part of tropical Australia have not offset climatic and geographical disadvantages, and the area remains to all intents and purposes unpopulated except for a few cotton farmers in an irrigated area on the lower reaches of the Ord River and a handful of pastoralists who raise lean beef on million-hectare holdings, support strong lobbies in both State and Federal Parliaments, and manage their leaseholds by using methods which cause a rapid and accelerating deterioration of natural vegetation and soil.

Ironically, the 'economic breakthrough' in the North West has been made in the arid and semi-arid division of the Pilbara, where vast iron ore deposits long known to exist but only recently surveyed, are now being exploited as a result of a change in Federal policy which until 1962 forbade export of iron ore from Australia on the ground that known reserves must be conserved to meet the requirements of the local iron and steel industry.

The iron ore mining companies, financed largely by American, British and Japanese capital, are contracted to supply Japanese steel mills with vast quantities of ore and pellets during the next 20 years. Mining and dispatch operations are highly mechanized and will, apart from the labour force required for construction works, offer direct and indirect employment for perhaps 5 000 permanent workers in settlements north of the 26th parallel.

Hope is nevertheless entertained by the West Australian Government that the current mining operations will lead to an integrated Australian iron and steel industry in the North West and that the facilities created by exploitation of the iron ore deposits will stimulate other mining ventures in a region known to be rich in many minerals.

The terrain of the North West is excitingly colourful and varied, but the traveller unfamiliar with inland Australia would do well to keep in mind the fact that the variety is compounded of ingredients of massive proportions. The Hamersley Range, for instance, is more than 320 kilometres long. Its scenery is superb and its changes of visual mood enthralling, but it is virtually lost in a limitless ocean of red sand and silver-grey spinifex and funereal mulga scrub.

Climate has been as potent a factor as distance in discouraging settlement of the areas which receive adequate and reliable rainfall. For perhaps seven months of the year the North West receives little or no rainfall. Its skies are cloudless, its days warm to pleasantly hot and its nights cool and bracing. In the remaining five months the heat is fierce and the rainfall, whether meagre or copious overall, is torrential. In the Pilbara and the adjacent coastal plains particularly, meteorological statistics of average precipitation are entirely deceptive. Years of complete drought may be followed by a season in which cyclonic storms deluge the parched countryside with as much as 70 centimetres of rain within 24 hours.

North of the cyclone belt, however, the monsoon country receives between 50 and 120 centimetres with fair reliability in a three or four month wet season.

Quite apart from the physical discomfort of living the year round in such a climate, the weather pattern poses formidable problems for settlers who try to farm or graze the land without the backing of large water conservation works. The North West therefore remains sparsely settled. So far only one large water conservation project has been undertaken. A diversion and a main storage dam have been built near Kununurra on the Ord River in East Kimberley and the stored water used to irrigate farms totalling about 90 000 hectares capable of yielding a variety of tropical crops. Large sums have also been spent already or allocated for roads serving pastoral holdings which raise beef cattle by the 'open range' method.

The North West may accurately be described as a region of strange, exciting forms, vivid colours and almost unbelievable spaciousness. The cycle of the seasons determines whether it appears beautiful or repellent. It has an incalculable potential for winter tourism—warmth and unfailing sunshine, superb coastal and mountain scenery entirely different from that of the eastern and southern seaboard and fishing probably unequalled anywhere in the world. Its 'vermin'—an excessive kangaroo population, wild buffalo, camels, donkeys, pigs, dingoes and crocodiles—and multitudes of feathered game give devotees of blood sports a scope that would be hard to match outside Africa.

It must be realized, however, that despite the recent marked improvement of main roads, access 'highways' still have hundreds of kilometres of rough and sometimes dangerous surface. Secondary roads are often suitable only for four-wheel drive vehicles (see Travel in the Outback).

Except for hotels and motels newly established at such boom centres as Port Hedland, Dampier, Mount Tom Price and Kununurra, the accommodation available to casual visitors is still fairly primitive. Service and organized entertainment are practically non-existent.

Probably the easiest and cheapest way of seeing the country is to take one of the numerous road coach or air tours now run regularly from southern capitals. Travel agencies and tourist bureaux will be able to advise. The more active and adventurous traveller may prefer to join a 'safari' tour or convoy, several of which make north-western circuits in the season.

Air transport even to the more remote centres of population is frequent and comfortable, but hire cars are scarce and expensive.

The North West as properly defined covers about one-sixth of the Australian continent. For convenience this *Guide* divides it into three are as: the Gascoyne district between the Tropic of Capricorn and the 26th parallel; the North West Coast and Pilbara; and the East and West Kimberleys.

GASCOYNE DISTRICT

CARNARVON

(Population 4 222)

Carnarvon is the main town of the Gascoyne district, 983 kilometres north-north-west of Perth on the North West Coastal Highway. The Gascoyne is a vast pastoral area with productivity declining in recent years because of over-grazing and erosion. Carnarvon's prosperity these days is due mainly to its highly profitable prawning industry, to the success of irrigated fruit and vegetable farms near the mouth of the Gascoyne River, and to the National Aeronautics and Space Administration tracking station at Brown's Range, 10 kilometres from town.

The big harvests from the tropical fruit and vegetable plantations, which are irrigated from shallow bores sunk in the river sands, have highlighted the potential of large water conservation schemes in the North West and studies are being made of the practicability of constructing two large dams upriver. A comparatively small area of river flats at present produces annual crops of bananas, mangoes, paw-paws and winter vegetables worth more than three million dollars. The main market is Perth.

The town of Carnarvon itself is not particularly attractive, but the district is full of fascination—particularly to the traveller who is in no great hurry.

History. In 1606 the Dutch navigator, Dirk Hartog, examined the coast and landed on the island which bears his name in Shark Bay, to the south of the river mouth. The Englishman William Dampier followed in 1699 and reported that the country seemed barren and useless.

Nearly 130 years later, however, the explorer George Grey discovered and named the Gascoyne River for his friend Lieutenant J. Gascoyne, RN. Grey thought the area had pastoral potential, but no attempt at settlement was made until another explorer, F. T. Gregory, examined the district in 1858 and again reported favourably. In the mid 1870s the first settlers, Aubrey Brown, J. H. Monger and C. S. Brockman, moved sheep into the Gascoyne and established stations. (Brown's original holding is now the site of the tracking station.) The township of Carnarvon was surveyed in 1883, with streets 40 metres wide to permit camel trains to turn in them—an admirable example of pioneering foresight because the town was to depend on camel train communications until the early 1920s. It was named in honour of the Secretary of State for the Colonies, Lord Carnarvon.

Bananas were first grown on the river flats in 1920, so successfully that the State Government established a research station to assist planters and help solve their irrigation problems. The acreage under cultivation increased rapidly, but is now limited because all available resources of unconserved waters have been put to use.

In 1950 a whaling station was established and continued operations profitably until 1962, by which time the annual catches had declined to an uneconomic level. Soon afterwards, however, the prawning industry was started and has been steadily expanding ever since.

Places of Interest. Marine Museum, on Babbage Island near the prawning works. **Gascoyne Agricultural Station** and experimental farm, 10 kilometres from town on the south plantation road. **Rotary Park,** picnic spot on river near Onslow Bridge. **Dwyer's Leap,** on Babbage Island, a good spot for water-skiing. **Oyster Creek,** about 8 kilometres south of town, is a rewarding fishing spot for small boats when the tide is right. **Miaboolya Beach,** on turnoff from road north to Quobba Station, about 10 kilometres from town. **The Blows,** on Quobba Station, 68 kilometres from Carnarvon; a stretch of rocky coast, with spectacular blowholes, and excellent fishing and oystering. (Road is treacherous after rain.) **Cape Cuvier,** about 24 kilometres beyond Quobba Station, with multicoloured 120 metre cliffs battered by the sea; scenically magnificent. **Kennedy Ranges,** 161 kilometres east on road to Gascoyne Junction, are the happy hunting ground for gemstone prospectors who can collect petrified wood, opalite, chalcedony and many kinds of semi-precious stones. **Rocky Pool,** 55 kilometres from town on the Junction Road, is a picturesque permanent waterhole, where interesting specimens may also be found. **Brown Range Space Vehicle Tracking Station,** operated for the Department of Supply by Amalgamated Wireless (Australasia) Ltd, tracked the first of many space vehicles in January 1964. It was an essential link in a worldwide chain of stations set up to help the Apollo Project put men on the moon. The station is open to visitors and conducted tours may be arranged through the Carnarvon District Tourist Bureau.

Sports. Tennis and badminton courts. Bowling greens. Tennis courts (winter only). Pony and polocrosse clubs. Rifle club. Water-skiing. Night basketball.

Fishing on this coast is almost incredibly good, particularly north of The Blows. Mangrove crabs and prawns can also be caught and rock oysters are plentiful. Big game fishing excursions for Spanish mackerel and sailfish may be arranged through the tourist bureau.

Accommodation. Three **hotels.** Preferred: Carnarvon, Olivia Terrace. Two **motels.** Recommended: Highway, West Street. Four **caravan and camping parks,** all facilities.

Transport. Express and tourist **coach** services from Perth and North West towns. Daily **air** services. **Aerial tours** available.

SHARK BAY (Population 323)

Denham, 911 kilometres from Perth, is the only town on Shark Bay where a large fishing industry is now based. The bay is popular with boating and fishing enthusiasts who have their own craft, but it is not yet developed as a resort.

Accommodation. One **hotel.** One **motel.** Three **caravan and camping parks,** limited facilities.

Transport. Road service. Twice weekly **air** service.

GASCOYNE JUNCTION (Population 100)

Gascoyne Junction is a small service centre for a large pastoral area in which the average size of holdings is 36 000 hectares. The nearby Kennedy Ranges are chiefly of interest to gemstone and mineral specimen prospectors, although the gorges contain beautiful rock pools in which good fishing may be had. Most points of interest are accessible only by four-wheel drive vehicles.

Accommodation. One **hotel.**

Transport. Road service and weekly **air service.**

NORTH WEST COAST AND PILBARA

EXMOUTH

(Population 2 638)

A model town built by the Commonwealth and Western Australian Governments as a service centre for the United States Navy's radio communications base at North West Cape, Exmouth is 402 kilometres north of Carnarvon and 1 375 kilometres north of Perth. It accommodates married naval personnel attached to the base and Australian civilians employed on the project.

The main point of interest is the very low frequency (VLF) transmitting station itself which has 13 lattice steel towers all more than 305 metres high to support the antenna canopy of the transmitters, which can communicate with fleet units anywhere in the Indian and Pacific Oceans. The installation cost $A80 million.

The base was named in 1968 for Harold E. Holt, Prime Minister of Australia at that time.

The region is semi-arid and badly eroded by over-grazing and pastoral mismanagement, but despite its grim appearance has much to interest tourists.

The fishing in Exmouth Gulf and on the open coast is probably the best in Australia. Marlin, sailfish, Spanish mackerel, tuna, giant sharks and rays are taken in the deep water off the mouth of the gulf and an incredible variety of smaller fish in the shallows. Crabbing, prawning and oystering are excellent. The sheltered waters are ideal for all kinds of water sports in winter and early spring.

Cape and Rough Ranges which form the mountainous backbone of the cape peninsula are not impressive when viewed from the highway, but are spectacular at close quarters. Many of the enormous canyons and caves contain examples of primitive aboriginal art. Roads which can be negotiated by four-wheel drive vehicles were built by oil exploration companies in the Cape Range, and some are being minimally maintained. They lead to unique and fascinating terrain.

Prawning is now a major industry on the gulf and a large fleet of trawlers is based on a processing plant near **Learmonth,** an RAAF wartime airfield about 48 kilometres south of Exmouth which is still serviceable.

Sports facilities in the new township are elaborate. There is a golf course and recreation areas developed for all kinds of games. Most are floodlit for night play.

Accommodation. Tourist accommodation is limited. One **hotel** (expensive but well equipped). Two large **caravan and camping parks,** all facilities, originally developed to accommodate construction workers.

It should be noted that climatic conditions are uncomfortable at Exmouth between early November and late April. The area is subject to violent cyclonic storms.

Transport. Road services and **air** service to Learmonth with connecting bus.

ONSLOW (Population 349)

Old Onslow, near the mouth of the Ashburton River, was a colourful mining and pearling port until 1926 when the settlement, after repeated heavy damage by cyclones, transferred to the site of the present town on Beadon Bay. The town was founded in 1883 and named after Sir Alexander Onslow, Chief Justice of Western Australia, about three years after the first settlers had established sheep stations in the district. Gold was discovered on the upper reaches of the river in the 1890s, but the area was so remote that only sporadic mining continued after the alluvial was worked out. The whole region is rich in minerals and large iron ore deposits have been discovered at Deepdale, about 96 kilometres east. Hopes are held that mining will be revived and offset the slow decline of the wool industry in the North West.

Onslow is the service port of the Barrow Island commercial oilfields. During the second world war the harbour was used as a base by US submarines and it was the main depot for the British force which tested nuclear bombs on the Monte Bello Islands in 1953. The new town suffered extensive cyclone damage in 1934, 1961 and 1963.

Accommodation. One **hotel. Caravan park,** some facilities. No camping.

Transport. Road and **air** services. **Shipping** service monthly.

ROEBOURNE (Population 1 395)

About 13 kilometres inland from the old pearling port of Cossack at the mouth of the Harding River, Roebourne is 1 746 kilometres from Perth on the North West Coastal Highway. The town was proclaimed in 1866 and named after J. S. Roe, Western Australia's first Surveyor-General. It was the headquarters of the Government Resident for the North West and enjoyed considerable prosperity as the pastoral industry boomed along the semi-arid coastal plain. Copper was discovered at Whim Creek, 80 kilometres east of the town, in 1872 and intensive prospecting began in the Pilbara.

Good pearling grounds were found in Nicol Bay and for a time Cossack was the most important and busiest port on the coast, despite the fact that the pearling fleet was virtually wiped out by a cyclone in 1873. Decline set in when the pearlers moved to Broome in the early 1880s, and the thin trade of the region had to be shared with rival settlements.

Cossack is reached by 8 kilometres of rough but normally passable track leading off the highway between Roebourne and Port Samson. Many of its buildings were beautifully designed and built of local stone by master masons. They remain basically intact to this day despite damage by weather and vandals. Some are now restored and used as holiday 'apartments' by town residents or mine workers from the hinterland iron fields. Inscriptions on gravestones in the nearby cemetery give intriguing glimpses of the dramatic history of the settlement.

Port Samson was the point of shipment for the blue asbestos won from the Wittenoom mines 290 kilometres inland, until they were closed down in 1967.

Accommodation at Roebourne. One **hotel. Camping and caravan park,** limited but adequate facilities.

Transport. Road, air and **shipping** services.

DAMPIER

(Population 3 558)

Dampier is the company town and port of Hamersley Iron Pty Ltd and lies a few kilometres west of Roebourne on King Bay, facing the unusual and beautiful islands of **Dampier Archipelago.** Five hundred houses have been built on the site—all ultra-modern, many air conditioned. The settlement was created for workers at the bulk loading terminal of the Mount Tom Price iron ore mines, 290 kilometres by rail inland in the Hamersley Ranges. Hamersley Iron is a consortium of the Kaiser Steel Corporation of America and Conzinc Riotinto of Australia.

The Dampier installations are now delivering 10 million tonnes of ore a year into giant ore carriers (up to 106 000 tonnes deadweight) for delivery to Japanese blast furnaces. A pelletising plant with a capacity of two million tonnes a year is in operation.

Domestic and industrial water is supplied to Dampier by a seawater desalination plant with a capacity of 1 820 000 litres a day.

Of Interest is the **Karratha** townsite under development as future regional capital.

Hotel accommodation is available at Dampier but permission to inspect the town should be sought from Perth headquarters of the Hamersley Company or inquiry made through the WA Government Tourist Bureau.

Note: The service road for the new standard gauge railway between the mines and the port may be used by private motorists at their own risk. It passes through harsh but extremely colourful mountain country to the west of the Wittenoom-Roebourne road.

PORT HEDLAND

(Population 7 172)

As main port for the Hamersley iron ore region and the great iron mines at Mount Goldsworthy and Mount Newman, Port Hedland is now one of the fastest growing towns in Australia.

Destined to become one of the greatest iron ore shipping centres in the world, the town is built on an island about 13 kilometres long and 1.6 kilometres wide. It is connected to the mainland by three long causeways over tidal creeks, with a fourth causeway recently constructed to give direct access to the bulk loading installations handling ore from Mount Goldsworthy.

As available land was inadequate for industrial and residential expansion, a new town has been built 8 kilometres inland beyond the tidal flats, and about 4 kilometres from the aerodrome. The iron ore berths accommodate carriers of up to 100 000 tonnes and other facilities in the inner harbour include wharves for large freighters to handle other mineral exports as well as output of the vast evaporation works of the Leslie Salt Company already established on the coast near the town. The salt produced is used for the hardening of steel.

Port Hedland's water supply comes from bores sunk in the Yule River sands to the east, but it will probably soon be necessary to install desalination plant. The average annual rainfall in the district is less than 280 millimetres.

Port Hedland is not happily situated, from a scenic or recreational point of view, but its enormous construction and industrial operations are of great interest. Organized tours of inspection are available.

Owing to the pressure on accommodation in the town, forward bookings for hotel and motel accommodation are absolutely essential.

History. The town was founded in 1863 and named by its surveyor, C. C. Hunt, after Peter Hedland, a master pearler who sailed up the coast in 1857 and discovered the harbour. Pastoral industry boomed in the region until the early years of the 20th century. The great Mundabullangana station, 80 kilometres west, was reported to have shorn as many as 120 000 sheep in one season; but after the turn of the century pastures began to decline.

For a time Port Hedland was an important pearling centre, though never as large as Cossack. Then in 1888 rich gold was discovered in the Marble Bar and Nullagine districts some 240 kilometres south-east, and the ensuing rush subsided only when the strikes on the eastern goldfields around Coolgardie attracted diggers from all over the continent in 1892-3. However, mining for gold and other metals in the Pilbara continued for many years, despite difficulties of climate, terrain and distance. In 1912 tin mining increased to such a degree that a railway was built from Port Hedland to Marble Bar.

During the second world war mining for tin, tantalite, beryllium, columbite, manganese and other strategic minerals was stepped up in the Pilbara and in 1942 Japanese aircraft bombed the port, which was used by Allied flying boats patrolling the Indian Ocean. Mining again declined after peace was restored and in 1951 the Marble Bar railway was closed. Later in the same decade, however, manganese deposits were discovered on the upper reaches of the Oakover River and considerable tonnages were shipped through the port. Tin mining also revived, but the future of the region remained uncertain until the great iron ore developments began in 1964.

Of Interest. **Pretty Pool** for swimming and shell collecting. **Annual race meeting,** mid August.

Accommodation. Three **hotels.** Recommended: Port Hedland Motor Hotel. One recommended **motel.** Two **caravan and camping parks,** all facilities.

Transport. **Road** services. Frequent **air** services from Perth via other North West towns.

MARBLE BAR (Population 391)

Marble Bar has the doubtful distinction of being the most consistently hot town in Australia on meteorological records taken over a number of years (although, when statistics have been compiled, it may yield place to the mining township at Mount Tom Price about 161 kilometres by air to the south-west).

Between October and March it is not uncommon for daily maxima to exceed 48°C. The longest heat wave on record was in 1923-4, a drought period, during which the maximum exceeded 38°C for 160 consecutive days. In winter, although day temperatures often approach the century, frosts can be experienced at night.

Despite its climatic extremes, the country around Marble Bar is in some places very beautiful with a wide range of flora and fauna and colourful and unusual rock formations. The low ranges in the vicinity of the town and to the east of the Oakover River are scenically delightful, particularly in late winter when masses of desert wildflowers are in bloom.

The town itself is a grim, lonely little settlement, typical of much of the Western Australian Outback.

History. See Port Hedland.

Places of Interest. **Marble Bar pool,** 5 kilometres west of town, where bars of multicoloured jasper are exposed in the river bed. Unfortunately the area has been damaged by vandals and made unsightly by tourists' litter. Fine stone **Government buildings** overlooking town. **Old Comet gold-mine,** on secondary road to the south of the town. **Tin workings** on Nullagine road. Motorists on this road should note that there is unusual scenery worth discovering on secondary roads running east from **Nullagine** hamlet itself.

Accommodation. One **hotel.** One **caravan and camping park,** some facilities. (Both for seasoned outback travellers.)

Transport. **Road** services. Thrice weekly **air** service.

WITTENOOM (Population 422)

Until 1966 a residential and service centre for miners working deposits of blue asbestos in the Hamersley Ranges, Wittenoom is a small, neat town in the heart of the Pilbara about 322 kilometres from Port Hedland and 299 kilometres from Roebourne. Hopes are still entertained that the asbestos mine which closed in 1966 will be reopened and that iron ore deposits in the region will be exploited, but in the meantime the settlement depends on the tourist trade to keep it going.

History. Blue asbestos was mined sporadically in the district during the 1930s and in 1939 the Yampire Gorge deposits were systematically exploited for the first time by the Asbestos, Molybdenum and Tungsten Co Ltd. In 1953 a subsidiary of the Colonial Sugar Refining Company set up a plant in Wittenoom Gorge and by 1950 was sole producer of blue asbestos fibre in Australia. The West Australian Government assisted the project by building a town for the miners and their dependants. The resultant improvement of roads and air communications encouraged winter tourist traffic to the ranges, which many travellers hold to be scenically superior to the mountain country in the vicinity of Alice Springs. The colour of the rock formations is undoubtedly more varied and vivid.

Places of Interest. **Wittenoom, Dale's, Hamersley, Jubilla, Colonial, Red** and **Yampire Gorges. Fortesque, Joffre and Cascade Falls.** Paperback forests, palm forests, lily ponds and large pools on the Fortesque River near **Millstream Station** (detour off Roebourne road). Tremendous panoramic views from the summit of **Mount Herbert** over which the road to Roebourne passes. **Python Pool,** to the south-east of Mount Herbert.

Accommodation. One **hotel. Camping and caravan park,** all facilities.

Transport. **Road** services. Daily **air** service. **Charter aircraft** and **hire cars** available.

Company Mining Towns in Pilbara

TOM PRICE (Population 3 370) south-west of Wittenoom in the heart of the Hamersley Ranges, and 290 kilometres from Roebourne.

PARABURDOO (Population 1 778), south of Tom Price.

NEWMAN (Population 3 889), south of Port Hedland (340 kilometres).

GOLDSWORTHY (Population 1 020), east of Port Hedland (132 kilometres).

THE KIMBERLEY REGION

BROOME

(Population 1 884)

Broome, once the prosperous and cosmopolitan centre of 'The West's' pearling industry, is on Roebuck Bay 2 020 kilometres by air north-north-east of Perth. It is now a scattered, sleepy little town from which most of the colour and romance has faded, although the comparatively recent establishment of a modern meatworks, justified by the increase in the price of export beef rather than by increased production by the cattle stations, has done much to restore its economy. The coastal plain behind Roebuck Bay is flat and monotonous, but the coast itself has attributes for people interested in shell collecting, fishing and marine life generally. Nevertheless, Broome's historical associations remain its chief attraction for tourists.

The town is busiest during the April to October beef-killing season, when the meatworks employs about 130 seasonal workers. Apparently in expectation that the cattle turnoff will increase as a result of upgrading of beef roads, which permits animals to be transported to the abbatoirs in road-trains rather than driven long distances on foot, a new jetty 823 metres long and providing two deepwater berths was recently constructed. Processed meat can be dispatched direct to overseas markets in ocean-going freighters instead of being transhipped at Fremantle from small coastal steamers, as was previously the case.

Provisions of adequate port facilities anywhere on the Kimberleys coast is difficult and expensive because of the tremendous rise and fall of the tides. The equinoctial variation is more than 9 metres at Broome and approaches 12 metres in the sounds to the north-east.

Although pearling as it was once known in Broome is dead, some luggers based on the port still fish or young pearl oysters to supply stock for cultured pearl farms at Kure Bay, 402 kilometres north-east, where a Japanese-Australian consortium has been operating since 1954. Broome is the supply base for this small but profitable industry.

History. Abel Tasman sighted the Australian coast near Broome in 1644 and William Dampier in 1699 landed on the coast somewhere near the town 11 years after his first visit to Cygnet Bay in 1688. His report of the land and its inhabitants was again so unfavourable that other mariners avoided the area for more than a century. Phillip Parker King sailed along the coast as far as Cambridge Gulf in 1819 and named Roebuck Bay after Dampier's ship. In the wake of the explorers John and Alexander Forrest, sheep and cattlemen pushed into the Kimberleys from both east and south-west in the early 1880s, but discovery of rich pearling grounds off the coast and lucrative trade in tortoise shell were responsible for the foundation of Broome township in 1883. It was named after Sir Frederick Napier Broome, then Governor of Western Australia.

The pearling industry expanded very rapidly in the next 30 years in spite of severe damage and loss of life caused by cyclones every few years. It probably reached its peak about 1925 when 350 luggers employing 3 000 men were working out of the port.

In the early years aborigines were employed as divers, often under squalid and oppressive conditions and for small wages, but the introduction of conventional diving dress about the turn of the century resulted in an influx of Asians, mainly East Indonesians (known as Koepangers), Filipinos and Japanese. Of these the Japanese were by far the most skilled and daring divers at depths of more than 10 metres. The death-rate among them was appallingly high, as the size of the Japanese sections of pearling port cemeteries will attest.

The industry began to decline in the 1930s and was, of course, entirely suspended during the second world war. There was a brief boom again afterwards, but the substitution of plastics for pearl shell in button manufacture brought about the collapse of pearling in the late 1950s. Pearls for jewellery were at all times a mere by-product of diving for shell, although many gems of great value were discovered and their romantic aura obscurred the sordid realities of a brutal and ruthless industry.

Places of Interest. Dinosaurs' tracks embedded in the sandstone at the base of the cliffs of Gantheaume Point. Scientists have vouched for their authenticity and believe that they were made by a species of carnivorous dinosaur about 3 metres high, which lived in the Cretaceous age about 130 million years ago. The tracks can be examined only at low spring tide. Concrete replicas are installed at **Gantheaume Point** (6.5 kilometres) which commands an excellent view of **Cable Beach** (5 kilometres), one of the most beautiful beaches near Broome (5 kilometres), so named because it was the terminus of the cable across the Timor Sea from Java. **Anastasia's Pool,** also at Gantheaume Point, is a small pool blasted or otherwise excavated in the solid sandstone by a pearler named Patrick Percy who decided to make a safe bathing place for his wife. **Pioneer's Cemetery,** near the abutment of the old jetty and the caravan park. **Japanese cemetery** at the end of Anne Street. A large column was erected in memory of 40 Japanese crewmen lost in the 1908 cyclone which drowned 150 men in the pearling fleet. **Buccaneer Rock** in Roebuck Bay at the entrance to Dampier Creek. It has a navigational beacon and is reputed to have been the place where Dampier careened the *Roebuck* in 1699. **Bedford Park,** containing the **War Memorial** and **Dampier's Chest,** erected by the Western Australian Historical society as a memorial to the English navigator. **Museum of Firearms** and convict irons at the police station. (Visitors are welcome.) The **wrecks of flying boats** sunk in the bay by Japanese bombers in 1942 can be seen at low tide. The cleaning and packing of pearl shell may be seen at **Streeter and Male's sheds** on their jetty. Arrangements may also be made to see cultured pearls from Kure Bay. The **meatworks** may be inspected between 9.30 am and 10 am and 1.30 pm and 2 pm during the season. Roman Catholic Missions at **Beagle Bay** (126 kilometres) and **Lombadina** (accessible only for four-wheel drive vehicles).

Sports. Golf club, reserved for members and associates on Saturday afternoon and Sunday. Tennis. Rifle club. Fishing. Swimming at Cable Beach and in the town pool near the old jetty.

Accommodation. Two **hotels.** Preferred: Continental. One good **motel** (unlicensed). **Caravan and camping park,** limited facilities.

Transport. **Road** and **air** services. **Taxis** and **hire cars** available.

DERBY

(Population 2 521)

Derby is the administrative centre of the North West. It is a small, simply laid out town on King Sound near the mouth of the Fitzroy River, 216 kilometres east-north-east of Broome. The centre for the beef cattle industry in the Fitzroy Valley and the King Leopold Ranges, it also serves to a lesser degree the BHP iron ore mining settlements on Cockatoo and King Islands in Yampi Sound about 130 kilometres north by air.

Forty-four kilometres north of the main road to Wyndham via Fitzroy Crossing and Hall's Creek, Derby is an excellent base from which to explore the legendary ranges and rivers of the East Kimberley which until a few years ago were regarded as inaccessible to all but experienced and intrepid outback travellers. Nowadays a trafficable fine-weather beef road has been built from Derby through the Oscar Napier and King Leopold Ranges to Gibb River, and is being extended northward another 320 kilometres to the Kalumburu Mission near the mouth of the King Edward and Drysdale Rivers which flow into Napier Broome Bay, close to Cape Londonderry, the most northerly point of the West Australian coast.

The construction of the road from Derby to Gibb River passes close to Mount House station, about 64 kilometres north-west of the much publicised Glenroy station, where an Air Beef scheme was inaugurated in 1949. An abattoirs for local beef was established at Glenroy and the dressed meat was air-freighted to Derby or Wyndham for chilling and export. Thus labour costs and loss of condition caused by overlanding to coastal meatworks were greatly reduced. The scheme was marginally an economic success, but in 1962 it was discontinued when the road to Derby had been sufficiently improved to carry road-trains of chiller trucks.

The abattoirs constructed at Derby in 1966 provides permanent employment for about 60 workers and a new 550 metre jetty can berth coastal vessels, although overseas freighters are prevented by the tide in the sound which has a rise and fall of 10 metres. The ships of the State Shipping Service of Western Australia are so constructed that they can lie on the bottom of the ocean without damage when the tide is out.

At one stage investigation of the practicability of harnessing the swift tidal flow for the generation of electricity was carried out in the Secure Bay area, but nuclear power stations now seem more economical.

History. The cattle country in the vicinity of Derby was pioneered by Hamlet Cornish in 1879 and by the much publicized Durack family who in 1883 overlanded cattle from Western Queensland in one of the most romantic droving enterprises in Australian pastoral history. The townsite was surveyed in 1883 and named for Lord Derby, Secretary of State for the Colonies in 1882.

Places of Interest. **Mowanjum Aboriginal Mission,** south of town, one of the most successful establishments of its kind in the North West. **Prison Tree,** off the main road 8 kilometres south of town. This ancient, hollow boab (bottle tree) is said to have been used as a lockup for chained native prisoners being brought into town for trial at the turn of the century. **Myalls Bore,** 180 metres from the prison tree, supplies a cattle trough at the stockyards where cattle are mustered and sprayed for tick before being shipped out of the port. The locals claim that their trough is the longest in the southern hemisphere. The **Fitzroy River** which discharges into King Sound near the town is a string of picturesque pools during the dry season and a raging giant during 'the wet'. **Shire Offices** and **Civic Centre,** unusually handsome modern buildings of local sandstone in a 3 hectare park which is being developed as a tropical garden. Two particularly fine boabs have been retained in the reserve. An avenue of these remarkable trees which flourish in the Derby district has been planted in the main street. When mature their trunks, which store water, assume grotesque, bottle-like shapes. **Windjana Gorge** and **Tunnel Creek** in the Oscar Napier Range, 96 kilometres east on the Gibb River beef road, in spectacular and historic country best visited with a local guide.

Derby celebrates an annual Boab Festival in early August. Events include a bushman's carnival, a corroboree, car trials and a native arts display.

Sports. Race track. Tennis courts. Swimming pool with outdoor restaurant. Nine-hole golf course. **Fishing for barramundi,** a tropical species confined to far northern estuary and river waters and regarded as a great delicacy.

Accommodation. Two **hotels.** Recommended: Boab Inn. **Caravan and camping park,** primitive facilities.

Transport. **Air** services from Perth and North West centres. **Air charters** available.

COCKATOO AND KOOLAN ISLANDS

These islands in Yampi Sound form part of the Buccaneer Archipelago. They have rich iron ore deposits which, unlike the new enterprises in the Hamersley and Ophthalmia Ranges, have been mined by BHP since 1951. The mining settlements on them are self-contained company townships and accommodation is available only for company guests. Return flights between Derby and the islands may however be arranged with the company's agent in Derby subject to space being available on the Pioneer aircraft. The coastal scenery of the region is superb and the mining operations are of great interest. Koolan Island reserves have been estimated at one hundred million tonnes. Both Cockatoo and Koolan have very limited natural water supplies and the settlements are supplied by back-loading water in ore carriers from the eastern States.

FITZROY CROSSING (Population 33)

This tiny roadside settlement comprising a store, hotel, police station, post office and mission hospital is 272 kilometres east of Derby on the road to Hall's Creek, at the point where it crosses the Fitzroy River about 400 kilometres by river from the mouth. There are a number of big, permanent waterholes in the area which sustain a great variety of fish and wildlife. Large sharks and sawfish which have adapted themselves to live in freshwater are often caught in the reaches and freshwater crocodiles (protected by law) are common. The Johnson crocodile is a fish eater and has never been known to attack human beings or land animals. It is distinct from the saltwater or estuarine crocodiles which live near the mouth of all Kimberley rivers and sometimes penetrate many kilometres inland during the wet season. Best known of the waterholes near Fitzroy Crossing lies in **Geikie Gorge,** possibly the most colourful and spectacular of all accessible river gorges in northern Australia excepting that in the Katherine River of the Northern Territory.

Picnic races and a bushman's carnival, where station workers gather from all over the Kimberley, are held at Fitzroy Crossing every September.

Accommodation. One **hotel.** (of good standard).

Transport. **Air** service from Perth and Derby.

HALL'S CREEK (Population 676)

The present town of Hall's Creek, 2 832 kilometres from Perth and 322 kilometres east of Fitzroy Crossing, is 16 kilometres from the original settlement near the gold strikes made by Charles Hall and James Slattery in 1885. It was the first payable gold found in Western Australia and a great rush set in, more than 2 000 diggers setting out through the bush from Derby and Wyndham in 1886. Scores perished of heat exhaustion, thirst and hunger and the diggings themselves were plagued by epidemic diseases. Although the Kimberley gold strike never paid well, prospecting and small-scale mining has continued in the region. Hall's Creek is in a low rainfall area on the northern fringes of the Great Sandy Desert.

Places of Interest. Mud-brick **ruins** of old town. **Meteorite Crater** at Wolf Creek, about 136 kilometres south. The crater, scientifically identified in 1947, is the second largest in the world—852 metres in diameter with an average depth of 49 metres. The meteorite is believed to have struck the earth about one million years ago.

Accommodation. One **hotel. Caravan and camping park,** all facilities.

Transport. **Air** service from Perth via North West settlements twice weekly.

WYNDHAM

(Population 1 496)

Wyndham is the most northerly port in West Australia and the terminus of the Great Northern Highway. A good beef road extends eastward into the Northern Territory, joining the Stuart Highway from Darwin to Alice Springs at Katherine.

Wyndham serves the East Kimberley cattle stations and is port for the new irrigation areas on the Ord River. Its meatworks, established in 1919, handle between 35 000 and 45 000 cattle in each killing season and have the capacity for 60 000. Most Kimberley cattle are of the Shorthorn breed, but a number of stations are building up Hereford, Santa Gertrudis and Brahman herds.

Wyndham port can berth vessels of 10 000 to 12 000 tonnes. The township is a strange mixture of old-fashioned corrugated iron buildings and modern houses. A new settlement is growing up 5 kilometres east of the old town. It is situated on Cambridge Gulf about 3 500 kilometres by sea from Perth. The summer climate is excessively hot and humid, and locals boast the highest per capita beer consumption in Australia.

Places of Interest. **Meatworks** during killing season. **The Grotto,** a deep rockbound waterhole near town. **Crocodile Lagoon** and **Marlgu** and **Police Lagoons,** which teem with bird life. **Telegraph Springs.**

Sports. Rough nine-hole golf course. Tennis courts. Bowling greens. Swimming pool. Good fishing beyond the tidal waters at Lacross Island. Deep sea fishing boats may be hired to take game fishermen as far afield as Admiralty Gulf.

Accommodation. Two **hotels.** Recommended: Wyndham Town House. **Caravan and camping park.** No information on facilities.

Transport. **Air** services (northbound four times weekly, southbound thrice weekly). **Taxi** and **coach** tours available. **Air** charters.

KUNUNURRA

(Population 1 496)

A modern, well planned town on the east bank of the Ord River about 100 kilometres east-southeast of Wyndham, Kununurra is the administrative and residential centre of the Ord River irrigation scheme. The surrounding country is mountainous beyond the river flats and scenically grand.

The Ord River project was first mooted in 1945 when the State and Commonwealth Governments jointly set up the Kimberley Research Station, a few kilometres from the present townsite, to investigate the possibilities of tropical agriculture on the alluvial blacksoil plains. Field tests showed that the land was potentially productive of a wide range of crops and by 1963 a diversion dam across the river had been constructed to service about 12 200 hectares of cropland planted mainly with cotton. The scheme succeeded economically and the Commonwealth Government went ahead with the construction of a main storage dam in the Carr Boyd Ranges, 40 kilometres upstream. The new dam covers an area of 64 000 hectares and conserves enough water to irrigate a further 32 200 hectares for the cultivation of tropical crops. A third developmental stage is planned in which a hydro-electric station will be constructed to supply the district's power requirements.

Farming techniques on the Ord are highly sophisticated and mechanized, and have special appeal for travellers with knowledge of tropical agriculture. The Ord Tourist Centre at Kununurra organizes launch tours on the dams and the river and coach tours of the town and successful farms. Lectures are given on the basic technicalities of the scheme, which may be the forerunner of similar developments in the Fitzroy Valley. The aboriginal word *kununurra* means 'big water'.

Places of Interest. **Cotton ginnery.** **Kimberley Research Station.** **Middle** and **Thompson Springs.** **Diversion Dam** and the new dam, **Lake Argyle.** **Kelly's Nob** lookout, for views of town. **Hidden Valley.** **Black Rock.** Native **rock paintings.**

Sports. Tennis courts. Golf course. Aquatic sports. Fishing. (Most good fishing spots are accessible only to four-wheel drive vehicles).

Accommodation. One **hotel** (excellent standard). One **motel,** also recommended. **Caravan and camping park,** all facilities.

Transport. **Road** and **air** services (three northbound and three southbound flights weekly).

Norfolk Island

NORFOLK ISLAND

Norfolk Island, is in the South Pacific Ocean, about 1 600 kilometres east of Sydney and 1 050 kilometres north-west of Auckland, New Zealand, at 29° South latitude and 167° East longitude. It is volcanic in origin and roughly elliptical in shape, about 8 kilometres long and 5 kilometres wide, and has 32 kilometres of precipitous coastline unbroken by beaches or inlets. The highest peaks, Mount Pitt and Mount Bates, are just over 300 metres above sea level. The flora and fauna are of great interest to naturalists because they have evolved in isolation from human habitation until comparatively recently.

The island is very beautiful, with fertile soil and mountain ridges still clothed with stands of the world-famous Norfolk Island pine trees which first brought it to the attention of the outside world. The climate approaches the European notion of the ideal, ranging between 9°C and 28°C, with a mean of 19°C. The average annual rainfall is about 1 320 mm. With this advantage and its lovely coastal and hill scenery, it has great tourist potential, but development has been retarded because it possesses no safe harbour and passenger shipping services have in any case deteriorated. Today the island is largely dependent on air services from Sydney and Auckland. Nevertheless, with the growth of air travel the number of holidaymakers is increasing. About 10 000 tourists now visit Norfolk Island every year. Every six weeks a ship leaves Sydney for the New Hebrides and Solomon Islands via Norfolk Island and every three weeks a ship bound for Noumea, New Caledonia, calls at Lord Howe Island and Norfolk Island on the way.

Industries other than tourism are slowly declining. Vegetable and flower seeds are still important to the economy, but production is reported to be diminishing. Vegetables, fruit, meat and dairy produce are grown for local consumption, but the supply is insufficient for the demand and imports are necessary. Small quantities of wool are exported.

Kingston, a small settlement on the south coast, is the administrative centre for the island's population of about 1 000 people. Civil affairs are run by the Norfolk Island Council, consisting of the Administrator appointed by the Governor-General of Australia, an ex-officio chairman and eight elected members who are residents of the island. The cost of administration and public works is met from local revenue derived mainly from customs duties, postal services, Crown land rents, and a small 'public works' tax levied on adult males. Residents are not liable to income tax on earnings within the Territory nor are death duties levied. The Commonwealth Government makes a grant-in-aid to the Territory every year.

The islanders are mainly the descendants of Pitcairn people who arrived at Norfolk in 1854, although there is now a considerable admixture of 'mainlanders'.

HISTORY Norfolk Island was discovered by Captain James Cook in 1774. He reported it fertile but uninhabited, although there were signs of previous residents probably of Polynesian origin.

In 1788 Captain Arthur Phillip, first Governor of New South Wales, sent Lieutenant King in HMS *Supply* to settle the island with a party of 23 soldiers and convicts, hoping to make it an agricultural supply base for the new colony of New South Wales. The island was, however, covered with dense subtropical forest and the work of clearing land for crops was arduous. By 1804 the population had grown to about 1 100, but the island was expensive to maintain. Its famous pine trees, which grow to a height of 45 metres, proved unsuitable for use as ships' masts and spars and its wild flax turned out to be of inferior quality. The Secretary of State for Colonies ordered the settlement to be wound up and its people transferred to Van Diemen's Land. Withdrawal was completed by 1813 and most buildings on the island were destroyed on the order of Governor Macquarie.

In 1825, however, it was re-opened as a punishment station for refractory convicts from New South Wales and substantial stone buildings including a gaol were erected. It became one of the most notoriously brutal prisons under a penal system of appalling cruelty and degradation.

Not until 1855 was the island abandoned as a prison settlement. Preparations were made for it to receive Pitcairn Islanders, the descendants of the *Bounty* mutineers, who had increased to such an extent that they were starving on their own tiny island.

Norfolk Island received in 1856 the entire population of 194 Pitcairners, who were transferred at their own request to a new home. Subsequently 46 elected to return to their original island, where their descendants live today.

In 1896 Norfolk Island, which had been given the status of a separate colony of the British Crown, became a dependency of New South Wales. In 1913 it became a Territory of Australia.

Extensive restorations of historic buildings in the Kingston settlement on the south coast were begun in 1973 and are proceeding.

Sports. Nine-hole golf course. Tennis. Swimming. Water ski-ing. Riding. Excellent angling and game fishing (boats and charter launches available). Bowling greens.

Accommodation. Five **hotels.** Recommended: Norfolk International, South Pacific. Four **guest houses. Caravan park,** all facilities. Holiday **flats** and **cottages.**

Transport. Air: Qantas operates three flights a week from Sydney en route to Auckland (Mon., Wed., Sat.). Air New Zealand operates two flights a week from Auckland (Sun., Thur.). **Sea:** Services from Sydney by Burns Philp and F. H. Stephens. **Road:** Rental cars and scooters, taxis and hire cars are available for local travel.

Miscellaneous. Currency: Australian and New Zealand currencies are of equal value. Visitors are advised to use travellers' cheques. **Shopping:** Norfolk Island is a free port and goods may be purchased duty-free. **Clothing:** Light tropical clothing is suitable for most of the year, but warmer clothes are advisable for June, July and August. **Communications:** Cables may be dispatched and received from Monday to Saturday noon.

Index